THE ULTIMATE BOOK OF

SPORTS

MOVIES

THE ULTIMATE BOOK OF

SPORTS
MOVIES

FEATURING THE
100 GREATEST SPORTS FILMS
OF ALL TIME

RAY DIDINGER AND GLEN MACNOW

FOREWORD BY
GENE HACKMAN

RUNNING PRESS
PHILADELPHIA • LONDON

9   8   7   6   5   4   3   2   1
Digit on the right indicates the number of this printing

Library of Congress Control Number: 2009921675
ISBN 978-0-7624-3548-7

Design by Joshua McDonnell
Edited by Greg Jones
Typography: Akzidenz Grotesk, Boton, and Mercury

Photographs courtesy of Everett Collection

Running Press Book Publishers
2300 Chestnut Street
Philadelphia, PA 19103-4371

Visit us on the web!
www.runningpress.com

DEDICATIONS

To Maria: My editor, my soul mate and my inspiration. You make all things possible.

To Emily: Welcome to the family. We could always use another good sports fan.

ACKNOWLEDGEMENTS

There are many people we would like to thank for their help in putting this book together. Greg Jones, our editor at Running Press, endorsed the project from the start and helped guide it along the way—despite his repeated lobbying that we include *The Big Lebowski*. And Josh McDonnell did a great job with the design.

Thanks to Phil Martelli, coach of the St. Joseph's University Hawks, for preparing a scouting report on the Hickory High Huskers.

Thanks to Frank Weimann, our agent at The Literary Group International, who helped find a market for a book about sports films.

Thanks to the many sports public relations directors who helped us gather quotes, including Zack Hill, Rich Burg, Mark Dalton, Rick Smith, Kevin Byrne, Pat Hanlon, Peter John-Baptiste, Rich Dalrymple, Jim Saccomano, Harvey Greene, Jack Brennan, Doug Miller, Dan Edwards and Craig Kelley. Also, Chip Namias, director of Athlete and Event Sports Public Relations, and Kathy Duva, who got us in touch with Buddy McGirt and Mark Breland. Thanks also to the athletes and others who provided the quotes.

Thanks to our interns, Brandon Kamin, Ben Seal and Chris DiFrancesco, who helped compile lists and contact sources—and offered advice beyond their years. Also, thanks to our meticulous fact checker Paul Jolovitz. (If you find any mistakes, blame him.)

Thanks to NFL Films producers Chris Barlow, Steve Seidman and Angela Torma who asked various narrators and interview subjects to name their favorite sports movies. Also, thanks to producers Ken Rodgers, Greg Smith, Gerry Reimel, Garrett Fittizzi, Steve Lucatuorto and Adam Ryan who debated the merits of the top 100 films over many lunches in the NFL Films cafeteria. (Sorry, Garrett, but *Over the Top* still didn't make it.) Thanks to David Plaut for providing research material from his personal library.

Thanks to Versus producer Kate Evans for helping to enlist Gene Hackman for the foreword.

CONTENTS

Movies have the ability to make us believe. If only we'd had that one little break, that indefinable moment of clarity where we saw that opening between tackle and guard and ran over the linebacker . . . then we could have scored, big time. If we'd just had that clear shot at the basket then it would have put us into the finals. We *coulda* been contenders.

Maybe you'll recognize this scene. *On the Waterfront* certainly wasn't a sports movie, but I love the metaphor. The camera focuses on two men arguing in the back seat of a taxi. The older brother had taken the odds to deliver his younger sibling to the bookmakers in the kid's big fight at the Garden. The younger brother had gone along and taken the dive. Some of the dialog went like this:

"Remember that night in the Garden, Charlie," Terry, the ex-boxer, tells his older brother. "You came down to the locker room . . . 'It ain't your night kid,' you said, 'We're going for the price on Wilson.' Remember that?" Terry implores. "I *coulda* taken Wilson apart. You *shoulda* looked out for me, Charlie. I *coulda* been somebody."

How many times have we heard "shoulda, coulda?" Most men, when asked if they played sports, will answer either with an equivocal "Yeah, I *coulda*, but I had to work after school." Or better yet, "I was really fast, I *woulda* scored, but they never threw me the ball."

In our memories at least, we seem to be just a smidgen away from that dream of glory Irwin Shaw described so well in his short story *The 80-Yard Run*. Way past his youth, Shaw's hero goes back to the practice field where he had that one spectacular run. He relives the moment, going through all the moves, once again breaking clear into the end zone. If he *coulda* just had the opportunity to do as well in a real game, he laments.

It doesn't seem to matter that a lot of people go on to be successful doctors, lawyers, politicians, writers, sales-men. There is still that lingering moment we have fantasized about, over the course of so many years. We think, surely it must be at least partially true; that "80 yard run," that clear shot at the basket. We've relived it so many times, how could it not be?

The movies solve so beautifully many of those fantasies for us. The quality of many lives, unfortunately, are predicated on how well they adjust to not having been selected to that all-important first team. The movies adjust that for us; we are able to lose ourselves in the pure joy of sport, and forget for the moment that destiny had other things in mind for us.

Film sets up the individual or the team with a conflict—the boxer's lack of connections, the skier's stubborn independence, the baseball player's field of dreams.

As viewers we sit watching, seeing clearly what our team or individual must do, praying that the actors show at least a modicum of athleticism, loving it. "Yeah, that one little break, go man go . . . yesss," and for the next two hours we get to live with the hero's manful quest to overcome his problems, learn something about himself, secure the admiration of girlfriends and town folk and watch him bathe in the camaraderie of his fellow competitors.

Maybe best of all we are able to empathize for just a few moments with fallen heroes like the ex-boxer as played by Marlon Brando in the back seat of that taxi with Rod Steiger.

"So what happens?" Brando says. "Wilson gets a shot at the title in the ballpark. What did I get? A one-way ticket to Palookaville. You *shoulda* looked out for me, Charlie. I *coulda* had class. *I coulda been a contender. I coulda been somebody.*"

Ahhh . . . the movies, we love them.

Chris Nashawaty of *Entertainment Weekly* calls Gene Hackman "maybe the finest actor alive" and, indeed, his credits include some of the most memorable film performances of the last half century.

He won the Academy Award for Best Actor in 1971 for his portrayal of detective Jimmy "Popeye" Doyle in *The French Connection*. He won his second Oscar as Best Supporting Actor for his chilling performance as Sheriff Little Bill Daggett in *Unforgiven*. That film also won Best Picture honors in 1992.

Hackman was nominated for Oscars on three other occasions for his work in *Bonnie and Clyde* (1967), *I Never Sang for My Father* (1970) and *Mississippi Burning* (1988). Yet to many movie-goers he is best remembered as Coach Norman Dale in *Hoosiers*, the sublime 1986 film about Indiana high school basketball.

"Many have said they can't imagine anyone other than Gene Hackman playing Norman Dale," wrote film critic James Berardinelli. "His performance is letter-perfect, from the competitive heat he shows during games to the reflective sadness that emerges in quieter moments. The film doesn't have to give us a detailed backstory for Norman: Hackman's acting provides us with a full definition of his personality."

Sports are a familiar backdrop for Hackman's acting talents. In addition to *Hoosiers*, he portrayed an Olympic skiing coach driving Robert Redford to glory in *Downhill Racer* (1969), a former football star turned private detective in *Night Moves* (1975) and an NFL head coach trying to win with Keanu Reeves at quarterback in *The Replacements* (2000).

We are honored that he agreed to provide the foreword for our book.

—Ray Didinger and Glen Macnow

INTRODUCTION

Drive past the Philadelphia Museum of Art and you will see them. People of all ages, people from around the corner and around the world, people drawn to the famed gallery not by the works of Goya or Wyeth, but by the spirit of Rocky Balboa, the fictional boxer who has inspired generations of underdogs.

They pose for pictures next to the Rocky statue and they climb the steps, huffing and puffing, maybe even stopping to rest halfway up, but eventually they make it to the top. Once there, they turn toward the city skyline, thrust their fists into the air and allow themselves a *Rocky* moment.

The image is decades old: Rocky, the lonely figure in Converse sneakers and tattered sweats, running up those steps, preparing for a title fight that no one thought he could win. Yet after all this time, people refuse to let go.

Actor and screenwriter Sylvester Stallone, who created the character of Rocky Balboa and portrayed him in the original film and five sequels, summed up the Italian Stallion's enduring popularity.

"When people cheer for Rocky," he said, "they're really cheering for themselves."

That is the power of a good sports movie. It doesn't matter if you are from South Philly or South Dakota, the message still lands with the force of a left hook to the heart. In this book, we examine that impact, why some films have it and others do not, why some sports films connect with audiences and others with bigger budgets and bigger stars miss entirely. We list and review what we consider the top 100 sports movies of all-time, and we also devote a chapter to the all-time stinkers. (Yes, Carrot Top makes an appearance.)

Sports and movies are a perfect artistic marriage. Sports feature big stars and storybook finishes; the same could be said for Hollywood. Sports produce drama on a regular basis: ninth-inning rallies, Hail Mary passes and sudden death overtimes. The movies have all that plus the advantage of a script, which means they can have the

hero sink that last-second three-point shot every time.

Critics say that makes sports movies predictable, even trite—and yes, some of them are. Was there ever a doubt that the high school football team coached by Goldie Hawn would win the big game in *Wildcats*? In a word: no. Was it a surprise when Elvis Presley put down his guitar and punched his way to the top in *Kid Galahad*? Hardly.

But the best sports movies don't pander. Like the teams and the athletes we root for, they don't always give us what we want. Remember, Rocky lost that first title fight. That may be why the original film, which won the Oscar for best picture in 1976, still resonates. It wasn't just a lot of Hollywood cotton candy. It felt honest. It felt real. The characters had flaws and fears just like the rest of us.

Some sports movies are frothy, silly fun. For example, the Marx Brothers' zany antics (banana peels on a football field?) in the 1932 film *Horse Feathers*. Other sports movies are as dark as Kafka. *Raging Bull* certainly fits that description. Some lift your heart (*Rudy*) and others break it (*Brian's Song*). The great ones such as *Million Dollar Baby* and *Hoop Dreams* do both.

Still, the classic sports movie theme is the triumph of the underdog, the scrappy athlete or team that prevails in spite of the odds. It has been a Hollywood staple for years. One of the best examples of the genre is *Hoosiers*, a 1986 film about a team from a tiny Indiana town that wins the state high school basketball tournament. The title game comes down to one last shot and when the star player looks at the coach and says, "I'll make it," he is really speaking for all of us.

Long before Rocky stepped into the ring against Apollo Creed, Charlie Chaplin laced up the gloves in *The Champion*, a silent film released in 1915. Harold Lloyd made a film entitled *The Freshman* in which he played a water boy who becomes a football hero. Buster Keaton competed in two sports (crew and track) in *College*, a

United Artists release from 1927.

When silent films gave way to "talkies," sports themes remained popular. In 1929, Warner Brothers released *The Forward Pass*, a football movie starring Douglas Fairbanks Jr. and Loretta Young. The advertising campaign promised: "The roar of the stands, the thud of flying feet racing to the most dramatic touchdown ever filmed and every seat is on the 50-yard line." Theater marquees read: "It's a real man's picture that women will love."

In 1932, Wallace Beery won the Oscar as best actor for his performance in *The Champ*. Beery played a broken-down prizefighter who makes a comeback to provide for his son played by Jackie Cooper. Beery wins the fight, but he collapses and dies in the dressing room. The film was re-made in 1979 with Jon Voight as the boxer and Ricky Schroder as his son. Same ending, same reaction. Audiences wept, even the men. Sports movies have that effect.

"I cried the first time I saw *Field of Dreams*," said Mike Golic, who played eight seasons in the NFL and now is an ESPN football analyst. "I still cry at *Brian's Song*. *Rocky* made me stand up and cheer. *Hoosiers* made me stand up and cheer. That's the great thing about a good sports movie: it brings out those emotions."

Men identify with sports movies in a way they don't identify with other films. How many men have been undercover cops? How many have been jet pilots or spies? When most men are watching, say, Matt Damon as Jason Bourne, there is a certain distance. But almost every American male once swung a baseball bat and dreamed of hitting the game-winning home run. So, when Robert Redford steps to the plate in *The Natural*, the men in the audience are right there in his spiked shoes.

It poses a greater challenge for the filmmaker. Because virtually everyone in the audience has either played the sport or watched it on TV, they are quick to spot a phony. Other than doctors, who knows what is really said in an operating room? But over the years, enough coaches and players have worn microphones on the field that even the casual fan knows how real jocks walk, talk, scratch and spit. If the director and writer don't get that part right, the whole film falls apart.

Bull Durham got it right. It was written and directed by Ron Shelton, who played five seasons in the Baltimore Orioles farm system, and it starred Kevin Costner, who had the swing and the swagger to make us believe Crash Davis really could've made it to The Show.

A good sports movie works across the board. Men, women, teenagers, seniors, they all get it. That's because sports are a metaphor for life. Sports are all about striving, about overcoming disappointment and finding a way to win. They are about heroes and fame and the price that must be paid for success. Those are the themes that have defined classic drama since the beginning of time, and they provide a sturdy framework for whatever story an author may want to tell.

When done well, sports movies do more than entertain—they reflect our culture and, in some cases, become woven into its fabric. We see these films, we discuss them, we benefit from them, and we even quote them in our daily lives. And so as part of our analysis we highlight both the quotes that "made" the movie, as well as those that have made it into our national lexicon. Also, we've quoted by transcribing directly from watching the films ourselves. In these times of fast-and-loose information dispersal via the internet, you never know if a film quote referenced in informal discussion is accurate. (Consider the most enduring movie misquote—"Play it again, Sam,"—which was never actually uttered in *Casablanca*. The real line was, "Play it, Sam, for old times. . . .")

In picking our top 100 films, we didn't factor in the box office. We included some films that were commercial duds, such as *Fat City* and *Wind*, and others that were in limited release, such as the cricket movie *Lagaan* and a film about Australian-rules football, *The Club*. We focused only on what was on the screen and we selected the 100 films we found the most interesting. We don't expect everyone to agree. Indeed, disagreeing is part of the fun.

We did not include the three highest-grossing sports movies of all-time: *The Waterboy* ($161 million) and the remake of *The Longest Yard* ($158 million), both starring Adam Sandler, and *Talladega Nights: The Ballad of Ricky Bobby*, starring Will Ferrell ($148 million). They fall into the category of Frat Boy Comedies and while they obviously were a big hit with the Saturday night mall crowd, they didn't do much for us. *Caddyshack* and *Happy Gilmore* did and that's why they made the list.

Sports movies—like baseball bonus babies—are a risky investment. Even a "can't miss" prospect will miss now and then. For example, Ferrell's 2008 release *Semi-Pro*, a parody of the American Basketball Association, was an air ball at the box office, grossing just $33 million. But the studios keep cranking them out because they know when a sports movie connects, it's usually a tape-measure home run.

"It's tougher now because people see so much [sports] on ESPN, it's like a continuous loop," said Mark Ciardi, who produced four successful sports films: *The Rookie, Miracle, Invincible* and *The Game Plan*. "What you have to do is give them a really good story that isn't just about sports. *The Game Plan* was really a father-daughter story; football was more or less in the background. That's what appealed to the Disney people [who financed the movie].

"You can't just make movies for guys anymore. You want the guys, but you also have to appeal to the wife, the girlfriend, the whole family. We've tried our best to do that. When we tested the films, we found they scored best with women over 25. I think what happened is *The Rookie* did so well [earning $75 million] that other studios tried to copy it. As a result, there were too many [sports] movies coming out, and the market was flooded."

"Movie people are fascinated with athletes," said Ernie Accorsi, who spent 40 years as a National Football League executive before retiring as general manager of the New York Giants following the 2006 season. "I believe all actors want to be athletes and all athletes want to be actors. Take a guy like George Clooney, I'm sure that is his secret lust. That's probably why he did *Leatherheads*.

"He had a thousand scripts on his desk, I'm sure, but he picked that one because it was his chance to be a pro football player. Lawyers, cops, soldiers—he has done all that. But the chance to be a pro football player was something he probably thought about since he was a kid. This was his shot so he took it."

Accorsi—who worked as a sportswriter prior to becoming a football executive—considers *Field of Dreams* the finest sports film ever made.

"Dick Stockton called me," Accorsi said, referring to the veteran TV broadcaster. "He said, 'You have to see this movie. If you don't see it tonight, our friendship is over.' The movie had just opened. I didn't know the first thing about it. He said, 'It doesn't matter. Just go.'

"I went that night and I loved it. It made me feel like I was 14 again. I was so moved, I flew to Chicago, rented a car and drove to the field in Iowa where they filmed it. It took me two and a half hours, the last 80 miles were on a two-lane highway, but it was worth it. It was magical, that's the only way to describe it.

"The field is exactly as you saw it in the movie. I stood there for an hour, just staring. Then I walked through the outfield and into the corn stalks, hoping I'd bump into Shoeless Joe [Jackson] and Dizzy Dean. You tell someone that story and they look at you like you're goofy.

"But then they see the movie, and they understand."

*　*　*　*　*

In the course of writing this book, we surveyed more than a hundred athletes, coaches and various celebrities and asked them to name their favorite sports movie. You will find their selections in the chapters that follow, but here is a sampling that reflects the diversity of opinion and, in some cases, how far some people stretch the definition of a sports movie.

Joe Buck, Fox broadcaster: "Baseball translates better (to the screen) than other sports because of the *mano a mano* battles between the pitcher and the batter. I love *The Natural* for that reason. I still get chills when that ball hits the light tower."

Phil Simms, former New York Giants quarterback, MVP of Super Bowl XXI: "I've probably seen every sports movie ever made, but *Field of Dreams* has a depth that sets it apart. So many things in that movie are so true about athletes: the relationships with your wife, your children, your father. Any athlete relates to the dynamics you have growing up and how it's really special. To have a chance when it's all over to go back and revisit it, oh my gosh, that's a beautiful thing."

Ray Lewis, Baltimore Ravens linebacker, MVP of Super Bowl XXXV: "I watch *Gladiator* all the time and I'm always inspired. It is about the evil people can do to each other. But it is good over evil and the satisfaction you can get by doing the right thing even when the masses are against you. It's about overcoming obstacles and taking care of each other. You can relate to the movie as a family man and as a team member."

Ric Flair, former world wrestling champion: "It's all about commitment which is why *Rudy* is a special movie. It focuses on the kid that no one thinks is going to make it, but puts his life on the line and perseveres to be his best. When it came out, I made my own kids see it because it was a special message. I've seen it so many times myself that I can't even count that high."

Joey Pantoliano, Actor: "I watched *Fear Strikes Out* as a young kid, and it always stuck with me. It was the first time I ever saw a movie about a famous person—an athlete—with a serious mental health problem. Later, I went to Yankee Stadium and saw Jimmy Piersall play live, and thought, 'Here's a guy who has the same issues as everyone else. He's a sports hero, but he's a human being with all the weaknesses of other people. That stayed with me."

Ken Griffey Jr., member of the 600 Home Run Club: "I really don't watch a lot of sports movies. Does *Jaws* count? That's my favorite movie. It's kind of about the sport of fishing, right? But the people are the bait."

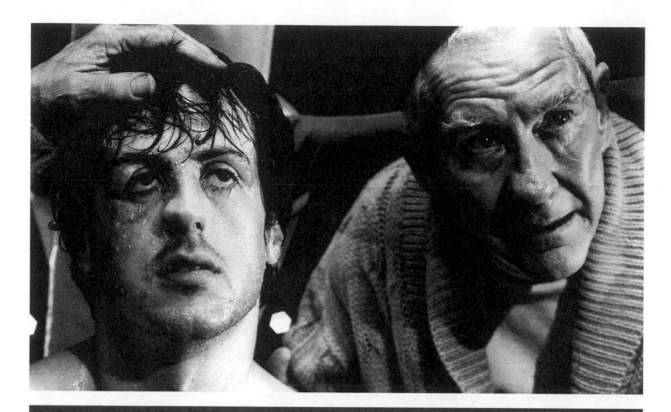

1 ROCKY (1976–PG)

SPORT: BOXING | **STARS:** SYLVESTER STALLONE, TALIA SHIRE, BURGESS MEREDITH
DIRECTOR: JOHN AVILDSEN

How do you choose the best sports movie ever made?

A difficult task. It's a question of judgment and taste, to be sure. But to be the champion among dozens of contenders, the top sports movie must meet five tough standards:

1. It needs to have a powerful story. The script is everything, as they say in Hollywood. There must be challenges and surprises, triumphs and setbacks.

2. It needs to have characters—three-dimensional heroes and bums, interesting folks who make you care about their lives.

3. It needs to have topflight sports action. A compelling story about an athlete who just stands there quickly stops being compelling. A great sports movie needs sweat and blood and speed and power. And the actors in the movie have to be better athletes than those middle-aged guys in your YMCA hoops league.

4. It needs to create goose bumps. There must be at least one scene in the film that sends shivers down your back or raises a lump in your throat.

5. It needs to be realistic—but not too much so. Because a powerful sports movie lets us stretch our imagination, allows us to dream. This is cinema's great advantage over real life.

"Apollo Creed vs. the Italian Stallion. Now that sounds like a damn monster movie."—Apollo Creed

More than any movie ever made, *Rocky* meets all five criteria. The script, written by Sylvester Stallone, is the touching story of a hardscrabble club fighter who takes his best shot. Stallone may not have invented the lovable-underdog saga, but he sure perfected it. *Rudy* is a spin-off of *Rocky*. So is *Miracle*, even if it is based on a true story. So is *Hoosiers*. Truth be told, dozens of movies listed in this book owe Stallone a nod.

Rocky is chock full of colorful characters. Paulie (Burt Young), the row-home loser who keeps nipping from a flask and trying to earn a buck off his best friend. Mick (Burgess Meredith), the rheumy-eyed octogenarian trainer seeking one last pass at the brass ring. Apollo Creed (former NFL linebacker Carl Weathers) the brash, angry Ali clone. Even the bit parts—like Gazzo the mobster ("What, you think I don't hear things?") and Buddy, Gazzo's wise-cracking driver ("Take her to the zoo. I hear retards like the zoo.")—add layers of grit to the story.

You want Grade A sports action? The brawl between Balboa and Creed that culminates the film is as good as it gets. From the moment late in the first round when the "badly outclassed challenger" shockingly floors the champ with a left, up through final bell, as the Italian Stallion buries one last hook in Creed's ribcage ("Ain't gonna be no rematch." "Don't want one."), Rocky will have you feinting and cheering for 25 minutes.

Need goose bumps? Watch Rocky in the training sequence performing those one-armed pushups as "Gonna Fly Now" kicks into high gear. Cut to him dashing through the streets of Philadelphia, a quick flash of the fighter punching the sides of beef, and then the iconic shot of Rocky in the gray sweat suit, arms aloft at the top of the Art Museum steps. If that doesn't create tingles, you must be unconscious.

Finally, *Rocky* is plausible—to a point. As most folks know, Stallone based his screenplay on the 1975 fight between Muhammad Ali and little-known Jersey brawler Chuck Wepner (aka "The Bayonne Bleeder"). Wepner never actually knocked down Ali (the champ tripped) and he was called out on a TKO with 19 seconds remaining in the 15th round. So Sly took the real life story and made it better.

Recalling the Ali-Wepner fight to *Playboy*, Stallone said, "The crowd is going nuts. Guys' eyes are turning up white. And here comes the last round, and Wepner finally loses on a TKO. I said to myself, 'That's drama. Now the only thing I've got to do is get a character to that point and I've got my story.'"

For all of those reasons, we deem *Rocky* the best of all time. Whenever we're flipping around the channels and discover it on one of the cable stations, we're hooked for the rest of the night.

"Women weaken legs!"—Mick

You may disagree with our ranking, which is certainly your right. But just don't hold against *Rocky* the five sequels that followed it—and which we find entertaining to various degrees (see the following chapter). The follow-ups diluted the franchise, often making people forget how intelligent and nuanced the original is, full of the tender little moments and layered dialog that make it worthy of its Best Picture Oscar.

While Ali-Wepner may have inspired the screenplay, *Rocky* really is a metaphor for Stallone's own story. Before this, he was a struggling actor who landed a few small roles—a subway mugger in Woody Allen's *Bananas*, a thug in *Death Race 2000*. Frustrated that he couldn't get a starring part—and coping with a pregnant wife and a $106 bank account—he decided to try writing his own vehicle.

He drafted the original version of *Rocky* into a spiral notebook in one coffee-fueled weekend. There were lots of revisions. In various drafts, Creed was Jamaican, Adrian was Jewish and Rocky used his loser's purse to buy a pet shop. One version even had Rocky throwing the fight.

When he finally got it right, Stallone pitched the project to United Artists. Producers Irwin Winkler and Robert Chartoff had been searching for a boxing project and liked the script. Just one problem: No one envisioned Stallone as the lead in his own screenplay. They offered him $20,000 for the rights. He declined. Then $100,000. Then $200,000. Stallone, saying he "had gotten used to being poor," told producers they could have the script for nothing—but he had to star in the film.

Finally, a compromise was reached. Stallone could headline his own project, but it would have a bargain basement budget of $1 million. He would get $20,000 for the script and—we're not kidding—would be paid $1,40 for four weeks of acting. He would also get a small pie of the action—if there was any.

"Why do you want to fight?"—Adrian
"Because I can't sing or dance."—Rocky

Director John Avildsen (*Lean on Me, The Karate* was hired even though, as he later told *Entertain Weekly*, "Boxing wasn't something that interested What sold him on the script? "By the third page, th is talking to his pet turtles, Cuff and Link. I got totally seduced."

The cast was hired (Meredith got the biggest check: $25,000) and the movie was shot in under a month during December 1975. Because of the shoestring funding, some grand ideas were scaled back. For instance, the wonderful scene of the first date between Rocky and Adrian (Talia Shire) was supposed to take place at a packed ice rink with hundreds of skaters enjoying a festive holiday season. But there was no money for extras, so it was rewritten as a closed, empty rink. As they say, necessity is the mother of invention—or in this case, great art.

The unlikely film with the puny budget opened in November 1976 to mixed reviews (Vincent Canby of the *New York Times* panned it, saying that Stallone's performance "reminds me of Rodney Dangerfield doing a nightclub monologue."). But audiences loved *Rocky*, rising for standing ovations at the finale as a blind, bloodied Italian Stallion embraces Adrian in the ring ("I love you." "Where's your hat?"). *Rocky* gained a buzz that made it the nation's smash movie that holiday season.

Ultimately, it took in nearly $120 million at the box office. Overall, it has earned more than $1 billion over the years—not a bad return on investment for United Artists. Stallone earned an estimated $6 million on his small piece of the profits.

"He doesn't know it's a damn show! He thinks it's a damn fight!"—Duke, Apollo's trainer

Rocky's Best Picture Oscar came over some worthy competition, including *All the President's Men, Taxi Driver* and *Network*. Years later, *Network* director Sidney Lumet remains a sore loser. "It was so embarrassing that *Rocky* beat us out," he told *Entertainment Weekly* in 2006. Lumet said he was skeptical when *Network* screenwriter Paddy Chayefsky predicted *Rocky*'s win on the flight out to the Oscars.

"I said, 'No, it's a dopey little movie.' And Paddy said, 'It's just the sort of sentimental crap they love [in Hollywood].' And he was right."

Well then, you can mark us down as sentimentalists as well. More than 30 years later, *Rocky* still holds up. Sure, the tempo is a little slower than movies made these days, but the story and sweetness still work.

"Before this, boxing in movies generally spoke to something negative," Talia Shire said in the American Film Institute's salute to the top 10 sports movies (which ranked *Rocky* second to *Raging Bull*). "But here it spoke to something spiritual, transcendent. He just wants to go the distance. That's America. That's what people want in this country."

To which we would only add. . . .
"Absolutely."—Rocky

🎞 **CHEERS:** One reason the action scenes work so well is that *Rocky* marked the introduction of the "Steadicam," a camera stabilizer that produces a smooth shot in turbulent surroundings, even when the cameraman is walking or running. The Steadicam was invented by Garrett Brown of Philadelphia, who also designed the SkyCam used in football games, the DiveCam used in Olympic diving and the MobyCam used to film underwater. The man deserves to be in a Hall of Fame somewhere.

👎 **JEERS:** Not much to dislike here, unless you want to blame *Rocky* for eventually spawning *Rocky V*.

✒ **WHAT THEY WROTE AT THE TIME:** "The story . . . has been told a hundred times before. A description of it would sound like a cliché from beginning to end. But *Rocky* isn't about a story, it's about a hero. And it's inhabited with supreme confidence by a star. His name is Sylvester Stallone, and he reminds me of the young Marlon Brando."—Roger Ebert, *Chicago Sun-Times*

☺ **GOOFS:** Check the background of the "sold out" arena during the title fight. Because producers could only round up 100 or so extras, most of the seats are empty.

✔ **REALITY CHECK:** In the famous training scene—as "Gonna Fly Now" builds toward a crescendo—the Stallion runs from South Philadelphia's Italian Market, up along the Schuylkill River, back down to the old Navy Yard on the Delaware River, and across town to the Art Museum. We know the guy's getting in shape, but Kenyan marathoners don't cover this much ground in a month.

◉ **REPEATED WATCHING QUOTIENT:** Infinity. How could you ever get sick of this gem?

PIVOTAL SCENE: The brilliant underlying point of *Rocky* is that he loses the fight but still wins the war for his own self respect. Understand, this is a guy who works as an enforcer for a local mobster, who is regarded as a lazy underachiever in the ring, who is berated as "Creepo" by neighborhood punks. But visiting the arena the morning before his title bout, Rocky has his moment of clarity and self-realization. He comes back to his apartment to reveal his inner thoughts to Adrian.

"I can't beat him," he says. ". . . I ain't even in the guy's league."

"What are we going to do?" asks Adrian. We love her here for using the word *we* rather than *you*.

Rocky tells her he has a new goal. "It really don't matter if I lose this fight. It really don't matter if this guy opens my head, either. Because all I want to do is go the distance. Nobody's ever gone the distance with Creed, and if I can go that distance, you see, and that bell rings and I'm still standing . . ."

Here it comes . . .

"I'm gonna know for the first time in my life, see, that I weren't just another bum from the neighborhood."

And a new man is born.

BET YOU DIDN'T KNOW: Stallone was so nervous about the above scene—and Avildsen's threats to cut it out—that he got drunk before filming it and nailed it in one take.

BET YOU DIDN'T KNOW II: Stallone, a strong believer in method acting, spent so much time punching the frozen sides of beef in the training scenes that his knuckles were permanently disfigured.

DON'T FAIL TO NOTICE: The moment where Gazzo the mobster pulls out an inhaler during the middle of a conversation with Rocky. It was not in the script and occurred only because actor Joe Spinell started having an asthma attack.

CASTING CALL: Imagine how the movie would have worked with this cast: Ryan O'Neal as Rocky, Bette Midler as Adrian, Lee J. Cobb as Mick and heavyweight fighter Ken Norton as Apollo. All of those actors came under consideration by a studio that projected the film as a vehicle for more established stars.

O'Neal—coming off the critically acclaimed *Paper Moon* and *Barry Lyndon*—was the first choice of United Artists studios. But Stallone, as we said, insisted on playing Rocky Balboa himself. Producers Winkler and Chartoff—unfamiliar with the obscure actor—asked to see a photo. An aide showed them a shot of the cast of *The Lords of Flatbush*, and their interest grew. Problem was, the producers had mistaken Stallone for another cast member—blond-haired, blue-eyed Perry King. When they later met Stallone, they almost backed off.

Midler turned down the role of Adrian. Susan Sarandon auditioned next, but was deemed "too beautiful and worldly" to play the part, according to Stallone. Cobb refused to read for the role of Mick, telling Avildsen, "The last prick I auditioned for was Arthur Miller and I ain't gonna read for anyone else." And Norton, a top heavyweight contender, was hired to play Apollo, but quit at the last minute to take a spot on ABC's jock-olympics show *The Superstars*. Bad career choice.

SPORTS-ACTION GRADE: A-plus. We concede that Balboa v. Creed may lack some pugilistic realism. Fact is, it's better than real boxing. Tell us you didn't leap from your chair cheering the first time you saw Rocky crack the champ's ribs.

What few people know is how choreographed the scene was. HBO boxing analyst Larry Merchant did a television feature on the movie soon after its release, taking Stallone and Weathers back into the ring to re-enact the bout.

"It was done like a dance," Merchant recalled. "You could hear them talking under their breath, giving instructions. 'OK, go to the ropes. Here comes the hook. Overhand right.' They talked all through it, but you never heard it in the film because of the crowd noise and the music. It was fascinating. Stallone told us how he wrote the fight. He thought through how it would go, and he announced it into a tape recorder. He did the actual blow by blow for 15 rounds. Then he put it down on paper."

There may not be a more exciting sports scene in the history of cinema.

99 **BEST LINE:** Mick: "You're gonna eat lightning and you're gonna crap thunder."

👀 **"I KNOW THAT GUY":** You need to be an old-timer (or a fan of *Nick at Nite*) to recognize this one, but the club fight announcer in the opening scene is played by Billy Sands. From 1955 to 1966, Sands had a good sitcom run, first as chirpy Pvt. Dino Paparelli in the *Phil Silvers Show*, and then as motor machinist mate Harrison "Tinker" Bell in *McHale's Navy*.

🎬 **IF YOU LIKED THIS, YOU'LL LIKE:** *Rocky Stories: Tales of Love, Hope, and Happiness at America's Most Famous Steps.* The book, by reporter Michael Vitez and photographer Tom Gralish, both of the *Philadelphia Inquirer*, tracks a full year of people bounding up the steps of the Philadelphia Art Museum to the Rocky statue. The site has become iconic since the movie, and the book captures moments ranging from marriage proposals to the triumphs of cancer survivors to an Iranian immigrant paying homage to Rocky Balboa, his can-do inspiration.

"You can't borrow Superman's cape," Stallone said during a 2006 visit to Philadelphia. "You can't use the Jedi laser sword. But the steps are there. The steps are accessible. And standing up there, you kind of have a piece of the *Rocky* pie."

🎬 **MY FAVORITE SPORTS MOVIE:** Actor and playwright Chazz Palminteri: "I'll never forget the first time I saw *Rocky*, the feeling I got—amazed, floored. The theater rose and cheered. Oh my God, it changed the whole genre of movie making. The characters were great, not cliché. Stallone did a masterful job. It's a classic."

🎬 **MY FAVORITE SPORTS MOVIE TOO:** Tim Tebow, Heisman Trophy-winning quarterback from the University of Florida: "I was probably 10 years old when I first saw it. Our family had a minivan with a TV in the back and we'd play tapes all day. I watched it over and over, I think because I kept hoping maybe this time he'll win. But as I look back on it, the ending was great because he lost—but he still won. One of these days I'm going to run those steps and I know I'll hear that music pounding in my ears."

DOWN FOR THE COUNT: ROCKY SEQUELS

SYLVESTER STALLONE'S ORIGINAL *ROCKY* WAS A BLUE-COLLAR ANTHEM FOR THE AGES. IT WAS ALSO A LOVE STORY WITH A SYMPATHETIC HERO, GRADE-A SPORTS ACTION, AND A DOZEN ICONIC SCENES THAT STILL STAND UP. IT DESERVES TO BE RECOGNIZED AS THE GREATEST SPORTS MOVIE EVER.

ROCKY MAY BE THE MOST IMITATED MOVIE EVER MADE. WHEN KURT RUSSELL AS COACH HERB BROOKS IN *MIRACLE* YELLS AT HIS TEAM, "YOU WERE BORN TO BE HOCKEY PLAYERS. THIS IS YOUR TIME!" HE'S CRIBBING FROM MICK SCREAMING, "YOU'RE GONNA EAT LIGHTNING AND YOU'RE GONNA CRAP THUNDER!"

FOR BETTER OR WORSE, *ROCKY* ALSO SPAWNED A SERIES OF FIVE SEQUELS—SO FAR—THAT STALLONE SHOT OVER THREE DECADES. THEY RANGE FROM ENTERTAINING TO INSIPID. MUCH OF THE ORIGINAL FILM'S BRILLIANCE IS NOW OBSCURED BY THE CARTOONISH MOMENTS THAT FOLLOWED—SUCH AS THE ITALIAN STALLION CRADLING A FADING APOLLO CREED IN HIS ARMS IN *ROCKY IV* AS IVAN DRAGO MUMBLES, "IF HE DIES, HE DIES."

TRUTH BE TOLD, WE LIKED THAT SCENE. AND IN A CERTAIN WAY WE ENJOY ALL THE *ROCKYS* (WELL, NOT *V*, BUT WE'LL GET TO THAT). THEY JUST SEEM TO GET CHEESIER AS ROCKY GROWS OLDER. THE BASIC FORMULA IS THIS: THE MORE PLASTIC SURGERY AND STEROIDS STALLONE ENDURED MAKING THE FILM, THE MORE FARFETCHED THE STORYLINE. AND YET, STILL ENDEARING.

SO LET'S GO THROUGH OUR HERO'S CAREER:

ROCKY II **(1979):** Starts right where *Rocky* leaves off and boasts the same cast of characters. In fact, the opening scene at the hospital—set right after the first fight—is downright brilliant. After all the camera crews and reporters have left, Balboa peeks his head into the champ's room.

"Apollo," he says, "I need to know. Did you give me your best tonight?"

"Yes," Creed grunts.

"Okay, thanks," Rocky says. He has received his validation.

The plot, in a nutshell, is this: Balboa is told that he can no longer box because of an eye injury. He begins a career as a commercial pitchman, which fails miserably given that he's functionally illiterate and can't read the cue cards. Rocky falls into being a slap-happy old joke, Adrian falls into a coma and the movie falls into a serious lull.

Eventually, Adrian snaps out of it and orders our hero back into the ring. ("You can do one thing for me: Win. Win!") Cut to Rocky doing one-armed pushups. Cue the song "Gonna Fly Now." All is well again.

The rematch between Rocky and Creed is not exactly *The Thrilla in Manila*. But its finish—the Double Knockdown—had moviegoers jumping out of their seats in 1979. And, of course, this is where Rocky first wins the Heavyweight Title.

All in all, a worthy sequel—although, to be honest, Adrian had become so overbearing that we almost were rooting for her not to wake up.

Best Line: Gazzo the mobster: "How about investing in condominiums? It's safe."

Rocky: "Condominums?"

Gazzo: "Yeah, condominiums."

Rocky: "I never use 'em."

ROCKY III (1982): Opens with a montage of Balboa easily disposing of pretenders to his belt. There's a fun interlude—inspired by Muhammad Ali's 1976 bout against Japanese wrestler Antonio Inoki—in which The Italian Stallion tussles with pro wrestler Thunderlips (Hulk Hogan). Then down to business. A new challenger has emerged—the Tysonesque Clubber Lang (Mr. T). Clubber taunts Rocky every way he can, including shouting at Adrian, "Hey woman, I bet you go to bed every night dreaming you had a *real* man, don't you?" Fighting words.

Gruff, lovable Mick dies along the way, and a retired

Apollo Creed transitions into being Rocky's new manager. (Warning: You'll cringe at the beach training scenes.) There's a great fight in which Rocky is dethroned, then an almost-slapstick rematch in which, of course, he wins the title back.

Best Scene: It's the ending, actually, in which Rocky and his opponent-cum-best-pal-and-trainer Apollo climb into the ring one more time in an empty gym—just to see who's the tougher man. The two fighters circle each other and each man unleashes an overhand right. The camera freezes with the punches just inches from their target and we're left to wonder what happened next.

A quarter-century after *III*, most of this movie is forgotten. But many of Clubber's lines entered the lexicon:

"I pity the fool."

"My prediction? Pain."

"You make me want to be a better man."

Well, two out of three anyway.

To some, *Rocky III* is where the series jumped the shark. "It was like [Stallone] had to make each movie more brutal than the one before," said former welterweight champion Mark Breland. "Was there a referee in any of those fights? I guess as the director he was trying to please the crowd, but I thought he went too far. Mr. T as Clubber Lang? That was the end for me."

ROCKY IV (1985): The Italian Stallion has now retired and unretired more than Roger Clemens (and probably taken as many injections along the way). He's just an affable corner man as this one starts—helping Apollo through an exhibition with Soviet robot Ivan Drago (Dolph Lundgren). Of course things go terribly wrong. The commie cheats and reneges on the deal—as commies always did back then. The exhibition ends with a kill shot to Apollo's head as Rocky throws in the towel in slow motion. Too little, too late.

You could figure out the rest even if you never saw the movie. Rocky must come back to avenge his friend's death. He trains by climbing a 20,000-foot mountain and screaming Drago's name into the ether. The 20-minute boxing scene is, by far, the least realistic of any *Rocky* movie, which is like debating the least-plausible season of *24*.

Indeed, by *Rocky IV*, there was no longer any serious attempt to achieve realism (if you don't believe this, listen to Brigitte Nielsen struggling to play Russian ice queen Ludmilla). But that's okay.

Anyway, Rocky vanquishes Drago ("He's chopping the Russian down!"). Then he grabs the mike to tell the Russian crowd, "During this fight, I've seen a lot of changing, in the way you feel about me, and in the way I feel about you. In here, there were two guys killing each other, but I guess that's better than 20 million. I guess what I'm trying to say, is that if I can change, and you can change, everybody can change."

Even the Politburo members stand and cheer. And you thought President Reagan had something to do with ending the Cold War.

ROCKY V (1990): Widely regarded as the Zeppo Marx of the *Rocky* series, the one that brings nothing to the table. We won't trouble you with a plot synopsis, except to say that Stallone pulled every hackneyed idea out of the closet: Rocky left broke by poor management; a lizardy Don King-like promoter (Richard Gant) pushing brain-addled Rocky back into the ring; a protégé turn-coat (Tommy Morrison) who makes the mistake of taking the old man for granted.

Particularly creepy is the appearance of Stallone's real-life son, Sage Stallone, as Rocky's wimpy offspring. And, is it just us or does Adrian grow increasingly annoying with each episode?

(For more on *V*, see the chapter "Worst Sports Movie Sequels.")

ROCKY BALBOA (2006): Once more, with feeling. Certainly it's tough—at age 60!—for Stallone to dust off the old act one more time. This is like Joe Montana, in his fifties, aiming to come back to win a fifth Super Bowl ring.

And yet, Sly pulls it off. It works because he rediscovers the sweetness that made this series so appealing in the first place. The South Philly good-guy palooka is back, as are some of the long-lost side characters, like cult hero Spider Rico and neighborhood chippie Little Marie. Even Bill Conti's theme, "Gonna Fly Now", is back in the rotation.

Trivia question: Who were the only two actors—other than Stallone—to appear in all six Rocky films?

Answer: Burt Young as Paulie and Tony Burton as Duke the corner man.

The plot in *Rocky Balboa* drips beyond treacly at times, such as when Rocky names his restaurant after the late Adrian, whose grave he visits daily. But sappy was always part of what made this thing tick, as well as increasingly implausible fight sequences. Just relax and let it roll over you. We just wish someone had let former light heavyweight champion Antonio Tarver (who plays Rocky's foe, Mason "The Line" Dixon) in on the joke. He's the only one here who doesn't seem to be enjoying himself.

Anyway, Stallone promised after *Rocky Balboa* that he will not make a *Rocky VII*. We're not taking him at his word.

MY FAVORITE SPORTS MOVIE: 2007 National League Rookie of the Year Ryan Braun: "All the Rocky movies are very motivational. They show what an underdog can accomplish with guts and determination. If they make Rocky VII, I'll be there. Most people say the sequels aren't as good, but you can say that about any sequel. I just know in every Rocky movie there's that moment when he starts training and the music starts to play and I get a chill down my back. It gets me every time."

2 HOOSIERS (1986–PG)

SPORT: BASKETBALL | STARS: GENE HACKMAN, DENNIS HOPPER, BARBARA HERSHEY
DIRECTOR: DAVID ANSPAUGH

Gene Hackman had his doubts when he was first hired to play embattled coach Norman Dale in *Hoosiers*. "No basketball movie had ever made it commercially," he recalled. "And we're going to make a *high school* basketball movie? I thought, 'We should have our heads examined.' "

Likewise, Dennis Hopper, cast as town drunk and hoops savant Shooter Flatch, was dubious during filming. He and Hackman wondered why David Anspaugh kept focusing on "all those damned basketball games."

"[Gene and I] were sitting on those wooden benches saying, 'Here's the big money. Why aren't they shooting us?' " Hopper mused.

It's said that during the filming of *The Godfather*, Francis Ford Coppola fretted that he had a disaster on his hands. If Hackman and Hopper had similar concerns, their fears were equally unfounded. Just as Coppola pro-

duced a masterpiece, so too did *Hoosiers* director David Anspaugh. The little Cinderella story about the Hickory High Huskers is a nearly perfect sports movie.

Hoosiers is a predictable David vs. Goliath tale without being cliché. It is emotionally stirring without being manipulative. It is heart-stirring without being mushy; a feel-good film without being preachy. It boasts brilliant performances—from Hackman and Hopper right down to the flannel-shirt-wearing bit characters in bad haircuts who seem like they just walked out of small-town America, circa 1952.

Add to that some rousing sports action, plus the fact that the film is based on a true story and, well, you've got an enduring classic on your hands.

We surveyed more than 100 prominent people for this book, asking them to name their favorite sports movie. No film was cited more than *Hoosiers*. From legendary golfer Arnold Palmer ("It had a lot of heart. It was a great portrait of America in the 1950s.") to Super Bowl XXXIV MVP Kurt Warner ("They weren't supposed to be there and they won it all. It is really like my story."). From Colorado Avalanche left winger Ryan Smyth ("Small-town people rising to win a championship in the big city.") to WNBA star Sue Bird ("Back in CYO we used to watch it before games to get psyched up."). From Red Sox third baseman Mike Lowell ("I love that Jimmy Chitwood *never* misses a shot.") to University of Wisconsin coach Bo Ryan ("How could anyone involved in basketball *not* love it?").

To, yes, even President Barack Obama, who calls *Hoosiers* "truly inspirational." We can almost imagine the president's next State of the Union Address to Congress: "If you put your effort and concentration into playing to your potential, to be the best that you can be, I don't care what the scoreboard says at the end of the game. In my book we're gonna be winners."

Okay, maybe not.

On the surface, *Hoosiers* is a simple tale about tiny Hickory High (just 64 boys) which sends its team all the way to the state title game against a school 20 times its size. Its template is the true story of the 1954 Milan Indians, who won the Indiana championship in a game that ranks up there with the U.S. Olympic Hockey "Miracle on Ice" in terms of improbable victories. Anspaugh and screenwriter Angelo Pizzo—Indiana U college buddies from the 1960s—embellished history with the subplots that any textured film needs. (By the way, the old frat brothers peaked here in their first collaboration. Their second film, *Rudy*, was a few notches down. Their third, *The Game of Their Lives*, was a bomb.)

In *Hoosiers*, Anspaugh and Pizzo take you to a time and place where high school hoops means everything to a small village. Sometimes that's positive—as when the caravan of townspeople cheerily follows the team bus to road games. Sometimes it's not—as when suspicious local hicks cross-examine the new coach on everything from his religion to his attitude on zone defense. Regardless, there is an organic sense of a real community throughout the film.

And there's something more, because *Hoosiers* isn't just about basketball or a long-gone America. It is also about redemption. The comeback of the small team sets the plot arc for the comeback of its coach, a puzzling 50-ish man with a shadowy past who seems a little too qualified for this outpost. It's also the chance of a comeback for Hopper's village drunk character. Once, 20-plus years ago, Shooter had his own chance for glory. But he missed the winning shot in a high school title game and his life since has been on a downward spiral. He is a disgrace to his son Everett (David Neidorf), one of the current players.

Coach Dale offers Shooter rebirth—over everyone's objections—in the form of an assistant-coaching job. The catch is that Shooter must remain sober. He manages for a few games and then stumbles into a critical semifinal contest bombed. It's a great scene, as the rowdy drunk humiliates his son, who then injures himself in a fistfight borne out of embarrassment. Hopper asked Anspaugh for a 20-second warning before his entrance into the scene. He then spun in circles so that he'd be able to reel around the hardwood like a true drunk.

Two other characters are worth mentioning here. The fabulously named Myra Fleener (Barbara Hershey) is the flinty teacher (and "flinty" is an extremely kind way of describing her) who has a lifelong grudge against high school hoops and seems intent in taking it out on Coach Dale.

Myra: "A basketball hero around here is treated like a god. . . . I've seen them, the real sad ones. They sit around the rest of their lives talking about the glory days when they were 17 years old."

Coach Dale: "You know, most people would kill to be treated like a god, just for a few moments."

Myra eventually comes around, leading to the only low point of *Hoosiers*. More about that later.

The other intriguing character is Jimmy Chitwood (Maris Valainis), the lights-out shooter who quit playing after the Huskers' previous coach died. Jimmy also apparently quit talking, since he doesn't utter a word in his first few scenes. Anyway, he, too, finally joins the ride, saving the coach's job and bringing peace and harmony to tiny Hickory.

It's at this point that *Hoosiers* really picks up. The first half of the movie focuses on Coach Dale's travails; the second half is the run to the state tournament. The final game, of course, ties it all together.

And the pep talk before the final game? Well, we rank the all-time top five movie locker-room scenes like this:

5. Tony D'Amato (Al Pacino) in *Any Given Sunday*: "We fight for that inch. On this team, we tear ourselves and everyone else around us for that inch. . . . I'm still willing to fight and die for that inch!"

4. *Rudy's* Dan Devine (Chelcie Ross, who also appears in *Hoosiers*) telling his Notre Dame seniors before their final home game: "Remember no one, and I mean *no one*, comes into our house and pushes us around." This clip has been played *ad nauseum* at every single NHL and NBA game over the past decade.

3. Bluto Blutarsky (John Belushi) psyching the *Animal House* Deltas for their day of revenge: "Over? Did you say over? Nothing is over until we decide it is! Was it over when the Germans bombed Pearl Harbor? Hell no!"

2. Knute Rockne (Pat O'Brien) channeling George Gipp in *Knute Rockne: All-American* with the "Win one for the Gipper" speech.

And #1:

Coach Dale: "We're way past big-speech time. I want to thank you for the last few months. They've been very special to me. Anybody have anything they want to say?"

Merle: "Let's win this one for all the small schools that never had a chance to get here."

Everett: "I want to win for my dad."

Buddy: "Let's win for coach, who got us here."

Preacher Doty: "Blah, blah, blah." (This part slows the whole thing down and should have been cut.)

Reverend Purl: "And David put his hand in the bag and took out a stone and flung it. And it struck the Philistine in the head, and he fell to the ground. Amen."

Coach Dale: "I love you guys."

All (clasping hands): "Team!"

Works every time.

There has always been debate about how strong a coach Norman Dale really is. Wrote Mike Vaccaro in the *New York Post*: "What do you get when you mix one part Dean Smith, one part Vince Lombardi, one part Casey Stengel and one part Red Auerbach? About half the coach that Norman Dale is."

Truth be told, Dale's game strategy is sometimes lacking much imagination beyond "Give the ball to Jimmy." But put us in those old black Chuck Taylor high tops and we couldn't name anyone we would rather play for. And no one, and we mean *no one*, comes into our house and suggests that any movie coach ever was a better motivator.

CHEERS: The original music by Jerry Goldsmith weaves together synthesized effects and a symphonic score to create one of the all-time great soundtracks. It's brilliant from the start—the opening five minutes of *Hoosiers* have no dialog, just visuals and Goldsmith's music. Notice late in the movie how he mutates the sound of the ball bouncing off the floor to create a backbeat for the music. By the way, Goldsmith was nominated for 17 Oscars during his career (including this one). He won just one, in 1976, for the *The Omen*.

JEERS: The romantic angle between Coach Dale and town crone Myra Fleener seems completely implausible, especially since she spends the first half of the movie trying to bury him. It reaches its low ebb 90 minutes in, during the let's-make-out-in-the-cornfield scene.

Norm: "Would you like to go to Deer Lick and take in a movie some time?"

Myra (reading from an old news clipping): "Norman Dale, coach of the Ithaca Warriors, was given a lifetime suspension for striking one of his players. . . ."

Hey, way to set the mood, Myra. And then we get the most uncomfortable movie kiss since Eddie Murphy made out with his own grandmother (also played by Eddie Murphy) in *Nutty Professor II*. Ugghhh.

"I KNOW THAT GUY": Sheb Wooley, who plays kindly but weak-hearted principal Cletus, made a career as a cowboy in Western classics such as *High Noon, The*

Outlaw Josey Wales and *Silverado*. His biggest success, however, came with the 1958 novelty hit song "Purple People Eater". Wooley also wrote the theme song for the long-running TV series *Hee Haw*. You shouldn't hold that against him.

📽 **PIVOTAL SCENE:** After getting off to a terrible start (either 1-3 or 0-4, it's impossible to tell), Coach Dale is hauled before the angry townsfolk who show up for the let's-fire-the-coach meeting carrying torches and pitchforks. Despite Myra's shocking last-minute appeal to give him a chance, the yokels vote 68-45 to send him packing.

But wait . . . here comes Jimmy Chitwood dribbling in from the dark parking lot to utter his first lines of the film. "I don't know if it will make any change," he says, "but I figure it's time for me to start playing ball."

Raucous applause. "I told you once we got rid of *him*," spouts village jackass George (Chelcie Ross), pointing to a humiliated Coach Dale. Then Jimmy shushes the rabble.

"One more thing," Jimmy says. "I play, coach stays. He goes, I go."

The mob grows quiet. Jackass George's smile dissolves. God—at least the local hoops god—has spoken. A quick re-vote takes place, and Coach is saved.

Quick cut to the next game, with Jimmy making five straight shots in slow motion. Yes folks, we are on our way.

✎ **WHAT THEY WROTE AT THE TIME:** "A goosebump ride through Indiana's legendary state basketball tournament—a ride that is so wonderfully corny you have to enjoy it. *Hoosiers* is about redemption and virtue rewarded, and about what it's like to live in a small town where basketball is your whole life."—Bruce Newman, *Sports Illustrated*

🎬 **CASTING CALL:** According to the 2005 Special Edition DVD commentary, Jack Nicholson was the first choice to play Coach Dale. A scheduling conflict opened the role for Hackman. Thank God.

One other casting note: Pizzo and Anspaugh originally auditioned California basketball players to portray the Huskers, but decided those actors lacked the proper basketball ability as well as Midwestern authenticity. "There are differences between someone who grew up in San Fernando Valley and someone who grew up in Brownsburg, Ind.," Pizzo told the *Bloomington Herald-Times*. "It shows in the way they walk, the way they look, the way they talk."

★ **SPORTS-ACTION GRADE:** An easy A-plus, from the opening practice shot of the boys dribbling around chairs to the chill-inducing state title game. That's not debatable.

☺ **GOOFS:** Although it's a great movie, *Hoosiers* has a plot hole large enough that Robert "Tractor" Traylor could drive through it. Follow this: In the first practice Buddy quits the team and persuades Whit to follow ("I ain't no gizzard."). A few scenes later, Whit apologizes and Coach Dale allows him to return. But Buddy? As far as we know, he's gone, perhaps off to Terhune High. Midway through the film, however, Buddy is suddenly playing for Hickory in a crucial game. When did he rejoin the team? What did he say to persuade the coach to let him back? How come none of this is explained?

The movie never clarifies it, but the Special Edition DVD release does. According to director David Anspaugh, the scene of a humble Buddy begging for forgiveness was cut because of studio heads' insistence that the film stay under two hours. That mystery scene is included in the new DVD. To be honest, it's not that good a scene.

✔ **REALITY CHECK:** Well, by our count, Jimmy Chitwood goes 34-for-39 during the film. Larry Bird would have killed for those numbers.

99 **BEST LINE:** So many great ones. We need to cite two:

First, in the game where Coach Dale gets ejected on purpose, it's up to Shooter to design the last-minute strategy. The old sod reaches into the depths of his foggy brain and comes up with this game-winner: "We're gonna run the picket fence at 'em. Merle, you're the swing man. Buddy, you're solo right. Merle should be open swinging around the end of that fence. Now boys, don't get caught watching the paint dry." Brilliant.

Second is the moment when the Huskers—most of whom, as the coach noted, have never seen more than a two-story building in their lives—first walk into the huge modern arena in Indianapolis before the state title game. They are visibly awed. Coach Dale has Buddy measure the distance from the backboard to the foul line, then puts Ollie on Strap's shoulders to hang his trusty tape measure from the rim to the ground.

Coach Dale: "How far?"

Buddy (with eye to ground): "Ten feet."

Coach Dale: "I think you'll find these exact same measurements as our gym back in Hickory."

How many thousands of coaches do you figure have copied this strategy since *Hoosiers* first came out?

◉ **REPEATED WATCHING QUOTIENT:** We're up to about 8,754 viewings, and we still love it.

♣ **BET YOU DIDN'T KNOW:** The original script called for Shooter to break out of the hospital detox ward and show up at the state title game to watch Hickory win. Hopper, a recovering addict, objected to the scene, saying it sent the wrong message. "Being an alcoholic, I felt that it was really destructive to have Shooter leave," he said in the book, *Dennis Hopper: A Madness to His Method* by Elena Rodriguez. "Maybe he'll never get sober, but he ain't going to get sober if he goes to that game. I said, 'Just do a shot of me in the hospital jumping up and down while listening to the game on the radio.'"

♣ **BET YOU DIDN'T KNOW II:** Steve Hollar, who portrays point guard Rade Butcher, played for DePauw University at the time of filming. The NCAA viewed his work as a violation of its policies and fined him five percent of his earnings for *Hoosiers*. The other Huskers were ex-high school basketball players, except for Everett Flatch (Neidorf, who was a professional actor) and—of all people—Jimmy Chitwood (Valainis, who was a college golfer). Actor Kent Poole, who plays Merle, committed suicide in 2003.

☞ **DON'T FAIL TO NOTICE:** The coach of the South Bend team that Hickory defeats in the state title game. That's Ray Crowe, who was actually the coach of Crispus Attucks High in Indianapolis, the team that Milan High beat for the 1954 championship. By the way, Oscar Robertson was a sophomore on that squad. Attucks High would go on to win the Indiana title in both 1955 and 1956.

⊛ **IF YOU LIKED THIS, YOU'LL LIKE:** If you want to watch another upbeat movie about Middle-America high school kids in the 1950s check out *October Sky*. It's the true tale of Homer Hickam, a coal miner's son who, motivated by Russia's launch of Sputnik, takes up rocketry and grows up to become a pioneering NASA engineer.

🎞 **MY FAVORITE SPORTS MOVIE:** Brian Billick, head coach of the Super Bowl XXXV champion Baltimore Ravens: "Anyone who coached any sport has to love that movie because it shows a man who, first of all, loves coaching and, secondly, understands that leadership is not a popularity contest. He has his beliefs about how the game should be played, how players should be treated, and he is very consistent. If he fails, he fails, but he will do it his way. It's a beautiful thing when you see the players buy into his program. That's what every coach strives for because that's when you know you have a chance to win."

🎞 **MY FAVORITE SPORTS MOVIE, TOO:** University of Florida football coach Urban Meyer, a two-time BCS National Champion: "We have a *Hoosiers* night at our house every year, where we all watch it together. We know every line of dialogue. There are so many great lessons, but the biggest one is the whole concept of team. The coach and players [at Hickory High] were a bunch of misfits. Individually, they were nothing. But together, they won it all."

A TOP NCAA COACH SCOUTS THE HICKORY HUSKERS

NOTE: PHIL MARTELLI HAS BEEN THE HEAD COACH OF THE SAINT JOSEPH'S UNIVERSITY MEN'S BASKETBALL TEAM SINCE 1995, GUIDING THEM TO FIVE NCAA TOURNAMENTS AND FOUR ATLANTIC 10 CONFERENCE TITLES. IN 2003-2004, MARTELLI'S HAWKS ADVANCED TO THE NCAA ELITE EIGHT AND FINISHED THE SEASON AT 30-2. HE AGREED TO WRITE UP A SCOUTING REPORT ON COACH NORMAN DALE'S HICKORY HIGH SQUAD.

Says Martelli:

They're coming off a 15-10 record last season, and have four starters returning. They've also got a new coach who has instituted a new system.

Offensive overview: Very patient. They will all make the extra pass. We need to make them play quicker; they can be turnover prone.

Defensive overview: Love to play man-to-man. They will trap in the half court along the sideline. Screens seem to hurt them. We can beat them with size in the low post.

Personnel:

No. 14—Buddy: Their best defender.

No. 53—Strap: Uses the head/shoulder fake. Has a good hook shot.

No. 21—Everett: A slasher.

No. 12—Merle: Runs the show.

No. 43—Whit: Not much to scout here.

No. 25—Rade: Shooter!

No. 13—Ollie: Deep sub.

No. 15—Jimmy: The superstar. He's fearless.

Offensive patterns:

2-2 with a runner.

UCLA cutter series.

Will pop the shooter off the elbow.

Picket fence.

AN INTERVIEW WITH MARIS VALAINIS
(JIMMY CHITWOOD IN *HOOSIERS*)

How often do you run into people who tell you that they watch* Hoosiers *to get psyched up before a big game or tournament?

All the time. I was in a bar one day and a six-foot-eight guy comes over and says, 'Thanks, we won the state tournament because of you.' And it's pretty humbling when a PGA golfer or NBA star tells me that, but it happens. I was fortunate enough to golf with Kobe Bryant recently, and he said that his high school coach used to show them *Hoosiers* all the time. Here I am with one of most famous people in the world and he was excited to be with me. That was weird.

In your mind, what happens to Jimmy Chitwood after the movie ends?

That's a fine question. I think he goes with the academic scholarship. I know that Bobby Plump (the Milan High star on whom Jimmy is based) went on to play at Butler University, but I think that Jimmy was more about the academics.

Two scenes we want to ask you about: The first is when Coach Dale (Gene Hackman) conducts a one-way conversation with Jimmy as you hit 12 straight shots on that outdoor court.

Yeah, that's a vivid memory for me. They were trying to get in one more scene that day before it got dark, so they told Gene and me to try to get it down in one take. There was a light rain and the sun was perfect. I started shooting and I wasn't listening to a word Gene was saying. I just concentrated on making the shots, and they kept going in. When he stopped talking, I figured the scene was over. I took one more shot, and that's the only one I missed.

The other scene is the game-winning shot at the state title game. Jimmy makes it and thousands of people rush the floor. How many takes did that require?

Just one, believe it or not. I kept missing as we were warming up, and that had me worried. The casting director came up and said, 'You know you're not even looking at the basket,' which was funny, because he knew nothing about basketball. I've got this big shot to take with everyone set to run onto the floor of the Butler Fieldhouse and I'm not feeling right. So we filmed it, and of course I got it on the first take.

Is it true that you never actually played high school ball?

Yeah. I went to a Catholic high school where the coach already picked out his team by my freshman year. It was kids that he'd recruited. I got cut twice. How about that? But I was kind of slow and really didn't grow [he's now six-foot-three] until my senior year. I'm probably a smarter and better player now at age 45 than I was back then.

You played some golf at Purdue and did some acting. Tell us about your post-Hoosiers career.

I moved out to California after *Hoosiers* and dreamed of acting. I appeared in a few movies [notably *Casualties of War* with Michael J. Fox and Sean Penn], but it's a tough business. My personality is kind of laid back for Hollywood. Then I was a golf pro for a long time, and now I am director of development for a construction company. I still love to play recreational basketball, though.

Do people recognize you as Jimmy Chitwood?

Yeah. Usually on the basketball court. They quote me the line, 'I'll make it.' But I'll never get tired of that. How could I? It's a compliment.

Do you still have that smooth shot?

Oh, I don't want to brag. I'm okay. I'm never the last guy chosen in pickup games. Of course, that might be on reputation from the movie.

How many times have you watched Hoosiers?

Fewer than you might think. Probably just a handful, honestly. I'll see bits and pieces when I turn on TV and it's there. I used to feel uncomfortable seeing myself on film, but I'm past that now. Now I look at the experience as something I was lucky to do. I know what the movie means and I feel fortunate to be a part of it. I'm looking forward to showing it to my daughters [now 5 and 3].

What was it like working with Gene Hackman?

He was terrific. He came out to Indiana two weeks early and gave all of us kids acting lessons. We sat around and he taught us technique—things like thinking of something that might make us cry, or singing a song in a certain mood. It was tremendous. He would always say, 'Do your best, because you're not going to be able to change it ten years from now.'

And Dennis Hopper?

Very dedicated. Every evening he'd lock himself in a screening room and look at the day's shooting. He would critique himself. With us, he was awesome. We used to hang around in the trailer playing cards with Dennis Hopper. I'm not sure I realized then how cool and special that was.

How much of the game action in Hoosiers was choreographed and how much was spontaneous?

Most of it was a bunch of guys just playing ball. One of the things that made Hoosiers successful was that the games were filmed with a Steadicam, which was very new and expensive back then. All they told us was, 'Don't bump into the camera.' We had some plays we had to run for specific moments, but most of the action was spontaneous.

When you were a 22-year-old shooting Hoosiers, did you have any sense that it would end up being an iconic movie?

Well, yes and no. It was funny because we were running around, and the director would say, 'Remember, whatever the camera shoots will be on film forever.' So we were well aware of that. And I knew it was a special story. Every kid from Indiana learned the story of Milan High growing up. When Hoosiers remained popular for a while, I thought that maybe it would be like the *Wizard of Oz*, popular long after it was made. And now it is.

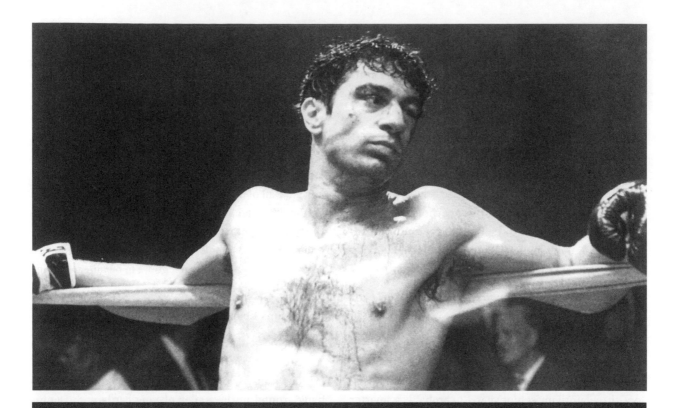

3 RAGING BULL (1980–R)

SPORT: BOXING | **STARS:** ROBERT DE NIRO, JOE PESCI, CATHY MORIARTY
DIRECTOR: MARTIN SCORSESE

Martin Scorsese never intended for *Raging Bull* to be another *Rocky*. He knew his film would not be embraced or loved because his central figure—we can't call him a hero—was Jake LaMotta, who is neither embraceable nor lovable.

Red Smith, the Pulitzer Prize-winning columnist, called the middleweight LaMotta, "A crumbum, a creep, a highly unappetizing specimen of the human race . . . a louse through and through, foul of speech, vile of temper, a bullying wife-beater, a pimp, altogether self-centered without a spark of decency."

Okay, Red, we get the picture, and so did Scorsese. He knew LaMotta, the former world boxing champion, was a violent, abusive man with a soul as dark as the night. He knew if he filmed LaMotta's story—no matter how brilliantly—it would not appeal to everyone. He was proven correct.

Raging Bull divided movie critics and audiences like few films before or since. It grossed $23 million at the box office, which was good but not great. It received some enthusiastic reviews—Vincent Canby of the *New York Times* called it "an achievement"—but it was hammered by other critics who were repelled by its characters, principally LaMotta.

Frank Deford, reviewing the film for *Sports Illustrated*, found it "so peopled with despicable human beings and so gratuitously violent that all the good stuff is cancelled out." Kyle Smith of the *New York Post* wrote, "If it leaves us with any feeling at all, it is smug superiority to its punishingly unpleasant, but not meaningful or important, central character."

Still, *Raging Bull* was nominated for eight Academy Awards, including Best Picture, Best Director, Best Actor (Robert De Niro), Best Supporting Actor (Joe Pesci) and

Best Supporting Actress (Cathy Moriarty). De Niro and Thelma Schoonmaker (Best Film Editing) won Oscars. Scorsese lost to Robert Redford, whose film *Ordinary People* also earned Best Picture honors.

Over time, *Raging Bull* has grown in stature. The American Film Institute ranked it among the top five American movies of all time. *Entertainment Weekly* placed it fifth on its list of the 100 Greatest Movies. *Halliwell's Film Guide* put it seventh on its Top 1,000. Yet Andre Soares of the *Alternative Film Guide* calls it "the most overrated American movie of the last 30—or 40 or 50—years.

"I'm not quite sure how far back one must go to find so much praise bestowed upon so much artifice," Soares wrote. "Much of the acting is as out of control as a bull running through the streets of Pamplona."

In boxing, the reviews would be called a split decision, but clearly Scorsese comes out ahead. *Raging Bull* is not the people's champion in the way that *Rocky* is and always will be, but it is widely recognized as the greater artistic achievement. Roger Ebert of the *Chicago Sun-Times* called *Raging Bull* the best film of the 1980s, and one of the four greatest movies ever made.

It is an unusual sports film in that we can't bring ourselves to root for the main character. That means there is no joy and no happy ending. It may leave you feeling as bruised and battered as one of LaMotta's opponents, but that's what Scorsese wanted. He wanted the audience to feel the punches and the rage that defined LaMotta. There are no soft edges, there is only a willful brutality that carries LaMotta to the top and then brings him down.

Author Joyce Carol Oates, who often writes about boxing, once talked about the boxer's "divided self," that is, the duality of a man who lives by one code in the ring and another in his personal life. Inevitably, a boxer suffers when he can no longer separate the two. In the case of LaMotta, there never was a separation: he was the same person inside the ring and out. In *Raging Bull*, De Niro brings that monster to life in a chilling and unforgettable way.

Canby called De Niro's Oscar-winning performance, "the best of his career, a titanic character, a furious original, a mean, inarticulate Bronx-bred fighter whom the movie refuses to explain away in either sociological or psychiatric terms. He is propelled not by his milieu, his unruly id or by his guilt, but by something far more mysterious. Just what that is, I'm not at all sure."

No one understood LaMotta, even those closest to him, including his five wives and his brother/manager, Joey. He was proud, yet self-destructive. He always said his toughest opponent was Sugar Ray Robinson, whom he fought six times (winning only once). But it would be more accurate to say Jake LaMotta's toughest opponent was himself, a point *Raging Bull* makes over and over again.

Scorsese, as he did in his previous films *Mean Streets* and *Taxi Driver*, brings the texture of New York City into the story. Scenes of Jake and Joey (Pesci) walking down the street on a summer day, past kids playing by an open fire hydrant, evoke a powerful sense of time and place. It is The Bronx in the '40s—men in sleeveless T-shirts, suspenders and dress pants sitting at the community pool, swapping dirty jokes and talking business with the Mafia wiseguys. You can almost feel the sweat on Jake's eight-ounce bottle of Coke.

Scorsese shot *Raging Bull* in black-and-white, in part, because he wanted his film to stand apart from the *Rocky* series, which had already cranked out two installments and was working on a third. Scorsese also felt black-and-white would be more effective in capturing the mood of LaMotta's time. As the director, he moved the point of view back and forth between objective and subjective in a way that enhanced, rather than confused, the narrative, which is not easy to do.

When Scorsese wanted to show the world as seen by Jake, he went to slow-motion. The scene in which Jake first sees Vickie (Moriarty), the 15-year-old blonde who becomes his obsession, is especially memorable. Vickie is sitting on the edge of the pool, her legs paddling in the water. As the camera lingers on her seductive figure, we know what's going on in Jake's mind and we can almost feel what's happening in his Fruit of the Looms.

In the fight scenes, Scorsese insisted on staying in the ring. He did not want to show the action from outside the ropes. He wanted the audience to experience the brutality, so he shot it tight, mixing film speeds and occasionally using a series of explosive stills. When LaMotta breaks an opponent's nose, you hear the crunch, you see the flesh collapse and the blood spray like water from a ruptured hose.

The violence shocked audiences when the film was first released, and it was reason enough for some critics to pan it. But the photography is spectacular (cinematographer Michael Chapman earned an Oscar nomination), and when the punches land, the sound is unlike anything we've heard before. The audio engineers mixed a variety of sounds—the splat of a melon being split, the crack of a gun being fired—and the effect is mesmerizing.

But for all of Scorsese's mastery, the film really belongs to De Niro. Much has been written about the actor gaining 60 pounds to play the bloated, middle-aged LaMotta and, granted, that's taking art to the extreme. But it is in the first half of the film, when he is the young LaMotta, twisted with ambition and jealousy, raging against the world, that he carries *Raging Bull* to the heights. He commands the screen, and his profane dialog with Joey is alternately funny and frightening.

The film shows LaMotta as a tough-as-nails middleweight contender who insists on doing things his way. He refuses to play ball with the mob—Mafia boss Tommy Como is played by Nicholas Colasanto, "Coach" on TV's *Cheers*—and as a result, he is denied a title shot.

Como tells Joey, "Your brother can beat all the Sugar Ray Robinsons and Tony Janeros in the world, but he's not getting a title shot. Not without us, he's not."

Reluctantly, LaMotta agrees to tank a fight against Billy Fox so the mob can make a killing betting against him. He is rewarded by getting a chance to fight Marcel Cerdan of France for the middleweight championship. LaMotta defeats Cerdan on a TKO to finally win the championship belt.

Lean and muscular thanks to months of training, De Niro looks like a world-class boxer. He studied tapes of LaMotta for hours, so he has the Bronx Bull's crouching, wade-in style down to perfection. There was nothing pretty or scientific about LaMotta. He was a brawler, plain and simple, and when De Niro lowers his shoulders and moves in on an opponent, you feel like it is 1948 and you're ringside at the old Garden.

Even more compelling is the character De Niro creates outside the ring. In the ring the violence is understood; blood flies, but there are rules. It is the rest of the time that LaMotta is the most frightening. There is a look of malevolence in his eyes, and you never know when it will erupt. He could lash out at any second. It could be something he sees or, worse, something he imagines. De Niro puts a very unsettling tick in that time bomb.

Much of LaMotta's rage is rooted in jealousy. He is convinced Vickie, his beautiful young wife, is unfaithful. He believes she's sleeping with the same Mafia guys he has hated for years. Later, he adds Joey to the list of suspects. When a brooding LaMotta walks into the bedroom and asks Vickie, "Where were you today?" we cringe because we know what's coming. There is no indication she has done anything wrong, but the look on his face says it doesn't matter.

"Jake, don't start, OK?" she says.

She has been through this dozens of times, deflecting Jake's questions about various men, including total strangers, such as Tony Janero whom she off-handedly refers to as "good-looking." When Jake meets Janero in the ring, he smashes his face to a bloody pulp and then smirks at Vickie as Janero falls to the canvas. It is unspeakably cruel, but for the Raging Bull, totally in character.

This time, Jake attacks Vickie, slapping her and throwing her to the floor. Then he storms into his brother's house, pulls him away from the dinner table and, while Joey's wife and kids look on, he knocks him through a glass door and pummels him. He is convinced the two are having an affair. Why? He didn't like the way Joey kissed Vickie earlier in the day. "You kissed her on the mouth," Jake says. That was enough to start him thinking.

Is it any wonder that, by the end of the film, Jake is alone? Vicky has left him and Joey has disowned him and when he finally goes to jail for pimping out an underaged girl in his seedy Miami nightclub, he has no one to call and nowhere to turn.

Raging but no longer bullish, the flabby ex-champion bangs his head against the wall of his cell, crying, "Why, why, why?" He pounds his fists into the concrete, the same fists that brought down the best middleweights in the world, but now it is just sound and fury signifying nothing.

"I'm not an animal," he says, sobbing. "I'm not an animal."

If it were anyone else, we would be sympathetic.

But it is Jake LaMotta. So we're not.

CHEERS: De Niro is at the top of his game, making LaMotta a fearsome force of nature. Pesci holds his own in their joint scenes, which is no small feat.

This was the first of three landmark Scorsese films featuring the two great stars. The chemistry among the three also lit up the screen in *Goodfellas* and *Casino*.

JEERS: It is a famous scene, but the end of the last LaMotta-Robinson fight is overdone. It is shown as a blinding flurry of punches that ends with LaMotta's blood dripping off the ring ropes. Yes, Robinson battered LaMotta in scoring the TKO, but it wasn't the savage butchering shown in the film.

WHAT THEY WROTE AT THE TIME: "Scorsese has made an unblinking study of authorized violence and the least sentimental boxing film of all time." —Ernest Schier, *Philadelphia Bulletin*

DON'T FAIL TO NOTICE: The scene in which LaMotta warms up in the dressing room, then makes the long walk through the tunnel to the ring in Briggs Stadium for the fight with Marcel Cerdan. Scorsese does it in one tracking shot. There are no cuts, no second or third cameras. It is one continuous shot that allows you to take that long walk with Jake and Joey and listen as the roar of the crowd grows louder.

Scorsese went on to use the same tracking technique for the famous nightclub scene in *Goodfellas*.

PIVOTAL SCENE: LaMotta agrees to throw the fight with Billy Fox, but he can't bring himself to hit the canvas. LaMotta never was knocked down, not once in his entire career, and he wasn't about to let the light-hitting Fox put him on the deck. So he leans against the ropes, drops his hands and lets Fox pound on him.

"Hit me, you bum," he mutters through his mouthpiece.

The referee stops the fight and the crowd boos.

LaMotta insists on doing it his way, even when he takes a dive.

BEST LINE: "He ain't pretty no more."—Tommy Como after LaMotta, in a jealous rage, brutalizes Tony Janero.

REALITY CHECK: In the film, LaMotta is shown battering Cerdan around the ring until the Frenchman finally quits on his stool after the 10th round. In reality, Cerdan was winning the fight until he tore a muscle in his right shoulder.

As Red Smith wrote, "With only his left, Cerdan fought on until his corner induced him to accept the inevitable and save himself for another night. Meanwhile, LaMotta was having hell's own time beating one side of Cerdan."

"I KNOW THAT GUY": Billy Fox is played by former WBA light heavyweight champion Eddie Mustafa Muhammad.

BET YOU DIDN'T KNOW: Robert De Niro broke two of Joe Pesci's ribs in the scene where they spar in the gymnasium.

SPORTS-ACTION GRADE: A-plus. The boxing scenes are very intense. They are shot so tight, you can almost feel the sweat and blood splash in your face. Thelma Schoonmaker's Oscar-winning editing keeps the pace suitably breathless.

REPEATED WATCHING QUOTIENT: *Raging Bull* is a great film, but it can leave you emotionally wasted. Rewatch it with caution.

MY FAVORITE SPORTS MOVIE: James Carville, Democratic strategist: "I love boxing. All the drama, the buildup, the brutality. I never miss a really good fight and you don't see many these days. *Raging Bull* is a tough movie to watch—it's so brutal—but it's magnificently done. The fight scenes are both carnivorous and ballet. And I wouldn't be the first to say that Robert De Niro's portrayal (of LaMotta) is one of the great acting performances ever."

4 THE NATURAL (1984–PG)

SPORT: BASEBALL | **STARS:** ROBERT REDFORD, GLENN CLOSE, WILFORD BRIMLEY
DIRECTOR: BARRY LEVINSON

When TriStar Pictures agreed to produce *The Natural*, many in the movie industry felt it was a mistake. The script, adapted from Bernard Malamud's 1952 novel, had been kicking around Hollywood for years. Jon Voight, Michael Douglas and Nick Nolte all expressed an interest at one time or another, but no studio was willing to invest in it.

Sports movies are a risky proposition. A few succeed at the box office, but more fail. Also, Malamud's original story was rather dark with overtones of Homer and Greek mythology. How were you going to sell that to baseball fans? And if a movie about baseball couldn't even attract baseball fans, well, what was the point?

But in 1983, Robert Redford saw the script. He was looking for an opportunity to work with director Barry Levinson and he knew Levinson had always wanted to make a baseball movie. They took the idea to TriStar, and

on the strength of Redford's name, and Levinson's success with the film *Diner*, the studio agreed to do the film.

Still, there were doubts. "Redford goes into *The Natural* with two strikes against him," wrote syndicated columnist Ivor Davis. "Baseball, that traditionally iffy film subject, and middle-aged disillusionment and failure in the character." There was a third potential strike: the 46-year-old Redford trying to pass for a major league ballplayer.

The producers resolved one issue—the disillusionment—by changing the story. In Malamud's novel, Roy Hobbs is a tragic figure who literally strikes out at the end. In the film, the script by Roger Towne (brother of Oscar-winner Robert Towne) has Hobbs hitting a mammoth home run to win the pennant. As endings go, that's a little more uplifting.

"The movie's tone is very different," producer Mark

Johnson said. "Ours is a story about a man who is given a second chance and what he does with it. The book is cynical, ours is hopeful."

On the other matter—Redford's credibility as a ballplayer—the producers and writers did not have to do a thing. Redford played a lot of baseball in his youth, and even in his forties he was in good shape, so he was believable as Roy Hobbs. Okay, it was a stretch when he played Hobbs as a teenager, but when he threw the ball, that smooth southpaw motion was a pleasure to watch. And when he picked up a bat as the older Roy, well....

"Robert Redford's swing is maybe the best acting he's ever done," wrote Wilfrid Sheed in the *New York Times*.

"Redford plays so authentically, you want to sign him up," wrote Roger Angell in *The New Yorker*.

The film opens with Hobbs as a boy, playing catch in the fields with his farmer father. One night, lightning splits a tree behind the house and young Roy carves a bat out of the wood. He engraves the name "Wonderboy" on the barrel.

It isn't long before Roy (now played by Redford) is 19 and riding the train to Chicago for a tryout with the Cubs. Along the way, he encounters "the Whammer" (Joe Don Baker), a thinly disguised version of Babe Ruth. The scout who found Roy bets sportswriter Max Mercy (Robert Duvall) that the kid can strike out the Whammer on three pitches. When the train stops, they find an open field and Roy does, indeed, blow three fastballs past the Whammer.

The mysterious Harriet Bird (Barbara Hershey) watches the contest and the next thing you know, she is sitting with Roy on the train asking, "Have you ever read Homer?" Right away, you get a bad feeling. She has a weird look in her eye and she is dressed entirely in black. You keep waiting for the alarm to go off in Roy's head, but he is so naive he tells this creepy stranger about his dreams.

"Someday when I walk down the street, people will say: 'There goes Roy Hobbs,' the best there ever was, the best there will ever be in the game,' " he says.

Roy doesn't realize it, but he has just walked into the black widow's web. In Chicago, Harriet invites him to her hotel room where she shoots him with a silver bullet. It seems Harriet is a deranged woman on a mission to kill "the best" in every sport. She planned to take out the

Whammer (she was giving him the eye on the train) but when she saw Roy in action, he became the target instead.

It is a bizarre scene—and not very well explained in the movie—but it is based on a true story. In 1949, a woman named Ruth Ann Steinhagen shot Eddie Waitkus, first baseman of the Philadelphia Phillies, in Chicago's Edgewater Beach Hotel. Police reports indicate she was a delusional baseball groupie who was infatuated with Waitkus. We've seen that stalker syndrome repeated many times.

Harriet Bird is a different story. She appears out of nowhere, shoots the hero and leaps to her death from the hotel window. We're left wondering: "What was all that about?" It is the weakest part of the movie, but it sets up the real story which is Roy's comeback.

Like Waitkus, Hobbs survives the shooting. Waitkus returned to baseball the following season and helped the Phillies win the National League pennant. Hobbs isn't as lucky. He drops out of sight for 16 years. He resurfaces in 1939 as a middle-aged rookie with the New York Knights, a last-place team in the National League.

When Hobbs reports, manager Pop Fisher (Wilford Brimley) doesn't want any part of him. "Mister," he says, "you don't start playing ball at your age, you retire." Hobbs will not discuss his past or why he was away from the game for more than a decade. He was playing outfield for a semi-pro team when a Knights scout saw him and signed him for $500. Fisher puts Hobbs on the bench and ignores him.

Finally, Fisher tires of the lackadaisical play of right fielder Bump Bailey (Michael Madsen). He benches Bailey and sends Hobbs up to hit for him. "Come on, Hobbs," Fisher says. "Knock the cover off the ball." Which he does—literally. Hobbs hits the ball so hard, the seams explode and the insides unravel. The outfielders are chasing a tangle of string while the winning runs cross the plate. The legend is born.

Given the chance to perform, Hobbs becomes the best player in baseball. But evil forces are at work. The team owner, the Judge (Robert Prosky), will gain full control of the ball club from Fisher if the Knights fail to win the pennant. It looked like a sure bet until Hobbs came along. Now the team is winning. The Judge offers Hobbs a bribe to tank the rest of the season. Hobbs flatly refuses.

But the Judge and his gambler sidekick Gus (Darren McGavin) have a Plan B. Actually, it's Plan Double B as in "Blonde Bombshell." They introduce Hobbs to Memo Paris (Kim Basinger). Just like with Harriet Bird, Roy ignores the warning signs. Even Pop Fisher, Memo's uncle, tells Roy, "She's a jinx." But it's too late, Roy is smitten. Pretty soon, he is scoring in the bedroom but striking out on the field. He falls into a deep slump and the Knights go into a tailspin.

The team goes to Chicago and his old girlfriend from back home, Iris (Glenn Close), surprises him by coming to the game. The sight of Iris in her shimmering white dress snaps Roy out of his funk. He hits the game-winning home run one day and hits four more homers the next. After the last game, he walks Iris home and tells her the whole story of what happened to him.

"My life didn't turn out the way I expected," he says.

"I believe we have two lives," Iris says. "The life we learn with and the life we live with after that."

Second chances, in other words.

Iris tells Roy she has a 16-year-old son whose father lives in New York. Hello, Roy? This is your son, get it? It takes awhile—in fact, Iris has to put it in the form of a note and send it to the dugout—but finally Roy figures it out.

The Knights' season comes down to the final weekend. They need one win to clinch the pennant. The Judge will do anything to stop them. At a party, Memo puts poison in Roy's drink and it causes the bullet wound to rupture in his stomach. The doctor tells Roy if he plays again, it could cost him his life. Without Roy, the Knights lose three in a row and it looks like the season is down the drain.

But on the final night, Roy shows up and with the blood seeping through his jersey, he hits a ball that clears the roof and crashes into the stadium lights, setting off a series of explosions, allowing Roy to do his final home run trot through a shower of fireworks.

"*The Natural* is a movie that stays with you," said actor Tom Selleck. "You think the movie is over when he hits the home run but then it goes to the shot of him playing catch with his son on the farm, and it adds another layer to it. His life has come full circle. Now he's back where he started as a boy and he's playing catch with his son.

That's how most people think of baseball—a game that links the generations."

Chase Utley, the Philadelphia Phillies All-Star second baseman who has been called "The Natural" by some baseball people, loves it as well. "It's old-school in a lot of ways, but I could relate to what [Hobbs] was going through and how much it meant to finally get a chance to play in the big leagues. He knew he might only have that one season, so when he says, 'You'll get the best I've got', you know he means it.

"Some things are exaggerated, obviously, like the part where he knocks the cover off the ball and they're throwing around a ball of string. But it's such a good movie, you don't mind. There's a part of you that says, 'That could never happen', but there's another part of you that says, 'That's pretty cool.' If you're really into the story, you go with it."

🏆 **CHEERS:** Redford is perfectly cast as Hobbs. He chose the number 9 for his uniform as an homage to his baseball idol, Hall of Famer Ted Williams.

🏆 **MORE CHEERS:** The camerawork of Caleb Deschanel was nominated for an Oscar, justly so. The shots of Roy pitching to the Whammer with the sun setting over his shoulder are pure visual poetry.

🏆 **JEERS:** Max Mercy, the sportswriter, is a shady character who doesn't ring true. At one point he tells Hobbs, "I'm here to protect this game from the likes of you." Later, he is supplying photographs to the Judge for the purpose of blackmailing Hobbs.

⚾ **BET YOU DIDN'T KNOW:** The baseball scenes were filmed in War Memorial Stadium, the former home of the Buffalo Bills. The stadium was abandoned at the time and it was torn down shortly after the film was completed.

⚾ **BET YOU DIDN'T KNOW II:** Some of the movie's best quotes are borrowed from real-life baseball stars. Roy's quote about being "the best there ever was, the best there will ever be in the game" is the mantra Ted Williams repeated to himself as a youth. And the line, "To be a ballplayer, you have to have a lot of little boy in you," comes from Hall of Fame catcher Roy Campanella.

🏆 **BET YOU DIDN'T KNOW III:** The day that Texas Rangers slugger Josh Hamilton put on his power show in the 2008 All-Star Home Run Derby, he watched *The Natural* in his hotel room. While he was viewing the movie, he was interrupted by a knock on the door. Baseball officials picked that moment for his random drug test. "Right when Redford's character was about to hit that final home run, the pee guy came in," Hamilton said afterward. "I told him, 'Hold on, I've got to watch this.'"

🏆 **BET YOU DIDN'T KNOW IV:** Glenn Close, who was nominated for an Oscar as Best Supporting Actress, passed time on the set by playing pepper with the guys. An avid softball player in her youth, Close said her skill with the bat earned her new respect from the crew.

✒ **WHAT THEY WROTE AT THE TIME:** "*The Natural* is an impeccably made but quite strange fable about success and failure in America."—*Variety*

☞ **DON'T FAIL TO NOTICE:** The bronze plaque honoring Bump Bailey is misspelled. It says, "In Memorium" instead of "In Memoriam."

✔ **REALITY CHECK:** Baseball historian Gene Kirby, who served as technical advisor on the film, told Wilford Brimley and Richard Farnsworth that no coach or player in that era had a mustache. Kirby felt they should shave for the sake of accuracy, but the actors had their mustaches for years and were allowed to keep them.

😎 **"I KNOW THAT GUY":** Former Cleveland Indian outfielder Joe Charboneau plays one of the Knights, and former Milwaukee Brave Sibby Sisti, a Buffalo native, plays the Pittsburgh manager.

99 **BEST LINE:** "My Dad always wanted me to be a baseball player," Hobbs says before the final game.

"Well, you're the best one I ever had," Pop Fisher says, "and you're the best goddamn hitter I ever saw. Go suit up."

📽 **PIVOTAL SCENE:** In his final at bat, Hobbs breaks his lucky (some might say enchanted) bat "Wonderboy." He turns to the bat boy and says, "Pick me out a winner, Bobby." He comes back with his own bat, "The Savoy Special," the one Hobbs carved for him. He says, "Use this one." Hobbs smiles, takes the bat and hits the pennant-winning home run.

"I know it's fairy-tale-ish," ESPN's Chris Berman says, "but the look on the kid's face, you don't get any better than that."

★ **SPORTS-ACTION GRADE:** A. Levinson brought in a former major league pitcher, Frank "Spec" Shea, to school the actors on how ballplayers looked in the '30s. Pitchers double-pumped in their windups, hitters had unusual stances and swings. With Shea's help, *The Natural* got it right.

🎞 **MY FAVORITE SPORTS MOVIE:** Tony Romo, Dallas Cowboys quarterback: "There was humor, suspense, great music and some very nice baseball scenes. How could you not love the way Robert Redford carried himself throughout the movie? He had confidence. He was cool. You just knew he was going to come through in the end."

🎞 **MY FAVORITE SPORTS MOVIE, TOO:** Super Bowl-winning coach Tom Coughlin: "I'm a sucker for a great ending. I like the All-American story. It's like the 2007 New York Giants—'Tell us you can't do it.' In this case, you had a guy who missed years of playing ball. All of a sudden, he appears on the scene. Everybody is trying to figure out who he is.

"At the end, he is at risk of serious injury, but he goes up to the plate and hits the home run. What else is there? That's what life is all about, isn't it? The drama of a moment in time being created and then producing."

5 BULL DURHAM (1988–R)

SPORT: BASEBALL | STARS: KEVIN COSTNER, SUSAN SARANDON, TIM ROBBINS
DIRECTOR: RON SHELTON

The standard rap on *Bull Durham* over the years has been that while it's a sexy and comedic love triangle, it's more of a chick flick than a sports movie. The portrayal of minor league baseball, some critics charge, just doesn't ring true.

So we asked some real ballplayers what they thought.

Brad Lidge, Philadelphia Phillies closer: "Of every baseball movie I've ever seen, it's the one that tells it like it is. The bus rides, the sweltering hot days, the knuckleheads you encounter along the way. Trust me, that was exactly what the minors were like."

Joe Morgan, Hall of Fame second baseman: "I played a season in Durham and watching *Bull Durham* made me feel like I was reliving it. The scenes of the players doing kid things like wetting down the field and sliding around in the mud is the way it is, basically, because most minor leaguers are kids."

Prince Fielder, Milwaukee Brewers first baseman: "My favorite scene is when the pitcher is called into the office and told he is going up to the majors. It reminds me of when I got the call up from Nashville. You just walk around with this big smile on your face."

Aaron Heilman, Chicago Cubs reliever: "Kevin Costner looks like the veteran guy who was stuck in the minors, kind of resigned to it, but still with enough pride to do the job. The scenes on the bus where the young guys are listening to him, trying to soak up his knowledge—that's how it is."

Good enough for us.

In the course of researching this book, we interviewed dozens of major leaguers, asking each his favorite sports movie. The one they mentioned the most? *Bull Durham*. In fact, more than a few players say they routinely slip lines from the film into their daily ballpark conversation.

Major League catcher Chris Coste—whose 10 years in the minors make him a real-life version of Costner's Crash Davis character—says, "The conversation at the pitcher's mound (from *Bull Durham*) actually became a running joke between (former Phillies teammate) Clay Condrey and me. Every time he came in, I would go out there and say, 'I hear candlesticks make a good wedding gift.' That kept things loose. It's amazing how accurate the dialog from that movie is."

Not surprising, however, since *Bull Durham* was written and directed by Ron Shelton, who spent five seasons in the Baltimore Orioles minor league system playing with future major league stars Don Baylor and Bobby Grich. When Shelton lovingly shows the quirks and daily patterns of life in the Class-A Carolina League, he does so from the vantage of a guy who's been there.

Bull Durham—the first (and best) of a half-dozen sports movies created by Shelton—is a rarity in the genre. First off, it combines sports, comedy and romance—a difficult triple play to pull off. It is neither sentimental nor reverential. It is not about superstars, but mostly the fringe players who scruff around in baseball's minor leagues. It doesn't end in tragedy, or in the underdogs rising to their shining moment. In fact, the hero of the film ends up getting cut. At the same time, it shows a love and respect for the game, embodied in Crash's impassioned creed calling for (among other things) a Constitutional ban on Astroturf and the designated hitter.

The set-up for the movie is this: Crash, the proverbial "player to be named later," is a 30-something minor league catcher who finds his Triple-A contract reassigned to the Single-A Durham Bulls. Seems the organization has a big-time prospect, brilliantly named Ebby Calvin "Nuke" LaLoosh (Tim Robbins), who possesses a "million-dollar arm and a five-cent head." In exchange for tutoring Nuke on and off the field, Crash gets to keep getting paid to play baseball.

His resentment is palpable. Crash is a guy who would cut off his arm to make it, who speaks of his brief stint in the majors as "the 21 greatest days of my life." His student, meanwhile, is a callow kid who defines success by his Porsche 911 with a quadrophonic Blaupunkt.

Still, Crash knows he must point Nuke toward "The Show." So he offers these lessons:

- Don't think. You can only hurt the ball club. Never shake off your catcher, or he may just tip off the hitter on what pitch is coming.
- When you get in a fight with a drunk, never throw a punch with your pitching hand.
- Don't try to strike everybody out. Strikeouts are boring, in addition to being fascist. Ground balls are more democratic.
- A player needs to learn his clichés before talking to the media. Study them, memorize them. They are your friends.
- You'll never make it to the big leagues with fungus on your shower shoes. Think classy and you'll be classy. If you win 20 in The Show, you can let the fungus grow back and the press will think you're colorful. Until you win 20, however, it just means you are a slob.
- Be cocky, even when you're getting beat. Play the game with fear and arrogance.
- Respect a streak. If you think you're suddenly winning because you are having sex, or not having sex, or wearing a woman's garter belt—well then, you are.

Speaking of sex, that's where Nuke's other teacher comes in. Annie Savoy (Susan Sarandon) is the ultimate groupie, a William Blake-quoting community college instructor who, each season, pledges her heart and body to a single player on the Bulls. Nuke—the future superstar—is the obvious candidate except, well, the older and wiser Crash keeps getting in the way. There's a brilliant scene early on, where Annie auditions the two men for the role of lover. Crash walks out on the opportunity for sex (something players *never* do), saying he's "been around too long to try out for anything." If he doesn't win her heart right there, he certainly wins her mind.

"And so this strange kind of ménage thing happens among the three of them," Sarandon said on a 2008 TV show in which the American Film Institute named *Bull Durham* the No. 5 sports movie of all time (hmmm, we agree). "Who does she choose? The young buck with lots of energy—not too much knowledge—but lots of raw talent? Or the guy who maybe doesn't have the talent as much, but has the brains and the love of the sport? He can still hit them out of the park, but isn't going to go any further."

The romantic triangle evolves over the course of the 1987 Carolina League season. While Annie keeps sleeping with Nuke (or not sleeping with him, so as to avoid jinxing a winning streak), she and Crash find themselves irresistibly pulled together. It all ends up in satin bathrobes, bathtub sex, dancing to the Dominoes' "Sixty Minute Man," and sharing a bowl of Wheaties. Very erotic stuff, trust us.

In the end, Nuke (thanks to lessons learned) gets promoted all the way from Single-A to the Big Leagues in one season—a bit of a stretch, to be sure. Crash gets released, plays out the string on another team (supposedly breaking the all-time minor league record for home runs), retires and comes back to Annie. Presumably, they are looking forward to a life together; he as a coach for Visalia in the California League and she, we suppose, as a composition teacher at the College of the Sequoias. You can start a good debate on the topic of whether they'd still be together after all these years.

Bull Durham captures the authenticity, the lingo and the funny side of baseball better than any other film ever made. If Annie Savoy is the high priestess of what she calls "The Church of Baseball," consider us devotees.

CHEERS:
This is a terrifically acted movie, which makes it astounding that not a single performer was nominated for an Oscar. Costner—coming off of *The Untouchables* and *No Way Out*—is in his prime here (Hey, remember when he *had* a prime?). Sarandon, at age 42, is at her sexiest since *Atlantic City* in 1980. And this was Robbins' breakout role—in addition to letting him meet his lifelong romantic partner in Sarandon.

Even the supporting actors are outstanding. Take note of the late Trey Wilson, who plays flustered manager Joe Riggins ("Lollygaggers!"), and Robert Wuhl, who steals a few scenes as pitching coach/wedding-gift advisor Larry Hockett. We still crack up every time we watch him execute that goofy run out to the mound with his hands shoved down his jacket pockets.

JEERS:
Yes, Robbins is a fine actor who nails the naïve bravado of a flame-throwing bonus baby. But his athletic skills are another matter. His delivery looks like a wounded giraffe trying Tae Bo and sneezing halfway through the routine. Robbins claims he hit 85 miles per hour on the speed gun during filming. "Not with that pitching motion he didn't," Arizona Diamondbacks pitcher Brandon Webb told us.

★ SPORTS-ACTION GRADE:
Solid A. Robbins aside, the actors in *Bull Durham* can really play. Costner, a former college player, "had very good throwing mechanics," says Webb. His batting isn't bad either—the switch-hitter actually knocked two homers with the cameras rolling. Most of the other actors in uniforms were college or minor-league players; in fact two of them—Butch Davis and Kelly Heath—made it to the majors. They were trained by real-life Durham manager Grady Little who, of course, went on to crush the hearts of Red Sox fans in the 2003 American League Championship Series.

✎ WHAT THEY WROTE AT THE TIME:
"Susan Sarandon is marvelous in a great role, and I hope she is remembered at Oscar time. She is required to play every position, if you will, and we're not talking just baseball. She is sexy and bright and funny. It is a full, wonderful character and she is equal to it."—Gene Siskel, *Sneak Previews*

☻ BET YOU DIDN'T KNOW:
The character of Nuke LaLoosh is loosely based on minor-league legend Steve Dalkowski. In a nine-year career, Dalkowski struck out an astounding 12.6 batters per nine innings—but he also walked 12.3. Unlike Nuke, he never made it to The Show.

☻ BET YOU DIDN'T KNOW II:
The pool hall scene in which Nuke tells Crash he is being promoted to the majors was re-shot a few weeks after production. The original had Crash in a black whorehouse playing the Righteous Brothers' "Unchained Melody" to a 60-year-old hooker when Robbins barged in to break the news. In that version, Costner told *Entertainment Weekly*, "I was drunk and . . . we went out and fought in the alley, with a bunch of black hookers cheering for me." Costner said the scene was redone, because, "The pool hall was somehow thought to be a better experience for the audience, because we didn't want to see (Crash) with a black woman, I guess. But it was perfectly in line with who he was."

MORE CHEERS: Make sure you get the 20th-anniversary DVD, which has outstanding commentary by Shelton. Among other things, we learn that Sarandon won the role by showing up for her audition in a sexy red-and-white dress; that Costner, despite his ability, had athletic insecurities; and that Robbins' Elaine Benes-style dance floor gyrations were choreographed by Paula Abdul.

GOOFS: In some of the game scenes—supposedly set in the balmy Carolina summer—you can see steam coming from the actors' mouths. That's because they were filmed during a November cold snap. Actress Jenny Robertson, who plays Annie's pal Millie, says on the DVD commentary that actors tried to prevent the effect by sucking on ice cubes right before shooting.

REPEATED WATCHING QUOTIENT: Extremely high. This is a richly textured film that reveals something new upon every new viewing.

DON'T FAIL TO NOTICE: The note Crash writes to Annie in the dugout does not say, "I want to make love to you," as Millie reads aloud. It says, "Let's fuck sometime," which you can see over Crash's shoulder as he writes it.

DON'T FAIL TO NOTICE II: Those aren't baseballs that Annie is hitting at the batting cage. They're tennis balls, tossed underhand from about 10 feet away to Susan Sarandon. Look closely and you can tell.

CASTING CALL: Kurt Russell, a friend of Shelton's who also played minor-league baseball, helped develop the script and wanted to play Crash Davis. The studio reportedly preferred Costner.

BEST LINE: Crash, when asked by Annie what he believes in: "I believe in the soul, the cock, the pussy, the small of a woman's back, the hanging curve ball, high fiber, good scotch, that the novels of Susan Sontag are self-indulgent, overrated crap. I believe Lee Harvey Oswald acted alone. I believe there ought to be a constitutional amendment outlawing Astroturf and the designated hitter. I believe in the sweet spot, soft-core pornography, opening your presents Christmas morning rather than Christmas Eve, and I believe in long, slow, deep, soft, wet kisses that last three days."

"I KNOW THAT GUY": Early on, Durham's manager calls a slumping player, Bobby, into his office, and tells the kid he is being released by the organization. Hey, wait. Isn't that Everett—Shooter's son—from *Hoosiers*? Actor David Neidorf didn't have much of a career, but he's the only guy who appears in two of our top-five ranked films.

REALITY CHECK: Much is made of Crash chasing the all-time minor league home run mark, but his total of 247 wouldn't crack the top 20 in real life. Hector Espino, who spent most of his career in the Mexican League, heads that list with 484.

MY FAVORITE SPORTS MOVIE: *Sopranos* star James Gandolfini: "I just watched it again, and what hit me was the look on Kevin Costner's face when he is cut by the team. These guys give up everything for the love of this game; they love what they do and all of a sudden, they can't do it anymore. It really showed on his face. There was a lot of funny stuff, too, about baseball and life, but I'll remember the look on Costner's face and how that kind of thing affects a person. I loved that."

MY FAVORITE SPORTS MOVIE, TOO: Seven-time NHL All-Star Mike Modano: "It's more about athletes' off-the-field lives than the sports themselves, and that's what I really like. It gives a great insight about what it's like to be an athlete. It's a staple on our team flights, and we throw around quotes in the dressing room all the time."

ALL-TIME MOVIE BASEBALL TEAM

WE'VE CHOSEN OUR ALL-TIME, ALL-MOVIE, ALL-STAR BASE-BALL TEAM. ONLY FICTIONAL CHARACTERS ALLOWED—SORRY, GARY COOPER, YOUR TURN AS LOU GEHRIG IN *THE PRIDE OF THE YANKEES* DOESN'T MAKE THE CUT. HERE'S WHAT THE SCOUTS HAVE TO SAY ABOUT OUR 25-MAN ROSTER:

C—Crash Davis (Kevin Costner in *Bull Durham*)
Smart veteran who still has a power swing well into his thirties and won't embarrass as a late-season call-up, having once spent 21 days in the bigs. Knows how to deal with media and handle young pitchers, although there is suspicion that he occasionally tips off hitters on what's coming.

1B—Jack Elliott (Tom Selleck in *Mr. Baseball*)
Former World Series MVP seemed washed up a year ago, and has tried to revitalize his career in Japan. His prima donna attitude first carried over to the Far East, but recent reports suggest a better attitude. One concern: Why does a guy playing for the Chunichi Dragons insist on wearing a Detroit Tigers cap?

2B—Marla Hooch (Megan Cavanagh in *A League of Their Own*)
"What a hitter!" Difficult to get good scouting reports, because the camera always seems so far away. Raised by her widowed father to be a great ballplayer, let's just say her beauty is in the inside. A distaff version of Dan Uggla—and we do mean Uggla.

3B—Benjamin Franklin Rodriguez (Mike Vitar in *The Sandlot*)
"The Jet" is a leader of young men who shows enough promise at age 12 that we predict he'll have a major league career into his 30s—albeit mostly as a pinch runner. Has enough speed to outrun an angry English Mastiff. One of two players on this list to literally hit the cover off the ball.

SS—Joe Hardy (Tab Hunter in *Damn Yankees!*)
Broke into majors by hitting .524 over his first half season with Washington. May be the best player in history, but we've got questions about his character. Who is this Mr. Applegate he keeps hanging out with? A steroid dealer? A fixer? Something doesn't seem kosher.

OF—Roy Hobbs (Robert Redford in *The Natural*)
Like Hardy, an older player who showed up out of nowhere to dominate the league. Best power hitter since "The Whammer," he also displays the kind of arm that once may have struck out baseball's top hitter. A bit mysterious; seems to be covering up a shady past.

OF—Willie Mays Hayes (Wesley Snipes in *Major League*)
Self-absorbed but enthusiastic. Has learned to use his great speed as an advantage—he tacks a sliding glove above his locker with each stolen base and, last we checked, he was nearing 100. Shows promise of developing Barry Bonds-like power in the future (like his doppelganger in *The Fan*).

OF—Kelly Leak (Jackie Earle Haley in *The Bad News Bears*)
Smooth-fielding power hitter who has got experience beyond his years (riding a motorcycle and picking up girls at age 13), but we fear that two-pack-a-day cigarette habit will stunt his growth and sap his wind. Definitely has issues with authority.

SP—Henry "Author" Wiggen (Michael Moriarty in *Bang the Drum Slowly*)
Intellectual righthander throws like Tom Seaver at his best. A bit of a snob, he's had trouble in the past connecting with teammates. Recently, however, he seems to have developed a great on-field, off-field chemistry with catcher Bruce Pearson.

SP—Bingo Long (Billy Dee Williams in *Bingo Long*)
Reminds scouts of Satchel Paige in his prime, getting by on trick pitches and guile. Certainly has guts—shoos his defensive teammates off the field for the first pitch of the game, his so-called "invite pitch." No one has ever hit it.

SP—Prof. Vernon Simpson/King Kelly (Ray Milland in *It Happens Every Spring*)
A brainiac with a rag arm who somehow managed to win 38 games last season plus three more in the World Series. He has passed every drug test, but somehow we think he must be cheating some way or another. Perhaps authorities should check his glove for illegal substances.

SP—Steve Nebraska (Brendan Fraser in *The Scout*)
Raw talent discovered in the Mexican jungle, he combines a 110-mph fastball with a Donovan McNabb-like case of nerves that prompts him to throw up on the pitcher's mound. It is not hyperbole to predict he will throw a 27-strikeout perfect game some day—in fact, we foresee it.

Closer—Rick Vaughn (Charlie Sheen in *Major League*)
The "Wild Thing" can hit 100 on the speed gun, even if he can't always see the plate through his Coke-bottle glasses. His background raises questions—there was that jail term and the fling with a teammate's wife. But if you can bring it like he does, we'll overlook anything.

6 SLAP SHOT (1977–R)

SPORT: HOCKEY | STARS: PAUL NEWMAN, MICHAEL ONTKEAN | DIRECTOR: GEORGE ROY HILL

When it first came out, the comedy *Slap Shot* was dismissed by critics as vulgar and trivial and a misplaced tribute to on-ice thuggery. Many theatergoers were appalled to hear such blue language from Paul Newman (even Butch Cassidy never used *those* words). Others couldn't relate to a two-hour paean to the garage sport of minor league hockey.

The movie pulled in $28 million at the box office, ranking it below sports-comedy stink-bombs of the era such as *The Main Event* and *Semi-Tough*. Within a matter of weeks, *Slap Shot* skated in and out of the theaters. It appeared destined to be forgotten.

Except. . . .

Except that somewhere along the way, this uproarious movie evolved from being an amusing throwaway into a cult classic—if we define cult classic as one whose fans see it dozens of times and gleefully recite every line.

"It's the best bus movie ever," said former Philadelphia Phillies catcher Chris Coste, referring to the films that teams like to watch on those 300-mile road trips. Coste, who played beer-league hockey as a young man in North Dakota (his missing front tooth serves as proof), added, "I've quoted every line from that movie millions of times—'putting on the foil' or, 'Eff-ing machine stole my quarter' or, 'Old-time hockey, like Eddie Shore and Dit Clapper.'"

And Toe Blake.

So how did *Slap Shot* grow in prestige over the years to the point that most sports fans (including us, obviously) place it on their top-ten lists?

We're not quite sure. But we figure that once people got past the obscenity (admittedly, it's tough to sail past "Hanrahan—Suzanne sucks pussy! . . . She's a dyke!") and accepted the minor-league theme (perhaps the success of *Bull Durham* opened minds), they discovered that *Slap Shot* might just be the most hilarious sports movie ever made.

Hey, the critics also panned *It's a Wonderful Life* when that first came out.

Granted, Newman's portrayal of Coach Reggie Dunlop isn't as heart-warming as Jimmy Stewart's George Bailey. But let's just say that it would be a tough Christmas Eve call if competing networks aired the bucolic idealism of Bedford Falls against the grimy games at the War Memorial Auditorium.

Slap Shot is set in the fictional town of Charlestown, PA. Newman's Reg Dunlop is the aging and unsuccessful player-coach of the Federal League's Charlestown Chiefs, who play uninspired hockey before sparse and hostile crowds.

The town's largest mill is set to close, which sparks rumors that the Chiefs will be shut down as well. So Dunlop is struggling to hold his team together and, at the same time, trying to ascertain the identity of the Chiefs' owner so that he can lobby for his players.

Meanwhile, the Chiefs' cheapskate general manager, Joe McGrath (Strother Martin), reaches down to the low-level Iron League to sign three siblings—the bespectacled, semi-adolescent Hanson Brothers. The boys bring their toy cars along on road trips and wrap their knuckles with aluminum foil before games, the better to pack a nasty punch.

Dunlop is initially horrified and won't even put the trio on the ice. When he eventually lets them play, the Hansons create chaos, brutalizing the opposition and thrilling Charlestown's long-suffering loyalists. Other Chiefs players follow their goonish lead—except for leading scorer Ned Braden (Michael Ontkean), a Princeton grad repulsed by the Cro-Magnon approach.

Anyway, the Chiefs start winning games, drawing crowds and inciting police actions. To old heads, this may sound a lot like the Philadelphia Flyers of the mid-1970s. So it shouldn't be surprising that Hockey Hall of Famer Bobby Clarke—the captain of those Broad Street Bullies—cites *Slap Shot* as his favorite film. "I started laughing during the opening scene and I never quit laughing during the whole movie," Clarke said.

And does Clarke see any parallel between the Chiefs and his Flyers? "Well . . . we only had two brothers on our team (Joe and Jimmy Watson)," he said. "They had three."

After watching *Slap Shot* for about the 874th time, we decided to list the reasons why it holds up better than ever three decades after its initial lukewarm reception:

1. For a farce, the screenplay rings extremely true to life. *Slap Shot* was written by Nancy Dowd (yes, a woman!) whose brother Ned played for the Johnstown (PA) Jets, the team on which the Chiefs team is based. Intrigued by Ned's tales, Nancy gave him a tape recorder to document life behind the scenes in minor league hockey. Dowd, by the way, shared an Oscar for best screenplay one year later for writing *Coming Home*, a super-serious film about returning Vietnam veterans.

Nearly every character, from barfing goalie Denis Lemieux ("Who own da Chief?") to toupee-wearing announcer Jim Carr ("Everyone is on their feet yelling, 'Kill! Kill!' This is hockey!") to reporter/stooge Dickie Dunn ("I tried to capture the spirit of the thing.") is based on a real person. Indeed, to this day, hockey players refer to a reporter who writes false rumors as a "Dickie Dunn."

"It's a spoof, but anyone who has spent time around hockey knows all those characters," said veteran broadcaster Gary Thorne. "That *is* the minor league hockey life. That's how those guys live, how they travel, how they talk. You walk through a locker room before a game and you'll hear guys say: 'I'm going to get so-and-so tonight.' Hockey people decried the movie and said it would hurt the sport. I think it actually helped the sport."

A couple of side notes here: First, Dowd originally planned her project to be a documentary. Director George Roy Hill convinced her it would work better as a full-length comedy. Second, the real-life Ned Dowd has a cameo in the movie, playing ultimate goon Ogie Ogilthorpe.

2. Newman's presence gives *Slap Shot* more than just star power. His acting chops (he appears in 80 percent of the scenes), help it graduate from being a series of goofy skits into a taut, plot-driven film. Okay, maybe we just exaggerated. But without Newman, this movie is *The Fish that Saved Charlestown*. With him, it's a film about broken dreams, working-class angst and love's longings—not to mention guys who flash the audience at fashion shows.

Newman said for years that he had more fun filming *Slap Shot* than any movie he ever made. "I always wanted to play for a team," he told *Time* magazine. "This gave me that chance." It also taught him how to curse like a player. "This is the raunchiest film I have ever done," he said in a promotional interview at the time of *Slap Shot's* release. "The language is heavy beyond blue, into purple almost. I think it will be tastefully vulgar."

The amazing thing to watch is how well Newman moves on the ice. He was 51 years old when *Slap Shot* was filmed (Dunlop is said to be 38), and the guy could flat-out skate. The only injury he sustained during filming came when he was sitting down. Watch the scene where Hanrahan (the goalie with the lesbian wife) dives into the penalty box to pummel Dunlop. Somehow, both actors managed to pull groin muscles at the same moment.

3. The marauding Hanson Brothers are the greatest auxiliary characters in the history of sports comedy, bar none. Better than Tanner Boyle in *The Bad News Bears*. Better than Pedro Cerrano in *Major League*. Better than Bob Barker in *Happy Gilmore*.

The look—stringy hair and black-rimmed coke-bottle glasses—is not contrived. That's who these guys were. The language, too, is genuine. Director Hill told the Hansons (actually brothers Steve and Jeff Carlson and David Hanson) to speak on camera as they spoke in real life. Even the toy racing cars are real.

The three, in fact, did play for the 1974-75 Johnstown Jets (as did a third genuine Carlson brother, Jack, who lost his part in the film when he was called up to the Edmonton Oilers). They finished 1-2-3 on the team in penalty minutes, started more than one brawl at the opening faceoff and, according to Jets coach Dick Roberge, really wrapped their fingers with aluminum foil until a league ruling outlawed taping their hands.

"They were very professional," Newman told *Sports Illustrated* in 2007. "And they were completely crazy. We drank a lot of beer."

The three Carlsons, plus Hanson, all eventually got to the NHL or its 1970s rival, the World Hockey Association. To this day they make a living by, well, being themselves—traveling to conventions and bar mitzvahs in full uniform and kibitzing with an adoring public.

And that's kind of the bottom line. More than 30 years after its release, *Slap Shot* is more popular than ever with the public. In a recent letter to the fan-based website *Slap Shot Nation*, Nancy Dowd wrote, "You wore the Halloween costumes, hosted the *Slap Shot* parties, memo-rized the lines, and laughed and laughed. That is the real measure of a motion picture, not the opening weekend grosses. When an object is embraced by a popular culture, it takes on a life of its own."

🍺 **CHEERS:** To George Roy Hill's insistence on hiring actors who knew their way around a hockey rink. In addition to the Hanson Brothers, Ontkean was a star player at the University of New Hampshire. And most of the thugs and extras were actual minor league skaters, right down to Andre "Poodle" Lussier, who, as you know, remains in semi-seclusion in Northern Quebec ever since the unfortunate Denny Pratt tragedy.

🍺 **JEERS:** Not that it ruins the movie, but near the end, *Slap Shot* dissolves from being a broad satire to being a *Three Stooges* comedy. The Native American war paint on Clarence "Screaming Buffalo" Swamptown is probably the tipping point.

✎ **WHAT THEY WROTE AT THE TIME:** "For all of its considerable merits, the film ultimately disappoints. It is a defect that *Slap Shot* shares with the current hit *Network*—a desire to present an editorial so corrosive that aesthetics, questions of form and proportion simply dissolve. . . . *Slap Shot* may have done a lot of fast skating and some solid body checking, but in the last period it makes a final costly slip—and misses its goal."—Richard Schickel, *Time*

☺ **GOOFS:** Ned Braden's legendary striptease defies the laws of physics—or at least film editing. Watch carefully. As he disrobes, Ned is clearly wearing a jockstrap *over* his long underwear. Near the end of the dance, the camera cuts away to show to show the referee handing Reg the league trophy ("Here you go, ya bum!"). When it cuts back to Ned, he is wearing only the jock—revealing his bare butt. Are we to believe that everyone was so distracted by the trophy presentation that Ned was able to slide off his underwear and put the jockstrap back on?

🗩 **BEST LINE:** Coach Reg Dunlop during a radio interview: "I have a personal announcement—I'm placing a personal bounty on the head of Tim McCracken. He's the coach and chief punk on that Syracuse team."

Radio announcer Jim Carr: "A bounty?"

Dunlop: "Yeah—a hundred bucks of my own money for the first of my men who really nails that creep. That's eight o'clock at the War Memorial."

👁 **REPEATED WATCHING QUOTIENT:** Don't take our word for it. Listen to comic star Mike Myers, who told *The Sporting News*, "To me, this is like *A Christmas Carol*. I watch it once a year."

☝ **DON'T FAIL TO NOTICE:** The player wearing uniform No. 7 for the Hyannis Port Presidents? That's Bruce Boudreau who—30 years later—became coach of the Washington Capitals. Boudreau got cast for the small role because he was playing for the Johnstown Jets at the time of filming.

"I was the little hog who stays in front of the net, because I knew where the camera was," Boudreau told the *Washington Post*. He even scores two goals in the movie's opening scene.

🎬 **PIVOTAL SCENE:** Initially, Reg is mortified by the Hanson Brothers and keeps them rooted to the bench. But in a game against Broome County, he needs to play them after another of his charges (Dave "Killer" Carlson) has his face rearranged in a fight. The first time the Hansons hit the ice, they become Tasmanian devils—fighting, wrestling, triple-teaming one poor sap and dragging a stick blade across the face of every player on the opposition bench. The Charlestown fans go crazy, and the beleaguered coach suddenly sees the future of his team. It certainly isn't "old time hockey."

⭐ **SPORTS-ACTION GRADE:** It earns a solid A. This really *was* minor league hockey in the 1970s.

😵 **"I KNOW THAT GUY":** Sex-crazed defenseman Morris Wanchuk (he of the Gene Simmons tongue) is played by actor Brad Sullivan. He went on to portray Al Capone's fur coat-wearing bookkeeper in *The Untouchables*, the guy who gets nabbed in the Canadian border raid and then shot by Frank Nitti in an elevator.

◀ **CASTING CALL:** Al Pacino expressed interest in playing Reg Dunlop, and Nick Nolte tried out for the role of Ned Braden. Both lost out because of their inability to skate.

🙂 **SIGN OF THE TIMES:** Oh, pretty much everything. The Afros on white guys. Reg Dunlop's leather jumpsuit. The clothes that all look like they shrunk four sizes in the wash.

🍎 **BET YOU DIDN'T KNOW:** The notorious character of Ogie Ogilthorpe—"the worst goon in hockey"—is based on Bill "Goldie" Goldthorpe, who played for 16 minor league teams between 1973-84. Goldthorpe earned 25 fighting majors his rookie season—*before Christmas*. "I couldn't wish anyone a Merry Christmas," he told a Canadian radio station. "My fists were too sore to shake hands." That same year he tried to throttle a young Bob Costas—broadcaster for his own team, the Syracuse Blazers—when Costas made a joke at his expense.

Goldthorpe was once arrested for fighting—his own teammate. The two got into a fracas at the Green Bay airport and Goldie didn't calm down even after police arrived. He spent the night in jail and was subsequently escorted across the border by Canadian immigration officials.

🎞 **IF YOU LIKED THIS, YOU'LL LIKE:** It's not a sports movie, but Paddy Chayefsky's *Network*, which came out three months before *Slap Shot*, lampoons TV news as hysterically as this movie sends up hockey.

🎟 **MY FAVORITE SPORTS MOVIE:** ESPN host Mike Greenberg: "It's one of the five funniest movies ever made in any genre. Paul Newman was never funnier in any movie, and I think it captured the texture of small-town small-time sports in a way no other movie I've seen has."

🎟 **MY FAVORITE SPORTS MOVIE, TOO:** Philadelphia Flyers forward Simon Gagne: "I watched it so many times growing up. It was dubbed in French, but not the type of French we spoke in Quebec. It was the French they speak in France, so some of the slang was tough to understand. Still, we figured out the good lines. Everybody I know still uses the good lines."

7 · THE LONGEST YARD (1974–R)

SPORT: FOOTBALL | STARS: BURT REYNOLDS, EDDIE ALBERT, MICHAEL CONRAD
DIRECTOR: ROBERT ALDRICH

How is it that we wind up rooting for Paul Crewe (Burt Reynolds)? When *The Longest Yard* opens, he is shown swilling down liquor and slamming his girlfriend against the wall. He makes off with her Maserati and drives it into a lake. He slugs a cop and is sent to prison where we learn he is a former NFL star who was banished for shaving points.

Clearly, this is not a nice guy. He is an abusive, selfish lout with no sense of decency or morals. So why is it that by the end of *The Longest Yard*, we're on our feet rooting for him?

Two reasons. One: the warden and the guards at Citrus State Prison are so evil, they make Crewe and his fellow convicts look almost saintly by comparison. Two: Burt Reynolds plays Crewe with a raffish charm that wins us over. We're willing to believe he has a good heart, even if there is plenty of evidence to the contrary.

Director Robert Aldrich did a similar good-guy/bad-guy flip-flop with *The Dirty Dozen* in 1967. The two films are very similar. You might even call *The Longest Yard* "The Dirty Eleven" because it uses the same thematic playbook: hardened criminals come together, develop a sense of pride and mission, spit in the eye of cynical authority figures and prove themselves on the field of battle—in this case, the gridiron.

Reynolds earned good reviews two years earlier for his performance in *Deliverance*, but *The Longest Yard* is the film that made him a star. In her *New York Times* review, Nora Sayre wrote, "[Reynolds] manages to make even the prison chains look like fashionable men's wear, as though he were modeling the latest in metal accessories." In other words, the man is very cool.

"I was very proud of the film, extremely proud," Reynolds told Bob Keisser of the *Los Angeles Herald-Examiner*. "It was a real entree for me and the rest of my career. We wanted it to be authentic. We wanted to get as much realism as possible."

In the film, upon arriving at Citrus State Prison, Crewe meets Warden Hazen (Eddie Albert) who greets him with a smile and the warm words, "It's nice to have you here." Crewe responds with a grunt and a limp handshake.

Hazen tells Crewe of his passion for football. He proudly shows off the trophies won by the prison guards, a beefy collection of sadistic brutes who amuse themselves by kicking around the prisoners when they're not practicing the power sweep. The guards play in a semi-

Hampton)—tells him, "Most of these old boys don't have nothing. Never had nothing to start with. But you had it all. Then you let your teammates down and got yourself caught with your hand in the cookie jar."

"Oh, I did, did I?" Crewe says.

"I ain't saying you did or you didn't," Caretaker replies. "All I'm saying is you could've robbed banks, sold dope or stole your grandmother's pension checks and none of us would've minded. But shaving points off a football game? Man, that's un-American."

To make Crewe pay for his disrespect, the warden orders him to assemble a football team from the prison population and play a game against the guards. Crewe wants no part of it, but he gives in when Hazen promises him an early parole.

POLICE OFFICER:

WHY'D YOU DRIVE HER CAR INTO THE BAY?

pro league and while they've won a lot of games, they have never won the national championship. The warden feels Crewe can put them over the top if he agrees to join the coaching staff.

"What do you think of semi-pro football, Mr. Crewe?" Hazen asks.

Crewe smirks. "Semi-pro is a joke," he replies.

The look on the warden's face is priceless. Crewe might as well have kneed him in the groin.

Hazen comes right to the point: Crewe can have easy duty and a (relatively) pleasant stay at Citrus State if he agrees to coach the team.

"I'm not interested in football anymore," Crewe says dismissively. "I just want to do my time and get out of here."

Seething, Hazen tells the guard, "Get him out of here."

Crewe is tossed into the cell block where he is not exactly welcomed with open arms. As one prisoner—a resourceful scrounger known as Caretaker (James

Crewe begins recruiting players. He enlists a giant weightlifter (Richard Kiel), a mass murderer (Robert Tessier), a dim-witted country boy (Wilbur Gillian) and others, all of whom welcome the chance to play against the guards. It is their one shot at payback for all the abuse they suffered.

Aldrich hired dozens of real players and divided them between the teams. Among the prisoners are Pervis Atkins, a halfback for the Los Angeles Rams; Sonny Sixkiller, a quarterback at the University of Washington; and Ernie Wheelwright, a fullback with the New Orleans Saints. The guards include former Minnesota Viking Joe Kapp (Walking Boss) and Rams linebacker Mike Henry (Lt. Rasmussen). Green Bay linebacker Ray Nitschke had no acting experience, but he has a featured role as Bogdanski, the biggest and meanest of the guards.

"Originally, Ray was supposed to be like the other [players] and be in the background," said Dave Robinson, Nitschke's Green Bay teammate who passed up a chance to be in the film to play another season in the NFL. "But when Ray met with the director, he took out his false teeth and put them on the table. Ray was really scary looking with his teeth out.

"The director said, 'This is the guy I want. And no makeup. I don't want any makeup. I want to be able to see all those scars.' So he wound up giving Ray quite a few lines. For a guy who wasn't an actor, Ray did a good job. You talk to anyone who saw the movie and they all remember Ray's character."

But most of all, people remember Reynolds as Paul Crewe. A former running back at Florida State, Reynolds has the fluid stride of a big-time player. He also has the attitude. Whether he is smooth-talking his fellow prisoners, facing off with the warden or making love to the

Reluctantly, Crewe agrees, but he gets a promise from the warden that the guards will ease up once they have the game in hand. Hazen gives his word, but of course he has no intention of honoring it. Crewe throws two interceptions and fumbles a snap allowing the guards to build a three-touchdown lead. But at that point the guards, on Hazen's orders, start playing even more viciously and send several prisoners off the field on stretchers.

Realizing he has been double-crossed, Crewe turns the tables on Hazen. He leads a fourth quarter rally that climaxes with Crewe scoring the winning touchdown on the final play, a one-yard run that takes one minute and 50 seconds of super, super, super slow-motion to complete. It truly is *the* longest yard.

Aldrich does not shortchange the football action. The

PAUL CREWE:

COULDN'T FIND A CAR WASH.

warden's secretary (Bernadette Peters in a memorable beehive hairdo), he is pitch-perfect as the cocky smart-ass who, even in handcuffs and leg irons, still swaggers like a one-time NFL MVP.

The Longest Yard builds to the big game between the guards and the prison team, which calls itself "The Mean Machine." With Crewe flashing his old moves at quarterback, the prisoners play the guards on even terms for a half. During intermission, the warden orders Crewe to tank the second half. He doesn't want the cons pulling off an upset and shaking the prison's power structure.

"I can't do that," Crewe says.

"You've done it before," Hazen replies, reminding Crewe of his earlier point shaving and threatening to implicate Crewe in the arson death of Caretaker. Crewe had nothing to do with it, but Hazen is ready to frame him for the crime. "You'll be with us until you're old and gray," Hazen says, telling Crewe he wants the guards to win by no less than 21 points.

big game lasts 47 minutes, more than a third of the film, but we aren't complaining. It neatly weaves comedy and drama and ends, fittingly, with Crewe handing the game ball to the ashen-faced warden.

"Stick this in your trophy case," he says with a go-to-hell grin.

Crewe disappears up the tunnel as the credits roll. We can only assume he is sent directly to solitary confinement where the warden sees to it that he spends the next 50 years living on bread and water. But we also get the feeling that Crewe would say it was worth it.

CHEERS: Reynolds' performance as Crewe is terrific, but Albert is equally good as the sinister warden. Michael Conrad, who later starred in *Hill Street Blues*, makes a strong impression as Nate Scarborough, a former NFL player who joins forces with Crewe on the Mean Machine.

JEERS: We cannot forgive the people behind the decision to re-make *The Longest Yard* with Adam Sandler in the Reynolds role. We don't care if the film did make $158 million at the box office—compared to the original, it was an embarrassment.

CASTING CALL: James Hampton (Caretaker) was originally cast as Unger, the creepy arsonist. After reading the script, Hampton asked to switch roles.

BET YOU DIDN'T KNOW: Aldrich encouraged the players to go all out in the game. "Guys were really tackling and hitting," Reynolds said. "Sometimes the defense knew where I was going, sometimes I went the other way on purpose. Put a helmet on Ray Nitschke and he thinks it's for real. I took some licks that were staggering."

WHAT THEY WROTE AT THE TIME: "The plot yields some dramatic tension because of what winning and losing represents. The prisoners are playing for their dignity and even the most reluctant spectator is forced to respond to that theme."—Nora Sayre, *New York Times*

REPEATED WATCHING QUOTIENT: Very high. There are several hilarious set pieces—for example, Crewe and Miss Toots getting it on in the warden's office—and the big game is a lot of fun. The scene where Crewe disables Bogdanski with two bullet passes to the crotch never fails to draw a cheer.

DON'T FAIL TO NOTICE: Joe Kapp wears No. 11 in the film, the same number he wore as a quarterback with the Minnesota Vikings in 1969 when he led the Vikings to Super Bowl IV.

REALITY CHECK: The dropkick field goal by Indian (Sonny Sixkiller) is actually wide right.

"I KNOW THAT GUY": Ed Lauter (Cpt. Knauer, head of the prison guards) was the hockey coach in *Youngblood*.

PIVOTAL SCENE: Crewe and Hazen meet in the shower at halftime with Hazen ordering Crewe to throw the game. As Hazen walks away, Crewe says, "There is only one thing I'm sorry about."

"What's that?" the warden asks.

"That you're not out there on the field with us, knocking heads," Crewe says.

"I'm afraid I'm a little old for that," Hazen replies.

"No," Crewe says, "you never had the guts in the first place."

SPORTS-ACTION GRADE: A. Even Brian Dawkins, a seven-time Pro Bowl safety, feels it looked and sounded like the real thing. "I love the tough football scenes," Dawkins said. "That's the way football ought to be played."

MY FAVORITE SPORTS MOVIE: Indianapolis Colts quarterback Peyton Manning: "Burt Reynolds was great. He was totally believable as a pro player. It was fun to see Ray Nitschke as one of the guards. It was just a real enjoyable movie. It was funny, but it had some drama, too. It was a great story with a great ending."

MY FAVORITE SPORTS MOVIE, TOO: *Monday Night Football* analyst and 1980 NFL MVP quarterback Ron Jaworski: "I go to movies to be entertained and have a good time. *The Longest Yard* did that. I still remember Burt Reynolds wore No. 22—a weird number for a quarterback—but he looked like a player. He played in college and it showed."

8 THE HUSTLER (1961-NR)

SPORT: POOL | STARS: PAUL NEWMAN, JACKIE GLEASON, GEORGE C. SCOTT
DIRECTOR: ROBERT ROSSEN

There was a time in this country when pool halls were as plentiful as McDonalds. They were populated not by college kids looking for a Friday night pick-up, but by murky characters of all ages angling to take your money over a game of nine-ball.

The Hustler returns you to those days. It is set in the early sixties, but really more closely resembles the Great Depression, when there were 40,000 billiard parlors across the country. There weren't glossy state lotteries to bet on back then. Working-class folks didn't shuttle to Las Vegas for $99 on the weekends. You wanted to wager a few bucks, you went downtown and picked up a cue stick and some chalk.

Paul Newman stars as Fast Eddie Felson, a young hustler from California. In the opening scene at a dingy watering hole, he sinks a nearly impossible shot, misses it the second time, then feigns drunken bravado and bets the predatory clientele he can make it one more time. Of course he does, departing with a fat wad of crumpled bills.

But Eddie is aiming for bigger game. He is hunting for Minnesota Fats (Jackie Gleason), the whale of a legend known in every seedy pool hall in the nation. The two meet soon enough and lock horns in a $200-a-game showdown.

What ensues is one of cinema's great scenes, backed by a jumpy jazz score, in which two great actors strut their stuff. Director Robert Rossen devotes a full 20 minutes to this one claustrophobic battle, trusting his audience's patience in a way that no director would today.

Initially, Fats controls the table, and Eddie is in awe. "He is great, that Fat Man," he says. "Look at him move, like a dancer. And those chubby fingers, that stroke, like he's playing a violin."

But Eddie finds his game and starts winning. He struts like Deion Sanders, boasting, "Fat Man, I've got a hunch that it's me from here on in. . . . I've dreamed about this game every night. . . . You know, this is my table. I own it."

The marathon match goes back and forth. After eight hours, Eddie is up $1,000. The stakes rise. After 25 hours, he's up $18,000. His manager (Myron McCormick) wants his player to leave ahead, but Eddie isn't here to take Fats' money—he's here to take his crown.

"The game ends when Fats says it does," he says.

Of course Minnesota Fats didn't become a legend by losing. More than a full day into the marathon, he sends out for booze, knowing that Eddie will follow suit. The veteran can handle his liquor, the kid cannot. Fats never sweats, never loosens his tie, never loses composure. Eddie, meanwhile, succumbs to drunkenness and exhaustion. After 40 hours, Fats has all the money and Eddie is broken—his skill undercut by his own demons and weaknesses.

The rest of the movie leads up to the inevitable rematch, traveling down a road of smoky flophouses and seedy bars. Eddie shacks up with the wrong dame, Sarah Packard (Piper Laurie), a broken woman who goes to college two days a week and drinks on the others. He gets his thumbs cracked by dock workers who spot him as a hustler.

He dumps one manager and finds another, the evil Bert Gordon, brilliantly played by George C. Scott as Satan in sunglasses. Gordon berates his new charge by calling him a loser and saying he lacks "character." The insults will either crush Eddie or prompt him to play better in anger. Gordon doesn't care either way; he's just as happy to bet against his man.

There's a pivotal seduction-rape scene between Gordon and Packard (off-camera, of course—this was 1961) that ends with Sarah's suicide at a Louisville hotel. That cements Eddie's transition into a hardened cynic as he returns to New York for the rematch with Fats.

The second showdown with Newman and Gleason is even better than the first. Both men glide around the table, shooting fast, as world-class players really do. Gleason's Minnesota Fats doesn't have a lot of dialog, but his grace and sad, expressive face are brilliant. Newman's Eddie, meanwhile, is in a zone borne of rage.

"How can I lose?" he shouts, at Gordon more than Fats. "It's not enough that you just have talent. You have

EDDIE: "FAT MAN, YOU SHOOT A GREAT GAME OF POOL."

FATS: "SO DO YOU, FAST EDDIE."

to have character, too. Right? I sure got character now. I picked it up in a hotel room in Louisville."

You can watch for yourself to see how it all ends, but the final exchange between the two main characters provides perfect punctuation:

"Fat Man, you shoot a great game of pool."

"So do you, Fast Eddie."

The Hustler was a minor box office success when it came out, spurring a brief resurgence in pool around the nation. It was more so a critical hit, winning Academy Awards for both Art Decoration Black-and-White and Cinematography Black-and-White. It was nominated for seven others, including Best Picture (losing out to *West Side Story*). All four of the major characters (Newman, Gleason, Scott and Laurie) were nominated for acting Oscars, although none won.

We would argue that Newman's performance in *The Hustler* makes his personal Mount Rushmore of excellence, along with those from *Hud, Cool Hand Luke* and *The Verdict*. It's interesting to note that although he was nominated for nine acting Oscars over his career, the only one he won was for playing Fast Eddie Felson the second time around, in 1986's *The Color of Money*. Consider that an honor handed out 25 years too late.

In *The Color of Money*, Newman plays a wiser and wizened version of Eddie. A young Tom Cruise, fresh off of *Top Gun*, plays his protégé. It's not bad but, like most sequels, it doesn't match up to the original.

🖝 **DON'T FAIL TO NOTICE:** As Fast Eddie warms up for his first game against Fats, his manager, Charlie, sits in front of a poster featuring 15-time World Champion Willie Mosconi. Just minutes later, the real Mosconi makes a cameo appearance as the guy who holds the bet money. Also, a hefty Jake LaMotta—Robert De Niro's model in *Raging Bull*—plays the bartender in the opening scene at Ames Billards.

🍺 **CHEERS:** To the amazing talent of Newman and Gleason – not just as actors, but at the pool table. Throughout *The Hustler* you see both attempt extremely challenging shots, and the drawn-out scenes with few camera cuts suggest that they often sunk several of them in one take.

Gleason was already a high-level player when he was cast for the movie. And Newman moved a table into his Upper East Side apartment and took daily lessons from Mosconi, improving to the point where, well, he could beat most anyone in your local billiards hall. Newman grew so confident of his skill that during a production break one afternoon, he challenged Gleason to a game of nine-ball – with a friendly $1 wager.

Newman won, so they played again. The young actor took another dollar from the old master. And then another. And then, full of bravado, Newman challenged Gleason to one more game – this time for $100.

"He whipped my ass," Newman later recalled. "He was hustling me. He was looking down my throat the whole time."

Newman paid off his debt the following day – entirely in pennies.

According to Shawn Levy, author of Paul Newman: A Life, "Gleason, of course, had been winning bets like this for years. He was in life very much like the man he was playing in the film. Newman was just imitating it."

📑 **JEERS:** To the 2007 DVD release, which bogs down this riveting movie with some of the most mind-numbing commentary this side of the IRS tax code. One example is this exchange with small-time actor Stefan Gierasch, who has the minor role of Preacher:

Q: "How did you get the part?"

A: "I read for the scene."

Well, who cares?

◉ **REPEATED WATCHING QUOTIENT:** It runs more than two hours and is dark in nature, so *The Hustler* may not be a movie you dive into every weekend. Still, it's one that, when you're clicking around the dial and land on it, the remote usually gets put down.

◀ **CASTING CALL:** Director Rossen said over the years he had hoped Frank Sinatra would play the role of Fast Eddie Felson—reviving his strung-out performance from *The Man with the Golden Arm*—but Old Blue Eyes was unavailable. Jack Lemmon turned down the gig, and Cliff Robertson auditioned but lost out to Newman. Lemmon, Robertson and Newman were all 35 years old at the time of shooting.

♦ **WHAT THEY WROTE AT THE TIME:** *"The Hustler* belongs to that school of screen realism that allows impressive performances but defeats the basic goal of pure entertainment."—*Variety*

✔ **REALITY CHECK:** When Fast Eddie is on a hot streak during his first match with Fats, one of his critical shots is actually illegal—his stick runs through the cue ball and hits the 13, which pockets another ball. We would have expected the Fat Man to notice that slip.

😎 **"I KNOW THAT GUY":** Big John, one of the pool hall degenerates, is played by Michael Constantine, a veteran Greek actor with the worst comb-over this side of Rudy Giuliani. Old heads will remember Constantine from his TV roles as the principal in *Room 222* or a gangster routinely getting roughed up in *The Untouchables*. More folks will remember him as Gus, the Windex-spraying dad in *My Big Fat Greek Wedding*.

★ **SPORTS-ACTION GRADE:** B-minus. Hey, it's pool we're talking about here. You can't exactly make a game against Minnesota Fats as exhilarating as a fight against Apollo Creed.

99 **BEST LINE:** Fast Eddie: "It's a real great feeling when you're right and you know you're right. It's like all of a sudden I got oil in my arm. The pool cue's part of me. You know, the pool cue, it's got nerves in it. It's a piece of wood, but it's got nerves in it. Feel the roll of those balls, you don't have to look, you just know. You make shots that nobody's ever made before. I can play that game the way nobody's ever played it before."

♥ **BET YOU DIDN'T KNOW:** Gleason's character of Minnesota Fats is not named after the famed real-life player—actually, it's the other way around. Rudolph Walter Wanderone Jr.—who was born in New York City and raised in Illinois—claimed to be the model for the movie's skilled hustler. But Walter Tevis, who authored the 1959 novel that is the basis for the film, wrote in 1976 that Wanderone's claim was "ridiculous. I made up Minnesota Fats—name and all—as surely as Disney made up Donald Duck."

Gleason, for his part, held Wanderone (who never won a national title) in utter contempt and resented that he co-opted the Minnesota Fats name. "I could beat him playing pool left-handed," the Great One told *Playboy* in 1986. "He can't play pool. He just wanted to cash in."

♥ **BET YOU DIDN'T KNOW II:** Piper Laurie, whose offbeat character in this film was typical of her roles, basically left acting after *The Hustler*, moved to Woodstock, N.Y., and didn't make another movie until 1976, when she scared the world as the maniacal mother in *Carrie*. In other news, Laurie is believed to have had a romantic affair with Ronald Reagan during the filming of *Louisa* in 1950, when he was 39 and she was 18.

🎞 **IF YOU LIKED THIS, YOU'LL LIKE:** *The Color of Money*, obviously, but as we said, it doesn't match up to *The Hustler*. Instead, check out *Pool Hall Junkies*, a 2002 tale of a troubled shooter starring Rick Schroder and Chazz Palminteri, with supporting spots from Rod Steiger and Christopher Walken.

🖐 **MY FAVORITE SPORTS MOVIE:** Actor Orlando Bloom (from the website full-bloom.net): "When I was 11 or 12, I watched *The Hustler*. It was black-and-white, and at first I thought, 'Ugh—I don't know if I'm going to be impressed by this.' But, of course, Paul Newman was so cool that I was incredibly impressed by him, and still am. That's the first time I remember thinking that maybe acting was something I'd like to do, too."

9 CADDYSHACK (1980-R)

SPORT: GOLF | STARS: BILL MURRAY, CHEVY CHASE, RODNEY DANGERFIELD, TED KNIGHT
DIRECTOR: HAROLD RAMIS

You probably couldn't get rivals Tiger Woods and Phil Mickelson to agree on much. But the top two golfers in the world see one thing the same: Both regard *Caddyshack* as the best movie ever made.

"It's my favorite by far," says Tiger. "It's just a classic." Woods so adores the film that he channeled greenskeeper Carl Spackler in a 2007 American Express commercial paying homage to many of *Caddyshack's* touchstone scenes.

Says Mickelson, "Every other movie is a couple of notches down." What most impresses Lefty is how much of *Caddyshack*—including the Dalai Lama scene, his favorite—was ad libbed. "That was pretty amazing. It

makes me more enchanted with the movie when I find out how it was made and the talent that was required."

The two Masters champs are not alone. Every weekend hacker adores *Caddyshack*, and has memorized dozens of classic lines from the film. In fact, we can't think of a single movie this side of *The Godfather* that has so influenced the vernacular of the American man.

Who doesn't quote from Bill Murray's "Cinderella story" monologue ("It's in the hole!") at least once a round? How often have you insulted a partner's garish clothing with Rodney Dangerfield's great putdown, "When you buy a hat like that, I bet you get a free bowl of soup, huh? It looks good on *you* though." Heck, you can even go to mini-golf and find some guy steadying his nerves over a putt while his taunting buddies yell, "N-n-n-n-ooooonan!"

Nearly 30 years after it was made, *Caddyshack* is that rare movie you can watch repeatedly and still glean new nuggets—hmmm, how come we never noticed how *funny* Doctor Beeper is? It boasts three great comics—Murray, Dangerfield and Chevy Chase—at the top of their game (and Ted Knight is no slouch himself). It satirizes class warfare, but also offers poop and booger jokes. All that plus pointless nudity.

And somehow, amazingly, critics panned it upon release. "Immediately forgettable," sniffed Vincent Canby of the *New York Times*.

Time has proven Canby wrong, don't you think?

"If you're still at the age when farting and nose-picking seem funny," offered the *Time Out Film Guide*, "then *Caddyshack* should knock you dead."

Okay, count us in.

This is the part of the chapter where we usually lay out the plot synopsis. But we're going to make a leap of faith here and assume you've already watched *Caddyshack* countless times. So, rather than lay out the ABCs of something you already know ("Danny Noonan wanted a golf scholarship . . . "), we're just going to tell you 10 things we love about it:

1. Most of *Caddyshack*, as Mickelson notes, was improvised. We're not just talking about a few lines here and there. Entire scenes were added on the fly following daily brainstorming sessions among first-time director Harold Ramis, head writer Brian Doyle-Murray (who also plays Lou, the caddy master) and several of the lead actors.

    The best addition, perhaps, came after Ramis realized there was no joint screen time between his two biggest stars—Chase and Murray. He hurriedly wrote a premise in which Ty Webb (Chase) sends an errant shot into Spackler's (Murray) ramshackle home/garage and wanders in to retrieve it. Everything after that—the inane conversation about cutting Judge Smails' hamstring, the joint smoking ("Cannonball!"), Spackler spitting on his own living room floor—was ad libbed. The scene has nothing to do with the overall plot, but is completely hilarious.

2. "So we finish the 18th and he's gonna stiff me. And I said, 'Hey, Lama, how about a little something, you know, for the effort?' And he says . . . 'There won't be any money, but when you die, on your deathbed, you will receive total consciousness.' So I got that going for me, which is nice."

3. The film was inspired by Brian Doyle-Murray's memories of working as a caddy from age 11, as well as

TY: "I DON'T PLAY GOLF FOR MONEY."

AL: "WHAT ARE YOU, RELIGIOUS OR SOMETHING?"

writer/producer Doug Kenney's recollections of growing up as the son of a country club tennis pro. Both Murray and Ramis also worked as caddies in their youth. Nearly all of the characters, from the despotic Judge Smails (Knight) to the sexy Lacey Underall (Cindy Morgan) to the fossilized Havercamps ("That's a peach, Hon.") were based on real people they encountered. So, too, were most of the setups, including the infamous Baby Ruth scene.

4. Judge Smails: "You know, you should play with Dr. Beeper and myself. I mean, he's been club champion for three years running, and I'm no slouch myself."

   Ty Webb: "Don't sell yourself short, Judge. You're a tremendous slouch."

5. There is a lot of creative tension at work here. First off, Chase and Morgan (a former model for Irish Spring soap, by the way) did not get along at all—which made their sex scene a challenge. "The bottle of massage oil he spilled on my back certainly wasn't in the script," Morgan said. "You can look in my eyes and almost hear me say, 'You son of a bitch, now the gloves are off.'"

   A few others in the cast didn't approve of the atmosphere on the set, which Clark Collis of the London Daily Telegraph described as "an 11-week party, legendary even by Hollywood standards." Knight, particularly, was troubled by what executive producer Jon Peters called "nightly debauchery."

6. Al Czervik (Dangerfield) owns the greatest golf bag in history. In addition to holding about 20 clubs, it boasts a beer dispenser, a stereo system that plays Journey, a phone (in the days before cell phones), a mini television, an ejector button that prompts all of his clubs to fly into the air and a putter with sonar tracking. We want that bag.

7. Judge Smails christening his yacht: "It's easy to grin / When your ship comes in / And you've got the stock market beat. / But the man worthwhile / Is the man who can smile / When his shorts are too tight in the seat."

8. Caddyshack is the final work of co-producer Doug Kenney, a comic genius. Kenney co-founded the 1970s satire magazine National Lampoon and wrote National Lampoon's Animal House, which became the top-grossing comedy in history upon its release in 1978.

   Kenney was a hugely important influence in moving humor from its tame form in the early 1970s, to the subversive, sophomoric and edgy form that emerged with the Lampoon, the early years of Saturday Night Live and the sometimes vulgar, often hysterical films that followed Animal House. One month after Caddyshack opened, his body was found at the bottom of a cliff in Hawaii. The death was ruled accidental. He was 32 years old.

9. Al Czervik to Judge Smails' wife: "Oh, this your wife, huh? A lovely lady. Hey baby, you must've been something before electricity. . . . You're a lot of woman, you know that? Yeah, wanna make 14 dollars the hard way?"

10. Call it a multiple tie. The lead song, I'm Alright, by Kenny Loggins. . . . Spackler overly enjoying the golf ball washer. . . . Spaulding Smails drinking the leftover liquor and barfing into Dr. Beeper's moon roof. . . . "Elihu, will you loofah my stretch marks?". . . . Spaulding picking his nose. . . . "Hey everybody, we're all gonna get laid!". . . . The water ballet scene during the lifeguard's swim session. . . . The Napoleon Dynamite-looking caddy who flashes eight fingers when Bishop Pickering says, "Put me down for a five.". . . . "You'll get nothing and like it!"

🍺 **CHEERS:** Murray, Chase and Dangerfield are the big names, but Ted Knight nearly steals the movie as tyrannical Judge Elihu Smails. With his stentorian delivery and dancing eyebrows, Knight is the perfect pompous blowhard. Who else could ever make you laugh with lines like, "I've sentenced boys younger than you to the gas chamber. Didn't want to do it. I felt I owed it to them."

🍺 **JEERS:** There isn't much to dislike here. If forced to criticize, we'll knock the cheesy animatronic gopher created by special effects master John Dykstra, whose other credits include Star Wars and Spiderman. The voice—literally stolen from Flipper the dolphin—just makes it worse.

WHAT THEY WROTE AT THE TIME: "One of the movie's problems is that the central characters are never really involved in the same action. Murray's off on his own, fighting gophers. Dangerfield arrives, devastates, exits. Knight is busy impressing the caddies, making vague promises about scholarships, and launching boats. If they were somehow all drawn together into the same story, maybe we'd be carried along more confidently."— Roger Ebert, *Chicago Sun-Times*

★ **SPORTS-ACTION GRADE:** D-minus. But that's not why you're watching.

✔ **REALITY CHECK:** In the final scene, Danny's putt (worth $80,000) freezes on the lip of the 18th hole. Then come the explosions created by Spackler trying to blow up the gopher. As chaos ensues, Lou, the match's referee, stays put and stares at the ball. Finally, after 53 seconds, the earth rumbles and the ball tumbles in—winning the match for the good guys. For what it's worth, Rule 16.2 of the USGA says that if a ball falls in more than 10 seconds after a player has reached the hole, the player must add a penalty stroke. Of course, that would have ruined the finish. And who wants to be a stickler?

◉ **REPEATED WATCHING QUOTIENT:** Endless. Once a week. For the rest of your life.

🎬 **PIVOTAL SCENE:** Well, nothing's exactly pivotal here, but there are several iconic moments. Most remembered—and most imitated—is Spackler's "Cinderella story" monologue as he swings through the mums.

"This unknown, comes out of nowhere to lead the pack. At Augusta, he's on his final hole. He's about 455 yards away. He's gonna hit about a 2-iron."

Whoosh!

"Oh, he got all of that. The crowd is standing on its feet here at Augusta. The normally reserved Augusta crowd going wild for this young Cinderella, coming out of nowhere. He's got about 350 yards, he's gonna hit about a 5-iron. He's got a beautiful backswing. . . . "

Whoosh!

"Oh, he got all of that one. He's got to be pleased with that. The crowd is just on its feet here. He's a Cinderella boy. Tears in his eyes, I guess, as he lines up this last shot. He's about 195 yards out and it looks like he's gonna hit an 8-iron. This crowd has gone deadly silent. Cinderella story, out of nowhere, a former greenskeeper. Now about to become the Masters champion."

Whoosh!

"It looks like a—it's in the hole! It's in the hole!"

Like Robert De Niro's "You talking to me?" speech in *Taxi Driver*, Murray improvised the scene based on one direction. Ramis told him to pretend he was a child announcing his triumph.

"It was a spur-of-the-moment idea," Murray wrote in his book, *Cinderella Story, My Life in Golf*. " 'Get me some flowers,' I said. 'Four rows of mums.' They still weren't sure where I was going. But the main idea was to cut down flowers. See, there is a weird thing that greenskeepers can't help but have that was a factor in Carl's persona: the anger over the class tension.

"Nobody wrote a word of script. It just came from my head into the camera. I did it in one take—but I knew it had worked."

◀ **CASTING CALL:** Initially, Murray and Dangerfield were written in for minor roles, but their brilliant improvisational skills brought them more lines and more scenes—much to the chagrin of some cast members whose parts ended up being cut.

👊 **BET YOU DIDN'T KNOW:** While this is the movie that launched Dangerfield's Hollywood career, the standup comic feared he was bombing during filming. Scott Colomby, who plays cooler-than-thou caddy D'Annunzio, told the *Mr. Skin* website (hey, we'll gather info wherever we can get it) that Dangerfield—accustomed to the instant audience response in nightclubs—had a tough time adjusting to movie acting.

"Between takes, Rodney was just sweating," said Colomby. "A lot. I went over to him and asked if he was all right. He just couldn't stop shaking.

" 'They're not laughing,' Rodney told me. 'Nobody's laughing. I'm dying up here!'

"I calmed him down. I told him that it wasn't like a comedy club and that everyone had to keep quiet while they were filming. He felt a lot better after that."

☻ **"I Know That Guy"**: Henry Wilcoxon, who plays the golf-addicted clergyman, was a veteran character actor from old Cecil B. DeMille epics. We doubt you own those DVDs, but you might have seen him as Pharoah's general, Pentaur, in the 1956 classic, *The Ten Commandments*. In *Caddyshack*, Bishop Pickering is playing the round of his life in a raging thunderstorm. He lifts his club heavenward and is felled by lightning—all to the theme from *The Ten Commandments*.

🕐 **Sign of the Times**: What does it say about society that comedic references made in 1980 are no longer appropriate in this more-Puritan age? Watching *Caddyshack* on over-the-air TV these days is like watching *Goodfellas* on Nick at Nite. Everything from Al Czervik's "Who stepped on a duck" line to the Ty Webb-Lacey Underall drinking/sex scene has been chopped out. Most of the edits involve the film's many drug jokes.

In the original, there is this encounter between club pro Ty and caddy Danny Noonan:

Ty: "Can I ask you a question? Do you do drugs, Danny?"

Danny: "Every day."

Ty: "Good boy."

In the version now shown on American television, the words "every day" have been replaced by "No." The rest of the dialog—including "good boy"—remain the same. In an effort to protect our minds, the gag is ruined.

👾 **"I Know That Gal"**: Danny's Irish-accented girl-friend, Maggie O'Hooligan, is portrayed by Sarah Holcomb. Two years earlier, she lost her toga and passed out drunk as Mayor DePasto's jailbait daughter in the equally hysterical *Animal House*. According to the book *The Real Animal House,* written by Chris Miller, Holcomb fell into serious drug use after *Caddyshack* and never made another movie.

🎞 **If You Liked This, You'll Like**: *Ghostbusters, The Blues Brothers, Stripes, National Lampoon's Vacation, Fletch, Coming to America, Planes, Trains and Automobiles*—any number of great comedies from the 1980s when *Saturday Night Live* alums knew how to be funny.

🎬 **My Favorite Sports Movie**: Super Bowl-winning coach Jon Gruden: "Bill Murray doing his 'Cinderella Boy' thing—you can't walk on any golf course in the world and not hear someone saying it. And the thing is, everybody knows where it came from. Then that person quotes a line and another person quotes another line and, pretty soon, you've got the whole movie going on. . . . I enjoy watching it with my sons now. I get a kick out of seeing them laugh at all the same jokes I laughed at when I was their age."

🎬 **My Favorite Sports Movie, Too**: New York Giants quarterback Eli Manning: "It is a movie you can watch over and over again and never get tired of it. You always can find a new line to quote and that keeps it interesting."

10 NORTH DALLAS FORTY (1979–R)

SPORT: FOOTBALL | STARS: NICK NOLTE, MAC DAVIS, BO SVENSON
DIRECTOR: TED KOTCHEFF

Football fans see only what happens on Sunday. They see the game, the cheering crowd, the adulation. They don't see Monday when the real price is paid by the players who must put their battered bodies back together. They don't see the politics of the front office, the mind games played by the coaches and the unspoken fear that grips each player who knows that any game could be his last.

Wisely, that's where *North Dallas Forty* begins. It doesn't start with Phil Elliott (Nick Nolte) scoring the winning touchdown for the North Dallas Bulls. It doesn't show him signing autographs for his adoring fans. Rather the film opens with Elliott, the morning after the game, waking up on a blood-stained pillow, wincing as he feels the effects of every hit he took the day before.

Elliott gulps some pain pills, washes them down with beer and slowly drags himself down the hall to the bath-

room. Every few steps he reaches for an aching body part and flashes back to a moment in the game: a hit that flipped him in the air, an elbow that hit him in the face, a tackle that twisted his head around. He remembers each blow. He will live with them all week, if not longer.

Finally, Elliott lowers his scarred and swollen body into a warm bath, and just when you are wondering why anyone would put himself through this, he begins to smile. Then he flashes back to the one-handed catch he made to win the game. Suddenly, the pain is gone. Elliott is back in that moment and that moment makes it all worthwhile.

It is a powerful scene, and it lets you know immediately that *North Dallas Forty* is not going to be your typical rah-rah football film. Based on the best-selling novel by former Dallas Cowboys receiver Pete Gent, *North Dallas*

Forty strips away the sugar-coating on the NFL to reveal a world that is brutal and dehumanizing. There are excesses in the film, some of the characters are exaggerated stereotypes, but there is a lot of truth here as well.

"Seeing Nick Nolte trying to get out of bed the morning after a game, I said, 'That's me,' " said Cris Collinsworth, who played eight seasons as a wide receiver with the Cincinnati Bengals. "I've tried to explain it to people, what it's like to go through that, and most of them have no clue. But that scene brings it home."

PHIL: "**ALCOHOL AND FEAR ARE A POTENT COMBINATION.**"

CHARLOTTE: "**WHAT ARE THEY AFRAID OF?**"

PHIL: "**FALLING ON THEIR ASSES IN CHICAGO MONDAY NIGHT.**"

"I played when the fields were all Astroturf and you had all the skin scraped off your arms and elbows. The morning after a game, I was stuck to the sheets because of all the turf burns. I was a skinny guy, and I'd be so beat up and sore I couldn't stand up most Mondays. I'd literally roll out of bed onto my knees and crawl to the bathroom."

The Cowboys, on whom Gent based the story, blasted the film. Team president Tex Schramm called it total fiction. Pete Rozelle, then commissioner of the NFL, dismissed it as "just a movie." But many players said otherwise. Jeff Severson, who played six years in the

league, said the film had "the authenticity of a newsreel." Carl Weathers, who played two seasons in Oakland before pursuing an acting career, said, "I think it's the film that comes closest to capturing the drama of what goes on in a locker room."

"Pete got the alienation part right, how the players hate the system and the crap that goes on," said Fred Dryer, who played in the league for 13 seasons before becoming an actor. "I never sat at my locker and talked with [teammate] Jack Youngblood about how to defend the 44 trap. I talked about kidnapping the general manager, taking him into the desert and burying him. That's what we talked about on the bus and walking to practice.

"One day we were taking a break in the shade. The coach sounded the horn and said, 'OK, let's go. Back to work.' I said to Jack, 'Don't you hate yourself for doing this? Here we are, trapped inside this world. Isn't it a shame?' Jack said, 'Yeah, you're right.' But then we got up and went back to practice. We hated it and we hated ourselves for doing it, but we did it. People would say, 'Why? The money, right?' No.

"Pete touched on it. There are those once-in-a-lifetime moments, those explosions of talent when it all comes together and you do something truly beautiful. For Pete, it was a catch. For me [a defensive end], it might be a tipped-ball interception. But those are the moments you live for. That's why you put up with the other stuff. It's the price you pay for the chance at one of those moments."

North Dallas Forty focuses on Elliott, a veteran wide receiver (Gent based the character on himself) who still enjoys playing the game, but hates the rules put in place by owners and coaches. Elliott is a rebel who smokes pot, mutters wisecracks under his breath in team meetings and sleeps with the fiancee of the owner's brother.

Head coach B.A. Strothers (a stern Tom Landry figure played by G.D. Spradlin) has benched Elliott because he doesn't like his attitude, but he won't cut him because Elliott can still make a big play when called upon.

When Strothers accuses him of immaturity, Elliott replies, "I've scored five touchdowns coming off the bench. That's pretty mature." The coach leaps from his chair. "You scored five touchdowns?" he says. "We let you score those touchdowns. It's a team game, it's not about the individual. When are you going to learn that?"

Elliott's best friend is quarterback Seth Maxwell (Mac Davis playing a character loosely—or not-so-loosely—based on Don Meredith). Maxwell is a good old boy who shares Elliott's distain for management, but unlike Elliott, he knows how to hide his feelings behind a wink and a smile.

"You better learn how to play the game," Maxwell tells Elliott, "and I don't mean the game of football. Give 'em what they want. Hell, I've been fooling them bastards for years."

"I can't do it, Seth," Elliott says. "You start acting like somebody else and pretty soon that's what you become, somebody else."

Elliott meets Charlotte Caulder (Dayle Haddon) at a team party. She is standing off to the side, appalled by the raunchy goings-on. Elliott, who is something of an outsider himself, is drawn to her. At one point, the hulking Jo Bob Priddy (Bo Svenson) hoists a terrified woman over his head while the other players and groupies cheer him on.

"Jo Bob is here to remind us that the biggest and the baddest get to make all the rules," Elliott says.

"I don't agree with that," Charlotte replies.

"Agreeing doesn't play into it," Elliott says.

Disgusted, Charlotte heads for the door, only to be intercepted by Jo Bob, who announces in graphic terms what he would like to do to her. Elliott intercedes, but Jo Bob, fueled by drugs and booze, turns on Elliott and begins choking him. Maxwell has to rush in and save him.

"What do you expect?" Maxwell says. "These girls know what goes on at these parties."

"She didn't seem like that to me," Elliott says.

He follows Charlotte home. Reluctantly, she lets him in. She explains she went to the party with a friend. "I thought it would be fun," she said. "Obviously, I was wrong." She is unlike other women Elliott has known. She cares nothing about football. To her, it is an alien world, violent and barbaric. What she saw at the party only confirmed that. But in Elliott she sees a decent guy—complicated, conflicted and maybe a little messed up, but basically decent. Soon, they are in bed together.

The film plays out over one week. That's one of the weaknesses of the film compared to the novel. Gent's book spanned an entire season so all the violence, treachery and debauchery was spread out over four months. In the film, it is compressed into seven days which makes it seem unrealistic. We don't doubt that Gent saw all the things he wrote about at various points in his five-year NFL career, but when he tries to cram a lifetime's worth of baggage into a two-hour screenplay, sometimes things get messy.

There are a few gratuitous shots at players who read the Bible and the team chaplain is portrayed as a hapless jock-sniffer, all of which is unnecessary. But when Gent sticks to the meat of the story, it is prime stuff.

The big game—the Bulls meet Chicago on Monday night television—is a savage affair with a Rambo-like body count. Jo Bob and O.W. Shaddock (ex-Raider John Matuszak) intentionally break the leg of Chicago's best lineman, Alcie Weeks (ex-Rams tackle Doug France). Wide receiver Delma Huddle (ex-Chiefs halfback Tommy Reamon) tears his hamstring and takes a vicious shot that shatters his cheekbone.

On the final play, Elliott catches a touchdown pass to pull the Bulls within one point of a tie, but the holder drops the snap on the extra point attempt and the Bulls lose to fall from championship contention. In the locker room Shaddock explodes when an assistant coach (Charles Durning) tells the players they lost because they didn't study the computer tendencies.

"That's all you give us, your computer tendencies and other chickenshit," Shaddock says. "You've got no feeling for the game."

"You're professionals," the coach says. "This is a business."

"Every time I call it a game, you say it's a business," Shaddock roars. "And every time I say it's a business, you call it a game."

Matuszak is no Olivier, but he delivers those lines with a passion that is totally convincing. You have to believe those are sentiments he felt many times in losing locker rooms and this scene was a cathartic experience, not just for Matuszak but for hundreds of NFL players watching and thinking, "Right on."

"Most of us [players] saw it as a movie about a sport that, when you look at it, is kind of absurd," Collinsworth said. "We're a bunch of adult men out there trying to kill each other. *North Dallas Forty* raises that question, 'Are these guys crazy?' It's a question I think we all asked ourselves at one time or another."

🍴 **CHEERS:** Nolte is very good as Elliott. He does not have the physique of an NFL wide receiver, but he has the rebel-bucking-the-system thing down cold.

🚩 **JEERS:** Country singer Mac Davis made his acting debut as Maxwell, and he is not convincing as a character and certainly not as an NFL quarterback.

🏈 **BET YOU DIDN'T KNOW:** Tom Fears, a Hall of Fame receiver with the Los Angeles Rams and a head coach with the New Orleans Saints, was the technical adviser on the film.

✒ **WHAT THEY WROTE AT THE TIME:** "The main thrust of *North Dallas Forty* is to indict the National Football League as an evil institution on the nether side of civilization."—Frank Deford, *Sports Illustrated*

⏲ **SIGN OF THE TIMES:** Elliott is shown wearing a T-shirt with the slogan: "No Freedom, No Football." That is the actual shirt the NFL players wore during the 1974 strike.

☝ **DON'T FAIL TO NOTICE:** Stallings, the lineman who is cut for missing a block, is Jim Boeke, who played guard for the Cowboys. Boeke had a similar experience, jumping offside at a critical moment in the 1966 NFL championship game. He was traded to New Orleans one year later.

👀 **"I KNOW THAT GUY":** The player who is getting his ankles taped next to Elliott before the big game is Harold Jackson, a wide receiver who played 16 seasons in the NFL.

🎬 **PIVOTAL SCENE:** When the coach lectures Elliott about giving something back to the game, Elliott lists his many injuries.

"There's pieces of me scattered from here to Pittsburgh on these football fields," he says. "Isn't that giving something back to the game?"

Strong stuff and effectively delivered by Nolte.

★ **SPORTS-ACTION GRADE:** B. A dozen former NFL players appear in the cast, so the stances and moves look authentic. The offensive line copies the Cowboys with linemen straightening up before dropping into a three-point stance. The one problem: Mac Davis throwing the football. If he's supposed to be Don Meredith, Dandy Don has grounds to sue.

👆 **MY FAVORITE SPORTS MOVIE:** Marty Brennaman, Hall of Fame broadcaster: "Pete Gent really depicted the inside story of the NFL, especially what the Cowboys were like back then. The movie, like the book, was one of the early tell-it-like-it-is stories. Those kinds of revelations were rather shocking back then. Since then, the insider's kind of story has been told many times, but *North Dallas Forty* was one of the first to tell it and it did it well."

👆 **MY FAVORITE SPORTS MOVIE, TOO:** Hall of Fame defensive end and broadcaster Howie Long: "The movie did a great job of capturing the pressures and kind of things players go through to get on the field. All of that stuff about fearing losing your job if you don't play is absolutely true. Even great players worry that they're just one injury away from being out.

"The only part that didn't ring true for me was the parties. People diving naked into swimming pools or sawing cars in half? Hey, I played in Oakland and Los Angeles and I never saw anything that good."

11 FIELD OF DREAMS (1989–PG)

SPORT: BASEBALL | STARS: KEVIN COSTNER, JAMES EARL JONES, RAY LIOTTA
DIRECTOR: PHIL ALDEN ROBINSON

There are many who regard *Field of Dreams* as the greatest sports movie ever made—a wondrous allegory about life, fathers and sons, lost dreams and a bygone America, all staged in an Iowa cornfield. It is, to reverential devotees, the modern version of *It's a Wonderful Life*.

"That movie had a mystical feel to it," says Pete Carroll, head football coach at USC. "It was very inspiring."

And then there are those who regard it as so much pap. *Premiere* magazine listed it among the 20 most overrated films of all time. "A gooey fable," declared Peter Travers of *Rolling Stone*.

Bill Simmons of ESPN wrote, "I think the world is separated into two kinds of people—people who loved *Field of Dreams*, and people who don't have a heart. If I were dating a woman and she said she didn't like *Field of Dreams*, I'd immediately dump her."

We agree. Certainly, Simmons offers a better method of judging a potential mate than the unlock-the-car-door

test in *A Bronx Tale*. Anyone—man, woman, child—who isn't touched by the innocence and fantasy of *Field of Dreams* is too much a grinch for us.

Writer and broadcaster Peter King, who has witnessed thousands of inspiring moments over his career, called *Field of Dreams* the most emotional sports movie he has ever seen.

"Every kid who grew up playing baseball at some point played catch with his father," says King. "You don't think of it as an emotional experience. But when your Dad is gone, you do think of it as an emotional experience. Every time I see that movie, I bawl. I can't help it."

So why doesn't it crack our Top Ten? Because, great as it is, that sweetness sometimes seeps into sappiness. Occasionally, the movie becomes just a tad too reverential for our taste—worshiping that deity called baseball. Moses saw a burning bush, Ray Kinsella (Kevin Costner) sees a vision of a baseball diamond in his cornfield. With a chorus of angels singing in the background, just in case you missed the subtlety.

Plus this: The entire movie leads up to the final seven-minute scene, the climactic reconciliation between Ray and his long-estranged dad, John Kinsella (Dwier Brown). The two had parted ways—emotionally and physically—when Ray was a teen, and never squared matters before Dad's early death. Years later, thanks to Shoeless Joe Jackson (Ray Liotta), they get that second chance out in the magical Iowa ball field.

We are told that Dad was a damned good catcher in his day. Now, as father and son meet again, there's some talk about Iowa and heaven and how easily the two are confused. As we watch, we're feeling the lump growing in our throat.

"Hey Dad," says Ray. "You wanna have a catch?"

We're welling up at this point.

"I'd like that," says John, as the music nears crescendo.

Ray picks up his glove, and we're totally verklempt. Searching for Kleenex in the pocket.

So Ray throws, in that convincing Costner-as-Crash-Davis overhand motion. Dad catches the ball, and then . . . well, he executes the feeblest toss this side of Biddy Ball. Pushes it like a nine-year-old girl.

Almost ruined the movie right there.

Okay, call us sticklers. We apologize. We don't want to get bogged down in the negative. As we said, we're willing to buy into the overall vision of *Field of Dreams*. Once upon a time, Hollywood regularly produced this kind of movie—usually starring Jimmy Stewart. Nowadays, such flights of fancy are too rare.

Twenty years after it first came out, *Field of Dreams* has been parodied so many times that it's easy to forget the original premise: An Iowa farmer, still wracked by guilt over that suspended relationship with his dad, is told by voices to plow under his field and build a baseball diamond. This leads to the appearance of his father's hero, the disgraced Shoeless Joe.

But it does much more than that. The voices then tell Ray to enlist reclusive writer Terence Mann (James Earl Jones, playing a character based on author J.D. Salinger), and track down Minnesota doctor Archibald "Moonlight" Graham (Burt Lancaster), who never got his full shot in the majors. And it concludes with our hero gaining peace of mind, closure with his father and financial success far beyond his imagination.

Director Phil Alden Robinson never really tries to explain the far-fetched plot twists, which is smart. Instead, he relies on the audience leading with its heart. "This story teaches you that you've got to have dreams," he said in a *Newsweek* interview soon after its release, "but you should keep yourself open to the possibility that a fork in the road may lead you to something just as good."

It all works. Well, almost all. We just wish they had taught the dad how to throw.

CHEERS: To the outstanding acting that makes a far-fetched story almost believable. Costner was in his prime here, wrapping up a four-movie streak of *The Untouchables, No Way Out, Bull Durham* and *Field of Dreams*. Not a bad string. Jones is as weighty and authoritative as ever, and Liotta does a good job making Shoeless Joe Jackson likeable but not antiseptic. Lancaster, in the final movie role of his 45-year career, remains poetry in motion.

"I wanted somebody [for the role of Doc Graham] who in his youth was a jock," Robinson says on the DVD's director's commentary. Lancaster worked as a circus acrobat as a young man and was a legitimate athlete in *Jim Thorpe—All-American*. "Doc ultimately performs such a lovely act in the movie that I wanted it to be a tough jock. It's much more interesting and touching when a tough guy does something sweet and gentle."

JEERS: To the over-the-top school board book-banning scene, particularly the verbal smackdown between hippy-dippy Annie Kinsella and Beulah "The Fat Cow" Gasnick.

"I just stopped the spread of neo-Nazism in the United States," boasts Annie, as she shadowboxes down the school hallway. In fact, making actress Amy Madigan a refugee from the Sixties—using words like "groovy" and "far out"—proved annoying throughout the film.

WHAT THEY WROTE AT THE TIME: "Poesy, pointlessness and baseball worship aside, the movie is easy to get along with. Costner is a likable lead, as plausible with his ghosts as Jimmy Stewart was with Harvey."—Rita Kempley, *Washington Post*

PIVOTAL SCENE: While Ray, his family and Mann cheer the players, Ray's evil brother-in-law Mark (Timothy Busfield) pressures him to sell the farm to save his family. Mark, cynic that he is, cannot see the game before him. "You've got no choice," he says, shoving a bank note under Ray's nose. "Sign the papers. You will be evicted. You will lose everything."

Mann, meanwhile, forecasts that it will all work out, that "strangers will line up" to pay $20 each to visit Ray's property.

Ray, torn between fear and fantasy, breathes deep, then mumbles, "I'm not signing."

The argument between Ray and Mark escalates into a tug-of-war over Ray's daughter (Gaby Hoffmann), who tumbles from the bleachers and stops breathing.

Enter Moonlight Graham. The young ballplayer walks to the foul line, pauses, and then steps over, morphing back into the elderly doctor. He rescues the girl from choking on a hot dog. But in doing so, he sacrifices his dream to play ball. Once you cross the line, Ray notices, "You can't go back."

Graham's action has one other effect. Suddenly, Mark can see the players. The greedy banker has become another fervent fan. "Do not give up this farm Ray!" he shouts. "You've got to keep this farm!"

It's a brilliant scene, with two huge plot turns—Mark's awakening to the vision and Doc Graham's irrevocable decision. It's well played by Costner and Busfield. But the scene is stolen by Jones and Lancaster, two Hall of Fame actors at their best here.

" BEST LINE: It's too easy to list, "If you build it, he will come." Or, "Hey, is this Heaven?" "No, this is Iowa."

So we'll go with Mann's ode to the sport in the above-described scene:

"The one constant through all the years, Ray, has been baseball. America has rolled by like an army of steamrollers. It has been erased like a blackboard, rebuilt and erased again. But baseball has marked the time. This field, this game—it's a part of our past, Ray. It reminds us of all that once was good and it could be again. Oh, people will come Ray. People will most definitely come."

BET YOU DIDN'T KNOW: Graham is based on a real ballplayer. Archibald Graham—described as "quick as a flash of moonlight"—debuted in right field in the bottom of the eighth for the New York Giants on June 29, 1905 (not 1922, as in the movie). He never touched the ball in the field, and was left on deck when the Giants made their third out in the ninth. In real life, as in the movie, Graham quit baseball to become a doctor in Minnesota.

Author W.P. Kinsella stumbled upon Graham's one-line entry while leafing through the *Baseball Encylopedia* in 1965. "How could anybody come up with that nickname?" Kinsella noted. "I was intrigued, and I made a note that I intended to write something about him. My approach to fiction writing is that when I need facts, I invent them. So I would have invented a background for Moonlight Graham, but I'm sure nothing as wonderful as the truth. It was a gold mine."

BET YOU DIDN'T KNOW II: The movie was shot in 1988, as Iowa was going through its worst drought since the Dust Bowl of the 1930s. Producers spent $25,000 watering the cornfield to keep it from dying. "We had the only corn for 100 miles in any direction," noted director Robinson.

DON'T FAIL TO NOTICE: Moonlight's 50-year quest to get that one at-bat against big-league pitching? Well, he's *still* waiting. If you recall, Graham finally gets the chance to step in against Ed Cicotte, star pitcher from the Black Sox. He takes a few high and inside, and then lofts a sacrifice fly.

In baseball, a sacrifice fly does not count as an official at-bat.

DON'T FAIL TO NOTICE II: For the final shot, an aerial view of cars driving to the farm, more than 1,500 locals volunteered to line up. Traffic got so heavy that most of the cars weren't moving. So Robinson—relaying instructions through a local radio station—told people to flash their high beams on and off, creating the appearance of traffic passing behind obstructions. If you watch closely, you can see the effect.

"I KNOW THAT GUY": Young Archie Graham is played by fresh-faced actor Frank Whaley. You may recall him as Brett from an early scene in *Pulp Fiction*. As in Big Kahuna Burger Brett. As in, "Check out the big brain on Brett." As in the late, unfortunate Brett.

If you missed the appearances of Matt Damon and Ben Affleck in this movie, perhaps you blinked. As teenagers, they were among thousands of Bostonians hired to play extras in the Fenway Park scene.

SIGN OF THE TIMES: Ray and Terence Mann walk right up to Fenway Park and buy tickets moments before game time. Try your luck with that these days. Once inside, they order two beers and two hot dogs—sum total: seven bucks. For what it's worth, two brews and two dogs cost $23 at Fenway in 2008. If you upgrade to the sausage dogs (highly recommended) add another $4.

GOOFS: In the game at Fenway, right before the scoreboard goes berserk with messages about Moonlight Graham, we see the stadium clock read 10:31 p.m. Then the camera moves to Ray, who's marking the plays on his scoresheet. It's the third inning. Either someone screwed up the timing, or that is one long ball game.

REALITY CHECK: In the movie, Shoeless Joe bats right and throws left. In reality, Jackson batted left and threw right.

Also, when the 1919 Black Sox first emerge from the cornfield, one of them is wearing catcher's gear. None of the eight banished players ever played catcher.

CASTING CALL: As great as Costner was, Robinson was reluctant to give him the lead because he was just coming off of *Bull Durham*, and the director worried that viewers would confuse this character with Crash Davis. Tom Hanks was initially offered the role of Ray, but turned it down.

Country singer Reba McIntire auditioned for the part of Annie.

The baseball scenes were coached by former USC head coach Rod Dedeaux and former major league outfielder Don Buford.

SPORTS-ACTION GRADE: No better than a B. For the ghosts of Hall of Fame players, these guys are just so-so.

REPEATED WATCHING QUOTIENT: Any time you need a good emotional pick-me-up.

IF YOU LIKED THIS, YOU'LL LIKE: *Shoeless Joe*, the W.P. Kinsella novel on which the movie is based. (There are several plot changes: in the book Ray is reunited with an identical twin brother and, of course, Mann is actually J.D. Salinger.) In fact, we recommend any of Kinsella's stories, especially *The Iowa Baseball Confederacy* and *The Further Adventures of Slugger McBatt*.

In the director's cut of the DVD, Robinson notes that the movie was originally going to be called *Shoeless Joe*, but a focus group thought that meant it would be a story about a homeless man. When *Field of Dreams* was proposed as a title, says Robinson, "I thought it sounded like a room deodorizer. But they test marketed it and it worked."

Robinson called Kinsella, expecting the author to be upset about the new name. Instead, Kinsella told him he had originally titled his novel *Dream Field*, but the publishing company changed it to *Shoeless Joe*.

MY FAVORITE SPORTS MOVIE: Mike Scioscia, California Angels manager: "I loved the scenes of the players on the field, working out. You could see how much they loved baseball and what it meant for them to play again. As someone who has spent his whole life in the game, it really connected with me. For Joe Jackson to have [baseball] taken away and then to have it back, it was like this wonderful gift. It made me appreciate the fact that I get to come to the park and put this uniform on every day. It is a gift and you shouldn't take it for granted."

MY FAVORITE SPORTS MOVIE, TOO: University of Connecticut men's basketball coach and two-time NCAA Tournament winner Jim Calhoun: "I grew up learning baseball and playing catch with my father. I lost my dad when I was 15, and that was very tough. When I watched *Field of Dreams*, and saw Ray playing catch with his father, I got goose bumps. That scene remains so special for me, and I think it's the same for millions of us who lost our fathers along the way."

ACTORS AS ATHLETES: WHO MAKES THE CUT?

IT SEEMS SO SIMPLE. IF YOU'RE CASTING A SPORTS MOVIE, WHY WOULDN'T YOU LOOK FOR ACTORS WHO CAN ACTUALLY PLAY THE SPORT? YET OVER THE YEARS HOLLYWOOD HAS DRAFTED AS BADLY AS THE DETROIT LIONS IN THIS REGARD.

KEANU REEVES AS AN NFL QUARTERBACK (*THE REPLACEMENTS*)? SCOTT BAKULA AS A COLLEGE FOOTBALL STAR (*NECESSARY ROUGHNESS*)? SONG-AND-DANCE MAN DAN DAILEY AS HALL OF FAMER DIZZY DEAN (*THE PRIDE OF ST. LOUIS*)?

WHAT WERE THEY THINKING?

IT'S OK IF THE ACTOR IS PLAYING THE ROLE FOR LAUGHS. RODNEY DANGERFIELD'S DISJOINTED GOLF SWING IN *CADDYSHACK* IS PART OF THE JOKE. WE'RE SUPPOSED TO LAUGH WHEN HE HITS A DRIVE THAT RICOCHETS OFF THE BALL WASHER. WE'RE NOT SUPPOSED TO LAUGH WHEN MAC DAVIS THROWS A TOUCHDOWN PASS IN *NORTH DALLAS FORTY*, BUT WE DO BECAUSE HE LOOKS SO OUT OF PLACE.

HERE'S A SCOUTING REPORT ON 10 ACTORS WHO MAKE THE CUT AS CREDIBLE ATHLETES. THEY ARE RANKED IN ORDER OF AUTHENTICITY:

1. Kevin Costner. He played a pitcher tossing a no-hitter in *For Love of the Game* and a catcher setting home run records in *Bull Durham*, and he was equally convincing in both roles. Also, he did not look out of place swinging a golf club next to pro Craig Stadler in *Tin Cup*. A true jock, he now competes in pro-am golf events.

2. Burt Reynolds. He was a halfback at Florida State and he still had all the right moves as Paul Crewe, the NFL star-turned-con in *The Longest Yard*. He needed them, because in the big game between the prisoners and the guards, the hitting was for real. Of the last play, when Crewe scores the winning touchdown, Reynolds said, "I probably scored on seven or eight takes and I got clobbered on fifty."

3. Robert Redford. He played a college track star (*The Way We Were*) and a world-class skier (*Downhill Racer*), but he's best remembered for his role in *The Natural*. "There's a way real ballplayers have of moving—smooth and easy—and [Redford] had it," said Mickey Vernon, who spent 26 years in the major leagues as a player, coach and manager. "The way he followed through on a throw, the way he turned his hips on a swing, even the way he adjusted his cap. I said, 'This guy is a ballplayer.' "

4. Robert De Niro. As a youngster, De Niro was so sickly and pale the other kids called him "Bobby Milk." He didn't play sports; he studied acting. But he trained in a boxing gym for a year to prepare for the role of Jake LaMotta in *Raging Bull*. De Niro studied film of LaMotta and learned his style so well that even at 36 (his age when the film was made), he looked like a real-deal middleweight contender.

5. Paul Newman/Jackie Gleason. We're putting them together for their brilliant work in *The Hustler*. Gleason, who plays the fictional Minnesota Fats, was an accomplished billiards player who circled a pool table with a grace that belied his girth. "That fat man moves like a dancer," Newman says. Lessons from world champion Willie Mosconi honed Newman's game to a point where he could make most of his own shots.

6. Wesley Snipes. His martial-arts background combined with the expert training of Emmanuel Steward turned Snipes into a convincing boxer. He is very good in *Undisputed*, and even better in the little-seen *Streets of Gold*. There is a scene in the latter film where Snipes demolishes an opponent with such vicious hooks and combinations that you'd swear you were watching Marvelous Marvin Hagler. He is that good.

7. Charlie Sheen. He was a ballplayer before he became an actor, and it is obvious just by the way he toes the pitching rubber. Sheen was a high school baseball star who passed up a scholarship to the University of Kansas to pursue an acting career. When he was filming *Major League*, his fastball was timed in the high 80s, and unlike his character Rick "Wild Thing" Vaughn, he knew where it was going most of the time.

8. Hilary Swank. She competed in the Junior Olympics as a swimmer and she ranked fifth in her native Washington state in gymnastics, but she trained even harder for the role of boxer Maggie Fitzgerald in *Million Dollar Baby*. She trained four hours a day, six days a week for three months. She pumped iron and drank protein shakes to add nearly 20 pounds of muscle. She also trained extensively at Gleason's Gym in New York, sparring with Golden Gloves boxers to develop the moves that helped her win an Oscar.

9. Tom Selleck. Born in Detroit (that's why his *Magnum, P.I.*, character wore a Tigers cap), Selleck was a three-sport athlete in high school. He attended the University of Southern California on a basketball scholarship, but his favorite sport is baseball. In the film *Mr. Baseball*, Selleck shows off a nice left-handed stroke. He once hit a ball over the wall at Camden Yards while taking part in a celebrity game.

"When we did *Mr. Baseball*, I spent part of spring training with the Tigers," Selleck said. "[Manager] Sparky Anderson promised me at least one at bat. He let me pinch hit in a game against Cincinnati. I hit for Rob Deer. The pitcher was Tim Layana. My claim to fame is I fouled off about six pitches before finally striking out."

10. Woody Harrelson. Harrelson is the most versatile actor/athlete, appearing in films involving five different sports: football (*Wildcats*), basketball (*White Men Can't Jump* and *Semi-Pro*), bowling (*Kingpin*), boxing (*Play It to the Bone*) and poker (*The Grand*). We have to assume he'll get around to baseball one of these days. *Major League IV*, anyone?

HERE ARE 10 ACTORS WHO WE PUT ON UNCONDITIONAL WAIVERS. THEY ARE RANKED IN ORDER OF FUTILITY:

1. Anthony Perkins. Before he was Norman Bates in *Psycho*, Perkins played Jimmy Piersall in *Fear Strikes Out* (1957), which was sort of a baseball psycho tale. Piersall was a Boston Red Sox player driven to a nervous breakdown by his demanding father (played by Karl Malden). Off the field, Perkins is effective in making us feel the young Piersall's anguish, but on the field, it is obvious he doesn't know the first thing about baseball. As former big leaguer Bob Uecker said, "When Anthony Perkins threw, I thought it was Millie Perkins."

2. John Goodman/William Bendix. How did it happen that the greatest baseball player of all time, Babe Ruth, was the subject of two of the worst baseball films? *The Babe Ruth Story* with William Bendix was dreadful, and Goodman's 1992 performance in *The Babe* was equally bad. Wrote Dave Kindred in *The Sporting News*, "[Goodman] can't swing a baseball bat. The word 'gawdawful' comes to mind. Goodman at bat as Babe Ruth is the visual equivalent of Roseanne Arnold in a bikini as Marilyn Monroe."

3. Charlton Heston. He could drive a chariot (*Ben-Hur*) and part the Red Sea (*The Ten Commandments*), but Heston couldn't throw a football. He proved that in the 1969 film *Number One*. He plays Ron Catlan, an aging quarterback with the New Orleans Saints. The aging part he could handle, but the quarterbacking was a problem. Heston never played football, so he asked the Saints quarterback to teach him how to throw a spiral. Unfortunately, the Saints quarterback at the time was Billy Kilmer, who couldn't throw a spiral, either. The results are some of the worst football scenes ever put on film.

4. Mac Davis. Davis was a country music star who made his acting debut in *North Dallas Forty*, and he was out of his element as an NFL quarterback. His character, Seth Maxwell, is based on Don Meredith, who played for the Dallas Cowboys. Davis has Dandy Don's country swagger, but when he throws the football, he looks like a farmer trying to heave a watermelon over a fence.

"I did like the scene where the players are in the weight room," said NBC analyst Cris Collinsworth. "The other guys are pumping iron and [Davis] has a little-bitty weight in one hand and a can of beer in the other. Quarterbacks are like that."

5. Ryan O'Neal and Barbra Streisand. We're putting them together because, well, they deserve it. Could there be anything less convincing than Ryan O'Neal as a prizefighter? How about Barbra Streisand as a boxing manager? Now try to imagine both in one film, *The Main Event*. On second thought, don't.

6. Robert De Niro. What? Wasn't he on our list of bests? Yes, he may have learned enough boxing moves to play Jake LaMotta in *Raging Bull*, but throwing hooks and jabs isn't the same thing as throwing a baseball. Prior to filming *Bang the Drum Slowly*, De Niro watched a lot of baseball, just as he did with boxing, but never achieved the fluid ease of someone who played the game his whole life.

As *ESPN.com* noted, "De Niro swings the bat like he is going after a pinata." He must have continued to practice, because when he played Al Capone in *The Untouchables*, he was much improved.

7. Corbin Bernsen. We can see why Bernsen was cast as Roger Dorn in *Major League*. The part called for someone handsome (check) with a strong diva quotient (check). But what about the part where Dorn has to play third base? Guess they left that part out of the audition. Bernsen reaches for every ground ball like it's a live grenade.

8. Glenn Ford. *Follow the Sun* was the story of golfer Ben Hogan, who came back from a crippling car crash to win the U.S. Open. Ford was well-suited to the role of Hogan, a man so aloof the other golfers called him "The Texas Iceberg." There was only one problem. "[Ford] didn't know how to play," Hogan's wife Valerie said. "He told them he did." The result was Ford, a novice hacker, playing the purest ball-striker the game has ever known.

9. Michael Caine. This Oscar winner looked totally out of place in *Victory* portraying a world-class soccer player leading a team of Allied POWs in a game against the Germans. Huffing and puffing, surrounded by real players such as Pele and Bobby Moore, Caine appears almost embarrassed. He is much better as a narrator in the World Cup highlight film, *Hero*.

10. Chevy Chase. In *Caddyshack*, Chase's Ty Webb is supposed to be an eccentric millionaire, ladies man and scratch golfer. OK, we'll buy the first two, but with that swing—sorry, we're not buying the third.

12 MILLION DOLLAR BABY (2004–PG-13)

SPORT: BOXING | STARS: CLINT EASTWOOD, HILARY SWANK, MORGAN FREEMAN
DIRECTOR: CLINT EASTWOOD

Million Dollar Baby is the most honored sports movie of all time. It was nominated for seven Academy Awards and swept four of the top prizes—Best Picture, Best Director (Clint Eastwood), Best Actress (Hilary Swank) and Best Supporting Actor (Morgan Freeman). It dominated the Oscars in a year when most predicted Martin Scorsese's lavish film *The Aviator* would clean up.

There must have been a lot of awkward foot-shuffling in the audience when the awards show turned into a *Baby* parade. Most of the big-name producers had the script on their desk at one time or another but rejected it. It was passed around to all the major studios. The executives would read a few pages and groan, "What, another boxing movie?" The project was tossed in every trash can in town.

Al Ruddy, who produced *The Godfather*, loved the story, but for four years he tried to find backers without

success. "I couldn't get anybody interested," Ruddy told *Sports Illustrated*, "and I'm talking about people who are friends of mine, people I've done business with for years. They'd tell me, 'Who wants to see a movie about two old grizzled guys and a girl fighter?' "

Finally, Ruddy found a believer in Clint Eastwood. "It's a downer," Eastwood said after reading the script, "but, God, it's gorgeous."

A year earlier, Eastwood proved he could take a painful subject and turn it into gold. His *Mystic River*, a film that dealt with death and child abuse, was nominated for six Academy Awards. Eastwood convinced long-time backers Warner Brothers and Lakeshore Entertainment that he could have similar success with *Baby*.

On Eastwood's word, the two studios agreed to split the $30 million production cost. Eastwood, one of Holly-wood's most efficient directors, completed the shoot in

37 days and brought the film in under budget. It wound up earning more than $200 million at the box office, in addition to winning two Golden Globes, two Screen Actors Guild awards and a New York Film Critics Award, as well as the four Oscars.

Kenneth Turan of the *Los Angeles Times* called *Baby*, "The director's most touching, most elegiac work yet . . . a film that does both the expected and the unexpected [with] the emotional daring of the great melodramas of Hollywood's golden age when films considered it a badge of honor to wear their hearts on their sleeves.

"What can be said about Clint Eastwood that hasn't been said before?" Turan wrote. "That he is American film's last and best classicist, a 74-year-old director who's aged better than a *Sideways* Pinot Noir? That his increasingly fearless and idiosyncratic choice of material has made him more of an independent filmmaker than half the people at Sundance? That he continues to find ways to surprise audiences, yet remain inescapably himself? It's all true, and never more so than in Eastwood's latest, *Million Dollar Baby*."

The screenplay was written by Paul Haggis, who combined two short stories authored by F.X. Toole, the pen name of veteran boxing cornerman Jerry Boyd. They were originally published as part of a collection entitled *Rope Burns*. They have since been re-published borrowing the title *Million Dollar Baby*.

The focus of the story is Maggie Fitzgerald, a 31-year-old waitress and amateur boxer who is determined to turn pro. She wants Frankie Dunn (Eastwood), a crafty old trainer, to teach her the ropes. She introduces herself one night at the arena and Frankie does his best to brush her off.

"I don't train girls," he says, never breaking stride. He keeps walking and Maggie keeps walking with him, telling him she won her bout earlier that night. Frankie hates the whole notion of women boxing. He calls it "the latest freak show out there." He leaves Maggie at the arena, drives off and assumes that's the last he will ever see of her.

The next day, Frankie is walking through the Hit Pit, the tattered old gym he owns in downtown Los Angeles, when he sees Maggie punching a heavy bag. "What are you doing?" he asks. Again, she tells Frankie she wants him to train her. Again, he refuses, but Maggie grins and we can see where this is headed. She is going to wear the old coot down.

If that was the whole of the story, it wouldn't be anything special. The reluctant mentor-irrepressible pupil story has been done a million times. The poor boxer-makes-good story has been done more than a million times. Just slapping one on top of the other like a slice of salami on a ham sandwich wouldn't make it a gourmet meal. But there are many layers to *Million Dollar Baby*, all beautifully rendered, and they combine to make the film truly memorable.

While Frankie is portrayed as a gruff and distant loner, there is a deep hurt in his life—his estrangement from his daughter. He writes to her every week and each letter returns to Frankie unopened. The look on his face as he picks up his mail and sees the latest letter in the stack, the quick flicker of pain you see in his eyes, is so sad. He never says a word but he doesn't have to. It is an eloquent silence.

We learn Maggie comes from a white trash background. She lost her father and did not have much of a relationship with her mother and siblings, so she took off for L.A. She is alone and looking for a father figure and Frankie has a void in his life due to the rift with his daughter—so it is clear they are destined to come together.

It starts with left jabs and right hooks, but becomes much more than that. Frankie and his sidekick Eddie "Scrap Iron" Dupris (Freeman) become Maggie's family, and Maggie becomes Frankie's surrogate daughter. The same material in the hands of less skillful performers could have become trite—especially with Freeman's character serving as an off-camera narrator, always a tricky device. But Eastwood, Swank and Freeman are so good, we want to see them through every crisis.

Swank is superb as Maggie—earnest, gutsy, yet so emotionally needy and vulnerable. When Frankie finally caves in and agrees to train her, she flashes a smile that seems to fill her entire face. When she says, "Boxing is the only thing I ever felt good doing," we believe her. As good as Swank was in her other Oscar-winning role in *Boys Don't Cry*, she is even better here.

Freeman's character is a former heavyweight contender whose career was ended by a ring injury that left him blind in one eye. Frankie was his manager and he still blames himself for letting it happen. Now Scrap Iron works at the Hit Pit, sweeping the floors and emptying the spit buckets, but his real job is serving as a common-sense dispenser for the irascible Frankie.

When a delusional but harmless kid wanders into the gym and announces he wants to be the next welterweight champ, Scrap Iron indulges him, allowing him to hang around and hit the bags even though it is obvious it is all a fantasy. The kid—whom Scrap Iron calls "Danger"—has no money, and he shows up every day in the same shirt and sweatpants.

Frankie asks Scrap Iron if Danger is paying gym dues. Scrap Iron leans on his mop and gives Frankie his "Are-you-serious?" look. "The boy can't even afford pants, Frankie," he says. "How's he gonna pay dues?" Frankie wants to kick him out, but Scrap Iron says, "Aw, he ain't hurting nobody. Let him be."

Frankie grumbles, but Danger stays.

Eastwood was nominated for Best Actor and did not win, but he is the equal of Swank and Freeman, which is saying a lot. Turan calls Eastwood's performance "the most nakedly emotional of his 50-year career." Eastwood and Freeman established a comfortable on-screen chemistry in *Unforgiven*, another Oscar winner, in 1992 and they find the same smooth old-buddy groove here.

But the real heart of *Baby* is the relationship between Frankie and Maggie and what happens once Frankie begins to manage her career. He takes her burning desire, adds his years of boxing knowledge and turns the thirtysomething diner waitress into a contender. Maggie wants to move the process along quickly, but Frankie is the cautious type. (Early in the film, we see a heavyweight prospect named Big Willie Little leave Frankie because he wants to step up in class. Frankie doesn't think he's ready.)

Frankie, who has been denied an emotional connection to his own daughter, develops one with Maggie. He still is her trainer and 24/7 taskmaster, but he smiles more and he listens when she talks about her life and her family. He has a robe made for her with the words "Mo Cuishle" on the back. It is Gaelic for "My darling, my blood" although he doesn't tell her that until the very end of the film.

Maggie gets her title shot in Las Vegas against the fearsome Billie the Blue Bear, the WBA women's champion, played by Lucia Rijker, a real-life kick-boxer whose scowl and brooding eyes would have intimidated Mike Tyson in his prime.

We won't reveal what happens next because if you haven't seen the film there is no way to address it without spoiling everything. It is as emotionally wrenching as any film you are likely to see. The ending caused a considerable uproar when the film was released and there was speculation it might hurt the movie's Oscar chances. Obviously that proved not to be true, but the final act is widely debated among movie critics and fans alike.

Andrew Sarris of the *New York Observer* said, "No movie in my memory has depressed me more than *Million Dollar Baby*." Meanwhile, Roger Ebert of the *Chicago Sun-Times* called it "a masterpiece, pure and simple."

"A movie is not good or bad because of its content, but because of how it handles its content," Ebert wrote in calling it the best film of 2004. "*Million Dollar Baby* is classical in the clean, clear, strong lines of its story and characters and it had an enormous emotional impact."

🏆 **CHEERS:** Hilary Swank trained with a boxing coach for three months and packed on almost 20 pounds of muscle to play Maggie. She is simply great, balancing the poor waif Maggie (scraping up the pennies and nickels that pass for tips in the diner) with the ferocious Maggie we see in the ring.

🏴 **JEERS:** Frankie's daily theological interrogations of the parish priest (Brian O'Byrne) don't make much sense. What is the point? If Frankie has that many issues with his faith, why bother coming to mass?

🎭 **BET YOU DIDN'T KNOW:** In addition to producing, directing and starring in the film, Eastwood also wrote the musical score.

✏️ **WHAT THEY WROTE AT THE TIME:** "Eastwood's darkly funny, surprising and immensely moving tale of ambition and disillusionment is as close to an anti-Rocky as any sports movie ever made."—Franz Lidz, *Sports Illustrated*

PIVOTAL SCENE: Maggie wins a bout out of town and on the way back to L.A., she asks Frankie if they can stop and visit her family. Maggie has been sending her mother and siblings a portion of her winnings ever since she started boxing.

Maggie finds her family hasn't changed at all. They are still redneck lowlifes—and ungrateful ones at that. Instead of thanking Maggie, her mother looks at the fresh bruise on her face and mocks her for boxing.

"People hear what you're doing and they laugh at you," the mother says.

Maggie leaves more determined than ever to win the championship, if only to prove something to her family.

GOOFS: When Scrap Iron tells Maggie the story about how he lost the sight in his eye, he talks about "going 15 rounds." It would have only been 15 rounds if it was a title fight and we already know Scrap Iron never fought for the title.

CASTING CALL: Sandra Bullock was originally cast as Maggie Fitzgerald, but dropped out before the filming began.

REALITY CHECK: We can't be sure because we weren't at the weigh-in, but we find it hard to believe that Maggie and Billie The Blue Bear are in the same weight class. Billie looks like a linebacker. Maggie is buff, granted, but she still looks at least 20 pounds lighter.

REPEATED WATCHING QUOTIENT: As good as this film is—and it is very good—it would be hard to sit through the whole thing more than once. And, frankly, there is no need. This film, especially the ending, will stay with you.

SPORTS-ACTION GRADE: B. The boxing scenes are well-staged and Swank throws a nifty combination, but some of the bouts would have been stopped by a referee or ringside physician. Swank is allowed to continue fighting with a busted, bloody nose. That would not happen in any responsible arena.

MY FAVORITE SPORTS MOVIE: Marv Albert, Hall of Fame broadcaster: "As one who has appeared in such basketball classics as *The Fish That Saved Pittsburgh*, *Celtic Pride* and *Eddie* [this had straight-to-DVD written all over it despite Whoopi Goldberg's efforts], I still maintain much faith in sports movies. The best I've ever seen is *Million Dollar Baby*, which was obviously more than a film about boxing. My feeling is most boxing movies have been over the top when it comes to the fight scenes—almost video-game-ish—but Hilary Swank's performance was remarkable as was Clint Eastwood's feel, both as a director and actor. *Million Dollar Baby* is a touching, beautifully crafted movie that, to me, is the best sports film of all time."

13 THE PRIDE OF THE YANKEES
(1942–NR)

SPORT: BASEBALL | STARS: GARY COOPER, TERESA WRIGHT, WALTER BRENNAN
DIRECTOR: SAM WOOD

Most movies don't age well. The plots and the dialog go stale. The clothes and the music become dated. The camerawork and sound isn't as good. This is especially true for sports movies. Today, the games are more sophisticated and the action is more visceral so it makes for better filmmaking.

But the truly great films retain their power and that is the case with *The Pride of the Yankees*. It is the only film in our top 15 that was made before 1960 and, really, it was an easy call. *The Pride of the Yankees* is a work of art and, as such, it is timeless. Black and white or color, it doesn't matter. The story of baseball legend Lou Gehrig, beauti-

fully played by Gary Cooper, still touches your heart.

It is interesting to watch *The Pride of the Yankees* now and consider the forces that shaped it. The film was made in 1942 when the United States was reeling from the attack on Pearl Harbor. The war was not going well for the Allies. President Roosevelt was calling for Americans to demonstrate their courage and strength. *The Pride of the Yankees* offered Gehrig as a symbol of those qualities.

To drive home the point, the film opens with a prologue written by Damon Runyon describing Gehrig as a man who "faced death with the same valor and fortitude that has been displayed by thousands of young Americans on the far-flung fields of battle."

RKO Studios also factored the war into how Gehrig's story was told. Typically, a baseball film appeals to a male audience, but since most American men were overseas, producer Sam Goldwyn and director Sam Wood shifted the focus. They made it more of a love story so it would appeal to women who were buying most of the movie tickets in 1942. In that sense, it was a forerunner of *Bull Durham* and *Jerry Maguire*.

The original movie poster shows Eleanor Gehrig

The Pride of the Yankees the finest sports film ever made.

"I saw it when I was 10 or 11 and it had a real effect on me," Dryer said. "I was living in California and I'd never seen major league baseball. The Dodgers didn't come west until 1958, so *The Pride of the Yankees* was my introduction to the mythology of baseball. It made the whole ballpark thing come alive for me.

"It hit me like a sledgehammer when Gehrig fell ill (in the film). I wasn't prepared for that. Back then, movies had happy endings. I thought, 'He's sick, but he'll come back.' When he didn't, when he said his goodbye at Yan-

ELEANOR: **"HOW'S TANGLEFOOT? HAS HE COME TO YET OR CAN'T YOU TELL?"**

LOU: **"WHAT DOES IT MEAN WHEN A GIRL SAYS YOU REMIND HER OF A NEWFOUNDLAND PUPPY?"**

(Teresa Wright) melting in the arms of her husband (Cooper). She is in a dress, he in a suit. There is no sign of baseball in the illustration or the tag line. ("It's the Great American Love Story.") When the film was re-issued after the war, the poster was changed to show Lou in a Yankees uniform swinging for the fences.

One can only imagine the impact the film had when it was first released less than a year after Gehrig's death on June 2, 1941. He was just 37 when he succumbed to amyotrophic lateral sclerosis (ALS), the crippling illness now known as Lou Gehrig's Disease.

Fred Dryer, who played 13 seasons in the NFL and later became an actor and producer in Hollywood, considers

kee Stadium and walked away, I couldn't believe it. Sad as it was, (the ending) made it very real and it made Gehrig very real to me.

"Years later when I played in Yankee Stadium (1969-71 with the football Giants), I walked around the field and thought about that. I thought about Gehrig, about the speech, about the emotion that must have been in the stadium that day. It was like daydreaming, but in black and white because the images in my mind were the images from the movie."

The Pride of the Yankees follows the standard rags to riches path. Gehrig is born in New York and attends Columbia, where he follows the wishes of his German immigrant parents and studies to be an engineer. He also excels in sports. The Yankees offer him a contract which he signs to help pay the bills incurred by his mother's illness. She is furious when she is told.

"You gave up everything we planned and for what? For you to play ball?" she says. She wants Lou to be an engineer like his Uncle Otto back in the old country.

"People have to live their own lives," Lou says. "Nobody can live it for you. Nobody could have made a baseball player out of Uncle Otto and nobody can make anything but a baseball player out of me."

After a brief stop in the minors, Lou is called up to the Yankees. He takes over one day when the regular first baseman Wally Pipp complains of a headache. The rookie goes in the lineup, and that's the end of Wally Pipp. Lou plays the next 2,130 consecutive games to set a major league record and he teams with Babe Ruth to give the Yankees the greatest one-two punch in baseball history.

The Pride of the Yankees contrasts the personalities of the swaggering, larger-than-life Babe (played effectively by The Babe himself) and shy, salt-of-the-earth Lou. A cynical sportswriter covering the team mocks Lou. "He's a chump, a rube with a batting eye," he says. "He plays the game, goes back to the hotel, reads the funny papers, gargles and goes to bed." The Babe, obviously, cut a wider and more colorful swath.

Gehrig and Ruth combine to hit more than 700 home runs and they help the Yankees win four world championships. After The Babe is dealt away in 1935, Gehrig plays another four seasons, wins one home run title and grows into the role of team captain.

In 1938, Gehrig notices he is slowing down. He thinks at 34 he is just feeling the effects of middle age. But the following season, he goes 4-for-28 in the first eight games and takes himself out of the lineup. He goes to the hospital for tests and learns he has a nerve disease for which there is no cure.

"Is it three strikes, Doc?" Lou asks.

"You want it straight?" the doctor replies.

"Yeah," Lou says.

"It's three strikes."

The Yankees honor him at the stadium. That's where Lou gives the speech in which he refers to himself as "the luckiest man on the face of the earth." In the film, they change the speech slightly (see "Reality Check" below) but it does not lessen the impact. Cooper delivers it with just the right feeling. He is emotional but not maudlin. Standing at the microphone in that baggy white uniform, Cooper actually seems to become Lou Gehrig.

The Pride of the Yankees was nominated for 11 Academy Awards, including Best Picture, Best Actor (Cooper) and Best Actress (Wright). It won one Oscar: Daniel Mandell for film editing. Cooper lost out to James Cagney (*Yankee Doodle Dandy*). The American Film Institute ranks *The Pride of the Yankees* #22 on its list of the top 100 most inspiring movies in American cinema. The "luckiest man" speech ranks #38 among greatest movie quotes.

There is some baseball in the film, but not a lot. In part, that is because the studio wanted the love story of Lou and Eleanor in the foreground. But there was another reason for limiting the baseball action: Gary Cooper wasn't much of an athlete. The 6-foot-3 Cooper was actually bigger than Gehrig. The Iron Horse was 6-0 and 200 pounds in his prime. Cooper also projected the stoic strength that was so much a part of Gehrig's character. But the similarity ended there. On the field, Gehrig was a natural and Cooper was the unnatural. Cooper did not play sports and he had a lot to learn taking on the role of Gehrig.

Lefty O'Doul, who played 11 years in the big leagues, worked with Cooper, teaching him the basics. Cooper only felt comfortable swinging the bat right-handed. Gehrig, of course, was left-handed. O'Doul tried to turn Cooper around without success. Director Wood came up with a solution. He filmed Cooper batting righty and flipped the negative so on the screen it appears he is a lefty. To make it work, the lettering on Cooper's cap and uniform had to be reversed and when he hit the ball, he ran to third base, not first. It sounds comical, but it worked.

"I saw the movie as a teenager and I was so impressed," said Robin Roberts, the Hall of Fame pitcher who broke in with the Philadelphia Phillies in 1948. "I had three sports idols: Whizzer White, the football player who became a Supreme Court justice; Otto Graham, who was a basketball and football star in college; and Lou Gehrig.

"When I got to the big leagues, I met a lot of people

who knew Gehrig. I asked them about Gehrig because I was curious. They all said the same thing: 'What you saw in the movie, that was Lou. He was a great ballplayer, but he was also a great man.' "

🍺 **CHEERS:** Among many nice touches in the film, the song that Lou (Cooper) and Eleanor (Wright) dance to the first time is "Always." It was the Gehrigs' favorite song.

🚩 **JEERS:** The character of Sam Blake (Walter Brennan) is based on New York sportswriter Fred Lieb. His on-screen relationship with Gehrig, which includes fixing him up with Eleanor and driving the happy couple to the ballpark after their wedding, seems a little unprofessional even for the 1930s.

✔ **REALITY CHECK:** In the film, Lou ends his famous speech by saying: "People say that I've had a bad break. But today I consider myself the luckiest man on the face of the earth."

In reality, that's how Lou began his speech. He said, "For the past two weeks, you've been reading about a bad break. Today, I consider myself the luckiest man on the face of the earth. I have been in ballparks for 17 years and have never received anything but kindness and encouragement from you fans."

After thanking his teammates and family, he closed by saying: "I might have been given a bad break, but I've got an awful lot to live for."

👆 **BET YOU DIDN'T KNOW:** Lou Gehrig starred in football as well as baseball at Columbia University.

☝ **DON'T FAIL TO NOTICE:** The bracelet Teresa Wright wears in the film is the bracelet Lou gave Eleanor on their fourth wedding anniversary. It has 17 medallions, each one representing a Yankee world championship or an All-Star appearance. The bracelet is now on display at the Baseball Hall of Fame in Cooperstown, N.Y.

🎬 **PIVOTAL SCENE:** In his final season, Lou topples off his stool while trying to tie his shoes in the clubhouse. Every eye in the room turns toward him, but catcher Bill Dickey (playing himself) holds up his hand as if to say, "Leave him alone." He knows Gehrig does not want to be the object of pity.

💬 **BEST LINE:** Ma Gehrig: "All baseball players are good for nothing loafers in short pants."

✎ **WHAT THEY WROTE AT THE TIME:** "A simple, tender, meticulous and explicitly narrative film, a real saga of American life, homey, humorous, sentimental and composed in patient detail."—*New York Times*

◉ **REPEATED WATCHING QUOTIENT:** It is worth seeing again, but make sure you have the tissues close at hand.

★ **SPORTS-ACTION GRADE:** C. There isn't much baseball in the film, but it is fun to see the real Babe Ruth (not William Bendix or John Goodman) playing pepper and trotting around the bases.

🎞 **MY FAVORITE SPORTS MOVIE:** Dusty Baker, Cincinnati Reds manager: "Think about him [Gehrig]. No alibis, no excuses, no complaining. He knows he's gonna die, but he's got no anger. Heck, he called himself lucky. That's a man's man."

🎞 **MY FAVORITE SPORTS MOVIE, TOO:** Terry Bradshaw, Hall of Fame quarterback: "If I'm going to watch a sports film, I usually want it to be a biography. The Lou Gehrig movie, *The Pride of the Yankees*, is my favorite. It's a wonderful story about a great Yankee and a great guy. I've watched it a bunch of times and I always love it as much as the first time."

14 HOOP DREAMS (1994–PG-13)

SPORT: BASKETBALL | STARS: WILLIAM GATES, ARTHUR AGEE
DIRECTOR: STEVE JAMES

"People always say to me, 'When you get to the NBA, don't forget about me.' Well, I should have said back, 'If I don't make it to the NBA, don't you forget about me."—William Gates, in the final scene of *Hoop Dreams*

Hoop Dreams is a movie about the 99.99 percent of those kids who grow up *not* to become Kobe Bryant. It is about two adolescent boys who work and sweat and imagine themselves as the next NBA superstar. It is about the impossible dream of escaping a grueling inner-city destiny by devoting yourself to basketball.

It may also be the most powerful sports movie ever made. Because it is all true.

This 1994 documentary follows the lives of William Gates and Arthur Agee, whom we meet as two 14-year-olds living in Chicago's Cabrini Green projects. From the jump, basketball is everything to them. They watch the

NBA All-Star Game on TV and then try to imitate Michael Jordan's tongue-wagging moves on a neighborhood court that has weeds growing through the asphalt. Each boy is certain that stardom awaits him. "I'm going to get my dad a Cadillac," pronounces Arthur, "so he can cruise to my games."

Both teens, in fact, are talented enough to be recruited to St. Joseph's High School, a private academy in the Chicago suburbs most famous as the alma mater of Isiah Thomas. When Arthur gets to play a little one-on-one with the Detroit Pistons superstar at a summer camp at St. Joseph's, you see him sizing himself up for a bright future.

But it is William, more mature emotionally and physically, who makes the better early impression. As a freshman, he wins a spot on the St. Joseph's varsity squad and even starts at point guard, the first time that has happened since . . . well, you know who.

"I think I may have seen the next Isiah Thomas," Chicago sports talker Bill Gleason proclaims on the show *The Sportswriters on TV*. Young William, he tells the audience, has the right stuff.

If you think this story is just about teens playing ball, you are wrong. From the start the boys are encircled by various characters and hangers-on—some aiming to be helpful, some no better than parasites. There are talent scouts, coaches, journalists and recruiters, all of whom want their piece of the action. Before he is even 15, William is shown opening a stack of brochures from top colleges—Marquette, Rice, Illinois. He glances over glossy pictures of well-scrubbed coeds and grassy quads that must look enticing to a youngster seeking to escape the concrete claustrophobia of the projects.

There is also family to deal with. William's older brother, Curtis, was once a talented athlete whose career peaked playing junior college ball. Bad breaks, he says. Uncoachable, others say. Now, Curtis sees his own failed possibilities being resurrected through his younger sibling. He is desperate for William to succeed. Admirable goal, except that it comes with the burden of unwanted pressure. "I always felt that Curtis should not be living his dream through me," William wisely notes.

Arthur must contend with tougher family issues. His father, Bo Agee, drifts between jobs and lapses into drug use. In perhaps the film's most wrenching scene, father and son play a good-natured game of one-on-one. They hug goodbye at the end and, as Arthur stays to practice his shooting, the camera follows Bo as he wanders to the shadows beyond the court and negotiates a crack deal. The camera pans back to Arthur and you see the pain in the 15-year-old's eyes.

Hoop Dreams pulls no punches. You watch the breakup of the 20-year marriage between Bo and Sheila Agee and learn later that he comes back to assault her. You peek inside the Agees' darkened apartment after the power is cut off by the electric company and they are living by the light of a lantern. But you also see hope: Sheila Agee enrolls in nursing school, aiming to pull herself from welfare. She graduates with the highest grade in the class, and you'll likely cry along with her at the graduation.

The power of *Hoop Dreams* is that it is at times dis-

turbing, at times uplifting and always compelling. Director Steve James and his crew shot more than 250 hours of film and edited it down to a 170-minute gut punch.

By sophomore year, the boys are going in separate directions. William is making honor roll and emerging as a player with college—and perhaps pro—potential. Because his family cannot afford St. Joseph's hefty tuition, a well-heeled alum appears as an angel to take care of his financial needs.

But not so Arthur. His family doesn't have the tuition money either. He sits home for two months, waiting—but, in his case, no fairy godmother shows up. And, he has fallen into disfavor with St. Joseph's coach Gene Pingatore. "Coach keeps asking me, 'When are you gonna grow?' " he notes.

Finally, he is forced to leave the posh academy and enroll at his local high school, located in a ramshackle neighborhood of broken houses and broken dreams. In a heart-rending moment, a wiser-than-his years Arthur suggests that Pingatore quit on him once his prospects as a star player faded. In the final irony, his family is forced to pay $1,300 in back tuition for St. Joseph's to release his transcript. The wealthy school that plucked him from the pond has thrown him back—with a debt to boot.

The coaches and faculty members at St. Joseph's were upset with their portrayal in *Hoop Dreams*, although every character gets his say on camera. School administrators later filed a lawsuit, saying they were promised the film was going to be a non-profit venture shown on PBS, rather than in theaters. We're not really sure why that would make a difference. Regardless, it grossed about $8 million, which ranks among the top 20 documentaries ever. Director James split the profits—about $200,000—with the Agee and Gates families.

By junior year, William is a nationally ranked prospect, getting recruiting mail from the likes of Duke, Georgetown and Michigan State. Everything seems perfect until he injures his knee in practice. The trip to the doctor will remind you of Boobie Miles' tragic moment in *Friday Night Lights*. The youngster, who has never been hurt before, believes he will spring right back. The doctor must tell him otherwise, and sitting for nearly a full season is a hard nut for an idealistic teen to swallow.

Still, William works his way back. The following summer, he wins an invitation to the prestigious Nike Camp in Princeton, N.J., where the top college coaches in the nation—Bob Knight, Mike Krzyzewski, Bobby Cremins—peer from the bleachers at the future of their programs. It all goes well, until William again injures his knee. As he writhes on the floor, you feel his pain.

Many of the coaches in *Hoop Dreams* are shown as manipulators, making promises to the young athletes while ignoring their parents' concerns about academic achievement. One coach who comes across better is Marquette's Kevin O'Neill. The camera is there as O'Neill visits the Gates household, and again as William makes his recruiting visit to the Wisconsin campus. O'Neill offers a four-year scholarship, saying it remains valid even if William's tender knee gives out.

William takes the offer, and celebrates at his 18th birthday party. "He's a great kid and some kids don't even live to this age," says his mother, Emma Gates. "He's 18 and he's lived this long and I'm very proud of him."

Arthur takes longer to find himself, but eventually gets there. As a senior, his high school finishes third in the state and he is a leading scorer. He wins a scholarship to Mineral Area Junior College in southern Missouri, which—truth be told—resembles a prison. All seven of the school's black students play on the basketball team and live together in one house.

Ultimately, of course, neither William Gates nor Arthur Agee became the next Isiah Thomas. Both played college ball (William at Marquette and Arthur, eventually, at Arkansas State). William got a degree in communications and Arthur later formed a foundation to help other kids get into college.

The journey we watch over five years is dramatic and revealing. It will both outrage and inspire you.

🏆 **CHEERS:** The real-life characters—friends, family, coaches and teachers—are as good as any fictional cast that could have been cooked up.

🏳 **JEERS:** Over nearly three hours, there is less than 20 minutes of real basketball action. We know the movie is a portrait of the boys' lives, but we would have preferred a little more hoop, a little less dreams.

✒ **WHAT THEY WROTE AT THE TIME:** "*Hoop Dreams* isn't about the triumph of the human spirit or any of the other top 10 favorite sports clichés. It's about something far rarer in the movies and of vastly greater significance—it's about real life."—Hal Hinson, *Washington Post*

◉ **REPEATED WATCHING QUOTIENT:** Check it every five years or so, just to see how powerful documentary non-fiction can be.

🎬 **PIVOTAL SCENE:** A second one-on-one game between Arthur and his father—dubbed "The Great Santini" scene by director James—occurs near the end of the movie. Bo Agee has been through crack addiction and prison, but has found religion and come back to his family. His son remains wary and resentful.

A few plays into their showdown, Bo tries to fudge the score and Arthur fumes. "Ain't no con game going on anymore, Dad," he says.

Arthur then reels off four straight baskets, leaving his father laboring under a summer sun.

"I'm older now," says Arthur.

★ **SPORTS-ACTION GRADE:** B-plus. It's top-flight high school basketball action. We just wish more of it was put into in the film.

💬 **BEST LINE:** "It became more of a job than a game to play."—William Gates at the end of high school.

😎 **"I KNOW THAT GUY":** Look closely at the aspiring college players during the scene at Nike camp. Two of them are teenaged Jalen Rose and Chris Webber, both of whom realized their own hoop dreams.

🎽 **BET YOU DIDN'T KNOW:** Today, William Gates is a pastor in his old neighborhood of Cabrini Green. He had a tryout with the Washington Wizards in 2001, which ended when he broke a bone in his foot. Arthur Agee has earned some money as a public speaker and tried launching a *Hoop Dreams* clothing line, but has yet to attain a successful career.

William's brother, Curtis, was murdered in 2001. Arthur's father, Bo, was murdered in 2004.

15 BRIAN'S SONG (1971–NR)

SPORT: FOOTBALL | STARS: BILLY DEE WILLIAMS, JAMES CAAN
DIRECTOR: BUZZ KULIK

In 2008, the web site eHarmony compiled a list of "20 Movies that Make Men Cry." *Brian's Song* finished No. 1.

Larry Csonka, the Hall of Fame fullback, admits he choked up watching *Brian's Song*. It's hard to imagine Csonka with that battle-scarred face and outta-my-way scowl getting all misty over a movie, but he swears it really did happen.

"I was breaking into the league around the time [Gale] Sayers and [Brian] Piccolo were playing in Chicago," Csonka said. "Like everyone else, I was shocked when Piccolo died. I heard they were doing this movie and I thought it would be one of those sappy TV deals.

"I was surprised at how good it was. I didn't know the depth of their friendship. I was watching it and thinking, 'Wow, this is really something.' The scene where Gale visits (Piccolo) in the hospital for the last time, the love

those two guys had for each other, it really hits you."

It is a tribute to the power of *Brian's Song* that a TV movie made almost 40 years ago still resonates with athletes and fans. When we surveyed people for their all-time favorite sports movies, *Brian's Song* was on most short lists. Csonka had it at No. 1, as did Rich Gannon, the former Oakland quarterback, and Brian Baldinger, the former NFL lineman, now a Fox network broadcaster.

"I was 10 when I saw it," said Baldinger, "and I decided that night that sports would be my life. That's how much of an impression it made on me."

"I saw it at my grammar school, St. Cecilia's in Philadelphia," said Gannon, the NFL's Most Valuable Player in 2002. "I was a kid who dreamed of playing in the NFL and that movie was my first behind-the-scenes look at pro football. It showed the training camp, the film study, guys rehabbing injuries, stuff I never thought about before. And, yeah, I cried."

The film stars Billy Dee Williams as Sayers and James Caan as Piccolo. They were unknowns at the time, although Williams would soon emerge as a romantic leading man, and Caan would create an unforgettable role as Sonny Corleone in *The Godfather*.

Brian's Song is the poignant story of two Chicago Bears who go from rookie rivals to best friends over the course of five seasons. The film ends tragically as Piccolo succumbs to cancer, but his courage inspires Sayers on and off the field.

It begins in 1965 as rookies Sayers and Piccolo join the Bears. Sayers is a first-round draft pick, an All-America from Kansas, a dazzling runner who is destined for greatness. Piccolo is a free agent from Wake Forest, short on talent but long on desire.

Director Buzz Kulik and writer William Blinn draw contrasting portraits of the two players. Sayers, for all of his acclaim, is painfully shy. Piccolo is an extrovert with a wry sense of humor. When they first meet, Sayers is on his way to see Bears coach George Halas (Jack Warden). Piccolo tells Sayers that Halas is deaf in one ear so he should keep that in mind.

Piccolo's story is nonsense, but Sayers believes him. When he meets with Halas, the coach is moving around his office, filing papers. Sayers keeps running circles around the coach, trying to stay on his "good" side. Perplexed, Halas says,"I know you have good moves, Sayers, but what are you doing?" Sayers realizes he's been duped.

Over the course of the summer, Sayers and Piccolo become friends. Gradually, Piccolo brings Sayers out of his shell. As the team prepares for the regular season, Halas asks the two men how they would feel about being roommates on the road. He explains it would be the first time in Bears history that a black player and a white player shared a room.

"It will be news," Halas says.

Sayers and Piccolo shrug. They're friends, their wives are friends, they go out together. Roommates? Sure, why not? So a racial barrier comes down and hardly anyone bats an eye. Given the context of America in the turbulent '60s, that's no small accomplishment.

Sayers has one of the greatest rookie seasons in NFL history, scoring 22 touchdowns, including six in one game against San Francisco (still tied for an NFL record). Over the next two years, he becomes the most celebrated player in the game, winning the rushing title in 1966. Piccolo plays sparingly. Mostly, he cheers on his roommate.

Sayers is off to another blazing start in 1968 when he suffers a devastating knee injury. Piccolo steps into Sayers' spot and plays well, including a 112-yard rushing performance against New Orleans. When Sayers recovers the following year, he is paired with Piccolo in the backfield. This is what they wanted, the chance to play together, but it is cut short when a malignant tumor is discovered in Piccolo's chest.

Piccolo's illness is not widely known until after the season, when Sayers accepts the Most Courageous Athlete award for coming back from his knee injury. He tells the audience that Piccolo is more deserving of the honor for his courage in battling cancer.

"I love Brian Piccolo," Sayers says, "and I'd like all of you to love him, too. Tonight, when you hit your knees, please ask God to love him."

It is an emotional scene, and Williams plays it very well. Overall, it is the acting of Williams and Caan that keeps *Brian's Song* from becoming maudlin. It is a pleasure to watch Williams as Sayers opens up. When he stands in the locker room and tells the team about Piccolo's illness, he is not the quiet kid we saw earlier. He is strong and confident, and we know it is largely due to Piccolo's influence.

Caan does his part by maintaining Piccolo's irreverence. Lying in the hospital, barely able to speak, he tells Sayers: "When you dedicate a game to someone, you're supposed to win it." (The Bears lost after Sayers' locker room speech). After Sayers gives him a blood transfusion, Piccolo says,"I'm developing this tremendous craving for chitlins."

The laugh the two men share is a touching reminder of happier times. And if it moves you to tears, well, you are not alone.

"That was the first sports movie I can remember where the people, not the games, were the most important thing," Baldinger said. "I watched it and thought, 'That's what sports should be about—friendship and teamwork.' When you get right down to it, that's what life should be about."

CHEERS: The Bears allowed Screen Gems to shoot at their training camp with many of the coaches and players appearing on camera. Since the film was made just one year after Piccolo's death, the Bears still had a strong emotional attachment to Piccolo, which made for a heartfelt movie.

"The first day I walked onto the field in Brian's No. 41 jersey, a lot of the players wept," James Caan said. "They really loved that guy."

JEERS: They foolishly re-made *Brian's Song* as a TV movie in 2001. It was a bad idea for many reasons, but most of all because younger viewers who only heard about the original film watched this lame imitation and wondered, "That's the movie I heard so much about?" No, it's not even close.

WHAT THEY WROTE AT THE TIME: "*Brian's Song* can melt the hearts of the coldest, most emotionally stunted men in the universe. It's the *Old Yeller* of adult males and no real man will ever fault another for getting a bit misty in its presence."—Brad Laidman, *Film Threat*

PIVOTAL SCENE: When Sayers returns home following his knee surgery, he finds Piccolo in the basement, assembling workout equipment. Sayers is irritated, and tells Piccolo he doesn't want to use it. Piccolo gives Sayers a verbal kick in the butt.

Piccolo tells Sayers how he went to Wake Forest, led the nation in rushing, and still was passed over in the draft because the scouts thought he was too slow. He came to the Bears as a free agent, fought for a spot on the roster, and then sat on the bench and waited for a chance to play. Sayers' injury gave Piccolo that chance.

"So next season if I beat you out, I want to know I beat you at your best," Piccolo says.

Piccolo pushes Sayers through his rehabilitation and Sayers comes back to win his second NFL rushing title.

BET YOU DIDN'T KNOW: This isn't in the movie, but NFL Commissioner Pete Rozelle spent Thanksgiving Day, 1969, at the hospital with Piccolo, watching the Lions-Vikings game on television.

IF YOU LIKED THIS, YOU'LL LIKE: *Something for Joey*, a 1977 TV movie about Penn State's John Cappelletti and his kid brother, Joey, who was stricken with leukemia. Cappelletti dedicated his 1973 Heisman Trophy to his brother.

★ SPORTS-ACTION GRADE: A. The producers used NFL Films game footage, so we see the real Sayers and Piccolo in action. It is clear why the other players called Sayers "Magic." No other runner in NFL history, with the possible exception of Barry Sanders, was that elusive.

MY FAVORITE SPORTS MOVIE: Clint Hurdle, manager of the 2007 NL Champion Colorado Rockies: "There are so many themes in that movie. It's the blue-collar guy who befriends the five-tool superstar. It shows how they bond, how they rely on each other, and how they change roles. It starts off with Brian helping Gale, and in the end Gale is helping Brian. It is the best film I've seen at showing the kind of bond that can develop between teammates."

MY FAVORITE SPORTS MOVIE, TOO: NFL Films President Steve Sabol: "Every football team is a group of men joining together to pursue a dream. *Brian's Song* followed that dream, and from it grew a special friendship that became more meaningful than the dream itself. *Brian's Song* was *Brokeback Mountain* with football helmets instead of cowboy hats—and minus the scene inside the tent."

16 MIRACLE (2004–PG)

SPORT: HOCKEY | STARS: KURT RUSSELL, PATRICIA CLARKSON, NOAH EMMERICH
DIRECTOR: GAVIN O'CONNOR

There are no surprises in *Miracle*. There is no M. Night Shyamalan twist at the end. Even those who weren't born in 1980 when the United States hockey team upset the seemingly invincible Soviets know the story. They have heard Al Michaels' famous call—"Do you believe in miracles? Yessssss!"—countless times.

It is familiar territory, we know exactly where we're going the whole time, but thanks to the uncanny performance of Kurt Russell as coach Herb Brooks and a convincing cast of young athletes/actors, we thoroughly enjoy the ride. Credit director Gavin O'Connor and screenwriter Eric Guggenheim for developing an insightful portrait of the team and what it overcame on its way to winning the Olympic gold medal.

Miracle establishes the context of the times during the opening credits. Newsreel footage of the Iran hostage crisis, the meltdown at Three Mile Island and the long lines at the gas pumps paint a picture of an America experiencing what President Carter called "a crisis of confidence." The Cold War is still going on and the Soviet invasion of Afghanistan is casting a dark shadow across the globe.

Against this backdrop, Brooks is given the task of assembling a U.S. hockey team to take on the world at the Winter Olympics. The American team will consist of college kids while other countries send their battle-tested veterans. The Soviets and Czechs still are operating behind the Iron Curtain so their top players have not yet found their way to the National Hockey League. They play for their national teams.

The Soviets have won the hockey gold medal in every Olympics since 1960, when the U.S. won. They routed the

NHL teams in a series of exhibition matches in the '70s and defeated a team of NHL All-Stars in a best-of-three series in 1979. The Soviets are the best hockey team in the world, a finely tuned machine that crushes everything in its path. If the North American pros are no match for them, what chance do a bunch of amateurs have?

But Brooks has a plan: He will beat the Soviets at their own game. For years, the North American teams have played their plodding dump-and-chase game against the Soviets. They shoot the puck into the corner and chase after it, hoping to outmuscle the Soviets along the

Olympics, but we'll be the best conditioned," Brooks says. He adds, "You don't have enough talent to win on talent alone."

Seventy of the top collegiate players in the country are invited to a tryout camp. On the first day, Brooks hands a sheet of paper to assistant coach Craig Patrick (Noah Emmerich).

"What's this?" Patrick asks.

"Twenty-six names," Brooks says.

He has already decided which players to keep and which ones to send home.

HERB BROOKS: "PUT YOUR STREET CLOTHES ON. I'VE GOT NO TIME FOR QUITTERS."

ROB MCCLANAHAN: "YOU WANT ME TO PLAY ON ONE LEG? HUH? I'LL PLAY ON ONE LEG."

HERB BROOKS: "THAT'LL GET 'EM GOING."

boards. But that strategy rarely worked because the Soviets were much faster. On the larger international ice surface, they would get to the puck first and with one or two crisp passes be back on the attack.

"You can't beat those guys playing that way," Brooks says. "I'm going to take their game and throw it right back in their face."

Brooks' blueprint calls for a team of hungry kids, not fat-headed all-stars, who are willing to learn a new style of play. They will have to endure a grueling training program. Brooks will make them skate until they're on their knees with their tongues hanging out.

"I can't promise you we'll be the best team at the

"You're missing some of the best players," Patrick says.

"I'm not looking for the best players, Craig," Brooks says. "I'm looking for the right ones."

Miracle does several things very well, which is why the film holds our interest even though we know the whole story before we even settle into our chairs. First, it takes us deep into the scheming mind of Brooks, who pushes every button and pulls every string to get the most out of his players. He gives written psychological tests and most of the time he seems as cold as the ice he stands on.

"I'll be your coach, I won't be your friend," he tells the players.

Deep down, of course, he cares deeply for them. He sees in them the same qualities that drove him when he was trying out for the 1960 U.S. Olympic team. He was the last man cut from that squad and was forced to watch on television as the team won the gold medal. Brooks has been trying to recapture that moment ever since.

The film also shows the rift that existed on the team and for awhile threatened to tear it apart. There was a split between the Eastern players (Boston University, Boston College and Harvard) and the Midwestern players (Minnesota, Wisconsin, North Dakota). They played against each other in junior tournaments and then in college so there was a lot of baggage that needed checking before they could come together as a team.

One reason Brooks was so hard on the players was he wanted them to bond and he felt the quickest way to do that was to have them unite against him. As the team doctor (Kenneth Welsh) says, "If they all hate him, they won't have time to hate each other."

So there was a method to Brooks' madness. As he told Sports Illustrated, "It was a lonely year for me. This team had everything I wanted to be close to, everything I admired: the talent, the psychological makeup, the personality. But I had to stay away. There wasn't going to be any favoritism."

Everyone agrees Brooks was fair. Tough, but fair. When he was named coach, most people assumed he would favor the players who helped him win an NCAA championship at the University of Minnesota. He did not. He played Jim Craig (Boston University) in goal ahead of Steve Janaszak (Minnesota) and he picked Mike Eruzione (Boston U.) to be the team captain. He cut Minnesota kids to keep players from other schools.

"I gave our guys every opportunity to call me an honest SOB," Brooks said. "Hockey players are going to call you an SOB at times anyway, in emotion. But they could call me an honest one because everything was up front."

Well, not everything. Brooks was always playing mind games. In the film, less than a month before the Olympics, Brooks brings in a new player. The other players, who have been together for seven months, are resentful. Several players, including Eruzione, fear losing their spot on the team to the newcomer.

A group of players, led by Eruzione, confront Brooks.

"This is crazy, bringing him in this late," Eruzione (Patrick O'Brien Demsey) says.

"The kid can flat-out play," Brooks says.

"And we can't?" says defenseman Jack O'Callahan (Michael Mantenuto).

"He's got the attitude I want," Brooks says. "Somebody here better tell me why I shouldn't be giving him a hell of a look."

"Because we're a family," says center Mark Johnson (Eric Peter-Kaiser).

"What?" Brooks says.

"We're a family," replies winger Rob McClanahan (Nathan West).

It is the validation Brooks has been waiting for—Eruzione and O'Callahan (Boston), Johnson (Wisconsin) and McClanahan (Minnesota), all standing as one. Brooks has his team. The new guy has served his purpose. He is sent packing and the U.S. squad heads to Lake Placid ready to shock the world.

"It's a wonderful film," wrote E.M. Swift of Sports Illustrated who covered the 1980 Winter Olympics. "My 11-year-old son also loved it, leading me to believe that another generation will fall under the team's magical spell. Who could have known that two superlative weeks of play by that group of fresh-faced kids would keep its hold on the American imagination for so long?

"[Brooks] brought out in them qualities they didn't know they had. And together as a team, they did the same for us. For Americans. I've always believed that was the miracle—that a hockey team could do such a thing."

CHEERS: Kurt Russell captures everything about Herb Brooks, from his Minnesota accent to his incessant gum chewing to his frightening array of plaid pants. "Brooks had all these sayings—'Herbie-isms,' the players called them—and Russell had them down to perfection," said Dave Anderson, the Pulitzer Prize-winning columnist who covered the 1980 Winter Olympics for the New York Times.

JEERS: The film shows Brooks telling his wife (Patricia Clarkson) that his team doesn't match up with the Soviets. In fact, Brooks was optimistic going into the game. He agreed the Soviets were better but they had not played their best in the tournament and he felt they were ripe to be taken.

🔊 **CASTING CALL:** The role of U.S. winger Buzz Schneider is played by his son Billy.

✔️ **REALITY CHECK:** Brooks did make the team stay on the ice and skate for an hour after a lackluster tie in Norway. But the punishment did not end the way it is shown in the film, that is, with Brooks asking, "Who do you play for?" and Eruzione replying, "I play for the United States of America." Brooks ended the drill on his own because he felt the players had suffered enough.

☺ **GOOFS:** After the Czech game, Brooks complains the press is overreacting to the team's success. He says, "We've won two games." In reality, the Americans had won only one game at that point, the one over the Czechs. They tied their first game against Sweden.

☞ **DON'T FAIL TO NOTICE:** While the patriotic theme of the USA defeating the Soviets is part of the story, the producers stop short of making the film political. You never see Brooks or the players talk about winning the game as a metaphor for winning the Cold War.

As center Mark Pavelich said later: "If people want to think that performance was for our country, that's fine. But the truth of the matter is, it was just a hockey game. There was enough to worry about without worrying about Afghanistan or winning it for the pride and glory of the United States. We wanted to win it for ourselves."

❞ **BEST LINE:** Brooks' speech to the team before the Soviet game is a classic. He gave his notes to the film's producers so they could get it exactly right.

"Great moments," Brooks says, "are born from great opportunity. And that's what you have here tonight, boys. That's what you've earned here tonight. One game. If we played 'em ten times, they might win nine. But not this game. Tonight, we skate with them. Tonight, we stay with them. And we shut them down because we can.

"Tonight, we are the greatest hockey team in the world. You were born to be hockey players, every one of you. And you were meant to be here tonight. This is your time.

Their time is done. It's over. I'm sick and tired of hearing about what a great hockey team the Soviets have. Screw 'em. This is your time. Now go out there and take it."

✎ **WHAT THEY WROTE AT THE TIME:** "To make a movie about that team and those games requires more than an ability to depict personal dramas or re-enact game highlights. It requires the re-creation of a world and a mindset and *Miracle* accomplishes both brilliantly."—Mick LaSalle, *San Francisco Chronicle*

😎 **"I KNOW THAT GUY":** Eddie Cahill, who plays goalie Jim Craig, is a regular in the TV series *CSI: New York*.

👁 **REPEATED WATCHING QUOTIENT:** Anytime you need inspiration, go to Brooks' speech before the Soviet game. You'll be ready to take the ice, even if you can't skate.

★ **SPORTS-ACTION GRADE:** A. "The game action is sensational," Swift wrote. "Gavin O'Connor wisely chose to cast hockey players—minor leaguers and collegians—instead of actors who could skate. The results are by far the best hockey scenes ever filmed—maybe the best sports scenes, period. The body checks are brutal. The passing and scoring sing with authenticity, having been carefully choreographed from actual footage of the U.S. team's games."

🎞 **MY FAVORITE SPORTS MOVIE:** Steve Spurrier, University of South Carolina football coach: "It's a great story about a group of young men—who at first want nothing to do with each other—uniting for a cause and their country. And, of course, I appreciate that the coach knows how to press the right buttons."

17 CHARIOTS OF FIRE (1981–PG)

SPORT: TRACK | STARS: BEN CROSS, IAN CHARLESON, IAN HOLM | DIRECTOR: HUGH HUDSON

When *Chariots of Fire* won the Oscar for Best Picture of 1981, it was a huge upset. The film was up against a strong field—*Raiders of the Lost Ark, Reds, On Golden Pond* and *Atlantic City* were the other nominees—and the tale of two British track stars seemed to have about as much chance as a sprinter with a pulled hamstring.

When Loretta Young opened the envelope to announce the winner, she could not hide her surprise. Her eyes widened and she paused for a second as if to make sure there wasn't a mistake. When she announced "*Chariots of Fire,*" it was hard to tell if the screams that followed were screams of delight or disbelief.

Even now, you can still start a lively debate asking people what they think of the film. Frank Deford of *Sports Illustrated* considers it the best sports film ever made. *Premiere Magazine* rated it one of the 20 Most Overrated Movies of All-Time. Many critics adored it—as

did many athletes. Dara Torres, the only American swimmer to compete in five Olympics, says it is her favorite movie ever.

It is easy to find fault with *Chariots*. The first half is downright boring at times. Certain plot points are repeated until they are beaten into the ground. Harold Abrahams feels persecuted because he is Jewish. Eric Liddell is devoted to his Christian faith. OK, we get it. Can we move the story along now?

For a movie about men who run fast, *Chariots* often seems stuck in molasses. And when Abrahams and Liddell finally do run, they are shown in slow-motion, which annoys even Deford. ("A ghastly cliche," he calls it.)

"It's a shame that once again, even in a movie as true and sophisticated as this one, the sporting scenes are marred by slow-motion sequences," Deford wrote in his review. "Can't people in movies run and jump and bat and throw at the same speed with which they do everything else?"

The reason the film works—and it really does work—is the actors (Ian Charleson as Liddell, Ben Cross as Abrahams) are so good they make you care about their characters. The fact that it is a true story, and the script—which won an Oscar for screenwriter Colin Welland—is pretty faithful to the real events, gives *Chariots* almost a documentary feel.

Abrahams, the son of a Lithuanian immigrant, enrolls in Cambridge. As one of the few non-Anglo-Saxons on the hallowed grounds, he feels like an outsider. He says he feels "a cold reluctance in every handshake." But it only makes him more determined to succeed. "I'm going to take them on, one by one, and run them off their feet," he vows.

Abrahams makes good on his promise. In one of the film's best scenes, he becomes the first student to run a complete lap around the Great Court in less time than it takes the steeple clock to strike 12 bells at midday. Looking on, the school master (Sir John Gielgud) says, "I doubt there is a swifter man in the kingdom."

That is the cue to introduce Liddell, the son of Scottish missionaries and a world-class sprinter. He enjoys the competition, but it is secondary to his religion. Liddell is shown winning races and preaching sermons to his adoring fans afterwards.

As the 1924 Olympics approach, Liddell's sister Jennie (Cheryl Campbell) accuses him of putting his training ahead of God's work. She says, "You are so full of running, you have no time for standing still." She is preparing to meet their parents at their mission in China. Eric is expected to join them, but he wants to run in the Olympics first. He tries to makes his sister understand that his athletic pursuits are really an extension of his faith.

"I believe God made me for a purpose, but He also made me fast," he says. "And when I run, I feel His pleasure."

Abrahams is running against prejudice. Liddell is running to honor his God. They are very different sorts of heroes, but by the time they climb aboard the steamer in London and set sail for the Olympic Games in Paris, you are rooting for both of them. You are also prepared to root against their jaunty American rivals, Charlie Paddock and Jackson Scholz, who are expected to kick butt in Paris.

Abrahams and Liddell are entered in the 100 meters, but as it turns out the qualifying heats are on Sunday. Liddell refuses to run on the holy day. The head of the British delegation pulls him into a meeting with the Prince of Wales and other politicians who try to pressure him into changing his mind. Staring into the eyes of the future king, Liddell stands his ground.

"God made countries," he says. "God makes kings and the rules by which they govern. And those rules say that the Sabbath is His. And I for one intend to keep it that way."

Another member of the British team offers Liddell his spot in the 400 meters which is scheduled for later in the week. Liddell, who has successfully competed at the longer distance, accepts. But word of his principled stance makes headlines back home and assures his sister that he still has his priorities in order.

When the Games begin, director Hugh Hudson faces a structural dilemma. Filmmakers talk about "delivering the moment"—that is, building the emotion to one climactic scene, one event that pays off everything that has gone before. Hudson is faced with *two* endings: Abrahams' quest for gold in the 100 *and* Liddell's race in the 400.

It is to Hudson's credit that the two scenes play so well. Abrahams' victory, which comes first, is not shortchanged and Liddell's triumph does not feel like an anticlimax. It is a neat bit of storytelling on the part of the director, who was nominated for an Oscar but lost to Warren Beatty (*Reds*).

Hudson makes it work by showing the two races from different perspectives. He lets us see Abrahams' victory through the eyes of his coach Sam Mussabini (Ian Holm), who is not allowed in the Olympic stadium because he is considered a professional. Sam stands at the hotel window, waiting to see which flag is raised for the medal ceremony. It is not until Sam sees the Union Jack go up that he knows his man has won the gold. All alone, Sam celebrates by punching his fist through his straw hat.

Liddell's victory is told in more straight-forward fashion with the runner—yes, in slow-motion—hitting the tape, his head thrown back, smiling as his words ("When I run, I feel His pleasure") echo above the roar of the crowd.

🍺 **CHEERS:** Ian Holm stands out in a fine supporting cast. *Chariots* received seven Oscar nominations, but Holm received the only acting nomination for Best Supporting Actor as the crusty coach who makes Abrahams a champion.

🍺 **JEERS:** The film is stuck in Cambridge for an awfully long time. We could have done with less tea and less Gilbert and Sullivan.

☞ **DON'T FAIL TO NOTICE:** In the credits, Dodi Fayed, the son of the Egyptian billionaire who was killed along with Diana, Princess of Wales, in a car crash in Paris in 1997, is listed as executive producer.

✒ **WHAT THEY WROTE AT THE TIME:** "A piece of technological lyricism held together by the glue of simpleminded heroic sentiment."—Pauline Kael, *The New Yorker*

✔ **REALITY CHECK:** The Olympic schedule was set a full month before the Games so Liddell knew about the 100 meter heats before the team ever left for Paris. The decision to move Liddell to the 400 meters was made well in advance. There was no secret meeting with the Prince of Wales.

✔ **REALITY CHECK II:** In the movie, Abrahams and Liddell race against each other (Liddell wins) in a meet in England. In real life, the two men never ran against each other until the Olympics when they both competed in the 200 meter final. Liddell took the bronze medal (third place) and Abrahams was sixth. Jackson Scholz of the United States won the gold.

😀 **"I KNOW THAT GUY":** In the film, Scholz is played by Brad Davis, the actor who starred in the harrowing *Midnight Express*, the 1978 film about an American student who is sent to a Turkish prison for smuggling hashish.

💬 **BEST LINE:** Harold Abrahams: "In one hour's time, I will raise my eyes and look down that corridor, four feet wide, with 10 lonely seconds to justify my whole existence. But will I? I've known the fear of losing, but now I am almost too frightened to win."

🎬 **BET YOU DIDN'T KNOW:** The opening scene of the British team running along the water was shot in St. Andrews, Scotland, near the famous golf course. The producers rounded up a dozen of the club's caddies, dressed them in track whites and had them run alongside the film's stars to shoot the scene. Today, there is a plaque marking the spot.

🎬 **BET YOU DIDN'T KNOW II:** The film's original title was *Running*, but Welland saw a line in a William Blake poem ("Bring me my spear, bring me my chariot of fire.") he liked better.

★ **SPORTS-ACTION GRADE:** B. All the slow-motion action becomes numbing. Hudson is much better capturing the tension before the race as the runners share one changing room and eye each other in a wary silence.

🎞 **MY FAVORITE SPORTS MOVIE:** Jerry Jones, Dallas Cowboys owner: "This movie was very inspirational for me because it captured the essence of athletes and their pride, both from an individual perspective and from the pride that a competitor feels when representing his country. It had all of the things that make up a great sports movie from the standpoint of determination and overcoming the odds. But it also added elements that you don't always see in a sports film, things such as ethnic bias, the political side of Olympic competition and spiritual conviction. *Chariots of Fire* did a wonderful job of capturing a bygone era in sports. It took you back in time to a day when athletes traveled by boat and train. The costumes, the landscapes, the uniforms and the sporting venues were all depicted so accurately. And the music was dramatic. Everyone knows that theme song. (The instrumental performed by Vangelis won the Academy Award). "It's one of the few movies that, if I see it on television in the house, I stop whatever I'm doing and watch it again."

18 BODY AND SOUL (1947–NR)

SPORT: BOXING | STARS: JOHN GARFIELD, LILLI PALMER, WILLIAM CONRAD
DIRECTOR: ROBERT ROSSEN

Body and Soul was the first boxing movie to shine a light on the sport's ugly underbelly. Previous boxing films were mostly tender love stories or lighter-than-air comedies, such as the popular *Joe Palooka* series. So when *Body and Soul* came out, it hit audiences like an uppercut to the chin.

Body and Soul took its lead from the New York State Senate inquiry into corruption in sports, specifically boxing. The investigation was attracting national headlines at the time and Americans were learning more about the shady dealings between gangsters and many boxing promoters. *Body and Soul* put real flesh and blood on those headlines. The film is more than 60 years old, yet it still is regarded as one of the best boxing movies ever made.

"Here are the gin and tinsel, squalor and sables of the Depression era, less daring than when first revealed in *Dead End* or *Golden Boy*, but more valid and mature because it is shown without sentiment or blur," wrote the *National Board of Review* in praising *Body and Soul* as a triumph for director Robert Rossen and star John Garfield.

Body and Soul is the fictional story of Charlie Davis (Garfield), a Jewish kid from New York's East Side who piles up an impressive record as an amateur boxer. His father runs a candy store and his mother wants Charlie to forget boxing and get an education. "That is no way to live, hitting people and knocking their teeth out," she says.

But when Charlie's father is killed (a bomb meant for the speakeasy next door takes out the candy store instead), his mother applies for welfare. When a woman from the agency comes to the house, Charlie throws her out. "We don't need your help," he says. He's too proud to take a handout.

"Do you think I did it to buy myself fancy clothes?" his mother asks. "Fool, it's for you. To learn, to get an education, to make something of yourself."

Enraged, Charlie tells his friend Shorty (Joseph Pevney) to get in touch with Quinn (William Conrad), a boxing manager, and tell him he's ready to turn pro.

"Tell Quinn to get me a fight," Charlie says. "I want money, you understand? Money, money."

"I forbid it," his mother says. "Better you should buy a gun and shoot yourself."

"You need money to buy a gun," Charlie shouts back.

What follows is the standard montage of Charlie, now a professional, knocking out one opponent after another. There are the usual shots of spinning newspaper headlines, pages flipping on a calendar and train wheels rolling down the tracks. This kind of storytelling was hardly new even in 1947.

what he wants.

Roberts gets Charlie his shot at champion Ben Chaplin (Canada Lee). Chaplin has a blood clot on the brain, the result of a previous bout, and he is just looking for one more payday. He takes the fight with Davis knowing he will lose, but with the assurance that Davis will take it easy on him. Roberts tells Chaplin and his manager they have nothing to worry about.

"Nobody gets hurt, you have my word," Roberts says.

But Roberts doesn't tell Charlie anything. Fighting with his usual ferocity, Charlie knocks out Chaplin and sends him to the hospital. Shorty overhears Chaplin's manager and Roberts arguing in the dressing room. Learning what happened, Shorty tells Roberts he's finished with him. "And when Charlie finds out, he'll quit, too," Shorty says.

But Charlie doesn't quit. He feels badly for Chaplin, he knows he got a raw deal, but Charlie also knows Roberts is where the money is. "I'm the champ," he says.

CHARLIE: "WHAT ARE YOU GONNA DO, KILL ME? EVERYBODY DIES."

But *Body and Soul* takes a sharp turn when a dapper mobster named Roberts (Lloyd Gough) shows up to get his piece of the action. Charlie has been piling up the wins, but they've all been in small towns for small purses. If he wants to break into the big time, he'll have to cut a deal with Roberts. Shorty sees through Roberts right away and tells Charlie that the mobster is bad news.

"He doesn't care about you," Shorty says. "He just wants his piece of the pie."

"What's the difference?" Charlie replies. "It'll be a bigger pie, more slices for everybody."

As soon as Roberts moves in, we see Charlie change. He becomes more greedy and ruthless. He dumps his girlfriend Peg Born (Lilli Palmer) for Alice (Hazel Brooks), a nightclub singer who was seeing Quinn. His relationship with Shorty becomes strained. But Charlie knows Roberts can pave his way to the title and that's

"If I walk away now, what will I do?" Disgusted, Shorty leaves Charlie. (He dies when he is struck by a car outside the nightclub.)

As the champion, Charlie succumbs to the pitfalls of wealth and celebrity. We see him dressed in flashy clothes, slurping down drinks with Alice, ripping up losing tickets at the race track and it's all subsidized by Roberts, who keeps handing him fat envelopes full of cash with a smile and a slimy, "Here ya go, champ."

Then one day Charlie comes around for his envelope and Roberts says, "Not so fast." Uh oh, the bill is coming due. Roberts wants Charlie to fight the top contender, a rising star named Jackie Marlowe. And that's not all. Roberts wants Charlie to lose.

"It's time, Charlie," Roberts says. "You don't like fighting anymore, you like living too much. Take the money from this fight and buy yourself a restaurant."

Charlie gets the picture. Roberts has his hooks in Marlowe; that's his new meal ticket. Charlie is yesterday's news. He is being tossed onto the trash heap as Ben Chaplin was before him. He doesn't like the idea of tanking his last fight and he balks until Roberts slaps another fat envelope on the table.

"Money's got no conscience, Charlie," Roberts says. "Here, take it." So he does.

Wrestling with his emotions and with no one else to turn to, Charlie reaches out to his mother and to Peg, his old girlfriend. When he tells them this will be his last fight, they are elated. But when he tells them it's fixed, the mood changes. Peg slaps him across the face and walks out. . . .

Now, we don't want to ruin the big fight, but suffice it to say, it brings *Body and Soul* to a rousing finish.

The film was a career highlight for Garfield, who was nominated for an Academy Award (he lost to Ronald Colman in *A Double Life*). It drew two other nominations—Best Original Screenplay (Abraham Polonsky) and Best Editing (Francis Lyon, Robert Parrish)—with Lyon and Parrish winning the Oscar.

Yet *Body and Soul* has a bitter legacy. Many of its cast and crew—including Garfield, Anne Revere, Gough, Lee and Polonsky—were called before the House Un-American Activities Commission for alleged affiliations with the Communist Party. All were blacklisted and their careers effectively ended.

🏆 **CHEERS:** Garfield is very good in a difficult role. He goes from an honest kid off the streets to a morally corrupted champion, yet he offers just enough glimpses of decency now and then that his awakening at the end is believable.

🚩 **JEERS:** Hazel Brooks, who played Alice, is a caricature as the nightclub vamp. Her billing—"And introducing Hazel Brooks"—suggests United Artists had big plans for her, but her acting career went nowhere after *Body and Soul*.

👑 **BET YOU DIDN'T KNOW:** Canada Lee, who plays Ben Chaplin, and Artie Dorrell, who plays Jackie Marlowe, were professional boxers. Lee fought a 10-round draw

with future middleweight champion Vince Dundee in 1928. Dorrell compiled a record of 38-9-6 and fought former welterweight champion Fritzie Zivic in 1944 (he was TKO'd in the 7th round).

99 **BEST LINE:** Shorty (Joseph Pevney): "Charlie's not just a kid who can fight. He's a machine that makes money."

🎬 **PIVOTAL SCENE:** While Charlie is visiting his mother, a delivery boy arrives with the groceries. He tells Charlie that all the people in the neighborhood are betting on him to defeat Marlowe.

"We are so proud," he says. "All over Europe, they are killing people like us (Jews), but not here. Here Charlie Davis is champion of the world."

Charlie, who has already agreed to throw the fight, doesn't know what to say. His guilty conscience is working overtime.

😎 **"I KNOW THAT GUY":** William Conrad (Quinn) was later the TV detective *Cannon*.

🎡 **IF YOU LIKED THIS, YOU'LL LIKE:** *Golden Boy*, a 1939 screen adaptation of a Clifford Odets play. Garfield played the lead on stage, but he lost the movie role to William Holden.

◎ **REPEATED WATCHING QUOTIENT:** Like most films of that era, it is pretty short (104 minutes), so it moves along briskly. The final fight is worth seeing again. The camerawork is also worth another look, as it was clearly ahead of its time.

★ **SPORTS-ACTION GRADE:** B. J Russell Peltz, a boxing promoter for more than 40 years, says the fight scenes in *Body and Soul* are the best ever put on film. Credit cameraman James Wong Howe who filmed the final bout on roller skates, moving in a tight circle around the two fighters with a handheld camera, moving as they moved. The technique put the audience closer to the action than it had ever been before.

BOXING MOVIES: THE WINNER AND STILL CHAMPION

The sport of boxing has been in decline for years. Too many sanctioning bodies, too many titles and too little star power have caused fans to drift away. But that has not stopped Hollywood from making movies about boxing. It has been a popular subject for more than a century (Thomas Edison filmed a James J. Corbett exhibition match in 1892) and it is likely to remain so whether anyone can name the current heavyweight champion or not.

Why?

For one thing, it is the easiest sport to film. There are two fighters, face to face, in a confined space. It is not like nine players spread out on a baseball diamond or 22 men in helmets and pads sprawling across a football field. For the purposes of lighting and camera placement, a boxing ring is the perfect stage. It makes for a quicker and therefore cheaper shoot.

But more than that, boxing lends itself to melodrama. It is about an individual, not a team, so the writer can focus on one storyline. There is also the backdrop of vengeful mobsters, double-crossing managers and other shady characters that populate the sport and provide a wealth of material for movies.

Columnist Jimmy Cannon called boxing, "the red-light district of sports." It is a good description and it accounts for why directors from Alfred Hitchcock to Martin Scorsese keep going back. It may be a dirty world, but it does not disappoint.

"Boxing is more disorganized than other sports and that's good for a movie," said J Russell Peltz, who has been promoting fights for more than 40 years. "Seth Abraham (a former matchmaker for HBO) said, 'In boxing, everyone flies the Jolly Roger,' and it's true.

"There are a lot of colorful characters and it makes for better stories. *Rocky* is one of the most popular movies of all time and it could only happen in boxing. Rocky was a club fighter, a guy off the street, but the heavyweight champ gave him a shot at the title. That happens. We've all seen fighters who aren't anywhere near the top 10 handed a title shot. You don't see it in other sports.

"The defending Super Bowl champion can't pick a 3-13 team [for a title defense]. There's a playoff system. In tennis tournaments, players have to win their way to the finals. But in boxing, there is no system, no checks and balances. It is a sport where people make up the rules as they go along."

Most critics would agree that more good movies have been made about boxing than any other sport. We have 14 boxing films in our top 100 and we could have included more. We left out *The Champ* with Wallace Beery (also the remake with Jon Voight), *Golden Boy* with William Holden, *City for Conquest* with James Cagney, *Somebody Up There Likes Me* with Paul Newman, *The Hurricane* with Denzel Washington and *The Great White Hope* with James Earl Jones because, for one reason, we did not want the final list to be too heavily weighted toward one sport. However, each of those films is worth seeing.

While it is true that many boxing movies are clichéd and others are embarrassing for other reasons (*Matilda*, a 1978 movie about a boxing kangaroo, did nothing to enhance the career of Elliott Gould), those that manage to rise above the stock characters and hackneyed scripts often achieve critical acclaim.

Boxing films are the most honored films of the sports genre. Three actors won Oscars for portraying fighters: Beery (*The Champ*), De Niro (*Raging Bull*) and Swank (*Million Dollar Baby*). Marlon Brando won for playing an ex-fighter (*On the Waterfront*). Morgan Freeman was voted Best Supporting Actor for his portrayal of Eddie "Scrap-Iron" Dupris, the broken-down pug who cleaned the gym in *Million Dollar Baby*.

Two boxing films won the Oscar for Best Picture—*Rocky* and *Million Dollar Baby*—and when the American Film Institute ranked the greatest American movies of all-time, it put *Raging Bull* in the top five alongside *Citizen Kane, The Godfather, Gone With the Wind* and *Casablanca*.

Film critic Leonard Harris called *Rocky* "Cinderella on a more active level." The movie, written by Sylvester

Stallone, who was then a virtual unknown, was a kind of physical fairy tale. Unlike other boxing films, which were full of bad guys and fixed fights, *Rocky* had an innocence that touched people's hearts. The film grossed $117 million, an enormous figure in 1976. Five sequels followed and while the character of Rocky Balboa went through many changes he remained a hero to underdogs everywhere.

Bill Curry spent 10 seasons in the NFL and played for Hall of Fame coaches Vince Lombardi and Don Shula. Yet when Curry became a college coach, he did not inspire his players with speeches borrowed from Lombardi and Shula. When Curry wanted to fire up his players, he would show them one of the *Rocky* films.

"My favorite was *Rocky IV*, the one where he fights the Russian champion," Curry said. "I'd show the film and ask the players: 'When was the fight over?' The fight was over when the Russian went back to his corner and said, 'He is not human.' He hit Rocky with everything, but Rocky was still coming at him. At that moment, the fight was over. You knew it.

"I'd tell the players, 'That's how we want our opponents to see us. We're not human. We'll never be broken.' It makes the point about what it takes to win, the pain you have to be willing to endure to succeed. People say, 'But, Bill, that's a boxing movie.' I say, 'No, it's a life movie.'"

Peltz, who was inducted into the Boxing Hall of Fame in 2004, decorated his Philadelphia office with posters from old boxing movies. He collected dozens of films on tape. His favorite is *Body and Soul*, a 1947 black-and-white classic with John Garfield as a kid who punches his way to the middleweight title, but in the process sells his soul to the mob.

"I liked the dialog so much, I put it on a tape and played it in my car," Peltz said. "One of my favorite scenes is where Garfield is trying to tell Lilli Palmer that the fight is fixed. She doesn't understand what 'fixed' means. He says, 'It's a racket. Don't you get it, Peg? That's why I want to bet the 50 grand.' She slaps him across the face.

"People think that's fiction, but that's the way boxing worked for years. The mob did control fighters, they pulled the strings. They would arrange for some guys to fight for the title and other guys never got a shot. If a fighter was controlled by the mob and he made a $100,000 purse, they weren't bashful about taking $90,000 or more.

"There wasn't much a fighter could do," Peltz said. "Even the ones who did know they were being cheated, what could they do? Call a cop? Write their Congressman? They couldn't do anything, so they did what they were told. There is a lot of truth in those old movies."

The newer films are less concerned with accuracy and more interested in star power. One example is *Ali,* a biographical film that was a showcase for Will Smith who played Muhammad Ali. He earned an Oscar nomination, but the film was disappointing.

Director Michael Mann—whose credits include *Heat, The Insider* and *Collateral*—offered what amounted to a series of sketches rather than a coherent portrait of the former heavyweight champion. Smith's performance held your interest, but in the end, the film did not tell you anything you didn't already know about Ali.

But when a boxing movie scores, either with a great scene or a great line, it has undeniable power. It comes down to the one-on-one nature of the sport. Lose and there are no teammates or coaches to blame. It is the fighter, stripped down to a pair of trunks, standing alone in the ring, facing his opponent and his fears.

In *Million Dollar Baby*, Morgan Freeman articulates it in this haunting voiceover: "If there's a magic in boxing, it's the magic of fighting battles beyond endurance, beyond cracked ribs, ruptured kidneys and detached retinas. It's the magic of risking everything for a dream that nobody sees but you."

19 REMEMBER THE TITANS (2000–PG)

SPORT: FOOTBALL | STARS: DENZEL WASHINGTON, WILL PATTON, RYAN HURST
DIRECTOR: BOAZ YAKIN

Remember the Titans is based on the true story of T.C. Williams High School in Alexandria, Va. The football team, the Titans, won the state championship in 1971, but accomplished much more than that. President Richard Nixon was quoted as saying, "The team saved the city of Alexandria."

That may be stretching the truth, but there is a reason why people remember the Titans. At a time when racial hatred was tearing the country apart, the coaches and players at T.C. Williams High School rose above it in an inspiring way. As Ben Morris wrote in the *Alexandria Gazette*, "It all came about through the hard work and sacrifice of these young men and their coaches who worked together, proving to everyone that different ethnic groups can mesh unanimously for a singular ambition."

That is the theme of the film: There is no limit to what people can accomplish when they recognize that their common dreams outweigh their differences. In the case of

the Titans, it is the coaches and players, black and white, who are thrown together when their schools are merged. They learn to work together and they learn to trust each other. In the end, they learn to love each other and their success sends a healthy message to the whole town.

The film was produced for Disney Studios by Jerry Bruckheimer, who is better known for his bombastic visuals (*Pearl Harbor, Armageddon*) than coherent storytelling. His heavy hand does slam down on *Titans* now and then—usually in the form of cartoonish football violence—but the acting is so good, especially Denzel Washington as head coach Herman Boone, the film stays solidly on course.

Titans is built on two storylines: One is the relationship between Boone and assistant coach Bill Yoast (Will Patton), the other is the relationship between Gerry Bertier (Ryan Hurst) and Julius Campbell (Wood Harris), the two best players on the team—one white, one black—who conquer their mutual distrust and become best friends.

This is familiar ground, rutted with cliches, and if a film hits too many of them, it can wind up in a ditch. *Titans* is able to avoid that by allowing the characters, especially Boone and Yoast, to think, speak and act like real people and not mere devices.

It would be easy, for example, to make Boone, the African-American coach brought in to take over the team, a man of unshakable conviction, a combination of Vince Lombardi and Martin Luther King. But writer Gregory Allen Howard puts enough rough edges on Boone that we watch him with keener interest because we never know just how he will react to any given situation.

He describes himself as "a mean cuss," and at times he goes out of his way to prove it.

In hiring Boone, the school board passes over Yoast, a long-time coach in the district. The move is designed to appease the African-American portion of the newly merged school district. "We have to give them something," a board member says.

No one spells it out for Boone, but he is smart enough to know what's going on. He knows Yoast is getting the shaft, yet Boone is ambitious enough to take the job anyway. Yoast ends up as his defensive coordinator.

When he moves in, Boone is welcomed as a hero by the African-American families. In a town where integration is greeted by picketers, racial taunts and bottle-tossing, the coach is seen as a symbol of hope, an authority figure who can exert an influence beyond the field and into the community. Boone, rather coldly, tells them he's not that kind of leader.

"I'm not the answer to your prayers," he says. "I'm not the savior, Jesus Christ, Martin Luther King, or the Easter Bunny. I'm just a football coach."

Boone is tough and does not play favorites. He is tough on everyone, including Yoast. Boone sees Yoast talking to one of the African-American players after Boone benches him for blowing an assignment. Boone accuses Yoast of coddling the kid, claiming he would not have done it if the player were white.

"I'm the same mean cuss with everybody out there on that football field," Boone says. "The world don't give a damn about how sensitive these kids are, especially the black kids. You ain't doing these kids a favor by patronizing them. You're crippling them. You're crippling them for life."

Yoast is a product of the Old South who isn't thrilled with integration, but he is trying to make the best of it. He talked the white players on team out of quitting (they were ready to walk off to protest the hiring of Boone) and he is juggling football with his duties as a single father. He doesn't like Boone (understandable since Boone took the job that should have been his), but he begins to understand him when some rednecks toss a brick through Boone's window one night when Yoast and his daughter are visiting.

"Maybe your little girl got a taste of what my girls go through," Boone says. "Welcome to my world, Yoast."

The relationship between the two men grows and they learn from each other. The same is true of Bertier and Campbell. Forced to room together at the training camp in Gettysburg, they can't stand each other (Bertier tells Campbell, "You're nothing but a pure waste of God-given talent") but they grow so close, Bertier winds up walking away from his foxy girlfriend (Kate Bosworth) when she tells him to choose between her and "Big Ju." (She won't even shake Campbell's hand).

"You've got your priorities all messed up," she tells Gerry.

"I don't think so," he says.

The bonding of the coaches and players is the real story, more than the touchdowns and the victories. In truth, the Titans were even better than the film suggests. They not only went undefeated (13-0) but they dominated. They outscored their opponents 357-45 and their defense, led by Bertier, posted nine shutouts. The producers built a few close games into the film for the sake of drama.

"That movie is all about unity," Arizona Cardinals receiver Anquan Boldin told us. "I am a huge believer in unity because that is what sports are all about. No matter what your race is, team unity and great teammates make sports something special to be a part of."

What made the film special—and a $115 million hit for Disney—is the emotional center embodied by Boone.

"Tonight we got Hayfield, like all the other schools in this conference they're all white," Boone says in one stirring locker room speech. "They don't have to worry about race, we do. Let me tell you something. You don't let anyone come between us. Nothing tears us apart.

"In Greek mythology, the Titans were greater even than the gods. They ruled their universe with absolute power. Well, that football field out there is our universe. Let's rule it like titans."

CHEERS: Denzel Washington is a riveting Herman Boone putting just enough menace in his character to keep us on edge. Example: The scene in which he approaches the rival coach who referred to him as a "monkey". We have no idea what Boone will do. Slug the guy? Offer a withering comment? Boone smiles and flips him a banana.

JEERS: Yoast's young daughter is one of those precocious, overly opinionated types who wears out her welcome in a hurry.

BET YOU DIDN'T KNOW: The original script was full of profanity, but Disney insisted Bruckheimer remove it. The studio wanted *Titans* to be a family film.

PIVOTAL SCENE: During camp, with the white players and black players refusing to work together, Boone takes the team on a 3 a.m. run through the Gettysburg battlefield. When they finish, he delivers a speech that pulls the team together.

"Fifty thousand men died on this field, fighting the same fight that we're still fighting among ourselves," he says. "Listen to their souls, men. You listen and you take a lesson from the dead. If we don't come together right now on this hallowed ground, we, too, will be destroyed."

BEST LINE: Herman Boone: "We will be perfect in every aspect of the game. You drop a pass, you run a mile. You miss a blocking assignment, you run a mile. You fumble the football and I will break my foot off in your John Brown hind parts and then you will run a mile."

GOOFS: When the Titan player picks up an opponent's fumble and runs for a touchdown, he is running the wrong way.

DON'T FAIL TO NOTICE: To ensure this football movie appealed to non-football fans (read: women) Yakin built in a soundtrack that quickly switches to upbeat '70s rock music every time something positive happens on the field for the Titans.

WHAT THEY WROTE AT THE TIME: "*Titans* rocks. It marries the verve and fireworks of a popcorn movie with serious social drama. It's a slick Hollywood product, but it also may be the most moving and entertaining movie so far this year."—Eric Harrison, *Houston Chronicle*

REALITY CHECK: In the playoff game, the opposing team lines up in the shotgun formation. One of the Titans says, "Who do they think they are, the New York Jets?" No NFL team was using the shotgun in 1971, and certainly not the Jets with Joe Namath at quarterback.

"I KNOW THAT GUY": Ryan Gosling has a small role as defensive back Alan Bosley. Gosling has gone on to become a leading man, and was nominated for an Academy Award for Best Actor in the 2006 film *Half Nelson*.

REPEATED WATCHING QUOTIENT: You might not plan your night around watching it again, but if you stumble across it while flipping channels, it's almost a guarantee that you'll stick with it for awhile.

SPORTS-ACTION GRADE: C-minus. The game action is way over-the-top and the real Titans did not dance onto the field. The cheesy choreography is a Hollywood invention.

MY FAVORITE SPORTS MOVIE: Tony Dungy, Super Bowl-winning coach: "I identify with the story because I went through something similar. My class [Parkside High School, Jackson, MI] was one of the first to integrate that school, so we had to face a lot of those issues. As players and coaches, we had to work through it before we could become a team.

"I thought the film delivered a really good message. When we [the Colts] won the Super Bowl, Coach Boone sent me a note to say congratulations. Coming from him, it meant a lot."

MY FAVORITE SPORTS MOVIE, TOO: Dirk Nowitzki, the NBA's 2006-07 MVP: "It's a great story about a team of diverse characters and backgrounds coming together for the common goal of winning a championship. That's a lot like what we try to do in the NBA."

20 BREAKING AWAY (1979–PG)

SPORT: BICYCLE RACING | STARS: DENNIS CHRISTOPHER, DENNIS QUAID, DANIEL STERN, JACKIE EARLE HALEY, PAUL DOOLEY | DIRECTOR: PETER YATES

Say the words "teen movie" and what comes to mind is a beer-soaked bacchanal that opens with overcharged high schoolers conspiring to lose their virginity while Mom and Dad are out of town, and ends with someone barfing in the pool.

Not that we didn't enjoy semi-classics such as *American Pie* and *Porky's*. But it would be nice, just once, to see a film about adolescents that goes beyond beer bongs, torturing the class nerd and the predictable jokes about masturbation.

Breaking Away is that movie.

This little film from 1979 explores issues like teen identity, parent-child relationships, self-confidence and class bias, and does so without bathing them all in alcohol and testosterone. Not once does it insult your intelligence. The result is one of the greatest coming of age movies ever

made. And, oh yes, the sports scenes are terrific.

Breaking Away focuses on four 18-year-olds, a few months out of high school, struggling to decide whether they want to spend their future hanging out together, finding a job or—perish the thought—moving on to college. They live in Bloomington, Indiana, where the tension between the snobby college kids and the working-class "cutters" (so known because their fathers cut the stones to build the university) leaves the locals feeling inadequate and resentful.

Dave Stoller (Dennis Christopher) is the most intriguing of the quartet, a restless kid who's obsessed with bike racing and inspired by the famous Italian Cinzano race team. He lives out his fantasy listening to opera, speaking with a faux-Italian accent and driving his father (Paul Dooley) crazy by changing the family cat's name from

Jake to Fellini. So immersed is he in this daydream that he begins an unlikely romance with a beautiful Indiana University coed (Robyn Douglass) by convincing her he is an Italian exchange student.

Mike (Dennis Quaid) is the former high school jock, embittered and afraid of the future. He aims to keep the group together, even if that means dead-end jobs for all of them. Cyril (Daniel Stern) is the wise-guy slacker, and Moocher (Jackie Earle Haley) is the undersized loner.

While the film focuses on the foursome's friendships and fear of the so-called real world, we learn that Dave, to everyone's amazement, has developed himself into a world-class cyclist. We get to see his talent—chasing down a truck on the interstate, and challenging his Italian heroes in a 100-mile race (accompanied by Rossini's *Barber of Seville* overture). It all leads up to the 12-minute climactic finale (predictable but still fist-pumping exciting), in which Dave takes on the frat-boy elitists in the Indiana University "Little 500" cycling race.

Every few years, a *Slumdog Millionaire* or *Juno* comes out of nowhere and becomes the little independent movie that could. *Breaking Away* was among the first of that sort. Its author, Steve Tesich, won the 1979 Academy Award for Best Original Screenplay. Overall, it was nominated for five Oscars, including Best Picture (won by *Kramer vs. Kramer*). In 2006, the American Film Institute placed it eighth on the list of America's 100 Most Inspiring Movies—second only to *Rocky* among sports films.

It may be second to none among coming-of-age films. We'll put it right up there with *American Graffiti, Breakfast Club, Boyz n the Hood* and *Basketball Diaries* in the pantheon of teen flicks that show respect for their characters—and audience—and go above and beyond rampant raunchiness and trivial nonsense.

On a side note, it's interesting to examine the long-term careers of the four aspiring actors in this movie. For Quaid, 24 at the time, *Breaking Away* was his breakout movie. He's all over this book. Stern, as well, went onto a long career, often playing characters with the same dry wit and Woody Allen outlook as he showed here with Cyril. Think of his character Shrevie in *Diner*.

The bantam-sized Haley was a successful teen actor (he plays Kelly Leak in *The Bad News Bears*), before disappearing into B-movies for a few decades. He re-emerged in 2006, earning a Best Supporting Actor Oscar nomination portraying a pedophile in *Little Children*.

It's Christopher, among the four, whose career ended with a flat tire. He followed up *Breaking Away* with a fine performance in 1981's *Chariots of Fire*. And then? Well, nothing notable, really, unless you want to include the freakish made-for-TV clown horror mini-series *It*. Which we won't.

So what happened? We figured it out recently by catching Christopher on an episode of HBO's *Deadwood*. At age 50, he still looks 18 years old, still looks like Dave Stoller about to slap on his bike helmet. In this case, staying youthful proved to be a bad career move.

CHEERS: To the world-class performance by Paul Dooley as Dave's perplexed but loving dad. Dooley plays a former stone cutter turned car salesman who just wants his son to stop shaving his legs and get a job. He rants that he didn't raise his son to be an "Eye-talian," and gets increasingly flustered as even the dinner his wife serves seems to be changing into "eenie foods."

"Zucchini, linguini, fettuccine. I want some American food, dammit! I want french fries!"

Consider it robbery that Dooley was not nominated for a Best Supporting Actor Oscar, while eight-year-old Justin Henry was for playing just another cute little kid in *Kramer vs. Kramer*.

JEERS: To the short-lived and awful 1980 television series based on this movie. *Friday Night Lights* it wasn't. Only Barbara Barrie (Mrs. Stoller) and Haley (Moocher) made the shift from movie to TV show. Teen pop idol Shaun Cassidy played Dave Stoller, which is like casting Milli Vanilli in a remake of *Brian's Song*.

PIVOTAL SCENE: Cycling down the highway, Dave spots a Cinzano Vermouth truck and begins to chase it, staying close by riding the tailwinds of the semi. The amused driver notices Dave in his rearview mirror and flashes four fingers to signal they are traveling 40 miles per hour.

The truck picks up speed, but Dave manages to keep up. Five fingers for 50 miles per hour, six fingers for 60. Then . . . well, we won't give away the scene's ending, but it will leave you both laughing and shaking your head in wonderment.

Director Peter Yates shoots this scene without dialog and, really, not a lot of action. But the sense of speed and fear of an imminent accident leave you riveted. Let us recall that Yates directed perhaps the greatest chase scene in history, in 1968's *Bullitt*. He didn't lose his touch here.

99 BEST LINE: Cyril: "Hey, are you really gonna shave your legs?"

Dave: "Certo. All the Italians do it."

Mike: "Some country. The women don't shave theirs."

✎ WHAT THEY WROTE AT THE TIME: "The cast is unknown, the director has a spotty history, and the basic premise falls into this year's most hackneyed category (unknown boxer/bowler/jogger hopes to become sports hero). Even so, the finished product is wonderful. Here is a movie so fresh and funny it didn't even need a big budget or a pedigree."—Janet Maslin, *New York Times*

☞ DON'T FAIL TO NOTICE: The lead character of Dave Stoller is based on a colorful Bloomington legend named Dave Blase, who also had an Italian fixation and once led a team to victory in the Little 500. The real Blase has a cameo here as the race's announcer.

◉ REPEATED WATCHING QUOTIENT: Very high. Good movie for women, good movie for kids. Good movie anytime you need a little encouragement and motivation.

★ SPORTS-ACTION GRADE: Solid B. There's only so much a director can do with a bike racing scene. It can never attain the nuance and excitement of, say, a goal-line stand or the last round of a title fight. Still, the aforementioned truck-chasing scene, and the two major races do get your heart pumping. The original reviews of *Breaking Away* suggested that theatergoers jumped from their seats and cheered. Feel free to do that from your living room sofa.

☙ BET YOU DIDN'T KNOW: Dooley and Christopher have played father and son three separate times—in this film, in Robert Altman's 1978 film, *A Wedding*, and in a 2001 episode of *Law and Order: Criminal Intent*.

☻ "I KNOW THAT GUY": Actor Hart Bochner, who plays snooty frat boy Rod (the perfect name) in this flick, has the kind of pretty-boy good looks that make you want to punch him in the face. That's why you always see him cast as an overconfident jackass, most memorably in *Die Hard*.

Surely you recall Harry Ellis, the cocaine-addled "can-do" guy ("Hey, sprechen ze talk?") who meets his end after thinking he can negotiate with terrorist Hans Gruber.

"Hans, Bubby. I'm your white knight."

Bang.

✖ IF YOU LIKED THIS, YOU'LL LIKE: *American Flyers*, an early Kevin Costner flick—which is to say before he started taking himself too seriously. Costner and David Marshall Grant star as brothers training for a bicycle race across the Rockies.

SIGN OF THE TIMES: Those crotch-hugging shorts? Clothes that all appear four sizes too small? The neon colors? The haircuts from hell? This movie could only have been shot in the 1970s, the black-hole decade for fashion.

21 WHEN WE WERE KINGS (1996–NR)

SPORT: BOXING | STARS: MUHAMMAD ALI, GEORGE FOREMAN | DIRECTOR: LEON GAST

Leon Gast was a young filmmaker who went to Zaire, Africa, in 1974 to chronicle an international Woodstock featuring artists from America, including James Brown, and performers from Africa, such as Miriam Makeba. The week-long festival would conclude with a heavyweight title fight: the undefeated champion George Foreman against former champion Muhammad Ali.

Originally, Gast was more interested in the music. He was known for filming concerts—he produced films on B.B. King and the Grateful Dead—not sports. But when Foreman suffered an eye injury in training, the bout was pushed back five weeks. To fill the time, Gast began trailing after Ali, watching him interact with the people of Zaire. He quickly realized he had a whole different kind of film on his hands.

In *When We Were Kings*, Gast has total access to Ali, and the former champ is at his audacious and boastful best, offering playful predictions such as: "You think the world was surprised when Nixon resigned? Just wait till I whip Foreman's behind." He delights the crowds with riffs that sound like modern rap. A sample: "I wrestled an alligator, I tussled with a whale. I done handcuffed lightning and thrown thunder in jail. I injured a rock, I murdered a brick. I'm so mean, I make medicine sick."

But Ali also has many introspective moments as he walks through the villages and bonds with the people. It is clear the trip to Africa touches an emotion deep inside him. "I live in America," he says, "but Africa is the home of the black man. I'm going home to fight among my brothers."

Desson Howe of the *Washington Post* describes Ali as

"a champion with grace, charm, an oversized ego, formidable fighting skills, a cheekily inspired sense of poetry, political savvy, religious conviction and defiantly independent opinions." At 32, Ali is all that. Gast's film shows the people of Zaire reaching out, touching his hands and face as if he were the Messiah.

Foreman, by contrast, alienates the people when he steps off the plane with his German Shepherd. He is unaware that German Shepherds were used against the citizens of Zaire by the Belgian military when they occupied the nation then known as the Belgian Congo. The sight of Foreman's snarling dog sends an ugly message to the populace and it is only reinforced by the champion's sullen manner. While Ali mingles with the people, Foreman stays secluded with his entourage.

This is not the affable George Foreman of today, the smiling grandfather who sells grills and appears in sitcoms. This is Foreman at 25, a dour and inscrutable wrecking machine fresh off devastating knockouts of Joe Frazier and Ken Norton, both of whom had wins over Ali. Foreman is a heavy betting favorite. Even Howard Cosell, an Ali loyalist, picks Foreman to win.

A French reporter asks Foreman what he would do if he lost to Ali. Foreman glares at the man. "I beg your pardon?" he says. The reporter nervously tries to rephrase the question, but Foreman cuts him off. "I beg your pardon?" he says, ending the interview.

Given the personalities of Ali and Foreman, plus the backdrop of a newly independent African nation, Gast has all the elements for a great documentary. He shot more than 300,000 feet of film—which helps to explain why it took him 22 years to edit it down to 90 minutes— so even if the fight had ended the way most people expected, with Foreman crushing Ali, Gast would have had an intimate character study of the two men.

But when the fight turns out to be the now-legendary "Rumble in the Jungle" with Ali shocking the world by knocking out Foreman in the eighth round, well, Gast has a film for the ages. *When We Were Kings* is the toast of the Sundance Film Festival and wins the 1997 Academy Award for Best Documentary Feature.

"*Kings* limns the meaning of the fight," writes David Armstrong of the *San Francisco Examiner*, "and shows why it transcends the parochial world of sports. The film-makers blend vintage interviews with a romantic young Ali who extols Islam and idealizes Mother Africa. . . . In the hands of director Gast and chief editor and interviewer Taylor Hackford, *Kings* becomes a rich social document."

There are many levels to the story, including the rise of Don King. The bombastic promoter makes the decision to stage the fight in Zaire when that nation's president, Mobutu Sese Seko, agrees to put up the $10 million purse. Mobutu sees the event, with the accompanying music festival, as a way of promoting his country, but some critics find it hard to justify spending $10 million on what amounts to a PR campaign when the nation itself is wracked by poverty.

Gast sets what is surely a bizarre scene. The fight is held in a 70,000-seat soccer stadium rumored to have been the site of mass executions during Mobutu's rise to power. Mobutu does not attend the bout, fearing an assassination attempt. The fight is scheduled for 3 a.m. Zaire time so it will be prime time in the United States. There are native drummers and witch doctors at ringside. As the fighters enter the arena, the crowd chants, "*Ali, boma ye.*" Translation: "Ali, kill him."

Gast uses assorted talking heads to reconstruct the round-by-round drama. Authors Norman Mailer and George Plimpton, who were at ringside, eloquently describe the mood, which bordered on dread for those who were rooting for Ali. Mailer says Ali's dressing room was "like a morgue." There was a feeling, even in Ali's camp, that Foreman was invincible. They feared he may demolish Ali and even humiliate him.

Mailer offers a vivid account (which is supported by Gast's footage) of Ali sitting on his stool after the first round, staring across the ring at the hulking Foreman and wondering if he could stand up to that power.

"The nightmare had finally come to visit [Ali]," Mailer says. "It was the only time I've ever seen fear in his eyes. He was up against a man who was younger and bigger and stronger than he was. A man who was not afraid of him. [Ali] had never been in this position before.

"Watching [Ali], you could see him nodding as if he were talking to himself, asking himself, 'Do you have the guts?' You could almost see him summoning the courage and as he nodded, saying, 'The time has come. I will find a way to master this man.' "

Ali mastered Foreman using the technique he called the "rope-a-dope," leaning back against the ropes, going into a defensive shell and inviting Foreman to pound away. At the time, it seemed suicidal. Plimpton recalls thinking, "The fix is in." It appeared Ali was making no attempt to fight back. But Ali let Foreman punch himself into a state of exhaustion. Then he chopped the big man down with a series of counterpunches, finally knocking him out with a straight right hand to the jaw.

With the stunning victory, Ali regained his heavyweight title, but more than that, he was once again an icon. He had done what no one else thought possible: he felled the mighty George Foreman. It was the high point of his career, and there is an undeniable sadness in seeing the film and comparing the charismatic Ali of Zaire with the sad figure of today, trembling with Parkinson's disease, his eyes glassy and unfocused.

But thanks to Gast, *When We Were Kings* stands as a vivid reminder of what he once was. As Desson Howe writes: "The movie is a metaphor for any of us who lament the passing of time, who remember when we were younger, quicker and more alert. Ali was magic; he was lightning in gloves. He was the best and the brightest. *Kings* proves it."

🔖 **CHEERS:** The film has no narrator. The story is told entirely through interviews and clips from the original broadcast, and it flows seamlessly.

🚩 **JEERS:** Gast introduces Zaire's president Mobutu and discusses the political climate in the African nation, but there is much more that could have been said about his rise to power.

💬 **BEST LINE:** George Plimpton describes Ali's rope-a-dope as resembling "a man leaning out his window to see if there is something on his roof." Plimpton also describes Don King as having "a great uprush of hair."

🎖 **BET YOU DIDN'T KNOW:** When *Kings* won the Oscar for Best Documentary Feature, Ali and Foreman joined Leon Gast on stage. They received a standing ovation.

"The sight of Foreman helping Ali onto the stage was so poignant," said Jeff Wald, executive producer of the TV series *The Contender*. "No one even noticed the producer [Gast], they were applauding the two fighters. Afterwards, the press asked George what he thought of the film. George said, 'I've seen it several times. I keep thinking the ending will change.'"

✒ **WHAT THEY WROTE AT THE TIME:** "[Ali] is one of the most perfect unions of thought and action anyone has ever seen. The conceptual beauty of his victory over Foreman is indistinguishable from the beauty of its execution. Athletes think with their bodies. Physically, Ali was able to express not just strength, but more intelligence and wit than any athlete ever has."—Charles Taylor, Salon.com

👓 **"I KNOW THAT GUY":** You may recognize one of Ali's sparring partners as a young, lean Larry Holmes.

⭐ **SPORTS-ACTION GRADE:** Solid A. Muhammad Ali is at the top of his game.

🎞 **IF YOU LIKED THIS, YOU'LL LIKE:** *Tyson*, the 2009 documentary about the former heavyweight champion, directed by James Toback. The film is one long monologue as Tyson discusses his rise and fall culminating with his 1992 rape conviction and three-year stretch in prison. Toback is sympathetic to Tyson so the film lacks balance, but it is compelling nonetheless. Hearing Tyson say "I never thought I'd live to be 40" explains a lot.

◉ **REPEATED WATCHING QUOTIENT:** It sure beats watching any heavyweight title fight today.

🎬 **MY FAVORITE SPORTS MOVIE:** Sportscaster James Brown: "What I found interesting about the film was the difference between the George Foreman of Zaire and the George Foreman I knew from hosting heavyweight title fights on HBO. When George fought Ali, he was seen as the villain. The guy I knew was nothing like that. He was incredibly gracious and warm. He would work a fight on Saturday and fly home immediately so he could be in church the next morning. It's hard for me to match that guy up with the one in Zaire."

22 A LEAGUE OF THEIR OWN (1992–PG)

SPORT: BASEBALL | STARS: TOM HANKS, GEENA DAVIS, MADONNA
DIRECTOR: PENNY MARSHALL

Most baseball seasons don't play out according to plan. Key players are injured and have to be replaced. Lineups are juggled and sometimes it turns out for the better. It can be the same way with baseball movies. Take *A League of Their Own*, for instance.

When Columbia Pictures began production on its film about the All-American Girls Professional Baseball League (AAGPBL), Debra Winger was cast in the role of Dottie Hinson, the star catcher of the Rockford Peaches. But Winger suffered a back injury and dropped out, so producers Elliot Abbott and Robert Greenhut had to find a replacement. They brought in Geena Davis.

It was a tough break for Debra Winger, but it worked out well for Columbia.

Watching the film now, it is hard to imagine anyone other than Davis, the statuesque, red-haired beauty, in the role of Hinson. She was the pinup girl of the AAGPBL, "The Queen of Diamonds," whose combination of baseball ability and good looks helped to sell the girls' league in America during World War II.

Winger may have been able to catch and throw, but she would not have looked as regal on the cover of *Life* magazine, and it is unlikely she could have played off co-star Tom Hanks as effectively as Davis. The on-screen chemistry between the leads—Davis as the star player, Hanks as the drunken slob of a manager—is one of the film's real strengths.

Davis joined the cast only days before filming was due to start. The other actors—Rosie O'Donnell, Madonna, Ann Cusack among them—had already completed the Hollywood equivalent of spring training. They worked with professional baseball coaches, including Joe Russo, the coach at St. John's University, to learn the fundamentals. "It sounds silly," Russo said, "but what I have to do is get them not to throw like a girl."

The cast bonded as a team during the experience.

When Davis came in, she was a bit of an outsider. She auditioned for the part by playing catch with director Penny Marshall in Marshall's backyard. Davis proved to be a good enough athlete that she was able to outperform the other actors within a matter of weeks. There never was a question about her acting ability: she won an Oscar for her role in *The Accidental Tourist* in 1988.

The script was written by Lowell Ganz and Babaloo Mandel, who have a way with witty dialog, as they demonstrated in *City Slickers*, *Splash* and the underrated *Night Shift*. As a director, Marshall tends to smear sentimental goo over her projects, and the result is like eating a cake with about eight inches of icing. *Big*, *Awakenings* and *The Preacher's Wife* are so sugary, they should come with a warning for diabetics.

A League of Their Own has its too-sweet moments—especially the bracketing device of opening and closing the film with a reunion of the AAGPBL alumni 50 years later at the Baseball Hall of Fame—but for the most part, Marshall keeps the sappy stuff in check. The result is a very pleasant two hours at the ballpark.

Vincent Canby of the *New York Times* called it "one of the year's most cheerful, most relaxed, most easily enjoyable comedies . . . a serious film that's lighter than air, a very funny movie that manages to score a few points for feminism in passing."

The film is a fictional account of the AAGPBL, a professional league for women which helped fill the void created when most major league stars went off to military service in World War II. There were four original teams—the Rockford Peaches, the Racine Belles, the Kenosha Comets and the South Bend Blue Sox. *League* focuses on the Rockford team, which is managed (sort of) by Jimmy Dugan (Hanks).

Dugan is a former major league star whose career was cut short by alcoholism. He takes the Rockford job because he needs the money, but he has no intention of actually managing the team. "Girls are what you sleep with after the game," he says, "not what you coach during the game."

So while Dugan gets drunk and dozes in the dugout, Dottie Hinson (Davis) runs the team. Hinson is a no-nonsense Oregon farm girl. A married woman whose husband is at war, she has no patience for the dissolute Dugan. She also has ambivalent feelings about baseball. She was talked into joining the league by her kid sister Kit (Lori Petty), a pitcher who knew she could ride Dottie's coattails into the AAGPBL.

But there is a part of Dottie that enjoys the game,

placed 54th, but there is no doubt it is repeated more often than half of the quotes ranked ahead of it. It is very funny, and the story Dugan tells about how he didn't cry when his manager Rogers Hornsby called him "a talking pile of pig shit" is a hoot.

There's no crying in baseball.

Thanks to Jimmy Dugan, we'll never forget that cardinal rule.

One of the most interesting aspects of the film is the understated way the relationship between Dugan and Dottie evolves. From the early scenes when Dugan is in a drunken haze and Dottie can barely tolerate the sight of him, they develop a respectful manager-player rela-

JIMMY DUGAN: **"I WAS IN THE TOILET READING MY CONTRACT AND IT TURNS OUT, I GET A BONUS WHEN WE GET TO THE WORLD SERIES. SO LET'S GO OUT THERE AND PLAY HARD."**

more than she is willing to admit even to herself. Dugan sees it and it helps bring him around. He sobers up (he never does get around to shaving) and he begins to function as a real manager, encouraging his players and, when necessary, chewing them out.

The most famous scene from *League* is Dugan ripping outfielder Evelyn Gardner (Bitty Schram) for throwing to the wrong base.

"Start using your head," he says. "That's the lump that's three feet above your ass."

Evelyn's lip quivers, then she begins to cry. Dugan, the hard-boiled baseball lifer, is aghast.

"Are you crying?" he says. "There's no crying in baseball!"

The American Film Institute put the "no crying" line on its list of the 100 greatest film quotes of all time. It

tionship and, finally, they become friends. They bond over baseball. Dottie keeps insisting the game isn't that important to her, but Dugan has seen her play and he knows better.

"I gave away five years at the end of my career to drink," Dugan says. "Five years, and now there isn't anything I wouldn't give to get back any one day of it."

"Well, we're different," Dottie says.

Dugan doesn't buy it.

"Baseball is what gets inside you," he says. "It's what lights you up, Dottie. You can't deny that."

When Dottie says the game is too hard, Dugan answers like a man who has been to the big leagues and won a home run title or two.

"It's supposed to be hard," he says. "If it wasn't hard, everyone would do it. The *hard* is what makes it great."

League was the No. 1 film in America when it opened in July 1992. It made $107 million domestic, and another $25 million overseas. Nice return for a film that cost just $40 million to make.

🍺 **CHEERS:** Jon Lovitz has a terrific role as Ernie Capadino, the sarcastic talent scout who discovers the Hinson sisters. When the girls hesitate about boarding the train, he says, "See, here's how it works. The train moves, not the station."

👎 **JEERS:** The scene with the Western Union delivery man barging into the locker room, saying, "I have a telegram from the War Department." It is inconceivable that someone could be so insensitive to stand in front of a roomful of women and say, "The least they could do is send someone in person to tell you your husband is dead."

👑 **BET YOU DIDN'T KNOW:** Hanks' character of Jimmy Dugan was loosely based on Hall of Famer Jimmy Foxx. After his playing career, Foxx went broke with a series of bad investments so he worked as a minor league coach and manager, including a stint with the Fort Wayne Daisies of the AAGPBL.

👑 **BET YOU DIDN'T KNOW II:** The original story was written by Kelly Candaele, whose mother played in the AAGPBL. Kelly's brother Casey played 9 seasons in the major leagues.

📣 **CASTING CALL:** Moira Kelly was signed to play the role of Kit Hinson, but she hurt her ankle filming the skating movie *The Cutting Edge*. Lori Petty replaced her. Also, Penny Marshall's daughter, Tracy Reiner, is Rockford outfielder Betty "Spaghetti" Horn.

✒ **WHAT THEY WROTE AT THE TIME:** "The movie has a real bittersweet charm. The baseball sequences, we've seen before. What's fresh are the personalities of the players, the gradual unfolding of their coach and the way this early chapter of women's liberation fit into the hidebound traditions of professional baseball."—Roger Ebert, *Chicago Sun-Times*

💬 **BEST LINE:** Ira Lowenstein (David Strathairn), an AAGPBL official, confronts Jimmy Dugan, who is showing up drunk for games and falling asleep in the dugout.

"Great game, Jimmy," he says. "I especially liked that move in the seventh inning where you scratched your balls for an hour."

Dugan replies, "Well, anything worth doing is worth doing right."

☞ **DON'T FAIL TO NOTICE:** Tom Hanks put on 30 pounds to play the bloated Dugan.

😎 **"I KNOW THAT GUY":** Eddie (the Big Ragu) Mekka, Penny Marshall's co-star from the *Laverne and Shirley* TV show, is Madonna's jitterbug dance partner. Another L&S alum, David (Squiggy) Lander, is the game announcer at the World Series.

★ **SPORTS-ACTION GRADE:** C. Even if we grade on a curve, allowing for the fact these are women, some of the swings don't look good enough to make it in slow-pitch softball.

🎬 **MY FAVORITE SPORTS MOVIE:** Pat Williams, senior vice president of the Orlando Magic and GM of the 1983 NBA Champion Philadelphia 76ers: "The chemistry between Tom Hanks and Geena Davis is terrific. And what an ensemble—Madonna, Rosie O'Donnell, Jon Lovitz. That's an all-star cast right there."

23 FRIDAY NIGHT LIGHTS (2004–PG-13)

SPORT: FOOTBALL | STARS: BILLY BOB THORNTON, DEREK LUKE, LUCAS BLACK
DIRECTORS: PETER BERG AND JOSH PATE

Turning a successful book into a movie can be tricky. Four hundred pages of plot don't always translate neatly onto film; readers may have preconceptions of their favorite characters; a downer of a story ending can spell box-office disaster.

Sometimes the adaptation works (*The Godfather, Jaws*). Sometimes it doesn't (*Bonfire of the Vanities, The Da Vinci Code*).

Friday Night Lights, the laser-sharp look at West Texas high school football, works magnificently. Based on the acclaimed 1990 best seller by H.G. "Buzz" Bissinger, the movie captures the culture of gridiron as a small town's identity, where 17-year-old boys become gods for a few months, but the humiliation of failure is worse than death.

It helps that one of the film's directors, Peter Berg, happens to be Bissinger's cousin. Clearly, Berg got the author's underlying unease over how an economically ravaged oil town can spend millions building a state-of-the-art stadium, when the school district itself is close to broke. Priorities. As one caller to a talk-radio show says during the movie, "It's about coaching. And you know what else? They're doing too much learning in that school."

But that's the way it works in Odessa, Texas, where the Permian High Panthers have won four state football titles (plus two more since the 1988 season about which the book was written). Half the town's men seem to wear championship rings from their youth, and most of them show up to watch the high-school two-a-days. "It is a religion," producer Brian Grazer says on the DVD commentary. "And people go to that church every Friday night."

That said, *Friday Night Lights* is not an attack on football. The practice and game scenes are outstanding, especially the final game, which was filmed at the old Astrodome in Houston. And the young men who play the game come off as likeable and sympathetic.

Consider Boobie Miles (Derek Luke), the cocky star running back who sits at his locker gazing through the glossy catalogs of the dozens of colleges aiming to recruit him. Miles destroys his knee early in his senior season, and suddenly yesterday's toast of the town is today's stale crust. His dreams are gone. As Bissinger says, "One millisecond changed his whole life."

We meet quarterback Mike Winchell (Lucas Black), an unsmiling, twitchy Peyton Manning look-alike who

the son of a high school basketball coach, Thornton was able to nail the role without having to do much research. "I mean he's a coach from Texas," Thornton told ESPN.com. "It's not like a stretch. It's not like they hired a British theatre actor to play a Texas football coach. They hired a guy from Arkansas."

Thornton's Coach Gaines is alternately fuming, compassionate, fearful and stoic. Much of his time is spent suffering through local boosters—everyone from the bank president to the school's janitor—who tell him how to coach and let him know that anything short of a state title will be considered grounds for dismissal. After one humiliating loss, Gaines and his wife return home to find

BRIAN CHAVEZ: "WE GOT TO LIGHTEN UP. WE'RE 17."

MIKE WINCHELL: "I SURE DON'T FEEL 17."

copes each day with an overriding sense of doom; tailback Don Billingsley (Garrett Hedlund), whose drunken failure of a dad tries to cure the kid's fumble-itis by duct-taping his arms around a football; and safety Brian Chavez (Jay Hernandez), the deep thinker of the team, who is the first to recognize that the glare of the bright stadium lights can burn a young man.

In one of the most telling scenes, those three seniors sneak off to the edge of town to relax by skeet shooting—and to consider the overwhelming pressure placed upon their bulked-up shoulders.

Chavez: "We got to lighten up. We're 17."

Billingsley: "Do you feel 17?"

Winchell: "I sure don't feel 17."

The young actors are genuine, but the movie belongs to Billy Bob Thornton, playing Coach Gary Gaines. As

a dozen for-sale signs propped on their lawn.

The Permian Panthers don't quite bring home the state title in 1988, but their journey will keep you enthralled. The back end of the film is dominated by on-field action, which is nothing short of superb. Plus, by that point, you know the characters and find yourself caring about them. There's a wonderful small moment right near the end between Billingsley and his abusive dad. And there's also one of those almost-cliché "where are they now" finishes, where we learn that the young men who spent their high school lives as supermen and scapegoats grow up to become lawyers, surveyors and insurance men.

The book works, the movie works. And of course, *Friday Night Lights* was turned into a television series by Berg and Grazer in 2006. The show, although a critical success, spent much of its first two seasons on the verge of being cancelled. While it strays further from Bissinger's original premise, it is well worth watching. Other than *Friday Night Lights* and *M*A*S*H*, we can't think of another worthwhile book-movie-TV series triple-play, can you?

CHEERS: From the opening title card, the soundtrack—by West Texas indie band Explosions in the Sky—sets exactly the right tone for *Friday Night Lights*. The score isn't quite football marching band and it isn't quite Texas C&W; it is searing guitar solos and bone-rattling drum shots that give the film an energetic, hard-driving backdrop.

JEERS: As we noted, it's impossible to distill a 416-page book into a two-hour movie without losing something. That said, the key element of Bissinger's story examining racism within the community should not have been ignored. For example, the book notes that the reason schools were originally desegregated in Odessa was to get blacks onto the football team.

SPORTS-ACTION GRADE: A-plus. Go ahead, name a football movie where the game scenes seemed more authentic. You can't do it. Allan Graf, a former stuntman and starting guard for the 1972 National Champion USC Trojans, coordinated the football action. He tried out more than 800 potential players, and settled on 41, whom he worked out for three weeks before shooting. Each actor/player had to memorize Permian's real 1988 playbook.

PIVOTAL SCENE: His career ended by injury, Boobie Miles makes one last trip to the Permian stadium to clean out his locker. He pulls out his team towel, his lucky black Nikes, his Mercedes-Benz catalog. He cracks jokes with teammates and encourages them to "go out and win states" without him. He exits with a strut and a smile.

But when he reaches his car in the parking lot, Boobie breaks down. "What are we gonna do now?" he sobs into his sympathetic uncle's shoulder. "I can't do nothing else but play football. We practiced. You told me we were gonna go to the pros. Now what are we gonna do?" He is inconsolable.

It's a powerful scene and true to the actual events. "Football was something that you love to do—and all of a sudden you can't do it no more," the real Boobie Miles says on the DVD commentary. "It was devastating. I couldn't get my family out of the ghetto being hurt. Football was my ticket."

BET YOU DIDN'T KNOW: Miles actually rushed for 1,385 yards in 1987—the year before his injury. Not bad, especially when you consider that he was a backup to senior feature back Shawn Crow—who rushed for a whopping 2,288 yards that 14-game season. Crow went to play at TCU, where he too blew out his knee. Chris Comer, who stepped in after Miles' injury (and who is portrayed in the movie by Lee Thompson Young), ended up rushing for 2,135 yards in 1988. Not too shoddy for a fill-in.

CASTING CALL: NFL wide receiver Roy Williams—who played for Permian from 1997-2000—can be seen on the sidelines as an assistant coach for Midland Lee. Also, in some of the game scenes where Luke (as Miles) is standing on the sidelines in crutches, the man standing next to him is the genuine Boobie Miles.

GOOFS: Down six points with 54 seconds to go in the state title game vs. Dallas-Carter, Winchell overthrows a receiver. The camera then cuts to the stadium clock, which is still running. C'mon, even a Pop Warner beginner knows that the clock stops after an incompletion.

BEST LINE: Coach Gaines' title game halftime speech to a team trailing 26-7 is the stuff of legends:

"Boys, it's real simple. You've got two more quarters and that's it. Now most of you have been playing this game for 10 years. You've got two more quarters and after that most of you will never play this game again as long as you live.

"You've all known me for a while, and for a long time now you've been hearing me talk about being perfect. Now I want you to understand something. To me, being perfect is not about that scoreboard out there. It's not about winning. It's about you and your relationship to yourself and your family and your friends. Being perfect is about being able to look your friends in the eye and know that you didn't let them down, because you told them the truth. And that truth is that you did everything you could. There wasn't one more thing that you could have done.

"Can you live in that moment? As best you can, with clear eyes and love in your heart? With joy in your heart? If you can do that, gentlemen, then you're perfect. I want you to take a moment, and I want you to look each other in the eyes. I want you to put each other in your hearts forever—because forever is about to happen here in just a few minutes."

✎ **WHAT THEY WROTE AT THE TIME:** "The only fake thing in *Friday Night Lights* is Billy Bob Thornton's hair. As Gary Gaines, the real-life coach of the Permian Panthers football team in Odessa, Texas, Thornton wears a piece and zips up his *Bad Santa* mouth.... Thornton gets inside the coach's skin. It's a subtle, soulful performance in a movie that otherwise goes for the jugular. Chronicling the team's 1988 season, the film is red meat for rabid football junkies."—Peter Travers, *Rolling Stone*

👁 **REPEATED WATCHING QUOTIENT:** Very high—the characters are deep, the dialog is gritty, the action is intense. We also highly recommend that you read Bissinger's book.

👓 **"I KNOW THAT GUY":** Well, Lucas Black is too well known to fit our normal definition of this category, but you may not have recognized him from the other movie he co-starred in with Billy Bob Thornton. Eight years earlier, Lucas played the bullied pre-teen whom Billy Bob, as Karl Childers, befriends and protects in *Sling Blade*.

✔ **REALITY CHECK:** The 1988 Permian Panthers did, indeed, end their season by losing to Dallas-Carter, but it was in the state semi-finals, not the title game. We have no problem with the film taking creative license here.

☞ **DON'T FAIL TO NOTICE:** At the end of the movie, Coach Gaines is seen adjusting his depth chart—taking down the name plates for departing seniors and moving

up some new starters. The quarterback replacing Mike Winchell is listed as "Case." That denotes Stoney Case, who would go on to lead Permian to a national high school football title in 1989 and have a four-season career as an NFL backup QB.

🎞 **IF YOU LIKED THIS, YOU'LL LIKE:** *The Last Picture Show*, Peter Bogdanovich's look at high schoolers coming of age in another dusty West Texas small town, set in 1951. The two young men, played by Timothy Bottoms and Jeff Bridges, even play football.

☝ **MY FAVORITE SPORTS MOVIE:** Stanley Cup-winning coach Ken Hitchcock: "The class and dignity that the Billy Bob Thornton character shows throughout the movie gives you a great sense of the combination of stress and pressures that comes with being a coach. Fans come up to him and say, 'Hey, we love you Coach, but if you lose, you're finished.' Back when I coached in junior hockey, people would talk to me like that every day."

AN INTERVIEW WITH H.G. "BUZZ" BISSINGER

H.G. "Buzz" Bissinger is a former Pulitzer Prize-winning investigative reporter for the *Philadelphia Inquirer*. His book, *Friday Night Lights*, spent 15 weeks on the *New York Times* best-seller list in 1990. He has been a contributing editor to *Vanity Fair* magazine since 1996.

How did you convince the people of Odessa, Texas to open up to you, an East Coast outsider, when you researched your book, Friday Night Lights?

They were very proud of the football program and respected that I wanted to spend time and live in their community for a year. If I had parachuted in for three days here and there, they wouldn't have given me the access. But I quit my job at the *Philadelphia Inquirer* and moved down there with my fiancé and twin kids. We rented a house, my kids went to school there. I went to every practice, and they admired that—particularly the players. They saw that I was serious about telling the story.

How did that story change from the time you conceived the book to when you wrote it?

Going in, I thought it would be more of a *Hoosiers* type of story about a community coming together over high school football in a larger-than-life way. I knew about the excesses—the $5.6 million stadium that seats nearly 20,000 people. What I wasn't prepared for was the racism and what a joke the classroom was. I thought I'd write about the intensity, but it was multiplied by 10.

When the book came out, there was a lot of talk that people in Odessa felt betrayed.

Well, the kids, to a fault, felt the book was honest and accurate. The players and students said, 'Hey, this is the way it is.' That's what carried me through the incredible controversy. Gary Gaines never talked to me until I went to see him, unannounced, on the eve of the movie's

release in 2004. I wanted to look him in the eye and say that, while I didn't regret anything I wrote, I wasn't out to hurt him. He showed great dignity and charm. It was a gratifying conversation. He confessed he never read the book, which I wish he had.

When did the idea of turning the book into a movie begin?

The rights were sold right after the book came out in 1990. Alan Pakula was the first director to get the rights to it. He decided not to do it. It passed through Ted Demme (*The Ref, Blow*), and Jon Avnet (*Fried Green Tomatoes, Risky Business*), and Richard Linklater (*The School of Rock, Before Sunset*), and Brian Levant (*The Flintstones*) who I suppose would have made Fred and Barney two of the players. Each script was worse than the rest, each time it kept moving further from the book.

So how did it finally get done?

Producer Brian Grazer turned to Peter Berg. It was a complete stroke of luck that had nothing to do with Pete being my cousin. He just was the right guy for the job—finally.

Explain your relationship with Berg.

We're second cousins who knew each other growing up. He was quiet, always the bad little kid getting into trouble one way or the other. We became close in the 1980s when he went to Macalester College and I was working for the *St. Paul Pioneer Press* in Minnesota. But I never foresaw that we'd do a project together.

Once you sold the book rights, what influence did you have over the movie script?

None. I had no contractual right to okay anything. They could have made these guys into elephants and I had no recourse. My fear was they'd end up making a *Fast Times at Ridgemont High* movie out of it and make the kids I wrote about look silly. The advantage I had with Pete as the director was he understood not to strip away the kids' honor—and not to change the script so that they won at the end. He stayed true to the story.

But the movie removes a lot of aspects of the book, most notably the racism you wrote about.

That's true, and I understand why. Pete told me, 'I can make a movie about racism and it won't play, with Universal Studios or the audience.' And I understood that. Within the constraints of Hollywood, the movie is very true to the book.

Is there anything about the movie that disappointed you as the author?

Two things bothered me. Tim McGraw was fantastic in his role as Charley Billingsley, but the real Charley wasn't nearly as dark as that. I remember calling Charley's house after the movie and his wife just hung up on me. I understand that entirely.

The other aspect that bothered me was how, at the end of the movie, Boobie Miles and the team live happily ever after. In real life, he quit the team midway through the season. In the movie, he's cheering them on at the final Dallas-Carter game, which was a little Hollywood schmaltz.

How did you feel about the casting?

The casting was fantastic. Billy Bob Thornton was very understated; he reminded me a lot of the real Gary Gaines. The kids were great, especially Lucas Black as Mike Winchell. Lucas never met Winchell until the premier, but his portrayal was dead on. He nailed Winchell's insecurity perfectly. The character who kind of got lost in the movie was Brian Chavez, played by Jay Hernandez. Pete Berg didn't particularly like his work, so a lot of his story got cut.

Do you keep in touch with any of the people you wrote about?

Yeah, several of the kids. I've stayed good friends with Brian Chavez and his father. Our families went to the College World Series together this year and I'm going to his wedding next year. I talk to Boobie Miles once a month or so, usually when something's happened to him—a problem with an ex-girlfriend, a speeding ticket, things like that. He's basically an ebullient person, but it's been a rough road for him.

Sounds like you're filling the role now that his uncle, L.V., fills in the book and the movie.

That's fair to say.

Now there's Friday Night Lights the TV show, which is further removed from your book. Do you still recognize your original product?

No, I don't recognize the television show as my book. I have little to do with it, not out of malice, because they do what works for TV. It makes sense, but it's not *Friday Night Lights* as I wrote it. But it still sells some books for me—I'll take the help where I can. I am proud that the book, the movie and the show are all critically acclaimed. You can't say that about too many projects.

One of your other writing projects, Shattered Glass, became a successful movie. Do you see any other of your books translating to screen?

There's been some interest by (actor) Kevin Pollak in my book, *Three Nights in August* (which is about St. Louis Cardinals manager Tony La Russa). What do you think, Ray Liotta playing La Russa? I think that would work.

24 THE WRESTLER (2008–R)

SPORT: PROFESSIONAL WRESTLING | STARS: MICKEY ROURKE, MARISA TOMEI
DIRECTOR: DARREN ARONOFSKY

There was a time early in his career when Mickey Rourke was compared to a young Robert De Niro. In his early roles—Boogie in *Diner*, Harry Angel in *Angel Heart*, Charlie in *The Pope of Greenwich Village*—he was both dangerous and delicate, confident but still a little vulnerable.

By all accounts, he was going to be a big star. And then. . . .

And then Rourke took a disastrous career path. He took inane roles in cringe-inducing films. He left acting for four years to become a boxer—winning a few fights, but taking shots that scarred his soulful eyes. He got arrested, more than once. His career—and his looks—died in a haze of temper tantrums, spousal abuse charges, rumors of drug use and undeniably bad plastic surgery. And then. . . .

And then he came back. A few small roles in decent films (Francis Ford Coppola's *The Rainmaker*, the graphic-novel *Sin City*) helped Rourke emerge from the depths. The De Niro comparisons were long gone, but the man could still act. And then. . . .

And then, in 2008, Rourke got his star vehicle, playing, well, in many ways, himself. In *The Wrestler*, he stars as Randy "The Ram" Robinson, a one-time pro wrestling icon who packed-in the fans at Madison Square Garden back in the 1980s but is now reduced to grappling third-rate opponents in half-empty VFW halls.

It's a story about faded glory. In his prime, Randy inspired action figures and video games. (There's a poignant scene where the aging wrestler implores a neighbor kid to play against him in a prehistoric Nintendo game that bears The Ram's likeness. "This is sooo old," gripes the kid.)

Now he lives in a grungy North Jersey trailer park, lugs boxes part-time at an overly fluorescent supermarket, and takes whatever matches he can get. He wears a hearing aid and reading glasses and limps through painful arthritis. Still, he'll do anything to continue in the business—including shooting steroids into his butt, or engaging in self-mutilation during matches. In one tragic scene The Ram sits at a nearly empty nostalgia show, surrounded by other broken down relics of the ring, hoping to hawk Polaroids of himself for a few dollars. Ahh, show business.

The sad story is made sadder when Randy suffers a heart attack right after a match. Wrestling is all he knows, all he wants to do. When a doctor tells him he must retire, he realizes he has nowhere to go. Somewhere along the way he neglected to come up with a Plan B.

The Wrestler is pumped full of clichés. But it works because Rourke is wonderful at portraying, as The Ram calls himself, "a broken down piece of meat." His appearance is startling—a puffy, reconstructed face, stringy hair made blond through trips to the beauty parlor and a muscled-up body that looks like it would fail any performance-enhancing-drug test. The growling voice is something off a Tom Waits recording. Seriously, if you were not told in advance that is Mickey Rourke on the screen, you would never guess who you are watching. Overall, it was impressive enough to earn Rourke the 2009 Golden Globe Award for Best Actor in a Motion Picture–Drama.

Anyway, Randy tries for awhile to adjust to life without wrestling which, of course, isn't going to work. There's a powerful (albeit obvious) parallel story in which he falls for a stripper named Cassidy (Marisa Tomei) who won't commit to any relationship that lasts longer than a lap dance. Just like him, Cassidy is trying to survive flaunting a body that isn't getting any younger. Just like him, she uses a stage name. Just like him, she is a pro at faking something that the fans want to pretend is genuine.

Tomei is terrific in the role. In fact, our only criticism would be that her body—extremely naked throughout much of the movie—looks too good to play a fading stripper. Trust us, we're not really complaining here.

There's an exchange in *The Wrestler*, when The Ram and The Stripper are sipping beers in a dive bar, as he tries to convince her to care for him. "Round and Round," the heavy-metal standard from the band Rat Attack comes on the jukebox, and both agree that, as Randy says, "The '80s ruled, man, before that Cobain pussy had to come along and ruin it." Really, for both parties here, it's not just the music that peaked decades earlier.

There have been previous efforts to put pro wrestling on the screen, but most were played for laughs. (Does anyone remember *The One and Only*, with Henry Winkler as a Gorgeous George clone?) *The Wrestler*, while eliciting a few chuckles along the way, is definitely not designed to show the fun and happy side of "sports entertainment," or whatever Vince McMahon calls his seedy empire these days. Rather, it's a magnifying glass aimed at the underbelly of the business—pills and shots, gruesome physical punishment, decaying hearts and bodies that give out before their owners hit age 50.

The Wrestler leads up to an ending that can be interpreted several ways—in fact, the two authors of this book debated exactly what it meant. That's a good thing. Nearly two hours in you will deeply care for Randy "The Ram," and worry about what happens to him. Credit writer Robert D. Siegel's layered script, credit director Darren Aronofsky. But mostly, credit Rourke, who creates an unforgettable character.

🏅 **CHEERS:** The movie gets the world of professional wrestling just right. Those who don't follow it may be repulsed by scenes of a man in tights inviting another to shoot his forehead with a staple gun. Or two guys falling

RANDY:

"THE SHIEK? LAST I HEARD HE WAS SELLING USED CARS."

backwards off an eight-foot ladder onto a table covered with barbed wire.

But this is what these men do to make a living. Beyond that, you'll be fascinated by the backstage shoptalk among the wrestlers, the surprising respect that supposed enemies show each other and the choreography, which can be as complex as a ballet or as simple as, "I'm the heel. You're the face. Done."

"That was so dead-on, man," former WWE champion Mick Foley told *Sports Illustrated*. "They nailed it."

🏳 **JEERS:** There is nothing interesting in the subplot about the broken relationship between Randy and his 20ish daughter Stephanie (Evan Rachel Wood). We get the cliché—she harbors a grudge because he missed a childhood birthday or two. From the anger to the tears to the aborted reconciliation, it all seems contrived and predictable.

✏ **WHAT THEY WROTE AT THE TIME:** "Darren Aronofsky has created a masterful vanitas-style portrait of a world in decline. Mickey Rourke is amazing as Randy 'The Ram' Robinson, a fading cartoon of a man. I went into this expecting a sleeper hold, and instead I got a sharp elbow to the face."—Screenwriter Diablo Cody (*Juno*) in *Entertainment Weekly*

💬 **BEST LINE:** In desperate need of money after the heart attack interrupts his wrestling career, Randy asks his supermarket manager for more hours.

Manager: "All I've got available is weekends."
Randy: "That works."
Manager: "Isn't that when you sit on other dudes' faces?"

🎬 **PIVOTAL SCENE:** Randy goes to work behind the deli

counter—Samson in a hairnet—slicing ham and slinging potato salad. Initially, the showman in him embraces the role as he kibitzes with the clientele ("You want two big [chicken] breasts? I'd like two big breasts."). But the work grows dreary as he copes with a hectoring boss and some patrons from hell.

He takes an order one day from a customer who looks at him quizzically. I'm sure I know you, says the man. Are you with the Teamsters? Do you play softball? No, Randy sheepishly insists, we've never met.

The man stares a little harder. "Randy the Ram?" he asks incredulously. "Ram Jam?"

Randy just turns away in humiliation.

"Wow," says the client. "You look just like that dude, that wrestler from the '80s. Only older."

Randy's temper wells up until he can take it no more. He punches the meat slicer, gashing his hand. He rampages, shoving the abusive manager and slapping cereal boxes from the shelves. "I quit!" he declares, leaving the hairnet fluttering in his angry wake.

Quick cut to the next scene of Randy on a payphone. "I want to do it," he implores his old promoter. "I want to wrestle again."

🔍 **"I Know That Guy":** Small-time wrestling promoter Scott Brumberg is played by Judah Friedlander, best known for his role on *30 Rock* as staff writer Frank Rossitano—the guy with the oversized glasses and trucker's hats with weird messages. He's a little tough to spot under that Gil Grissom beard and Trenton Devils jersey.

★ **Sports-Action Grade:** A-minus, assuming that you'll buy into pro wrestling as a sport. We just wish there was more than 12 or so minutes of ring action in the movie.

🍎 **Bet You Didn't Know:** The Bruce Springsteen song that closes the film came about because of an old friendship between Rourke and The Boss. The two had lost touch during Rourke's "lost years," Aronofsky told MTV, "but Mickey wrote Bruce a letter—a very long, heartfelt letter—and sent him the script."

Springsteen loved the project. He wrote the song about "a one-trick pony, a one-legged dog" while on tour in Europe and debuted it for Aronofsky backstage at Giants Stadium. Make sure you notice the poster of Springsteen on the wall of The Ram's trailer.

◀ **Casting Call:** At one point, Rourke was fired from the project and Nicolas Cage was set to replace him, until Aronofsky had a change of heart.

Most of the wrestlers in the movie are played by veterans of the real circuit, including Ernest "The Cat" Miller, Dylan Keith Summers (aka Necro Butcher) and Ron "The Truth" Killings.

✴ **If You Liked This, You'll Like:** *All the Marbles*, a 1981 Peter Falk vehicle in which he plays the greasy manager of a women's tag team called the "California Dolls."

You may also want to check out the 1999 documentary *Beyond the Mat*, which Rourke used as a resource material.

"We watched and saw what happens at the end of somebody's career," he said. "You know, what they looked like then and what they look like now, or the guys who are still trying to hang in there. We really wanted to pay homage to the sport in its due course as the movie went along. Sure, we exposed certain things that wouldn't be in a *Rocky* movie, you know? But we weren't making that kind of movie."

◎ **Repeated Watching Quotient:** If you know where to find *WCW Monday Nitro* on your television dial, it's probably limitless. If not, *The Wrestler* is worth a few viewings, just to see how Rourke abused his body and Tomei took care of hers.

25 THE SET-UP (1949–NR)

SPORT: BOXING | STARS: ROBERT RYAN, AUDREY TOTTER, GEORGE TOBIAS
DIRECTOR: ROBERT WISE

Shot in 20 days and only 72 minutes in length, *The Set-Up* is a small film, but it packs a heavyweight wallop.

It was overshadowed by *Body and Soul*, the John Garfield classic which was released two years earlier and earned four Academy Award nominations, and *Champion* with Kirk Douglas, which came out the same year and picked up six Academy Award nominations. *The Set-Up* wasn't nominated for anything, yet it is arguably the superior film.

Body and Soul and *Champion* were more traditional films. They told an entire life story, following Charlie Davis (Garfield) and Midge Kelly (Douglas) from their dirt-poor youth to their reign as world champions. We

saw the hard times and we saw the high times, the wealth, the flashy clothes, the hot babes, all the trappings of success.

The Set-Up has a more narrow focus. The entire story takes place in one night. In fact, it takes place in just 72 minutes. When we first see the clock, it is 9:10 p.m. The film ends at 10:22 P.M., which means the story unfolds in real time. All the action takes place in a two block stretch of a seedy town where Stoker Thompson (Robert Ryan) is scheduled to fight that night.

We don't see any montages of Stoker's career. We don't see any flashbacks to how he got started or how high he climbed in the heavyweight rankings. We don't see any of the glory, if there was any. All we see is the present and the present isn't very pretty.

Stoker is a 35-year-old pug with scar tissue around his eyes and a brain that's turning to tapioca pudding. There is the suggestion that once upon a time he was a decent fighter, maybe even a borderline contender, but that was many years and many miles ago. Now he is what promoters call "an opponent," a guy who goes from town to town fighting whatever local boy they put in front of him. He lives on chump change and memories.

Stoker still has his pride, and he clings to the belief that he is just one win away from getting back in the big time. He hasn't totally lost his skill—he still has knockout

"You were just one punch away from a title shot then. Don't you see? You'll always be just one punch away."

"But if I don't do this, what would I do?" he asks.

"I don't care," she says. "It's better than seeing you hurt. It's better than having you dead."

Julie refuses to go with him so he leaves her ticket on the bureau. He walks across the street to the rundown arena. It is such a low budget operation there are only two locker rooms so Stoker shares a dressing space with four other fighters: a nervous teenager who is making his pro debut, a punchy old-timer who still dreams of winning a title and the two headliners who are ripe with bravado. As Stoker undresses, he studies the others in the

STOKER:

"I'M JUST ONE PUNCH AWAY."

JULIE:

"DON'T YOU SEE? YOU'LL ALWAYS BE JUST ONE PUNCH AWAY."

power in his right hand—but he is old and slow and his reflexes are gone. He takes too many punches and usually finishes the night flat on his back.

His wife Julie (Audrey Totter) wants him to quit but he refuses. As he packs his gear in his shabby hotel room, preparing to walk across the street to the arena, he says he has a feeling he is going to win this fight. And a win, he says, will earn him a main event spot next time out.

"I'm just one punch away," he says.

Julie has absorbed all the emotional punishment she can stand. On this night, she finally tells Stoker the truth.

"I remember the first time you told me that," she says.

room and sees his own career from how it began to where it is headed.

What Stoker doesn't know is his manager Tiny (George Tobias) has sold him out. His opponent Tiger Nelson (Hal Baylor) is an up-and-comer and the mob boss who owns Nelson doesn't want to take any chances on Stoker landing a lucky punch. They slip Tiny $50 for a guarantee that Stoker will throw the fight. But Tiny is so certain that Stoker will lose, he doesn't bother to tell him he is supposed to take a dive.

"There's no percentage in smartening up a chump," Tiny says. He knows Stoker has lost his last four fights, all by KO. He also knows there is no way Stoker would agree to take a dive. Tiny pockets the money and waits for Nelson to send Stoker to dreamland. No one will be any the wiser and Tiny will be $50 richer.

But Stoker, stung by Julie's words and feeling more alone than ever, sees the fight as his last stand. He goes toe-to-toe with Nelson and after three rounds of savage fighting, it is clear Stoker isn't taking a dive. The mob boss (Alan Baxter) is giving Tiny that "so-you-want-to-wind-up-in-the-river?" look. Before the final round, a desperate Tiny tells Stoker about the arrangement. He begs Stoker to go down.

"You gotta do it," Tiny says. "You can't double-cross these guys."

The look on Stoker's bloody face—a mix of disbelief, bewilderment and finally anger—is unforgettable. We don't want to spoil the ending, but we promise it will bring a lump to your throat.

Director Robert Wise, who later would win Oscars for the musicals *West Side Story* and *The Sound of Music*, makes the dingy arena so real, you can almost feel the peanut shells crunching beneath your feet. He cuts between the violence in the ring to the people in the audience, all screaming with blood lust, and makes the sport seem as barbaric as anything staged in ancient Rome.

🍺 **CHEERS:** Robert Ryan is superb as Stoker Thompson. He was 40 when he made the film, so he looked like an old warhorse and he had the boxing background to handle the moves in the ring. Ryan was a heavyweight boxing champion at Dartmouth (5-0, three knockouts) and later in the Marine Corps.

🏳 **JEERS:** Some of the fans are just a little too sadistic, in particular the blind guy who is sitting ringside with a friend who provides a blow-by-blow description of what's going on. When the blind guy says, "Nelson should keep working on Stoker's [cut] eye," it is downright creepy.

🍎 **BET YOU DIDN'T KNOW:** Hal Baylor, who plays Tiger Nelson, was the California state heavyweight boxing champion. He had a professional record of 52-5.

99 **BEST LINE:** A fan waiting outside the arena strikes his match on the poster announcing the fight card. He sees Stoker Thompson's name.

"Is he still fighting?" the guy asks. "I remember him when I was a kid."

😎 **"I KNOW THAT GUY":** The bespectacled ringside fan is Herbert Anderson, who played Dennis Mitchell's father in the TV series *Dennis the Menace*.

🎬 **IF YOU LIKED THIS, YOU'LL LIKE:** *Somebody Up There Likes Me*, another black and white boxing film directed by Robert Wise. It is the true story of former middleweight champion Rocky Graziano, nicely played by Paul Newman.

✎ **WHAT THEY WROTE AT THE TIME:** "The Set-Up is arguably Robert Ryan's finest starring film."—*New York Times*

★ **SPORTS-ACTION GRADE:** Solid A. Both Ryan and Baylor are experienced boxers and it shows with the way they move and throw punches.

◉ **REPEATED WATCHING QUOTIENT:** The film is only 72 minutes so it is ideal for watching a second or even third time. The final fight scene really is a knockout.

🎞 **MY FAVORITE SPORTS MOVIE:** HBO boxing analyst Larry Merchant: "I've probably seen every boxing movie ever made, but the one that stands out in my mind is *The Set-Up*. It was a 1940s *film noir*, but I think of it as a *fight noir* because the scenes are so dark with all the bad guys lurking in the shadows. Robert Ryan looked like a real boxer. I've been ringside for a lot of fights and most movies don't come close, but *The Set-Up* does. It's sort of a forgotten movie, but I think it's a classic."

26 MAJOR LEAGUE (1989–R)

SPORT: BASEBALL | STARS: TOM BERENGER, CHARLIE SHEEN, CORBIN BERNSEN
DIRECTOR: DAVID S. WARD

We did not have very high hopes for *Major League*. The previews made the film look like a bad slapstick comedy and the plot read like a rip-off of *Bull Durham*. Let's see, we have the wise old catcher, the rookie pitcher with control problems, the first baseman who practices voodoo, the crusty manager. I mean, haven't we seen this before?

When the team reports to spring training, we see the players living in military-style barracks with bunk beds. It's all we can do not to flee the theater. Major league ballplayers don't live like that. Most of them have million-dollar condos on the beach. The rookies might stay in a hotel, but sleeping in a barracks? What utter nonsense.

But if you stay with *Major League* awhile, the strangest thing happens. You get sucked in. Maybe it's the first few wisecracks from play-by-play announcer Harry Doyle (Bob Uecker). Maybe it's Rick "Wild Thing" Vaughn (Charlie Sheen) throwing fastballs that look like real fastballs. It's hard to say why, exactly, but you find yourself settling in for the full nine innings.

Major League isn't as good as *Bull Durham*. It isn't as cleverly written and the romance between catcher Jake Taylor (Tom Berenger) and Lynn Wells (Rene Russo) lacks the sizzle of Crash Davis (Kevin Costner) and Annie Savoy (Susan Sarandon). But there are a lot of fun moments and when the woeful Cleveland Indians turn it around and make their late season run for the pennant, you are on the Wahoo bandwagon.

The movie was written and directed by David S. Ward, who also wrote *The Sting*. Ward is a life-long Indians fan and his screenplay draws much of its humor from the team's bleak history. (Doyle says, "Remember, fans. Tuesday is Die Hard Night. Free admission for anyone who was actually alive the last time the Indians won the pennant.")

The film opens with Rachel Phelps (Margaret Whitton) inheriting the team from her late husband. Rachel is a former showgirl who has no interest in baseball and no love for Cleveland. She wants to move to sunny Miami and finds a clause in the stadium lease which allows her to relocate the franchise if season attendance falls below 800,000.

To ensure that happening, she assembles a team of misfits, including the broken down Taylor, the fresh-from-prison Vaughn and the voodoo man Pedro Cerrano (Dennis Haysbert). She hires manager Lou Brown (James Gammon) who spent 30 years knocking around the bush leagues. When they call to offer Brown the job, he is selling tires. "Can't talk now," he says. "I got a guy on the other line who wants to buy four whitewalls."

The Indians start the season losing games in an empty stadium. For Rachel, everything is going according to plan. The general manager, whose sympathies lie with the players, tells Brown about the owner's scheme. Brown tells the players, saying: "Once she moves the team to Miami, she'll get rid of all of us for better personnel."

"There's only one thing to do," Taylor says. "Win the whole fucking thing."

The inspired Indians go on a tear, climbing from last place to a tie for first in the American League. The season comes down to a one-game playoff against the New York Yankees with Rachel watching glumly from the owner's box. In what hardly qualifies as a surprise, the Indians pull out a victory in the bottom of the ninth.

If it sounds like the re-working of a tired formula, well, it is. But it does so with just enough irreverence to keep you entertained. There is a great scene in which Rachel, in her silk blouse and stiletto heels, walks through the clubhouse, patting players on the butt and snapping their jock straps. With her naughty strut and withering stare, she's the perfect She-Devil owner, a cross between George Steinbrenner and Morgan Fairchild.

"It takes all the little moments and actions of baseball

and makes them funny," says Boston Red Sox closer Jonathan Papelbon. "Hey, those stupid things do happen. There are players who act like that. It's a stretch—but not too much."

Uecker, the former big league catcher who now calls games for the Milwaukee Brewers, provides the most laughs with his portrayal of Doyle, the tippling announcer. His call on a Vaughn wild pitch—"Jusssst a bit outside"—is now widely imitated throughout baseball.

Early in the season, when the Indians are in last place and the cavernous ballpark is deserted, Doyle is wrapping up another loss. "For the Indians, no runs, one hit . . . That's all we got, one goddamn hit?" His broadcast partner slaps his hand over the microphone. "Harry, you can't say goddamn on the air." Doyle says, "Don't worry, nobody's listening anyway."

Among the players, only Sheen as Vaughn looks like the real thing, but he is so good he makes up for the rest. As a youth, Sheen attended the Mickey Owen Baseball School and in high school, he was scouted by the pros.

One of the few flaws in *Bull Durham* was the casting of Tim Robbins as pitcher Nuke LaLoosh. There was nothing in his mechanics that suggested he could throw a ball hard enough to knock a tin can off a fence. In the film, when they talk about Nuke hitting 100 on the radar gun, we roll our eyes and say, "Yeah, right."

With Sheen as the Wild Thing, we believe it. And when he comes in to get the final out in the playoff game with the Yankees and he throws that high cheese past the cleanup hitter, we're right there with him.

Former Dodgers catcher Steve Yeager was technical advisor for the film and he has a small role as Indians coach Duke Temple. But even Yeager could not make Corbin Bernsen into a believable major league third baseman. Bernsen's Roger Dorn, a prima donna who worries more about his stock portfolio than infield practice, is the weak link in the cast.

CHEERS: The Indians play "Wild Thing" when Vaughn enters the game. The Chicago Cubs and later the Phillies copied the idea for reliever Mitch "Wild Thing" Williams.

JEERS: When the Indians win the pennant, the Cleveland media is shown celebrating in the press box. We know it's been a long time since the Indians won, but it still does not allow for cheering in the press box.

WHAT THEY WROTE AT THE TIME: "As long as it sticks to the field and the clubhouse, the script doesn't falter. But there is time to go out for popcorn during the clichéd love scenes between Berenger and Russo."—*Variety*

REPEATED WATCHING QUOTIENT: Once a summer when the home team is losing and you need a laugh.

BET YOU DIDN'T KNOW: *Major League* was a bigger box office success ($49 million) than *The Natural* ($47 million).

CASTING CALL: Yankee slugger Clue Haywood is played by former major league pitcher Pete Vuckovich. In the film, Haywood leads the American League in home runs. Vuckovich never hit a home run in his 11-year career, although he did win a Cy Young Award.

"I KNOW THAT GUY": Dennis Haysbert, who plays Cerrano, is the President of the United States in the TV series *24*. Chelcie Ross, who plays aging pitcher Eddie Harris, is the overreaching assistant basketball coach fired by Norman Dale (Gene Hackman) in *Hoosiers*.

BEST LINE: Harry Doyle (Uecker): "In case you hadn't noticed—and judging by the attendance you haven't—the Indians have managed to win a few ball games and are threatening to climb out of the cellar."

SPORTS-ACTION GRADE: A-plus when Charlie Sheen is on the mound. C-minus the rest of the time.

MY FAVORITE SPORTS MOVIE: Ohio State University football coach Jim Tressel: "I spent my entire life rooting for my Indians to win, and this movie made it happen. That plus a few laughs along the way. My Tribe, my Tribe!"

AN INTERVIEW WITH BOB UECKER

BOB UECKER, WHO PLAYS THE CLEVELAND INDIANS PLAY-BY-PLAY ANNOUNCER HARRY DOYLE, PLAYED SIX SEASONS IN THE MAJOR LEAGUES AND WON A WORLD SERIES RING WITH THE 1964 ST. LOUIS CARDINALS. HE BECAME A NETWORK BASEBALL BROADCASTER WITH ABC IN THE 1970S AND HE IS NOW THE VOICE OF THE MILWAUKEE BREWERS. HIS IRREVERENT SENSE OF HUMOR IS REFLECTED IN THE TITLE OF HIS AUTOBIOGRAPHY, CATCHER IN THE WRY.

How did you get to play in Major League?

David Ward [writer/director] sent me the script. He said he wanted me to be Harry Doyle. It wasn't much of a stretch. I had done the TV series [Mr. Belvedere] for five years and I was a play-by-play man for the Brewers so I knew a little something about acting and I obviously knew baseball. I thought, 'This [film] looks like fun' and it was.

How many lines were scripted and how much did you ad-lib?

David let me go. He said, 'I want you to be Harry Doyle. Say whatever comes into your head.' He gave me general directions, like, the team is down, the team is rallying, [Rick] Vaughn can't find the plate, things like that. Then he let me go. I'd say stuff like, 'This umpire is giving us a hose job' and David would say, 'That's it. Do more stuff like that.'

Was it hard to come up with material?

Heck, no. Most of it was stuff I heard guys say in dugouts and clubhouses. Like the line about the Pete Vuckovich character leading the American League in home runs and nose hair. Ballplayers rag on each other like that all the time.

Do you have a favorite line?

The line everyone remembers is when Charlie Sheen [Vaughn] throws a wild pitch and I say, 'Juuuuust a bit outside.' I hear that constantly. The joke is I'm doing the games on radio and I'm bull-shitting the fans. They can't see the game and I'm working for the team so I'm just making stuff up, trying to make them sound better than they are.

Describe a typical shooting day.

The team in the film is Cleveland, but most of the movie was shot in Milwaukee. We'd finish the [Brewers] game and then start setting up for the movie. They would empty the stadium and all the actors and extras would come in and we'd shoot through the night. It sounds brutal, but it was really a lot of fun.

What was the hardest part of your role?

When they filmed my scenes, there was nothing happening on the field. I'd be in the booth describing home runs and double plays and getting all excited and it was all made up. David would say, 'Action,' and off I'd go. It was a little weird at first, but I got used to it.

You played six years in the majors. How would you rate the film's actors as ballplayers?

Charlie [Sheen] was really good. He could've played pro ball. He has a hell of an arm. Tom [Berenger] hadn't played much baseball, neither had Corbin [Bernsen] but I give them credit, they worked at it. Steve Yeager [former Dodger catcher] worked with Tom for a month, teaching him to crouch, how to set a target, how to throw. Tom learned enough to get by, although in the movie when you see the catcher throw out a runner, that's Yeager throwing the ball.

What about Bernsen?

He took lots of infield [practice] and he took a lot of hard ground balls off his shins, which is no fun. But he kept working at it. That's true of all the [actors]. They weren't prima donnas. They really did become like a team.

Were you pleased when you saw the film?

This will shock you, but I've never seen the film from beginning to end. I've seen bits and pieces of it over the years, but I've never sat down and watched the whole thing. I know how I am. If I watched it, I'd think about all the things I could have done better and it would bug me. I'm happy to know the film was a success and it's nice when people say I made them laugh. That's enough for me.

How did you make the leap from baseball announcer to actor?

I was doing a lot of sports banquets and I worked up a routine which basically poked fun at my playing career [he was a career .200 hitter]. I was in New Orleans and Al Hirt, the great trumpet player, said, 'You're wasting your time doing banquets. You should be on *The Tonight Show*.' I said, 'Yeah, right. Johnny Carson is just dying to have me.' But Al called somebody and a week later *The Tonight Show* contacted me. After that, things just started rolling.

How did you feel walking onto the stage for The Tonight Show?

Scared to death. I stepped through the curtain, the band was playing and there was Johnny Carson and Ed McMahon. I thought, 'Holy shit, what do I do now?' But Johnny was great. He let me do my thing, he laughed at my stories, I had a blast. When I left, he asked Ed, 'Did he really play baseball?' Johnny had no idea. But I did the show dozens of times after that. Really, that made my career, that and the Miller Lite commercials.

How did the beer commercials come about?

I have to credit Bud Selig (current baseball commissioner and former owner of the Brewers). Pabst was our main sponsor and I thought it might be a conflict for me to do commercials for a competitor. I told Bud what Miller was offering and he gave the OK. He said it was too good to pass up. It ran for 17 years, the longest running commercial series in history. It's part of Americana. I can't go anywhere without someone saying: "You must be in the front rowwwwww."

What were your emotions in 2003 when you were inducted into the Baseball Hall of Fame for your broadcasting career?

It meant a lot to me, obviously, but I couldn't play it straight. When I got up to speak, I said, "I hope this doesn't come off as sour grapes, but I really think I should be going in the Hall as a player."

27 KNUTE ROCKNE ALL-AMERICAN
(1940–NR)

SPORT: FOOTBALL | STARS: PAT O'BRIEN, RONALD REAGAN, GALE PAGE
DIRECTOR: LLOYD BACON

The Gipper is fading fast. The strep throat was bad enough, but now pneumonia has set in. The doctors have given way to priests at his bedside. It's only a matter of time, they say.

Rockne is there, of course. They've been in tough spots before, the Gipper and the Rock. There was the Notre Dame-Indiana game in 1920. The Gipper had a separated shoulder that day. The Irish fell behind 10-0, but the Gipper brought 'em back. They pulled it out, they always did.

But this time it's different. The Gipper and the Rock both know that. Gipp asks his coach to lean forward. He has something to say, but it's hard. His voice is almost gone.

"Sometime, Rock," the Gipper whispers, "when the team is up against it, when things are going wrong and

the breaks are beating the boys, tell them to go in there with all they've got and win just one for the Gipper. I don't know where I'll be then, Rock, but I'll know about it and I'll be happy."

It is one of the classic movie moments of all time. Pat O'Brien in a fake, flat nose is the Rock—Knute Rockne, head football coach of the Fighting Irish. Ronald Reagan, his pompadour sinfully lavish by Notre Dame standards, is the Gipper—George Gipp, the team's All-American halfback. Together, they spilled enough tears to float the Golden Dome.

The film, *Knute Rockne All-American*, might not have launched Notre Dame's national stock, but it surely enhanced it. The movie was a hit with football fans and non-fans, men and women, just about everyone except avowed Notre Dame haters. The scene set in the 1928 season where Rockne gives his "win one for the Gipper" speech at halftime of the Army game has been repeated—and parodied—so often, it is part of our cultural identity.

Who doesn't know "Win one for the Gipper"? We've all heard it, we've all repeated it and some of us probably voted Reagan into the White House because of it. As David Casstevens wrote in the *Dallas Morning News*: "Ronald Reagan is said to have immortalized George Gipp. A more accurate statement is that the role of George Gipp immortalized Ronald Reagan."

It is true. Throughout his public life, Reagan was referred to as "The Gipper." Political opponents used it mockingly, suggesting Reagan was a shallow wanna-be jock. Allies used it with affection, because they felt Gipp and Reagan shared an All-American, can-do spirit that was instrumental in their success. Even now, years after his death, when people talk about Reagan regardless of the context, they usually slip in a reference to "The Gipper."

Considering how the role defined him, it is worth noting that Reagan almost didn't get the part. The film's producer, Hal Wallis, considered William Holden, John Wayne (a former football player at Southern Cal), Robert Young and Robert Cummings for the role. He also tested actor Dennis Morgan, who was a bigger name than Reagan at the time, but Reagan made such a passionate pitch for the role, Wallis hired him. Also, Pat O'Brien liked Reagan and lobbied with the producer on his behalf.

"I've always suspected that there might have been many actors in Hollywood who could have played the part better," Reagan said in a 1983 interview. "But no one could have wanted to play it more than I did. And I was given the part largely because Pat O'Brien kindly and generously held out a helping hand to a beginning young actor.

"I'd been trying to write a screenplay about Knute Rockne," Reagan said. "I didn't have many words on paper when I learned the studio that employed me [Warner Brothers] was already preparing a story treatment for the film."

Reagan got remarkable mileage out of very little screen time. *Knute Rockne* runs 98 minutes, and Reagan is on the screen for approximately eight minutes. He has only four scenes, but all are memorable.

Scene One: Gipp (Reagan) is walking across the field in street clothes, picks up a loose ball and punts it out of the stadium. "What's your name?" Rockne asks. "George Gipp," the freshman replies. "What's your's?"

Scene two: Gipp is stretched out on the practice field, bored, possibly sleeping, when Rockne sends him in to play against the varsity defense. On his first carry, Gipp breaks away on a spectacular touchdown run. When Rockne meets him in the end zone, Gipp flips him the ball and says, "Guess the boys are just tired."

Scene three: Gipp is now the best halfback in the nation, having completed a record-setting senior year which saw him outgain the entire Army team (332 yards) in a 27-17 victory. When the coach's wife (Gale Page) praises him for his great career, the cocky Gipper turns all mushy.

"No, Bonnie, Rock's the rare one, not me," he says. "There will be new fellows coming along year after year, a lot them much better football players than I ever was. There will never be but one Rockne, here at Notre Dame or anywhere else. He gives us something they can't teach in schools, something clean and strong inside. Not just courage, but a right way of living that none of us will ever forget.

"Don't tell Rock I said that, Bonnie," the Gipper says. "He'll think I was an awful sap."

Gipp coughs, but brushes it off as "just a little sore throat." We know better.

Scene four is the Gipper's dying request to Rockne.

If you're only going to have four scenes in a movie, those are four pretty good ones. Reagan rode them to the Governor's Mansion in California and, finally, to two terms in the White House.

"I have a copy [of the film] and I told President Reagan about it," said Jack Kemp, a former Buffalo Bills quarterback and U.S. Congressman (R-NY). "He asked, 'What's your favorite scene?' I said it was when Rockne sends him in and tells him to run. He [Reagan] asks in a cocky way, 'How far?' Then he runs for a touchdown. To me, it was very much like Reagan. He had the same sort of optimism, that's what made him a great leader."

While historians value the film more for its ties to Reagan, it stands up as a fitting tribute to Rockne, who still holds the record for the highest winning percentage of any Division I football coach (.881). In 13 seasons at Notre Dame, his teams won 105 games and lost 12, with five ties.

They were undefeated five times, and in one five-year stretch, Rockne's team lost just once in 40 starts.

The film traces Rockne's story from his arrival in the United States as a boy emigrating from Norway. With little money, Rockne (O'Brien) has to work four years in a Chicago post office to earn enough to afford the tuition at Notre Dame. He is 22 when he finally enrolls and he shows as much promise in chemistry class as he does on the football field.

Father Callahan (Donald Crisp) asks Rockne to stay on as a graduate assistant in the chemistry department, but Rockne says his heart is in coaching. "You think I'm making a mistake, don't you?" Rockne asks. "Anyone who follows the truth in his heart never makes a mistake," the priest replies.

Combining creative brilliance with a dynamic personality, Rockne builds Notre Dame, a small Catholic school in Indiana, into a major force in American sports on a par with the New York Yankees. Millions of people—many of whom never graduated high school or ever set foot in Indiana—became fans of the Irish. That passion still exists among the so-called "Subway Alumni" and it all started with the charismatic Rockne.

Knute Rockne All-American was released in 1940, nine years after Rockne's death in a plane crash. In 1997, the film was deemed "culturally, historically or aesthetically significant" by the United States Library of Congress and selected for preservation in their National Film Registry.

CHEERS: The use of old newsreel footage allows today's audience to see Notre Dame legends—such as the real Four Horsemen—in action.

JEERS: The film goes a little overboard in burnishing the Rockne legend. It shows Rockne (O'Brien) and quarterback Gus Dorais (Owen Davis, Jr.) introducing the forward pass to college football. Schools such as Michigan and Minnesota were throwing the ball before Rockne ever enrolled at Notre Dame.

BET YOU DIDN'T KNOW: Knute Rockne was only 43 years old when he died.

CASTING CALL: James Cagney tried to convince Warner Brothers to cast him as Rockne. He felt he was typecast as a gangster and saw this role as a chance to break out. However, the studio chose O'Brien.

PIVOTAL SCENE: Rockne attends a Broadway show, and while watching the dancers move about the stage, he is inspired to create the "shift." That was an innovation in which the backfield would line up in one formation and shift to another formation just before the ball was snapped. That was the Notre Dame offense until the 1940s, when coach Frank Leahy went to the T-formation.

WHAT THEY WROTE AT THE TIME: "Through it all runs the theme of Rockne's whole purpose in life—molding boys under his care to become good Americans who are conscious of their responsibilities and opportunities."—*Variety*

BEST LINE: Knute Rockne: "The secret is to work less as individuals and more as a team. As a coach, I play not my eleven best, but my best eleven."

SPORTS-ACTION GRADE: C. Scenes with the actors, including Ronald Reagan, playing the Irish varsity won't convince even the most rabid Notre Dame fan.

MY FAVORITE SPORTS MOVIE: Marv Levy, Hall of Fame coach, Buffalo Bills: "I saw it when I was in elementary school and it made me want to be a football coach. I enjoyed playing, but seeing Pat O'Brien as Rockne was so inspiring, it made me think about becoming a coach one day. One [Rockne] quote really resonated with me. I used it throughout my coaching career. He said,'Don't tell me about the will to win. Tell me about the will to prepare.' "

28 BANG THE DRUM SLOWLY (1973–PG)

SPORT: BASEBALL | STARS: MICHAEL MORIARTY, ROBERT DE NIRO
DIRECTOR: JOHN D. HANCOCK

Mark Harris wrote the best-selling novel *Bang the Drum Slowly* in 1956, but it wasn't made into a motion picture until 1973. Why the delay? Well, most people in Hollywood thought the story—the friendship between two major league ballplayers, one of whom is dying—was too depressing. They didn't think audiences would pay to see it.

However, the success of tear-jerkers such as *Love Story* (1970) and *Brian's Song* (1971) made the studios reconsider. *Love Story* was a box office smash and was nominated for seven Academy Awards. *Brian's Song* is one of the most popular made-for-TV movies of all time. So if you have the right story, people will watch, even if it means stocking up on Kleenex.

Bang the Drum Slowly is certainly a compelling story. It is, in essence, *Brian's Song* in baseball, the major differ-

ence being *Brian's Song* was based on a true story and *Drum* is fiction. But the themes of friendship, teamwork and—dare we say it?—love are much the same. Audiences and critics alike embraced the film.

Drum features a young Robert De Niro as Bruce Pearson, the catcher who is dying of Hodgkin's Disease. Michael Moriarty is Henry Wiggen, Pearson's roommate. Pearson is a country bumpkin with limited baseball skills. Wiggen is an All-Star pitcher and Renaissance man who writes books and sells insurance when he is not winning games for the New York Mammoths.

They are an odd couple whose paths never would have crossed if it were not for baseball. Pearson chews tobacco and wears a smiley face T-shirt under his sports coat. Wiggen is a bit of a snob, intellectually superior to the other players and rather aloof. His teammates call

Wiggen "Author," but Pearson is so dim, he doesn't get the joke. He calls the pitcher "Arthur."

Pearson is an easy target for clubhouse pranks and the other players pass the time by ragging on him. When he learns he has Hodgkin's Disease, Pearson turns to Wiggen, whom he considers a friend. He begs his roommate to keep his illness a secret. He fears the team will get rid of him if it finds out.

Wiggen, who serves as the film's narrator, says in a voiceover, "Suddenly, you're driving along with a man who's been told he's dying. It was bad enough rooming with him when he was well."

Wiggen, who merely tolerated Pearson earlier, becomes his protector. He sympathizes with this simple, good-natured soul who made it to the big leagues only to learn that he has less than a year to live. As Pearson's father (Patrick McVey) tells Wiggen, "I swear, my son's

son making visits to the Mayo Clinic and explaining them away as fishing trips. They even invent a story about Pearson having to see a specialist for a case of the clap. It's a tricky thing going for laughs in a film about terminal illness, but it is done to good effect in *Bang the Drum Slowly*. Those moments—which usually include Dutch sucking on a cigarette and arching a suspicious eyebrow—give the audience some needed relief from all the sadness.

Wiggen finally tells a few teammates about Pearson's illness. They feel ashamed for all the times they needled and mocked Pearson. They close ranks around him and—here is where the film gets a little sticky—the Mammoths launch an inspired pennant drive with Pearson playing the best baseball of his career. He is dying, but somehow he turns into a combination of Carlton Fisk and Johnny Bench.

DUTCH: "SKIP THE FACTS. JUST GIVE ME THE DETAILS."

been handed one shitty deal."

Wiggin nods in agreement.

When Wiggen negotiates his new contract with the Mammoths, he insists the team include a guarantee that Pearson will not be released or sent to the minors. Wiggen convinces management that he pitches better when Pearson is behind the plate. Since he is the ace of the staff, they give him what he wants.

As the season goes along, Wiggen and Pearson are inseparable. People begin to, shall we say, wonder. What's up with those two guys? Manager Dutch Schnell (Vincent Gardenia) hires a private eye to follow them around. Dutch, an old-school baseball man, won't stand for any hanky-panky on his ball club.

There are some funny scenes with Wiggen and Pear-

It is a stretch, especially given De Niro's awkward attempts to swing a bat. He never played baseball as a kid, and it shows. When he was cast in the role of Pearson, he went to the Cincinnati Reds training camp and studied the catchers, including Bench. He picked up a few things—he is very good at chewing tobacco and spitting, for example—but he isn't convincing as a player. Pearson is supposed to be a fringe big leaguer, but De Niro isn't even that good.

Moriarty, on the other hand, is very good as Wiggen. His right-handed throwing motion is smooth and his little tics on the mound—the way he fingers the ball, the way he fiddles with his cap and looks in for the catcher's sign—are those of someone who played a lot of baseball. Moriarty also impressed as a hockey player in *The Dead-*

liest Season (1977) before joining the original cast of the TV series *Law and Order*.

Bang the Drum Slowly walks a fine line between solid storytelling and sentiment. There are a few slips into the sugary stuff, but for the most part director John D. Hancock keeps things on course. Late in the film, Pearson—his health deteriorating—staggers under a pop fly. It's a scene that could have been maudlin, but it is handled delicately and well. (De Niro, the method actor, ran in circles to make himself dizzy before each take.)

The film ends with Pearson's inevitable passing, and Wiggen, as the narrator, gets the final word. His tribute to his late roommate is understated, but it stays with you for that very reason.

"He wasn't a bad fellow," Wiggen says. "No worse than most and probably better than some. And he wasn't a bad ballplayer when they gave him half a chance."

"From now on," Wiggen says, "I rag nobody."

🍺 **CHEERS:** There is a running gag, a card game called Tegwar—"The Exciting Game without Any Rules." It is played in hotel lobbies by Coach Joe Jaros (Phil Foster) and Wiggen, who lure unsuspecting suckers and take their money.

Jaros and Wiggen make up the rules as they go along, slapping down their cards and shouting things like "That's a Double Honeybee" and "Oh, a Coney Island Tatey." The other players have no idea what's going on. Foster, an old Vaudeville comic, is right at home ad-libbing lines like: "A natural banjo. Why, I haven't seen one of those since Joe DiMaggio had one in St. Petersburg."

📋 **JEERS:** The musical score by Stephen Lawrence does not show the same restraint as the screenplay or the direction. It tries to wring a tear out of almost every scene.

🍎 **BET YOU DIDN'T KNOW:** Vincent Gardenia earned his only Academy Award nomination for Best Supporting Actor with his portrayal of Dutch Schnell, the Mammoths manager. He lost to John Houseman (*The Paper Chase*).

🍎 **BET YOU DIDN'T KNOW II:** When the film was released, many reviewers compared the character of Henry Wiggen to Tom Seaver, the New York Mets all-star pitcher. Some people, believing the story was based on fact, thought Mets catcher Jerry Grote had a terminal illness.

💬 **BEST LINE:** Dutch Schnell: "When I die, the newspapers will write in their headline: 'The Sons of Bitches of the World Have Lost Their Leader.' "

✒ **WHAT THEY WROTE AT THE TIME:** "Part of what made the catcher so appealing was the gentleness with which De Niro filled him. If Moriarty's pitcher seemed a product of baseball brought to the modern city, De Niro represented baseball as it started out and as we still like to think it can be, unsullied and idyllic in its lack of self-awareness, even in an age of Astroturf and polyester jerseys."—Jay Carr, *Boston Globe*

👓 **"I KNOW THAT GUY":** One of the Mammoth benchwarmers is Danny Aiello, who later starred as Sal the pizza shop owner in Spike Lee's *Do the Right Thing*, among other notable roles. This was his acting debut.

★ **SPORTS-ACTION GRADE:** C. Moriarty makes the grade as a pitcher, but De Niro looks overmatched at the plate.

✋ **MY FAVORITE SPORTS MOVIE:** Pitcher Curt Schilling: "It's a great example of one teammate looking out for the other. The pitcher is so good, he really doesn't need to worry about others, but he takes the catcher under his wing and looks out for him. That's how teammates ought to watch out for each other."

29 JERRY MAGUIRE (1996–R)

SPORT: FOOTBALL | **STARS:** TOM CRUISE, CUBA GOODING JR., RENEE ZELLWEGER
DIRECTOR: CAMERON CROWE

Jerry Maguire is actually two movies in one. Men will watch it and see a solid sports film. Women will enjoy a delightful chick flick. The great thing is—it works for both.

So we had He and She sit down together and take notes on this Tom Cruise vehicle about an idealistic sports agent (boy, there's an oxymoron) and the woman and wide receiver who love him for different reasons.

He: "This might be the best movie ever about sports business. It shows the seamy side of football as an industry, without destroying your love for the game. Plus, did you catch all those great cameos? Give a big thumbs up to Drew Bledsoe and Troy Aikman and Warren Moon and—"

She: "What are you talking about? Jerry Maguire is about relationships. It's about a man who is everybody's friend, but can't show intimacy. It's about a woman—and bravo to Renee Zellweger as Dorothy Boyd—who loves him for the man he wants to be or, as she says, 'I love him for who he almost is.' "

He: "Yeah, well, she does a fine job, I guess. But let's be honest—the best character in this movie is Rod Tidwell. Cuba Gooding Jr. won the Best Supporting Actor Oscar for portraying Tidwell as the proud, hot-dogging, sometimes angry wide receiver that we've seen so many times in the NFL. He's Chad Johnson, or Terrell Owens. Gooding nailed the role. I challenge you to name any actor ever who so accurately got into the skin of the modern athlete."

She: "Funny, I though Gooding was great, but more for how he displayed all that love for his family, more than all that preening. And, good as he was, the character who steals *Jerry Maguire* is Jonathan Lipnicki as Dorothy's son, Ray. That little boy with the glasses was adorable. Didn't you notice how Jerry falls in love with him before he falls in love with Dorothy? And how about how Ray walks around saying, 'Do you know the human head weighs eight pounds?' How endearing was that?"

He: "Ah, you give any little kid a couple of funny lines and he'll try to steal the movie. Let's get to the part that really surprised me about *Jerry Maguire*. The football scenes are terrific—I give it an A-minus on sports action. That pivotal scene—where the Cardinals play the Cowboys on *Monday Night Football*—seems lifelike. Yes, some of it actually was clips of Aikman and Emmitt Smith making plays. But the shot of Tidwell catching that touchdown pass in traffic, being dumped on his head, laying there unconscious and—finally—getting up to perform the greatest touchdown dance ever? That was phenomenal action."

She: "You call that action? I'll give you A-plus action—the pivotal scene, which takes place on Dorothy's front porch after her first date with Jerry. He breaks the strap on her dress (maybe accidentally, but I don't think so), and when he goes to fix it, it evolves into one of the great foreplay scenes in movie history."

He: "To be honest with you, I found Jerry's fiancé, Avery Bishop (Kelly Preston), a lot hotter than Dorothy. But that's just how a guy looks at things. We tend to like sexy more than cute. Anyway, let's get to some of these issues we're supposed to debate. Best line? Easy. When Rod says to Jerry, 'Show me the money.' Sure, we all grew tired of the line after it became a cliché. But that's every self-centered pro athlete talking."

She: "I suppose it is, but it's not as good as two lines right near the end of the film. Jerry comes home to win back his wife. He gives her the whole close-the-deal love speech, leading up to 'You complete me.' Ooh, that was romantic. And she stops him right there and says, 'Shut up. Just shut up. You had me at hello.' How great was that moment?"

He: "Not as good as it would have been if they didn't exchange those lines in a room full of bitching divorcees. Actually, that'll be my thumbs down—those repeated scenes of the cackling manhater's club. It seems like the henhouse where Dorothy and her sister (Bonnie Hunt) live is permanently inhabited by those shrews."

She: "You know what? We can agree on that—but I take a little umbrage at your characterization there. Let's just say that those scenes with the angry women could have been cut way down. By the way, the older woman who talks about 'getting in touch with my anger?' That's director Cameron Crowe's mother."

He: "Hey, can I give another compliment here? Jay Mohr was perfect as Bob Sugar, the oily, despicable anti-Jerry agent who reminds me of every Scott Boras/Drew Rosenhaus greed-hound polluting sports these days."

She: "Okay, if despicable is what you're looking for. I'll give my 'cheers' to the soundtrack. Everything from Springsteen to Nirvana to Paul McCartney to Charlie Mingus. Best soundtrack since *Ghost*. Speaking of which, I'd list *Ghost* under the category of, 'If you liked this, you'll like . . .' but I know you want me to name another sports movie here. So I'll say *Cinderella Man*. Another movie about a good-hearted man in a tough business who wins over Renee Zellweger."

He: "Not a bad choice. I'll watch that with you any time. But I have to say that if you like this, you'll like *Any Given Sunday*, which is also a critical look at the business side of sports. As far as 'repeated watching quotient,' I'd say I could see *Jerry Maguire* about once a year."

She: "I'm with you. You bring the popcorn, I'll bring the hankies."

✎ **WHAT THEY WROTE AT THE TIME:** "A good love story and a good football movie in one neat package? . . . Just think of all those guys who were able to convince their girlfriends to actually go out and see a sports flick."—Kevin Jackson, ESPN.com

☞ **DON'T FAIL TO NOTICE:** By our count, there are at least three NFL owners, three coaches, six national broadcasters, two prominent agents and 13 NFL players with walk-ons in this film. Plus Katarina Witt. See how many you can spot.

☺ **GOOFS:** In the scene where the Cardinals play the Philadelphia Eagles, the surface in Philadelphia's stadium mysteriously turns from artificial turf to grass and then back to turf again.

◣ **CASTING CALL:** This was a big-time release with a big-time director, so many other stars were considered for the leading roles. We won't list all of them, but how different would *Jerry Maguire* have been with Tom Hanks as Jerry, Jamie Foxx as Rod and Winona Ryder as Dorothy? Ryder actually did a screen test with Cruise, but Cameron Crowe rejected her, saying the two looked too much like brother and sister to be convincing on-screen lovers.

👓 **"I KNOW THAT GUY":** The character of Arizona Cardinals general manager Dennis Wilburn is played by Glenn Frey, guitar player and vocalist for The Eagles.

✔ **REALITY CHECK:** Various sports agents and other assorted hangers-on are shown running all over the sidelines during NFL games. Trust us, getting field passes during the regular season is tougher than walking into the White House unannounced. No agent would be allowed to stand by the end zone—as Jerry did—while his player lay there injured.

♟ **BET YOU DIDN'T KNOW:** *Jerry Maguire* grossed more at the box office—$154 million—than any sports drama in history. It marked the fifth consecutive Tom Cruise movie to crack the $100 million mark, following *A Few Good Men*, *The Firm*, *Interview With the Vampire* and *Mission: Impossible*.

🎞 **MY FAVORITE SPORTS MOVIE:** Miami Heat superstar Dwyane Wade: "It's an entertaining movie with good football scenes, and it's inspiring as well—a man trying to do the right thing. I've probably watched it dozens of times."

30 DOWNHILL RACER (1969–NR)

SPORT: SKIING | STARS: ROBERT REDFORD, GENE HACKMAN | DIRECTOR: MICHAEL RITCHIE

There is much to admire in *Downhill Racer*, director Michael Ritchie's taut study of the World Cup ski circuit. There is the camerawork, which conveys the speed and danger of the sport. There is the spectacular scenery. There is the acting of Robert Redford as skier David Chappellet and Gene Hackman as Eugene Claire, coach of the U.S. team.

But what is most intriguing about the film is its portrait of the world-class athlete. In this case, the athlete is Chappellet, and behind the blonde hair and perfect smile is what? An All-American hero? Uh, no. Chappellet is a ski bum with little in the way of education, a shallow narcissist incapable of carrying on a conversation or sustaining a relationship. Think Bode Miller, toothy smile and all.

"All you ever had was skis," Claire (Hackman) says, "and that's not enough."

Well, for Chappellet (Redford), it is. His life has been defined by one thing: his ability to ski downhill faster than anyone else. He discovered that talent at an early age and spent years developing it—to the exclusion of everything else. He is a skier, but he could be a swimmer, a gymnast, a skater or a fencer, and it would be the same thing. The dedication required to reach the elite level is the same across the board.

"This is the point we miss when we persist in describing champions as regular, all-around Joes," wrote Roger Ebert in the *Chicago Sun-Times*. "If they were, they wouldn't be champions."

This is not to say all Olympic athletes are like that, but some are. Chappellet is one of those who operate in a narrow tunnel, but Ritchie and writer James Salter don't condemn him for it. They make it clear that if he were a regular, all-around Joe, he'd still be on the family farm in Idaho Springs, Colorado. He wouldn't be tearing up the slopes in France and signing fat endorsement deals with ski manufacturers.

Chappellet is ego-driven and selfish, which leads to clashes with Claire, who runs the U.S. team with a football coach's "we're-all-in-this-together" mentality. Chappellet is standoffish with the other skiers, and his rivalry with the other top American, Johnny Creech (Jim McMullan), contributes to Creech crashing and wrecking his knee.

"He's not a team man," Claire says angrily.

"Well, this isn't exactly a team sport," another coach points out.

He is not trying to defend Chappellet, exactly, but he makes a valid point. Chappellet is a skier. He's not a point guard or a tight end. When he is careening down the hill at 90 miles per hour, he is all alone. Can you really blame him if he is all about himself?

"His world is that international society of the well-exercised inarticulate, where the good is known as 'Really great' and the bad is signified by silence," wrote Roger Greenspun of the *New York Times*. "In appreciating that world, its pathos, its tensions and its sufficient moments of glory, *Downhill Racer* succeeds with sometimes chilling efficiency."

Ritchie and Salter draw the character of Chappellet in subtle strokes, some of which make him sympathetic. He doesn't say much, and when he does speak, his conversations tend to trail off. He seems incapable of explaining himself, or maybe there just isn't that much to explain. Perhaps he is uncomfortable around the other skiers, most of whom are rich kids with college educations. Maybe that's why Chappellet keeps to himself. We're left to wonder.

There is a poignant scene when Chappellet, now a rising star on the ski circuit, goes back to visit Idaho Springs. When he returns to the farm, his father (Walter Stroud) practically ignores him. There are long stretches of silence and, painful as they are, they help explain why Chappellet is so cut-off from those around him. At one point, he tries to make his father understand his competitive desire.

"I'll be a champion," he says.

His father barely looks up. "The world's full of them," he grunts.

The moment is as chilling as a head-first tumble into a snow bank. From then on, you view Chappellet a little differently. He is still a cynic—he'd sneer at having his face on a Wheaties box, but he'd gladly pocket the money—and he has a hollow affair with a French woman who works for a ski company, but what lingers is the sense that he has no life away from the slopes. As glamorous as it is, it is also rather empty and sad.

"Some of the best moments in *Downhill Racer* are moments during which nothing special seems to be happening," Ebert wrote. "They're moments devoted to capturing the angle of a glance, the curve of a smile, an embarrassed silence. Together they form a portrait of a man that is so complete and so tragic that *Downhill Racer* becomes the best movie ever made about sports without really being about sports at all."

CHEERS: The skiing action is expertly shot, much of it with a hand-held camera so the audience sees the downhill course just as the skier sees it. "It's good stuff with the terrain whizzing by, the flags a blur and the blinding white turning vision into pure instinct.—Ernest Schier, *Philadelphia Bulletin*

CREECH: **"HE'S NOT FOR THE TEAM. HE NEVER WILL BE."**

JEERS: The relationship between Chappellet and Carole Stahl (Camilla Sparv) is more of a puzzle than a romance. When she leaves, Chappellet doesn't know why and to be frank, neither do we.

BET YOU DIDN'T KNOW: Robert Redford did most of his own skiing in *Downhill Racer*. Ritchie only used a double (former ski racer Joe Jay Jalbert) for scenes that required Chappellet to take a tumble.

CASTING CALL: Paramount wanted Roman Polanski to direct *Downhill Racer*. It would have been his first American film, but he chose to do *Rosemary's Baby* instead. The studio took a chance on Michael Ritchie, a successful TV director who never had done a major motion picture. Although *Downhill Racer* was a disappointment at the box office, it was widely praised by critics and it launched Ritchie's career in Hollywood. He and Redford teamed up again in *The Candidate*, a scathing political satire.

DON'T FAIL TO NOTICE: Ritchie used 16-millimeter and 35-millimeter cameras to shoot the skiing action. Cutting back and forth between two types of film makes it look more like a documentary than a movie, which is what Ritchie wanted to achieve.

WHAT THEY WROTE AT THE TIME: "Good movies about sports have been few and far between, so when one comes along as breezy and smartly photographed as *Downhill Racer*, it is an event worth noting."—Ernest Schier, *Philadelphia Bulletin*

IF YOU LIKED THIS, YOU'LL LIKE: *Snow Job*, a 1972 film starring French skiing champion Jean-Claude Killy. The story is nonsensical—a robbery in which the thieves use snowmobiles—but Killy does all of his own skiing, and much of it is spectacular.

REPEATED WATCHING QUOTIENT: On a hot summer night when the air conditioner is broken, pop it in and before you know it, you'll be whooshing down the slopes and feeling cool all over.

SPORTS-ACTION GRADE: A. Even if you've never skied, you will feel like you did after seeing this film. Jalbert skied right behind Redford, carrying a 50-pound camera to get the first-hand perspective of downhill racing. It is a noisy, bumpy, terrifying blur.

MY FAVORITE SPORTS MOVIE: Kenneth Turan, film critic, *Los Angeles Times*: "It gives you that rush of victory, but it's very honest and very accurate about athlete/coach relationships and how those things work. Football films have a harder time doing that. They can't resist the lure of the cornball. I thought *Downhill Racer* was a very honest film."

31 HE GOT GAME (1998–R)

SPORT: BASKETBALL | STARS: DENZEL WASHINGTON, RAY ALLEN | DIRECTOR: SPIKE LEE

Do you remember LeBron James's senior year of high school in 2003? The national ESPN-fueled mania over an 18-year-old with a regal nickname; the premature parallels to Jordan; the unconfirmed stories of illegal gifts and shady hangers-on; the debate over whether King James should go pro or spend a year at college? Remember?

Well, take that story, turn it into a Spike Lee film (or "joint," as the director calls it), add Denzel Washington for depth, a dynamite soundtrack and a few extraneous subplots, and you've got *He Got Game*. This story is more about temptation than about basketball, more about greed than about sport. And it works—in large part because Lee loves hoops enough to both embrace it and shine a light on its dirty underbelly.

"It's my favorite movie," says Cleveland Cavaliers guard Delonte West, "because it really shows the reality of making the move from high school basketball to the next step. It shows the other side of basketball—pressure—that people don't get to see."

The story opens with Jake Shuttlesworth (Denzel) shooting jumpers on a run-down court at the Attica Correctional Facility in upstate New York. Jake is serving a lengthy sentence for murdering his wife—although we later find out there's more to that story. Meanwhile, the son he left behind, Jesus (Ray Allen), has grown to become the top-ranked high school player in the country.

Jake is summoned to see the warden (Ned Beatty), who offers a proposition: If Jake can convince his son to play at the governor's alma mater, Big State, The Guv will agree to reduce Jake's interminable sentence. Jake is given a cheap hotel room in the old neighborhood on Coney Island, a week's time and a letter of intent he must persuade Jesus to sign.

The problem is that Jesus is not happy to see the man who killed his mother. The more Jake tries for reconciliation, the more he is resisted. And, soon enough, Jesus comes to regard his father as one more slimy bloodsucker trying to latch onto him to achieve his own ends.

Which, of course, is true. In fact, the movie is populated by smarmy characters who praise Jesus as their ticket to the main chance. They include—and give us a little space here to roll out this roster—the conniving girlfriend (Rosario Dawson) who's convinced she'll be left behind; the pedophile uncle who quotes Don Fanucci from *The Godfather II* ("All I'm asking is that you let me wet my beak."); the oily sports agent who dangles a platinum Rolex in the kid's face; the viscous high school coach who lays $10,000 on the table; the holy-roller coach of Tech U (John Turturro); the swaggering college star (Rick Fox) and the silicon-enhanced "recruiters." And, of course, the tainted governor of New York. We think his name was Spitzer.

Throughout the betrayal, Jesus tries to stay pure. He accepts no graft (well, very little . . . what man could turn down those nubile twins at Tech?) and repeatedly tells everyone he is weighing his options. The more he demurs, the more pressure is exerted on him.

It's all a little black and white, and we don't just mean that in the way you might expect from a Spike Lee film (yeah, yeah, "joint."). *He Got Game* would be improved if Lee introduced one or two sympathetic characters to his story. And never mind the Coney Island hooker with the heart of gold (Milla Jovovich) who takes a liking to Jake Shuttlesworth. We still can't figure out what she had to do with the story.

But overall, this is one of the better basketball movies ever made—not in a lead-up-to-the-big-game *Hoosiers* kind of way, but in an athletes-as-commodities kind of way. And if you think the movie is a big stretch on the truth, listen to the words of Sacramento Kings guard Tyreke Evans, who spent one year at Memphis University after being a high school basketball phenom in Chester, PA.:

"I felt I was watching my own life when I saw that movie. Everything that happened in *He Got Game* really happens. Trust me."

And give Spike Lee credit for taking risks. Casting Allen—a great player, but a novice actor—works, because his inexperience on screen plays well to the character's innocent persona. The sound track combines Public Enemy with Aaron Copland in a way some critics hated, but, well, we always loved the "Beef. It's what's for dinner" song, whatever that's called.

🍺 **CHEERS:** To Denzel, as usual. The great actor turns himself into a weary, desperate loser. Other than his portrayal of Rubin Carter in *The Hurricane*, it's the most sympathetic character he's ever played.

🍺 **JEERS:** To the very last scene, which defies both logic and physics. We won't give it away, but after 134 minutes of gritty realism, why did Lee decide to end it with a cheap trick that doesn't do justice to a film school freshman?

✔ **REALITY CHECK:** For what it's worth, this *is* New York, where the closest they've got to "Big State" would be the State University of New York at Albany. The Great Danes play basketball in the America East Conference and have sent exactly zero players to the NBA. Chances that Jesus would play there are about the same as him playing at the Barbizon School of Beauty.

📢 **CASTING CALL:** Spike Lee sure knows how to call on friends. Cameos come from more than a dozen top-shelf NCAA coaches, as well as an NBA Dream Team of Shaquille O'Neal, Scottie Pippen, Reggie Miller, Charles Barkley and Michael Jordan (the only one in the movie who actually utters, "He got game."). Jesus' high school teammates include Travis Best, Walter McCarty and John Wallace. No wonder they won the city title. And it's always good to catch the great Jim Brown, here stealing all the good lines as a mean-spirited probation guard.

😊 **GOOFS:** All of those great cameos of coaches—Dean Smith, John Thompson, John Chaney—hailing Jesus on ESPN. Well, in real life those comments would disqualify their schools from landing the kid. Every college coach this side of Kelvin Sampson knows he's not allowed to publicly discuss potential recruits during the signing period. And let's also slap a fat NCAA violation on Tech U for inviting the kid for a visit within days of the signing deadline.

★ **SPORTS-ACTION GRADE:** A-minus, because most of the actors in the movie—including Denzel—obviously know their way around a basketball court. Surprisingly, there are virtually no scenes of actual games. It's prison yard ball, schoolyard ball—and great schoolyard ball at that.

🎬 **PIVOTAL SCENE:** The entire movie sets up to one last confrontation between father and son. Jake, his week of semi-freedom up, makes Jesus an offer: He'll play him one-on-one, with the letter of intent as the stakes. It is a test of manhood, a rite of passage set at night on a brightly lit blue asphalt court.

Initially, Jake dominates—schooling his son in the low post and hitting a few long jumpers. As the trash talk grows nastier, Jake loses his edge—and his energy. Jesus is bigger, faster and, ultimately, mentally stronger. The icier Jesus gets, the more he dominates. In fact, he is using the lessons we saw Jake teach him years ago. Even as he slays his father, he is validating him.

The contest ends with Jake gasping for air on the ground, and his son looking down at him, for the first time, with pity.

🍎 **BET YOU DIDN'T KNOW:** The original script called for Jesus to win that showdown, 11-0. Lee says he instead told Denzel and Allen to play it for real. The 11-5 score represents their actual game. At least that's their story.

99 **BEST LINE:** Jake Shuttlesworth explaining that his son is named not after Jesus of Nazareth, but after hoops legend Earl Monroe, whose more familiar moniker, "The Pearl," was not his first nickname.

"They called him Jesus, 'cause he was the truth," says Jake. "Then the white media got hold of it, and they got to call him Black Jesus. You know, he can't just be Jesus. He's got to be Black Jesus. But still, he was the truth. So that's the real reason you've got your name. Not Jesus of the Bible, but Jesus of the playgrounds. Jesus of North Philadelphia."

👓 **"I KNOW THAT GUY":** If you were a fan of *The Wire*, make sure you don't miss the four-line appearance of young Jamie Hector, who portrayed the stoically terrifying drug dealer Marlo Stanfield on HBO's landmark series. Hector plays one of the many blood suckers trying to get something out of Jesus—in his case, Nikes. His character is billed in the credits as "Leech."

🎞 **MY FAVORITE SPORTS MOVIE:** NFL great Michael Strahan: "I was surprised at how good an actor Ray Allen was. It could not have been easy because he had a lot of emotional scenes with Denzel, who is a great actor. My favorite movies are the ones about fathers and sons. Those movies just get to me, and the relationship between Denzel and Ray was really good."

REQUIEM FOR A HEAVYWEIGHT
(1962–NR)

SPORT: BOXING | STARS: ANTHONY QUINN, JACKIE GLEASON, MICKEY ROONEY
DIRECTOR: RALPH NELSON

Before Rod Serling launched his landmark TV series *The Twilight Zone*, he wrote the powerful screenplay *Requiem for a Heavyweight*. Serling, who did some boxing in his younger days, painted a bleak picture of the fight game. *Requiem* is a brilliant piece of work, but, man, is it depressing.

It was first produced for *Playhouse 90*, a live TV show, on October 11, 1956. Jack Palance played the boxer Mountain McClintock, Keenan Wynn was his unscrupulous manager Maish, and Ed Wynn was the faithful trainer, Army. The show won four Emmys, and Serling's script earned a Peabody Award.

One year later, British television produced the show (changing the title to *Blood Money*) with the pre-James Bond Sean Connery in the lead. The story also has been revived a few times on Broadway, most recently in 1985 with John Lithgow as the broken-down fighter and George Segal as the manager. Segal's Maish was so hateful, *New York Times* theatre critic Frank Rich described him as "serpentine."

So *Requiem* has been around for a long time, and some talented actors have taken on the roles, but it is hard to imagine anyone else in those parts once you've seen the 1962 film with Anthony Quinn, Jackie Gleason and Mickey Rooney. They are so good, they blow you away.

Quinn and Gleason were at their peak in 1962 when the film was made. Quinn was fresh off two hits, *The Guns of Navarone* and *Lawrence of Arabia*, and Gleason had just earned an Academy Award nomination for his performance in *The Hustler*. The *film noir* tone of *Requiem* was right in step with *The Hustler* and Gleason stepped seamlessly into the role of Maish.

The film represented a comeback for Rooney, whose movie career had faded. He does not have many lines—Army is a quiet sort who serves as caretaker as well as trainer of Mountain Rivera (Quinn)—but when he finally tells Maish off, the diminutive Rooney cuts the hulking Gleason off at the knees.

"You fink," he says. "You dirty, stinking fink."

Nothing more needs to be said. It is a killer line and Rooney drives it home with the force of a sledgehammer.

Requiem is the story of a fictional heavyweight who was once ranked fifth in the world, but after 17 years in the ring he is battered and used up. The film opens with Mountain Rivera (Quinn) in the ring against Cassius Clay (Muhammad Ali in his film debut). The viewer sees the fight through Rivera's eyes as the lightning-fast Clay throws a flurry of punches into the camera lens en route to a knockout victory.

In the dressing room, the doctor examines Rivera's bloody eye and tells him it's all over. If he fights again, he likely will go blind. "Tell him to buy a scrapbook," the doctor says with little sympathy. He obviously has delivered this message before.

Maish and Army have been Mountain's manager and trainer from Day One. The three men have been a team, traveling the country together, drinking and playing cards. They were in the big time for awhile when Mountain was a contender, but those days are long gone. Things have been sliding downhill for years, and now they're at an end. So what are the three men to do?

Mountain would seem to face the toughest road. He is 37 and punch drunk, with a face that has been beaten into a mask of pulpy scar tissue. He has no education and no skills other than fighting. But Maish has even greater problems. He has lost a ton of money to local mob boss Ma Greeny (a truly scary Madame Spivy), and he has no way of repaying her now that Mountain, his meal ticket, is out of business.

Army takes Mountain on a series of job interviews, hoping to find something the big guy can do. He almost gets a job as an usher in a movie theater, but they don't have a uniform to fit him. He goes to an employment agency where kindly counselor Grace Miller (Julie Harris) takes an interest in him. She sees that beneath the misshapen nose and cauliflower ears, Mountain is really a gentle soul with a good heart. She suggests a job as a counselor at a summer camp. She arranges for Mountain to meet the camp director for an interview.

Maish, meanwhile, is frantically trying to save his butt. He makes a deal with a sleazy promoter (Stan Adams) for Mountain to become a professional wrestler. He will wear a feathered head dress and wrestle as "Big Chief Mountain Rivera." It's humiliating, but it is a paycheck and once Maish gets his cut, he can pay off Ma Greeny.

Maish tells Mountain about the wrestling offer. Mountain wants no parts of it. He had 111 professional fights and never took a dive. He has too much pride to get involved in a freak show. He tells Maish about the job interview. Maish pretends to be happy for him. He suggests they celebrate. Maish gets Mountain drunk so that when he goes to meet the camp director, he is an incoherent, falling-down mess.

Grace is heartbroken by Mountain's humiliation. A spinster, she feels drawn to him—and he feels the same for her—but it is awkward. Neither one knows how to move beyond the first tentative kiss. As Grace is leaving Mountain's room, she runs into Maish. She slaps him for double-crossing Mountain. He responds with a look that says, "Lady, you really don't get it."

"Do you really want to help him?" Maish asks. "Here's how you can help him. Leave him alone. If you gotta say anything to him, tell him you pity him. Tell him you feel so sorry for him you could cry. But don't con him. Don't tell him he could be a counselor at a boys' camp. He's been chasing ghosts so long, he'll believe anything, any kind of ghost. Championship belt, pretty girl, maybe just 24 hours without an ache in his body. It don't make any difference. It all passed him by."

Like we said, *Requiem* is depressing. But it's also one of the finest boxing films ever made.

🏆 **CHEERS:** It would have been easy to make Mountain Rivera a pathetic caricature, all slurred speech and confusion, but Anthony Quinn invests him with a range of emotions—sadness, anger, love, shame. We really feel the fighter's pain.

👎 **JEERS:** The scene in which Mountain saves Maish's butt by flattening two of Ma Greeny's hoods is so poorly staged -- punches that clearly fail to connect send the bad guys reeling -- that it loses its dramatic power.

💬 **BEST LINE:** Mountain Rivera: "Mountain Rivera was no punk. Mountain Rivera was almost Heavyweight Champion of the world."

🎬 **PIVOTAL SCENE:** Maish admits to Mountain that toward the end of his career, he made money by betting against him. Mountain cannot believe the betrayal.

"Why, Maish?" he asks. "Why did you bet against me?"

"Would it have made any difference?" Maish replies. "Would it have made any difference if I hocked my left leg to bet on you? You're not a winner anymore, Mountain. There's only one thing left and that's make money from the losing."

"In all the crummy 17 years I fought for you, I wasn't ashamed of one single round, not one single minute," Mountain says. "Now you make me ashamed."

😎 **"I KNOW THAT GUY":** An old-time boxing fan will have a field day picking out familiar faces. In the bar where Mountain meets Grace, the camera pans across the room to show former champs Barney Ross, Gus Lesnevich and Willie Pep.

✒ **WHAT THEY WROTE AT THE TIME:** "As Mountain Riviera, Anthony Quinn, in memorable make-up including a broken nose, cauliflower ears and battered eyebrows, again is a Quasimodo-like brute who nevertheless elicits sympathy."—A.H. Weiler, *New York Times*

⭐ **SPORTS-ACTION GRADE:** B. There is only one boxing scene, but it is a doozy—a snarling young Cassius Clay throwing a blur of punches into the camera. You'll be reaching for the smelling salts when it's over.

👁 **REPEATED WATCHING QUOTIENT:** Only for manic depressives.

33 PHAR LAP (1983–PG)

SPORT: HORSE RACING | STARS: TOM BURLINSON, RON LEIBMAN, MARTIN VAUGHAN
DIRECTOR: SIMON WINCER

Phar Lap is to Australia what Seabiscuit is to America—a racehorse whose rise to prominence during the Depression lifted the spirits of a nation. Both horses overcame humble beginnings to gallop into legend. Eventually, both horses were immortalized in books and motion pictures.

Seabiscuit, the movie, made more money and earned more praise, including seven Academy Award nominations, but we think *Phar Lap*, a much smaller film made in Australia, is better. Even if you don't have the slightest interest in horse racing, the story is so beautifully told that you will be cheering.

The film is directed by Simon Wincer, who also directed the American TV series *Lonesome Dove*. It is photographed by Russell Boyd, whose other credits include *The Year of Living Dangerously*, *Tender Mercies* and *Gallipoli*. David Williamson (*The Club*) provides the screenplay. Their combined talents make *Phar Lap* a film you won't soon forget.

Phar Lap died in 1932, yet the big chestnut colt still is revered in Australia. His enormous heart—which weighed 6.2 kilograms compared to 3.2 kilograms for most horses—is on display in the National Museum of Australia. In fact, it is the object visitors ask to see most often. His body is stuffed and mounted in the Australia Gallery at the Melbourne Museum. Fans still cry and leave flowers at his feet.

"In my opinion, there is nothing maudlin in a nation

mourning the loss of a racehorse when that horse is Phar Lap," said Sir Hubert Opperman, Australia's champion cyclist.

In the film, Phar Lap is purchased sight unseen by American sportsman David Davis (Ron Leibman) on the recommendation of Australian trainer Harry Telford (Martin Vaughan). Telford feels the horse has a winner's bloodlines. But when Phar Lap arrives in Australia from his native New Zealand, he looks like a dud. He is gangly and shows little promise on the track.

"He looks like a cross between a sheepdog and a kangaroo," Davis says.

The horse loses its first five races, and Telford's wife, Vi (Celia De Burgh), tells him to sell the worthless nag and be done with it. But the trainer believes he can turn the horse into a winner, and he does so with the help of stable boy Tommy Woodcock (Tom Burlinson).

The horse literally rips the shirts off the other stable boys, but he bonds with the kindly Woodcock. Phar Lap trusts Woodcock, and the stable boy's patience unlocks the horse's potential. When Woodcock tells him to run, he runs like the wind.

Telford and Woodcock disagree on how to train the horse. Telford trains him hard, almost to the point of cruelty. Woodcock, who loves the horse and calls him by the pet name "Bobby," prefers a gentler hand. When Woodcock objects to Telford's methods once too often, the old trainer fires him. However, Phar Lap becomes depressed and stops eating, so Telford is forced to bring Woodcock back. The horse immediately perks up.

"Your trouble is you think horses are human," Telford tells Woodcock as the boy slips Phar Lap another sugar cube. "You can't train them that way. You ease up and they'll take advantage of you."

"Bobby is different," Woodcock says.

Phar Lap begins winning races and setting track records across Australia. In 1930 and '31, he wins 14 consecutive races. The fans love him because, like Seabiscuit, he is an underdog, a horse that came from nowhere to dominate the sport. But the stuffed shirts who run the racing industry aren't nearly as fond of him. Phar Lap is so good, they say, he is taking the competition out of the sport. He is also costing the bookmakers a bundle because the adoring public keeps betting on him and he keeps cashing their tickets.

At one point, a promoter takes Davis aside and says, "Look, Dave, if something is good, that's OK. But if something is too good, it upsets the entire system." In other words, look out.

One morning, Phar Lap is out for his morning romp and a shotgun blast is fired from a passing car. The horse is not injured, but Davis and Telford agree to move him to a secret location and hire guards for protection.

Things aren't much better on the track. Racing officials try to handicap Phar Lap by putting lead weights in his saddle to slow him down. They keep increasing the weight until Woodcock and jockey Jim Pike (James Steele) are almost in tears. "I've never had a horse die under me," Pike says. "I don't want Phar Lap to be the first." Yet the horse—which the press dubs "The Red Terror"—keeps winning.

Williamson's script makes the point that Phar Lap isn't a horse that runs fast. Rather, he is a horse that runs as much with his heart as with his legs. Like any great athlete, he has an innate competitive drive that carries him beyond exhaustion and beyond pain. He runs one race on a cracked hoof and as he comes down the stretch, the camera focuses on his bloody leg wrappings, yet Phar Lap never breaks stride until he crosses the finish line.

"He's a freak," a rival owner says.

In 1932, Davis takes Phar Lap to Mexico to race in the Agua Caliente Handicap for the largest purse in North American track history. The horse wins again in track record time, and Davis pockets a cool $50,000.

OK, here is the spoiler alert. If you haven't seen Phar Lap but you have an interest in the film, you might want to stop reading now, because we're about to discuss the ending.

After his win in Mexico, Phar Lap is sent to a ranch in California, where he will stay while Davis lines up a series of races for him in the United States. One night Woodcock is awakened by the sound of moaning from Phar Lap's stall. The horse is terribly ill and there is nothing the doctors can do. He dies the next morning, just 16 days after his spectacular run at the Agua Caliente Stakes.

While the film does not come out and say it, it certainly implies that Phar Lap was the victim of foul play. It is believed the horse was killed either by professional gamblers or jealous rivals. Tests found Phar Lap's stomach and intestines inflamed, which suggests poisoning, most likely arsenic.

It is interesting to note the film was edited differently for Australian and American audiences. The version that played in Australia opened with Phar Lap's death and then told his story in flashback. The Phar Lap that played in America opened with Davis and Telford purchasing the colt and followed his rise to stardom.

Why the change? Well, the studio knew that in Australia most people were familiar with the story and if the film was structured in the traditional way, audiences would spend the whole night waiting for—and dreading—the sad ending. It was better, the producers felt, to get it out of the way early. The American audience was less likely to know the story, so the ending would come as a surprise.

Regardless of which version you see, be forewarned: The sight of Tommy Woodcock crying "Bobby" as he hugs the dying Phar Lap will rip your heart out.

🍷 **CHEERS:** Russell Boyd's camera work is stunning. Some of the most spectacular scenes are those of Telford training Phar Lap by riding him up steep sand dunes. It is brutal and beautiful at the same time.

🍺 **JEERS:** There are several occasions where the music undercuts the drama. The horses are dueling down the stretch and just when you think this might be the race where Phar Lap finally breaks down, the victory trumpets kick in and the suspense is gone.

💬 **BEST LINE:** Jim Pike: "If anything catches us today, mate, it'll have to have wings."

✏️ **WHAT THEY WROTE AT THE TIME:** *"Phar Lap* isn't a surprising movie; it has too much dialog on the order of 'That horse is going to be a champion, can't anyone understand that? He's going to be a champion!' for that. But in its own way, it's a winner."—Janet Maslin, *New York Times*

★ **SPORTS-ACTION GRADE:** B. Director Simon Wincer, as he demonstrated in *Lonesome Dove* and *The Lighthorsemen*, knows how to film a story on horseback.

✸ **IF YOU LIKED THIS, YOU'LL LIKE:** *The Black Stallion*, a 1979 film about a relationship between a boy and a horse with an excellent performance by Mickey Rooney as the trainer.

◎ **REPEATED WATCHING QUOTIENT:** If you're an animal lover—and even if you're not—you'll want to skip the last act. It's that painful.

34 THE ROOKIE (2002–G)

SPORT: BASEBALL | STARS: DENNIS QUAID, RACHEL GRIFFITHS, BRIAN COX
DIRECTOR: JOHN LEE HANCOCK

The story behind the making of *The Rookie* is almost as improbable as the story itself. You find it hard to believe that a 35-year-old high school teacher could become one of the oldest rookies in major league history? Well, that is the tale of Jim Morris, who had a brief but inspiring career with the Tampa Bay Devil Rays in 1999-2000. But how that story made it to the screen is just as unlikely.

It began with a young film producer named Mark Ciardi flipping through a magazine at the doctor's office. He saw an article about a Texas school teacher who was signed to a professional baseball contract after throwing 98 MPH fastballs in an open tryout.

"I saw the picture and said, 'That's Jimmy Morris,'" Ciardi said.

Ciardi and Morris were both signed by the Milwaukee Brewers in 1983. They roomed together in spring training. Ciardi made it to the big leagues (he pitched four games for the Brewers in 1987) but Morris did not. He had a series of arm injuries that ended his career in 1989. Ciardi quit around the same time. Morris went back to Texas, Ciardi went to Hollywood.

A decade later, their lives intersected again, this time with Morris' dramatic resurrection as a ballplayer. When Ciardi saw the article, Morris was pitching for the Devil Rays' top farm team in Durham, N.C.

"My first thought was, 'This is a movie,'" Ciardi said. "My second thought was, 'I want to make it.'"

Ciardi and his business partner Gordon Gray still were trying to establish themselves in the movie industry. They were working out of a garage, searching for just the right project. The Jim Morris story, they felt, was it.

Ciardi called the clubhouse in Durham and spoke with Morris. He was excited about the idea of a movie and referred Ciardi to his agent to work out the details.

"We were up front with him," Ciardi said. "We told him we didn't have much money, but we knew people who would write the check. We took the idea to Disney

and they loved it. They agreed to back us 100 percent. We tried to get back to the agent to sign the deal, but he was away. We couldn't contact him."

That weekend, Morris was called up to the Devil Rays. He made his first major league appearance in Texas and struck out the first batter he faced (Royce Clayton). The team went to California a few days later and a writer from the *Los Angeles Times* did a front page profile on Morris. The headline read: "This Should Be a Movie." The piece caught the eye of every studio executive in town. Pretty soon, Morris and his agent were flooded with offers.

"I thought we were sunk," Ciardi said. "When we reached (the agent), he kept cutting out to take other calls. He got over 200 calls in three days. Every major studio wanted in. But Jim and his agent stuck with us. They said we came to them first so it was only right that we get the first crack. Thank goodness for loyalty."

The Rookie was a hit, taking in more than $75 million at the box office. It launched the careers of Ciardi and Gray, who produced two more inspirational sports films, *Miracle* (2004) and *Invincible* (2006) and the father-daughter football comedy *The Game Plan* (2007). Ciardi and Gray have long since moved out of the garage. They are now major players in Hollywood and it all started with the story of Jim Morris.

Set in a dusty West Texas town called Big Lake, Morris (Dennis Quaid) teaches science and coaches baseball at the local high school. He was once a hot pitching prospect (the No. 4 overall pick in the 1983 amateur draft) but four arm surgeries later, he was given his release. Now 35, married with three children, he is doing OK, but that lost opportunity still nags at him. At night, he throws pitch after pitch into the rusty backstop on the high school diamond.

One day while pitching batting practice to his team, Morris is goaded into putting a little "something" on the ball. OK, he says. He tugs on his cap, cranks up the old left arm and throws a fastball that explodes into the catcher's mitt. The kids can't believe it. Neither can Morris, who says, "Gee, I forgot how good that sounds."

The Big Lake kids are headed for another losing season when Morris lectures them on never quitting. "If you don't have dreams," he says, "you don't have anything."

One of the kids asks, "What about your dreams, Coach?" Another says, "Yeah, you're the one who should be wanting more."

They strike a deal: If the team wins the district championship, Morris will take another shot at the big leagues. In what seems like a totally implausible storyline (except it really happened), the Big Lake team catches fire and wins the district title. When they pin the newspaper clipping on the bulletin board, one of the players writes on it, "It's your turn, Coach."

Morris hears about a tryout in nearby San Angelo. His wife (Rachel Griffiths) is going out that day so he tosses the kids in his pickup truck and drives to the field where he is surrounded by a hundred hard-throwing studs half his age. The Tampa Bay scouts take a look at Morris and wave him to the back of the line.

When they finally call his name, Morris is in the middle of changing his baby's diaper. He rushes onto the mound, flexes his arm and uncorks a heater that lights up the radar gun. The great mystery is how Morris, after four arm surgeries, can throw in the high 90s when he topped out in the 80s ten years earlier. Asked to explain it, Morris shrugs. He still doesn't know how it happened, it just did.

The Devil Rays offer Morris a minor league contract which he signs only after his wife first objects ("You can't eat dreams, Jim") and then relents, knowing she can't deny him another shot at pro ball. He starts in Double-A Orlando, earns a promotion to Durham and finally gets the call to The Show.

Only the worst kind of cynic would point out the Devil Rays were an awful team in 1999 and that Morris was only added when the rosters were expanded in September. That's all true, but it's beside the point. So is the fact he pitched in just 21 games over two seasons and his statistics—no wins, no losses, a 4.80 ERA in 15 innings—are unremarkable. The mere fact that he got there at all is what makes his story worth telling.

CHEERS: There is a cool scene along a deserted highway where Morris (Quaid) uses the "You are going this fast" radar sign to time his fastball. Stay tuned to the end of the movie to see the plot twist on this.

JEERS: Director John Lee Hancock lets too many scenes drag, especially the high school baseball. *The Rookie* runs more than two hours, too long for a family film.

DON'T FAIL TO NOTICE: The G rating. Hard to believe you can make a baseball movie without profanity, sex and tobacco, but *The Rookie* did it.

BET YOU DIDN'T KNOW: After his first major league appearance, Jim Morris asked Texas catcher Ivan "Pudge" Rodriguez for his autograph.

REALITY CHECK: Morris struck out first hitter Royce Clayton on four pitches, one of which was a foul ball. In the film, they show Morris (Quaid) blowing Clayton away on three straight fastballs.

PIVOTAL SCENE: Morris calls his wife from a pay phone in Durham and asks her to meet him in Arlington. "I need you to bring my blue blazer," he says. She looks puzzled. He explains, "They have a dress code in the big leagues."

Her reaction when the words sink in is one of the best moments in the film.

BEST LINE: Morris' minor league teammates enjoy teasing him about his age. Two of the better lines: "So what was it like watching The Babe play?" And "How many fans did you lose when they raised the ticket prices to 50 cents?"

WHAT THEY WROTE AT THE TIME: "I found myself tearing up over *The Rookie* on a crowded cross-country flight. Goofy plastic headphones, head and neck at a decidedly unhealthy angle, no elbow room, no foot room and none of it mattered because when Jim Morris was reaching over the bullpen wall to hug his wife and kids I was right there with him, the water running."—Eric Neel, ESPN.com

★ **Sports-Action Grade:** B. Quaid worked with former major league pitcher Jim Gott to improve his mechanics. His stride still seems a little short for a guy throwing in the high 90s, but considering he had not set foot on a ball field since Little League, Quaid is pretty good.

🎞 **If You Liked This, You'll Like:** Two more baseball movies geared to a younger audience, *Angels in the Outfield* and *Rookie of the Year.*

◉ **Repeated Watching Quotient:** Once a summer ought to do it, preferably during a kids' sleepover.

🎬 **My Favorite Sports Movie:** Brett Myers, veteran Major league pitcher Brett Myers: "It is an awesome story. It's not one of those make-believe or fantasy stories. *Field of Dreams* was OK, but I watched it once and I was done with it. I could watch *The Rookie* over and over because it's something that really happened. It's a great story about perseverance, a guy who thought [baseball] was over for him, but he got his shot and made it."

AN INTERVIEW WITH JIM MORRIS

JIM MORRIS MADE HIS FINAL MAJOR LEAGUE APPEARANCE ON MAY 9, 2000. HIS ARM PROBLEMS RECURRED AND TAMPA BAY RELEASED HIM, BUT HIS INSPIRATIONAL COMEBACK STORY LED TO A BOOK (*THE OLDEST ROOKIE*) IN ADDITION TO THE FILM. HE NOW TRAVELS ALL OVER THE COUNTRY AS A MOTIVATIONAL SPEAKER.

How accurate was the tryout scene in the film, The Rookie?

Very accurate. I did have my three kids with me and, yes, I was the last one to throw. When I went to the mound, people were packing up their stuff and leaving. Then I started to throw and a crowd began gathering behind the backstop. I thought, 'I'm either doing really good or really bad.' When I saw the scouts go from one radar gun to two and finally three, I thought that was a good sign. But I was shocked when they told me I was throwing 98 miles an hour.

How can you explain that you were able to throw harder at age 35 than you were when your pro career ended a decade earlier?

There is no logical explanation for it. I really think it was God's way of getting my attention. When I made the bet with my high school team, I didn't think there was any way [the tryout] would lead to anything. But I do have faith in God and I believe things happen for a reason.

In the film, they show you agonizing over the decision to sign the contract. Did you really consider turning it down?

At the time, I had a good job offer [teacher and coach] at a bigger high school. I could either take that or I could follow a dream [pro baseball] that I had already failed at when I was much younger. I was taking a pay cut going back to baseball with no assurance that it would lead to anything. I mean, I was a 35-year-old guy going to Double-A ball. But I always told my students if they had a dream, they should chase it. How would it look if I didn't do the same?

Do you remember how it felt when you were called up to the majors and walked in the Tampa Bay clubhouse for the first time?

I walked in and saw Wade Boggs, Fred McGriff and Jose Canseco and I thought, 'I'm not in the classroom anymore.' At that point, most of the players had heard about me and knew I was called up [from the minors]. Wade Boggs came over and said, 'Man, that is the best story I've ever heard.' I'm thinking, 'You're Wade Boggs, you're on your way to the Hall of Fame.' I'll never forget that moment.

How much time did you spend on the movie set?

Quite a bit. I had one of those director's chairs with my name on it. I remember the first time I walked on the set, Rachel Griffiths [who played Lorri Morris, Jim's wife] was filming a scene and she sounded just like a good old Texas girl. They said, 'Cut' and she came over, gave me a hug and said, 'It's nice to meet you' in her Australian accent. Five minutes later she was back in character talking like a Texan.

Did the director and cast ask for your input?

They asked all the time. They'd finish a scene and John Lee or Dennis would ask what I thought. I'd say, 'Why are you asking me? You're the movie guys.' I thought they did a phenomenal job.

Were you there when they filmed the scene of your first major league game?

Yes, it was quite an experience. The scene where Dennis warms up in the bullpen, then gets called into the game was filmed during an actual [Texas Rangers] game. They filmed it during the seventh inning stretch so we only had four or five minutes. Dennis had to run from the bullpen to the mound. He said, 'I hope I don't fall down.' I said, 'That's funny. That's exactly what I was thinking that night.'

Did the filmmakers change many things in your story?

The one thing they made up was the scene where I clock my fastball by throwing it past a highway radar sign. It's a scene that people love, but I never did it because I never thought of it. But I've heard from some people who say, 'Do you know how many dented radar screens we have now because of you?'

Did the film's success surprise you?

I think it surprised everyone. Disney thought it might be a small hit, but it exceeded all expectations. For me, the best part was seeing the effect it had on audiences. I remember attending one of the early screenings. I saw a father and son come into the theater and they weren't even speaking to each other. When they came out, they had their arms around each other. I think it had that effect on a lot of people.

How did you feel when The Rookie won the ESPY Award as best sports movie of 2002?

It was another one of those 'Can-you-believe-this?' moments. I've had so many of them, it's hard to describe. After the ceremony, Dennis hugged me and said, 'You turned my life around.' I'm thinking, 'You're Dennis Quaid, you've made a hundred movies.' But this film obviously had a special meaning for him. He did a wonderful job.

Do you still follow your old team, the Rays?

Of course, they'll always be my team. I'm really proud of what they accomplished this season (2008). They're young, they're talented and they're hungry. I love watching them play.

35 HEAVEN CAN WAIT (1978–PG)

SPORT: FOOTBALL | STARS: WARREN BEATTY, JULIE CHRISTIE, JACK WARDEN
DIRECTORS: WARREN BEATTY, BUCK HENRY

Heaven Can Wait is, in a sense, a precursor of many sports movies that followed, including *Bull Durham*, *Jerry Maguire* and *Fever Pitch*. Call it a romantic comedy focused around a sports theme. The sports element works well; the screwball romance works even better.

The story centers on Joe Pendleton (Warren Beatty), a veteran quarterback for the Los Angeles Rams—and, yes kids, there was a real NFL team in Los Angeles once upon a time. Joe is struggling to come back from injury to start for a Rams squad that seems bound for the Super Bowl. From the start, we see that Joe is an earnest guy who treats everyone well, plays an off-key clarinet and feeds his body liver-and-whey milkshakes, with a little spinach mold tossed in.

Joe also goes on long bike rides, which proves to be a problem when he pedals through a tunnel and is broadsided by a vehicle.

Well, almost. Turns out that the angel (Buck Henry) assigned to oversee Joe's life anticipates the accident and—aiming to spare him the pain—sends him to heaven a second too early. With his quick reflexes, it turns out, Joe would have avoided the accident. He is due another 50 years on Earth. What to do?

The case is appealed to Mr. Jordan (James Mason), the director of heaven's way station. He offers to send Joe back—except that the poor quarterback's remains have already been cremated. So Joe is returned to Earth in the body of wingnut billionaire Leo Farnsworth, whose wife and top aide are scheming to murder him and who owns a canning-plastics-nuclear-energy company apparently responsible for most of the planet's pollution.

Now, Joe's got two aims. One is to win the love of British activist Betty Logan (Julie Christie), which he can do by halting the ecological plunder. The other, more difficult challenge, is to get Farnworth's soft body into football shape so that he can return to the Rams. He hires team trainer Max Corkle, played perfectly by Jack

Warden, and throws a lot of passes to clumsy butlers. Soon enough, his skills return.

Of course, the Rams aren't about to give the job to a wacky industrialist, so Joe—now Farnsworth—buys the team and installs himself as first stringer. Sure he does. Hey, some movies ask you to take a leap of faith. *Heaven Can Wait* asks you to vault the Grand Canyon.

Anyway, everything seems perfect until the heavenly escorts return with more bad news: The murder plot against Farnsworth is about to succeed. Another new body is needed. All that arduous training—for nothing.

Then comes a wacky murder investigation, a few plot twists, the Super Bowl, and they all live happily ever after. Needless to say, it all works out for Joe's third persona. Did you expect Beatty—who produced, co-wrote and co-directed this movie—to end it any other way?

A critical sports fan may dismiss some of the far-fetched plot twists as naïve pap. Certainly they are. But, you know, sometimes there's nothing wrong with a corny ending.

CHEERS: To the sweet nature and uplifting story of *Heaven Can Wait*. Most family films are torture for at least one member of the family; this one works for men, women, kids, everyone.

JEERS: To the over-the-top, scenery-chewing scenes between murder conspirators Julia Farnsworth (Dyan Cannon) and Tony Abbott (Charles Grodin).

REALITY CHECK: Well, a billionaire buys a football team on a whim, the week before the Super Bowl. There is no background check by the NFL, and no outrage when he announces his plan to start himself at quarterback. So you can begin with that.

REPEATED WATCHING QUOTIENT: Once every five

years should suffice. Or when the NFL puts a team back in Los Angeles.

🎬 **PIVOTAL SCENE:** Joe, as the ghost of Leo Farnsworth, is watching girlfriend Betty Logan being framed for his murder (of course, being a ghost, no one sees him). At the same time, the Super Bowl is on television in the background (follow us here, because this is confusing). Joe watches Rams quarterback Tom Jarrett get sacked so hard that he loses consciousness on the field. Suddenly, Joe realizes this is his opportunity to take over Jarrett's body to fulfill his dream of playing in the Super Bowl. But he's conflicted because he wants to rescue his girlfriend.

You'll have to watch the rest for yourself.

✴ **IF YOU LIKED THIS, YOU'LL LIKE:** *Here Comes Mr. Jordan*, the 1941 romantic comedy that served as inspiration for this film. In essentially the same plot, Robert Montgomery stars as Joe Pendleton, a boxer this time around.

🏆 **BET YOU DIDN'T KNOW:** Beatty originally wanted to stay true to the boxing theme and tried to cast Muhammad Ali as Joe. But Ali declined, saying he needed to train for his pending title fight against Earnie Shavers.

❞ **BEST LINE:** Joe Pendleton: "They don't have a football team in heaven so God couldn't make me first string."

🎞 **CASTING CALL:** About a half-dozen NFL players from the era play members of the Rams, including Les Josephson, Marv Fleming and the great Deacon Jones. In addition, Dick Enberg, Curt Gowdy and Al DeRogatis appear as broadcasters at the Super Bowl.

☞ **DON'T FAIL TO NOTICE:** The high-rise Afro on young Bryant Gumbel, who makes a brief appearance as a Los Angeles sportscaster. The follicle elevation would do Dr. J proud.

★ **SPORTS-ACTION GRADE:** C-plus. Beatty's not bad for a 40ish actor who never made another sports movie in his life. Still, he throws a football like your neighbor's dad and sprints like a guy who couldn't outrun Drew Bled-

soe. On some of the long pass plays, it's clear that a body double is being used.

Beatty received some pointers from Ron Jaworski, who was the Rams' backup quarterback at the time. "He wanted some background about playing the position," Jaworski said. "He seemed like a nice guy." That was the end of it, until the movie came out, and Joe Pendleton was wearing his No. 16 Rams jersey. "I got a kick out of that," said Jaws.

Did he get anything else? "No, not a consultant's fee. I didn't even get a free ticket."

And how would Jaworski assess Beatty as a quarterback? "He wasn't a very good thrower, let's put it that way."

😎 **"I KNOW THAT GUY":** John Randolph, who plays the Rams owner who sells the team to Farnsworth, appeared in more than 100 films during his 50-year acting career. You may recognize him as Clark Griswold's father in *Christmas Vacation* or the police chief in *Serpico*. And if you watched *Seinfeld* from its inception, you'll recall him as the original Frank Costanza. When the show was put into syndication, his scenes were re-shot with actor Jerry Stiller.

✎ **WHAT THEY WROTE AT THE TIME:** "The surprise is that *Heaven Can Wait* is as much fun as it is when it has to waste so much energy in the service of a gimmick that we would now endure only in a pilot film for a projected television series titled *I Dream of Joey.*—Vincent Canby, *New York Times*

SIGN OF THE TIMES: It's a hoot to see Joe set up an old eight-millimeter projector to watch game films, and to watch him work out on prehistoric exercise equipment. But the best laugh comes when the former owner tells of selling his team for $67 million, noting, "It has a book value of $19 million."

These days, NFL franchises are priced at upwards of $1 billion.

📽 **MY FAVORITE SPORTS MOVIE:** ESPN broadcaster Suzy Kolber: "It's a movie about pro football and it's a love story. It combines my two favorite things—football and romance."

36 HEART LIKE A WHEEL (1983–PG)

SPORT: DRAG RACING | STARS: BONNIE BEDELIA, BEAU BRIDGES
DIRECTOR: JONATHAN KAPLAN

Shirley Muldowney was the first woman licensed by the National Hot Rod Association to drive a gas-powered car, and in 1977 she rose to the top of that high-octane macho world by winning an NHRA points championship. She was called a pioneer and was often compared to Jackie Robinson, who broke the color line in major league baseball.

But to Shirley, it was never about being a pioneer. As she said in a 2003 interview, "It was always about the racing." That was it, pure and simple. She loved the roar of the engines and the competition. Most of all, she loved the winning.

She was a drag racer, all guts and grease, just like Don (Big Daddy) Garlits, Connie (The Bounty Hunter) Kalitta, Don (The Snake) Prudhomme and the rest of the male hot rodders. She didn't do it for Gloria Steinem or the women's lib movement. She wasn't out to prove any point except that she could drive really fast.

"I didn't have to put up with all that chauvinism," she once said. "I chose to put up with it. This life just suited me. I've always loved everything about this sport."

Heart Like a Wheel, the story of Muldowney's life, makes that clear. The film opens with Shirley as a little girl, sitting in her daddy's lap, clutching the steering wheel as they drive the back roads in upstate New York. She loves driving the car, and when she begs her dad (singer Hoyt Axton) to go faster, we're seeing a glimpse of the future.

At 16, Shirley (Bonnie Bedelia) drops out of school and marries Jack Muldowney (Leo Rossi), a mechanic who competes in local drag races. One night Shirley convinces Jack to let her drive. She wins that race and that whets her appetite. Pretty soon, she is urging Jack to let her try the NHRA circuit. He tells her there is no way that the other drivers will let a woman crack their fraternity.

Shirley will not be deterred, however. She goes to an NHRA event, where she is told she needs the signature of three drivers to get her license. She goes from pit to pit, paper in hand, asking the drivers to sign. Most laugh her off, but Garlits sees it as a way to bring new fans to the sport so he signs. Kalitta also signs—although the way he eyes Shirley, it's clear his motives aren't the best—and he strong-arms another driver into providing the third signature.

Shirley competes in her first NHRA event and in her qualifying run, she sets the track record. She wants to hit the circuit full-time, but Jack resists. He still sees racing as a hobby; he doesn't believe they can make it work as a career. They argue and Shirley takes off.

Shirley hooks up with Kalitta (Beau Bridges), who helps her get a car and a sponsor. They become romantically involved as Kalitta remakes Shirley's image, outfitting her in white boots and hot pants and giving her the nickname "Cha Cha."

But Kalitta is a world-class horn dog who spends most of the film with his arm around various women, telling them, "You're the number one thing in my life." Shirley knows what Kalitta is up to, but he is her business partner as well as her paramour, so she hangs in longer than she should. Finally, she reaches her limit and breaks off the relationship.

Without Kalitta's backing, Shirley's career suffers. She loses her sponsorships and she is forced to work with a young, inexperienced crew. She goes through two lean years on the circuit before rebounding.

Kalitta returns to driving and in 1980, the NHRA top fuel championship final comes down to a race between the former lovers. Shirley beats Kalitta to claim her second world title. As she removes her helmet, she looks at Kalitta and says, "Not bad for an old broad in a used car, eh?" He laughs, she smiles and it seems like they put their differences behind them.

Well, maybe not entirely.

In a 2003 interview, Shirley was asked to pick a career highlight. She picked the 1980 victory over Kalitta. "I don't think I ever got as much satisfaction as I did in beating Connie after our falling out at the end of the '77 season," she said, still sounding like a woman scorned.

One year after the release of *Heart Like a Wheel*, Shirley was involved in the worst crash of her career. She was in a qualifying run at the Sanair Speedway near Montreal when the front wheels of her dragster locked, sending her car tumbling 600 feet down the track.

She suffered two broken legs, a fractured pelvis and two broken hands. The doctors needed six hours working with wire brushes to clean the dirt and grease from her skin before they could operate. She was hospitalized for two months and required five more surgical procedures, including a skin graft, over the next two years.

Even racing enthusiasts were surprised when Shirley returned to the track in 1986 and resumed her career. Why risk a comeback at age 46? She simply said, "I missed it. It's what I did best."

She finally retired in 2003 at the age of 62. The following year, she was inducted into the International Motorsports Hall of Fame along with Indianapolis 500 winner Bobby Rahal.

🍺 **CHEERS:** Bonnie Bedelia, a talented actress best known for her supporting roles as Bruce Willis' wife in the *Die Hard* series, earned a Golden Globe nomination as Best Actress for her portrayal of Shirley Muldowney.

🍺 **JEERS:** For a film about drag racing, there really isn't enough racing. Director Jonathan Kaplan spends most of his time with Shirley's soap opera life away from the track.

◀ **CASTING CALL:** Actresses Jamie Lee Curtis, Susan Lucci and Kathryn Harrold were all considered for the lead, but the producers chose Bedelia, who bears a strong resemblance to the real Shirley.

SIGN OF THE TIMES: While Shirley is hospitalized following a crash in 1973, she is watching the Bobby Riggs-Billie Jean King tennis match on TV.

✔ **REALITY CHECK:** Shirley hated the nickname "Cha Cha" and dropped it immediately after her break-up with Kalitta. "There is no room for bimbo-ism in drag racing," she said.

🍎 **BET YOU DIDN'T KNOW:** When Shirley Muldowney retired in 2003, she sold her pink top-fuel dragster for $350,000.

✎ **WHAT THEY WROTE AT THE TIME:** "This biographical film is something out of the ordinary. Its story is unusual, but it's told in a style that is immediate and understandable and that never opts for heroism at the expense of authenticity. The movie doesn't concentrate on glorifying its heroine. It simply tries to make her seem reachable and real and it succeeds."—Janet Maslin, *New York Times*

⊕ **IF YOU LIKED THIS, YOU'LL LIKE:** *Greased Lightning*, a film about Wendell Scott, the first black driver to win a NASCAR race. Comedian Richard Pryor plays Scott, who overcomes racial prejudice to succeed on the stock car circuit. Beau Bridges co-stars in this film as well.

★ **SPORTS-ACTION GRADE:** B-plus. The scene in which Shirley's car blows up during a 1973 race in Pomona, culminating with Shirley running down the track in flames, is chillingly real.

🎬 **MY FAVORITE SPORTS MOVIE:** NASCAR racer Mark Martin to *The Sporting News*: "I thought *Heart Like a Wheel* was pretty cool. I watch it every chance I get."

37 JIM THORPE–ALL-AMERICAN (1951–NR)

SPORTS: FOOTBALL/TRACK AND FIELD | STARS: BURT LANCASTER, CHARLES BICKFORD, PHYLLIS THAXTER | DIRECTOR: MICHAEL CURTIZ

John Riggins learned the story of Jim Thorpe by reading a book he checked out of the library at his grammar school in Centralia, Kansas.

"I stumbled upon a true American hero," said Riggins, who read the book as a third-grader and went on to become a star running back with the New York Jets and Washington Redskins. "The book made him larger than life and the film, *Jim Thorpe—All-American*, gave him life.

"It's a film I could watch every day just because Jim Thorpe was the real deal," said Riggins, who now occupies a space alongside Thorpe in the Pro Football Hall of Fame. "And Burt Lancaster gave an authentic performance of the Indian superstar."

Lancaster was well coached. That's because the real Jim Thorpe was on the set every day serving as technical advisor. Lancaster said it was the only time in his career that he felt intimidated.

"Imagine how I felt," Lancaster recalled in a 1983 interview, "trying to do all the things Jim Thorpe did with the man himself sitting just a few feet away. He was very gracious. He kept saying, 'You're doing fine, young man.'"

Lancaster was an accomplished athlete. He competed in baseball, track and gymnastics at New York University. He performed as a trapeze artist with Ringling Brothers. He could handle most of the sports scenes. The one thing he couldn't do was throw the discus.

"My footwork was all wrong," Lancaster said. "One day Jim got up, took off his jacket and said, 'Here, let me show you.' He was in his 60s, I'm sure he hadn't touched a discus in 30 years, yet he threw it flawlessly. We were speechless. Then we began to applaud."

Lancaster and Thorpe became friends during the filming and they stayed in touch until Thorpe's death in 1953. Lancaster had many memorable roles in his acting career, but Thorpe remained one of his favorites. "I'll always remember the look in his eyes," he said. "There was great pride, but also a lot of sadness."

Thorpe did not have a very happy life; the film makes that clear. It shows his triumph at the 1912 Olympics when he won two gold medals, only to have them later taken away. It shows him earning All-America honors in football, but it also shows him hitting rock bottom late in his career. This is a bittersweet portrait of the man chosen as the greatest athlete of the first half of the 20th century.

Like many sports films, *Jim Thorpe* is told in flashback with Thorpe's college coach, the legendary Glenn "Pop" Warner (Charles Bickford), as the narrator. It opens with Thorpe being honored at a dinner in his native Oklahoma. From there, it rolls back in time to the turn of the century and a young Thorpe, an Indian from the Sac and Fox Nation, running across the reservation with the speed and endurance of a stallion.

Jim's father sends him to the Carlisle (Pa.) Indian school to learn the skills of the white man's world. The students, who range in age from six to 25, spend half the day learning to read and write, the other half in the shop learning a trade. Jim is an indifferent student, but he is excited by his introduction to organized sports. He has no training and no grasp of the rules, but he is blessed with natural ability. Soon, he is excelling in both track and football.

The real Thorpe was just over six feet tall and weighed 200 pounds, with the speed of a sprinter. The Carlisle Indians had only 12 players on the football squad—with names like Jesse Young Deer, Little Boy and Sunny Warcloud—but Thorpe made them a national power. In four seasons, Carlisle won 43 games and lost only five, with two ties. As a senior, Thorpe scored 198 points and 25 touchdowns in 14 games.

In the film, Thorpe (Lancaster) pursues a coaching job after college, but he is passed over, presumably because he is an Indian. Pop Warner suggests Thorpe take a crack at the 1912 Olympics. He enters the decathlon and the pentathlon and wins the gold medal in both. King Gustav V of Sweden presents Thorpe with a laurel wreath and says, "Sir, you are the greatest athlete in the world."

Thorpe returns home a hero, but his joy is short-lived. A sportswriter discovers that he played two summers of semi-pro baseball for which he was paid $2 a game. By the rules of the time that makes him a professional, and therefore ineligible for the Olympics. Even though Thorpe apologizes, explaining he was unaware of the rules, the International Olympic Committee strips him of his medals.

Thorpe suffers an even greater loss a few years later when his son, Jim Jr., whom he adores, dies of infantile paralysis. Devastated, Thorpe begins drinking heavily and his bitterness drives away his wife (Phyllis Thaxter). He continues his athletic career—he helps launch the first professional football league in 1920, starring for the Canton (OH) Bulldogs—and while he still is a big name, his performance tails off due to his boozing and disruptive behavior.

Thorpe ends up a shabby figure, walking into a practice and asking, "Do you need a back?" The coach first brushes him off, then he notices the initials J.T. on his bag. He realizes who this is. "Can you still go, Jim?" he asks. Thorpe says, "Give me a chance." In his first scrimmage, Thorpe breaks into the clear but collapses from exhaustion. He is carried off the field for the last time.

After that, he becomes a sideshow act, calling out the contestants in a marathon dance contest. Barely able to stand and slurring his words, Thorpe is an embarrassment. "This guy is laying the biggest egg since the dinosaurs left town," the promoter says as he prepares to give him the boot.

Thorpe is in the dressing room, pouring himself a drink when Warner walks in. The old coach gives him a tough-love lecture about being a quitter and feeling sorry for himself and Thorpe, looking in the mirror, knows he is right.

Warner invites Thorpe to join him for the opening

ceremonies of the 1932 Summer Olympics in Los Angeles. When Thorpe enters the Coliseum, he receives a hero's welcome. Basking in the applause, the gleam returns to his eyes and he appears ready to get his life back on track.

In reality, Thorpe continued to have ups and downs. He earned a living through personal appearances and remained a prickly character. He feuded with Warner Brothers over the handling of the film. He said the studio paid him just $7,000 for the rights to his story. He also was paid $250 a week for his role as technical advisor. "But when they take the taxes out," he said, "I get $211."

Thorpe boycotted the premiere of the film in Muskogee, Ok., because they would not pay him an appearance fee. "Warner Brothers," he said, "are a bunch of damned stinkers."

Despite Thorpe's bitterness, many viewers have found the movie inspiring over the years. Among them was Herman Edwards, a 10-year NFL player and, later, head coach of two NFL teams. "Jim Thorpe made me want to become an athlete," Edwards recalled. "I was about 10 years old, flipping around the channels and I saw this black and white movie. I said, 'You gotta be kidding me. He was the best track man *and* football player?' And look at what he overcame.

"I knew if I was going to go anywhere in life and make something of myself, I'd have to do it through athletics, the way Jim Thorpe did. I loved the scene where he raced his Dad home. Twelve miles, his Dad's driving a truck and Jim's running, but Jim gets there first. I think he's the greatest athlete of all time."

CHEERS: In 1983, the International Olympic Committee restored Thorpe's gold medals. They presented replicas of the medals to his family. It was long overdue.

JEERS: The writing—the dialog in particular—is as sweet and sticky as maple syrup.

BET YOU DIDN'T KNOW: Director Michael Curtiz won an Academy Award for directing the classic *Casablanca* (1942).

WHAT THEY WROTE AT THE TIME: "The story is not all peaches and cream. [It] shows Thorpe on the skids, depicts his irritability, his heavy drinking, his divorce, his shifting from one team to another and finally the bottom rung with the former champion scratching out a living as a truck driver."—Laura Lee, *Philadelphia Bulletin*

CASTING CALL: The young Jim Thorpe was played by Billy Gray, who later starred as Bud Anderson in TV's *Father Knows Best*.

IF YOU LIKED THIS, YOU'LL LIKE: *The Joe Louis Story* (1953), an honest look at the life of the former heavyweight champion. Real-life boxer Coley Wallace is quite good as the Brown Bomber.

SPORTS-ACTION GRADE: C. The track scenes are well done, aided by Lancaster's athleticism. The football action, however, is pretty crude.

MY FAVORITE SPORTS MOVIE: Actor Dennis Quaid: "I saw Jim Thorpe several times as a kid and it deeply affected me. First of all, the story of the man's skill versus his fight for justice is compelling. Secondly, Lancaster was a terrific performer. And what a great athlete in his own right."

Charles Bronson and James Coburn made some classic films together, including big-budget epics *The Magnificent Seven* and *The Great Escape*. *Hard Times* was their third pairing, and while it was a much smaller film—shot in just 38 days—it may have been the most enjoyable.

In *The Magnificent Seven* and *The Great Escape*, Bronson and Coburn were secondary characters in large ensemble casts. In *Hard Times*, they are front and center and playing to their strengths—Bronson as the stoic loner, and Coburn as the fast-talking hustler who always has a smile on his face and a trick up his sleeve.

Roger Ebert of the *Chicago Sun-Times* is right on when he calls this "a definitive Charles Bronson performance." Bronson himself said it was one of his favorites. He was a man of action, and in *Hard Times* his character—a bare-knuckles fighter named Chaney—is all action. He has very little dialog. Mostly, he speaks with his eyes and his fists.

Bronson said he spoke fewer than 500 words in the entire film. We haven't counted them—you can if you want—but that seems about right. It suits his character, a drifter with one name who rolls into New Orleans on a freight train looking to make a few bucks in the Big Easy's underground boxing scene.

Chaney is a mystery. He has the gray hair and weathered face of a middle-aged man, but he has the muscular torso of a welterweight contender. So how old is he? He doesn't say. Where is he from? He doesn't say. Is he a former boxer? He doesn't say. Is he on the run from the law? From the mob? From an ex-wife? He doesn't say.

Writer-director Walter Hill reveals nothing of Chaney's past and that—combined with Bronson's inscrutable persona—makes him even more interesting. He gives no hint of how long he plans to stick around, or where he may be going next. Each time he finishes a fight and pockets his winnings, there is a chance he'll just hop the next freight and vanish into the night. He keeps everyone, including the viewer, guessing.

Hard Times is set, appropriately, in the 1930s during the Great Depression. When Chaney first meets Spencer "Speed" Weed (Coburn), a New Orleans gambler and wheeler-dealer, he is just off the train with six dollars in his pocket.

"I suppose you've been down the long, hard road," Speed says, eyeing the shabbily dressed stranger.

"Who hasn't?" Chaney replies.

"Every town has somebody who thinks he's tough as a nickel steak," Speed says. "But they all come to old Speed for the dough-re-me."

Speed manages bare-knuckles fighters (they are called "hitters") in illegal matches held on barges and in warehouses. It just so happens the night Chaney arrives, Speed's hitter loses to a hitter managed by another gambler, Chick Gandil (Michael McGuire). Chaney tells Speed he can beat Gandil's guy. Speed is skeptical until

SPEED: "YOU KNOW WHAT THEY SAY, CHICK, THE NEXT BEST THING TO PLAYING AND WINNING IS PLAYING AND LOSING."

Chaney says he will bet his last six dollars on himself.

When Chaney steps in the ring, his burly young opponent sneers. "Hey, Pops," he says, "you're a little old for this, ain't ya?" Chaney, who is outweighed by at least 50 pounds, knocks the big guy stiff with one punch.

Speed realizes he has struck gold with this grizzled hobo. He tells Chaney he will set up the matches and they will split the winnings. Chaney agrees, but tells Speed not to count on a long-term partnership. "I'm just looking to fill a few in-betweens," he says.

Chaney derives no pleasure from fighting. He doesn't take pride in being the toughest guy in town. To him, it is just a way to make a buck. He tries to explain it to Lucy (Jill Ireland, his real-life wife), a woman he meets in New Orleans.

"What does it feel like to knock somebody down?" she asks.

"It makes me feel a hell of a lot better than it does him," Chaney replies.

"That's a reason?" she says.

"There's no reason about it," Chaney says. "Just money."

Chaney knocks off every hitter in New Orleans and takes out a few more in the Bayou. There is no one left for Chaney to fight, so he is preparing to leave when Chick brings in the best hitter from Chicago, a man named Street (Nick Dimitri). Chaney isn't interested. He has enough money and he is ready to move on. Chick and Street find Chaney in a bar, drinking a beer.

"There's no point in avoiding this thing," Chick says. "It's going to happen."

"I could start it right here and now," Street says.

"Yeah, but you won't," Chaney replies.

"You don't think so?" Street says.

"You're not going to do it for free," Chaney says, finishing his beer and heading for the door.

He is right, of course. He and Street aren't two macho knuckleheads looking to flex their muscles in a bar. They are professionals, they fight only for the cash. But we all know it's inevitable that Chaney and Street will square off to answer the question of who's better.

As Ebert writes, "They fight in a steel-mesh bullpen, and there's a certain nobility about them. They may seem to be animals, but they're craftsmen in a way and they respect each other. The real animals are the spectators."

CHEERS: Cinematographer Philip Lathrop, who shot the classic gambling film *The Cincinnati Kid*, uses the same lighting effects to bring just the right atmosphere to the fight scenes.

JEERS: Strother Martin is a great character actor—his blustery general manager in *Slap Shot* is a riot—but he is wasted in *Hard Times*. His character—a medical school dropout who is addicted to opium—seems like he wandered in from another movie.

BET YOU DIDN'T KNOW: Charles Bronson was 54 years old when he filmed *Hard Times*.

DON'T FAIL TO NOTICE: Chick Gandil is the name of one of the Chicago Black Sox who threw the 1919 World Series.

WHAT THEY WROTE AT THE TIME: "Put Charles Bronson in modern clothes and he's a hard-bitten tough guy, but with that cap on he's one of the dispossessed, an honest man who's known hunger."—Pauline Kael, *The New Yorker*

BEST LINE: Speed Weed: "To the best man I know. To the Napoleon of Southern sports. Me."

"I KNOW THAT GUY": Robert Tessier, who plays Chick's henchman, was Shokner, the shaved head convict in *The Longest Yard*.

SPORTS-ACTION GRADE: B-plus. This is Walter Hill's directing debut, and he displays a knack for filming a fight scene. The big fight between Chaney and Street took a week to film, but it was worth it. Bronson and Dimitri (a veteran stuntman) are so into it, you almost wonder if they are fighting for real.

IF YOU LIKED THIS, YOU'LL LIKE: *Fighting*, a 2009 release, with Terrence Howard as a street hustler who recruits a naive hunk (Channing Tatum) into New York's underground fight circuit. The bare-knuckles action is well staged by director Dito Montiel.

39 THE BINGO LONG TRAVELING ALL-STARS & MOTOR KINGS (1976–PG)

SPORT: BASEBALL | STARS: BILLY DEE WILLIAMS, JAMES EARL JONES, RICHARD PRYOR
DIRECTOR: JOHN BADHAM

Billy Dee Williams plays a Satchel Paige spin-off and James Earl Jones evokes Josh Gibson in a funny and sometimes poignant look at black baseball before integration of the major leagues.

The two are stars in the Negro National League, a throwback to the 1930s when players on opposing teams joked with each other during games and socialized off the field in a close-knit society. Quickly, they grow tired of their owners' cheapness and mistreatment of players. Led by Jones's character, slugging catcher Leon Carter (who quotes W.E.B. Du Bois about self determination), they decide to quit working for others and form their own barnstorming team—known as the Bingo Long Traveling All-Stars & Motor Kings. Problem is, the owners of existing black teams won't play them. And white crowds in small towns in the South and Midwest react angrily to seeing their local nine soundly beaten by the visiting "coloreds."

What to do? Bingo (Williams) decides to play it all for laughs, and soon enough the All-Stars and Motor Kings become hardball's version of the Harlem Globetrotters—batting backwards, tossing out exploding balls and playing with enormous gloves.

There's a fine line between humor and humiliation, and the story sometimes crosses it, such as the scene where Bingo pitches in a gorilla suit. But the point that's being nailed home here (albeit heavy-handedly) is that the black players of the era must do whatever they must to survive.

The screen chemistry between Williams and Jones is terrific. Hell, we'll take it any day over their work in *The Empire Strikes Back*. Bingo is impulsive, creative and romantic; Carter is methodical and intellectual. But perhaps the best performance in the movie comes from Richard Pryor, who plays a light-skinned black man so

intent on getting to the big leagues that he tries posing first as a Spanish-speaking Puerto Rican (taking the name Carlos Nevada) and then as a Mohawk-wearing Native American (calling himself Chief Takahoma).

CHEERS: To the "shadow ball" routine, in which the All-Stars take pre-game infield practice in pantomime. They toss around an invisible ball, field imaginary pop-ups, even make diving catches of a Rawlings that doesn't exist. To fans in the stands—and viewers of the movie—it all looks quite real.

JEERS: Wedged into this upbeat story is a violent scene in which Charlie Snow (Pryor) is kidnapped and slashed with a straight razor. He escapes and reels onto the ballfield covered in more blood than the unfortunate Mr. Orange (Tim Roth) from *Reservoir Dogs*.

PIVOTAL SCENE: In the final scene, the All-Stars' rawest player, Esquire Joe Calloway (Stan Shaw) tells the others he has just signed with the Brooklyn Dodgers. Initially, his teammates are resentful—each has accomplished more and paid dues longer. But, of course, the Dodgers are most interested in a young player with the most upside potential.

Their anger fades as they appreciate that the dream they have all held forever will be realized by at least one of them. It's a bittersweet moment that foretells the erasing of baseball's color line—but also the collapse of the Negro leagues.

It's such a great scene that we won't mention this: The movie occurs in 1939 and only covers one season. Wish it weren't so, but that's a full eight years before Jackie Robinson became Major League Baseball's first black player.

99 BEST LINE: Bingo to Leon Carter, after again walking in on his catcher in bed with a floozy: "You keep giving autographs away so freely, and you're gonna run out of ink."

♣ BET YOU DIDN'T KNOW: In the opening scene, the supremely self-confident hurler Bingo stands on the field alone—his teammates lined up in foul territory—and challenges the opposition's leadoff batter to "hit my invite pitch." Of course, any ball hit into fair territory would almost certainly go for a home run.

The bit was inspired by Satchel Paige, who reportedly started games for more than a decade with this combination of showmanship and arrogance. Paige swore no one ever connected with that first pitch.

✔ REALITY CHECK: To thwart an intentional walk, Carter steps over home plate and smacks the ball. That's an automatic out in any league. We're surprised that the umpire— played by former major league ump Emmett Ashford—didn't know that rule.

☞ DON'T FAIL TO NOTICE: All the terrific vintage cars in this movie. The real Satchel Paige was a lover of fancy cars, particularly Packards. In tribute, Bingo drives a bright red convertible in which the main seat is taken out and replaced with an easy chair.

☺ GOOFS: James Earl Jones's weight seems to yo-yo up and down about 30 pounds throughout the movie. In the director's commentary, John Badham explained that when Jones learned during filming that he'd be doing a scene bare-chested, he resolved to get in shape and went on a rigorous diet. Problem is, the movie was not shot chronologically, so the buff Jones scene is inserted about 20 minutes in. In the next shot, ostensibly the day after, he appears to have swallowed a small goat.

◀ CASTING CALL: Well, directing call, anyway. Producers were close to hiring Steven Spielberg for the project in 1975—just as the summer blockbuster *Jaws* was released. Spielberg's huge success with the shark film gave him the opportunity to pursue any movie he wanted. He instead chose to direct *Close Encounters of the Third Kind*.

👀 "I KNOW THAT GUY": The All-Stars centerfielder/ backup catcher, Isaac, is played by Tony Burton. You better know him as Duke, loyal corner man to Apollo Creed and then, Rocky Balboa. Burton is the only actor—other than Burt Young and Sylvester Stallone, of course—to appear in all six *Rocky* movies.

👀 EVEN BETTER "I KNOW THAT GUY": Injured and mute bat boy Rainbow is played for laughs by DeWayne Jessic. Fortunately, he gains his voice back two years later in order to play frathouse party singer Otis "My Man" Day in *Animal House*.

★ SPORTS-ACTION GRADE: No better than a C-plus. Former major league outfielder Leon Wagner lends credibility as "Fat" Sam Popper (he should have kept his real nickname, "Daddy Wags"), as does former Negro leagues alum "Birmingham Sam" Brison. There's even a genuine midget catcher and one-armed first baseman from the Indianapolis Clowns, the team that inspired this story.

Those two both play better than James Earl Jones. "I'm six-foot-one and I know nothing about sports," Jones admitted in an interview with the Baseball Hall of Fame in 2006. "I'm flat footed. I couldn't hit a ball. I had to fake hitting a ball."

✪ IF YOU LIKED THIS, YOU'LL LIKE: Well, unless you count *The Jackie Robinson Story* (1950), or one episode of Ken Burns's PBS *Baseball* documentary, there's never been another worthy movie made about the Negro leagues. We think they deserve a fresh tribute.

◉ REPEATED WATCHING QUOTIENT: Once every 5.6 years—the average length of a major league baseball career.

SEAN PAYTON LOVES THE FILM *ONE FLEW OVER THE CUCKOO'S NEST*. "IT'S JUST AN AMAZING MOVIE THAT I CAN WATCH ANYTIME," SAID PAYTON, HEAD COACH OF THE NEW ORLEANS SAINTS. "I'M A HUGE FAN OF JACK NICHOLSON. THE WHOLE CAST WAS GREAT. IT'S A TRUE CLASSIC."

PAYTON CONSIDERS *CUCKOO'S NEST* AT LEAST PARTLY A SPORTS MOVIE. THAT'S BECAUSE THERE ARE SEVERAL KEY SCENES WHICH INVOLVE SPORTS. ONE IS THE MOMENT MENTAL PATIENT RANDALL MCMURPHY (NICHOLSON) BEGINS HIS REVOLT AGAINST AUTHORITY WHEN NURSE RATCHED (LOUISE FLETCHER) REFUSES TO TURN ON THE TELEVISION FOR THE WORLD SERIES.

FINALLY, MCMURPHY SITS IN FRONT OF THE BLANK SCREEN AND BEGINS CALLING HIS OWN PLAY-BY-PLAY: "KOUFAX LOOKS DOWN. HE'S LOOKING AT THE GREAT MICKEY MANTLE. HERE COMES THE PITCH. MANTLE SWINGS. IT'S A FUCKING HOME RUN."

THE OTHER PATIENTS GATHER AROUND, CHEERING AS MCMURPHY CONTINUES CALLING THE IMAGINARY GAME. ANOTHER MEMORABLE SCENE IS MCMURPHY ORGANIZING A BASKETBALL GAME AND GETTING THE GIANT INDIAN (WILL SAMPSON) TO STAND UNDER THE BASKET. MCMURPHY TOSSES HIM THE BALL AND SHOUTS: "PUT IT IN THE BASKET, CHIEF." THE INDIAN DUNKS THE BALL AND FOR THE FIRST TIME, A SMILE CROSSES HIS FACE.

SPORTS PLAY SUCH A SIGNIFICANT ROLE IN OUR LIVES THAT MANY FILMS—MURDER MYSTERIES, ROMANTIC COMEDIES, EVEN BIBLICAL EPICS—INCLUDE SCENES OF ATHLETIC COMPETITION. PAYTON GAVE US ONE THOUGHT. WE CAME UP WITH A FEW OF OUR OWN.

TEN MEMORABLE SPORTS SCENES FROM NON-SPORTS MOVIES

Strangers on a Train (1951). Written by Raymond Chandler and directed by Alfred Hitchcock, this is a classic suspense film. Tennis pro Guy Haines (Farley Granger) meets Bruno Anthony (Robert Walker) on a train. At first, Anthony seems nice enough, but the more he talks, it is clear he knows far too much about Haines (a bad marriage, a wife who is pregnant with another man's child, a romance with a senator's daughter). Anthony has his own issues involving his father. He wants the old man dead.

He makes Haines a proposition: He will kill Haines' wife if Haines agrees to kill his father. That way there is nothing linking them to the victim so they will get away with the crime. Haines thinks it is just a sick joke and leaves with a casual, "Whatever you say, Bruno."

He doesn't think any more of it until his wife is found murdered. Haines now realizes he has made a Faustian deal with a psychopath. Soon, Anthony is demanding to know when Haines will carry out his part of the arrangement. He tells Haines if he backs out, he will frame him for his wife's murder.

The famous scene takes place at a tennis match. Anthony, who is stalking Haines, is in the crowd. The spectators are following the flight of the ball, their heads moving back and forth, all except for Anthony who is staring straight ahead, his eyes locked on Haines. It is a haunting shot, one of Hitchcock's best.

Ben-Hur (1959). The chariot race in Ben-Hur was filmed half a century ago long before the advent of computer-generated special effects, which makes its breath-taking power all the more remarkable. The 18-acre set was built outside of Rome and 8,000 extras were hired for the big scene. Seventy-eight horses were trained for the five-week shoot.

There were rumors that at least one stunt man was killed during the filming, but director William Wyler denied it. He said three life-sized dummies were used and that is what the audiences saw being trampled. The danger was real, however. An infirmary was built on the set, but Wyler said most of those treated there had nothing more serious than sunburn.

Wyler shot so much film of the race that the ratio of footage shot to footage used was 263 to one—thought to be the highest ratio ever for a 65mm film. The MGM studio spent $15 million (a record at the time) to produce *Ben-Hur*, but it was rewarded with a $75 million box office and 11 Academy Awards.

M*A*S*H (1970). The film directed by Robert Altman is a dark comedy set in a Mobile Army Surgical Hospital (MASH) during the Korean War. Like many Altman films, it has an episodic quality with a lot of disjointed scenes—some work, some don't—but one scene that definitely works is the football game.

It is supposed to be a friendly game between two MASH units, but to spice things up they put $5,000 in a pot, winner take all. The 4077th brings in a ringer: Oliver "Spearchucker" Jones (Fred Williamson), an Army neurosurgeon who previously played for the San Francisco 49ers. The other side imports its own ringers, including Noland Smith, Tom Woodeshick and Jack Concannon, all NFL players in cameo roles.

Also on the 4077th team is Corporal Judson (Timmy Brown, a star running back with the NFL Eagles). The 4077th wins the game when the center uses the Hidden Ball Trick to score the deciding touchdown. Meanwhile their opponents pass a marijuana joint down the bench.

It is worth noting while the film is set in a war zone the only gunshot heard is the referee's pistol at the end of the game.

Black Sunday (1977). This is the first disaster movie filmed against the backdrop of a live event: Super Bowl X at the Orange Bowl in Miami. Adapted from a best-selling novel, the film tells the story of Arab terrorists vowing to hit America "where it hurts." They hijack the Goodyear blimp, arm it with explosives and head for the Super Bowl with a psychotic former Vietnam POW (Bruce Dern) at the controls.

Joe Robbie, the late owner of the Miami Dolphins, appears briefly in the film, rejecting pleas from an Israeli officer (Robert Shaw) to call off the game. "Cancel the Super Bowl?" he says. "That's like canceling Christmas."

CBS broadcasters Pat Summerall and Tom Brookshier have cameos and the game-winning touchdown scored by Pittsburgh's Lynn Swann can be seen from behind the end zone in one of the scenes.

The Great Santini (1979). Marine pilot "Bull" Meechum is a complex character, a man who preaches discipline yet is unable to control his own temper. Screenwriter Lewis Carlino uses a scene with Bull (Robert Duvall) and his son Ben (Michael O'Keefe) on the basketball court to reveal the demons within the man.

Ben, a high school jock, is playing one-on-one against Bull. What starts as a friendly game turns nasty when Ben drives past his father to score the winning basket. It is the first time anyone in the family has ever beaten Bull at anything. As his wife and two daughters congratulate Ben, Bull snarls, "You gotta win by two." When his wife protests, Bull slaps her.

"Who the hell asked you anything?" he says.

Ben refuses to play, saying the game is over. Bull begins bouncing the ball off the boy's head as he follows him into the house. "Whaddya going to do, cry?" he says. "Go ahead, cry, momma's boy."

The scene is so well acted (both Duvall and O'Keefe scored Academy Award nominations) and feels so real, it is almost painful to watch. Yet it says everything about what lies ahead for the doomed Bull and his inability to separate life in the Marine Corps and life with his family.

Diner (1982). Director Barry Levinson tells the story of four friends coming of age in 1950s Baltimore. Part of the movie involves their love affair with the Colts. Eddie (Steve Guttenberg) decides to get married, but his girlfriend (Ellen Barkin) must first pass a test proving her knowledge of the football team.

As she takes the oral exam, Eddie's buddies listen through the door. When Eddie asks her, "Who set the record for the longest run from scrimmage by a rookie?" one of the guys blurts out, "Alan Ameche."

"I heard that," Eddie shouts. He pulls the question from the quiz, despite his fiancée's insistence that she knew the right answer. Ultimately, she fails—by one point. Eddie emerges from the room, shaking his head.

"The wedding's off," he solemnly announces.

Levinson, a Baltimore native, wrote the original test and sent it to Ernie Accorsi, the Colts general manager at the time. Accorsi told Levinson the questions were too easy. He put together a new, tougher quiz. Example: What were the Colts' original colors? Answer: green and gray. Accorsi's test is the one used in the film.

Triumph of the Spirit (1989). This film tells the story of Salamo Arouch (Willem Dafoe), a Greek boxing champion who is captured by the Germans in World War II and sent to the Auschwitz concentration camp.

The Germans learn of Arouch's background and arrange a series of boxing matches for their entertainment. Arouch is ordered to fight other prisoners as the SS officers place bets. The prisoners are literally fighting for their lives because the loser is sent to the gas chamber. For Arouch, it is an impossible situation. If he wins, he sentences his opponent to death. If he loses, he dies himself.

Arouch won enough fights to survive the Holocaust and knowing it is a true story makes it especially gripping. It was shot on the site of the Auschwitz camp (the first film to do so) and the details are so carefully observed (wooden shoes on the prisoners) it is a film that stays with you long after you've left the theater.

Forrest Gump (1994). Chased by bullies, Forrest Gump (Tom Hanks) dashes through an open gate and runs right through a football practice being conducted by a man in a houndstooth hat. Forrest outruns not only the bullies but all the football players. "Who is that?" asks the man in the hat, who is obviously supposed to be Alabama football coach Paul "Bear" Bryant.

"Just a local idiot," an assistant coach replies.

The next time we see Forrest, he is wearing an Alabama uniform and returning a kickoff for a touchdown. In his voiceover, Forrest says, "And can you believe it? I got to go to college." He runs through the end zone, through the band and disappears into the tunnel.

"He must be the stupidest SOB alive," the coach says. "But he sure is fast."

Buffalo 66 (1998). Vincent Gallo always wanted to make a film with a football theme and since he grew up in Buffalo, it figured that the Bills would be the heart of the story. Make that broken heart. Gallo wrote the script for *Buffalo 66* after watching the Bills lose to the Giants in Super Bowl XXV.

"I needed that win, I needed to shake off the feeling that I'd always be from a loser town," Gallo said. "But they lost in the same way Buffalo loses all the time. They lost in the way all my friends from high school lost in their jobs, their marriages. It was all together. I can't tell you how painful it was."

Gallo pours all that pain into the script for *Buffalo 66*. Billy Brown (Gallo) loses ten grand betting on the Bills in the Super Bowl. When he can't come up with the money, he repays the bet by taking a fall for the bookie (Mickey Rourke). He does a five-year stretch in prison and returns home to see his mother (Angelica Huston) who still hasn't forgiven him for causing her to miss the last title that the Bills won—the 1965 AFL Championship Game. She went into labor with Billy that day.

"I've hated him ever since," she says.

***The Year My Parents Went on Vacation* (2008).** This is the story of a 12-year-old boy (Michel Joelsas) so immersed in the World Cup that he does not see the turmoil around him. The film is set in Brazil, 1970, when the nation was under totalitarian rule.

Year begins with the boy's parents driving him to Sao Paulo. He is told he will stay with his grandfather while Mom and Dad "go on vacation." However, it is clear the parents are political dissidents on the run from the government. They may not be coming back at all, but the boy grasps none of it. He is too busy reading about Pele.

The parents drop him off at the grandfather's flat not knowing the old man died that morning. An elderly neighbor takes the boy in and introduces him to a new life in the Jewish enclave. When he is not staring out the window waiting for his parents, the boy is rooting for the Brazilian soccer team. It is the one thing in his world that he can count on.

The most affecting scenes are those showing the people of Sao Paolo—all ages and nationalities—crowded around televisions watching the World Cup. Director Cao Hamburger seems to be making a point about the power of sport, that is, it can overcome even tyranny, if only for awhile.

40 THE ROCKET: THE LEGEND OF MAURICE RICHARD (2005–PG)

SPORT: HOCKEY | STARS: ROY DUPUIS, STEPHEN MCHATTIE, JULIE LEBRETON
DIRECTOR: CHARLES BINAME

The year is 1955 and the city of Montreal is engulfed in a riot. Cars are aflame, angry people fill the streets and the issue is . . . hockey?

Indeed it is, and if you're not a devotee of the sport, the opening of *The Rocket* will have you wondering: Why would otherwise level-headed folks lose their sanity over what we learn is the suspension of their star player by the National Hockey League commissioner?

The so-called "Richard Riot" serves as the opening and closing bookends for this marvelous movie. Maurice Richard, star winger for the Montreal Canadiens, was punished with a season-ending ban for slugging a referee. What *The Rocket* explains is why Richard acted as he did and why the good people of one of North America's great cities followed suit in their rage.

The record books show Richard to be one of the all-time superstars of his sport, perhaps the most dynamic player of the NHL's pre-expansion era. But he was more than that. He was, to French Canadians, an icon—an ethnic hero in an age when Quebecois were regarded as second-class citizens, even in a city where they were the majority. That he emerged from humble beginnings in Montreal only served to make him more of a superman to the local working class.

The prejudice even carried into the locker rooms. In one notable scene, Canadiens coach Dick Irvin (Stephen McHattie) berates his players: "You Frenchies are all alike—nothing but cowards. It's in your blood. You're nothing more than chicken droppings." They are not even allowed to speak French on the bench.

Richard, who is modest and stoic, absorbs the insults through most of his career. He overcomes a double-whammy reputation of being brittle (sort of an Eric Lindros of his era) and afraid to fight (conquered when he kayos a New York Ranger tough guy) to eventually become a star with the blend of skill and determination rarely seen in sport.

And, over time, he gains the courage to speak up off the ice. In one memorable scene, Richard (played magnificently by Quebec native Roy Dupuis) spills his guts to a newspaper columnist, creating a national buzz with his stories of the taunting and slighting of French-Canadian players.

The politics in *The Rocket* are certainly interesting. But the blood-and-guts portrayal of the sport of hockey in the era is what makes this movie. "These guys were hurt all the time," director Charles Biname told Matthew Hays of the Canadian Broadcast System. "It was routine. And they were exhausted. We talked a lot about (Ridley Scott's) *Gladiator*. And I really wanted to capture hockey the way (Martin) Scorsese captured boxing with *Raging Bull*."

Biname succeeds. *The Rocket* is not without flaws—the character of Richards's wife, played by Julie LeBreton, doesn't get to do much more than fret and stare over two hours. In addition, the movie was filmed with some actors speaking English and others speaking French, so half of it is clumsily dubbed for either audience.

Overall, however, it terrifically evokes a time when sport and society were much different. Dupuis, unknown to American audiences, seems to have been born to play this role.

Any sports fan should enjoy *The Rocket*. Hockey fans will marvel at it. Fans of the *bleu, blanc et rouge* will be overcome with joy.

CHEERS: To the accurate re-creation of hockey from the era. From the old lamps suspended over the ice surface to the white wool sweaters on referees, everything is designed to take you back to an NHL that few fans today got to see. Goalies have no masks (although they sport lots of facial scars), players use straight-bladed sticks and undersized pads. Hell, even the bottles of Molson have old-time labels.

JEERS: To some of the voices used in the French-to-English dubbing. Several of the characters sound straight out of a 1950s Japanese horror film.

SIGN OF THE TIMES: An early newspaper column critiquing Richard reads: "The concern was that he was just too fragile. Now it certainly looks like the Canadiens are stuck with a lemon—yes, a lemon that's so simple to crush. If he were to finish on top, it would be on top of a trash heap." They sure don't write 'em like that anymore.

PIVOTAL SCENE: Once labeled as soft and injury prone, Richard is taken down by a cheap shot in Game 7 of the 1952 Semi-Finals against the Boston Bruins. Concussed and unconscious, he is carried off the ice and stitched up in the locker room, even as his bleary eyes struggle to focus on the attending trainer. He returns to the game—blood-stained jersey and all—with just minutes left and the score tied, 1-1. Of course, he scores the series-winning goal on a phenomenal play.

You could label it sappy and implausible. Except that it's true.

DON'T FAIL TO NOTICE: The Stanley Cup, before that wedding cake of a trophy had all the engraved tiers of names tacked to it. The trophy Richard carries overhead is less than half the size of the three-foot-high Cup that teams win today. By the way, Richard had lots of practice holding it—he won the Stanley Cup eight times.

WHAT THEY WROTE AT THE TIME: "You get the same isolated sounds and images of violence in the crushing body checks and on-ice fights as you do in the boxing scenes in *Raging Bull*. Ultimately, however, *The Rocket* shares more in common with films such as *Cinderella Man* or *Rocky* in the sense the protagonist becomes a symbol for the working class."—Erik Floren, *Edmonton Sun*

REALITY CHECK: The Canadiens wear white jerseys both at home and on the road in the same season. In the 1950s NHL, teams wore white at home and colored jerseys on the road.

DICK IRVIN: **"YOU FRENCHIES ARE ALL ALIKE — NOTHING BUT COWARDS. IT'S IN YOUR BLOOD. YOU'RE NOTHING BUT CHICKEN DROPPINGS."**

⊙ REPEATED WATCHING QUOTIENT: At two hours-plus, it could stand to lose a good 20 minutes of hand-wringing moments between Richard and his wife. But if you stumble on one of the game scenes, you're not going anywhere.

★ SPORTS-ACTION GRADE: A-plus. The on-ice action is the best we've ever seen and really captures the style of hockey from the era. The shots in slow-mo, from low angles, high angles, even looking up from under the ice are evocative of the creative work done by NFL Films. We only wish there had been more game sequences.

◀ CASTING CALL: You could start a decent team with the real-life NHL players making cameos in this film: Vincent Lecavalier, Mike Ricci, Ian Laperriere, Stephane Quintal. Our favorite was Sean Avery (former boyfriend of Elisha Cuthbert), who appears as Bob "Killer" Dill, an undersized (five-foot-eight) goon for the New York Rangers in the 1940s. One year after making the movie, Avery became, in real life, an undersized (five-foot-nine) goon for the New York Rangers.

99 BEST LINE: Coach Dick Irvin: "Check your skates for cement, Richard. Something's slowing you down. Maybe you're too old. Maybe we need to get you a walker—with some skate blades on it."

And that was during a season in which Richard scored 38 goals.

👓 "I KNOW THAT GUY": McHattie, who can be nasty and cutting as Coach Irvin, knows how to do cruel. He was the sadistic killer who meets his end with a coffee pot to the head early in *A History of Violence*, also filmed in 2005.

⊛ IF YOU LIKED THIS, YOU'LL LIKE: *The Sweater*, a 10-minute 1980 cartoon about a Quebec lad who adores Maurice Richard. The boy endures great shame when he receives a Christmas gift of the jersey of the Toronto Maple Leafs, the favorite team of Canada's English-speaking population.

🎞 MY FAVORITE SPORTS MOVIE: Marty Biron, veteran NHL goalie and native of Lac St. Charles, Quebec: "The movie really shows what an important and heroic figure Maurice Richard was to all French-Canadians at the time. It shows what hockey meant, and what the Rocket meant to the people of Quebec."

41 **EIGHT MEN OUT** (1988–PG)

SPORT: BASEBALL | STARS: DAVID STRATHAIRN, JOHN CUSACK, D.B. SWEENEY, CHARLIE SHEEN | DIRECTOR: JOHN SAYLES

It's the fall of 1919 and the Chicago White Sox have just clinched the American League pennant. First baseman Chick Gandil (Michael Rooker) is celebrating at a South-side tap room when he is offered a dangerous proposition by gambler "Sport" Sullivan. The out-of-town fixer wants Gandil to round up a half-dozen teammates willing to drop the World Series for $10,000 apiece.

"You can go back to Boston and turn seventy grand at the drop of a hat?" asks Gandil. "I find that hard to believe."

"You say," counters Sullivan, "that you can find seven men on the best club that ever took the field willing to throw the World Series? I find *that* hard to believe."

"Well," says Gandil, "you never played for Charlie Comiskey."

So begins *Eight Men Out*, director John Sayles apolo-

gia for the worst scandal in baseball history. Sayles wrote the screenplay off of the highly acclaimed 1963 book by Eliot Asinof.

In this accounting of the infamous 1919 Black Sox, characters come in several easy-to-identify stereotypes. Baseball's owners, led by Charles Comiskey (Clifton James) are greedy and as blind as Mr. Magoo. Reporters (played by Sayles himself and by real Chicago newspaper legend Studs Terkel) are cynical, yet wise. And players are either too angry at ownership to fret about the fix, or too dumb to understand the consequences. Put outfielder Shoeless Joe Jackson (D.B. Sweeney) and third baseman Buck Weaver (John Cusack) in that last category.

The only character with real depth is aging pitcher Eddie Cicotte (David Strathairn), the nominal star of the film. Cicotte agrees to the bribe after Comiskey ostensibly cheats him out of a $10,000 bonus, but his sense of guilt is such that he can't even tell his wife the truth. In one of the best scenes, Cicotte turns over his hotel pillow to find rolls of cash freshly delivered by the fixers. He just stares at the money, too ashamed to even pick it up.

Overall, much of the movie comes across as an excuse for eight men whom—regardless of how oppressive and penurious management might have been—conspired to lose sport's biggest event. You almost get the sense that if Sayles were doing a movie on baseball's recent steroid scandal, Roger Clemens would be a victim of all that Congressional bullying and Mark McGwire would become Shoeless (or Witless) Mark.

What *Eight Men Out* fails to address (and what history appears to have forgotten) is how widespread game fixing was in baseball's early days. According to baseball author Bill James, at least 38 players were involved in the scandals of the era. More than 20—not just these eight—were banned from the sport after Judge Kenesaw Mountain Landis became commissioner. Huge names, like Ty Cobb and Tris Speaker, were rumored to be on the take. The shock is not so much that the 1919 World Series was rigged, it's that such a thing hadn't occurred earlier.

There is also historical debate over whether Jackson was involved in the fix or just an innocent bystander. Sayles argues that Shoeless Joe was pushed into the conspiracy by peer pressure, agreed to take money but received none of it, and—by hitting .375 in the Series—did nothing but give his all. Hey, we don't know. We weren't there.

This is not to say that this isn't a worthwhile movie. The settings and old-time baseball scenes are terrific, from the baggy, tobacco-stained flannel uniforms to the National Anthem singer using a megaphone to pump up the volume. Small details are perfect, such as how pitchers' windups were different then than they are today. Notice how the outfielders leave their gloves on the field at the end of each inning. They really did it that way up through the 1940s.

The off-field scenes, as well, take you back to a boozy ragtime era of speakeasies, cigars and street urchins. Before TV, before radio, drinking men would gather at so-called "gentlemen's clubs" (this is before strip joints co-opted that phrase). As a telegraph wired the game's progress, workers would move cutouts of players around a big wooden board. Hey, it wasn't exactly ESPN.com's "Real Time Scores," but it was the best they could do at the time.

Here's the bottom line: *Eight Men Out* is a worthy watch, full of the color and texture of old-time baseball. The guilty players are misunderstood and management is truly evil. There's a good story here. We just think it could have been told better.

CHEERS: To veteran actor Michael Lerner's portrayal of fixer Arnold Rothstein as an unsmiling stoic who dines alone and talks on a solid-gold telephone.

"I was the fat kid they wouldn't let play," Rothstein explains. " 'Sit down, fat boy; learn something.' Well, I learned something. Pretty soon, I owned the game."

JEERS: We kept asking ourselves—if the reporters recognize that the games are fixed, and the fans suspect that the games are fixed, how come manager Kid Gleason (John Mahoney) takes so long to catch on? Not until Game Seven, with his team down four games to two (they played best-of-nine games that year), does Gleason question Cicotte. And he sure does it damned gently for a guy whose career is going down the tubes.

WHAT THEY WROTE AT THE TIME: "If John Sayles were a ballplayer, they'd call him Lefty—not for his pitching arm but for his politics. The devoutly liberal filmmaker's political point of view is certain. It's his dramatic focus that sometimes gets fuzzy, as in the diffuse baseball drama."—Rita Kempley, *Washington Post*

GOOFS: Not that we're sticklers for this kind of thing, but left-handed hitter Eddie Collins (Bill Irwin) bats right here, and southpaw Dickey Kerr (Jace Alexander) throws righty.

PIVOTAL SCENE: The night before the verdict in the game-fixing trial, Cicotte—without ever actually admitting guilt to his wife—explains to her the roots of his bitterness.

Cicotte: "I always figured it was talent that made a man big. If I was the best at something. I mean, we're the guys they come to see. Without us, there ain't a ball game.

"Yeah, but look at who's holding the money," he continues, "and look at who's facing a jail cell. I mean talent don't mean nothing. And where's Comiskey . . . and Rothstein? Out in the back room cutting deals. That's the damned conspiracy."

Wife: "You would have won, too. You would have beat those guys easily."

Cicotte: "Well, won't nobody ever know that now."

✔ **REALITY CHECK:** Kerr tells his manager, Kid Gleason, that, in the first game he ever attended as a boy, he saw Gleason throw a no-hitter to beat Cy Young. In fact, Gleason never threw a no-hitter. Beyond that, Gleason permanently moved from the mound to second base in 1896, when Kerr was three years old.

◉ **REPEATED WATCHING QUOTIENT:** Once for the story; once more for the 1919 atmosphere.

🖐 **MY FAVORITE SPORTS MOVIE:** Hall of Fame catcher Yogi Berra: "I liked *Eight Men Out* because it showed that Shoeless Joe Jackson didn't bet on any games. He knew about [the fix] and didn't do anything about it and it kept him out of the Hall of Fame. That scandal hung over the game for years. When I broke into the big leagues [1946], we weren't allowed to talk to the fans before a game. If we got caught, we got fined. They were afraid that we might be talking to gamblers. That all went back to the Black Sox."

42 THE FRESHMAN (1925–NR)

SPORT: COLLEGE FOOTBALL | STAR: HAROLD LLOYD
DIRECTORS: FRED C. NEWMEYER, SAM TAYLOR

The first truly successful sports movie churned out of Hollywood and the only silent film in this book, *The Freshman* still holds up more than 80 years later for its endearing comedy and well-choreographed football scenes.

Harold "Speedy" Lamb (Lloyd) arrives at Tate University desperate to become the most popular student on campus. Problem is, he's a total geek, from his Harry Potter glasses to the fast-step jig he performs whenever he is introduced. In an effort to make friends, Speedy buys the entire student body an ice cream cone (well, this *was* the Prohibition era), and hosts a party, where he winds up the butt of jokes by the campus troublemaker (Brooks Benedict). About the only person not taking advantage of the well-meaning sap is pretty Peggy (Jobyna Ralston), who finds his naiveté endearing.

In a plotline that combines *Rudy* and *Revenge of the Nerds*, Speedy tries out for the varsity eleven at Tate, a school described as "a large football stadium with a college attached." Hmm, sounds a lot like an early version of USC.

Naturally, he's awful—punting the ball backwards over his head, whiffing on the tackling dummy and steamrolling the head coach. Although the coach (Pat Harmon) appears to have a sadistic streak bordering on Frank Kush ("so tough he shaves with a blowtorch"), he takes a liking to the overeager freshman. Speedy stays on as the waterboy, but is allowed to believe he is actually a substitute. He even wears jersey No. 0.

It all leads up to the big game against top-ranked Union State, in front of what appears to be 90,000 fans. Injuries deplete Tate's bench, and in comes our hero. Speedy, of course, scores the winning touchdown (we suspect you saw that plot spoiler coming), gets the girl and becomes—as he aimed to be—the Big Man on Campus.

If you've never watched a silent movie, *The Freshman*

is a good place to start. Think of it as an extended Benny Hill skit. Lloyd was second only to Charlie Chaplin among silent screen comics of the 1920s, the Red Sox to Chaplin's Yankees. This movie grossed $3 million when it came out, which was considered pretty good. Chaplin's *Gold Rush* grossed $4.2 million, which was the record-setting comedy at the time.

CHEERS: Speedy gets four touches in the game—a pass reception, a run on a fake punt and two punt returns. Judging from our estimate, he combines for 205 yards on the four plays—a better average than Forrest Gump. Why wasn't this guy drafted?

JEERS: Good luck finding a print of this movie that doesn't seem like it was stored underwater for the last few decades.

SIGN OF THE TIMES: College comedies sure were nothing like *Old School* or *Animal House* back in the 20s. Tate University seems mostly like a country club, with spoiled white kids strolling around toting tennis rackets, golf clubs and ukuleles. And what's with all those beanies?

BEST LINE: The Coach exhorting his squad: "You dubs are dead from the dandruff down." Hey, it isn't much, but it's the most they could fit on a caption card.

REALITY CHECK: With seconds to go in the game, and holding a slight lead, Union State gets the ball first-and-ten at their own one-yard line. What's their strategy? Punt the ball. Huh? Someone alert Amos Alonzo Stagg.

DON'T FAIL TO NOTICE: Lloyd blew off his right thumb and forefinger when a prop bomb exploded during filming of another movie in 1920. He apparently spent a fortune for a prosthetic glove, which is clearly visible in several of the game scenes.

☺ **GOOFS:** On Speedy's game-winning punt return, we counted at least 18 opponents trying to tackle him.

◉ **REPEATED WATCHING QUOTIENT:** *The Freshman* was added to the National Film Registry in 1990. It is listed at No. 79 on the American Film Institute's "100 Funniest Movies" list. So, sure, why not?

✸ **IF YOU LIKED THIS, YOU'LL LIKE:** Seventy-five years later, Harold Lloyd's granddaughter, Suzanne Lloyd, sued the makers of *The Waterboy* for copyright infringement. A judge ruled against her, saying the similarities were too general. We're not legal geniuses, but having watched both, we get the feeling that Adam Sandler must have studied *The Freshman* with a notebook in his hands.

★ **SPORTS-ACTION GRADE:** Solid B. Not bad, considering the times. Lloyd, five-foot-ten but pretty scrawny, was a terrific athlete. The football scenes were filmed on the field at the Rose Bowl, and the crowd scenes were shot at California Memorial Stadium during halftime of a game between UC Berkeley and Stanford. Players from USC portrayed members of both Tate and Union, which makes it appear more realistic.

43 MURDERBALL (2005–R)

SPORT: WHEELCHAIR RUGBY | STARS: MARK ZUPAN, JOE SOARES
DIRECTORS: HENRY ALEX RUBIN, DANA ADAM SHAPIRO

The first clue you get that *Murderball* is not the typical overly sympathetic film about disabled people occurs in its opening minutes. Joe Soares, coach of the Canadian wheelchair rugby team, is shooed from the sidelines of a game between two other countries by a female official.

"Fuck you," Soares mutters. "Bitch."

Later in the movie, one of the American players is insulted when a guest at a wedding confuses him for a competitor in the Special Olympics—rather than the 2004 Paralympics.

"We're not going for a hug," he snaps. "We're going for a fucking gold medal."

This is not to say that *Murderball* is a documentary about angry young men (well, some of them are). Rather, it's a look at extremely competitive world-class ath-

letes—who can be as intimidating and foul-mouthed as most extremely competitive world-class athletes—but happen to be confined to wheelchairs.

Simply said, *Murderball* is an intimate (sometimes *really* intimate) look at the lives of members of the American and Canadian Paralympic quadriplegic rugby teams over a two-year period leading to the 2004 Paralympic Games in Athens, Greece. It is as entertaining as any documentary you will ever see, more revealing than any A&E biography, and as dramatic as most of the scripted sports movies in this book.

It covers an ultra-violent sport that few know exist. Wheelchair rugby defies the standard belief that people who cannot walk should be handled with care. Rather, the competitors—some paralyzed, others missing limbs—strap themselves into armored chariots, which they propel into each other at high speeds. The game is played on a basketball court, and points are scored when a player crosses the opponent's end line holding the ball. But mostly, it seems, they collide like souped-up bumper cars. As one player says, "It's basically kill the man with the ball."

Indeed, the title of the movie comes from the original name of the sport, which really bears little resemblance to traditional rugby. But, as American star Mark Zupan, one of the subjects of the movie, notes, "We had to change the name. You really can't market something called 'murderball' to corporate sponsors."

Unfortunately, it's equally difficult to market something titled *Murderball* to filmgoers. The movie grossed less than $2 million in theaters after its 2005 release. Perhaps some people equated the name with a *Mad Max*-like futuristic thriller. Others, it seems, were not intrigued about a sports documentary about the disabled.

That's a shame, because there's so much more here. *Murderball* is at its best when it profiles the men who have already won one huge battle in their lives—the mental war of coming to terms with their damaged bodies. That said, this movie is less about people who overcome disability than it is about guys who like banging into other guys, drinking beer, swapping lies about sex and creating a culture of brotherhood.

There are two central characters here. One is Zupan, a Type-A Texan decked out in tattoos and a menacing red goatee. He's got a compelling personality, an attractive girlfriend (who speaks openly about her attraction to handicapped men) and a brutally honest way of speaking.

Zupan's story begins with the injury that occurred when he was in high school. His best friend's drunk driving caused the accident that threw Zupan into a canal and paralyzed his lower body. Their friendship ended that night—Zupan seething with anger and the friend wracked with guilt. Now, 10 years later, the two attempt a reconciliation. We watch as the nervous friend travels to a tournament to watch Zupan compete, unsure if he can cope with the sight of his old buddy in a wheelchair. You find yourself feeling pain for both men.

If Zupan is the film's hero, the antagonist is Joe Soares, who has been in a wheelchair since his childhood bout with polio. The sport's Babe Ruth from the 1990s, Soare's best playing days are over. After being cut from Team USA, Soares—a Tampa Bay resident—latches on as coach of the Canadian team (taking the American playbook with him). And this provides *Murderball's* spark: The Yanks view him as quad rugby's Benedict Arnold, while Soares is on a vengeful mission to beat the guys whom he believes abandoned him.

Soares, 42 when the movie began filming, resembles a young Robert Duvall, which is perfect since his personality mirrors Bull Meechum from *The Great Santini*. He is manically intense with his men. At home, he seems almost bullying toward his son, a bookish, viola-playing 13-year-old whose aversion to sports seems to embarrass Soares.

Midway through the film, Soares suffers a heart attack. This is amazingly filmed stuff, with the camera peering right into the emergency room. As he recovers, Soares softens, leading to an emotionally touching scene between father and son.

There is no softening, however, on the court. The story arc in *Murderball* leads up to a medal-round match between America and Canada at the 2004 Paralympics. And that's where this terrific movie becomes a terrific sports movie. We won't give away the ending, except to say the old ABC show *Wide World of Sports* could have easily used footage from the game for its "thrill of victory, agony of defeat" montage.

🍺 **CHEERS:** In recent decades, Hollywood has portrayed the disabled—along with Native Americans and Southern blacks—as completely virtuous, entirely sympathetic and typically victims. This film does not fall into those cliches. As Zupan's friends explain in a scene at his 10-year high school reunion, "Mark was an SOB before the accident, and he's an SOB now." Hey, boys will be boys, even when they happen to be sitting in wheelchairs.

🍺 **JEERS:** It's rewarding to witness the triumphs and travails of these young men, including a discussion of the challenges in their sex lives. But did the directors really need to insert a graphic sex instructional film that is shown to rehabilitating disabled people? Maybe this wouldn't have bothered us so much if we hadn't taken our 75-year-old mother to the film.

WHAT THEY WROTE AT THE TIME: "*Murderball* is a *Rocky*-esque sports saga with a rowdy, irascible cast of characters who demonstrate conclusively that being in a wheelchair does nothing to dampen the spirit of balls-out macho competition."—Andrew O'Hehir, Salon.com

PIVOTAL SCENE: A before-and-after side plot to the movie follows a young man named Keith Cavill, a dead ringer for Jeff Gordon who is paralyzed in a motocross race and undergoes 10 months of painful rehabilitation. You watch over Cavill's shoulder as he moves out of rehab into a modified apartment—sadly absorbing the impact that he will never again be able to use a normal toilet and shower.

Later, Cavill is introduced to Zupan at a quad rugby demonstration. He climbs into one of the souped-up wheelchairs. Suddenly, the former racer is reinvigorated. "It's unreal," he says with a smile. "I could run into anything." As nervous nurses hold him back, Cavill feels his old competitive juices stirring. "This is great," he says. "I want to go hit stuff."

DON'T FAIL TO NOTICE: The most honest questions posed to the athletes come not from adults in the film—some of whom seem intimidated by the wheelchair athletes—but from children. During a visit to a grade school, one little boy asks quadruple amputee Bob Lujano, "How do you eat pizza with your elbows?"

"I just pick it up," says Lujano. "No arms, no legs, no problem." And both he and the little boy smile.

SPORTS-ACTION GRADE: B-plus. While odds are that you know nothing about the rules and strategies of quad rugby, the game sequences can be downright thrilling. The directors rigged cameras onto the players' chairs to give viewers a direct point of view into the speed and violence of the sport.

BEST LINE: Zupan, summing up his rivalry with Soares: "If Joe was on fire on the side of the road, I wouldn't piss on him to put it out."

"I KNOW THAT GUY": If you followed NFL games on NBC or CBS in recent years you may recognize Beasley Reece. He's here as a Tampa-area sports reporter doing a standup report on Soares. These days, Reece is the sports director of CBS's Philadelphia affiliate.

BET YOU DIDN'T KNOW: When the movie was first screened at the 2005 Sundance Festival, Zupan was asked whether—if he had the power—he would turn back the clock to undo his paralyzing injury. Zupan said, "No, I don't think so. My injury has led me to opportunities and experiences and friendships I would never have had before. And it has taught me about myself . . . In some ways, it's the best thing that ever happened to me."

REPEATED WATCHING QUOTIENT: The message comes through the first time. You probably won't need a second viewing.

44 THE BAD NEWS BEARS (1976–PG)

SPORT: BASEBALL | **STARS:** WALTER MATTHAU, TATUM O'NEAL
DIRECTOR: MICHAEL RITCHIE

Ahh, the memories of Little League. Alcoholic coaches passed out on the pitcher's mound. Violent parental abuse. Dysfunctional pre-adolescents. Ethnic and racial slurs that would make Howard Stern wince.

What? Your Little League experience wasn't quite like that? No matter. *The Bad News Bears* skewers that most American of youth activities by turning a population of pipsqueak players into a potty-mouthed roster of anarchists. On one level, it's stinging satire. On another, it's downright funny.

To categorize *The Bad News Bears* as a children's movie is not quite right. Most of the actors are kids, of

course, and it centers on a youth activity. But the themes—being an outcast, winning at all costs—are definitely adult in nature. This movie comes by its PG rating honestly.

Indeed, sometimes it pushes that rating to the limit. *Bears* came out in 1976, before the nanny-fication of America, when a movie could have a scene of two pre-teens riding a motorcycle—without helmets!—and the nation wouldn't go into shock. We're not saying that was better; just a sign of the times. So, we get scenes here in which an adult teaches a 10-year-old to mix martinis, a father whacks his son in public and a cupie-cute little boy refers to his teammates as . . . well, we won't say it, but it's every epithet you ever heard for blacks, Hispanics, Jews and gays. And no one even blinks.

That's the irony. Much as it seems we live in an increasingly crude society, *The Bad News Bears* is a movie that could not be remade these days. Oh, wait a second. It was, in 2005. But trust us, the second version is much tamer (and less funny) than the original. More about that later.

First, the storyline: Morris Buttermaker (Walter Matthau) is a broken down, alcoholic ex-minor league pitcher who's hired to coach a youth team of non-athletic misfits known as the Bears. Initially, he has no interest

North Valley League championship. Which is kind of like the Little League World Series, assuming all the coaches were win-at-all-costs jerks and all the parents were blithering idiots.

Director Michael Ritchie made a career in the 1970s of lampooning American institutions, including politics (the biting *The Candidate*), beauty pageants (the underrated *Smile*) and pro football (the disappointing *Semi-Tough*). He takes a machete to youth baseball here in a way that the establishment still doesn't appreciate all these years later. "That film is something that doesn't portray Little League as it is," the organization's public relations director Lance Van Auken said recently. "It is

BUTTERMAKER: **"ALL SEASON LONG, YOU'VE BEEN LAUGHED AT, CRAPPED ON. NOW YOU'VE GOT A CHANCE TO SPIT IT BACK IN THEIR FACES."**

beyond collecting a paycheck, and watches impassively as his squad loses the first game 26-0. In one inning.

But soon, the familiar Matthau gruff-with-a-heart-of-gold character emerges (see: *The Odd Couple* and *Grumpy Old Men*), and he decides to actually teach the kids some old-school fundamentals. He recruits two ringers—a talented pitcher named Amanda Whurlitzer (Tatum O'Neal, coming off her Oscar in *Paper Moon*), as well as a pint-sized slugger-turned-juvenile-delinquent named Kelly Leak (Jackie Earle Haley).

Of course, the Bears pull off the biggest turnaround this side of the 2004 Red Sox and end up playing for the

not something Little League would be proud of."

Perhaps not. But it remains funny. The script was written by Bill Lancaster, son of Burt Lancaster, who said he modeled Coach Buttermaker's personality after his father. Not exactly a tribute to dear old dad.

The Bad News Bears was a success when it came out, grossing $32 million—good enough to inspire two sequels (and almost a third), a spin-off TV show and that 2005 remake. Let's briefly review each of them:

The Bad News Bears in Breaking Training (1977) was a moderately entertaining second effort done without Matthau and O'Neal, which is like redoing the Beatles without Paul and John. Still, it's worth seeing.

The strangest development in *Breaking Training* is that the central character of the fat catcher, Engleberg (played by Gary Lee Cavagnaro in the original), was replaced with another actor (Jeff Starr). Same character name, same persona, no explanation—just a different actor, like revolving Darrins on the TV show *Bewitched*. Cavagnaro later explained that he lost weight after the first film and wasn't willing to put it back on for a movie role. Rather than rewrite a slender catcher into the script, producers axed him.

The Bad News Bears Go to Japan (1978) is a completely unwatchable effort reviewed elsewhere in this book. Don't waste your time seeing it. There were plans for a fourth film, set in Cuba, but Paramount Studios looked at the puny box-office receipts from *Japan* and pulled the plug. Too bad in one sense: The producers had hoped to get Fidel Castro to play a small role as a Cuban coach in Version Four.

In 1979, the movie was made into a TV series starring Jack Warden, and with eight-year-old Corey Feldman as one of the kids. As far as we could determine, not a single person ever watched this show.

Finally, the entire thing was remade, starring Billy Bob Thornton as Morris Buttermaker. It's not bad, and some in the under-15 set might relate better to the lines and characters in this version than the original. But trust us, the politically incorrect snap of the 1976 *Bears* makes that the one worth watching.

🏅 **CHEERS:** Matthau, of course, makes this film go with his grumbling, stumbling persona. That's obvious. So we'll give you another positive: The soundtrack, comprised of arrangements from Bizet's *Carmen*, is brilliant throughout.

🏴 **JEERS:** We know they're kids and all, but some of the acting here is as bad as the ball playing. That's got to be why just two child cast members went on to have any semblance of a career—O'Neal and, to a far-lesser degree, Jackie Earle Haley. In his *New York Times* review, Vincent Canby said of Haley, "There's something about him that makes you suspect he may actually be an aged Munchkin, exiled from Oz for crimes that must remain unspeakable."

✔ **REALITY CHECK:** We never heard of a kid's league without a mercy rule. Our hunch is that someone would have stepped in to stop that first game before the score reached 26-0 in the first inning.

🎬 **PIVOTAL SCENE:** Early in the championship game, Coach Buttermaker is downright abusive to his team. He orders one player to get hit by a pitch and shoves another in the dugout. He sends sore-armed Amanda out to pitch another inning. When the team falls behind, he screams, "All season long, you've been laughed at, crapped on. Now you've got a chance to spit it back in their faces and what do you do? You're out there like a bunch of dead fish—not listening, bonehead plays, mistakes. I mean, don't you want to beat those bastards?"

The players—petrified by his loss of perspective—just stare back. The camera pans from one hurt face to another, and gradually Buttermaker gets it. Their goal is to win, yes, but more than that it is to have fun. Seeing it, the manager morphs back from a tyrannical Billy Martin to a docile Terry Francona. It all occurs a bit quickly, but, hey, it's the movies.

😀 **GOOFS:** That ain't Tatum O'Neal blowing those strikes past opposing hitters. Most of the shots of her pitching are taken from behind. Look carefully and you may discern that the pitcher is actually a teenaged boy wearing a wig.

☞ **DON'T FAIL TO NOTICE:** Speaking of shots from behind, late in the movie there is a moment when the opposition coach's wife (Shari Summers) walks away from the camera. In short-shorts and platform shoes. Slowly. Oh, my. Ms. Summers had an all-too-brief acting career, but we would nominate her keister for enshrinement on the Mount Rushmore of great 1970s derrieres.

🎬 **CASTING CALL:** Jodie Foster was originally given the role of Amanda, but dropped out to shoot *Taxi Driver*. Slightly different film, eh?

★ **SPORTS-ACTION GRADE:** D-plus. If you've ever watched 11-year-olds play Little League, you know how brutal it can be.

BET YOU DIDN'T KNOW: To keep the film at its 102-minute length, several scenes were deleted. Most would have added context to the film. They include:

- Some back-story of the relationship between Buttermaker and the man who hires him to coach, Councilman Whitewood. Turns out they were minor-league roommates years ago, and Buttermaker several times saved Whitewood from sticky situations. Now, Whitewood is repaying his debt.
- An explanation of the scene where the stadium scoreboard is dedicated to a boy who apparently passed away. In the cut scene, we learn that the boy was killed by a wild pitch the previous year. That almost makes it understandable when evil Yankees Coach Roy Turner (Vic Morrow) goes ballistic on his own son for beaning an opponent.
- A second air hockey scene. In the movie, Amanda loses a game (and a wager) to Kelly, meaning she has to go on a date with him and allow him to "do anything." In the deleted scene, Buttermaker (retaining some of his old athletic abilities) avenges Amanda's air hockey loss—turning around the original bet and winning a wager that forces Kelly to play for the team.

BEST LINE: Amanda Whurlitzer: "I'm almost 12 and I'll be getting a bra soon . . . well, maybe in a year or so. So I can't be playing no dumb baseball."

"I KNOW THAT GUY": Brandon Cruz, who plays Coach Turner's son and distraught Yankees pitcher Joe Turner ("Let go of the ball, Joey!"), peaked about five years before *Bears* as adorable Eddie Corbett in the TV Land favorite, *The Courtship of Eddie's Father*. Two of his most recent credits are for *Motorcycle Diaries* in 2004 (in which he's billed 51st as a "Chilean miner"), and in the TV show *Viva La Bam*, in which he's listed as "various crew." Not exactly a great career arc.

REPEATED WATCHING QUOTIENT: Once for yourself, once with your kids.

IF YOU LIKED THIS, YOU'LL LIKE: Any of the films listed in the chapter following this one.

MY FAVORITE SPORTS MOVIE: Director Quentin Tarantino, who says he still watches *The Bad News Bears* about once a month (as quoted in the *New York Times*): "I was in the sixth grade—the end of my first time. I was held back; I was in the sixth grade twice. But my first time in the sixth grade, toward the very end, I went and saw *The Bad News Bears*, and I fell hopelessly in love with Tatum O'Neal. I mean, so much in love with Tatum O'Neal. I'm embarrassed to tell you how much in love I was with her."

FAMILY MOVIE NIGHT: SPORTS FLICKS FOR KIDS

THIS BOOK IS BURSTING WITH MOVIES THAT ARE GREAT FOR CHILDREN. *THE BAD NEWS BEARS* IS ONE OF THOSE RARE FILMS THAT CAN DELIGHT BOTH SIX-YEAR-OLDS AND 60-YEAR-OLDS. *THE SANDLOT* MIGHT NOT ONLY EVOKE YOUR CHILDHOOD, IT MIGHT REMIND YOUR SON OF THE ONE HE IS LIVING NOW.

THE *KARATE KID* TEACHES CONFIDENCE. *REMEMBER THE TITANS* TEACHES TEAMWORK AND TOLERANCE. *THE ROOKIE* TEACHES PERSEVERANCE. *COOL RUNNINGS* TEACHES . . . WELL, NOTHING REALLY, BUT IT'S A HOOT NO MATTER YOUR AGE.

BEYOND THOSE IN OUR TOP 100 WHICH ARE AIMED AT MULTIPLE AGE GROUPS, HERE ARE 10 MORE (LISTED ALPHABETICALLY) THAT WE LIKE WHICH ARE GEARED SPECIFICALLY TOWARD KIDS:

Angels in the Outfield. There are two versions of this film, one made in 1951 with Paul Douglas and Janet Leigh, and a 1994 remake with Danny Glover. We'll tell you that the original is better, but good luck getting a kid to watch a black-and-white film with the slower pace of an earlier era.

Both versions have essentially the same plot: Orphaned children pray for their favorite losing baseball team, and angels appear on the field to intervene. Both have the gruff manager, who eventually becomes a true believer. Two sweet movies with a bit of a religious bent.

Cars. Down the road, we may come to regard this era as the golden age of animation. There are so many terrific creations by Dreamworks and Disney's Pixar that it's tough to keep track of them.

Cars, which won the 2007 Golden Globe for best animated film, gives human personalities to NASCAR autos and sends one, named Lightning McQueen, on a road toward friendship and redemption. Take two parts redneck, one part schmaltz; add voiceovers by the likes of Darrell Waltrip, Richard Petty and other legendary drivers; create awesome animation, and you've got an engaging little film.

Ice Castles. If you're searching for something to watch with your 13-year-old daughter, this 1978 weeper might be the best suggestion in this book. *Ice Castles* is a melodrama about a young girl (well played by professional figure skater Lynn-Holly Johnson), whose dreams of becoming a champion end when an accident takes her sight. You can figure the rest: She mourns for herself, but is pulled out of her malaise by a dreamy young hockey player (Robby Benson). Together, they work to achieve her goal.

Predictable? You bet. Manipulative? Absolutely. But you'll still end up trying to conceal that lumpy throat and those tearing eyes from your daughter.

Johnny Tsunami. Made for Disney TV in 1999, this simple little movie tells the story of a Hawaiian teen surfing sensation whose father gets a job transfer to snowy Vermont. Talk about a fish out of water. Things get worse when Johnny's dad enrolls him in a snooty private school full of skiers, when Johnny wants to go to the regular-guy public school full of snowboarders.

There's a strong message of tolerance here, and a nice subplot about families learning to compromise. There's also a lot of slang that no one over age 25 will understand. *Johnny Tsunami* is about as challenging as a bunny hill, but it is an enjoyable ride.

Little Giants. Rick Moranis—an underrated comic actor—plays the nerdy dad whose daughter is cut from the peewee team coached by his bullying brother (Ed O'Neill). So father and daughter form their own team with all the castoff kids and, of course, challenge O'Neill's evil corporate-like entity. You can bet on some last-second heroics. Think of *The Bad News Bears* in football pads.

We love that the team names—Giants and Cowboys—represent one of sport's great rivalries. We enjoyed the cameos by NFL biggies like Emmitt Smith, Bruce Smith and John Madden. And we snicker every time we recall the super-duper secret play, "The Annexation of Puerto Rico."

The Longshots is based on the true story of Jasmine Plummer, an 11-year-old from Chicago who in 2003 became the first female to quarterback a team to the Pop Warner Super Bowl. The film stars Keke Palmer, the gifted young actress who played a spelling whiz in *Akeelah and the Bee*. Ice Cube does well in a difficult role as the down-and-out uncle who rehabilitates himself as he teaches Jasmine the X's and O's.

The football action is awkward—unlike the real Jasmine, Palmer throws, well, like a girl—but youngsters in the audience aren't likely to care. *The Longshots* isn't a sports story as much as it is a story about a shy girl who's trying to fit in. The scene of Jasmine trying to put on her football uniform for the first time—puzzling over the pads, recoiling at the sight of a jockstrap—is better than anything that happens on the field. There isn't a word spoken, yet it says everything.

The Longshots has a healthy message about courage, tolerance and family, and delivers it in a way that doesn't feel preachy. An interesting footnote: The film was directed by Fred Durst, once the front man for the rock group Limp Bizkit.

The Mighty Ducks. Same notion as *Little Giants*, but a different sport. This time the castoffs are in ice skates, and their coach is a self-absorbed attorney (there's a redundancy) played by Emilio Estevez. He is convicted of drunk driving and ordered by the judge to coach a dreary youth hockey team. Same basic plot as *The Bad News Bears* and *Little Giants*, with the same gaggle of misfit kids—the fat one, the painfully shy one, the cocky one, the girl who gets put down by the boys. And same ending, where the coach gets to avenge his own demons by beating an old enemy.

Still, it works. The hockey scenes, particularly, are well shot. However, if you pick up this film in a video store, be forewarned: DO NOT get the sequels, *D2* or *D3*. They are *D-ismal*.

National Velvet. Most consider this 1944 film a classic, and there are generations of American women who still list it as a favorite from their youth. It has been copied and recycled many times over the years, but the original still stands up for its beauty and its sweetness.

Velvet features 11-year-old Elizabeth Taylor (who became an immediate international star) and squeaky-clean Mickey Rooney, as a jockey and trainer working together to win the Grand National steeplechase race. There is a great supporting cast (watch for a young Angela Lansbury) and an uplifting story. The American Film Institute placed *National Velvet* as No. 24 on its list of 100 Most Inspiring Movies.

Rookie of the Year. Far-fetched fluff about a Little League klutz who breaks his arm, only to discover that after surgery tightens his elbow tendons, he can suddenly hurl a 100-mile-per-hour fastball. He quickly becomes the Chicago Cubs' best pitcher this side of Mark Prior and—alas—ends up with the same flash-in-the-pan career.

The comedic cast includes John Candy, Daniel Stern and Gary Busey. Several major leaguers make brief appearances, including Barry Bonds, who pulls five facial muscles trying to crack a smile. It's all a lot of light-hearted nonsense, and there are plot holes larger than Bonds' cranium. But there are a lot of laughs. And your kid may want to go out and have a catch afterward, which is always nice.

Space Jam. Put *Roger Rabbit* in basketball sneakers, add the majesty of Michael Jordan, and you've got this film, a well-done combination of animation and live action. *Space Jam* takes the familiar Looney Tunes characters and casts them as Jordan's teammates in an intergalactic game against aliens who want to hold them as slaves (we're not kidding). So Bugs Bunny replaces Toni Kukoc, which seems a push to us.

The basketball scenes are great, often aided by the freedom that animation gives everything. Lots of slapstick humor, as expected from the Looney Tunes gang. And, again, lots of big-time cameos from the likes of Charles Barkley, Larry Bird, Patrick Ewing and Shawn Bradley.

Shawn Bradley? Who invited him?

45 SEABISCUIT (2003–PG-13)

SPORT: HORSE RACING | STARS: JEFF BRIDGES, TOBEY MAGUIRE, CHRIS COOPER
DIRECTOR: GARY ROSS

It is difficult to imagine the hold that a boxy, bow-legged five-year-old had on America in 1938. At a time when Babe Ruth had left the stage and Joe DiMaggio was entering it, when both Joe Louis and Jesse Owens were destroying the myth of Aryan superiority, the most popular athlete in this country was . . . a horse.

Seabiscuit, an undersized thoroughbred with the humblest of beginnings, was a national sensation. The influential columnist Walter Winchell listed the horse among his top ten newsmakers of the year, right below Roosevelt and Hitler. Seabiscuit had more endorsements than Peyton Manning could ever dream of, hawking everything from fresh fruit to ladies' hats. Thousands

swarmed race tracks to cheer him. Millions fiddled with their radio tuners to hear him run.

It boggles the mind, in this era, to recall that horse racing was once so huge that one of its stars—an animal, not a jockey—could be as popular as Michael Jordan or Tom Brady would later become. But that was the case. You can learn the details by reading Laura Hillenbrand's best-selling book, *Seabiscuit*. Or you can get the quicker version—well, 141 minutes worth—in this movie based on her work.

Seabiscuit the movie tells the story not just of one of the history's most remarkable horses, but also the three men responsible for his success. In fact, if the movie is guilty of anything (beyond running too long) it's that Seabiscuit himself becomes almost a secondary character. Indeed, 45 minutes pass before we even get to meet the title star.

Rather, the film focuses on the three men who create the legend. We meet Seabiscuit's owner, gregarious West Coast automobile magnate Charles Howard (Jeff Bridges). There's an interesting irony—oft pointed out—that Howard's fortune comes from making horses obsolete in American life ("I wouldn't spend more than five dollars for the best horse in America," he tells a potential car buyer early in the film). Howard's salesmanship and flair for publicity—he's Don King with a nice haircut and better ethics—help turn Seabiscuit into America's obsession.

We meet trainer Tom Smith (Chris Cooper), a taciturn, mysterious horse whisperer who sees potential in young Seabiscuit when others just see an unruly loser. Smith doesn't relate much to other humans, but he communicates with animals better than Dr. Dolittle. In one scene, he adopts a broken-down horse about to be euthanized for an injured leg. Asked by Howard why he's wasting his time with an injured animal, Smith says, "You don't throw a whole life away just because he's banged up a little."

And we meet Red Pollard (Tobey Maguire), who has failed both as a jockey and a prize fighter, and regards Seabiscuit as his one last chance for success. Pollard's parents—loving and literary—are ruined at the start of the Depression. As a 16-year-old, he is effectively sold into apprenticeship as a jockey and (as far as we can tell) never sees his family again. He is oversized at five-foot-seven and blind in one eye—which later comes into play.

Each man carries deep wounds. Howard mourns the death of his 11-year-old son (ironically, in a car accident) and the ensuing breakup of his marriage. Pollard grieves the separation from his family. And Smith, well, we're never quite sure of his story, but he sure seems off-kilter about something.

Together these damaged men are brought together by a damaged horse. And that's the story.

Smith is the one who puts everything together, spotting the stumpy Seabiscuit and "seeing greatness in his eyes." He also takes to Pollard, knowing that, despite the jockey's poor history (or maybe because of it), he has the potential to get the most out of a mistreated, troubled horse.

Understand, all of this makes up the first half of the movie. Then we get to the racing. And then *Seabiscuit* shifts into gear.

In rapid time, Seabiscuit goes from being a 70-1 underdog at Santa Anita to the hottest thing on four legs. The undercurrent is that Americans, ravaged by the Depression, regard this unlikely winner as a hero for tough times.

"The movie did a great job of depicting the era and the way people were struggling just to live," said Dick Jauron, the Buffalo Bills head coach who lists this as his favorite sports movie. "It was a total underdog story—the horse, the owner, the jockey—and the whole country identified with them."

It all leads up to a match race with Triple Crown winner War Admiral, the so-called unbeatable horse. Imagine Rocky vs. Apollo Creed. Hickory High vs. South Bend Central. USA hockey vs. USSR. We've seen this plot line many times before, and yet we still get suckered in. As Howard (Bridges) says, "Sometimes when the little guy doesn't know he's the little guy, he can do great things."

The buildup is terrific and the on-screen race against War Admiral may be the best horse racing scene in the history of film. *Seabiscuit* was nominated for seven Oscars (it won none), and most—like editing and cinematography—must be tied directly to the racing moments.

If the film has a flaw, it's that it tries to be *too* complete. Hillenbrand's book is 480 pages in paperback. Director/screenwriter Gary Ross tries to cram as much as he can into the movie, so 20 minutes after the first climactic scene, we get another one. And then another. Then a lot of hand wringing. And then a postscript.

Hey, that's a minor quibble. Seabiscuit is a good story well told and brilliantly filmed. The movie, like the horse himself, has a lot of heart.

CHEERS: Actor William H. Macy is a hoot in the role of manic (and fictional) radio sportscaster Tick Tock McGlaughlin. He tortures Greek mythology and toots a train whistle to provide comic relief to a movie otherwise lacking humor.

"Gary Ross, our writer and director, used my character in a very cagey way because I start off calling the horse a nag and useless," Macy told About.com. "And as I grow to love him, so does America grow to love him. I'm sort of the Greek chorus of this film."

Yeah, well that, plus he cracked us up each time he appeared on the screen with that fake mustache.

🏳 **JEERS:** Truth is, the movie should have ended after Seabiscuit's battle with War Admiral. Roll credits, turn up the lights, look at the tears rolling down people's faces. The entire last half hour was unnecessary.

✒ **WHAT THEY WROTE AT THE TIME:** "If the story of Seabiscuit hadn't been true, a Hollywood screenwriter might have concocted it and been laughed out of every studio pitch meeting for writing something so far-fetched. Truth isn't always stranger than fiction, but it's more inspiring. Even when Ross, as writer and director, veers toward the overly sentimental or downright unbelievable, one can't help but admire these characters and the rousing movie built around them."—Steve Pearsall, *St. Petersburg Times*

☺ **GOOFS:** Ten different horses shared the role of Seabiscuit. We're sure the ASPCA approved that no one was overworked, but the problem is that Seabiscuit seems to change color during the film, from a honey brown to a dark red and several shades in between. Hey, maybe our star spent time under a tanning lamp.

🎞 **PIVOTAL SCENE:** Smith, the trainer, first lays eyes on Seabiscuit—and falls for his stubborn heart—as he watches the enraged horse wrestle with a half dozen handlers trying to calm him. Seconds later, he turns around and sees an angry Pollard fighting off an entire crowd. The horse and the jockey share a sense of rage, and Smith is wise enough to put them together.

★ **SPORTS-ACTION GRADE:** An easy A. The races are breathtaking, with sweat dripping from riders and horses, and clods of dirt flying through the air. You see jockeys whipping the animals and each other, shouting and fighting from their mounts. Cameras are posted everywhere—above, below, between the horses—giving you a real sense of the danger of this sport.

◎ **REPEATED WATCHING QUOTIENT:** Fire it up once a year on the eve of the Kentucky Derby (held on the first Saturday of May).

◀ **CASTING CALL:** Hall of Fame jockey George Woolf—who becomes Seabiscuit's second jockey in the movie—is portrayed by Hall of Fame jockey Gary Stevens.

♣ **BET YOU DIDN'T KNOW:** Seabiscuit and War Admiral were actually related. Seabiscuit's grandfather, the great Man o' War, was War Admiral's sire. Which means that War Admiral was Seabiscuit's uncle, as it were.

☞ **DON'T FAIL TO NOTICE:** At least one of the seemingly wild mustangs that Smith is chasing down early in the movie appears to be wearing horseshoes.

✹ **IF YOU LIKED THIS, YOU'LL LIKE:** The PBS special, *American Experience: Seabiscuit*. Like this movie, it leans heavily on Hillenbrand's book. Less drama, but you'll get to see what the main characters really looked like.

🗨 **BEST LINE:** Jockey Red Pollard: "Everybody thinks we found this broken-down horse and fixed him. But we didn't. He fixed us. Every one of us. And I guess in a way, we fixed each other, too."

😎 **"I KNOW THAT GUY":** Eddie Jones, who plays War Admiral's owner, Samuel Riddle, is a veteran character actor you may recognize as the loving father of homely second baseman Marla Hooch in *League of Their Own*.

🏇 **MY FAVORITE SPORTS MOVIE:** Philadelphia Phillies pitcher and 2008 World Series MVP Cole Hamels: "It's the kind of movie that could motivate anyone. There aren't too many things that can make me cry but that movie came close. When I was a kid, I heard my grandmother talk about Seabiscuit. She had seen the horse run on the West Coast. But I just knew the name. I didn't know the story until I saw the movie. I thought it was great."

46 THIS SPORTING LIFE (1963–NR)

SPORT: RUGBY | STARS: RICHARD HARRIS, RACHEL ROBERTS
DIRECTOR: LINDSAY ANDERSON

At this point, we're figuring that you're weary of all those uplifting scrappy-longshot-becomes-courageous-hero flicks. How many underdogs can you cheer for, after all? So now for something completely different:

How about a depressing portrait of British working-class angst, centering on a brutish rugby player and his romantic frustration with his emotionally crippled landlady? Now that's a plotline unlike any other on our Top 100.

Trust us, *This Sporting Life*, a 1963 black-and-white British film, is a worthy watch. It may be the most downcast movie in this book (well, perhaps next to *Million Dollar Baby*), but there's a great texture and story to it and the sports action is riveting in its barbarism.

It tells the story of Frank Machin (Richard Harris), a coal miner in England's industrial midlands. In an early scene, Frank picks a bar brawl with the captain of the local rugby club. He gets beaten senseless, but his bravado impresses the team's manager, who invites him to try out.

Frank hasn't got much grace, but his scuffling style thrills the fans and impresses club owner Gerald Weaver (Alan Badel), who sees him as the type of player who will help sell tickets. Frank is a roughneck, bashing elbows and tossing punches in the middle of the scrum. He's Sean Avery, Rodney Harrison and Bill Laimbeer all rolled into one. And in a sport dominated by upper-crust college boys, Frank becomes the working-class hero.

Still, he's an angry young man. Frank comes to view himself as just a commodity for others to exploit. His recently widowed landlady Margaret Hammond (Rachel Roberts) uses him for sex, but denies him any emotional affection. Weaver, who owns the local factory as well as the rugby club, lets it be known that his players carry no more value than his industrial equipment. And in the film's creepiest scene, Weaver's wife (Vanda Godsell)—a cross between Agnes Moorehead and Camilla Parker

Bowles—tries to seduce him, and then belittles him when he rejects her advances.

Not a lot of yucks here.

The more Frank succeeds on the field, the more indolent he becomes. Although he views Weaver as his oppressor, he starts emulating the millionaire boss—buying a Bentley and a snazzy camelhair overcoat. In one of *This Sporting Life's* best scenes, he takes Mrs. Hammond to a ritzy restaurant, and then creates a stir by insulting the waiters and putting his shoes up on a chair. The low-rent kid cannot fit in at a high-rent establishment.

Richard Harris was a rising star at the time of this movie, and his performance drew comparisons with young Marlon Brando in *On the Waterfront*. Harris and Brando had just worked together in *Mutiny on the Bounty*, so it's likely there was some influence from the great Mr. Mumbles. Regardless, Harris' raging performance won him an Oscar nomination for Best Actor (Sidney Poitier won the award for *Lilies of the Field*). Roberts, too, got an Oscar bid for Best Actress (Patricia Neal took it for her role in *Hud*), playing the most emotionally repressed character this side of Frasier Crane's wife.

Give lots of credit, also, to director Lindsay Anderson, who went on to film *If . . .* and *O Lucky Man!*, two other great films about class consciousness. Here, Anderson takes you to a grim industrial Britain—post-World War II, pre-Beatles—where a young man's resentment stems from leaving row homes blackened by smoke only to go underground into the coal mines. There are lots of cigarettes and booze and bad teeth. Ah, England!

The best moments are the rugby scenes. The camera takes you directly under the scrum, as dirt flies up and blood and sweat drips off players' faces. Rugby is literally a foreign sport to most Americans, but following the rules of the game isn't important to appreciating *This Sporting Life*. Anderson wants you to see rugby as *Raging Bull* portrays boxing, with a violence that alternately draws you in and then repels you.

The movie leads up to a tragic finish. Mrs. Hammond dismisses Frank as "just a great ape on a football field," he punches her in the face and, well, things spiral downhill from there. If you're looking for a *Hoosiers* happy ending, Jimmy Chitwood's jump shot is nowhere to be found. There is no Adrian coming to reassure Rocky. Ray Kinsella and his dad are not going to reconcile over a game of catch.

But, if you're looking for a stark, provocative sports drama, *This Sporting Life* fits the bill.

🍺 **CHEERS:** As we said, the rugby scenes are exciting and tremendously realistic. How realistic? Harris broke a bone in his leg during the scene where he tries out for the team.

🚩 **JEERS:** The movie is shot in time-arcing flashbacks that take place as Frank is in a dentist's chair, under anesthesia following a punch that knocks out his front teeth. Between the time traveling and the mumbling British accents, it's sometimes difficult to follow what's going on.

✒ **WHAT THEY WROTE AT THE TIME:** "The football scenes have a live authenticity. Harris gives a dominating, intelligent performance as the arrogant, blustering, fundamentally simple and insecure footballer."—*Variety*

☺ **GOOFS:** Because a tight budget didn't allow for the hiring of many extras, hundreds of wooden dummies are placed among the spectators during the game scenes. Look carefully and you'll see them.

👁 **REPEATED WATCHING QUOTIENT:** Not too high unless you're in the mood to depress yourself.

◀ **CASTING CALL:** Young Glenda Jackson makes her film debut with a tiny role as a singer at the rugby club's Christmas party. Jackson would go on to be nominated for four Oscars and win two.

★ **SPORTS-ACTION GRADE:** A violence-packed A. Any director planning a sports movie could learn a lot by studying the camera angles and editing techniques used during *This Sporting Life's* rugby scenes.

☕ **BET YOU DIDN'T KNOW:** Director Anderson, who—because of the times—kept his homosexuality hidden, developed an unrequited crush on his lead actor. In his diary on April 23, 1962, during the filming of the movie, Anderson wrote: "I have grown to love Richard dearly—too dearly of course, with the result that I lack absolutely the detachment that would allow me to weather the storms of his temperament without suffering."

😎 **"I KNOW THAT GUY":** William Hartnell, who plays rugby scout "Dad" Johnson, went on to become the original *Doctor Who* in the cult sci-fi drama that ran for 26 years on British television.

🎞 **IF YOU LIKED THIS, YOU'LL LIKE:** *The Loneliness of the Long Distance Runner*, a 1962 British film about a rebellious young man who battles authority even as he finds salvation as a track star.

🎞 **MY FAVORITE SPORTS MOVIE:** British actor Ray Winstone (*The Departed*, *Indiana Jones and the Kingdom of the Crystal Skull*) to the website filmmonthly.com: "I watched Richard Harris in that movie and it did honestly change my life. Before then, most British movie actors were chappies from a different class. But that really opened the doors for working class actors like me."

47 CINDERELLA MAN (2005–PG-13)

SPORT: BOXING | STARS: RUSSELL CROWE, RENEE ZELLWEGER, PAUL GIAMATTI
DIRECTOR: RON HOWARD

Cinderella Man was released one year after *Seabiscuit* and it offered the same theme: The triumph of an underdog sports hero lifts America's spirits during the Great Depression. It prompted some snide comments, including critics referring to Ron Howard's boxing film as *Fistbiscuit*. Anthony Lane in *The New Yorker* wrote, "There's so much faith charging around in this picture that it could break your nose."

That may account for why *Cinderella Man* was such a disappointment at the box office. The film earned $61 million in the United States, well short of expectations for a movie with an Academy Award winning director (Howard) and two Academy Award winning stars—Russell Crowe and Renee Zellweger. Moviegoers may have decided after seeing *Seabiscuit* that the Depression was, well, just too depressing.

There were other theories, such as the film should not have been released in the summer when it was up against the big action blockbusters. Crowe may have hurt the film with his bad boy behavior during the publicity tour, which included throwing a telephone at a desk clerk at a New York City hotel. The tabloids wrote more about that incident than the release of the film.

Cinderella Man also was slammed for its unflattering—and inaccurate—portrayal of Max Baer, the champ that James J. Braddock (Crowe) dethrones for the heavyweight title. The film makes Baer look like a bloodthirsty monster, and his family (including *Beverly Hillbillies* alum Max Baer Jr.) claimed it was a gross distortion. We'll discuss this in greater depth later, but the Baer issue was a cloud that hung over the film throughout its entire run.

Cinderella Man was generally well-reviewed—Mick LaSalle of the *San Francisco Chronicle* called it "easily the best American film of the year"—yet it never found an audience. AMC Theaters offered a full refund to any ticket buyer who was dissatisfied with the film. Cine-mark Theaters made a similar offer. Still, the film played to mostly empty seats.

It is hard to put a finger on why, but *Cinderella Man* just didn't connect with the public. Maybe *Seabiscuit* stole its thunder, maybe Crowe turned people off, maybe America had its fill of boxing movies. It may have been a combination of all those things. But putting the cash register aside and just looking at *Cinderella Man* as a film, it is quite good. In some ways, it is very good.

"As a boxer," said 10-time world titlist Oscar de la Hoya, "I found it completely inspiring."

It is based on the life of Braddock, a journeyman pugilist who lucks into a few fights and winds up taking the crown from Max Baer. Damon Runyon gave Braddock the name "Cinderella Man" and it was a fit. It is well-documented by Runyon and others that Braddock, like Seabiscuit, became a symbol of hope for millions of Americans suffering through the Depression. He was an uncommon hero, but those were uncommon times.

When we first see Braddock (Crowe), he is handsome and cocky in a three-piece suit riding through Manhattan with his manager Joe Gould (Paul Giamatti) after flattening another opponent at Madison Square Garden. Gould is counting the night's winnings and vowing, "We're going straight to the top, Irishman."

Four years later, it is a totally different picture. The stock market has crashed and Braddock is among the millions who have lost everything. His family lives in a tiny basement apartment and his wife Mae (Zellweger) waters down the milk to make it last. The heat is shut off and as the three children huddle in bed, you can see their breath.

Braddock may have lost his bank account, but he has not lost his honor. When his oldest son steals a salami from the butcher shop, Braddock does not berate him. He takes him by the hand and walks him back to the shop to return it. "No matter what happens," he says, "we don't steal. Not ever." When his daughter says she is hungry, Braddock gives her the one slice of meat from his plate. "It's OK," he says, "I'm full."

His boxing career appears over. He broke his right hand, but continued fighting because he needed the money. Basically fighting with one hand, he loses 20 of 30 bouts and he is so ineffectual the New York boxing commission pulls his license.

Braddock has only one place to go and that's the New Jersey docks where every morning he stands with hundreds of other desperate men outside the gates, hoping to be chosen for the day's work. The film is particularly effective in conveying the feeling of helplessness that grips the men who push and shove and plead as the foreman approaches. He picks a few and slams the gate on the others, saying, "That's it."

Braddock has no celebrity status. He is rejected as often as he is selected. He is forced to go on relief but still doesn't have enough to feed his family, so in one of the film's most painful scenes he goes to Madison Square Garden and asks the promoters gathered there for money. He circles the room, hat literally in hand, as the men dig into their pockets for change. (This really happened. Braddock said it was the lowest point of his life.)

But Braddock's luck changes. A fighter pulls out of a match with the No. 2-ranked heavyweight Corn Griffin. No real contender will take the fight on such short notice so they have to find someone who will. The Garden is desperate enough to give Braddock back his license if he will take the match. They offer him $250, peanuts for a main event, but a windfall for Braddock. He takes the fight even though he has not trained in months and is given no chance at winning.

Braddock shocks everyone by knocking out Griffin. He discovers his left hand, which he rarely used earlier in his career, is a powerful weapon, thanks to working on the docks. The win leads to another bout, which he wins. That leads to another bout, which he also wins. Runyon dubs him "Cinderella Man" and next thing you know, he's signing to fight Baer for the title. At the press conference, Braddock is asked what he's fighting for.

"Milk," he says.

Crowe makes Braddock, the noble working stiff, totally believable. *Variety's* Robert Koehler writes, "As Braddock, Crowe's eyes have never seemed so full of unspoken sadness and ferocity with his body language ranging from spent hopelessness to a single muscle preparing to strike."

Crowe spent a month working with veteran trainer Angelo Dundee, preparing for the role. They studied tapes of Braddock's fights and Crowe sparred with then WBA super middleweight champion Anthony Mundine of Australia. Crowe dislocated his shoulder during one sparring session and needed arthroscopic surgery to repair it. Production was shut down for weeks while he recovered.

Cinderella Man does a fine job of explaining Braddock. Howard leans a little too heavily on the violin bow now and then, but that's OK. The problem comes with the introduction of Baer (Craig Bierko). The film portrays Baer as a sneering savage who revels in the fact he has killed two men in the ring. When he meets the Braddocks, he eyes Mae and says, "You're far too pretty to be a widow." Not content to leave it at that, he says, "Maybe I can comfort you after he's gone." Mae throws a drink in his face.

None of this is true. Yes, Baer did kill one opponent, Frankie Campbell. Another, Ernie Schaaf, died but it was after a bout with Primo Carnera. Schaaf was defeated by Baer before he fought Carnera and it was speculated the injuries he suffered in the bout against Baer had more to do with his death than the fight with Carnera, although that was never proven. However, it was common knowledge that Baer was haunted by the deaths of the two men. In fact, he donated part of his earnings from several bouts to the Campbell family to pay for the children's education.

Baer was never the same fighter after those tragedies. Later in his career, he was more of a clown than a fighter, slapping opponents and playing to the crowd. Newspaper accounts indicate that's how he lost to Braddock. He coasted through the bout, mugging and waving to the fans. Braddock, a 20-1 underdog, landed just enough punches to earn the decision.

There was no need for screenwriters Cliff Hollingsworth and Akiva Goldsman to demonize Baer. Long before the title fight, we were in Braddock's corner; we didn't have to think he was fighting Satan to root for him. Besides, the real villain isn't Max Baer, it's the Great Depression.

CHEERS: Paul Giamatti was the only cast member to earn an Oscar nomination and it was well-deserved. As Ty Burr wrote in the *Boston Globe*, "In his hands, Joe Gould becomes a quintessentially 1930s mixture of pep and desperation."

JEERS: The portrait of Baer is cruel. Alan Ward, who covered boxing for the *Oakland Tribune*, wrote of Baer: "It is incongruous that such a gentle, ingratiating man should have been a fighter. He had no mean streak at all."

BET YOU DIDN'T KNOW: Frankie Campbell, the boxer who died as a result of injuries sustained in a bout with Baer, was born Francisco Camilli. His brother was Dolph Camilli, who played for the Brooklyn Dodgers and won the National League home run crown in 1941.

CASTING CALL: Matt Damon, Ben Affleck, Billy Bob Thornton, Clive Owen and Mark Wahlberg all were considered for the part of Braddock, but Ron Howard picked Crowe because of their partnership in *A Beautiful Mind*.

WHAT THEY WROTE AT THE TIME: "I've never seen a boxing movie that has so convinced me I was seeing a pro bout both real and sustained."—Mike Clark, *USA Today*

GOOFS: Veteran trainer Angelo Dundee, who has a cameo as Braddock's cornerman, is wearing a pair of modern eyeglasses in the final fight scene.

BEST LINE: James J. Braddock to fight promoter Jimmy Johnson: "You think you're telling me something? Like, what, boxing is dangerous? You don't think working triple shifts and at night on a scaffold isn't just as likely to get a man killed?"

"I KNOW THAT GUY": Bruce McGill, who plays Johnson, excelled in other sports films, playing Yankees manager Ralph Houk in the HBO movie *61** and golfing great Walter Hagen in *The Legend of Bagger Vance*. Still, we'll always best remember him as motorcyclist-frat boy Daniel Simpson Day—D-Day—in *Animal House*.

SPORTS-ACTION GRADE: B. The big fight is well shot, but inaccurate. The film makes it look like an action-packed affair when in reality it was a dull 15 rounds with Baer coasting and Braddock fighting cautiously.

MY FAVORITE SPORTS MOVIE: Two-time Super Bowl-winning coach Bill Parcells: "I'm a boxing guy and a Jersey guy, so I loved *Cinderella Man*. I've seen it three or four times. I know some guys in North Jersey who are involved in the fight game who knew [James] Braddock so I've heard them talk about him. He was what Jersey people call a 'stand up guy,' just an honest, good guy. I could relate to the scenes of him working on the docks. Where I grew up, there were three or four families in our neighborhood where all the men worked on the docks. It's a tough life. For Braddock to go from where he was to the heavyweight championship of the world, he really was The Cinderella Man."

48 ROUNDERS (1998–R)

SPORT: POKER | STARS: MATT DAMON, EDWARD NORTON, JOHN MALKOVICH
DIRECTOR: JOHN DAHL

Just like the classic *The Hustler* sparked a pool-hall resurgence in America in the early 1960s, *Rounders* is often cited as a key factor in this country's recent mania over poker—particularly Texas hold 'em.

We're not so sure. We would argue that the lipstick camera—which makes it possible to see a player's down cards—has more to do with making Texas hold'em a TV sensation and, subsequently, a mainstream sport. But we recognize that two recent World Series of Poker champions, Chris Moneymaker and Jamie Gold, said that *Rounders* ignited their interest in the game. And we can't argue with this stat: The year the movie came out, there were 350 entrants in the WSOP Main Event; in 2008 there were 6,844.

These days you can't spend five minutes at a table in Vegas or Atlantic City without some wannabe quoting a few lines from the movie.

"It's immoral to let a sucker keep his money," some sunglasses-wearing tourist from Middle America will snicker. And we'll all know where he got his material. If nothing else, that tourist has good taste in movies. Because *Rounders* is an engaging character study, a solid story well told and the best damn poker film ever made.

It stars Matt Damon as Mike McDermott, a third-year law student trying—not so successfully—to avoid the lure of New York City's mysterious underground poker scene. Damon was on a roll when he shot *Rounders* in 1998, following his work in *The Rainmaker, Good Will Hunting* and *Saving Private Ryan*. That's a run any card player would admire.

Strong performances also come from Edward Norton as Lester "Worm" Murphy, an ex-con more attracted to the hustle than the actual game; from Famke Janssen, as a Russian gambler/vixen named Petra; from John Turturro, as career grinder Joey Knish, and—especially—from John Malkovich, as scenery-chomping Russian mobster Teddy KGB. More about Malkovich later.

The film opens with Mike getting wiped out by Teddy KGB to the tune of $30,000. He agrees to give up the gambling life and please his annoying girlfriend (Gretchen Mol) by sticking to his law studies and working part-time as a delivery driver. That works for nine months—during which time Mike is completely miserable.

He becomes more miserable when old buddy Worm gets out of jail, visits Mike's favorite club and runs up a massive debt in his name. Making things worse, the debt is owed to the Russian mob. Teddy—and his slovenly enforcer Grama—give Mike and Worm a quick deadline to raise the money. Or else.

And that sets up the second half of the movie, in which the two schemers (they once fixed high school basketball games together) travel from New York's Turkish baths to a preppie cigar bar to a cop's game in Binghamton, N.Y. (bad idea, as it turns out) to win enough money to save their lives. It's not an *Ocean's Eleven*-style caper film, but you'll be rooting for the rascals.

Rounders culminates in a showdown, in which Mike McD must return to the worst site of his card-playing life and try to topple the bully Teddy KGB. It's young Sugar Ray Leonard seeking a rematch against Roberto Duran in 1980, or the Red Sox against the overly smug Yankees in the 2004 ALCS.

There's a lot of nuance here, and if you don't understand the intricacies of poker you may get lost along the way. But the final face-off has as much tension as any Hitchcock film. And it will definitely have you wanting to make that late-night romp to the casino.

Rounders grossed just $23 million at the box office. Director John Dahl suggested that the studio, Miramax, had expected a date film (along the order of *Good Will Hunting II*), and failed to promote the film on its release. Regardless, it is a terrific guy movie and a cult film among millions of card players. It will take you to an intoxicating world.

CHEERS: As Russian kingpin Teddy KGB, John Malkovich is alternately intimidating and unintentionally hysterical. He primps, he taunts, he makes obscene gestures, he chomps Oreos, he rules his gambling den in a hand-me-down sweatsuit from the CCCP hockey team. The best part is Malkovich's vowel-bending accent. It may sound contrived, but he actually learned it by having a Russian woman read his lines into a tape recorder and then imitating her voice:

"I feel so unsyeetisfied. Jus' lyike a yunk man comming een for a qveeckee."

Worth the price of the rental right there.

JEERS: Animated as Malkovich is, Gretchen Mol is more wooden than Al Gore playing Mike's drippy girlfriend. How *she* ends up dumping *him* is beyond comprehension.

WHAT THEY WROTE AT THE TIME: "Is there a greater opening line in movie history than this one?: '*Listen, here's the thing. If you can't spot the sucker in your first half hour at the table, then you are the sucker.*' Bingo. I'm hooked. If I'm flicking channels and hear that line, I'm cooked for the next 100 minutes. Put a fork in me. This movie actually made me start playing poker in casinos against people who were missing teeth, for God's sake." —Bill Simmons, ESPN.com

REALITY CHECK: Hmm, Mike is the son of a janitor, slaving his way through law school as a delivery driver, avoiding poker (at least at first) after dropping $30,000 on one hand. And he's got that killer apartment? In New York City? We've heard of rent control, but that's a $4,000-a-month place, minimum.

REPEATED WATCHING QUOTIENT: Very high. We know a guy who heads to Atlantic City once a month to play in big-money tournaments. He watches *Rounders* every time, just before heading there, just to stoke himself up.

Pivotal Scene: Facing imminent defeat to Teddy KGB—and an inevitable beating by Teddy's thug, Grama—Mike must turn the game around quickly.

"You must be kicking yourself," Teddy bullies (we'll lose the accent for now), "for not walking out when you could. Bad judgment. But don't worry, son, it will all be over soon."

They are playing hold 'em. An ace, three and five show on the table. Mike holds an ace and five underneath, giving him the best two pairs possible.

He's about to push a big stack of chips to the middle. But—suddenly—he spots Teddy's tell. We won't give the secret away, but suffice it to say, it's a gesture Teddy made several times prior in the film. When Mike spots it, you'll see it as well.

Mike folds, knowing—through Teddy's tell—that he just avoided being suckered into losing against an Ace-five straight. But Mike does more. He shows Teddy KGB the cards he was holding underneath.

"It's a monster hand I've got," Mike says, "and I'm gonna lay that down, because you've got a two and four, and I'm not gonna draw against a made hand."

Teddy is stunned. How could Mike have read his hand? Is Mike in his head? What else does he know? At that point Teddy is rattled. Soon the game turns.

Don't Fail to Notice: When Worm checks out of jail early in the movie, he gets back all the possessions he had on him when he went in—including a toothpick in a plastic Baggie. He immediately puts the old toothpick back in his mouth.

Casting Call: If you're doing the seminal movie on poker, who better to step in for a cameo than Johnny Chan—winner of 10 bracelets in the World Series of Poker? Playing himself. Very cool.

Best Line: Mike walks in on The Judges Game involving his law dean (Martin Landau) and five other legal beagles. He glances around the room for about five seconds and then insists his reluctant dean raise the pot. How can he be so sure, asks another player, that the dean has the best hand?

"Well," says Mike, "you were looking for that third three, but you forgot that Professor Green folded it on Fourth Street and now you're representing that you have it. The DA made his two pair, but he knows they're no good. Judge Kaplan was trying to squeeze out a diamond flush but he came up short and Mr. Eisen is futilely hoping that his queens are going to stand up. So like I said, the Dean's bet is $20."

Geez, we don't want to ever play against *that* guy.

Sports-Action Grade: B. Hey, there's no running, no jumping, no hitting. But, for sheer competitive tension, *Rounders* is right up there.

Bet You Didn't Know: Edward Norton's inspiration for the role of Worm? Try Bugs Bunny.

"Worm is like Bugs dressed up as Keith Richards," Norton told the *Fort Lauderdale Sun-Sentinel*. "You always need to find a line in on a character, and Bugs Bunny is always scheming, always two steps ahead of a beating and always laughing."

"I Know That Guy": Actor Tom Aldredge, who plays moot court Judge Marinacci (one of the dean's poker pals), spent a career performing Shakespeare on Broadway and getting nominated for five Tony Awards. You likely don't know that, but we'll venture that you will recognize him as Hugh DeAngelis, Carmela's father in *The Sopranos*.

If You Liked This, You'll Like: *The Gambler*, the 1974 downer featuring an in-his-prime James Caan as a degenerate bettor. You may not enjoy it that much as *Rounders*, but it's worth seeing as a counterpoint to this compulsive-gambling-is-fun film.

My Favorite Sports Movie: Atlanta Braves catcher Brian McCann: "I consider it a sports movie because it's all about the competition. I'm not a huge card player, but I love the story, love the atmosphere of those underground poker games. Plus, Edward Norton is always great. I don't think he's ever made a bad movie."

49 BEND IT LIKE BECKHAM (2002–PG-13)

SPORT: SOCCER | STARS: PARMINDER NAGRA, KEIRA KNIGHTLEY, JONATHAN RHYS-MEYERS | DIRECTOR: GURINDER CHADHA

Bend It Like Beckham set box office records when it was released in Great Britain. It was the first film by a non-white Briton to reach No. 1 in that country. It became the top-grossing British-financed film ever. It was a triumph for writer-director Gurinder Chadha.

Still, no one expected *Bend It Like Beckham* to find an audience in the United States. It is, after all, a film about soccer and the cast was unknown in this country (although the radiant Keira Knightley has become a major star since then). But the movie was the talk of the Sundance Film Festival and generated enough buzz to make $32 million during its American run.

Simply put, *Bend It Like Beckham* is a charming film that will play anywhere.

"We showed it on our Ebert and Roeper Film Festival at Sea," wrote Roger Ebert in the *Chicago Sun-Times*. "The audience ranged in age from 7 to 81, with a 50ish median, and it was a huge success. The hip Sundance audience, dressed in black and clutching cell phones and cappuccinos, loved it, too. And why not, since its characters and sensibility are so abundantly lovable."

The hero is Jesminder "Jess" Bhamra (Parminder Nagra), a London teenager whose parents fled from Uganda to build a new life in England. They are a strict Sikh Punjabi family which means Jess is expected to attend school, learn how to cook and settle into a marriage (most likely arranged) with an Indian boy. Her sister Pinky (Archie Panjabi) is doing exactly that.

But Jess has different ambitions. She wants to play soccer—"football," as they call it in England. Her idol is David Beckham and her bedroom is a shrine to the Manchester United superstar. Her parents do not approve. Her father (Anupam Kher) scowls at the Beckham poster over her bed. "That bald man," her father calls him. He does not even care enough to learn his name.

But Jess is more than a fan; she has a gift for playing the game. She plays in the park with the boys and routinely dominates. Juliette "Jules" Paxton (Knightley) sees Jess in action and invites her to tryout for the Hounslow Harriers, an all-female club which plays a very serious brand of soccer.

Jess shows up for practice in her running shoes and gym shorts and the coach (Jonathan Rhys-Meyers) is convinced he is wasting his time even looking at her. Jules persuades him to give Jess a chance and, even without proper equipment, she puts on a show, weaving through the defense and making brilliant passes to set up Jules for easy goals. It is clear nothing can stop Jess—except her family.

Her father and mother (Shaheen Khan) do not want Jess playing soccer. "You have played enough, running around showing your bare legs in front of men," her mother says. "You must start behaving like a proper woman."

Beckham benefits by the insight Chadha brings to the story. She grew up in the same Southall neighborhood in a Sikh Punjabi family. She wasn't an athlete, but her interest in filmmaking put her at odds with those around her. That experience allows her to write scenes that feel very natural.

Example: The mother is telling Jess that a woman needs to focus on important things, such as cooking. "What's the good in knowing how to run around kicking a ball," she says, "if you don't know how to make round chapattis?" Meanwhile, Jess is behind her bouncing a head of cabbage from one knee to the other. It is a neatly drawn portrait of a mother and daughter sharing a kitchen yet living in different worlds.

Chadha does a neat balancing act of her own, having fun with Jess's parents, yet never allowing them to become caricatures. She writes them in such a way that you understand they are good people who are doing what they feel is in the best interest of their daughter. The father was a top cricket player in Uganda, but he was discriminated against when he moved to England.

"They would not let me play, they made fun of my turban," he says. "I don't want my daughter to be disappointed as I was."

Jess continues to play, but keeps it a secret. Of course, her parents find out and put a stop to it. The Harriers coach tries to convince them to let her play, saying an American coach is coming to scout the final match and there is a good chance he will offer Jess a college scholarship. As it turns out, the match is scheduled for the same day as Pinky's wedding so Jess is forbidden to play.

During the wedding reception, Jess's father softens and allows her slip away to play the second half of the game. When she arrives, she sets up Jules for the tying goal, then scores the game-winner on a penalty kick. On the final shot, she curves the ball around the defense, "bending it" like Beckham. Her father watches, now fully realizing her true potential.

"I saw her play and she is brilliant," he tells his wife. "It would be wrong for us to stop her."

Jess and Jules accept soccer scholarships to Santa Clara. The film ends with their families waving goodbye as the girls leave Heathrow Airport for the United States.

CHEERS: Chadha weaves together the wedding and the climactic soccer game, cutting between the dancing feet at the wedding reception and the feet kicking the soccer ball. The scene is beautifully edited to the festive Indian music.

JEERS: The romantic triangle between Jess, Jules and the coach is the weakest part of the story. The attraction between Jess and Joe seems to come out of nowhere.

WHAT THEY WROTE AT THE TIME: "There is a reality underneath *Beckham's* easy humor, an impeccable sense of milieu that is the result of knowing the culture intimately enough to poke fun at it while understanding its underlying integrity."—Kenneth Turan, *Los Angeles Times*

REPEATED WATCHING QUOTIENT: Pretty high if you are a soccer fan or if you have youngsters (especially girls) who play. The message—be true to your dreams—is delivered in a way that is pleasant, not preachy.

"I KNOW THAT GUY": Jonathan Rhys-Meyers, who plays the Harriers coach, has a splashier role as the tennis pro who beds and then murders Scarlett Johansson in Woody Allen's *Match Point*.

BEST LINE: Jules' mother (Juliet Stevenson) worries about her tomboy daughter's passion for soccer. She says, "There is a reason why Sporty Spice is the only one without a boyfriend."

IF YOU LIKED THIS, YOU'LL LIKE: *Gracie*, a 2007 film based on the life of actress Elisabeth Shue, who played youth soccer against boys while growing up in South Orange, N.J.

SPORTS-ACTION GRADE: C-plus. Most of the action goes like this: Ball is kicked. Cut. Ball is headed. Cut. Ball goes in net. There are not enough wide shots and not enough flow. Jess, however, looks like the real deal handling the ball.

50 LONG GONE (1987–NR)

SPORT: BASEBALL | STARS: WILLIAM PETERSEN, VIRGINIA MADSEN
DIRECTOR: MARTIN DAVIDSON

Of every movie in this book, *Long Gone* may be the least viewed and the most difficult to obtain. Created and aired by HBO in 1987, the film fell out of release and is nearly impossible to find these days in video stores or online rental clubs.

And that's a shame. Because, 20-plus years after it aired, this forgotten project remains an entertaining, funny and realistic look at low-level minor league baseball back in the '50s. Take three parts *Bull Durham*, two parts *Slap Shot*, add a dose of *Bingo Long* and a pinch of the *The Longest Yard* and you've got *Long Gone*.

Those ingredients have made it somewhat of a sports cult movie. While writing this book, we checked Amazon.com for its availability. Not a single copy could be found. Still, 32 people had rated the movie at the site—and 29 of them gave it the maximum five stars.

We would agree. This is an evocative movie, set in the South in 1957, with a smart script and well-staged baseball action. While it did not serve as a star vehicle for either of its main players—William Petersen or Virginia Madsen—both show here why they later went on to become stars. Petersen, of course, is best known as head investigator Gus Grissom on *CSI: Crime Scene Investigation*. And the beautiful Madsen stole the film *Sideways* as Paul Giamatti's out-of-his-league love interest.

Here, Petersen plays Cecil "Stud" Cantrell, pitcher, slugger and manager of the Tampico Stogies, a fictional Class-D franchise on Florida's Gulf Coast. Once, long ago, he was considered a prospect by the St. Louis Cardinals. But first Stan Musial stood in his way, and then World War II. Now he manages a team that must wear dirty uniforms because the owner is too cheap to have them laundered.

Cantrell is part Crash Davis, part Reggie Dunlop (and if those names don't register, you've skipped ahead in this book). At age 38, he lives by three rules:

1. All girls fuck.
2. Fuck 'em if they can't take a joke.
3. You're the asshole that you have to look at in the mirror.

The third rule, by the way, is often neglected as Cantrell drinks and carouses his way through three Southern states. At a dusty ballpark in Crestview, Ala., he seduces the National Anthem singer, the magnificently named Dixie Lee Boxx (Madsen), who was just elected Miss Strawberry Blossom of 1957. Cantrell thinks he is in for a one-nighter, but Miss Boxx becomes his Annie Savoy—despite his best instincts, he falls hard for her. One year before the release of *Bull Durham*, HBO's *Long Gone* had the Baseball Annie theme down quite well.

The last-place Stogies, meanwhile, get some unexpected help. First, an ambitious teenaged second baseman named Jamie Weeks (Dermot Mulroney) comes knocking. He's a topflight fielder and smart hitter—and also as naïve as he is young. You get a sense he is looking at a naked woman for the first time when he visits Cantrell's hotel room and sees Boxx sprawled across the bed.

Next, the Stogies add Joe Louis Brown (Larry Riley), a power hitter and strong-armed catcher. Problem is, Brown is black. And this is the Jim Crow South of the 1950s. Cantrell decides to pass off Brown as a Spanish-speaking Venezuelan—Jose Luis Brown (a gimmick borrowed from *The Bingo Long Traveling All-Stars & Motor Kings*)—and no one (save a few local Klansmen) is any the wiser.

With the influx of talent, the Stogies go on a winning streak. On the verge of the pennant, however, we learn that Tampico's owner (*Laugh-In* alum Henry Gibson) is as corrupt as he is penurious. Cantrell is given the *The Longest Yard* ultimatum: Lose the championship game, and he will get his chance to hook on as a coach with a major league organization. Win the game, and his career is finished.

There aren't many surprises in the script, and there's nothing original in a story about a scrappy underdog coming out on top. But the screenplay, written by Michael Norell based on a novel by Paul Hemphill (an Atlanta novelist who had a brief minor league career) crafts terrific quirky characters. And director Martin Davidson (*Eddie and the Cruisers*) does a great job of setting time and place, right down to Dixie's daily breakfast of Jax Beer.

We're likely frustrating you by touting a movie that hasn't been on the market since people still used VHS. So we're hoping this little push might convince HBO to re-release *Long Gone*—preferably with some DVD commentary. HBO has a legacy of outstanding movies and mini-series—*Band of Brothers, 61*, Recount* and many others. Before all of those, there was *Long Gone*. It should not be forgotten to history.

🍺 **CHEERS:** Stud Cantrell's constant warbling of Hank Williams Sr.'s *Long Gone Lonesome Blues* sets up a great country soundtrack that reminds us how Southern the sport of baseball was back in the day.

🍺 **JEERS:** We understand that the good boy-good girl relationship between Weeks and local Bible-toting teen Esther Wrenn is set up to counterbalance the Stud-Boxx affair. But it's as silly and sappy as an old ABC *After School Special.*

✔ **REALITY CHECK:** Joe Brown confounds an intentional walk by standing on home plate and socking a home run. Any umpire would call him out for that illegal trick.

◉ **REPEATED WATCHING QUOTIENT:** High, but you're going to have to find it first.

☞ **DON'T FAIL TO NOTICE:** The ingenious way in which Cantrell manages to get on base facing a pitcher against whom he is 2-for-68 lifetime.

📣 **CASTING CALL:** Jack Nicholson had read the original novel and was interested in playing Cantrell. When this project rolled around, however, he was busy filming a Western comedy called *Goin' South*. We suspect that had

Nicholson been available, the movie would have gone to the big screen rather than cable.

★ **SPORTS-ACTION GRADE:** B-plus. Mulroney, in his 1950s crew cut and baggy uniform, looks like Bill Mazeroski on second base. And Petersen is a surprisingly good athlete with a smooth pitching delivery (especially when compared with, say, Tim Robbins).

💬 **BEST LINE:** Cantrell, explaining the facts of life: "When God made man, He made him out of string. He had a little left, so He left that little thing. When God made woman, He made her out of lace. He didn't have enough, so He left that little space. Thank you, God."

😎 **"I KNOW THAT GUY":** Teller, the silent half of the comedy duo Penn & Teller, has quite a few funny lines as Hale Buchman, Jr. (also known as Asshole, Jr.), conniving son of the club owner. He was cast in the role because of his physical resemblance to Henry Gibson.

✒ **WHAT THEY WROTE AT THE TIME:** "Like the Amazin' Mets of old, *Long Gone*, a made-for-cable movie, came out of nowhere, and came out a winner. It's far and away the most entertaining and artful fictional work yet produced for a cable television network."—David Bianculli, *New York Post*

🍎 **BET YOU DIDN'T KNOW:** Petersen turned down a role in *Platoon* to make this movie. Although being in the Oscar winner for Best Picture of 1986 might have enhanced his career, Petersen insists he has no regrets. "Making *Long Gone* was like being on a regular baseball team for eight weeks," he told *TV Guide*. "We really had a great team of actors who could play ball. We lived in the same motels, drank together, ate together, partied together and played ball."

Probably more fun than two months in a Vietnam jungle.

51 THE KARATE KID (1984–PG)

SPORT: KARATE | STARS: RALPH MACCHIO, PAT MORITA
DIRECTOR: JOHN G. AVILDSEN

The Karate Kid is one of the most predictable and implausible sports movies ever made.

It's also one of the most enjoyable.

It is a movie that requires you to suspend your critical thought process and accept unlikely premises on faith. Like that a five-foot-seven, 105-pound weakling could develop into a martial arts master in a matter of weeks—mostly by painting fences—and then beat down the linebacker-sized bullies who have been wrecking his life. That plus get the best-looking girl in school who, of course, is on the rebound from dating the most sadistic of the bullies.

If you can just kind of let that all flow by, if you can just say, "Well, sure, it's perfectly reasonable that this old Japanese guy can heal a torn ACL just by touching it,"

then you'll have two hours of fun with *The Karate Kid*. If not? Well, there are plenty of movies in this book that tell more believable tales. Like, say, the one where the corn stalks tell the Iowa farmer to build a baseball field.

Daniel LaRusso (Ralph Macchio) is a pint-sized New Jersey teenager whose mother takes a job in California, the main attraction of which appears to be that it sinks them to the poverty level. Daniel seems to be a nice enough kid, but everyone west of Newark apparently hates his guts. In fact, he gets roughed up four times within the first 30 minutes of the movie.

His main tormentors are a pack of rich Aryan-Nation-in-training types who study karate under psychotic sensei John Kreese (Martin Kove) at the perfectly named "Cobra Kai" studio. Their mantra is, "Strike first! Strike hard! No mercy—*sir!*" They repeat it often. In unison.

Daniel has just two friends. One is high-school hottie Ali Mills (Elisabeth Shue), who doesn't mind that Daniel is friendless, penniless, frail, socially inept and goes out on dates with his mother, driving a jalopy that needs to be pushed down the street to get it started. No, Ali loves him for his . . . well, we're not sure, except that it makes her country-clubbing parents uncomfortable. Sometimes that's enough.

His other friend is the handyman at his apartment complex, an aging Okinawan named Mr. Miyagi (Pat Morita), who tries to catch flies with chopsticks and, in one of the movie's best scenes, incapacitates five of the neo-Nazis in about 30 seconds. This persuades Daniel (henceforth known as "Daniel-San") that rather than flee, he must learn to fight.

And learn to fight he does. Kind of. Mr. Miyagi's rigorous training method has Daniel-San sanding his deck, staining his fence, waxing his cars and painting his house. Somehow, we eventually see, the pipsqueak has learned to defend himself through indentured servitude. Meanwhile, Mr. Miyagi's got some great urban renewal going on.

The Karate Kid leads up to a terrific climactic scene, the standing-room-only All-Valley Karate Tournament, in which Daniel-San must defeat the meaner men from Cobra Kai. First, the bullies taunt him with lines like, "What's the matter, Danny, mommy's not here to dress you?" And, "Put him in a body bag, yeah!" Then one of them takes a deliberate disqualification by snapping Daniel's fibula in half (a violation, we are told, of the all-important Rule 31-point-2).

But our hero isn't done. After Mr. Miyagi lays his healing hands on the kid like the Rev. Benny Hinn, Daniel-San must face the evilest of the Cobra Kai, Johnny Lawrence (magnificently played by William Zabka, who made a career out of portraying jackasses). Let's see, Johnny is 60 pounds heavier, ten times nastier and has studied martial arts for a decade. Plus, he's got his psychotic sensei offering coaching advice like, "Sweep the leg, Johnny. Do you have a problem with that? No mercy."

Now, who's gonna win?

It leads up to one of the great sports movie climaxes, the Crane Kick to Blond Boy's face. A quick flash of a foot

and we're done. Cue music, show the girlfriend leaping from the stands, roll credits. Perfect, perfect ending.

In fact, you'll see it all coming a lot quicker than the unfortunate Johnny. This movie telegraphs more than Samuel F.B. Morse. But, hey, don't let that ruin the fun.

CHEERS: To the great performance by Pat Morita as Mr. Miyagi. It's right up there with Gene Hackman (Norman Dale) and Burgess Meredith (Mick) in the realm of all-time fantastic coach portrayals. It even earned him an Oscar nomination, which isn't bad for an actor whose previous high had been playing malt shop owner Arnold on *Happy Days*.

JEERS: If you're a fan of music from the 80s (easily the worst decade for rock), you'll tolerate the soundtrack put together by Bill Conti, who peaked with his work in *Rocky*. But if your taste has evolved since, say, Menudo, you'll find the songs cringingly bad. Survivor? Bananarama? Joe Esposito? ("You're the best . . . around . . . Nothing's gonna keep you down!") The music here is as dated as carbon paper.

BEST LINE: We've got to go with, "Wax on, wax off." It's right up there with, "There's no crying in baseball," and "If you build it, he will come," among the iconic lines in sports movies.

PIVOTAL SCENE: After spending day after day as Mr. Miyagi's personal slave, Daniel-San finally loses his temper.

"I've been busting my ass and haven't learned a goddamn thing," he shouts.

"You learn plenty," counters Mr. Miyagi.

"I learn plenty, yeah. I learn how to sand your decks, maybe. I wash your car, paint your house. Paint your fence. I learn plenty."

The angry student storms out, but is called back by his master, who squares off to fight. As Miyagi throws punches and kicks, Daniel-San instinctively blocks them all with the same wax on-wax off and paint up-paint down motions he used on household chores. Miraculously, he has mastered self defense without even knowing it.

We invite you all to try that teaching technique with your teenaged sons.

✏ **WHAT THEY WROTE AT THE TIME:** "All hail the Crane Kick, liberator of self-doubting wimps over bullies, redeemer of lost causes, winner of Elisabeth Shue's heart."—Phil Villarreal, *Arizona Star*

✔ **REALITY CHECK:** Every. Single. Minute.

◉ **REPEATED WATCHING QUOTIENT:** Fairly high. And you'll certainly get the opportunity, because some cable network or another airs *The Karate Kid* nearly every single day.

☞ **DON'T FAIL TO NOTICE:** Dutch, the albino-looking Cobra Kai fighter who breaks Daniel's leg, is played by Chad McQueen, son of the great Steve McQueen. Dad's career included *The Great Escape* and *Bullitt*. Chad kind of peaked here and stumbled on to appear in *Indecent Behavior II* and *Sexual Malice*, movies seen only after midnight way at the end of your TV dial. Steve and Chad McQueen; kind of like Yogi and Dale Berra.

★ **SPORTS-ACTION GRADE:** B-minus. It's a C right up until the last 30 seconds. The ending warrants an A.

◀ **CASTING CALL:** Chuck Norris was offered the role of evil sensei Kreese, but turned it down because he didn't want karate instructors presented in a bad light.

✷ **IF YOU LIKED THIS, YOU'LL LIKE:** *The Karate Kid II*, which starts exactly where *The Karate Kid* left off. Of course, two years passed between the shooting of the original and the sequel, so try not to notice how much older Daniel looks as he hoists the trophy he supposedly won seconds earlier. The setting then moves to Japan, where Daniel finds himself as immediately unpopular as he is in California.

Also, be sure to check out the music video "Sweep the Leg," by No More Kings, at sweeptheleg.com. It's a hilarious send up of life after *The Karate Kid* ends, largely from poor Johnny's perspective. Most of the original cast—including Macchio and Zabka—make appearances.

Do not make the mistake of renting *The Karate Kid III*, filmed in 1989. And under no circumstances, other than torture, should one be subjected to the Macchio-less *The Next Karate Kid*.

THE WORST SPORTS SEQUELS AND REMAKES EVER MADE

1. *Rocky V.* We have this theory that sometime, back around 1975, young Sylvester Stallone made a deal with the Devil. Sly would get to write and star in one of cinema's masterworks (*Rocky*, of course), and in return, would have to spend the rest of eternity humiliating himself with the likes of *Judge Dredd* and *Stop! Or My Mom Will Shoot*.

And this all-time stinker. By the time the fifth episode of the same story rolled around, The Italian Stallion was in his mid-forties and looked like a white version of Buster Douglas (this, apparently, before Stallone discovered HGH and botox).

In the first four movies, the story arced through Rocky's battles with an arrogant Ali-esque champion, a Mohawk-wearing thug and a steroid-inflated Soviet cyborg. There was really nothing left to wring out of the series—once Mick died the spirit of the thing was gone. But with *Rocky IV* grossing $300 million worldwide, well, who was going to turn off the tap?

And so it was done. Director John G. Avildsen returned after a three-*Rocky* hiatus, but failed to instill any of the nuance or humanity that made the original so, well, original. Real-life boxer Tommy Morrison, cast as the protégé-turned-foil, was wooden enough to make Mr. T seem like Mr. Laurence Olivier by comparison. And somehow, Stallone—regressing back to the porkpie hat and row home—

didn't seem as charming 14 years later.

Sly himself, in a 2007 interview with British TV host Jonathan Ross, admitted this episode was "inferior" to the others. We think he's being too kind. Certainly it was inferior at the box office, grossing just $120 million worldwide. Do the math: At an average of, say $6 a ticket (1990 prices, after all), there are 20 million people who will never get those two wasted hours back.

We only wish Stallone had stayed with the ending he first wrote, in which Rocky drops dead after beating Tommy Gunn in their street fight. At least our misery would have ended a few minutes earlier.

2. Caddyshack II. Eight years after the original changed the vocabulary of weekend hackers forever, writers Harold Ramis and Brian Doyle-Murray tried to cash in with this disaster, which is about as funny as eczema.

We won't waste your time trying to describe the plot, except to say there's nothing in it about caddies, and no golf at all for the first hour. You won't last that long.

Jackie Mason is a pale Xerox of Rodney Dangerfield, as the crude self-made millionaire clashing with the country club snobs. And Dan Aykroyd is at his most annoying, trying to channel Bill Murray as the gopher-hating groundskeeper. The gopher puppet returns from the 1980 original. He's the best member of the cast.

3. Slap Shot 2: Breaking the Ice. Or breaking the DVD, which would be a better idea. This is another example of taking a great original comedy—with story and substance—and trying to re-create its success with slapstick and crudeness. In this case, they waited 25 years, ripped off the plot of *Major League*, cast the weakest of all Baldwin brothers (Stephen) in the lead, and forced the original Hanson Brothers to skate around like they were still interested.

The only thing that could have made it worse would have been an appearance by Adam Sandler. Speaking of which . . .

4. The Longest Yard. This time, instead of trying to come up with a sequel for the 1974 classic, they just shot it all over again with essentially the same script. Except that instead of former Florida State star Burt Reynolds as

quarterback Paul Crewe, it's Sandler—which is kind of like replacing Brett Favre with Pauly Shore.

Reynolds takes the supporting role as Coach Nate Scarborough, which proves that at this point of his career it is impossible to find any film he will turn down (if you don't believe us, rent *The Dukes of Hazzard*.) Meanwhile, Snoop Dogg and Gary Oldman both dropped out during filming, which proves some actors still have their limits.

Like the REAL *The Longest Yard*, this 2005 version features some actual former NFL players, including Michael Irvin, Brian Bosworth and Bill Romanowski. On the plus side, each of them appears quite comfortable in the prison scenes.

It is shocking to realize that some filmgoers under 40 may know only this version of the movie. If you're among them, rent the 1974 version. Immediately. Seriously, put down this book and go get it.

Now.

5. Rollerball. The 1975 Sci-Fi original presented a frightening look at sports in an ultra-violent and corporate-controlled future. This 2001 remake came after TV studio creations like *Slamball, American Gladiators* and mixed martial arts inured us from any form of sports future shock. So it doesn't work on that level.

And it sure doesn't work replacing the brooding and athletic James Caan with Chris Klein, whose acting range appears to extend from goofy (*American Pie*) to vacuous (*Election*). We're supposed to buy him as a tough-guy rebel? That's like casting Adam Sandler as a real football player. Oops.

6. The Bad News Bears Go to Japan. They really needed to follow up on *The Bad News Bears in Breaking Training*? That stinker of a sequel wasn't evidence enough that you couldn't recreate the chemistry without Morris Buttermaker and Amanda Whurlitzer?

Apparently not, so Version III was released on June 30, 1978 and, by any account we could find, disappeared by Independence Day. Nothing remotely interesting happens in this film. No comedy. No action. There is a five-minute scene in which the kids take off their shoes. We're not kidding.

Tony Curtis stars, fresh off his performances in the dreadful *Sextette* (a sex romp with 85-year-old Mae West) and *The Manitou* (in which he plays a psychic whose girlfriend has a lump growing in her back that's the reincarnation of a 400-year-old demonic spirit). Come to think of it, this might have been Curtis's best film of 1978.

7. *The Next Karate Kid.* The fourth of the series came out in 1994, and by this time, Mr. Miyagi's philosophical musings didn't seem quite so poetic. "Sun is warm, grass is green." Plot is tired.

The twist here is that the new star student is—*what?*—a 15-year-old girl, played by 20-year-old Hilary Swank. If it's worth watching for anything, it's seeing Swank before she apparently took any acting lessons. Something tells us that the boxed DVD of this dog does not sit on her living room mantle between her two Oscars.

8. *Body and Soul.* We're sure this seemed like a good idea at the time. The 1947 original, starring John Garfield and Lilli Palmer, was a forgotten masterpiece by 1981. What better idea than to steal the script, update the cast to reflect how boxing had become an African-American sport, and even hire Muhammad Ali to play himself?

To further ensure commercial success, producers cast Sugar Ray Leonard look-alike Leon Isaac Kennedy and his wife, bombshell sportscaster Jayne Kennedy for the leads, wrote a ton of nudity into the script and arranged for a five-page spread in Playboy, which we fondly recall to this day.

How could it miss?

Well, miss it did. Leon was a former disc jockey from Detroit who broadcast under the moniker "Leon the Lover." As a boxer, well, let's say he was a better disc jockey. His fighting style evoked Shemp from *The Three Stooges*. And, for some inexplicable reason, he was given final say on the script. So it is replete with sappy stereotypes, like the crippled kid sister, as well as yawning plot holes.

On the other hand, Jayne Kennedy looked really good naked.

Leon left showbiz altogether in the 1980s. Last we read, he became a preacher. He ought to pray that no one in his flock ever sees him in this stinker.

9. *Major League: Back to the Minors.* *Major League* (1989) was clever, funny and had characters that reminded you of players you had known. The sequel, *Major League II* (1994), had most of the original cast, including Charlie Sheen and Tom Berenger. It lacked the clever story, but still could be called marginally funny.

This 1998 movie has none of that. It becomes worse when you consider that the talent level of the players on this team appears less than your beer league softball squad. And by the time they filmed this third version, pretty much everyone had abandoned the series except for future President Dennis Haysbert and Corbin Bernsen, who apparently had nothing else to do.

10. *Cannonball Run II.* Not that the original was anything great, but it had a boozy irreverence that made it a country-fried version of the old Rat Pack films. The sequel? Just boozy, in that the entire cast appears to be in the midst of a six-week bender.

There is an amazing cast of party animals on hand, from Burt Reynolds to Dean Martin to Cheech Marin to Foster Brooks. You get the feeling there's a really good time going on. It's just that you, as a filmgoer, aren't invited to the fun.

The movie is memorable for several things, none of them positive. Dom DeLuise unleashes the worst Brando-as-Godfather impression in cinema history, mumbling about a dead cat. And, sadly, this is the final film appearance of Frank Sinatra. There is something terribly wrong with that.

In *It Happens Every Spring*, Ray Milland plays a nutty professor (no, not *that* one) who accidentally creates a potion that causes a baseball to be repelled by wood. Armed with his discovery, he becomes a major league pitcher and lifts the St. Louis Cardinals to the World Series.

When the chicanery is discovered, the professor is hauled before a Congressional committee and barred from baseball by Commissioner Bud Selig.

Okay, we lied about the last part. But the rest pretty much outlines the plot. It is a totally silly, utterly preposterous film, but it's also great fun and a delight for audiences of all ages.

While Milland, Jean Peters and Paul Douglas are the names on the marquee, the real star of the film is Fred Sersen, who created the special effects. Sersen was one of Hollywood's most celebrated artists. He won two Academy Awards and was nominated on six other occasions. He created the catastrophic fire in *Old Chicago* (1938) and the floods in *The Rains Came* (1939).

Sersen was one of the pioneers of cinematic illusion. He was making cities burn, waters rise and sea creatures attack long before computers made such trickery routine. So when director Lloyd Bacon needed someone to make a baseball leap over a bat, he knew there was only one man for the job. He called Sersen, who had just finished working on *Down to the Sea in Ships* with Lionel Barrymore.

It Happens Every Spring was a different sort of venture for Sersen. In most of his films, Sersen—who worked on more than 200 motion pictures—sought to make the effects realistic. In this film—a fantasy played for laughs—Sersen could have some fun. He made the dancing baseball a comically crude device. It jumps over the bat and into the catcher's mitt with an exaggerated "Whoooosh." You can imagine Sersen chuckling as he put it on film.

Viewed today, the special effects are—well, the word *cheesy* comes to mind. But that only makes the film more amusing. And Ray Milland's pitching motion, which resembles a man falling off a ladder, makes it funnier still. If Milland looked more like a real pitcher and the special effects were slicker, *Spring* wouldn't be nearly as much fun.

Originally a short story written by Shirley Wheeler Smith in 1923, *It Happens Every Spring* was adapted into a screenplay by Valentine Davies, who won an Oscar for writing the Christmas classic *Miracle on 34th Street*.

Spring was such a quirky tale that no one knew how it would be received when it was screened for a test audience in Riverside, Ca. But as Davies wrote to Smith, "There was so much laughter that some of the funniest lines were completely drowned out. The [comment] cards were also most enthusiastic and what pleased us most was that the women and girls seemed to be no less enthusiastic about the picture than the men."

The film's hero is Vernon Simpson (Milland), a nerdy chemistry professor with a crush on Deborah Greenleaf (Peters), daughter of the school president. Vernon is developing a chemical compound designed to keep insects away from wood. One day a baseball crashes through his lab window and lands in a tub filled with the liquid.

While he is cleaning up the mess, Vernon notices something odd. Each time the ball comes near a piece of wood, it veers away. Vernon, a baseball freak, immediately sees the possibilities. If he rubs his secret compound on the ball, the ball will be repelled by the wooden bat and therefore be unhittable.

He tries it out with two members of the varsity baseball team, and when they helplessly flail away at his offerings, he is emboldened to ask the Cardinals for a tryout. When he mows down their best hitters, he is signed to a contract. He takes the name King Kelly, and with a stash of Methyl Ethyl Propin Butyl hidden in his glove, he becomes the top pitcher in baseball.

He wants to keep his identity a secret, so he refuses to be photographed or interviewed, which becomes a real hassle as he piles up win after win. Meanwhile, he is MIA at the university. The professor has disappeared and no one knows why. When he sends Debbie a diamond ring, her parents conclude that he must have turned to a life of crime. It is zany stuff, it doesn't make a whole lot of sense, but it is very entertaining.

It Happens Every Spring is typical of the screwball romantic comedies that were so popular in the 1940s. Cary Grant and Clark Gable made many. But this film was a departure for Milland, who was best known for his performance as an alcoholic writer in *The Lost Weekend*, a role which earned him the Academy Award in 1946.

Milland is good in *Spring*, especially his chemistry with Paul Douglas, who plays his dim-witted catcher and roommate Monk Lanigan. When Monk sees the bottle of Butyl in the bathroom, Vernon tells him it is hair tonic. Monk applies it to his scalp and when he tries to use a wooden brush on his hair, it is time for more of Sersen's special effects.

Over the years, some deep-thinkers have analyzed the film and questioned whether it is a good thing that it celebrates cheating in baseball, as if Gaylord Perry saw *Spring* and that is how he got the idea to smear Vaseline on the ball and become a Hall of Famer.

Lighten up, guys. It's only a movie.

⬆ **CHEERS:** The scene in which Monk tries to pick up the ball while wearing a wooden splint on his finger is hilarious.

⬇ **JEERS:** It is hard to find fault with anything in this 87-minute gem. Ray Milland looks nothing like a ballplayer, but that's part of the joke.

🍎 **BET YOU DIDN'T KNOW:** The movie was filmed in Wrigley Field in Los Angeles, home of the minor league Angels. The ballpark was later used for the 1950s TV show *Home Run Derby*.

👓 **"I KNOW THAT GUY":** Alan Hale Jr. is the catcher for the on-campus tryout. He is best known as the Skipper in *Gilligan's Island*, so it has a familiar ring when he calls out to Milland, "Hey, Professor. . . ."

🗣 **BEST LINE:** The tag line from the movie poster: "The guy who invented the ball nobody could hit. And the girl with the curves nobody could miss."

✎ **WHAT THEY WROTE AT THE TIME:** "Immensely silly, but quite charming."—Charlie Patton, *Jacksonville Times-Union*

★ **SPORTS-ACTION GRADE:** D. No one in the film looks like he belongs on a big league ball field, but so what? We're laughing the whole time.

🎞 **MY FAVORITE SPORTS MOVIE:** Mark Bowden, author of *Black Hawk Down* and *The Best Game Ever*: "I saw it on TV when I was growing up outside Chicago in the 1950s, probably on a rainy Sunday afternoon. It was funny, and the depiction of the Cardinals locker room and the players was fascinating. It seemed authentic enough to a kid who adored baseball. . . . And it holds up. I saw it again a few years back and was transported."

53 WITHOUT LIMITS (1998–PG-13)

SPORT: TRACK | STARS: BILLY CRUDUP, DONALD SUTHERLAND, MONICA POTTER
DIRECTOR: ROBERT TOWNE

Robert Towne is a man of considerable influence. He won an Academy Award for his script on *Chinatown*. He received three other Oscar nominations for screenwriting so he had the clout to sell a studio on a film project it might otherwise ignore. *Without Limits* was that kind of project.

Let's count up all the reasons why *Without Limits* was a lousy investment. First of all, it was a movie about track, a sport only a handful of Americans care about. Second, it was the story of a guy who competed in one Olympics and didn't even win a medal. Third, it was tried one year earlier—different studio, different cast—and flopped at the box office.

But Towne, a track enthusiast, had such a passion for the story of Steve Prefontaine, the charismatic American distance runner, that he was able to convince Warner Brothers to throw its millions behind the film. It helped that Tom Cruise signed on as producer and briefly considered playing the lead before deciding he was too old.

If we go strictly by the bottom line, *Without Limits* was an utter dud. The film cost $25 million to make and it grossed less than $1 million. If Cruise had played Prefontaine—even if he needed an oxygen tank to run the 5,000 meters—it would have sold tickets. But the lead, Billy Crudup, was an unknown, and the title was a head-scratcher, and as a result, the film went nowhere.

However, if we evaluate *Without Limits* strictly as a piece of art, it is quite good. Janet Maslin of the *New York Times* called it "the most stirring and unmistakably personal film [Towne] has directed." Owen Gleiberman of *Entertainment Weekly* called it "incisive and enthralling, as deft on its feet as the athletes it's about." Paul Tatara of CNN said it was "one of the best sports movies I've ever seen."

It is fitting in a way because Towne surely viewed this film the way Prefontaine viewed his career on the track, that is, it's not about the bottom line. It's not even makes the character of Prefontaine both understandable and admirable.

Towne tells much of the story in narration written for Donald Sutherland, who plays Prefontaine's coach Bill Bowerman. Towne's writing is lean, yet powerful, and Sutherland's read hits just the right notes. A typical line: "From the beginning, I tried to change Pre. He tried not to change. That was our relationship." Three short sentences, 17 words total, but it sums up everything we need to know about the two men.

Prefontaine (Crudup) is a track star of the 1970s. He

PREFONTAINE: "YOU CAN CALL A RACE ANY GODDAM THING YOU WANT, BUT I WOULDN'T CALL IT A PERFORMANCE."

BOWERMAN: "WHAT WOULD YOU CALL IT?"

PREFONTAINE: "A WORK OF ART."

about winning, it's about the art. It's about pursuing a higher standard than mere victory or dollars. That was Prefontaine's ethos and Towne was faithful to it in telling his story.

Even without an Olympic medal, Steve Prefontaine will be remembered as a great runner. And even without a big box office return, *Without Limits* will be remembered as a well-crafted piece of film-making, rich with feeling and insight. Towne's gift for writing is one of the film's strengths. With his well-chosen words, Towne

holds the American record at every distance from 2,000 meters to 10,000 meters. However, "Pre," as he is known, drives his coaches—Bowerman in particular—crazy by refusing to race strategically. He refuses to pace himself. He insists on pushing himself to the limit. That means going to the front of the pack and staying there. Bowerman tells Pre he'll never be able to defeat the world's best runners that way. Pre refuses to bend.

"I don't want to win unless I know I've done my best," Pre says, "and the only way I know how to do that is to run out front, flat out until I have nothing left. Winning any other way is chickenshit."

Handsome with sun-bleached blonde hair, Pre is like a rock star in the track hotbed of Eugene, Oregon, where he attends college. He is cocky and narcissistic and, frankly, at times he is not all that likeable. It's fine to be an iconoclast—it isn't like distance running is a team sport—but Pre takes it to irritating lengths when he says things like: "I can endure more pain than anyone you've ever met. That's why I can beat anyone I've ever met."

But when he is spiked during a race and we see him coming down the final straightaway with the blood soaking through his shoe, we can appreciate the fact that this is a guy who is defined by something more than stopwatches and medals.

Without Limits is at its best when it focuses on the relationship between the headstrong Pre and the coach/psychologist Bowerman. At first, Bowerman thinks he can change Pre simply by ordering him to do so. Then Bowerman realizes Pre is not just another runner, therefore he cannot be coached like one. The coach must find other ways to reach him, and although Towne does not belabor the point, it works as a metaphor for what was going on between the generations in America at the same time.

In the end, the coach and the runner find an understanding and a mutual respect. As Bowerman says in another voiceover: "Pre thought I was a hard case. But he finally got it through my head that the real purpose of running isn't to win a race, it's to test the limits of the human heart. That he did. No one did it more often. No one did it better."

🍺 **CHEERS:** Donald Sutherland's performance as Bill Bowerman earned him a Golden Globe nomination for Best Supporting Actor. "Sutherland hasn't completely involved himself in all his parts, but he's done so here," wrote Kenneth Turan in the *Los Angeles Times*. "The result is a commanding, almost hypnotic performance that is among the actor's best."

🏳 **JEERS:** The romance of Prefontaine and fellow student Mary Marckx (Monica Potter) is underdeveloped. Towne seems to lose interest once the story leaves the track.

◀ **CASTING CALL:** Towne originally wanted Tommy Lee Jones to play the part of Bill Bowerman, but Jones turned it down.

✏ **WHAT THEY WROTE AT THE TIME:** "Sutherland, updating the eternal myth of the tough-love coach/drill sergeant/Mr. Miyagi figure, gives a performance of triumphant, winking intelligence. [He] breaks Pre as if he were a beautiful horse."—Owen Gleiberman, *Entertainment Weekly*

☞ **DON'T FAIL TO NOTICE:** The running shoe that Bowerman develops during the film. It is the prototype of what became the Nike empire.

💬 **BEST LINE:** Steve Prefontaine: "I'd like to work it out so that at the end, it's a pure guts race. If it is, I'm the only one who can win it."

🐛 **BET YOU DIDN'T KNOW:** Steve Prefontaine competed in the 1972 Summer Olympics in Munich and finished fourth in the 5,000 meters. He was killed in a car crash in Eugene three years later.

👓 **"I KNOW THAT GUY":** Jeremy Sisto, who plays American marathoner Frank Shorter, is Detective Cyrus Lupo on TV's *Law and Order*.

★ **SPORTS-ACTION GRADE:** B. The track scenes are well shot and Crudup has the lean, sinewy stride of a distance runner.

✴ **IF YOU LIKED THIS, YOU'LL LIKE:** *Prefontaine*, which was released in 1997. It stars Jared Leto as Pre and R. Lee Ermey, the scary drill sergeant from *Full Metal Jacket*, as Bowerman. Not bad, but *Without Limits* is better.

54 THE HARDER THEY FALL (1956–NR)

SPORT: BOXING | STARS: HUMPHREY BOGART, ROD STEIGER, JAN STERLING
DIRECTOR: MARK ROBSON

The Harder They Fall is noteworthy because it was Humphrey Bogart's final screen appearance. Bogart was battling lung cancer, and it was a struggle for him to make it through the long days of filming. But he turned in a moving performance as Eddie Willis, a sportswriter who sells out to the syndicate.

The film is based on a novel by Budd Schulberg, who wrote the screenplay for *On The Waterfront*. The movies are similar in look and feel: gritty black-and-white *films noirs* shot in and around New York with Rod Steiger cast as the mobbed-up heavy. Ads for *The Harder They Fall* read: "If you think *On The Waterfront* hit hard, wait until you see this one."

The Harder They Fall did not reach the heights of *Waterfront*. It earned one Academy Award nomination, and that was for photography (Burnett Guffey). Bogart and Steiger were passed over, although both were deserving. The film earned mixed reviews. Some critics found it heavy-handed. Boxing apologists ripped it as dishonest. But others were blown away by the story, which painted an ugly picture of the fight game.

Sportswriter Reid Cherner of *USA Today* ranks it No. 1 on his all-time list of sports movies. "Bogart and Steiger make this gritty film a success," Cherner wrote.

The film was a thinly disguised biography of former heavyweight champ Primo Carnera. It was so thinly disguised, in fact, that Carnera sued Columbia pictures, claiming the film makes him look like a fraud. However, most boxing experts agree the film is an accurate account of Carnera's improbable rise to fame.

Carnera was a muscle-bound oaf imported from Italy who was—shall we say—carefully carried up the heavyweight ladder. His nicknames—"Satchel Feet" and "The Ambling Alp"—will give you some idea of his ring artistry. Nat Fleischer of *Ring* magazine described Carnera as "a crude fighter with little skill . . . one of the poorest heavyweight champions." Yet, in 1933-34, he held the title.

In *The Harder They Fall*, the fighter is Toro Moreno (Mike Lane), a 6-10, 270-pound circus strongman, brought in from Argentina to join the boxing stable of Nick Benko (Steiger). There is only one problem: he can't fight. The first time he spars, he's knocked on his butt by a broken-down old pug named George (Jersey Joe Walcott).

"Powder-puff punch and a glass jaw, great combination," says Willis (Bogart), who attends the workout. "That's some discovery you have there, Nick."

Benko has invested a lot of money in Toro, so he refuses to write him off. He asks Willis, an unemployed sportswriter, to sign on as Toro's publicist. His job will be to sell the big galoot, create a phony backstory and use the press to build Toro into a contender.

"Oh, I get it—Toro Moreno, Wild Man of the Andes," Willis says sarcastically.

"Perfect," Benko says.

"But what happens when you put him in the ring?" Willis asks.

"I'll take care of that," Benko says.

In other words, he'll pay Toro's opponents to take a dive.

Willis has spent years in the newspaper business, working to expose guys like Benko. His instincts are telling him to walk out, but his paper just folded and he needs the money. He stands there agonizing.

"Don't fight it, Eddie," Benko says. "What are you trying to do, hold onto your self-respect? Did your self-respect help you hold onto your job? Did your self-respect give you a new column?"

Reluctantly, Willis takes the job and begins selling a fighter who he knows can't fight a lick. They travel the country on a bus with Toro's likeness on the side. It's like a carnival act with Willis cranking the calliope as Toro piles up one bogus knockout after another.

Willis' conscience continues to nag him, especially as he grows closer to Toro. The big guy is a gentle soul who has no idea what's going on. He thinks he's winning these fights on the level. He is the only one who doesn't know it is a sham. He also is unaware Benko and his crooked associates are stealing his earnings. Willis knows where this is headed and so do we.

Thanks to Willis' publicity campaign and Benko's wheeling and dealing, Toro gets a shot at the heavyweight champion, Buddy Brannen (Max Baer). Here is where art meets life. Baer fought Primo Carnera in 1934, knocking him down 11 times to take his title. In the film, his character does the same thing, pulverizing the helpless Toro who is too proud to follow Willis' advice and take a dive. Toro keeps absorbing punishment until finally he is flat on the canvas, his jaw broken and his face a bloody mess.

After the fight, Willis goes to Benko's office to pick up Toro's purse. "I told him I'd bring it to him in the hospital," he says. Benko's accountant (Nehemiah Persoff) goes through the books and tells Willis that after this deduction and that deduction (all of them phony but notarized) Toro's share of the million dollar gate is $49.07.

That's the last straw. Willis gets Toro out of the hospital, gives him his own share of the purse ($26,000) and puts him on a plane back to Argentina. Then Willis returns to journalism. The last thing we see are the keys of his typewriter pounding out: "Professional boxing should be outlawed in the United States if it takes an act of Congress to do it."

Willis is writing an expose that presumably will put Benko and the rest of his lowlife ilk out of business. OK, so it didn't work out. Last time we looked, boxing was still around. But, hey, it was a cool way to end the film.

CHEERS: Bogart and Steiger did not get along, and it may have helped the film. You feel the tension when they share a scene and it's effective because it fits the relationship of the two characters. They are terrific together.

JEERS: The final fight doesn't make sense. Willis and George are begging Toro to "go down and stay down" rather than take more punishment. Hey, guys, all you have to do is throw in the towel. Did you forget?

✒ **WHAT THEY WROTE AT THE TIME:** "The portrait it draws of a promoter is so harsh and despicable that it makes one shudder to imagine there might be such a man loose in the world. As played by the relentless Rod Steiger, he has the charm of a knife-nicked grizzly bear."—Bosley Crowther, *New York Times*

😎 **"I KNOW THAT GUY":** Harold J. Stone, who plays TV reporter Art Leavitt, was Rocky Graziano's abusive father in *Somebody Up There Likes Me*.

🎬 **PIVOTAL SCENE:** Willis tells Toro the truth: he can't fight, all of his victories have been set-ups and now he is fighting the heavyweight champion who is eager to destroy him. Willis tries to convince Toro to take a dive and spare himself a beating.

"What will people think of me?" Toro asks.

"What do you care what a bunch of bloodthirsty, screaming people think?" Willis says. "Did you ever get a look at their faces? They pay a few lousy bucks hoping to see a man get killed. To hell with them. Think of yourself. Get your money and get out of this rotten business."

💬 **BEST LINE:** After Toro's defeat, Willis and George are alone in the dressing room. Willis asks, "Why didn't he fight like we told him to? Why did he take that awful beating?"

George says, "Some guys can sell out, other guys just can't."

Willis falls silent, his face heavy with guilt. He is one of those guys who sold out—and he hates himself for it.

★ **SPORTS-ACTION GRADE:** B-plus. The graphic black and white photography earned Burnett Guffey an Oscar nomination. For realistic sound, director Mark Robson recorded Baer and Walcott punching a ham, and he used that as the effects track for the big fight.

IF YOU LIKE THIS, YOU'LL LIKE: *Kid Galahad*, a 1937 boxing film, also starring Humphrey Bogart, except this time he plays the mobster.

🖐 **MY FAVORITE SPORTS MOVIE:** Buddy McGirt, former world welterweight champion: "I've studied boxing history and anyone who knows their history knows *The Harder They Fall* is really the story of Primo Carnera. It shows how he was exploited and taken advantage of and left with nothing. Humphrey Bogart is great as the one guy who stands up to the mob. I also like the movie because Jersey Joe Walcott is in it. He's my favorite fighter of all time."

SPORTSWRITERS IN SPORTS FILMS

Generally speaking, journalists have a low opinion of sports movies. They point to contrived storylines (Whoopi Goldberg coaching the New York Knicks in *Eddie*), distortion of facts (demonizing Max Baer in *Cinderella Man*) and impossible-to-swallow action (Keanu Reeves playing quarterback in *The Replacements*). Yes, there is much to scorn.

But there may be another reason why the press box critics dismiss the sports movie genre, and that's because of how they are portrayed in most films. They are either seen as cynical jackals nipping at the feet of the hero or hapless toadies, only too happy to sell their souls for a seat on the team charter. Either way, it is not a flattering portrait.

Eddie Willis, the sportswriter turned press agent in *The Harder They Fall*, is a sad figure, a man with a conscience but also bills to pay who sells out to a crooked boxing promoter. In the end, Willis (Humphrey Bogart) can no longer tolerate the lying and cheating so he returns home to write an expose about corruption in the fight game. He has seen the light and even though he is prepared to take on the mob, it is hard to view him as a hero. He has strayed too far.

For years, the best-known sportswriter on the screen

was Oscar Madison, a character from the Neil Simon comedy *The Odd Couple*. Walter Matthau played Oscar in the movie and Jack Klugman inherited the role on TV. Oscar was a New York scribe whose character was defined not by his column but by the gravy stains on his sweatshirt. Oscar was a slob, a womanizer and a serial litterbug—and made no apologies for it.

In the '70s, while America was swooning over the der-ring-do of Robert Redford and Dustin Hoffman as *Washington Post* reporters Bob Woodward and Carl Bernstein in *All the President's Men*, Oscar became the slacker face of the newspaper business. You could hardly blame sports guys for feeling a little put out. But, OK, that was a comedy.

What really troubles sports journalists is how they are portrayed in other, more serious films. Why does Hollywood insist on making the sports reporter so unappealing when news reporters are typically cast as heroes?

It is not that hard to explain. In movies like *All the President's Men* and *The China Syndrome*, the reporters are working to bring down a corrupt presidency or evil corporation. The reporters are the good guys. It is the other way around in sports films. The athlete is the hero and the reporters are the ones trying to knock him off his pedestal. They are usually lurking around corners, making snide comments and digging for dirt.

In the HBO film *61** two writers are shown interviewing Yankee star Roger Maris. A shy man, Maris (Barry Pepper) is uncomfortable with the media so he answers the questions with shrugs and cliches. As he walks away, one reporter cracks, "M-V-P. Most Vacant Personality."

In the original *Rocky*, Apollo Creed (Carl Weathers) and Rocky (Sylvester Stallone) are facing a roomful of reporters as they announce their title fight. Creed owns the stage in the manner of Muhammad Ali. Rocky, the small-time club fighter who can't quite grasp what is happening, sits at the table, not saying a word.

Finally, a reporter directs a question at Rocky. He asks, "Do you have anything derogatory to say about the champ?"

Rocky looks befuddled. "Derogatory?" he says. "Yeah, he's great."

Only in the movies would a reporter ask such a ridiculously worded question, but that's how it goes in Hollywood.

HERE ARE SOME OTHER NOTABLE CINEMA SCRIBES:

Dickie Dunn (M. Emmet Walsh) in *Slap Shot*. Covers the Charlestown Chiefs hockey team. Coach Reg Dunlop (Paul Newman) reads Dickie's florid prose aloud at the bar: "Their blue jerseys streaking across the milky white ice." Reg says, "Oooh, that's good writing, Dickie." Dunn replies: "I was just trying to capture the spirit of the thing."

Max Mercy (Robert Duvall) in *The Natural*. Roy Hobbs comes out of nowhere to lead the New York Knights to the pennant while Max watches from the press box, trying to remember where he saw him before. Years earlier, Hobbs was a hot-shot prospect who bumped into Max and the Whammer (Joe Don Baker) on a train, but Max can't quite put it together. Still, he keeps digging.

Max approaches Roy before a game.

"Looking for a scoop, Max?" Hobbs says, lacing up his spikes.

"You read my mind," Max replies.

"That took all of three seconds," Hobbs says.

Al Stump (Robert Wuhl) in *Cobb*. Stump was a real writer who contributed pieces to *The Saturday Evening Post*. In 1960, he agreed to collaborate with Ty Cobb on a book about his baseball career. Traveling with Cobb, Stump discovers the Hall of Famer is no hero, but a vile, misogynistic racist. But Stump has agreed to be his ghostwriter which means Cobb expects him to tell the world what a swell guy he is. This is what's known as an ethical dilemma.

In a sense, Stump cops out. He goes ahead with the original book, jotting down Cobb's self-serving recollections. But when he is alone, Stump records all the hateful things he has seen in the old man. Cobb has roughed up and belittled Stump as well as assorted waitresses, desk clerks, floozies and regular folks, all for no particular reason.

Stump finally lashes out, saying, "I put up with your bullshit. I give words, I give life to your bullshit. And you give me nothing but grief."

Cobb (Tommy Lee Jones) sneers, "You've never been this close to greatness in your short life, son. And you love it."

Stump winds up writing two books—the sanitized account of Cobb's life entitled *My Life in Baseball* published in 1961 and a warts-and-all book, *Cobb: A Biography* published in 1994. The latter book becomes the basis for the film, written and directed by Ron Shelton (*Bull Durham*).

Sam Blake (Walter Brennan) in *The Pride of the Yankees*. The character is based on Fred Lieb, a New York sportswriter who was a close friend of Yankee star Lou Gehrig and his wife Eleanor. In the film, Sam is shown leaning over the railing talking to Gehrig (Gary Cooper) while he is in the on-deck circle, urging him to court the lovely Eleanor.

Even if Sam's heart is in the right place, this poses some problems. First of all, he should be in the press box, not sitting next to the dugout. Secondly, he wouldn't be chit-chatting with a player while he is getting ready to hit. And third, he shouldn't be playing Cupid for someone he is paid to write about. It doesn't matter if it is the 1930s, it is still a conflict of interest.

Lexie Littleton (Renee Zellweger) in *Leatherheads*. A hotshot reporter from the *Chicago Tribune* circa 1925 is sent to dig up dirt on football star Carter Rutherford (John Krasinski). Her editor has a tip that Carter is not the war hero he is cracked up to be. It would be fine if the editor told Lexie to find the truth, but instead he instructs her, "Get this guy."

Lexie makes a deal with the boss. If she gets Rutherford, she gets promoted to assistant editor. Talk about having an agenda. Anyway, Lexie flirts shamelessly with her subject until he finally lets down his guard and tells his story. As it turns out, his legend is exaggerated, but through no fault of his own. No matter, Lexie files the story and Carter is made to look like a fraud.

The team tries to shoot down the story and Lexie winds up in hot water, but that's OK because by now she is in love with the coach (George Clooney) and planning to quit the newspaper and marry one of the guys she has been writing about all season. Still with us? We didn't think so.

Sam Simon (Seymour Cassel) in *61**. With his silver mane and acerbic personality, the character of Sam Simon is clearly based on veteran New York columnist Dick Young. Sam is a prickly, old-school type who has few friends but much influence.

In one scene, Whitey Ford (Anthony Michael Hall) asks Mickey Mantle (Thomas Jane): "Did you see Sam Simon's column today?" Mantle replies: "Aw, you know I don't read that shit." Mantle pauses and says, "What did he say?"

Anyone who has ever worked a sports locker room knows how true that is. Players always say they don't know what's written about them and don't care. It's a lie. They know and they definitely care.

Michael O'Neal (Dermot Mulroney) in *My Best Friend's Wedding*. We know this isn't a sports movie. Heck, it's a chick flick, but we don't care. This guy is our hero. He is a freelancer and we never see a single word he writes, but so what? Cameron Diaz and Julia Roberts spend the whole movie fighting over him. Finally, a sportswriter, not an athlete, is a sex object. Long overdue, we say.

SPORT: BASEBALL | **STARS:** ALGENIS PEREZ SOTO | **DIRECTORS:** ANNA BODEN, RYAN FLECK

Every baseball fan knows of the great Dominicans who have made it in the major leagues: from old-timers like Juan Marichal and the Alou family to current stars who dominate the game—Robinson Cano, Manny Ramirez, Jose Reyes, Hanley Ramirez, and so on. These days, nearly one in seven big leaguers hails from the tiny island nation of fewer than 10 million people.

Less known are the stories of the hopefuls from the Dominican Republic who come over with dreams of playing in Yankee Stadium and driving a Cadillac, but fall short. *Sugar*, a sweet movie filmed mostly in Spanish, focuses on one such young man.

The movie follows the path of Miguel "Sugar" Santos, a 19-year-old pitcher from impoverished San Pedro de Macoris whose noon-to-six knuckle-curve earns him a ticket to Class-A ball with hopes of climbing much further.

Santos is assigned to Bridgetown, Iowa (looking at the abbreviation IA, he wonders, "Where is *Ee-yah*?"), but he might as well be sent to Mars. With no knowledge of the English language or middle-American customs, everything becomes an exotic, often daunting experience—from visiting a diner (he repeatedly orders french toast because that's all he knows to say), to turning on his hotel TV and discovering in-room porn, to dealing with the chaste farm girl (Ellary Porterfield) who flirts with him and then drags him to a Presbyterian youth group meeting.

For a few weeks, Santos is a star pitcher for the Bridgetown Swing. He's signing autographs, pointing at his name in the paper (he can't read the rest of the article) and gaining extra attention from his coaches. But he injures his foot on a fielding play and subsequently loses control of his pitches. He gets knocked out of a few games early. Soon after, his best friend is cut from the team. Santos lacks the maturity and support system to cope with adversity, so he takes a fungo bat to the water cooler and then goes AWOL.

We won't reveal where the movie goes, but suffice it to say that Santos does not realize his goal of starting an All-Star Game and lifting his family from poverty. On the other hand, he does not return home as a defeated man. And he discovers that he can love the sport, even if he may never be pictured on a baseball card.

Sugar is at its best showing Santos as the stranger in a strange land. That, in itself, is a well-traveled movie path, but the story of Latin teens trying to survive in an ultra-competitive sport, while at the same time combating social disorientation, has been vastly underreported over the years. For every one who makes it, there are a dozen who fail because they are homesick, or don't understand what their manager is saying, or spend their entire paycheck (and gain 30 pounds) at the local McDonalds.

True story: Back in the 1980s, I (Glen Macnow) spent time covering baseball in the Dominican Republic. One day, I shared a ride with a young catcher named Francisco Cabrera, who was toiling at the Toronto Blue Jays academy near Santo Domingo. Cabrera had just been handed papers assigning him to play for the Jays' farm team in St. Catherine's, Ontario.

"What is St. Catherine's like?" asked Cabrera, who went on to play parts of five seasons in the majors. "Is it cold? Last year I played in Bradenton [Fla.]. That was freezing. Is this place as cold as Bradenton?"

I didn't have the heart to tell him.

If *Sugar* has a weakness, it's that the movie aims to be inherently neutral about many aspects of Dominican recruitment that warrant a harsher spotlight. The movie refers to the talent brokers known as *buscones* who illegally sign up prospects as young as 12, hide players to keep others from scouting them, and alter birth certificates. But it fails to really delve into the subject. Likewise, *Sugar* makes one quick allusion to drug use, but ignores the large issue of commonplace steroid abuse among players seeking to cross the Caribbean.

"Any industry where there's a lot of money to be made and there are poor people involved, there's going to be some exploitation on some level," co-director Ryan Fleck told the *New York Times*. "But we really didn't want to focus on that."

Too bad. A good movie might have become a powerful movie.

Regardless, *Sugar* is a worthy addition to any list of first-rate movies about baseball. It is original, thoughtful and authentic. If you can handle a film done mostly in subtitles, it is well worth two hours of your time.

CHEERS: Dominican native Algenis Perez Soto does a terrific job of creating a sympathetic character—especially for someone who never acted in his life. Soto was an infielder who tried out for the film on a whim (he was among 500 who auditioned) and got the lead role largely because of his warm, expressive face and his ability to throw a baseball. He spent two months training to become a convincing pitcher. The acting? That came naturally.

"When I was reading the script, I was like, 'I know this guy. I know this history,'" Soto told the *Los Angeles Times*. "I have a lot of friends who come to the United States to play baseball."

JEERS: *Sugar* needs more dramatic ups and downs, perhaps a subplot or two running through it. At times the movie comes across more as a documentary (it is fictional) than a feature film.

WHAT THEY WROTE AT THE TIME: "Santos is a hard worker trying his best to make a life for himself and the impoverished family he left behind. And that, ultimately, is what *Sugar* is about: What it means to be poor with a dream of glory, and how, even if that dream is shattered, America provides other opportunities. As such, *Sugar* is one of the finest, and most realistic films ever made about the immigrant experience."—Lewis Beale, *The Hollywood Reporter*

REALITY CHECK: Frustrated by failure, Santos tries a performance-enhancing drug. In his very next start, he is unhittable through four innings and then hurls a beanball to start a brawl. Hey, we know that steroids can affect both performance and behavior, but we doubt that one sample would have such an immediate impact.

CASTING CALL: That's 1990 World Series MVP Jose Rijo playing the head of the fictional Kansas City Knights' Dominican baseball academy.

BET YOU DIDN'T KNOW: Shortly before the film's release, Rijo was fired from his job as special assistant to the Washington Nationals amid a federal investigation into whether he and other baseball officials took kickbacks from signing bonuses promised to Dominican prospects.

SPORTS-ACTION GRADE: B-minus. Soto has a credible pitching motion and most of the other players are convincing. But there are not enough game scenes to earn a higher grade.

BEST LINE: Well, it's a series of lines, actually, when the teens at the Dominican academy recite back baseball phrases like so many Berlitz students.

"I got it!"

"Ground ball!"

"Line drive!"

"Home run!"

And then a pidgin-English chorus of "Take Me Out to the Ball Game."

REPEATED WATCHING QUOTIENT: Not very high. You'll get the story in one viewing and there's not enough action to prompt you into two.

"I KNOW THAT GUY": Those who grew up watching *Little House on the Prairie* should recognize actor Richard Bull (well, an older version of him), who played henpecked store owner Nels Oleson. Here he portrays Earl Higgins, a genial Iowa farmer who takes Santos into his home and lectures him in a Midwestern Spanglish, "No *chicas* in the bedroom. No *cervezas* in *la casa*."

MY FAVORITE SPORTS MOVIE: Boston Red Sox slugger David "Big Papi" Ortiz, quoted in the *Sarasota Herald-Tribune*: "It's a really accurate representation of what the players go through, of the hardships they face adjusting to the cultural differences they encounter in America."

56 MYSTERY, ALASKA (1999–R)

SPORT: HOCKEY | STARS: RUSSELL CROWE, BURT REYNOLDS, HANK AZARIA
DIRECTOR: JAY ROACH

Any true hockey head could envision living in Mystery, Alaska, a remote outpost where you skate for miles on frozen rivers and drive to school on a snowmobile. Each weekend, the hamlet's 633 residents gather for the "Saturday game," in which the most talented local men divide into two teams and play pond hockey on natural black ice. The Saturday game has been serving for decades as Mystery's source of identity and pride.

That is, until the town's prodigal son, Charlie Danner (Hank Azaria), writes a *Sports Illustrated* feature extolling the quirky local custom. Despite its hackneyed prose ("legendary players born on skates in a world permanently covered with ice and snow . . ."), the *SI* article prompts the NHL to devise its best marketing gimmick

since the glowing puck: The New York Rangers will travel to Alaska to take on the fierce locals in a nationally televised game of shinny.

Yeah, sure they will. The entire premise of *Mystery, Alaska* is far-fetched (similar to, say, a South Philly tomato can being invited to fight for the heavyweight championship), and requires you to suspend critical disbelief. But if you can move beyond the fanciful nature of the script, this is a fun, albeit hokey, hockey movie.

Russell Crowe stars as town sheriff John Biebe, who learns at the film's start that, after 13 years, he is being bumped from the Saturday game for a high school phenom. Crowe must deal with all kinds of conflicted emotions here—how he feels about the kid taking his spot, how he feels about being asked to coach instead, how he feels about his cute wife (Mary McCormack) flirting with former boyfriend Azaria. At one point, he starts babbling like John Nash in *A Beautiful Mind,* while taking out his frustrations on a life-sized metal cutout of former Montreal Canadiens goalie Ken Dryden.

Still, it's a typically solid Crowe performance. Lots of mumbling and pained expressions and a strong physical presence. And, since we don't think we're giving much away here by telling you he ends up lacing them up again to face the Rangers, we'll add that it's fun to see Crowe suffering through the most pain and bleeding he's endured this side of *Gladiator.*

We also learn that he probably didn't play much hockey growing up Down Under. Crowe moves on skates in a lumbering-old-NHL-Moose-Vasko kind of way, at one point using his stick as a rudder. Not as easy as your beloved Australian Rules Football, eh Rusty?

But back to the script. After initially being thrilled by the chance for glory, a few of the locals start to sense that they're being set up for the most lopsided hockey game since Japan played Sweden in the 1960 Winter Olympics (final score: 19-0). Stodgy town judge Walter Burns (Burt Reynolds) implores the Mysterians to back out, saying, "Two things we've always had: Our dignity and our illusions. I suggest we protect them both."

Of course, he's overruled. There wouldn't be a movie otherwise.

That sets up the next crisis. The spoiled pros from New York, naturally, have no interest in filling their few days off during the NHL schedule by flying to the Arctic Circle to get cross-checked by a bunch of yokels. They file a suit to stop the game. In one of the film's best scenes, Mystery's only attorney, Bailey Pruitt (Maury Chaykin), flies to New York, convinces a judge not to pull the plug and then drops dead of a heart attack.

And so, the disgruntled and freezing Rangers finally arrive.

Like any good sports movie, it all leads up to the big game. And by then, you're fully invested in the quirky underdogs. We won't give away the ending (we probably don't have to), but the actual hockey scenes are well choreographed and offer several highlights that should prompt you to rise from the Barcalounger. Someone

among the triumvirate of producer David E. Kelley, head writer Sean O'Byrne and director Jay Roach knows his hockey.

Actually, the best moments are those in the locker room. Anyone who ever played the game (or any sport, really) will appreciate the bits of clubhouse camaraderie, taping up sticks and swapping lies about sexual conquests. The locker-room language, we suppose, earned this film its R-rating, although there's really nothing here that would be objectionable to anyone over age 12.

In truth, *Mystery, Alaska* comes off like the pilot for a solid television sitcom, and we hope that isn't damning it with faint praise. Producer Kelley is the King of the Emmys, who has created quirky shows with oddball ensemble casts, like *Ally McBeal, Boston Legal* and *Picket Fences.* Place them in the remotest town on Earth, put them in skates and, well, it's better than 90 percent of the junk on TV.

🍺 **CHEERS:** To the National Anthem. Actually, both the American and Canadian anthems, which have never been used to such a strategic advantage. Aiming to add to the positive exposure, the folks of Mystery fly in singer Little Richard, who, of course, blends in like Joe Pesci in *My Cousin Vinny.* Then, with the temperature hovering around minus-10, they add to the exposure of a different sort by having the rock legend warble through the two anthems as slowly as possible as the Rangers stand idle and shivering.

🍺 **JEERS:** Burt Reynolds's face. We realize he has had a few bouts of cosmetic surgery since his *Longest Yard* days. But still, his skin is pushed up so tight here that the old man appears to be wearing a fiberglass goalie mask.

REALITY CHECK: In the buildup to the game, Charlie (Azaria) boasts that "the network figures on a 14-share minimum" for the national broadcast. Trust us, the NHL would kill for such numbers. The last five Stanley Cup Finals-deciding games have averaged a seven share on American television.

🎬 **PIVOTAL SCENE:** After a brutal second period, the boys from Mystery are slumped in the locker room, battered and disconsolate. Their early lead has turned into a 5-2 deficit, and the Rangers seem unstoppable.

Coach Burns sidles up to his captain, Biebe, and lays out his plan for the third period: Dump the puck, don't press the forecheck, focus on defense. It is a strategy not for victory, but just to keep the score close.

"If it's not a rout," the coach offers, "we can go home winners. . . . We're already beaten."

Biebe, hurting but proud, is outraged.

"We're not beaten," he insists. Jumping up, he shouts, "I'm not beaten. We're in this game. Is anybody here tired?"

His teammates start to sense his passion.

"The Rangers are starting to breathe through their mouths," Biebe yells. "Their strides are getting shorter. Do not give these guys too much respect! They didn't pull a dogsled, did they? They didn't skate the river, did they? Forget about that fucking circus out there! That's still black ice! This is still our pond!"

The players rise, shout and run back for the third period like they just got the "Pearl Harbor" speech from Bluto Blutarsky.

As they leave, the coach pulls his captain aside. "Nice assist," he says, a twinkle in his eye.

Suddenly it becomes clear that he's just used the best reverse psychology since Lou Holtz insisted his Notre Dame powerhouse couldn't beat Navy.

99 BEST LINE: Skank Marden (Ron Eldard): "I play hockey and I fornicate, because those are the two most fun things to do in cold weather."

◀ CASTING CALL: Strong cameos from ESPN puck-heads Steve Levy and Barry Melrose, along with Hall of Famer Phil Esposito, who sniffs at Mystery's odds by declaring, "Their top scorer is a grocer, their fastest skater is a high school kid, and the captain is the town sheriff."

But the fun stuff goes to Mike Myers, who channels Canadian Cro-Magnon Don Cherry in his role as crusty analyst Donnie Shulzhoffer. "This isn't exactly rocket surgery," he declares. "If you don't play the game with a big heart and a big bag of knuckles in front of the net, you don't got dinky-doo."

REALITY CHECK II: At movie's end, Mystery's top two young players are signed by the Rangers and invited to play for the club's farm team in Binghamton, N.Y. It's all very uplifting—but we suspect the other 29 NHL franchises might insist, as the rules stipulate, that the boys first go through the league's entry draft.

57 RUDY (1993–PG)

SPORT: FOOTBALL | STARS: SEAN ASTIN, JON FAVREAU, CHARLES S. DUTTON
DIRECTOR: DAVID ANSPAUGH

It is often said that no one is neutral about Notre Dame. You either love the Irish or you can't stand them. You either tear up at the sound of the Notre Dame victory march or you leave the room. That's the way it is with *Rudy*, the film about a spunky runt named Daniel "Rudy" Ruettiger whose whole life was built on the dream of playing football for the Irish.

Rudy placed fourth in a 2005 ESPN viewers poll of the top sports movies. Leonard Klady of *Variety* lavished it with praise, calling it "a film that hits all the right emotional buttons, an intelligent drama that lifts an audience to its feet cheering."

Other reviewers hated it. Andrew Payne of *Starpulse Entertainment News* called *Rudy* the most overrated sports movie of all-time. "*Rudy* stinks," he wrote. "It is an awful, overly sentimental movie filled with more processed cheese than a supermarket danish."

It is a wide split of opinion based partly on the viewer's feelings about Notre Dame. If you don't buy into the mystique of Rockne and the Gipper, you aren't going to buy into *Rudy*. The only way you can relate to Rudy's story is if you believe there's something special about playing football under the Golden Dome. But if you believe that, even a little bit, *Rudy* will get your Irish up.

The film opens with Rudy as a little kid living in a blue-collar Catholic home in Joliet, IL, where watching Notre Dame football is an autumn ritual. His father, Dan Sr. (Ned Beatty), is parked in his favorite chair every Saturday, and Rudy sits on the floor next to him as they watch the Irish on TV. Rudy's room is decorated with Notre Dame pennants, and he can recite every Knute Rockne pep talk from memory.

Rudy's dream is to attend Notre Dame and become part of that football tradition. The trouble is, he doesn't have the size (he is 5-6 and 170 pounds) or the grades (he is a C student). Even his father tells him: "Notre Dame is for rich kids, smart kids, great athletes. It's not for us. You're a Ruettiger."

Rudy (Sean Astin) joins his father, his brother Frank (Scott Benjaminson) and his best friend Pete (Christopher Reed) working in the steel mill. He isn't happy about it, he still has thoughts about going to Notre Dame, but he is beginning to think, well, like a Ruettiger. He dons his hard hat and heads to the plant every day. "Chasing a dream can only cause you heartache," his father says.

But Pete sees the wistfulness in Rudy's eyes. For his birthday, he gives Rudy a Notre Dame jacket. "You were born to wear that," Pete says. Rudy tells him, "You're the only one who ever took me seriously." Pete replies: "You know what my Dad said: Having dreams is what makes life tolerable."

Pete understands Rudy better than his own family, certainly more than Frank who ridicules his younger brother. "As long as he talks this crazy Notre Dame shit he deserves anything that comes his way," Frank says.

When Pete is killed on the job, Rudy decides he must pursue his dream for both of them. He hops a bus for South Bend, walks onto the Notre Dame campus and announces he wants to enroll. He tells his story to a kindly priest (Robert Prosky) who gets him into a junior college. He tells Rudy he could gain admission to Notre Dame if he shows sufficient academic progress.

Of course, just getting into Notre Dame is only part of Rudy's dream. The other part is earning a spot on the football team which will be next-to-impossible for a defensive end (Rudy's high school position) who is smaller than the ball boys.

That's the second half of the film: Rudy's hard work in the classroom to get the grades (it's a struggle, but he makes it with the help of tutor Jon Favreau), then earning a spot on the practice squad where he joins other walk-ons to serve as human tackling dummies for the Irish regulars. The scenes of a bloodied Rudy being driven into the mud by men twice his size will make you wince, but his tenacity earns the respect of coach Ara Parseghian.

Practice squad players don't dress for games, they sit in the stands with everyone else. Rudy desperately wants to come out of the tunnel at Notre Dame Stadium just once so his family can see that he really is part of the team. (Frank continues to doubt him, saying: "I see the games every week, but I never see you.")

Parseghian promises Rudy that he can dress for a game in his senior year, but then the coach resigns. The new coach, Dan Devine, has no knowledge of the promise and no particular interest in Rudy. To Devine, he is just another faceless body in a blue practice squad jersey. He has no intention of letting Rudy dress for a game until the other players on the team rally behind him.

Rudy is given his chance to dress for the final home game of the 1975 season. As the players gather in the tunnel, co-captain Roland Steele asks Rudy: "Are you ready for this, champ?" Wide-eyed, Rudy replies, "I've been ready for this my whole life."

"Then you lead us onto the field," Steele says.

The slow-motion shot of Rudy coming out of the tunnel, pointing to his family in the stands while the Notre Dame band plays the victory march, should strike a chord even in those who aren't huge fans of the Irish. And when Rudy finally gets a chance to play, as *SI.com* wrote: "Don't be surprised if you find yourself chanting, 'Rudy! Rudy! Rudy!'"

Rudy would seem to be a movie made for the underdog audience, but like *Rocky* it has universal appeal. Chris Long of the St. Louis Rams is certainly no underdog. The son of Hall of Famer Howie Long, an All-America defensive end at Virginia and second overall pick in the 2008 NFL draft, Chris is no Rudy, yet he relates to his competitive spirit.

"Rudy works for his dream," Long said, "and even though in the end it's just a couple of plays which really isn't that big of a deal, it's huge for him. I loved it."

CHEERS: Charles S. Dutton is very good as Fortune, the stadium groundskeeper who takes Rudy in and provides the tough love to keep him going.

🚩 **JEERS:** Rudy's brother Frank is such a spiteful antagonist, he ceases to be interesting pretty quickly. We can understand a little brotherly jealousy, but Frank's character is ridiculous.

👑 **BET YOU DIDN'T KNOW:** Charlie Weis opened his first team meeting as head coach at Notre Dame in 2005 by showing the film *Rudy* and asking the real Rudy Ruettiger to address the squad. Rudy's message: "You cannot ever quit on yourself."

✔ **REALITY CHECK:** The scene where the varsity players all drop their jerseys on Devine's desk and say, "Let Rudy dress in my place," well, it never happened. Devine said he alone made the decision to let Rudy dress for the final home game.

☞ **DON'T FAIL TO NOTICE:** In the big game, Notre Dame is playing Georgia Tech, but there are fans in the stands wearing Boston College colors. Why? The scenes were shot at halftime of a Notre Dame-Boston College game.

✎ **WHAT THEY WROTE AT THE TIME:** "Anyone who is not moved by this film has something else in their chest where their heart ought to be."—Robert Roten, *Laramie Movie Scope*

99 **BEST LINE:** Fortune to Rudy: "You're five foot nothing, a hundred and nothing and you hung in with the best college football team in the land for two years and you're going to walk out of here with a degree from the University of Notre Dame. You don't have to prove nothing to nobody."

😎 **"I KNOW THAT GUY":** Chelcie Ross, who plays Dan Devine, is the wanna-be coach who is chased off by Norman Dale (Gene Hackman) in *Hoosiers*. Both films were directed by David Anspaugh and written by Angelo Pizzo.

★ **SPORTS-ACTION GRADE:** B-plus. The football scenes were shot by NFL Films, so the coverage is first-rate. Anspaugh hired NFL Films because he knew he had a limited amount of time to shoot his game scenes (it all had to be done in the 15-minute intermission of the Notre Dame-BC game) so the cameramen had to get every shot right the first time. NFL Films crews deal with that pressure every week.

"The football scenes in *Rudy* were the best I've ever seen and I'm a tough critic," said George Martin, who played 14 seasons at defensive end for the New York Giants. "You could almost feel the hits. (Rudy) kept getting knocked down and getting back up. It was sheer brutality, but that's what it's like on the practice field. It's about survival and Rudy is a survivor."

🎞 **MY FAVORITE SPORTS MOVIE:** Gold Medal-winning gymnast Kerri Strug: "*Rudy* shows how if you really work hard and want something, you can make it happen. Not everyone is a star, but that doesn't mean you can't be successful. You know, we pay so much attention to the record holders, but we need to also pay attention to the people who struggle to make the team. Sometimes, they're just as inspiring."

58 KINGPIN (1996–PG-13)

SPORT: BOWLING | STARS: WOODY HARRELSON, BILL MURRAY, RANDY QUAID
DIRECTORS: BOBBY AND PETER FARRELLY

Not many folks are ambivalent about *Kingpin*. You either abhor this gross-out comedy (as does one of this book's two authors), or you love it (as does the other). In order to make the second category, you must find humor in the following:

• A sex romp with a skanky yellow-toothed landlady that leaves our protagonist barfing.

• A scene where a city slicker drinks fresh "milk" from a bucket—only to learn that the farm has no cows, only a bull. Think about it.

• A cross-dressing striptease involving a 240-pound man licking a dance pole.

And then there's the *really* distasteful stuff. Kingpin has prosthesis gags, stuttering gags, bong-smoking Amish gags, misuse of urinal gags and everything else that could be thought up at the frat house over the course of a beer-soaked weekend. That's why we love it—well, at least one of us.

Kingpin represents the first—and perhaps the best—of the recent genre of frat boy sports comedies. *The Waterboy, Talladega Nights, Blades of Glory* and *Dodgeball* all followed, and all grossed over $100 million at the box office (*Kingpin* grossed $25 million). All owe their success to this Farrelly Brothers story of a down-on-his-luck one-handed bowler who finds his second chance in a

Pennsylvania Dutch phenom. Kind of like *The Color of Money* meets *Dumb and Dumber*.

The movie opens with the story of young Roy Munson (Woody Harrelson), winner of the 1979 Iowa Odor-Eaters Championship, who heads out to make his name on the professional bowling tour.

He's a natural with a bright future. After his first tournament (which he wins), Roy is tutored in the seamy underbelly of bowling survival by veteran Ernie McCracken (Bill Murray in cinema's greatest-ever combover)—which involves hustling the locals. The hustle goes sour, however, and as McCracken burns rubber escaping, the angry victims feed young Roy's hand to the ball return. Think the wood chipper in *Fargo*.

Fast forward 17 years. We catch up with Roy living in a dilapidated rooming house in Scranton, Pa., drinking rotgut for breakfast and trying to make a living by selling fluorescent condoms ("You don't have a novelty machine in the men's room? And you call yourself a bowling alley?"). He wears a hook where his right hand used to be and also has a screw-on cheap rubber hand that displays his old state championship ring. How the ring survived that reset machine baffles us, but let's not be sticklers.

One day Roy stumbles upon Ishmael Boorg (Randy Quaid), an Amish galoot with great natural talent. The movie slows down a little in the middle as Roy coaches Ish, persuades him to join the tour, teaches him to floss his teeth and readies him for the $500,000 Reno Open. There's also a secondary plot arc involving a fallen woman with a heart of gold (Vanessa Angel) which doesn't add much to the movie beyond providing the opportunity for a half-dozen good breast jokes.

Act III of the movie heads for Reno, where Roy meets up with his old nemesis. Big Ern is now the sport's top superstar—introduced by Chris Schenkel as "a guy who has done for bowling what Muhammad Ali has done for boxing." You know that the tournament (which has several of the PBA's top stars in cameos) is going to end in a showdown between McCracken and the Amish Kid, and *Kingpin* does not disappoint.

Let's say here that Murray is at his comedic apex in *Kingpin*'s final 30 minutes. *Caddyshack, Groundhog Day* and *Stripes* all provided moments of glory for our favorite *Saturday Night Live* alum, but his portrayal of McCracken, the cocky, smarmy narcissist, borders on genius. The Farrellys gave Murray the opportunity to improvise most scenes, and his off-the-head victory speech near the end of *Kingpin* ("Now I can buy my way out of anything! Big Ern is above the law!") should have at least earned him a Best Supporting Actor Oscar nomination in 1996. Hell, who remembers Armin Mueller-Stahl in *Shine* anyway?

Harrelson is also terrific as the once-idealistic, now-cynical schmo. He's such a perpetual victim that he inspires a nationwide verb—to be "munsoned," as the movie says, is to have the world in the palm of your hands and then blow it. And Roy finds a way to blow it every time.

If you're a fan of the Farrelly Brothers, you'll recognize other regular members of their troupe, many of whom could not act their way out of a middle-school musical, but are funny enough to deliver a kick-in-the-pants sight gag. There are also some wooden cameos by jocks, although none approaching Brett Favre's inadvertent fall-down funniness in *There's Something About Mary*. Keep an eye open for pro golfers Brad Faxon and Billy Andrade and a certain steroided-up former major league pitcher with a bad attitude. And make note that the harmonica-playing Amish singer in the final scene is John Popper of Blues Traveler.

The jokes come fast here. Some will make you snicker (like the "Jeffersons on Ice" show at the Reno hotel), some which made you shudder (like the over-exuberant effort to remove a horse's shoes). There's physical humor, stupid jokes, groaners and throwaways coming at the pace of five a minute for all 113 minutes—which totals 565 jokes. If the Farrellys get you 50 percent of the time, that's a lot of laughs.

CHEERS: To the little movie tributes interspersed throughout *Kingpin*. In one, a nod to *Indecent Proposal* (which also starred Harrelson), Roy dreams that the wealthy casino gambler (Chris Elliott) offers to pay him $1 million to sleep with Ishmael. In another—to the tune of Simon and Garfunkel's "The Sounds of Silence"—Roy's post-coital nausea is filmed through the stocking-clad leg of his landlady, a takeoff on Mrs. Robinson's seduction scene in *The Graduate*.

JEERS: While the other performances here rival Olivier (or, at least, Jerry Lewis), Randy Quaid is a let down as Amish innocent Ishmael. We know Quaid can do comedy (he's great as Cousin Eddie in the *Vacation* movies). So how does he fall so flat in a role with such potential? Better leave the sports work to brother Dennis. By the way, Randy's credits include *Major League II*, *Caddyshack II* and *The Slugger's Wife*. Has there ever been an actor who appeared in three sports movies as awful as those? We can't think of anyone.

WHAT THEY WROTE AT THE TIME: "With maybe 25 belly laughs, the brazenly crude *Kingpin* is often uproarious, but be forewarned that its creators apparently conceived it underneath a limbo bar. How looow can a funny guilty pleasure go?"—Mike Clark, *USA Today*

DON'T FAIL TO NOTICE: The crowd's apparently genuine reaction as McCracken hits three straight strikes in the Reno tournament. Murray—a fine bowler—actually got the three strikes in a row, prompting the audience of extras to go wild.

CASTING CALL: Jim Carrey was the first choice to play Big Ernie McCracken. He was tied up filming *The Cable Guy*.

BEST LINE: As Roy prepares to bowl the final frame in his first tournament, you hear what appears to be an announcer in the background. Instead, it's his opponent:

McCracken: "It all comes down to this roll. Roy Munson, a man-child, with a dream to topple bowling giant Ernie McCracken. If he strikes, he's the 1979 Odor-Eaters Champion. He's got one foot in the frying pan and one in the pressure cooker. Believe me, as a bowler, I know that right about now, your bladder feels like an overstuffed vacuum cleaner bag and your butt is kind of like an about-to-explode bratwurst."

Munson: "Hey, do you mind? I wasn't talking when you were bowling."

McCracken: "Was I talking out loud? Was I? Sorry."

"I KNOW THAT GUY": The muscled-up white trash trucker named Skidmark who wants to punch out Ishmael at the redneck bar? Why, isn't that Roger Clemens in his funniest appearance this side of a Congressional subcommittee?

SPORTS-ACTION GRADE: D-minus. Hey, it's bowling, after all.

IF YOU LIKED THIS, YOU'LL LIKE: Any of the Farrelly Brothers' films. We'd recommend *There's Something About Mary* as the best.

REPEATED WATCHING QUOTIENT: High. If you like it the first time, you'll enjoy it just as much the tenth time.

MY FAVORITE SPORTS MOVIE: NFL Pro Bowl tackle Jon Runyan: "It was nonsense but I love that stuff. Slapstick comedy is my favorite. Put on a drama and I'm asleep in five minutes. The Bill Murray character was a riot. I loved that four-foot combover. I'm not a bowler, but they need to make more movies about bowling."

ALL THE RIGHT MOVES (1983–R)

SPORT: FOOTBALL | STARS: TOM CRUISE, CRAIG T. NELSON, LEA THOMPSON
DIRECTOR: MICHAEL CHAPMAN

Tom Cruise was fresh off his success in *Risky Business* when he crossed over to sports films with *All the Right Moves*. Instead of dancing to Bob Seger in his undies, he plays football for Ampipe High School. Cruise describes himself as a "5-foot-10 white cornerback" which seems, oh, about three inches too generous, but that's OK.

Cruise shows real acting chops in his portrayal of Stefen "Steff" Djordjevic, a kid who sees football as a way to earn a college scholarship and escape his depressed Pennsylvania steel town (the movie was shot in Johnstown). His father and brother both work in the steel mill, and unless he gets away, he is going to wind up spending his life there, too.

"I want to study engineering," Steff says. "I want to be the first Djordjevic to have something to say about what happens to the steel after it leaves here."

Steff has the brains to succeed in the classroom and the ability to excel on the football field, but he has an attitude, which irritates Coach Nickerson (Craig T. Nelson). Nickerson is a typical football tyrant who cannot correct a player without first grabbing him by the facemask. When he chews out a player, Nickerson expects the player to say only, "Yes, sir."

Steff is more likely to say, "But I made the play. . . ."

Or worse, he'll listen to the instructions and ask, "Why?"

High school coaches, especially the ones in movies, hate players like that. So when Nickerson ends practice by telling the players to take five laps, he grabs Steff and says, "You do ten." It's a scene heavy with symbolism—Steff jogging alone in the twilight with the smoky steel mill looming in the background, the destiny he is trying to escape.

Everyone wants out of Ampipe. Steff's best friend, Brian Riley (Chris Penn), has scored a full scholarship to play football at Southern Cal. Steff's girlfriend, Lisa (Lea Thompson), dreams of going away to college to study music. Even Nickerson is angling for a college coaching job, and he thinks an upset win over Ampipe's unbeaten rival, Walnut Heights, will cinch the deal.

"We're getting out of here" is a phrase we hear repeated over and over again. At times, it seems like a little much. I mean, Ampipe (or Johnstown) doesn't look like Palm Springs, but the way the characters are acting, you'd think it was the Turkish prison in *Midnight Express*. OK, we get it. It's a blue-collar town. The economy isn't exactly booming. But enough already.

Some talented people came together to make *All the Right Moves*. Director Michael Chapman was the cinematographer on *Raging Bull*, so he knows how to shoot sports action. Jan de Bont was director of photography, and he went on to direct *Speed*, which was a big hit (and earned three Academy Award nominations) in 1994. The result is a film that looks good, especially on the field, but sometimes stumbles in the storytelling.

The dialog is the weakest part of the film.

But when Chapman and de Bont let the pictures move the story along, they do so very nicely. The scene in which the Ampipe team rides the bus to Walnut Heights for the big game is a good example. Not a word is spoken as the coaches and players sit on the bus, staring out the window at the rain, each alone with his thoughts. One player fingers his rosary, another squeezes a football, another studies the game plan. Chapman allows the tension to build with just images and music.

When the Ampipe team gets to the locker room, one of the coaches puts a half-deflated football on a table by the door. On the ball is written: Ampipe High, State Champs, 1960. One by one, each player touches the ball for luck as he enters. You never see the players' faces, only their hands, but that makes it more effective. The audience identifies with the team, not the individuals.

The silence in the room as the players go through the ritual of taping and getting dressed knowing what is at stake—for the players, a college scholarship; for the coach, a chance at a better job—resonates more than any pep talk.

👍 **CHEERS:** Steff has the best speech in the film when he tells off Nickerson after the coach kicks him off the team for insubordination.

"You sit in your office and you decide, 'Scholarship here, no scholarship there,' " Steff says. "Who the hell gave you that power? You're not God, Nickerson. You're just a typing teacher."

👎 **JEERS:** It's hard to swallow the ending when Nickerson, after squabbling with Steff the entire film, offers him the chance to join him at Cal Poly on a full scholarship. It is hard to imagine these two personalities surviving another four years together, or that Nickerson would choose to do so.

🍎 **BET YOU DIDN'T KNOW:** Director Michael Chapman asked both Cruise and Lea Thompson to go back to high school "undercover" for a month to get in the right mood for the film. Cruise was recognized the first day. Thompson lasted four days before another student recognized her—and asked her out. (She declined).

🍎 **BET YOU DIDN'T KNOW II:** Walter Briggs, who plays the Ampipe quarterback known as "Rifleman", went on to play college football at Montclair State and played one game for the New York Jets as a replacement player during the 1987 NFL strike. His pro stats: two pass attempts, one incompletion, one interception.

✒ **WHAT THEY WROTE AT THE TIME:** "Craig T. Nelson's coach Nickerson is Bobby Knight-abusive in a way that makes R. Lee Ermey's drill instructor from *Full Metal Jacket* look like a girl scout."—Walter Chaw, *Film Freak Central*

😎 **"I KNOW THAT GUY":** Craig T. Nelson, of course, is most often identified for playing a more humane version of a football coach in the TV series *Coach*.

⭐ **SPORTS-ACTION RATING:** B. The strategy in the big game is totally illogical—why is Walnut Heights, a running team, throwing the ball in a monsoon?—but Chapman and de Bont know how to film the action.

👁 **REPEATED WATCHING QUOTIENT:** The last play of the Walnut Heights game is worth another look, especially if you have fond memories of the "Miracle at the Meadowlands."

🏈 **MY FAVORITE SPORTS MOVIE:** Six-time major league All-Star closer Billy Wagner: "I played quarterback in high school at 135 pounds. [*All the Right Moves*] was about all the things you go through in high school—trying to get into a college, dealing with girls and teachers, coaches and friends. My high school coach was just like the coach in the movie, grabbing everybody by the face mask. One time he grabbed for my face mask and broke my nose. I wanted to show how tough I was so I went in the game anyway. On the second play I broke my collarbone. That was a bad night."

60 FAT CITY (1972–NR)

SPORT: BOXING | STARS: STACY KEACH, JEFF BRIDGES, SUSAN TYRRELL
DIRECTOR: JOHN HUSTON

Stockton, California is not a fat city; far from it. The opening shots in *Fat City* of down-on-their-luck guys hanging on street corners and sitting on fruit crates set the mood. This is one of those places where dreams come to die. The flop houses and gambling halls are full of life's losers, people who are here because, well, they have nowhere else to go.

Walking amid this human wreckage is Billy Tully, a brooding drifter who was once a decent prizefighter but now, at age 29, spends his days in a boozy haze. When we meet Tully (played by Stacy Keach) he has been fired from his job as a short-order cook and he is forced to work in the fields, picking lettuce for 90 cents an hour.

Tully starts working out in the local gym with the thought of returning to the ring. He meets Ernie Munger, a naive teenager who is competing as an amateur. Tully befriends Munger (played by Jeff Bridges) and talks him into turning professional. Tully introduces the kid to his old manager, Ruben (Nicholas Colasanto, best known as Coach in the TV series *Cheers*), who is happy to take him on.

"I have a good-looking white kid," Ruben tells his wife. He sees Munger as a box office draw on the small-town circuit from Stockton to Reno, where most fighters are black or Hispanic. He gives him the ring name "Irish Ernie Munger" even though he knows the kid isn't Irish. It's all about the marketing.

There was a time when Ruben thought Tully would be his meal ticket, but it didn't quite work out. He lost a few tough fights, then it was a downhill slide to skid row. Tully now lives in a world of "what-might-have-beens." Most nights, he loses himself in shots and beers and bitterness.

Things don't improve when Tully moves in with Oma, a drunken harpy played by Susan Tyrrell. She does nothing but guzzle sherry and whine all day. Sitting in bed, wrapped in Tully's boxing robe, she scolds and belittles

him as he cooks dinner. When he throws up his hands and heads for the door, she bursts into tears and accuses him of leaving her. He can't win and he knows it.

Fat City makes it clear from the beginning there won't be any happy endings. Tully is at a dead end when we meet him and that's where we will leave him when it's all over. Yet for all the heartache, the story is so well told by director John Huston and screenwriter Leonard Gardner (a Stockton native who adapted the script from his novel) you will remember it for a very long time.

The film is beautifully shot by cinematographer Conrad Hall, who won Oscars 30 years apart for *Butch Cassidy and the Sundance Kid* (1969) and *American Beauty* (1999). His photography of the migrant workers and derelicts that wander the street creates an atmosphere that allows us to feel the desperation of people like Tully and Oma.

When Tully talks Ernie into turning pro, he tells him, "Don't waste your green years, kid. Before you know it, your life has slipped away, down the drain." Tully's eyes—sad and hollow—make it clear he is speaking from experience. Tully is only 11 years older than Ernie, but he is weighed down by so much sadness and regret, he seems like an old man.

Ernie needs the money because he marries his pregnant girlfriend Faye (Candy Clark) and he has some success with Ruben and trainer Babe (former welterweight contender Art Aragon) guiding his career. *Fat City* traces the lives of both fighters, but Tully is the more interesting story because Keach makes it so. He takes a complex—and not very likeable—character and makes him worth rooting for.

Some critics called *Fat City* Huston's most underrated film and compared it to his classics *The Maltese Falcon*, *The Asphalt Jungle* and *The African Queen*. Huston, who was a successful amateur boxer (and less successful pro), threw himself into the project and was disappointed when *Fat City* flopped at the box office. It is one of the best boxing films ever made, yet it is almost forgotten.

The most memorable scene comes late in the film when a Mexican fighter named Lucero arrives for a bout with Tully. Lucero (played by Sixto Rodriguez, a light heavyweight contender in the '60s) gets off the bus alone carrying a gym bag. Walking to his fleabag hotel, he sees a poster advertising the fight. He stares at it blankly for a few seconds and walks on.

Lucero was once a ranked contender, but now he is on the downside of his career. He travels from one tank town to another, fighting whatever local favorite they put in front of him. In Stockton, it will be Tully. In his hotel room, Lucero goes to the bathroom and as he urinates, the toilet bowl fills with blood. He has kidney damage from a fight in another town just like this one. He shouldn't be going back into the ring, but he will because it is the only way he knows to make money.

In the big fight, whenever Tully pins Lucero against the ropes and pounds him with body punches, you can't help wincing because you know what's happening to the poor guy's insides and you also know what his next trip to the bathroom will be like.

What separates *Fat City* from other boxing films is its lack of glamour. Most films build to a championship fight in a sold-out stadium with millions of dollars at stake. Here, the dimly lit arena is half-empty, the crowd is grungy and the winner's purse is $100. There is nothing to celebrate, really, no promise of a brighter tomorrow. It's just another night in Stockton—and that's not pretty.

🍺 **CHEERS:** Susan Tyrrell earned an Oscar nomination for Best Supporting Actress for her outstanding performance as Oma. She lost to Eileen Heckart (*Butterflies Are Free*).

🍺 **JEERS:** The saccharine ballad "Help Me Make It Through the Night," written and performed by Kris Kristofferson, is used as the movie's theme. In a film where so much feels natural, the music and lyrics just try too hard.

✎ **WHAT THEY WROTE AT THE TIME:** "Huston has confronted a piece of material perfectly suited to his insights and talents. The result is one of his best films in years ... a lean, compassionate, detailed, raucous, sad, strong look at some losers and survivors on the side streets of small-city Middle America."—Charles Champlin, *Los Angeles Times*

👀 **"I KNOW THAT GUY":** Former welterweight champion Curtis Cokes made his acting debut playing Oma's one-time lover, Earl.

★ **SPORTS-ACTION GRADE:** A-minus. The scenes with Keach and Rodriguez are very convincing. Bridges isn't quite as good.

👒 **BET YOU DIDN'T KNOW:** Huston carefully staged the fights beforehand, but once the cameras started rolling, he said, "All right, boys, now we're going to have two minutes of boxing. Go out there and fight."

Keach, who was in the ring with Sixto Rodriguez, a real fighter, was terrified. He told interviewers that the shot in the film of Rodriguez landing a solid right to the jaw and Keach dropping to the canvas was the real thing. Both Keach and Bridges were bloodied during the filming.

👁 **REPEATED WATCHING QUOTIENT:** You can skip over the scenes of Tully and Oma bickering, but the final bout between Tully and Lucero is worth a second and third look.

61 61* (2001–NR)

SPORT: **BASEBALL** | STARS: **BARRY PEPPER, THOMAS JANE** | DIRECTOR: **BILLY CRYSTAL**

For actor/comedian Billy Crystal, directing the film *61** for HBO was a labor of love. Crystal grew up a fan of the New York Yankees and Mickey Mantle in particular. In the film *City Slickers*, Crystal's character, Mitch Robbins, says the best day of his life was when his dad took him to Yankee Stadium for the first time.

"And Mickey hit a homer," he says, as if all his childhood fantasies were fulfilled at once.

Crystal says that scene was borrowed from real life. It happened just that way. To him, Yankee Stadium was a sacred place, and the Mick stood on a pedestal, then and always. So it was no surprise when Crystal did a film about the 1961 baseball season and the home run race between Mantle and teammate Roger Maris.

"I've been in pre-production on this film for 40 years,"

said Crystal, who was 13 years old in '61 and hanging on every pitch that season.

The film *61** succeeds largely because Crystal cared so deeply about it. For him, it was like re-opening an old scrapbook, or waving his hand over his baseball card collection and having all of his favorites come alive. It was a chance to relive a wonderful time in his life and it is clear he had a ball.

It is to Crystal's credit that he does not gloss over the failings of his idol. The Mick (Thomas Jane) is shown to be a hard-drinking, foul-mouthed womanizer who is actually less admirable than the straight-arrow family man Maris (Barry Pepper). Crystal does try to put Mantle's self-destructive lifestyle in context, but he does not excuse it.

In the film, Maris confronts Mantle about his drinking and skirt-chasing. Mantle is sharing an apartment in Queens with Maris and teammate Bob Cerv. The arrangement is Maris's idea. He thinks it is better than Mantle living in Manhattan and hanging out at Toots Shor's bar every night. But even in Queens, the Mick can't stay on the wagon and finally Maris loses patience with him.

"Did you ever stop and think if you took better care of yourself, you wouldn't be getting hurt all the time?" Maris says. "You're Mickey Mantle, for Christ's sake."

"What the fuck is that supposed to mean?" Mantle snaps. "You think you know me. You don't know shit about me."

Mantle tells Maris that his father, uncle and grandfather all died of Hodgkins Disease before the age of 45. He assumes the same fate awaits him.

"I'm gonna live my life the way I want," Mantle says. "So get off my back. Call your wife and cry to her about it."

The scene provides some understanding and perhaps some sympathy for Mantle, but the way he takes his teammate's concern and throws it back in his face is pretty cold. It's one of many occasions in the film when Mantle acts like a jerk and Maris comes off as a nice, well-intentioned guy.

Of course, the focus of 61* is the duel between Mantle and Maris to break the major league home run record of 60 set by Babe Ruth in 1927. Even the casual sports fan knows how that turned out: Maris hit 61 to break the record, and Mantle finished with 54. Crystal wisely keeps his eye not on the ball, but on the two men and how they deal with the pressure of chasing down the sport's most hallowed record.

Most Yankee fans are rooting for Mantle. He is one of their own, signed and brought to New York in 1951 to succeed Joe DiMaggio in center field. Blonde and movie-star handsome, Mantle is every man's idol and every woman's crush. Maris is seen as an outsider, acquired in a trade from Kansas City in 1960. Shy and uncomfortable in the big city, Maris is not warmly received by the New York fans and media.

The pressure causes Maris to start losing his hair and break out in a rash. He snaps at the sportswriters who crowd around him every day, calling them "bloodsuck-

ers." But even in his worst moments, Maris remains a sympathetic figure: a decent guy who finds himself thrust onto a stage he really did not want.

The asterisk in the title refers to the controversy over the record. Ruth hit his 60 homers in a 154-game season. There was sentiment among some traditionalists that since Maris did not hit No. 61 until the 162nd game that his mark should go into the record books with an asterisk. It did not. There never was an asterisk attached to the Maris record except in some people's minds.

However, the controversy sets up an interesting scene in the film. In the 154th game, Maris needs one more home run for 60. On his last at bat, Baltimore brings in knuckle-ball pitcher Hoyt Wilhelm to face him. To make it realistic, Crystal hired major league knuckleballer Tom Candiotti to play Wilhelm.

"We shot the scene at the L.A. Coliseum," Candiotti said. "I was there for six days. I had my own trailer just like the stars. They gave me tapes of Wilhelm to study. His nickname was 'Tilt' because he held his head at an angle and he wore his cap a little crooked. I had to get all the details right. Billy was a stickler for that stuff.

"[Crystal] wanted to show how a real knuckleball dances around. The trouble was Barry [Pepper] couldn't hit it and the catcher couldn't catch it. I threw 17 knucklers. Seventeen times Barry swung and missed. Billy came to the mound and said, 'We have a problem. It's called film. We're running out.' He asked if I could lob a slow one so Barry could at least get his bat on it. I blooped one up there and it hit him in the ribs.

"He went down and everyone came running in to see if he was all right. He said, 'How hard was that?' I said, 'It was about fifty miles an hour.' I mean, it was nothing. I'd hate to think what would've happened if he got hit by somebody throwing ninety.'"

It required several more takes, but finally Pepper got his bat on one of Candiotti's flutterballs. He hit a soft pop foul, Crystal yelled "Cut," and that was it. "He just needed to see Barry make contact," Candiotti said. "He took two or three shots from different angles, put them together and he got what he needed." (Maris was retired on a ground ball.)

"It was an education, seeing how a movie is made," Candiotti said. "Something as simple as me walking in from the bullpen, we shot that scene 30 times. Billy would shoot it from one angle, then another and another. I'd walk to the mound, go back to the bullpen, walk to the mound and back to the bullpen, over and over."

Late in the season, Mantle was hospitalized with a viral infection and an abscessed hip. One of the better scenes in the film is Maris visiting Mantle's bedside. At this point, the race to break Ruth's record is down to one man. Mantle's run is over. Only Maris remains.

What makes the scene effective is that writer Hank Steinberg resists the urge to give either man lines that are eloquent or profound. We know by now that Mantle and Maris are rather inarticulate, so the scene is written with a lot of awkward silences as the two fumble around trying to figure out what to say. But their mutual respect comes through loud and clear.

"I can't play no more," Mantle says. "I'm wore out. Done. I'm out of the race."

"You would've done it, too," Maris says, assuring Mantle that he, too, would have surpassed The Babe.

"Ah, bullshit," Mantle says. "It was you, Rog. You did it, you son of a bitch. Nobody can ever take that away from you. That record is yours."

🍺 **CHEERS:** Crystal certainly paid attention to details. In addition to Candiotti as Wilhelm, check out the actors who portray Jim Bunning (Detroit) and Dick Hall (Baltimore). They have the same sweeping sidearm delivery as those two pitchers.

🍺 **JEERS:** The film shows Babe Ruth's widow cursing as she watches Maris hit a late-season home run. The truth is Mrs. Ruth and Maris had a cordial relationship. She visited him after he hit No. 60 and he told her, "Don't feel badly, no one will ever replace The Babe."

🎬 **CASTING CALL:** Crystal hired Pepper after seeing him in *Saving Private Ryan* and noting his uncanny resemblance to Maris. He hired Jane because he looked so much like Mantle. Crystal felt that was more important then their athletic ability. Pepper had played very little baseball and Jane hadn't played at all, but Crystal believed with multiple takes and good editing, he could make them look like ballplayers. But he couldn't make them look like Mantle and Maris unless they really did.

✏ **WHAT THEY WROTE AT THE TIME:** "Billy Crystal made no mistakes in the depiction of the home run chase between Mantle and Maris. It's a classic story about their friendship and their rivalry. It's a great movie."—Christopher Russo, Sirius Satellite Radio

★ **SPORTS-ACTION GRADE:** B. Pepper and Jane must have spent a lot of time studying the batting stances of Maris and Mantle because they have them exactly right. Also, Pepper has the Maris home run trot, shuffling quickly around the bases, head down, looking almost embarrassed by the cheers of the crowd.

👁 **REPEATED WATCHING QUOTIENT:** Once a summer, or as often as you can stand the Yankees.

🎞 **MY FAVORITE SPORTS MOVIE:** Major league pitcher Jered Weaver: "I knew all about Roger Maris and Mickey Mantle as ballplayers, but this movie helped me to know them as people. What I found interesting was that they were such different people. As a ballplayer, I could understand how the pressure affected Maris in 1961. What I found most interesting was that the two men actually shared an apartment during that amazing season. You'd never see that today."

62 INVINCIBLE (2006–PG)

SPORT: FOOTBALL | STARS: MARK WAHLBERG, GREG KINNEAR
DIRECTOR: ERICSON CORE

Take a pinch of *Rudy*, mix in a dash of *The Rookie*, add a '70s rock score (Bachman-Turner Overdrive anyone?) and you have *Invincible*, the story of Vince Papale, the 30-year-old free agent whose raw desire earned him a spot on the Philadelphia Eagles.

The film was produced by Mark Ciardi and Gordon Gray, who previously had success with inspirational sports films *The Rookie* and *Miracle*. They saw an NFL Films feature on Papale and felt his story had all the elements of a feel-good family movie. The only difference was this time the sport was football.

They got the support of the National Football League, who had not partnered on a film since *Jerry Maguire* in 1996. The NFL liked the story—it was wholesome with a positive message—so it allowed them to use the real team names and uniforms, which added authenticity.

The real coup was landing two major stars, Mark Wahlberg and Greg Kinnear, to play Papale and Eagles coach Dick Vermeil. Ciardi and Gray took a shot with a first-time director, Ericson Core (he was head cinematographer on *The Fast and the Furious*) and he delivered a crowd-pleasing film that some compared to *Rocky* in shoulder pads.

That was one of the ironies of Papale's story: he made the Eagles roster as a long shot rookie in 1976, the same year that *Rocky*—Sylvester Stallone's tale of the underdog Philadelphia pug—won the Oscar for Best Motion Picture. Papale was so much like Stallone's character—Philly guy, Italian Stallion, kicked around and written off—that Rocky became his nickname.

Writers Brad Gann and Mike Rich shifted a few locales—they put Papale in South Philly, he actually lived outside the city—and they rewrote a few characters—Vince's love interest Janet (Elizabeth Banks) wasn't related to the bar owner Max. The real Janet was a gymnastics coach who met Vince after he retired from football.

Also, the film makes it appear Vince had no football background other than the rough touch he played with Max and the boys. That's not true either. He played a year with the semi-pro Aston Knights of the Seaboard Football League and two seasons with the Philadelphia Bell of the World Football League before he tried out for the Eagles. So he wasn't quite the rank amateur that *Invincible* suggests.

But those are fairly minor points. The heart of the story is Vince's Rocky-like determination to make it with the Eagles. Like Rocky, he knows he has one shot and one shot only at the brass ring, and while he is fully aware the odds are against him, he's going for it anyway. That spirit comes through.

"There isn't a day that goes by that someone doesn't come up to me and say how much they loved that movie," said Vermeil, who coached the Eagles from 1976 through 1982. "It touched a lot of people. It wasn't 100 percent factual, but so what? It was a great story about someone pursuing their dreams."

Invincible opens with Vince living in a South Philly row house, scuffling to make ends meet after losing his teaching job. His wife walks out, leaving behind a note that tells Vince he's a loser who never will amount to anything. He tends bar at the neighborhood saloon owned by his buddy Max, and he plays rough touch football with his friends on a vacant lot.

The downtrodden Eagles hire a new coach, Dick Vermeil (Kinnear) who holds an open tryout for anyone interested in joining the team, regardless of age or experience. Vince's buddies convince him to go even though he's 30 years old and never played college football. (In real life, Vince attended St. Joseph's University on a track scholarship.)

Several hundred candidates show up, but only Vince catches Vermeil's eye. He runs the 40-yard dash in 4.5 seconds and catches every ball thrown his way. "Where did you play college ball?" Vermeil asks. "I didn't play college ball," Vince replies. Vermeil knows it is a reach, but he invites Vince to join the full squad at training camp.

Most of the film focuses on Vince's daily battle to survive at camp. Vermeil puts the players through two grueling practices a day with lots of hitting and no mercy. The new coach works the players hard because he wants to weed out the weak and uncommitted. Things are particularly rough for Vince because the veterans resent him (some view him as a publicity stunt) and go out of their way to test him with cheap shots and insults.

There are other storylines—Vince's romance with Janet; his love for his blue-collar father who still talks about watching the Eagles win the NFL title in 1948; a strike that puts his buddies out of work—but, really, it all comes back to Vince and Vermeil.

With Vince, the story is about his willingness to pay any price necessary to make the team, and Wahlberg is very good at conveying his quiet, yet unflinching resolve. With Vermeil, it is about his understanding of what Vince represents. He knows Vince won't be a major contributor on the field—he will be a backup receiver and a special teams player—but Vermeil values the passion he brings to the locker room.

Vermeil tells the Eagles that he believes a team with better character can defeat a team with better talent. In Vince, he sees that character, which is why he decides to keep him while his assistant coaches favor a veteran who has more experience, but less heart.

On the day of the final cut, Vince is called into Vermeil's office. He is convinced he is a goner. "Thanks for sticking with me this long," he says as he slides his playbook across the desk to Vermeil.

Vermeil slides it back to him. "Why don't you hang onto that for a few months," he says. "Welcome to the Philadelphia Eagles."

🏛 **CHEERS:** Kinnear is a dead ringer for Vermeil circa 1976. The actor spent two weeks following Vermeil around during his training camp with the Kansas City Chiefs in 2005. Said Vermeil: "My son Richard said, 'Dad, he nailed you.' (Kinnear) did a great job."

🚩 **JEERS:** The scene in which Vince plays a rough-touch game just days before the Eagles home opener is laughable. One week into his pro career, he would risk an injury to help Max and the boys win a beer league game? Sure, that makes sense.

✔ **REALITY CHECK:** Vince did not score a touchdown on the fumble recovery against the New York Giants, as the movie shows. Yes, he recovered the loose ball and ran it into the end zone, but because it was a punt, it was ruled a muff which cannot be advanced.

✏ **WHAT THEY WROTE AT THE TIME:** "Mark Wahlberg is not only tough, but working class, a quality more difficult to fake than actors think."—Kyle Smith, *New York Post*

☞ **DON'T FAIL TO NOTICE:** The Eagles uniforms are accurate down to the smallest detail. The Liberty Bell patch on the sleeve was worn only for the 1976 season. It was in honor of the Bicentennial Celebration.

☺ **GOOFS:** Vince tells Janet about his all-time favorite Eagles player, Tommy McDonald. He says, "Tommy McDonald, All-American wide receiver, University of Oklahoma." McDonald was an All-American halfback at Oklahoma. He switched to wide receiver when he came to the Eagles.

👓 **"I KNOW THAT GUY":** Michael Rispoli, who plays Max, was the frighteningly evil Jackie Aprile in *The Sopranos*. Also, Stink Fisher—who plays Vince's roommate, Denny Franks—was Warren, the hospital orderly who looked after Uncle Junior in *The Sopranos*.

★ **SPORTS-ACTION GRADE:** B. Wahlberg helped with the realism by refusing to use a stunt double. When you see No. 83 take a crushing hit, you can see Wahlberg's contorted face inside the helmet.

🎬 **MY FAVORITE SPORTS MOVIE:** 2008 NCAA Defensive Player of the Year Rey Maualuga: "*Invincible* shows that even in a world of millionaire superstar athletes, a guy with desire can win out. I met Vince at an awards dinner and I told him, 'Man, you're an inspiration.'"

AN INTERVIEW WITH VINCE PAPALE

VINCE PAPALE PLAYED THREE SEASONS WITH THE PHILADEL-
PHIA EAGLES (1976-78) AND WAS THE SPECIAL TEAMS CAP-
TAIN IN 1977. IN A 2007 FAN VOTE, HE WAS NAMED TO THE
EAGLES 75-YEAR ANNIVERSARY TEAM AS THE OUTSTANDING
SPECIAL TEAMS PERFORMER. HE STILL LIVES IN THE
PHILADELPHIA AREA WITH JANET (NOW HIS WIFE) AND THEIR
TWO CHILDREN.

How did the idea for the movie Invincible come about?

It was November, 2002, and NFL Films did a feature on
me. It aired on ESPN before an Eagles-49ers Monday
night game. We had some friends at the house, we
watched the piece and it was very cool. Two days later,
we started getting calls from people in L.A. who saw it
and wanted to turn it into a movie. It was totally out of
the blue.

How long did it take to get the deal done?

Less than two years, which is pretty remarkable. Disney
bought the rights in October, 2004. I'll never forget it. I
was in the car with my two kids and got a call. It was (co-
producer) Ken Mok. He said, 'Hey, Disney just bought
your script.' I started crying. My kids thought somebody
died. I said, 'Guys, Disney is going to make our movie.' It
was our dream come true.

What was it like walking onto the movie set the first day?

I was as nervous walking onto the set as I was going out
to play my first game in the NFL. Disney had built props
to make Franklin Field look like Veterans Stadium. There
were all these extras in the stands, Mark Wahlberg was
wearing a jersey with my name. I thought, 'This is really
happening.' When I walked on the field, I got a standing
ovation from the extras, the crew, everyone. I couldn't
understand it, I hadn't done anything. But one of the
guys said, 'Hey, we're all here because of you.' It just blew
me away.

How did you feel about Mark Wahlberg's performance?

He just climbed into my body. He totally shared my
enthusiasm and passion for life. We spent a lot of time
together. He came to my house, spent time with my family. He's a great guy, totally down-to-earth. He promised
me he would give the role all he had and he did that. He
didn't just make me proud. He made me prouder. Now
we're like brothers. We're bonded for life.

How did he handle the bumps and bruises during the football scenes?

I give Mark a lot of credit. He didn't use a stunt double.
All the hits you saw in the movie, he took them for real.
Mark is in very good shape, a good athlete, but he had
never played organized football, so he was learning every
day. When he took the big hit, the one where he gets
blindsided and sent flying out of bounds, God, you
should've heard it. Everyone on the set held their breath,
they were afraid he was dead. But he bounced up and
finished the play. He tried to tell me it didn't hurt. I said,
'Come on, gimme a break.'

Do you have a favorite scene in the film?

I love the scene where Mark and Kevin Conway, who
plays my father, are talking and Mark is saying how he
doesn't think he is going to survive the next cut. Up to
that point, my father has been trying to downplay the
whole thing because he didn't want me to take it too
hard if things didn't work out. But in this scene he says,
'Vince, when I was telling you not to get your hopes up,
it didn't mean that I wasn't.' I was there when they
filmed it and it really got to me because my father was
such a big part of my life. Kevin totally nailed it.

In the film, the veteran players treat you badly in that first training camp. How accurate is that?

Very accurate. I think the veterans saw me as a publicity stunt, a 30-year-old rookie, a guy from the 700 level [the upper-deck at the Eagles' former home, Veterans Stadium] brought in for a tryout. I tried to earn their respect by working hard in practice, but even that caused problems. Every time I'd catch a pass, I'd sprint all the way to the end zone and that would tick off the defensive backs because they thought I was trying to show them up. They'd say, 'Yeah, you're an all-pro practice player. We can't wait to see what you can do in a game.' It took awhile, but I finally won them over.

How did Dick tell you that you made the team? Did it really happen the way it happens in the movie?

No, Dick didn't call me into his office. We were on the field, we knew it was cut-down day and we were counting heads, trying to figure out how many guys were still there and how many had to go. I was stretching and Dick came walking toward me. I thought, 'Uh oh, this is it. He's going to cut me right here.' But he gave me a big smile and said, 'Congratulations, old man. You're a Philadelphia Eagle.'

What happened next?

What do you think? I went bonkers. I said, 'Coach, can I make a phone call?' Dick said, 'Who are you gonna call, the Associated Press?' I said, 'I want to call my Dad.' He laughed and said, 'Go ahead.' I ran up the tunnel to the pay phone outside our locker room and I made a collect call to Westinghouse. I got the shop steward on the phone. I said, 'Hey, Slim, this is Vince. Tell Kingy—that's what everyone called my Dad—his little boy is a Philadelphia Eagle.' In the background, I could hear the plant erupting in cheers.

How has your life changed since the film was released?

I'm doing motivational speaking full-time, speaking to corporate groups. My message, basically, is one of hope. I was this kid from the projects, didn't come from the right school, didn't have the right pedigree. All I had was a dream, but I was able to make it happen. *Invincible* isn't about me. It's about anyone who has a dream, but has obstacles put in front of them. You can't give up, you have to take your best shot. I did, and look what happened.

63 ROLLERBALL (1975–R)

SPORT: ROLLERBALL | STARS: JAMES CAAN, JOHN HOUSEMAN
DIRECTOR: NORMAN JEWISON

The future world of Norman Jewison's *Rollerball* is one without crime or disease, poverty or racism. Plus, all the women look like fashion models. That's the good news.

On the other hand, freedom of choice has been replaced by fealty to the corporate states that now rule the world (Hello, Microsoft). And with no wars to stir the masses, the corporations mollify the human bloodlust by televising a brutal soporific sport that's a combination of roller derby, pinball and Ultimate Fighting.

Welcome to *Rollerball*, a science fiction nightmare set in 2018. The irony here is that Jewison intended for his movie to be a paean to anti-violence. Nice thought. But after it came out (as the horrified director explains on the DVD commentary) some filmgoers so loved the action that there was talk of forming real rollerball leagues.

Even now, what sells this movie is the Roman orgy of plasma and broken bones. Jewison tried to play the brutality so over-the-top that audiences would be repulsed. How could he have anticipated that, 30-plus years later, Americans would become blasé to the mayhem of Grand Theft Auto IV?

The sport of rollerball was invented by writer William Harrison in a short story for *Esquire* in 1973. It was translated to film as an anything-goes game where players in spiked gloves try to throw a softball-sized steel orb into a magnetized goal. Motorcycles race around the elevated oval and any form of defense is allowed—including cracking skulls. At times it's difficult as a viewer to grasp exactly what's taking place, but we'll admit that if Spike TV ever gets its act together, we'd waste a Friday night or two watching this stuff.

There's a melodramatic plot to *Rollerball*, ostensibly about one man's attempt to find freedom in a world devoid of it. Jonathan E (James Caan) the world's top star, is ordered to retire from his Houston-based team by conglomerate bigwig Bartholomew (John Houseman). It seems that Jonathan's success and popularity is undermining the complacency of the world's citizens. As Bartholomew says, Rollerball was designed "to demonstrate the futility of individual effort."

Jonathan refuses to quit, which presents a problem for world leaders, who spend most of their time video conferencing. That must have seemed very futuristic back in 1975.

To be honest, the plot flatlines early in the film. And both Caan and Houseman act with an annoying drugged-out stoicism that, we suppose, is meant to represent the lack of emotion in the future. So, take our advice and don't get hung up on the messagy stuff. Instead, enjoy the ferocious white-knuckle action sequences. *Rollerball*, to be honest, is at its best when Caan, in clunky skates and a 70s bike helmet, is beating the tar out of people.

Another way to enjoy the film is to look at its view of 2018 which, as of now, isn't that many years away. It's always fun to watch antiquated sci-fi to see how accurate its vision was. For example, how come every look at the future has men wearing white jumpsuits?

Anyway, let's run a checklist:

✔ Conniving corporate honchos will destroy the economic markets? Check.

✔ Public address systems will be everywhere you go, blathering in a feminine monotone? Not on our subway system.

✔ TVs will be wall-mounted flat screens, furniture will be ergonomic and Plexiglas will be the foundation of all interior décor? Check, check and . . . well, no.

✔ Superstar athletes will get the hottest girls and break all the rules? Check. Some things never change.

✔ Computers will evolve from handheld devices to mini-van-sized appliances? No. Although, on the other hand, they'll still crash at the worst times.

✔ Guns will shoot fireballs that set an entire forest to blazes? Please, we hope not.

✔ Librarians will be the sexiest women on Earth? Um, not where we live.

CHEERS: Considering this is a fictitious sport with virtually no rules, the in-game announcing is terrific. Jewison auditioned baseball's Mel Allen and a few NFL announcers, but found they couldn't keep up with the speed of the game. He finally hired hockey broadcaster Bob Miller of the Los Angeles Kings and Dick Enberg, who was 39 years old at the time.

"Jewison allowed me to create things on the fly," Enberg explained. "He said, 'This isn't football or baseball. We're not bound by any rules. If you think of something that sounds good, just say it.' So I did. I created things like the 'Flying Diamond' formation and the 'Flying Triangle.' It wasn't scripted, I just came up with it."

JEERS: We know Caan was proud of his hairy chest, but—just once—could he button his shirt?

BEST LINE: P.A. Announcer: "Your attention please. Rule changes for tonight's World Championship Game: No substitutions, no penalties . . . and no time limit."

REPEATED WATCHING QUOTIENT: Watch it once and then put it on the schedule again for 2018 to see what actually comes true.

CASTING CALL: Jewison says on the DVD commentary that he chose Caan to play the lead here after watching him star as Brian Piccolo in *Brian's Song*.

☞ **DON'T FAIL TO NOTICE:** At one point, Jonathan E's list of all-time records is recited, including most points in a game (18) and greatest number of players put out (13). There is also talk of the legendarily bloody contest between archrivals Rome and Pittsburgh, in which a Rollerball record nine players were killed. Archrivals Rome and Pittsburgh?

👓 **"I KNOW THAT GUY":** Burt Kwouk, the Japanese doctor who tries to pressure Jonathan to turn off another player's life support, played Peter Sellers' karate-smart sidekick, Cato, in the old *Pink Panther* movies.

★ **SPORTS-ACTION GRADE:** B-plus. You may not understand the rules, but it is exciting, well-shot stuff.

SIGN OF THE TIMES: For a movie about the future, a whole lot of things look dated in this film. Start with the lace-'em-up shoulder pads that wouldn't serve a Pop Warner team these days. Add to that the bulky four-wheel skates. They couldn't have anticipated in-line skates back in 1975?

🍎 **BET YOU DIDN'T KNOW:** Only one Rollerball rink was constructed, in Munich, Germany. It was repainted throughout the movie to suggest rinks from different cities.

🎞 **IF YOU LIKED THIS, YOU'LL LIKE:** *The Running Man*, Arnold Schwarzenegger's 1987 sci-fi thriller set in 2019. Not a sports movie, but it sure seems to "borrow" a lot from *Rollerball*.

Do not, under any circumstances, consider watching the 2002 remake starring Chris Klein.

64 THE PROGRAM (1993–R)

SPORT: FOOTBALL | STARS: JAMES CAAN, OMAR EPPS, CRAIG SHEFFER, HALLE BERRY
DIRECTOR: DAVID S. WARD

More than 15 years after its release, *The Program* is best remembered for what you *don't* see on the current DVD release.

The original movie had a scene of drunken college football players testing their courage by lying in the street as traffic whizzes by. That scene prompted copycat behavior, and four teenagers from Pennsylvania and Long Island were killed or critically injured trying to similarly prove their bravado. Touchstone Pictures recalled the film and deleted the "dotted-line chicken" moment.

Certainly, that was the necessary move at the time. Unfortunately, those episodes seemed to overshadow the rest of the movie. And that's a shame. Because *The Program* is a film that both takes a serious look at the pressures of big-time college athletics, and offers some excellent football scenes.

The movie follows the 1993 season of Eastern State University (we never are told *which* state), a perennial Top 25 program that has failed to make a major bowl game the two prior years. Coach Sam Winters (James Caan) is warned by his athletic director that ESU's alumni and the state legislature are restless, "and they both wield their checkbooks." In other words, win this season—or else.

Winters has hope, in the form of Heisman Trophy-candidate quarterback Joe Kane (Craig Sheffer) and freshman running back Darnell Jefferson (Omar Epps), who appears to be the second coming of Adrian Peterson—if he can just hold onto the football.

Speaking of Peterson, the Minnesota Vikings star, who attended Oklahoma, lists *The Program* as his favorite sports film. "It gives you a taste of what big-time college football is like," he said. "People might think it's not like that, but it is like that."

In some respects, *The Program* parallels the classic sports-movie formula, following a team through its ups and downs, leading up to the must-win game that can salvage its season. That movie template has been copied dozens of times.

But *The Program* also adds human sub-dramas that flash a harsh spotlight on the world surrounding major college athletics. Kane, the star quarterback, is plagued by generations of alcoholism within his family and winds up climbing into a bottle to escape the Heisman hype. His backup, Bobby Collins (Jon Pennell), is an academic dud who beds the coach's daughter and then gets caught having her take his placement test. Enraged, Winters tosses the kid from his squad. But when Kane's foibles push him into alcohol rehab, the coach must swallow his pride and reinstate the backup who humiliated him and his daughter.

Hmmm, perhaps this is starting to sound a little like *The Edge of Night*. Truth be told, there are some soap opera elements here, and many critics initially panned *The Program* as nothing more than a melodrama in shoulder pads. True enough, some of the dialog seems best suited for weekday afternoon TV (like this romantic line: "I've seen a lot of shitty things in my life, Autumn. That's how I know when I see something good."). Okay, maybe afternoon cable TV.

But we'll disagree with those who quickly dismissed *The Program*. For one, many of the melodramas here pack a punch. The subplot about desperate defensive end Steve Lattimer (Andrew Bryniarski) turning to steroids ("Hey, I just gained 35 pounds in the gym.") is both provocative and tragic—from the coach who closes his eyes ("Let the NCAA do its job," says Winters. "They test, we don't."), to the booster who essentially forgives, even when Lattimer, in a 'roid rage, attempts to rape his daughter.

Plus, there's terrific football action. The producers of *The Program* got the NCAA to sign off on using real college uniforms and stadiums. So when the ESU Timber

Wolves are playing the Iowa Hawkeyes, well, you can almost envision old Hayden Fry on the sidelines. The game shots are superbly choreographed and edited, raising the quality to the level seen in *Friday Night Lights* and *Jerry Maguire*.

"For someone like me who was still in high school and just thinking about playing college football, *The Program* gave me a chance to see what to expect," said Brian Westbrook, the star running back of the Philadelphia Eagles. "It was exaggerated in some ways. I didn't see any [players] getting paid at Villanova. But the action, the hitting and the intensity on the field was pretty authentic."

Except. . . .

Well, except that we're not buying actor Craig Sheffer as a big-time college quarterback. For one, he's got the worst throwing motion since Bernie Kosar. And secondly, you'd think a guy cast in a sports movie might have hit the weight room for a few weeks before filming. Sheffer's got no shoulder/neck muscles at all and his arms are the width of Slim Jims. We're supposed to accept this guy as a *Sports Illustrated* cover boy? Hell, he makes Doug Flutie look like Daunte Culpepper.

On the other hand, Sheffer can act and adroitly pulls off the "young man fighting his demons" role pretty well. Epps, also, is convincing as the cocky freshman who you just know is going to end up as Ricky Watters some day.

Caan doesn't have any heavy lifting here, mostly serving as the base character around whom everything revolves. Mostly, he's asked to react. Fortunately, his face can still move, since he filmed *The Program* before embarking on a decade-long binge of facelifts that left him looking like an escapee from Madame Tussauds.

◀ **CASTING CALL:** Chris Berman, Lynn Swann and Bo Schembechler all picked up paychecks for playing themselves.

🍻 **CHEERS:** *The Program* is an extremely popular movie among athletes, which gives it some street cred. Miami Dolphins running back Ronnie Brown said, "I loved the way it showed the team element, how the players really cared about each other and what it meant to be on a team."

Jacksonville Jaguars defensive end Paul Spicer said he first saw the movie back in high school and, "I can watch it to this day and still get hyped up about it." And Orlando Magic power forward Rashard Lewis added, "I'm from Texas and I'm a big football fan. I grew up watching football and playing football. That is one great football movie."

Those endorsements have to count for something.

🚩 **JEERS:** The in-game banter—supposedly TV commentary but really designed to keep movie watchers up to speed—is flat and clichéd. "That was a great clutch throw under pressure," Schembechler gasps at one play. "You just can't do better than that." Gee, thanks, Bo.

🎬 **PIVOTAL SCENE:** Coming off a suspension for steroid use, Lattimer tries to play clean. But, in the final seconds against Iowa, he is bulled over at the 1-yard line to lose the game. In the next scene, he is alone in his dorm room, pushing a large needle into his buttocks. "No problem," he reassures himself, as he picks up a barbell and starts compulsively lifting.

☞ **DON'T FAIL TO NOTICE:** The SEC banner hanging over Eastern State U's stadium at home games. That's because the action footage was filmed at the University of South Carolina's Williams-Brice Stadium, at halftime of several of the Fighting Gamecocks' 1992 contests. In fact, the movie never establishes which conference the Wolves play in. With a schedule that includes Mississippi State, Michigan, Iowa, Boston College and Georgia Tech, we sure couldn't figure it out.

✎ **WHAT THEY WROTE AT THE TIME:** "The film is one big cliché: A veteran coach who needs to make a bowl game to save his job, boosters giving players envelopes after games, a Heisman Trophy-candidate quarterback with working-class roots, a defensive end on steroids who smashes his head through car windows, a trash-talking All-American linebacker who suffers a season-ending injury and, of course, two tailbacks competing for the starting job—and Halle Berry."— Norman Chad, *Washington Post*

★ **Sports-Action Grade:** B-plus. The game scenes, as we said, are terrific. Their credibility is hurt, however, by lengthy conversations between players *during* plays. Such as this one:

Offensive lineman: "We're running doggies in the end zone and the trail runs right over your ass."

Defensive lineman: "You'll never be half the man your mama was."

Offensive lineman: "It's your misfortune now, big boy."

All this cleverness as they're running around. To get all those brilliant words in, director David S. Ward had to show things in slow motion. Only the mouths, apparently, move in real-time speed.

☝ **Bet You Didn't Know:** The scene in which Lattimer is visited by a "piss dealer"—who siphons out his drug-tainted urine and injects a clean sample—was inspired by an episode allegedly involving several members of the Philadelphia Eagles in the mid 1980s.

🙿 **Best Line:** Coach Winters in practice: "Lattimer, you cut out that necktie tackle crap. What, are you trying to make a highlight reel? That man left you hugging air. You take this helmet and put it right in his numbers. Drive it through their guts. I don't want to see nothing but snot bubbles in his nose."

⊗ **If You Liked This, You'll Like:** *Saturday's Hero*, a 1951 release starring John Derek (who went on to marry Ursula Andress, Linda Evans *and* Bo Derek—although not simultaneously) as a college football star coping with injuries, alumni handouts and corruption.

◉ **Repeated Watching Quotient:** A good watch at the start of every new college season.

🖐 **My Favorite Sports Movie:** Cy Young Award winner CC Sabathia, who was once offered a football scholarship by the University of Hawaii: "When I was playing football in high school, we used to watch it the night before our games. It got us psyched up and ready to play. The action was intense, but that's football."

ALL-TIME MOVIE FOOTBALL TEAM

WE ASSEMBLED OUR ALL-TIME, ALL-MOVIE, ALL-STAR FOOTBALL TEAM, AND THEN RAN THE ROSTER BY SOME EXPERTS. HERE IS THEIR SCOUTING REPORT:

OFFENSE

QB—Paul 'Wrecking' Crewe (Burt Reynolds in *The Longest Yard*)

Has some definite character issues—he's been tossed from pro football for shaving points. Throws a tight spiral with great accuracy—particularly at a prison guard's genitals. Capable of rallying a ragtag team of inmates to victory from a 35-13 deficit. Can even drop kick.

QB Backup—'Steamin' Willie Beamen (Jamie Foxx in *Any Given Sunday*)

Good scrambler. Like Donovan McNabb, he barfs too much.

QB Backup—Joe Pendleton (Warren Beatty in *Heaven Can Wait*)

Versatile; has performed magic in three different bodies.

RB—Gavin 'The Grey Ghost' Grey (Dennis Quaid in *Everybody's All-American*)

A Heisman Trophy winner at Louisiana University who finished his career in less-than-stellar fashion with the Denver Broncos—perhaps the result of those 40 pounds of gut he appears to have added. Runs with both power and speed. Still, debate remains over whether he ever beat local black high school legend Narvel Blue in a footrace.

RB—Julian Washington (LL Cool J in *Any Given Sunday*)

Talented but showboating power back, whose workload appears to be shrinking with the Miami Sharks' increased emphasis on the passing game. Shows signs of being more obsessed with money and image—"Kiss my Armani ass"—than he is in winning.

FB—Ray Griffen (J. Leon Pridgen II in *The Program*)

Still bitter over being displaced by Darnell Jefferson as the lead tailback, but appears to have made adjustment to new role as lead blocker. Has perfected the "thunder right" sweep for the ESU Timberwolves.

WR—Rod Tidwell (Cuba Gooding Jr. in *Jerry Maguire*)

A selfish, preening hot dog—in other words, just like every other WR in the NFL. Great hands and quickness, not afraid to go over the middle despite being undersized. Shows up big for prime-time games. His agent desires to make him the highest-paid receiver in the league. Make sure to check him for post-concussion syndrome.

WR—Phil Elliott (Nick Nolte in *North Dallas Forty*)

Smart possession receiver. May have the best hands in the league. Not afraid to play through pain. Red flags: Has some discipline issues, is not a true team player and seems to be in jeopardy of failing his next drug test.

TE—Roberta Muldoon (John Lithgow in *The World According to Garp*)

Former starter for the Philadelphia Eagles known for strength and "quick hands." Six-foot-four, although weight is down from 235 to 180 pounds. That may be a result of her post-career sex-reassignment surgery.

OL—Louie Lastik (Ethan Suplee in *Remember the Titans*)

Kind of slow, kind of dumb, but has a great attitude. Reportedly has strained back from carrying around "yo' mama."

OL—Ed Lawrence (John Goodman in *Everybody's All-American*)

Pro opportunities looked bright after a stellar career at LSU, but disappeared in a swirl of alcohol, gambling and self-destructiveness. Loyal teammate; would do anything for his star running back.

OL—Bud-Lite Kaminski (Abraham Benrubi in *The Program*)

Huge country-boy tackle for ESU who is pretty good at trash talk for an offensive lineman. "We're running doggies in the end zone and the trail leads right over your ass."

OL—Samson (Richard Kiel in *The Longest Yard*)

Has that real mean streak (almost criminal) that you look for in a lineman. Has perfected the clothesline takedown. "I think I broke his fucking neck."

OL—Jo Bob Priddy (Bo Svenson in *North Dallas Forty*)

Has some temper issues, often aimed at teammates insulting him by questioning his off-field plans to open a restaurant. Knows how to shut down a tougher opponent, even if it means breaking his leg. He and linemate O.W. Shaddock team up for the best pre-game ritual in football.

DEFENSE

DE—Julius Campbell (Wood Harris in *Remember the Titans*)

Off-field leader who knows how to unite teammates and cut through racial tensions. Terrific pass rusher with tons of natural talent. "Left side! Strong side!"

DT—Andre Krimm (Sinbad in *Necessary Roughness*)

Strong player languishing with the Texas State Fighting Armadillos. Big and strong, despite vegetarian diet. Moonlights as a professor of celestial mechanics—easily making him the smartest player on this squad.

DT—Phillip Finch (Tab Thacker in *Wildcats*)

Huge 400-pound load who can clog up the middle. Difficult to move, but more difficult to motivate. Knows a bit too much about gambling. Good on special teams—he can block a field goal.

DE—Steve Lattimer (Andrew Bryniarski in *The Program*)

Well-cut 6-foot-5, 280-pound specimen prone to wearing scary face paint and going into rages. A monster on defense. Suspected steroid abuser who will, apparently, go to gruesome lengths to beat the test.

LB—Luther 'Shark' Lavay (Lawrence Taylor in *Any Given Sunday*)

Aging former star—worried about his future and his legacy—who can still rise up to make a game-saving tackle on fourth-and-short. Team doctors, citing risk of paralysis, recommend immediate retirement. "If you don't be the man, you're just another punk."

LB—Bogdanski (Ray Nitschke in *The Longest Yard*)

Good motivator ("I'll see you on the field, superstar"), who can also cope with a spiral or two to the family jewels. Often displays a nasty side—almost sadistic—that seems about right for a prison guard.

LB—Charles Jefferson (Forest Whitaker in *Fast Times at Ridgemont High*)

Rumor has it that he hasn't attended a single class this season and flies in just for games. Still, his talent is second to none. Plays best when he's really mad. Still mourning the loss of his sports car, allegedly vandalized by boosters from rival high school. Check with Jeff Spicoli on that one.

LB—Bobby Boucher (Adam Sandler in *The Waterboy*)

Most dominating linebacker in NCAA history, capable of producing double-digit sacks in a single game for SCLSU. Single-handedly took a team that had not won in years and brought them to a bowl game. Also carries the team's refreshments.

DB—Stefen Djordjevic (Tom Cruise in *All the Right Moves*)

Hard-hitting cornerback packs a load, despite his apparent five-foot-two frame. Currently a free agent, after being framed and kicked off his high school team.

DB—Dr. Death (Vister Hayes in *The Best of Times*)

Intimidating, violent cover man for Bakersfield High, currently on parole from a recent jail stint. He has perfected bump-and-run coverage into bump-and-assault. Gave up just one catch in critical contest against Taft High's Jack Dundee (Robin Williams) which, unfortunately, turned into the game winner.

DB—Petey Jones (Donald Faison in *Remember the Titans*)

Great speed and cover skills. Overly sensitive since losing his job as starting quarterback. Considers football to be "fun," which might require coach to wipe the smile off his face.

DB—Levander 'Bird' Williams (Mykelti Williamson in *Wildcats*)

Another converted quarterback. He displays great hands, appearing to intercept a pass and return it for a touchdown in every game for Central High. Will need to make adjustments after playing for a female coach.

K—Lucy Draper (Kathy Ireland in *Necessary Roughness*)

Outstanding leg—in fact, two of them. Form is faulty, but who cares? Replaces Ray Finkle (Sean Young in *Ace Ventura*) who is currently serving time for kidnapping Dan Marino.

P—Clark Kent (Jeff East in *Superman*)

Young Clark has punted just once, but sent the ball into outer space. His parents appear to have forbidden him from playing for some reason. Are they hiding something?

Returns—Forrest Gump (Tom Hanks in *Forrest Gump*)

What he lacks in brains, he makes up in athletic ability. Just hand him the ball and point him in the right direction. "Run, Forrest, run!"

65 THE BOXER (1997-R)

SPORT: BOXING | STARS: DANIEL DAY-LEWIS, EMILY WATSON, BRIAN COX
DIRECTOR: JIM SHERIDAN

The Boxer is Danny Flynn (Daniel Day-Lewis), a man fighting battles that extend far beyond the ring. As a teenager in Belfast, Flynn was active in the IRA and winds up serving 14 years in prison. When he is released, he wants no part of the on-going violence. He wants to return home to resume his boxing career.

Of course, it is not that easy.

Flynn is caught between splintering factions of the IRA, one side led by Joe Hamill (Brian Cox), who is ready to end the sectarian war, the other side led by Harry (Gerald McSorley), a Sinn Fein officer who is determined to continue the bloodshed. Flynn tries to distance himself from the politics, but that is impossible in a city where armed troops patrol the streets and military helicopters swoop overhead.

Director Jim Sheridan (who teamed with Day-Lewis in *My Left Foot*) establishes Flynn's character in the opening shot. He shows Danny alone in the prison yard, shadow boxing. Dressed in a hooded sweatshirt, dwarfed by the gray walls and guard towers, Danny is a solitary figure. It is the day of his release, yet he is going through the same routine he has followed every day for 14 years. It is the portrait of a hard and stubborn man.

When Danny rebuilds his old gym with the intention of opening it to both Catholics and Protestants, he lights the fuse on an emotional powder keg. It finally explodes on the night of his comeback bout when a car bombing sets off a bloody riot in the streets. The night ends with the gym—and Danny's dreams of a peaceful life—going up in flames.

Adding to the tension is Danny's reunion with his former love Maggie (Emily Watson), who married his best friend while Danny was in prison. The husband, who also was involved in the IRA, is now behind bars and when Danny and Maggie see each other again, it is clear the old feelings are still there. The trouble is, if an IRA wife is unfaithful it is considered an act of treason and

there are dire consequences.

The Boxer is three stories in one: a political film, a boxing film and a love story. It is to Sheridan's credit that he weaves the three together as well as he does, although the politics become muddled at times. Day-Lewis carries the film with his usual beautifully nuanced performance. With his sharp features and piercing eyes, he is well-suited to the role of the distant and embittered Danny, but he is particularly good in several scenes with Maggie where he tries to articulate his feelings.

At one point, he describes the isolation of prison. "At first, you hold onto all the old voices in your head," he says. "Kids you knew in school, friends. When those fade, you talk to yourself. After awhile, it's as if your own voice doesn't belong there. Silence becomes your best friend."

He looks at Maggie and says, "I've lived with your face in silence."

"Those are great lines by any standard," wrote Edward Guthmann in the *San Francisco Chronicle*. "With Day-Lewis speaking them and Watson reacting, they are poetry."

The Boxer has a real life parallel in former featherweight champion Barry McGuigan, who rose to prominence during the Northern Ireland conflict. McGuigan was able to do what Danny Flynn tried to do, that is, use his success in the ring to bring Catholics and Protestants together. He refused to wear the colors of either side. Instead, he entered the ring under a blue flag adorned with a dove, the symbol of peace.

McGuigan served as technical advisor on the film. He worked with Day-Lewis for three years, teaching him how to move and throw a punch. McGuigan said they sparred more than a thousand rounds. The result is some of the most realistic boxing action ever put on film.

In the best scene, Danny goes to London to fight at a swanky dinner club where the spectators wear formal attire and drink champagne. Danny is matched with an

African fighter and after several bloody rounds Danny lands a vicious left hook. The African sags against the ropes, out on his feet. Rather than punish him further, Danny drops his hands. The crowd boos and the referee barks, "Fight."

"The fight's over," Danny says, walking away.

Watching on TV, the Sinn Fein officer Harry—who resents Danny for turning his back on the IRA— says, "What do you expect? He's a quitter."

Maggie says nothing, but the look in her eyes says she knows better.

👍 **CHEERS:** Daniel Day-Lewis, who won Oscars for his work in *My Left Foot* and *There Will Be Blood*, is superb as Danny Flynn. As David Denby wrote in *New York* magazine: "Silent and wary much of the time, he bursts out now and then in tirades of memorable bitterness."

👎 **JEERS:** The first half of the film drags and Sheridan telegraphs some of his punches. Russell Smith in the *Austin Chronicle* wrote: "The parrot-voiced lady who sat behind me presciently announced each major plot turn. 'My God! That car's gonna blow up.'"

🎬 **PIVOTAL SCENE:** Danny Flynn is released from prison and spends his first night at a homeless shelter where he bumps into his former trainer Ike (Ken Stott). Danny tells Ike he intends to resume his boxing career. Ike scoffs at the idea, reminding Danny he spent the last 14 years behind bars.

"I'm 32 years old," Danny says. "Archie Moore fought for the world championship when he was 42."

Ike smiles.

The next morning, the two men are re-opening the old gym and going back to work.

✎ **WHAT THEY WROTE AT THE TIME:** "*The Boxer* is a complex web of a movie and at first it seems odd that the main character should be someone so close to the center. But the center is the perfect place from which to explore the ironies and similarities of the left and the right." —Marty Mapes, *Movie Habit*

99 **BEST LINE:** Staring out the window at his Belfast neighborhood, frustrated that his efforts to rebuild his life have been thwarted by IRA violence, Danny says, "I'm not a killer, Maggie, but this place makes me want to kill."

★ **SPORTS-ACTION GRADE:** B-plus. The boxing scenes are first-rate, but there aren't that many of them.

◉ **REPEATED WATCHING QUOTIENT:** Worth revisiting, but we recommend fast-forwarding through the political monologues. Any scene with Day-Lewis is worth seeing again. He is totally convincing in a very difficult role.

SPORT: BASKETBALL | STARS: WOODY HARRELSON, WESLEY SNIPES, ROSIE PEREZ
DIRECTOR: RON SHELTON

White Men Can't Jump had all the ingredients to be a masterpiece. When it came out in 1992, writer/director Ron Shelton was still basking in the glow from his landmark *Bull Durham*. Actor Wesley Snipes was riding the wave of two powerful films—*Jungle Fever* and *New Jack City*. And Woody Harrelson was making the transition from television after seven years as likeable lug Woody Boyd on *Cheers*. With that collection of talent, creating a slick, hip-hop comedy-drama about the hustle of Los Angeles playground basketball—well, how could it not be superb?

Unfortunately, the finished product does not add up to the sum of its parts. Like the Dallas Mavericks of the past decade, it underachieved despite all that talent. While *White Men Can't Jump* is entertaining and occasionally provocative, there is nothing special about it, nothing that pushes it into the pantheon of champions.

Maybe we're being too harsh. Hey, the Mavericks, after all, are a fun team to watch and by most standards have been a success in recent years. Likewise, *White Men* rang up $76 million at the box office, making it the second all-time grossing movie ever about basketball (behind *Space Jam*, but we won't comment on that). Most critics applauded it initially, with Hal Hinson of the *Washington Post* calling it, "a self-celebrating form of verbal jazz."

We're just kind of stuck on what could have been.

White Men takes place on the playground courts of Los Angeles, where crumpled twenties are bet on the outcome of two-on-two basketball games. Sidney Deane (Snipes) is a world class hoops hustler who successfully destroys opponents by getting into their minds with nonstop bragging and mockery. Billy Hoyle (Harrelson) is the outsider with the backwards cap and Reebok Pumps who uses his geeky looks (and street ball's racial bias) as the lure. Everyone, after all, assumes that a white guy—particularly one appearing this dopey—can't keep up with the blacks.

Billy initially cons Sidney, who cons him back, which leads to a series of back-and-forth revenge games which, quite frankly, grow repetitive. Eventually, the two must join to survive (despite Billy's clever protestation that, "I don't hustle with people who are dishonest."). Sidney needs money to move his wife and son from their oft-robbed apartment at the Vista View ("There's no vista. There's no view," he notes). And Billy, well, he's got to pay off some not-so-goodfellas who threaten to kill him for reneging on a deal to fix a schoolyard game after an opponent taunted him.

Taunting is a huge part of this movie. As important as the game is, destroying your opponent verbally is even more so. Or is supposed to be. Every derivative of every four-letter word is turned into a dagger and any player's warts are there to be exploited, as when Sidney jeers a skinny challenger with, "Shut your anorexic malnutrition tapeworm-having overdose on Dick Gregory Bahamian diet-drinking ass up."

Sometimes the catcalls work, sometimes they just seem contrived. The racial gibes, particularly, grow weary.

What doesn't tire is the performance of Rosie Perez as Sidney's girlfriend, Gloria, a Puerto Rican one-time disco queen. Gloria believes her destiny is to become a *Jeopardy!* champion, so she crams her mind with endless amounts of useless information—such as foods that begin with the letter Q. With her bombshell body and Muppet voice, Perez steals the movie.

There are other elements to enjoy here. Any soundtrack that includes Duke Ellington, James Brown, Isaac Hayes, Cypress Hill and Jimi Hendrix gets our attention—although, according to Sidney, "White people can *listen* to Hendrix, but they can't really *hear* him."

In the end, however, *White Men Can't Jump* proves to be not much more than an engaging two-hour diversion.

Shelton, who did such a great job of bringing minor league life to the screen in *Bull Durham*, doesn't quite put the ball through the hole in his follow-up.

🍺 **CHEERS:** Make sure you get the bonus DVD containing the music video featuring Harrelson, Snipes and Perez. We're not saying that it's fine art; we're just saying that it's entertaining.

🚩 **JEERS:** Even back in 1992, most of these playground insults had to sound trite. "Your mama is so slow, she takes two hours to watch *60 Minutes*." Come on, really. Or this one: "You wouldn't know a behind-the-back pass if it hit you in the face. All you know is passing gas." Who wrote that line, a 12-year-old? The putdowns too often sound like rejected ideas from a brainstorming session for And 1 tee-shirt slogans.

✏️ **WHAT THEY WROTE AT THE TIME:** "I laughed out loud at the comic trash talk on the courts. I adored Rosie Perez. . . . The basketball was mesmerizing, done in slow motion set to music that matched the game's urgent, elegant flow. . . . Loved it so much, I saw it twice."—Dave Kindred, *The Sporting News*

👁 **REPEATED WATCHING QUOTIENT:** If you're headed out to a two-on-two tournament, *White Men Can't Jump* will help psyche you up. Other than that, stick with it again only if there's nothing better on.

☝️ **DON'T FAIL TO NOTICE:** Early in the film, Billy makes a joking reference to the last words of Lee Harvey Oswald ("It wasn't me, it was the—*bang!*"). In real life, Harrelson's father, Charles Harrelson, was a convicted hitman who boasted several times that he was involved in the conspiracy to kill President John F. Kennedy in 1963.

📣 **CASTING CALL:** Former NBA players Freeman Williams and Marques Johnson make appearances as street ballers. Gary Payton is also rumored to be an uncredited extra, but we sure couldn't spot him.

★ **SPORTS-ACTION GRADE:** C-plus. Believing that guys with the limited basketball skills of Harrelson and Snipes

could beat topnotch street players requires a stretch of logic. According to the film's publicity package, the duo's instructors—including the legendary Bob Lanier—insisted that Harrelson and Snipes became good enough to be able to start for an NCAA Division III team. Hmm. Woody might be able to hold his own in a juco contest. Wesley? Sit down and keep score, son.

🍎 **BET YOU DIDN'T KNOW:** Inspired by the movie, the real TV show *Jeopardy!* actually used the category "Foods that begin with the letter Q" in 1997. The answers: quail, quiche, quinine, quince, quahog. What, no quesadilla?

😎 **"I KNOW THAT GUY":** Sidney's playground pal Junior is played by Kadeem Hardison, who was in the midst of a six-year run on the *Cosby Show* spinoff *A Different World* when *White Men* was shot. Just as Jerry Lewis was once inexplicably a huge idol in France, Hardison's Dwayne Wayne character in *A Different World* was all the rage in Holland. His geeky eyeglasses became that country's top fashion statement in the early 1990s.

SIGN OF THE TIMES: Wow, once upon a time "boo-yah" was a cutting edge playground exclamation. It's sad to see ESPN's Stuart Scott still hauling it out nearly two decades later.

⊕ **IF YOU LIKED THIS, YOU'LL LIKE:** The *White Men Can't Jump* game released for the Atari Jaguar system in 1996. Actually, you probably won't. The game got terrible grades for muddy graphics and confusing rules. The video review website seanbaby.com termed it "so bad that some electricity might refuse to power it."

67 JUNIOR BONNER (1972–PG)

SPORT: RODEO | STARS: STEVE MCQUEEN, ROBERT PRESTON, JOE DON BAKER
DIRECTOR: SAM PECKINPAH

Steve McQueen plays Junior Bonner, a past-his-prime rodeo champion looking to settle down in his hometown of Prescott, Az. He quickly discovers that his father Ace (Preston) has gambled away his inheritance, and his greedy brother Curly (Baker) is selling off parcels of the family's land to open a mobile home retirement community.

There are all kinds of family dynamics here, and symbolic Old West vs. New West tension, but the real reason to watch the movie is McQueen. At age 42 (although he looks older) he nails the role as aging athlete aiming for one final moment of glory. Think Crash Davis in chaps and spurs.

Bonner signs up for the hometown July 4 rodeo. He's flat busted, and doesn't do anything to enhance his fortunes in the first two riding events. But although he needs the money, he more so needs to regain his pride. So, for the finale, he signs up to ride the prize bull Sunshine—a snorting, slobbering, intimidating menace that no one has ever tamed. Kind of like Mike Tyson circa 1987, if Tyson had a nose ring and was a little better behaved.

We don't want to give away the ending, except to say that in professional bull riding, the magic number appears to be eight seconds. Stretch that out into super-slow-motion, and you can make it last several minutes.

The film moves languidly, in the style of a lot of 1970s westerns. And despite the opportunity to show cowboys impaled on wild animal horns, it's the least violent film of Sam Peckinpah, the man who directed *The Wild Bunch* and *Bring Me the Head of Alfredo Garcia*. Or was that Damaso Garcia? Anyway, we suspect Peckinpah started feeling guilty about that halfway through the film, because he inserts a gratuitous bar brawl scene that serves no purpose beyond getting a little blood onscreen.

Watch for a brief cameo by genuine cowboy legend Casey Tibbs, who was known as "The Babe Ruth of Rodeo," and whom, we learned from his official bio, died at his home on Jan. 28, 1990, while watching the Super Bowl. It only makes sense that he foolishly bet on the Broncos.

CHEERS: There really is a rodeo event called "wild cow milking," in which two-man teams of cowboys try to subdue a stampede of female livestock let loose in the arena. This becomes a Demolition Derby among several breeds of mammals—one cowboy grabs the horns, the other aims to squeeze out the uncooperative cow's milk. The first team to fill a bottle wins.

We can't imagine that PETA is down with all this.

In what is both the most funny and tender scene in the film (although not for the cattle, we suspect), Ace and Junior Bonner—the rascal dad and the drifter son—team up, hoping to wrestle their way to a few bucks and a restored relationship. It may not be quite as heartwarming as the father-and-son scene in *Field of Dreams*, but it works.

JEERS: The first rodeo action scenes—thrilling as they are—don't come until you're 64 minutes into the movie. You must first sit through more than an hour of character development and long, panning scenes of country roads. Although we do get to see Junior knock his jackass of a brother through a window with a single punch.

✔ REALITY CHECK: Well, the roping-and-wrestling scenes were filmed using real riders at the Frontier Days rodeo in Prescott, so they ring true. The only problem is that McQueen—while able to impressively mount a horse (or motorcycle for that matter)—was smart enough not to get on the back of an angry 1,500-pound bull. It's all too apparent that a stunt double is being used for his money shots.

241

99 BEST LINE: Rodeo promoter Buck Roan (Ben Johnson): "You know something? Old Junior's gonna spoil all my horses if he don't stop blindfolding them with his ass." We don't even know what that means, but we love it.

99 SECOND-BEST LINE: Junior's nephew, Tim: "You could ride anything with hair on it, Uncle Junior." Now that just sounds creepy.

◀ CASTING CALL: Joe Don Baker was a big and physical man, who showed in *Walking Tall* that he knew how to swing a stick. So how come his only forays into sports films were a one-scene triumph as "The Whammer" in *The Natural*, and his supporting role here as the conniving and wimpy brother? Somewhere along the way, this man should have been cast as an offensive lineman.

👓 "I KNOW THAT GUY": Dub Taylor, who plays the rodeo riders' favorite saloon keeper, appeared in—get this—127 westerns during his career, usually doffing a bowler hat and the top half of his long johns as a shirt. He is so much the prototype for this subject that his life was chronicled in a 2007 feature-length documentary titled, *That Guy: The Legacy of Dub Taylor*.

⚙ IF YOU LIKED THIS, YOU'LL LIKE: *J.W. Coop,* which also came out in 1972 and starred Cliff Robertson as the bronco-riding title character. It's surprising there haven't been more rodeo movies over the years, given how easily the excitement of the events translate to film.

👁 REPEATED WATCHING QUOTIENT: Once is enough. Or else, just fast forward through the first half to get to the good rodeo scenes.

68 BLUE CHIPS (1994–PG-13)

SPORT: BASKETBALL | STARS: NICK NOLTE, SHAQUILLE O'NEAL, ED O'NEILL
DIRECTOR: WILLIAM FRIEDKIN

Blue Chips is one of Ron Shelton's earliest writing efforts. He completed the screenplay a decade before *Bull Durham* and *White Men Can't Jump* and it shows. The characters are more one-dimensional and the dialog doesn't have the same snap. It is a lot more conventional than his later films.

But the subject matter—corruption in big-time athletics—is meaty stuff and the performances by Nick Nolte (expectedly) and Shaquille O'Neal (surprisingly) are very good. The basketball action looks authentic, which makes sense since director William Friedkin has real players—Rodney Rogers, Allan Houston, George Lynch and Calbert Cheaney, among others—pushing the ball up and down the court.

Friedkin said he basically just rolled the ball out on the floor and let the guys play while the cameras rolled. Sometimes the best directing, he said, is not directing at

all. It would not work in every film—it would not have worked in *The French Connection*, for which Friedkin won an Oscar—but it worked well here.

Blue Chips is the story of coach Pete Bell (Nolte), who won two national championships at Western University, but now has fallen on hard times. He is coming off his first losing season and the alumni are restless. They want Bell to do what other Division One schools are doing—that is, break the rules and buy the best players.

Reluctantly, Bell succumbs to the pressure. He goes off to recruit an Indiana hotshot named Ricky Roe (Matt Nover). The kid comes right to the point: "I'm a white, blue chip prospect," he says, "and that should be worth $30,000 in one of those athletic bags." He also wants a new tractor for his father's farm.

Bell swallows hard, but says OK.

Butch McRae (Penny Hardaway) is a black inner-city

kid from Chicago. He wants a new home with a lawn for his mother. Bell makes it happen. Neon Bodeaux (O'Neal) is a seven-footer with enough game to take any team to the Final Four. He signs with Western and just like that he is driving a new Lexus. All the "gifts" are courtesy of a sleazy alum named Happy Kuykendall (J.T. Walsh).

Kuykendall is a caricature of an unprincipled booster, but he delivers one of the film's better speeches when he tells Bell there is nothing wrong with paying off the players. "Damn it, we owe these kids," he says, pointing out how much money a winning team brings into a university. Shelton seems to be saying the NCAA rules are a sham. A fair point, but he allows Kuykendall to become such a hateful figure it is impossible to take his side on anything.

With his new recruits, Bell begins piling up the victories and Western is once again a national power. But as the team climbs in the polls and the smiling alumni fat cats pat him on the back, he is overcome with guilt. It doesn't help that sportswriter Ed Axelby (Ed O'Neill) is snooping around looking for the dirt on Bell.

The Western team goes all the way, defeating Indiana (coached by the real Bobby Knight and with Bobby Hurley, the former Duke star, at point guard) and Texas Western (coached by Rick Pitino). But when it is all over, Bell spills his guts at the press conference, admitting to his recruiting violations and lamenting the fact that he traded his principles for a few victories.

If it sounds like a contrived ending, well, it is. As Desson Howe wrote in the *Washington Post*: "I've seen subtler semiology on *Sesame Street*."

But even when *Blue Chips* stumbles, Nolte holds your interest. He makes you feel his pain as he sells his soul to the hustlers and wheeler-dealers he once despised. There is never a doubt that in the end his conscience will win out and he will come clean, but Nolte is so good that he keeps you watching.

Among the players, Shaq brings more depth to his character than you would expect. He is a lot more believable here than he was in, say, *Kazaam*.

🍺 **CHEERS:** Nick Nolte followed Bobby Knight for part of the 1992 basketball season, and it shows. His Pete Bell has Knight's body language as well as his sweater and temper.

🚩 **JEERS:** The subplot involving Jenny, the coach's ex-wife (Mary McDonnell), is a waste of time.

🎬 **PIVOTAL SCENE:** Pete (Nolte) has a classic post-game meltdown. He rips the team and storms out of the room, only to return and rip them again. He stalks out, then comes back a third time, screaming, "I can't tell you how sick I am of basketball today." He proceeds to toss chairs and knock over the water cooler as the players cower in their lockers.

✒ **WHAT THEY WROTE AT THE TIME:** "A deafness-inducing but otherwise ho-hum would-be exposé of shady recruiting practices by college basketball programs."— Todd McCarthy, *Variety*

😎 **"I KNOW THAT GUY":** In his acting debut, at age 65, Celtics Hall of Famer Bob Cousy plays Vic Roker, Western University's athletic director. He is very good as the administrator who looks the other way as the rules are being broken.

99 **BEST LINE:** Coach Bell, coming clean, says, "Boys, the rules don't make much sense. But I believe in the rules. Some of us broke them. I broke them. I can't do this. I can't win like this."

★ **SPORTS-ACTION GRADE:** A-minus. Friedkin brought in real college players and so the games look real. It is just a little jarring to see Bobby Hurley, however, wearing Indiana red.

👁 **REPEATED WATCHING QUOTIENT:** Worth checking out if only to remember how Shaq looked in his prime.

🏃 **MY FAVORITE SPORTS MOVIE:** Philadelphia Phillies shortstop Jimmy Rollins: "I love that it paints a true portrait of what goes on in college sports. The coach doesn't want to get into the dirt, but he is forced to. Same thing with Shaq's character. They fall into the corruption because that's the system. That stuff really happens. Hey, how do you think the big schools stay good year after year?"

ATHLETES WHO COULD ACT

IT BEGAN, AS FAR AS WE COULD FIND, BACK IN 1917, WITH TY COBB STARRING AS A SMALL-TOWN BANK TELLER-TURNED-BALLPLAYER IN *SOMEWHERE IN GEORGIA*. OVER THE COURSE OF 30 MINUTES HE GETS KIDNAPPED, BREAKS FREE, BEATS UP HIS CAPTORS AND WINS THE BIG GAME. HE GETS THE GIRL, AS WELL.

IN THE 1930S, MULTI-SPORT STAR PAUL ROBESON CROONED THROUGH *SHOW BOAT* AND OLYMPIC SWIMMER JOHNNY WEISSMULLER YODELED HIS WAY THROUGH TOO MANY *TARZAN* REMAKES. AND FROM THERE, HUNDREDS OF PRO ATHLETES HAVE REPLACED EYE-BLACK WITH ACTOR'S MAKEUP, WITH VARYING DEGREES OF SUCCESS.

HERE ARE A DOZEN WHO IMPRESSED US. WE LEFT OUT ACTORS WHOSE SPORTS CAREERS ENDED IN COLLEGE (BURT REYNOLDS, TOMMY LEE JONES), AS WELL AS PROFESSIONAL WRESTLERS (DWAYNE JOHNSON, ANDRE THE GIANT), BECAUSE, HEY, THEIR SO-CALLED SPORTS CAREERS WERE ALL ABOUT ACTING ANYWAY.

1. Arnold Schwarzenegger. The ultimate multi-career performer who's still wowing them in Sacramento. The world-class bodybuilder broke through with 1977's *Pumping Iron* and grew, arguably, into the top action-movie icon ever.

Consider this: Arnold had just 16 lines in the original *Terminator*, and not a whole lot more in the sequel. Yet his trademark lines—"I'll be back" (originally written as "I'll come back") and "Hasta la vista, baby"—became part of the lexicon of our times. That's what you call screen presence.

2. Jim Brown. The greatest running back in NFL history, his film career might have peaked in his 1967 breakout role as an ill-fated tough guy in the ultimate guy's movie, *The Dirty Dozen*. But we've still enjoyed him in drama (*Ice Station Zebra*), comedy (*Mars Attacks!*) and sci-fi (with Schwarzenegger in *Running Man*). He even did a strong turn as football coach Montezuma Monroe in *Any Given Sunday*.

Here's an amazing story: Brown was wrapping up shooting *The Dirty Dozen* in England in the summer of 1966, when it came time to report to Cleveland Browns training camp. Brown—who had led the NFL in rushing eight of his nine pro seasons—called owner Art Modell to say he would be a week or two late.

"Get here on time, or don't bother to report," said Modell, figuring he could strong-arm his star running back.

"Well then, I retire," retorted Brown. And he did. Never looked back.

No one gives Jim Brown an ultimatum.

3. Alex Karras. He's appeared in more than a dozen movies and several sappy television series. But his seminal role will always be as the misunderstood, slow-witted lug Mongo in *Blazing Saddles*, delivering lines like, "Mongo only pawn in game of life," in a way that would do Richard Burton proud. Then he decks a horse with one punch.

4. Woody Strode. Never heard of him, you say? That's a shame, because Jackie Robinson's former UCLA Bruins teammate was among four African-Americans to break pro football's color line in 1946, joining the Los Angeles Rams. On screen, Woodrow Wilson Woodwine Strode (there's a name, eh?) was a presence in the 50s and 60s, playing tough-guy roles in classic westerns like *The Professionals, Once Upon a Time in the West* and *The Man Who Shot Liberty Valance*. If you're any kind of film fan, you'll certainly remember the greatest gladiatorial scene ever filmed, where, as the mammoth Draba, he dueled Kirk Douglas in *Spartacus*.

Spartacus: "What's your name?"

Draba: "You don't want to know my name. I don't want to know your name."

Spartacus: "Just a friendly question."

Draba: "Gladiators don't make friends. If we're ever matched in the arena together, I have to kill you."

Yeah, that guy.

5. Fred Williamson. Notice how many on this list are football players? We're not sure why. Maybe it has to do with them being the most receptive to coaching. "The Hammer" was a showboating defensive back for the Kansas City Chiefs in the '60s. He bombed on *Monday Night Football*, but played a great badass in the blaxploitation films of the 1970s.

"There are two things I demand of my scripts, and they're the same things my audiences demand," said the never-modest Williamson. "First, I have to get the girl. Second, I have to win all the fights."

We'll always love him from the scene in 1996's *From Dusk Till Dawn* when he morphed from a tough-guy trucker into a vampire.

6. Ray Allen. Finally, a basketball player. It wasn't much of a stretch for Allen to play a hoops star in *He Got Game* and, later, the dreadful *Harvard Man*. But we'll agree with Roger Ebert of the *Chicago Sun-Times* who called him "that rarity—an athlete who can act."

Allen was actually director Spike Lee's third choice for the role, behind Allen Iverson and Stephon Marbury. Those two, however, wanted to land the role of Jesus Shuttlesworth without auditioning. So Lee turned to Allen, who was humble enough to try out and agreed to weeks of acting lessons before the shooting. It kind of makes you root for him.

7. Carl Weathers. You probably don't remember his career as a linebacker for San Diego State, the Oakland Raiders or the Canadian Football League's British Columbia Lions. But you sure know him as Apollo Creed from the first four *Rocky* movies (a better set of pecs never existed), and as Chubbs Peterson, the one-handed golf teacher in *Happy Gilmore*. Or as Arnold's sidekick in *Predator*. We also spotted him as a military cop in *Close Encounters of the Third Kind* (isn't it fun to recognize an actor you know in a bit part?).

Did you catch the little inside joke in *Happy Gilmore*? Early on Happy (Adam Sandler) asks Chubbs, "Why didn't you play a real sport—like football or something?"

Replies Chubbs: "My mom wouldn't sign the permission slip."

8. Chuck Connors. Sure, he was TV's *Rifleman* to everyone who grew up in the '60s, and appeared in more than a dozen westerns, including William Wyler's *The Big Country*. But he was more than a cowboy. Connors played pro basketball with the Boston Celtics before switching to baseball and playing two seasons at first base for the Brooklyn Dodgers and Chicago Cubs. And he showed his acting chops in the sci-fi thriller *Soylent Green*, and a sense for comedy in *Airplane II*. He was also in *Trouble Along the Way*, featured in our "Lost Treasures" chapter.

9. Fred Dryer. A college All-American at San Diego State (where he played one season with Weathers) and a Pro Bowl defensive end with the Los Angeles Rams, Dryer retired to the CBS broadcast booth in 1981. He quit 10 games in, saying the job was too constraining.

Instead, he went to acting school. He was a finalist in 1982 for the role of Sam Malone in *Cheers*, and then got his break two years later, landing the title role in the NBC detective series *Hunter*. That show ran for seven years, with Dryer eventually learning to direct and also forming a production house.

In other news, Dryer was born on July 6, 1946, the same exact day as George W. Bush and Sylvester Stallone.

10. Merlin Olsen. Another All-Pro defensive lineman who went to TV. Olsen was a member of the Rams famed "Fearsome Foursome," but his dramatic roles went entirely opposite of that image. He was the six-foot-five teddy bear on *Little House on the Prairie*, as Jonathan Garvey, the poor farmer whose barn seemed to burn down every season. That character somehow evolved into a priest and was spun-off into the short-lived series, *Father Murphy*.

11. Kareem Abdul-Jabbar. Although he was known as a tough self-critic in his basketball days, Jabbar sure took acting roles in some stinkers—including *BASEketball*, *Troop Beverly Hills* and *D2: The Mighty Ducks*. But all of that slop is forgiven for his kick-boxing turn with Bruce Lee in *Game of Death* (1978) and, mostly, for his deadpan work as co-pilot Roger Murdock in 1980's *Airplane!* We love the moment when he steps out of character to debate a 9-year-old brat visiting the cockpit.

Joey: "I think you're the greatest, but my dad says you don't work hard enough on defense. And he says that lots of times, you don't even run down court. And that you don't really try, except during the playoffs."

Murdock: "The hell I don't. Listen kid. I've been hearing that crap ever since I was at UCLA. I'm out there busting my buns every night. Tell your old man to drag Walton and Lanier up and down the court for 48 minutes."

12. Tex Cobb. At six-foot-three, 230 pounds, with a gap-toothed grin and a face that has met too much leather, Randall 'Tex' Cobb seems a bit typecast as the bad guy.

He played Skull in Jim Carrey's *Liar, Liar*, and steals the movie *Raising Arizona* as evil bounty hunter Leonard Smalls, also known as The Lone Biker of the Apocalypse. He broke into Hollywood in 1979 as Jon Voight's opponent in the remake of *The Champ*.

"I made a whole lot more money not bleeding than bleeding," Cobb said, "and it was a whole lot more fun."

For all his fights and all his acting gigs, Cobb's greatest contribution to society came—unfortunately for him—when he received a 15-round beating from Larry Holmes in 1982. The one-sided heavyweight title match prompted broadcaster Howard Cosell to permanently swear off boxing. And for that we thank you, Tex.

ATHLETES WHO COULD *NOT* ACT

OUR TEMPTATION HERE IS TO NOMINATE ROGER CLEMENS FOR HIS EYE-DARTING, BODY-SHIFTING TESTIMONY IN THE 2008 CONGRESSIONAL STEROID HEARINGS, WHICH REMINDED US OF THE OLD "PATHOLOGICAL LIAR" CHARACTER PLAYED BY JON LOVITZ ON *SATURDAY NIGHT LIVE*. ROCKET'S PERFORMANCE WAS THE LEAST BELIEVABLE IN HISTORY.

BUT THAT WAS NO MOVIE. AND CLEMENS'S MOST NOTABLE FILM ROLE, PLAYING HIMSELF IN ADAM SANDLER'S *ANGER MANAGEMENT* (NOW THERE'S A GREAT IRONY), WAS SHORTER THAN HIS INFAMOUS FUSE.

SO HERE ARE A DOZEN WHO PERFORMED BETTER ON THE FIELD THAN ON THE SCREEN.

1. Dennis Rodman. His taste in movie roles was worse than his taste in wedding gowns. 'The Worm,' as he once was known, has polluted movie screens in *The Minis* (the plot outline reads: "Dwarves playing basketball . . . with Dennis Rodman") and *Simon Sez*. Reviewing his performance, *Austin Chronicle* critic Russell Smith wrote, "He fares as well as an actor as Sean Connery would trying to set a pick on Dikembe Mutombo."

But the all-timer is his performance in the 1997 buddy-action movie *Double Team,* alongside Jean-Claude Van Damme, the Muscles from Brussels. Rodman plays a flamboyant spandex-garbed arms dealer who . . . hell, why waste our time explaining the plot? Suffice it to say, Rodman won three Razzie awards for this trash: Worst Supporting Actor, Worst New Star and (along with Van Damme) Worst Screen Couple.

2. Brian Bosworth. Here's a good debate topic: Which was more dismal, The Boz's three-year Seattle Seahawks career or his dozen-film attack on Hollywood? Tough call, but his performance as a monosyllabic state trooper in *Stone Cold* might be even more embarrassing than that oft-replayed moment when Bo Jackson bulldozed over him on the way to the end zone. Especially when you add in the multicolored mullet that he brought to the big screen.

In a 2007 NFL Network countdown of all-time draft busts (The Boz rates No. 3), Bosworth hinted that acting is just his way of passing time until he can get back into the game. "This is not my passion," he said from the set of *Down and Distance*. "My passion is football. That's what I want to do—in some way, shape or form be part of it. Until I figure that out, I'm going to be that cloud floating around." Too bad he can't get back his gig as a color analyst for the XFL.

3. Brett Favre. He's done about 10 movie/TV appearances, usually portraying himself. And he can't even pull that off convincingly. The highlight was Favre's five-line appearance in 1998's *There's Something About Mary* ("Brett Favvv-ray?"), where he loses Cameron Diaz to Ben Stiller, which seems even more humiliating than tossing six interceptions in one playoff game.

Watch closely as Favre recites his line, "That's right, Mary, I'll always be true to you." We swear we can see him reading a cue card in the background.

4. Joe Namath. Another dynamic quarterback who turns to wood when exposed to celluloid. On the heels on his Super Bowl III stunner over the Colts, Namath tried to convert his swaggering image to film with *C.C. and Company*, in which he played a motorcycle gang leader who goes straight after falling in love with good girl Ann-Margret. Yeah, right.

Problem is, Broadway Joe portrays a Hell's Angel as convincingly as Hugh Grant would play a heavyweight boxer. Surrounded by a cast of tough guys right out of *Con Air*, he's the class nerd struggling not to be noticed, lest someone steal his milk money.

5. Shaquille O'Neal. Not bad in *Blue Chips*, where he essentially portrays himself. But Shaq's acting in *Kazaam* (he plays a hip-hop genie) and *Steel* (a jive-talking comic book superhero) prove that his acting skills are lamer than his free-throw-shooting efforts.

The problem, as we see it, is the Big Aristotle's vanity. He was executive producer of these two stinkers, so it's likely that no one in the cast or crew had the nerve to tell him that his rapping sounded like Dr. Seuss on quaaludes.

6. Ken Norton Sr. Appeared in about a dozen movies, but the one we'll always remember is 1975's *Mandingo*, a trashy potboiler (literally, as we'll soon explain) ostensibly about American slavery, but mostly about casting actors of all races, ages and genders in salacious sex scenes. Norton, who was in his boxing prime at the time, plays a "Mandingo" slave from Upper Niger who boxes for the entertainment of his owner (Perry King) while also secretly bedding his wife (Susan George).

Norton's not bad when he's boxing or, um, bedding. But he seems bored when he needs to read lines (which, let's face it, isn't as fun as the two other activities). It all ends badly for The Jaw Breaker when George delivers his baby and King submerges him in a cauldron of boiling water. All in all, a weird, disturbing movie not likely to turn up on TV anytime soon.

7. O.J. Simpson. It's almost too easy now to crack jokes at his expense, but The Juice, truly, lacked any credibility on the screen. He was passable in the *Naked Gun* series, playing an easygoing schlemiel. But when it came to dramatic efforts—like *The Towering Inferno* or *Capricorn One*—his lack of personality and/or serious acting chops shined through. As critic Dorothy Parker once wrote about Katherine Hepburn, of all people, "The performance spanned the range of emotions from A to B." We're not sure O.J. ever made it to "B."

According to IMDB.com, Simpson was originally considered for the title role in *The Terminator*, but the producers feared he was too nice to be taken seriously as a cold-blooded killer.

8. Tonya Harding. In her wedding night video. Trust us.

9. Roosevelt Grier. "Rosey" was a terrific defensive lineman at Penn State and as a member of the Los Angeles Rams' "Fearsome Foursome." We'll always honor him as the hero who ripped the gun from the hand of Robert Kennedy's assassin in 1968. He also wrote a book called *Needlepoint for Men*. Fascinating guy.

But Grier makes the Bad Acting Hall of Fame for his roles in two 1970s stinkers. The sci-fi bomb *The Thing with Two Heads* is aptly described by its tagline: "They put a white bigot's head on a soul brother's body!" Yes they did—in this case, Ray Milland, who squeezes into a fat suit with Grier and barks insults at him for 93 minutes. And in *The Glove*, Rosey plays an ex-con getting his revenge on sadistic guards by beating them to death with a steel-plated glove when he's not using it so play some soulful guitar. Onscreen in these two schlockfests, Grier seems disjointed and embarrassed. Can't say we blame him.

10. Mickey Mantle and Roger Maris. It's amazing how inept some athletes are just at playing themselves (see Brett Favre). The M&M Boys tried their hands in 1962's *Safe at Home!*, a youth morality tale about a Little League braggart which, unfortunately, fell from the Sunday afternoon TV rotation a few years back. On screen, Mantle looks bored and in need of a Jack Daniels, while a nervous Maris sweats like Sacha Baron Cohen in the wrestling scene from *Borat*.

If you want to see Mantle and Maris act more realistically, check them out in HBO's *61*. Wait, that's not really them?

11. Howie Long. We loved him as a Raider, currently enjoy him as a broadcaster and didn't even mind those endless Radio Shack commercials. But Long's attempts as an action movie hero in the late 1990s kind of proved the Peter Principle, which proposes that everyone rises to his level of incompetence. Long's worst effort was 1998's *Firestorm*, in which he's a multitasking fire chief trying to stamp out a forest blaze, save the girl and stop a prison break, all at the same time.

Wrote Stephen Holden of the *New York Times*: "His expressionless face and monotone delivery make even Arnold Schwarzenegger at his most robotic seem like a hypersensitive crybaby."

12. Kurt Thomas and Mitch Gaylord. A double entry for two American champion gymnasts who aimed to become pint-sized movie heroes before disappearing into oblivion. Thomas tried his hand in *Gymkata*, cast as—surprise—a champion gymnast. He is sent by the U.S. Government to the savage country of Parmistan to secure a missile site by competing in a sport that combines gymnastics and kung fu. So bad that it's funny.

Gaylord, an Olympic gold medalist in 1984, fared no better in *American Anthem*, a beefcake bonanza that attempted to appeal to teenaged girls. He plays a retired gymnast working in his dad's bike shop who falls hard for Janet Jones, later known as Mrs. Wayne Gretzky.

Gaylord spends lots of time appearing shirtless and trying to channel James Dean. And it's not easy for a guy who made his living on a pommel horse to re-create James Dean.

Worst Ensemble. The tagline for 1974's *The Black Six* was "Six Times Tougher Than *Shaft!* Six Times Rougher Than *Super Fly!*" How about, Six Times Worse Than *Rocky V*? The movie, about an avenging black motorcycle gang, features some incredible NFL talent—Mean Joe Greene, Lem Barney, Willie Lanier, Mercury Morris, Carl Eller and Gene Washington. That's four Pro Football Hall of Famers, 12 combined Super Bowl appearances and zero notices for good acting. Unspeakably awful.

69 HORSE FEATHERS (1932–NR)

SPORT: FOOTBALL | STARS: THE MARX BROTHERS
DIRECTOR: NORMAN Z. MCLEOD

The university suffers from a sagging reputation. The incoming president, eager to turn the school around, reasons that beefing up the football team is the easiest way to instant credibility.

Problem is, successful college football doesn't come cheap. Nor do players. So the president siphons off academic funds and hires a shady duo of operators to go out and "buy me some winners."

Sounds like the plot of a 21st Century expose? Could be. But instead, it is the opening of *Horse Feathers*, a Marx Brothers vehicle that is as hilarious nearly eight decades after it was made as it is prophetic. Hey, who knew that college athletics was a cesspool back then? And never mind those rumors that George Gipp was a paid professional.

Groucho Marx stars as Professor Quincy Wagstaff, newly installed head of troubled Huxley University. Within his first few days in office, he boots a boring biology professor out of the classroom, makes a pass at every pretty young coed and decides that, well, academics aren't going to keep good old Huxley solvent.

Speaking to his deans, Wagstaff says, "I tell you gentlemen, this college is a failure. The trouble is, we're interrupting football for education."

"Have we got a stadium?" he asks.

Yes, the deans reply.

"Have we got a college?"

Yes.

"Well we can't support both. Tomorrow we start tearing down the college."

Wagstaff visits the local speakeasy (Remember, this movie was made during the Prohibition era) and enlists bumblers Baravelli (Chico Marx) and Pinky (Harpo Marx) to find "real players" to help win the upcoming game against Darwin University. Turns out, archrival Darwin—which is just as corrupt—has already beaten him to the ringers. So Wagstaff hires the duo to kidnap Darwin's top recruits.

Needless to say, the plan goes awry. The middle part of *Horse Feathers* centers on some double-crossing, a subplot with a so-called "college widow" (which we gather to be 1930s talk for a loose woman), and at least a dozen wonderful sight gags. You can probably figure out one, during a poker game, when someone invites Harpo to "cut the cards."

We wind up at the big game, in front of what appears to be 70,000 fans, and all three Marx Brothers in uniform (Groucho's is under a tuxedo waistcoat). The climactic 10-minute football scene, we would argue, is one of the three funniest in movie history—right there with the original *The Longest Yard* and *M*A*S*H*. Lots of banana peels, a ball on a string and taunting of priggish referees. Groucho—at quarterback—lights a match on the center's rump and winds up to pass like a baseball pitcher.

And then it really gets silly. Some of the best stuff is Chico's signal calling:

"Humpty Dumpty sat on the wall, Professor Wagstaff gets the ball."

Or, "Hey diddle diddle, the cat and the fiddle, this time I think we go through the middle."

For those too young to have seen a Marx Brothers movie—and we're talking to most of you here—take our advice and rent *Horse Feathers*. Comedy often doesn't hold up through the ages. We can only wonder how the humor in *Kingpin* or *Happy Gilmore* will translate into popular culture around the year 2060.

But this choppy black-and-white film plays well today. With Groucho's searing wit, Chico's wordplay and Harpo's gift of pantomime, *Horse Feathers* remains a laugh riot even now.

CHEERS: To the barrage of one-liners and insults that tumble from Groucho Marx's brain over the course of 68 minutes. Speaking by phone to that college widow, he says, "Come right over to my office. You can't? You're in bed? Well, in that case, I'll come over to your office."

Groucho also breaks through the so-called "fourth wall" of drama, speaking directly to the audience. When Chico sits down to play the piano (as he got to do once in every movie), Groucho approaches the camera and wisecracks: "I've got to stay here, but there's no reason why you folks shouldn't go out into the lobby until this thing blows over."

🚩 **JEERS:** Why, oh why was youngest sibling Zeppo allowed into the family business? The unfunny Marx Brother plays Frank, a Huxley student and the son of Professor Wagstaff. To say he's superfluous is putting it nicely. In fact, Zeppo was dropped from the act in 1933. When a studio executive wanted to trim the remaining brothers' salary, Groucho said, "Why? We're twice as funny without Zeppo."

☺ **GOOFS:** Not sure we'd call it a goof, but you'll certainly notice some jumpy cuts throughout the movie, especially in the scene where all the brothers visit the college floozy's apartment. Right before release, federal censors removed about four minutes of risqué material (well, risqué for 1932), and the scenes were sloppily edited. No version of the uncut negative seems to have survived.

◉ **REPEATED WATCHING QUOTIENT:** Very high. In fact, the jokes zip by so fast, we suggest viewing it a few times to catch all the laughs.

✒ **WHAT THEY WROTE AT THE TIME:** "The Marx Brothers are not human, not mythological—they are completely fantastic and they seem completely mad. Again and again, the Marx Brothers act as we act in dreams, or as we would act if we dared."—Gilbert Seldes, *The Dial Magazine*

☞ **DON'T FAIL TO NOTICE:** Midway through filming, Chico Marx broke his kneecap in an auto accident. He limps in some of the late scenes. In the final football vignette, where the brothers chase down a dog and go for a ride in a garbage-can chariot, it is clear that a stand-in has replaced Chico.

🗨 **BEST LINE:** Flirtatious girl: "Professor, you're full of whimsy."

Wagstaff: "Can you notice it from there? I always get that way after I eat radishes."

Cracks us up every time.

★ **SPORTS-ACTION GRADE:** B-plus. There's nothing realistic about the football here, but it certainly is hysterical.

SIGN OF THE TIMES: Some of the players wear football helmets, others do not. Helmets did not become mandatory in college football until 1939.

🍎 **BET YOU DIDN'T KNOW:** Thelma Todd, who plays the wanton love interest, died of carbon monoxide poisoning in 1935 at age 30. Although her death was ruled a suicide, many believed she was murdered by mobsters seeking financial control of a Hollywood night club she owned.

✹ **IF YOU LIKED THIS, YOU'LL LIKE:** *Duck Soup* or *A Night at the Opera*. Really, any of the movies made during the Marx Brothers' prime—1929 to 1937—is worth a watch.

70 WE ARE MARSHALL (2006–PG)

SPORT: FOOTBALL | STARS: MATTHEW MCCONAUGHEY, MATTHEW FOX, DAVID STRATHAIRN | DIRECTOR: MCG

In November 1970, a charter flight carrying the Marshall University football team crashed, killing all 75 people aboard. The tragedy devastated the school and the town of Huntington, WV, where it is located. *We Are Marshall* is the story of how a new coach (Matthew McConaughey) rebuilt the football program and helped the community heal.

Some critics, like Connie Ogle of the *Miami Herald*, loved the film. Ogle wrote: "Equally thrilling and wrenching, [it] is an absolute must for anyone who loves sports and an eloquent explanation for those who don't understand what the fuss is about."

Other critics found it sappy and manipulative. Joseph Williams of the *Boston Globe*, who played football at the University of Richmond, ridiculed the "broadly drawn characters, unlikely scenarios and cornier-than-Iowa dialog." By the end, Williams said, "I wanted to throw my $4 soda at the screen." Easy there, big fella.

Yes, the film is heavy-handed at times and anyone familiar with the sports movie genre can see certain plot points coming a mile away. Yet there is something to be said for a movie that is so unabashedly heartfelt.

Watching *We Are Marshall*, you get the feeling it was a labor of love. It may have been just another gig for the cast and crew when they signed on, but in the course of filming on location and meeting the people who still live with the memory of the horrific crash, they clearly became emotionally involved. That caring, which is obvious throughout, is what keeps the movie afloat.

Director McG (real name Joseph McGinty Nichol), whose previous work included two *Charlie's Angels* films and some music videos, allows us to feel the texture of Huntington. Whether the characters are standing in front of a blast furnace, sitting in a booth at the diner or walking across campus, it has just the right look and feel. In gentle ways, McG paints the portrait of a small town where everyone knows everyone and a tragedy such as this is particularly painful.

There were 37 players and eight coaches on the doomed flight. There were also many boosters and friends, including a city councilman, a state legislator and four of the town's six physicians. Seventy children lost one parent in the crash, another 18 were orphaned. It was a trauma that will be felt for generations.

McConaughey plays Jack Lengyel, an outsider brought in to rebuild the football team. Matthew Fox, best known as Dr. Jack Shephard on *Lost*, plays assistant coach Red Dawson, the lone survivor from the previous staff. Dawson skipped the ill-fated flight to go on a recruiting trip and he has been dealing with guilt issues ever since.

Paul Griffen (Ian McShane), the head of the school board whose son died in the crash, opposes the plan to field a football team. He argues that it is disrespectful to the victims, but in reality he is so caught up in his own grief, he fears the return of football will only add to his suffering. He tries to oust the university president (David Strathairn) who feels football can help the school move forward.

Lengyel knows his team of freshmen and walk-ons will be outmanned and may not win a game, but he also knows the worth of the season cannot be measured on the scoreboard. After the team is crushed in its first game, Lengyel tells Dawson, "Winning is the only thing. I said it all my life and I really believed it. Then I came here and I realized it's not true. Winning doesn't matter. It doesn't even matter how we play the game. What matters is that we suit up and play."

The climax of the film is Marshall winning its first home game, upsetting Xavier on a touchdown pass on the final play. Watching the coaches and players celebrate—and Lengyel is right in the middle of it—you get the feeling that maybe winning does matter, just a little bit.

CHEERS: McConaughey isn't normally an actor we associate with subtlety, but he is very good here finding the balance between the tough football coach and sensitive father figure.

JEERS: The music is over the top. It is the one area where the film pulls a little too hard on the heartstrings.

PIVOTAL SCENE: The morning of the Xavier game, Lengyel takes the team to the gravesite where the remains of six deceased players are buried. He tells the team, "This is our past, gentlemen. This is where we have been. This is how we got here. This is who we are. How you play today, from this moment on is how you will be remembered. This is your opportunity to rise from these ashes and grab glory. We are. . . ."

The players respond: "Marshall."

Lengyel repeats: "We are. . . ."

The players answer in one powerful voice: "Marshall." You get the feeling Xavier might be in trouble.

✔ **REALITY CHECK:** The game-winning touchdown pass was actually a perfectly executed bootleg and the receiver, Terry Gardner, went into the end zone untouched. In the film, it is a desperation pass with the receiver making a spectacular catch. The coach, Jack Lengyel, who was on the set, told the director he should show the play as it really happened. But when Lengyel saw the film, he said, "They were right. The dramatic finish really helps tell the story."

WHAT THEY WROTE AT THE TIME: "Director McG contrasts highly stylized football action and the emotionally charged plane crash with an unobtrusive approach to the dramatic scenes. It's a tactic that provides the film with a particularly attuned sense of pacing and keeps the sentiment in check."—Kevin Crust, *Los Angeles Times*

BET YOU DIDN'T KNOW: Kate Mara, who plays Annie Cantrell, the fiancée of one of the crash victims, is the granddaughter of Wellington Mara, the late owner of the New York Giants. A singer and actress, she performed the National Anthem at the first Giants home game following her grandfather's death in 2005.

SIGN OF THE TIMES: The men's clothes fairly scream "Seventies." Wrote Ogle in the *Herald*: "McConaughey has apparently wandered into Paul Newman's all-plaid, all-the-time wardrobe from *Slap Shot*." Also, the soundtrack—"Peace Train," "Ventura Highway," "Cracklin' Rosie"—will have you thinking about your old eight-tracks.

"I KNOW THAT GUY": Ian McShane, who plays the distraught father, is the sadistic sheriff in HBO's Western series *Deadwood*. You may find him difficult to recognize without his mustache and foul mouth.

★ **SPORTS-ACTION GRADE:** C. Like many Hollywood directors, McG goes overboard in the football scenes. Too much slow motion, too many bodies cartwheeling through the air, every hit sounds like a bolt of lightning splitting a telephone pole. Lighten up, man.

REPEATED WATCHING QUOTIENT: Fair. A pleasant enough way to spend a quiet evening at home.

MY FAVORITE SPORTS MOVIE: Don Shula, Hall of Fame coach: "It was very inspiring. It showed how coaching is a lot more than diagramming plays. It is about leadership and helping people grow."

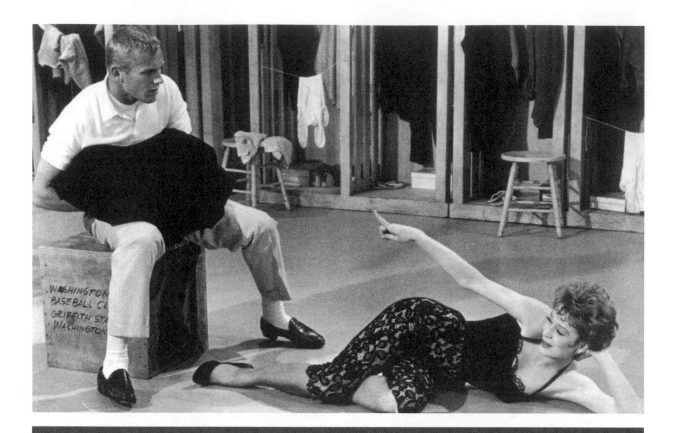

71 DAMN YANKEES (1958–NR)

SPORT: BASEBALL | STARS: TAB HUNTER, GWEN VERDON, RAY WALSTON
DIRECTORS: GEORGE ABBOTT, STANLEY DONEN

Damn Yankees opened on Broadway in 1955. It was a wonderful play; the critics loved it. There was only one problem: no one was buying tickets. On a good night, the theater was half full. After one month, the play was on the verge of closing.

Desperate, the producers decided to change the billboard. They were using a photo of the show's star, Gwen Verdon, in a Yankees jersey, sweatpants and sneakers. They replaced it with a shot of Verdon in character as the seductress Lola in a bustier and high heels.

Almost immediately lines began to form, comprised mostly of guys with their tongues hanging out. But they bought tickets. Oh, how they bought tickets. *Damn Yankees* ran for 1,019 performances. When they said the play had legs, they were talking about Gwen Verdon.

In 1958, when Warner Brothers brought *Damn Yankees* to the big screen, they knew what photo to put on the poster. It was Verdon as Lola reprising her vamp routine. It worked once again. The film was a big success.

New York Times critic Bosley Crowther gushed over Verdon's performance which he called "sizzling." He described Verdon as a "long-legged, swivel-jointed siren [who] manufactures her own strong brand of sex." Wow, you can almost see Bosley mopping his brow between paragraphs.

Verdon's spirited dancing—choreographed by her husband Bob Fosse—spices up a delightful baseball fantasy which still entertains today. Even the premise still applies: the Yankees win all the time and the Washington team stinks. The only difference is now the Washington franchise is in the National League.

The story, written by George Abbott and Douglass Wallop, is a 1950s version of the Faustian deal-with-the-Devil legend. Joe Boyd (Robert Shafer) is a middle-aged guy who lives in D.C. and roots for the Senators. The trouble is the Senators are a last-place team.

One night Joe cries out, "One long ball hitter, that's all we need. I'd sell my soul for one long ball hitter."

Suddenly, a stranger appears in Joe's living room. He introduces himself as Mr. Applegate, but he's really Satan (Ray Walston). He offers to turn couch-potato Joe into that young stud of a slugger who will lead the Senators to glory. All it will cost him is his soul.

Joe accepts the deal, but he puts in an escape clause. If he wants out, he can say so by a certain date and return to his former life. The Devil isn't worried. He will come up with a dirty trick to close the loophole. I mean, he's the Devil, for crying out loud.

What's in this for the Devil? He figures if the Senators win the pennant, it will cause millions of people to freak out. There will be heart attacks and apoplexy galore. "Just like the good old days," he says wistfully.

Joe is transformed into the power-hitting sensation Joe Hardy (Tab Hunter), a blonde Adonis who tears up the American League. Reporters start asking, "Who is this guy? Where did he come from?" Mr. Applegate creates the back story: Joe is a shy farm boy from Hannibal, Missouri. (Cue the song, "Shoeless Joe.")

Joe keeps smacking home runs and the Senators keep winning, but he misses his wife and wants to go home. Fearing Joe will invoke his escape clause, the Devil calls in his version of the closer, the sexy Lola (Verdon). Her job is to shimmy around until Joe's eyes are so glazed over, he forgets all about going home.

What follows is a tender tug of war for Joe's heart and soul with the forces of good—with an unexpected assist from Lola—finally winning out.

The film features 10 songs, including the classics *"You've Gotta Have Heart," "Shoeless Joe"* and *"Whatever Lola Wants."* The latter song was written for Verdon to sing while performing a semi-striptease. She did the number more than a thousand times on stage, but Warner Brothers felt it was too racy, so they toned it down. In the film, Verdon does the dance, but without the bumps and grinds.

The film featured virtually the entire Broadway cast. The only change was in the role of Joe Hardy, where Hunter, a '50s matinee idol, replaced Stephen Douglass. Hunter was not a trained singer or dancer, but he was good enough to get by.

"I saw the original on Broadway," Hunter said, "and I was thrilled when Jack Warner bought *Damn Yankees* for me as a make-up gift. I had been on suspension from the studio, so it was sort of a kiss and make-up gift, a damn good one. I was suspended because I had turned down a [previous] role at the studio."

🏆 **CHEERS:** Walston's Mr. Applegate has some great comic moments; for example, the scene in which he drops coin after coin after coin in a pay phone trying to place a call to Hell.

🚩 **JEERS:** Most critics agree that *Damn Yankees* worked better on stage. The dance numbers lose something with the camera cuts.

🎩 **BET YOU DIDN'T KNOW:** The Mambo dancer who joins Gwen Verdon in the *Who's Got The Pain* number is Bob Fosse.

✒️ **WHAT THEY WROTE AT THE TIME:** "If you're one of those aging admirers of old Fanny Brice or Lucille Ball, you'll delight in discovering Miss Verdon is a little of both in this show in addition to being a dancer who is probably as deft as any now in films." Bosley Crowther, *New York Times*

"I KNOW THAT GAL": Sister, the noisy neighbor, is played by Jean Stapleton, who later became famous as TV's Edith Bunker. Stapleton played Sister on Broadway. This was her film debut.

⭐ **SPORTS-ACTION GRADE:** It is a musical, not a hard-core sports-action film. There are a few black and white clips of the Yankees in action, but that's about it.

GREAT SPORTS/DATE MOVIES

IF *BULL DURHAM* INVENTED THE SPORTS-MOVIE/CHICK-FLICK GENRE, *JERRY MAGUIRE* PERFECTED IT. EVERY WOMAN WE KNOW EXITS THAT MOVIE DABBING HER EYES OVER TOM CRUISE'S "YOU COMPLETE ME" DECLARATION TO RENEE ZELLWEGER. AND EVERY MAN EXCITEDLY LISTS ALL THE NFL PLAYERS MAKING CAMEOS, OR DEBATES THE EXCESSES OF ROD TIDWELL'S (CUBA GOODING) TOUCHDOWN DANCE.

IN REALITY, CREATING A TWO-GENDER SUCCESS IS NO EASY FEAT. FOR EVERY *ROCKY* OR *THE NATURAL*, WHICH FLAW-LESSLY PULL OFF THE SPORTS-ROMANCE DOUBLE ANGLE, THERE ARE TOO MANY LIKE *FEVER PITCH* OR *SUMMER CATCH*, WHICH DO LITTLE MORE THAN TRY TO DISGUISE A SLOPPY TEARJERKER BY THROWING IN A FEW BASEBALL SCENES.

CONVERSELY, *HOOSIERS*, WHICH WE RANK AS THE SECOND-GREATEST SPORTS MOVIE EVER, HAS JUST ONE FLAW: THE CRINGE-WORTHY KISSY-FACE SCENE BETWEEN COACH NOR-MAN DALE (GENE HACKMAN) AND FRIGID SCHOOLMARM MYRA FLEENER (BARBARA HERSHEY). IT'S A HOOPS FLICK, DAMMIT! LET MYRA REMAIN HER ICY SELF, AND LET'S GET BACK TO SHOOTER, JIMMY CHITWOOD AND THE BOYS.

IT'S A FINE LINE. SOMETIMES SPORTS AND SEDUCTION BLEND PERFECTLY IN A FILM; SOMETIMES THEY GO TOGETHER ABOUT AS WELL AS GRAPEFRUIT JUICE AND CHOCOLATE CAKE.

THIS BOOK INCLUDES MANY FINE ROMANTIC TALES, INCLUDING *THE PRIDE OF THE YANKEES, HEAVEN CAN WAIT, CINDERELLA MAN, TIN CUP* . . . EVEN *YOUNGBLOOD*.

IF YOU'RE LOOKING FOR MORE, HERE ARE A HALF-DOZEN OTHERS THAT DON'T QUITE MAKE OUR TOP 100, BUT ARE SOLID RENTALS THAT OUGHT TO PLEASE BOTH HE AND SHE:

Finding Forrester (2000). Described by the *New York Times* as "The latest in a rising tide of shameless male weepies" upon its release, *Finding Forrester* is not a romance. Still, softies of both sexes will enjoy the story of an inner-city kid from the Bronx (Rob Brown) who forms an improbable friendship with a reclusive Pulitzer Prize-winning author (Sean Connery). The kid is a prodigy at both writing and basketball so, naturally, he is resented by the establishment at his swank New York prep school. Anna Paquin plays the obligatory flirtatious rich girl. It's a lot like *Good Will Hunting*—which was also directed by Gus Van Sant—if you were to recast the misunderstood genius as a 16-year-old black kid, add some dynamite hoops scenes and almost ruin the whole thing with a trite soap-opera ending.

Love & Basketball (2000). Or, as some have called it, *He and She Got Game.* Produced by Spike Lee and directed by Gina Prince-Bythewood, this smart movie tells the parallel tales of two young basketball stars, played by Omar Epps and Sanaa Lathan. The film covers 12 years—from age 11 to age 23—for the two characters, during which time they fall in love with basketball, fall in love with each other, and experience triumphs and failures in both departments. A smart, character-driven film that probably succeeds a little more as a sports flick than a chick flick. Just try to ignore that Epps looks at least a decade too old for the role he's playing.

One on One (1977). Years before he became the voice of the Beast in Disney's *Beauty and the Beast,* Robby Benson was regarded as a young Hollywood heartthrob. Here he stars as a small-town basketball star who finds himself overwhelmed at the demands and the corruption of big-time college sports—especially since he never learned to read. Fortunately, a sympathetic and sexually willing tutor shows up in the form of Annette O'Toole. And as they make out, a Seals & Crofts song plays in the background just to remind you this is, indeed, a chick flick. Every college girl in the 70s and 80s had at least three Seals & Crofts albums in her collection; by contrast, no guy we know could ever stand the soft-rock duet. Watch for appearances by G.D. Spradlin, who channels Bobby Knight in his most loathsome role since Sen. Pat Geary in *The Godfather II*, and by a then-unknown Melanie Griffith as a hitchhiker.

The Cutting Edge (1992).

D.B. Sweeney plays a one-time Grade A hockey prospect whose career ends when he is cheap-shotted in a game against West Germany. Moira Kelly plays a talented pairs figure skater with the personality of Judge Judy. As the tagline says, "The King of the Rink is about to meet America's Ice Queen." The *Odd Couple* plotline between society girl and blue-line bruiser is predictable, as is the dialog:

Kelly: "What do you shower, once a week?"

Sweeney: "Is that an invitation?"

You know where the movie is going and you know that Sweeney's gruff charm will eventually thaw Kelly's iciness. Listen, figure skating barely fits the definition of a legitimate sport in our book (Judges? Costumes?), but still, the two actors have an on-screen charm and chemistry that makes them easy to root for. "Toe pick! Toe pick!"

For Love of the Game (1999).

The plot line here sounds like a surefire hit: An over-the-hill 40-year-old pitcher (Kevin Costner playing a righty Tom Glavine, more or less), starting what could be the final game of his career, and working toward a perfect game. Meanwhile, his mind keeps drifting to his on-and-off girlfriend (Kelly Preston), who has just informed him she's leaving for good. A strong supporting cast is led by John C. Reilly, plus there's the bonus of Vin Scully calling the game. Add to that some well-filmed game scenes. So why wasn't this movie a bigger success? Well, the romance angle doesn't work, and the constant flashbacks to happier times with Preston become downright annoying. If your date is willing to fast-forward through the sappy stuff, you may enjoy this movie more.

Wimbledon (2004).

Tennis may be the only sport for which no great movie has ever been made. Skiing, bicycling, even bowling have received better cinematic treatment than tennis, a sport still waiting for its *Chariots of Fire*—or even its *Caddyshack*—to come along. *Wimbledon*, which stars Paul Bettany and Kirsten Dunst, is not that defining film, but it does have enough action to qualify as a sports movie and enough romance to qualify as a chick flick. Bettany plays the one-time prodigy who's fallen to 119th in the rankings, and Dunst plays the bitchy-but-luscious bad girl of tennis who's there to rescue his career. All that, plus lots of locker-room nudity (unfortunately not Dunst).

72 THE JERICHO MILE (1979–NR)

SPORT: TRACK | STARS: PETER STRAUSS, BRIAN DENNEHY
DIRECTOR: MICHAEL MANN

You may find yourself, one late night, clicking around the dial, zapping past the 16th repeat of *SportsCenter* or an infomercial plugging hair replacement, when you stumble on a 30-year-old made-for-TV movie about a prison lifer running sub-four-minute miles.

Put down the remote. *The Jericho Mile*—which occasionally airs during the insomnia hours on ESPN Classic or your local UHF station—is worth pushing back bedtime for a while. It is a gritty, unromantic look at prison life, racism, institutional corruption and—oh yeah—the joy of running. Invest 97 minutes (plus whatever commercial time) in the entire movie and you'll wonder why you haven't heard about it until now.

The Jericho Mile is the directorial debut of Michael Mann, which is enough reason to watch it. Mann went on to produce TV classics *Miami Vice* and *Crime Story*, and direct movies like *Heat, The Insider* and *Collateral*. Here, you can see his talent in the formative stage, and catch early hints of his trademarks—such as his sympathetic approach to criminals or his use of hard-driving rock music. We've got issues with the music, but we'll get to that later.

There's also a first-rate cast, led by Peter Strauss (coming off his hit-making TV miniseries role as Rudy Jordache in *Rich Man, Poor Man*) and Brian Dennehy (before he appeared in every single movie produced during the 1980s). Dennehy—in slicked-back hair, tight jeans and a black T-shirt—looks like a refugee from *Grease*, but he plays the role of a cold-blooded prison-yard bully (named Doctor D) with an evil perfection.

Strauss stars as Rain Murphy, a man serving a life sentence at Folsom Prison in California for killing his abusive father. He is a loner, barely talking to other prisoners and balking at any kind of rehabilitative therapy. His own brand of therapy comes from obsessively running the inside of the prison yard perimeter. It allows him—at least for an hour each day—to escape the grim reality that surrounds him.

In another movie, an overzealous tower guard might take a shot at our fast-moving track star. But in *Jericho Mile*, he is instead noticed by a do-gooder psychologist, who decides to time the lifer moving so feverishly in sweat pants and Keds. As it turns out, Murphy is running a prison mile (defined as eight times around the trash cans) in 3:59.

This is brought to the attention of the warden and, well, let's just say that this guy is the flipside of Warden Hazen from *The Longest Yard*. This one is from the school of positive reinforcement. So he hires Murphy a track coach (speaking of *The Longest Yard*, the coach is played by Ed Lauter, whom we fondly remember as Captain Knauer) and tries to arrange for an Olympic tryout.

Not surprisingly, state officials balk at allowing a cold-blooded murderer to go on furlough. So our Mister Rogers of a warden simply buttons up his cardigan sweater and asks for prison volunteers to build an IOC-quality track inside the yard.

"He can be an example to all the other prisoners," suggests Warden Warm-and-Fuzzy, while failing to notice that the Aryan Nation sect within his walls has just shivved Murphy's only buddy, R.C. Stiles (played by Richard Lawson before he got all gooey in *How Stella Got Her Groove Back*).

The middle part of the movie focuses on the internecine racial battles among prison sects. Give praise to ABC—for a show that aired in 1979, the violence and language are fairly brutal. Eventually, an uneasy coalition of black and Latin prisoners kick Dennehy's butt and decide to work together to build that track.

A qualifying race is arranged, and nervous-looking college runners enter the prison to challenge Murphy. Of course he blows them away, running a 3:52 mile. Los Angeles Olympics, here we come.

It's all leading up to a glorious inspirational ending. We can envision Bob Costas (or, Jim McKay back then), lauding our reformed father-shooter as he ascends the medal stand. Except . . . well, give Mann and writer Patrick J. Nolan credit for not going with the obvious and uplifting.

Stick around to the end, even if most networks don't

start airing *The Jericho Mile* until 2 a.m. There's a dramatic showdown scene about 90 minutes in, where Murphy must measure his dreams against his principles. And the final coda (which relates to the title of the movie) is so thought provoking, it may just keep you up for the rest of the night.

It's worth the sleep deprivation. Consider yourself forewarned.

⚜ **CHEERS:** The movie really was shot within the walls of Folsom, a maximum-security prison built in 1880. Many of the frightening-looking dudes in each scene are actual inmates, which gives it a genuine feel. In fact, Folsom's three power groups—Aryan Nation, Black Muslims and Latin Kings—agreed to a truce during filming. They even worked together to build the track used in *The Jericho Mile*, which remains there today.

⚑ **JEERS:** The film's opening montage sets the tone as a funky version of the Rolling Stones' *Sympathy for the Devil* plays in the background. At least we thought it sounded exactly like *Sympathy for the Devil*—driving bass line, conga drums and all. Instead, the closing credits list the composer as Jimmie Haskell, best known as the guy who wrote the theme song for *The Adventures of Ozzie and Harriet*. Somebody needs to tell Mick and Keith that they're being ripped off.

SIGN OF THE TIMES: Check out the vintage powder blue three-piece suit on Warden Gulliver (Billy Green Bush). His tailor should have been imprisoned.

📺 **PIVOTAL SCENE:** Murphy—despite running in a time that qualifies for the Olympic Trials—must convince a civilian board that he is reformed enough to be allowed out of prison. The head of the board insists that Murphy show fealty, as well as remorse for killing his father—even though we learn that the murder occurred after Murphy discovered the old man molesting his 14-year-old sister.

"If you were in the same circumstances, in the same place, would you commit the crime again?" the panel chairman demands. "Would you do it again, Mr. Murphy? I think people would like to know that."

Murphy struggles with the answer, knowing that if he gives the honest response, his Olympic hopes are over.

And so. . . .

We'll let you wait until you watch it yourself.

★ **SPORTS-ACTION GRADE:** B. Strauss, who was 31 when *The Jericho Mile* was shot, worked hard to get into shape and reportedly could run a 4:35 mile. We don't know about that, but he looks pretty convincing in shorts and track shoes. Kudos to Mann for not falling into the hoary cliché of filming runners in slow motion.

✎ **WHAT THEY WROTE AT THE TIME:** "Mann is probably a weekend runner himself, because he manages to capture, in one skillfully edited scene, what running (and, therefore, the character of Murphy) is all about. Officials bring two distance runners to prison to compete against Murphy; it's a pretty big deal, and hundreds of prisoners (real prisoners) gather around the dirt track to watch the race. As the three runners take off, the crowd screams its encouragement and the soundtrack blares out an insistent beat. Then it happens: Mann cuts to a shot of the three runners, and all sounds and music disappear, save the sounds of feet hitting gravel and breath being inhaled and exhaled. The runners are oblivious to the crowd, just as Murphy, when he runs alone, is oblivious to his prison walls."—David Bianculli, *Fort Lauderdale News*

☺ **GOOFS:** The mile run has never been an event in the modern Olympics. Instead, runners qualify for and race in the 1,500 meters.

👓 **"I KNOW THAT GUY":** The leader of the prison's black inmates—the magnificently named Cotton Crown—is played by Roger E. Mosley. You ought to recognize him as T.C. Calvin, Tom Selleck's best buddy from the 1980s series *Magnum, P.I.* More recently, Mosley has been recognized as O.J. Simpson's best buddy on golf courses around America.

♟ **BET YOU DIDN'T KNOW:** Mann received such positive acclaim in his first directorial effort (as well as a writing Emmy) that he quickly received more than 20 movie offers. He chose to direct *Thief*, a solid 1981 release starring James Caan as a safecracker trying to quit the mob.

◉ **REPEATED WATCHING QUOTIENT:** Hey, it's tough enough to find it once.

73 CHAMPION (1949–NR)

SPORT: BOXING | STARS: KIRK DOUGLAS, ARTHUR KENNEDY, RUTH ROMAN
DIRECTOR: MARK ROBSON

Kirk Douglas took a chance on the film *Champion*. At 32, Douglas still was trying to crack the big time in Hollywood. He was offered the lead in a big-budget MGM film, *The Great Sinner*, but turned it down to do this smaller *film noir* based on a short story by Ring Lardner. He saw *Champion* as a greater risk, but also a greater opportunity.

The role of Midge Kelly, the penniless hobo who achieves fame in boxing, was unusual for its time. Midge is not a hero, quite the opposite. He is a heel, a selfish brute who uses and abuses everyone around him, even his crippled brother Connie (Arthur Kennedy).

Douglas took the part and absolutely nailed it. He received his first Academy Award nomination and the film, which was released with little fanfare, earned six nominations in all. *Variety* called it "a stark, realistic study of the boxing rackets."

The Great Sinner? It was one of the year's biggest disappointments, fizzling at the box office despite a cast that included Gregory Peck and Ava Gardner.

Douglas's gamble paid off. His portrayal of the ruthless boxer made him a major star. It allowed him to break free of the studio system and pick and choose his own films, which he did very well through the '50s and '60s. Midge Kelly may have been a bad guy, but he was very good to Kirk Douglas.

Champion opens with Midge and Connie hitchhiking across the country. Short of cash, Midge agrees to box on a tank town fight card. A total novice, Midge takes a beating, but his toughness impresses veteran trainer Tommy Haley (Paul Stewart). He tells Midge to call if he ever decides to take the sport seriously.

The brothers find work washing dishes at a diner. Midge has a fling with the owner's daughter Emma (Ruth Roman). When the owner finds out, he forces them into a shotgun marriage. Midge has no intention of spending the rest of his life slinging hash, so he takes off

and leaves Emma. Connie has fallen for Emma, but tags along with Midge because, well, that's what orphaned brothers do.

With no better options available, Midge decides to call Tommy Haley. Connie tries to talk him out of it. Boxing, he says, "is a rotten business." Midge, who's getting harder and colder by the minute, tells his brother, "Lay off."

"It's like any other business," Midge says. "Only [in boxing] the blood shows."

Tommy agrees to train Midge and soon he is climbing the middleweight ladder. One night in the dressing room, Connie again expresses his misgivings about his brother's involvement in the sport. Midge is now so full of ambition and lust, he refuses to listen.

"For the first time in my life, people are cheering for me," he says. "Were you deaf? Didn't you hear them? We're not hitchhiking any more. We're riding."

Midge is matched against a top contender, Johnny Dunne, but it is with the understanding that Midge will take a dive. When Tommy tells Midge of the terms set down by the mob, he flies into a rage. "I work like a slave," he says, "and then the fat bellies with the big cigars tell me I'm still a bum."

Midge agrees to throw the fight, but pulls a double-cross by knocking out Dunne. The mobsters get their revenge by pummeling Midge, Tommy and even poor Connie in the empty arena afterwards. But the win over Dunne makes Midge a star. He is approached by another manager, Jerry Harris (Luis Van Rooten), who claims he can do more for his career than Tommy. Jerry is richer and slicker, with a fancy office and a hot young wife (Lola Albright), all of which appeals to Midge.

Midge dumps Tommy without a second thought and signs on with Jerry. At this point, he is so consumed with greed that even Connie leaves him. Midge gets his title shot and wins it while beginning an affair with Jerry's wife. Jerry gets Midge to break it off by offering him cash (see "pivotal scene" below) as he prepares for a fight against a revenge-minded Johnny Dunne.

Midge reaches out and asks Tommy to come back and train him for the Dunne fight. Reluctantly, Tommy agrees. Midge also tries to patch things up with Connie, inviting him to training camp. Connie arrives with Emma and announces they plan to marry. There's a slight complication: Emma never bothered to divorce Midge. He agrees to step aside so Connie and Emma can marry. You start to think that maybe the no-good louse is finally coming around, but the first time they're alone, Midge forces himself on Emma.

The next night in the dressing room, Connie confronts Midge, asking, "Why did you do it? Did you have to prove you were still the champion?" Midge slugs Connie and knocks him to the floor, then throws Connie's cane at him as he puts on his robe and heads for the ring.

In the fight, Midge takes a bloody beating, but just as he is about to be counted out, he looks at the faces at ringside, all the people he stepped on who now are smiling as they watch him brought down to earth. Enraged, he climbs off the canvas and KO's Dunne to retain his title. But in the dressing room, Midge collapses and dies of a brain hemorrhage.

In the final scene, Connie and Emma are surrounded by reporters who ask for a statement on Midge's death. Here is the opportunity to get even. All they have to do is tell the press what a lowlife Midge was. Connie, ever the loyal brother, cannot do it. Instead, he lies through his teeth, saying, "He was a champion. He died like a champion. He was a credit to the fight game right to the very end."

Connie and Emma leave the arena and Midge is allowed to pass into history as a hero.

🍻 **CHEERS:** Arthur Kennedy is superb as Connie. He is nominated for an Academy Award as Best Supporting Actor, the first of five nominations in his distinguished career.

📛 **JEERS:** The fight scenes are ragged in spots, especially the first fight with Johnny Dunne. The knockout punch misses Dunne by at least a foot, which would not have been so bad but they replay it in slow motion and it is almost laughable.

✒ **WHAT THEY WROTE AT THE TIME:** "Douglas plays Kelly with a carnivorous lust for fame, sex and respect. There are moments when he comes on like such a Lucifer, your impulse is to turn your eyes from the screen."—Carmen Ficarra, *Moviemaker*

💬 **BEST LINE:** Tommy Haley: "Midge is getting a shot at the title and he's got a new manager. A blonde."

🎬 **PIVOTAL SCENE:** Jerry learns Midge is sleeping with his wife. He tells her Midge is simply using her as he uses everyone else. To prove it, he makes Midge an offer: He'll let Midge keep his manager's commission from the Dunne fight ($65,000) if he agrees to break off the affair.

Midge looks at the wife and says, "You're his wife, I never should have come between you in the first place." Meanwhile, he is stuffing the money in his pockets.

She is speechless. For the first time, she sees how craven Midge really is.

⭐ **SPORTS-ACTION GRADE:** C. Douglas, a high school wrestler, is physically convincing, but the fight scenes are not.

74 LET IT RIDE (1989–PG)

SPORT: **HORSE RACING** | STARS: **RICHARD DREYFUSS, TERI GARR, DAVID JOHANSEN**
DIRECTOR: **JOE PYTKA**

Every $2 bettor who ever spent an afternoon at the track has dreamed of that winning streak, that day when solid tips plus heaven's help allows him to parlay his last few bucks into an instant fortune.

Of course, those days never come. That's how tracks stay in business.

But *Let it Ride* allows us to watch and root as one lifelong loser at the betting windows has that day of days. And we get to enjoy riding along.

Richard Dreyfuss stars as Jay Trotter, a sad-sack Miami cabbie who has just promised his wife (Teri Garr) that he will cut down on his compulsive betting to save their marriage. The opening scene of their reconciliation at a Chinese restaurant ends with him cracking open a fortune cookie that reads, "Sometimes you can be walking around lucky and not know it."

Of course, he immediately receives inside info on a sure thing and heads to the track the next day with his last $50. "This isn't gambling," he rationalizes. "Gambling includes risk. This is just taking advantage of an extraordinary business opportunity."

His horse comes through, returning $710 on his investment. Trotter, who never wins on this kind of long shot, decides that this day is different, and lays down all his earnings on the next race. He wins again. And again, after asking everyone around him which entry to bet on—and going the other way.

His $50 grows to $69,000 and, now, the lifelong schlepper is the hero of Hialeah, attracting buxom, willing women and his own personal bodyguard. Not sure whether he is being guided by divine intervention or just plain luck, he decides to parlay it all on one last pony run. When a horse on its way to the track literally winks his way, he figures he's got his winner.

We won't give away the ending, except to say the final race is a terrific nail-biter. And Dreyfuss makes the whole thing work with his usual likeability and nervous energy. He yips with joy or desperation at his fortunes, snaps his fingers, pulls on his tie like Rodney Dangerfield and makes us root for the rascal who hasn't finished ahead in a decade. Anyone who ever spent time poring over the *Daily Racing Form* can commiserate.

"In order to have a bad feeling, you need to have a good feeling first," he lectures a fellow track degenerate. "So you have no frame of reference."

The movie is held back by an annoying supporting cast. Garr is more of a nag than the horses as the clingy wife, and David Johansen is over-the-top obnoxious as the best friend who's the only guy in America with worse luck than Trotter. Only Robbie Coltrane, as the cynical ticket seller and a youthful Jennifer Tilly (more about her shortly) give you anyone else worth watching.

Let it Ride is based on a book by Jay Cronley, who covers horse racing for ESPN. The screenplay was written by Nancy Dowd, most famous for penning *Slap Shot,* who is clearly going for a Damon Runyanesque feel here. Often it works, occasionally it falls short.

It also marks the directorial debut of Joe Pytka, who mostly is known for commercials and Michael Jackson videos. In fact, Pytka went on to direct just one more movie, *Space Jam*. We don't know if that stinker was enough to convince him to leave the field.

CHEERS: Well, the real co-stars here are Jennifer Tilly's spectacular breasts, which seem determined to pop out of her skintight red dress through the entire film. We dare you to look away.

At one point, Vicki (Tilly) grabs Trotter from behind and squeezes him tight.

"Guess who?" she asks.

"A football salesman?" he replies.

JEERS: To the marketing campaign that helped turn this likeable movie into a box office flop.

"When it first came out, the studio just dumped it," Tilly told the film website *twoonethree.com*. "It was in the theater for less than a week."

Consider the advertising tagline: "He drinks. He smokes. He gambles. He curses. He thinks about committing adultery. You'll love him."

Yeah, that'll pull in the masses.

PIVOTAL SCENE: About to embark on his big day of gambling, and clutching onto his last $50, Trotter pauses in a grungy dive-bar men's room and kneels in front of the toilet to pray for a helping hand.

"I don't belong with these losers, God, you know that," he says, hands clasped in front of him. "I belong in the Jockey Club, around guys with all their teeth. Just let me win this once."

Every day, at every racetrack in the world, a scene like this takes place.

★ **SPORTS-ACTION GRADE:** B-plus. The races, at the classic Hialeah Race Course in Florida, are beautifully filmed. That two of them end in photo finishes only adds to the excitement.

✎ **WHAT THEY WROTE AT THE TIME:** "It would like to be a farcical, nonmusical update of 'Guys and Dolls.' . . . But the movie is so witless and confused in tone that its seedy racetrack clientele only emerge as dim, inarticulate cartoons."—Stephen Holden, *New York Times*

☺ **GOOFS:** The action all takes place on a September Saturday, but the TVs in the Jockey Club are showing live NFL games. The NFL never plays on Saturdays early in the season.

◉ **REPEATED WATCHING QUOTIENT:** Only if you're holding a Richard Dreyfuss film festival.

❞ **BEST LINE:** Trotter (betting his entire winnings of $69,000 on a 40-1 shot): "Let it ride."
Ticket seller: "You've got all kinds of balls."
Bodyguard: "Mostly crystal."

👓 **"I KNOW THAT GUY":** Or gal, in this case. Cynthia Nixon, also known as the only unsexy one on *Sex and the City*, appears here as a braces-wearing 19-year-old dreamer turned on by her first visit to the track.

✺ **IF YOU LIKED THIS, YOU'LL LIKE:** *On the Nose*, a 2001 British flick about a university janitor who finds a preserved Aboriginal head in a jar that allows him to pick winners at the track. Really. That movie stars Scottish comic Coltrane, who so marvelously plays the ticket seller in *Let it Ride*.

♟ **BET YOU DIDN'T KNOW:** While director Pytka only shot one other film, you've certainly seen his work hundreds of times. His commercials include the Ray Charles "Uh-huh" campaign for Pepsi, Larry Bird and Michael Jordan playing H-O-R-S-E for McDonalds and the "This is your brain on drugs" public service announcement.

75 THE EXPRESS (2008–PG-13)

SPORT: FOOTBALL | STARS: ROB BROWN, DENNIS QUAID, OMAR BENSON MILLER
DIRECTOR: GARY FLEDER

The Express is the story of Ernie Davis, the Syracuse University halfback who was the first African-American to win the Heisman Trophy. Davis was the top pick in the 1962 NFL draft but he died of leukemia before he ever played a down of professional football.

It is a compelling story and thanks to a fine performance by Rob Brown as Davis, *The Express* will prove enlightening to those who are too young to know the tragic tale. But this is really a film about two men—Davis and his coach Ben Schwartzwalder—and their relationship during that racially divisive time in America.

Dennis Quaid takes on perhaps his most challenging role as Schwartzwalder. He could have played him as the typical hard-nosed, my-way-or-the-highway football coach that we've seen a million times. But Quaid brings a depth to Schwartzwalder that makes the coach a far more interesting character.

Most of Quaid's other jock roles—Jim Morris (*The Rookie*), Cap Rooney (*Any Given Sunday*), Gavin Grey (*Everybody's All-American*)—are straightforward types, men with a strong sense of self who never waver in their beliefs, even when life kicks them in the teeth. His Schwartzwalder is a far more complex figure and Quaid does a very good job portraying a man who begins to question his values for the first time.

Early in *The Express*, we see Schwartzwalder and Jim Brown, his first All-American, in an uncomfortable conversation. It is clear the two had a difficult relationship: Brown, one of the first black athletes to speak out about race, and Schwartzwalder, the crusty ex-paratrooper who isn't comfortable with players speaking out about, well, anything.

Brown (Darrin Dewitt Henson) has finished his college career and is preparing to leave for Cleveland where he will become a superstar with the Browns. Schwartzwalder asks Brown if he would go with him to

Elmira, N.Y., to meet with a high school phenom, Ernie Davis. Schwartzwalder is hoping to sell the kid on attending Syracuse and possibly filling Brown's famed No. 44 jersey.

The coach won't say it straight out, but Brown knows the real story. Davis is black and Schwartzwalder feels Brown would be a more effective salesman. Brown agrees to make the trip and succeeds in convincing Davis to pick Syracuse over Notre Dame and 50 other schools bidding for his services.

Brown tells Davis that Schwartzwalder isn't the easiest man to get along with, but he will make him into the best football player he can possibly be. Davis is swayed by Brown's honesty and accepts the scholarship to Syracuse.

Once Davis reports to campus, *The Express* follows the traditional sports movie playbook. He clashes with hostile upperclassmen who are slow to accept the highly touted newcomer and he bonds with the hulking Jack Buckley (Omar Benson Miller), a fellow African-American who becomes his friend and protector. It is all familiar stuff, competently rendered.

What lifts *The Express* above the pack is the role reversal. In most films, it is the coach who changes the player. Here, the player changes the coach. Davis isn't as outspoken as Jim Brown, but he is equally aware of what's going on around him, such as segregated hotel accommodations on the road. He knows it's wrong and he can't understand why an authority figure like Schwartzwalder just shrugs and goes along with it.

When the Syracuse team—with its handful of black players—travels to West Virginia, Schwartzwalder warns them to expect trouble. "Keep your helmets on," he tells them in the tunnel. As the Orangemen take the field, the redneck crowd pelts them with bottles, garbage and racial taunts.

When Davis carries the ball to the one-yard line, the coach replaces him with a white halfback who scores the touchdown. Later in the game, the same thing happens. Davis carries the ball to the one and the coach sends the same substitute onto the field. This time Davis waves him off. He stays in the game and scores the touchdown as the West Virginia fans shower him with debris.

Schwartzwalder confronts Davis and the two finally have it out. The coach says he is thinking about the safety of the entire team. He fears the sight of a black player scoring a touchdown could set off a full-scale riot. Davis tells the coach that by bowing to that kind of hate, he is only reinforcing it. Sooner or later, Davis says, a man has to stand against it.

"We're willing to do it," Davis says, "but it doesn't mean a thing unless you're with us."

Quaid allows us to see Schwartzwalder's conscience at work. The way he fiddles with his glasses, the way he addresses the team, not quite as sure of himself, we can see that he is thinking about what Davis said.

Clearly, Schwartzwalder is not a racist. Indeed, he was recruiting black players before most major college coaches. But typical of many white Americans of that time, his idea of tolerance only goes so far. For example, when he sees Davis exchange flirty smiles with a white cheerleader, he calls the player into the office.

"There are certain lines you don't cross," the coach says sternly.

By the time the Orangemen travel to the Cotton Bowl to face Texas—with their race-baiting players and fans—Schwartzwalder knows it is much more than a football game. Even with a national championship and unbeaten season on the line, he sees the larger picture.

When Syracuse wins the game—which features an ugly brawl initiated by the cheap shots and racial taunts of the Texas players—they are told the trophy presentation will take place at a private club in Dallas. No blacks, in other words. When the white players tell the Cotton Bowl officials to shove their trophy and their club, Schwartzwalder nods in approval.

The Express focuses almost entirely on that season, 1959, which was Davis' sophomore year. It flashes forward to his senior season when he becomes the first African-American to win the Heisman Trophy. In his acceptance speech, Davis thanks Schwartzwalder for being "a good coach and a good man."

"I spoke with Jim Brown about his relationship with Ben," Quaid said, "and he told me that Ben was obsessed with football and only football, X's and O's. He and Jim butted heads over racial issues, but that's because Ben didn't want the civil rights movement spilling over onto his field. He didn't want to hear about it.

"But Ben changed, thanks to people like Jim Brown

and Ernie Davis. One of the greatest compliments the film received came from Jim Brown who said he gained new respect for Ben watching the movie. Ben was one of the soldiers who stormed the beach at Normandy. He wore those combat boots at practice, that's who he was. He brought that military experience to his coaching. Jim Brown and later Ernie Davis got Ben to reveal that he actually did have a soft, creamy center."

🍺 **CHEERS:** Quaid steals the film with his portrayal of Schwartzwalder. Michael Granberry of the *Dallas Morning News* wrote: "Quaid has quietly become one of America's finest actors. [He] can say more with a single facial expression than most can with 100 pages of dialog."

🚩 **JEERS:** The film is poorly paced. It drags in the middle, then rushes the ending. Davis wins the Heisman, meets President Kennedy, is drafted by the Washington Redskins, traded to Cleveland, then develops leukemia and dies all in what seems like a matter of seconds.

✒ **WHAT THEY WROTE AT THE TIME:** "As Davis, Rob Brown (*Finding Forrester*) is in possession of a kind face and an athletic grace that easily wins over audiences."— Michael Rechtshaffen, *The Hollywood Reporter*

🍎 **BET YOU DIDN'T KNOW:** A statue of Ernie Davis was unveiled on the Syracuse campus in October, 2008. The statue had a Nike swoosh on its jersey and Nike cleats on its feet, but Nike wasn't founded until 1972, nine years after Davis' death. The sculptor corrected the errors.

💬 **BEST LINE:** "I bet about now you're wondering what happened to that nice gentleman who came to your house and asked you to play for Syracuse."—Jack Buckley (Omar Benson Miller) talking to Ernie Davis (Brown) after Schwartzwalder drove them through a tough practice.

😄 **"I KNOW THAT GUY":** In this case, it is a voice. Clancy Brown, who plays assistant coach Roy Simmons Sr., is the voice for Mr. Krabs on *SpongeBob Squarepants*.

★ **SPORTS-ACTION GRADE:** C+. The action is filmed well enough and Rob Brown has the graceful stride of a football player, but the hits are over the top. Only in Hollywood does every hit on the football field sound like a nuclear explosion.

AN INTERVIEW WITH DENNIS QUAID

AFTER HIS BREAKOUT ROLE IN *BREAKING AWAY* (1979), DENNIS QUAID HAS GONE ON TO BUILD AN IMPRESSIVE RESUME AS A LEADING MAN AND SUPPORTING ACTOR, OFTEN IN SPORTS MOVIES. IN FACT, FIVE OF HIS FILMS MADE OUR LIST. A COMPETENT ATHLETE IN REAL LIFE—HE'S A NEAR-SCRATCH GOLFER AND ONCE HAD A 200-PLUS BOWLING AVERAGE—HE ADMITS HE'S PROBABLY NO MATCH FOR HIS BIGGER BIG BROTHER, RANDY. AND THOUGH HE HAILS FROM TEXAS, HE NEVER MADE MUCH OF AN EFFORT TO PLAY FOOTBALL, SAYING, "I HATE GETTING HIT."

WE SAT DOWN WITH DENNIS TO TALK ABOUT HIS SPORTS MOVIES, INCLUDING THE RECENT *THE EXPRESS* (2008), AS WELL AS HIS CAREER IN FILM OVERALL.

Of all the sports movies you have made, which one meant the most to you?

Oh, *The Rookie*. It was a baseball movie, but like all sports movies I do it had to transcend the sport. It had to be about something else, something universal that everyone can relate to. *The Rookie* was about second chances in life—and it was a second chance for me in a way. I had finished my first act as far as my career goes. Sure, I was working in the 90s but I really had to dig for good roles.

Are you saying your career hit a lull?

Yeah, the great roles stopped coming. I was being offered second, third, fourth roles—not the leads anymore. I'm not complaining about it—I've had a really good life. But when *The Rookie* came along, it just sort of paralleled my life in a way. It was a second chance for me as it was for Jim Morris. Making the movie itself felt very magical, and then what happened with it was very magical. That's why I told Jimmy Morris that what he did in real life changed my life.

How could making a movie feel magical?

Hey, I had not been on a pitcher's mound since Little League. Luckily, I was a lefty like Morris. To train, [former major league pitcher] Jim Gott came to my house every day, and we'd throw. Once a week, I'd go to Dodger Stadium and pitch off the mound. How much fun can you have?

Were you able to get any speed behind your pitches?

Ha! Let's just say that contrary to popular belief, I can't throw 99 miles per hour. I never checked it out on a speed gun. That would have been embarrassing. I just didn't want to look like Anthony Perkins [in *Fear Strikes Out*] out there.

Do people tell you that movie breaks them up?

Oh yeah, I know it does. When I read the script it broke me up. *The Express* does the same thing to me. It hits me in a place where I have no words emotionally.

You've made sports movies playing characters both real and fictional. Morris and Coach Ben Schwartzwalder in The Express were real people. How is it different portraying a fictional character and an actual person?

I feel like I have an added responsibility to the person—whether he is alive or dead—to capture his spirit. I may not look like Jimmy Morris or Coach Schwartzwalder, but I try to be real to the character. And I try to do it honestly—not idealistically. I really feel the warts-and-all approach is the best way to make your character approachable and human.

Your breakout role came in 1979 as the angry young man in Breaking Away. What did that movie do for your career?

Well, it made it a lot easier to get jobs. Before that movie I was a struggling actor, new to the scene, going from audition to audition. That movie gave me something for the resume. Beyond that, it remains one of my favorite movies I've done. Peter Yates, who directed it, became a mentor in my life. He was an Englishman. Steve Tesich, who wrote it, was a [Serbian] immigrant. And it's this great American story.

Why do you think it works so well?

Its innocence, maybe. They started making a lot of youth movies in the 80s and I think this was one of the first. There is an innocence and joy about it. A joy of life.

Yes, it's that rare teenage movie that's not about losing your virginity or getting stoned. It's a movie about nice, sympathetic kids trying to find their way.

They're real. I was 24 when we shot it, but playing an 18-year-old. Most people at that age don't know what to do with their lives. They don't know where they're going, or how good they might be. So, when those kids—the cutters, the dropouts—win the Little 500 race, it's a great success for them.

Okay, your next sports movie was Everybody's All-American, based on the great book by Frank Deford. It's a story of a man with great talent, but ultimately a sad story. Do you see it that way?

Yeah. Ultimately *Everybody's All-American* was about the death of the South, but it also related to what really happens to all athletes, even the greatest ones. You spend your entire life on a field, or around all the guys in the locker room. Then, when you're in the prime of life, at the height of your powers, they take away your ball and they send you home. So you sit there and wonder, 'What do I do with the rest of my life?'

Actors are luckier. You can work many more years.

If I'm lucky, I can go until I'm an old man. But what if they took it away in my late 30s? That's tough to swallow. That's one of the reasons I understand what Brett Favre went through [in 2008] when the Packers didn't want him anymore. That's why I'm pulling for him so hard [with the New York Jets] and want to see him go all the way. I really do. Brett's my guy now.

Let's talk about Any Given Sunday. It certainly is a darker look at sports than your other films.

Well, that's [director] Oliver Stone. That movie, to me, is a look at the difference between the beauty of the game and the business of the game. It reminded people of *North Dallas Forty*, I think. Oliver Stone showed a real visceral experience. Watching it, you felt like you were there on the field feeling the violence.

You play an aging quarterback, trying to hang onto his job against a hotshot kid.

Yeah, and getting bitch-slapped by my [movie] wife, Lauren Holly. She wants me to get out while I can. You know, I think that movie is really about survival of the fittest.

I know that asking you to name the favorite among your own films may be like asking you to name your favorite child, but is there one that meant the most?

I know I'm supposed to say this because I just finished it, but I have to say *The Express*, which is a beautiful story of Ernie Davis, a man whose life was short, but well lived. I base my feelings on the message of the movie and how making it affected me personally. So, I'd have to say that *The Rookie* and *The Express* are my favorites.

They're certainly the most uplifting of your films.

Yes, and who doesn't like uplifting experiences? I mean, I really like *Everybody's All-American*. But I was in a place in my life with those two other films, and they became a special experience for me. Even watching them was different. When I watch one of my own movies, I'm looking at it technically. But when I saw *The Express* and *The Rookie*, both times the emotion came up in me. I really don't have words for it.

Choked up?

Yes. And, you know, that's my favorite kind of movie. That's why I like *The Natural* so much. You sit there, watch it and let the experience go over you. The scene at the end when [Robert] Redford realizes he has a son. . . . Oh, I'm getting choked up thinking about it. I do, I like emotional stories.

Your brother, Randy Quaid, has been in a number of sports movies as well—not always good ones. Who's the best athlete in your family?

Well, I'm a good golfer—a six handicap—but Randy's bigger and stronger. He's six-foot-five. He'd win any competition between us that relies on size. Plus, as my big brother, he's still got that psychological edge. That never changes.

76 THE CINCINNATI KID (1965–NR)

SPORT: POKER | STARS: STEVE MCQUEEN, EDWARD G. ROBINSON, ANN-MARGRET
DIRECTOR: NORMAN JEWISON

Four years after *The Hustler* shined a spotlight on the seedy world of pool hall gambling, Hollywood decided to turn another pulp novel into a film that would do the same with side-street poker games. Richard Jessup's *The Cincinnati Kid* became that movie.

The two films have striking similarities. Both are stories of a brash young gambler trying to topple his underground sport's reigning king. Both feature charismatic blue-eyed stars in the lead—Paul Newman vs. Steve McQueen—as well as veterans dripping with gravitas as "The Man"—Jackie Gleason vs. Edward G. Robinson.

Both have a meaty "bad girl" role—Piper Laurie vs. Ann-Margret (who even chomps on an apple here, just in case you miss the point)—as well as a corrupting devil figure—George C. Scott vs. Rip Torn. And there's more: marathon games, sleazy side shows, endless cigarette smoke, redemption followed by failure.

The comparisons—well pointed out when *The Cincinnati Kid* was initially released—hurt this movie with critics. It never could reach the classic status that its older brother achieved. Likewise, in recent years, *The Cincinnati Kid* has become the "forgotten" poker movie since the 1998 release of *Rounders*, a grittier story told at a quicker pace.

It's all a bit of a shame. On its own, this is a terrific film. If you can watch it without making the inevitable comparisons, you'll enjoy a hard-boiled story with great action, surprising plot twists and the honky-tonk atmosphere of New Orleans in the 1930s.

Steve McQueen stars as Eric Stoner—"The Cincinnati Kid"—a crackerjack five-card stud player eager to be seen as the best around. To get there, he must topple Lancey Howard (Robinson)—AKA "The Man"—the incumbent champion. In many ways, this feels like a classic Western, with the young gunslinger stalking Wild Bill Hickok.

The game is arranged through a mutual friend named Shooter (Karl Malden), who agrees to be the dealer. Meanwhile, side deals are made, loyalties tested and Shooter's wife, Melba (Ann-Margret) aims to sleep with every man in Louisiana.

There are some great side characters here, led by Hollywood veteran Joan Blondell portraying a brassy poker player named Lady Fingers who has some sort of history with Lancey Howard. Also terrific is a young Rip Torn (you won't recognize him as the same guy from *Men in Black*) as the spoiled rich boy who tries to buy 'em when he cant beat 'em.

And, of course, there is McQueen. In the Hall of Fame of Cool, he is a unanimous first-ballot inductee.

The Cincinnati Kid is at its best when it sticks to the poker table (some of the side scenes are downright tedious). Poker is clearly not the most cinematic of sports, but director Norman Jewison makes it work through alternating tension and humor, and showing the reactions of players—all trying so hard not to show their sweat and their tics.

In the DVD commentary, Jewison talks about how tough it was to film a five-hand poker game, and how many of his colleagues in the business told him that no movie about card playing would ever find appeal among audiences. "But poker is about winning," says Jewison. "That's why it's so popular in America, because America is about winning."

🍺 **CHEERS:** Make sure you stick around through the closing credits. There's an original song, same title as the movie, written and performed by the great Ray Charles.

🚩 **JEERS:** There's a scene halfway through—designed to establish characters—in which The Kid tracks down his girlfriend (Tuesday Weld) at her family farm. The girl's parents appear to be extras from the movie *Deliverance*, and the scene becomes both monotonous and squirm-inducing. Sad to say, you will never get back those eight minutes of your life.

✏️ **WHAT THEY WROTE AT THE TIME:** "It's strictly for those who relish—or at least play—stud poker. Here is a respectably packaged drama of a young card sharp, played by Steve McQueen, with a capable enough cast, that pungently projects the machinations and back-room temperatures of the side-street professional gambling world and little else. . . . The film pales beside *The Hustler*, to which it bears a striking similarity of theme and characterization."—Howard Thompson, *New York Times*

😐 **GOOFS:** At the start of the big game, Shooter, the dealer, announces, "No string bets." Yet, throughout the night, players repeatedly declare that they will call, and then raise the pot—the definition of a string bet.

✔️ **REALITY CHECK:** Without revealing the climactic moment, let's just say that the chance of the game going down as it did on film is less than your chance of winning a date with Scarlett Johansson. To take her to the Cubs World Series parade. On Mars. In his book *Big Deal: A Year as a Professional Poker Player*, Anthony Holden wrote that the odds of the The Kid's and Lancey's hands occurring on the same deal are about 45 million-to-one. Further, since both hands need tens to be successful (again, we're aiming not to give much away), the chance of both appearing on one deal jumps to 300 billion-to-one. "If these two played fifty hands of stud an hour, eight hours a day, five days a week, the situation would arise about once every 443 years," wrote Holden.

◎ **REPEATED WATCHING QUOTIENT:** Once a year or so, just to remind yourself of how great Steve McQueen was.

☞ **DON'T FAIL TO NOTICE:** The running commentary on the DVD extra features, hosted by Phil Gordon and Dave Foley of Bravo's *Celebrity Poker Showdown*. The two analyze characters' playing styles and point out a few blunders made in the film.

🎞 CASTING CALL: Spencer Tracy was originally cast as Lancey, but had to drop out for health reasons. And Mitzi Gaynor auditioned for the role of Lady Fingers. Rumor had it that she didn't land the role because of tension between Gaynor and Ann-Margret.

★ SPORTS-ACTION GRADE: D. Until they make poker a full-contact sport, you can't expect a higher grade than this.

🖐 BET YOU DIDN'T KNOW: After bombing in the movie *Baby the Rain Must Fall*, McQueen took a year off from filmmaking—riding his motorcycle around the world and having an affair with sexpot Mamie Van Doren. (Not a bad way to kill time.) *The Cincinnati Kid* marked his return. Although it wasn't a smash at the box office, McQueen gained traction and went on to film *The Sand Pebbles*, *The Thomas Crown Affair* and *Bullitt* in rapid succession.

💬 BEST LINE: Lancey Howard—The Man—has just beaten The Kid in a huge hand by betting against the odds and all reason.

Lancey: "That gets down to what it's all about, doesn't it? Making the wrong move at the right time."

Cincinnati Kid: "Is that what it's all about?"

Lancey Howard: "Like life, I guess. You're good, Kid, but as long as I'm around you're second best. You might as well learn to live with it."

😎 "I KNOW THAT GUY": The fifth player at the big table is the great Cab Calloway, a famed big band leader and jazz pioneer. If you don't recognize him from his old recordings ("Minnie the Moocher," "St. James Infirmary"), perhaps you'll remember him as Curtis from *The Blues Brothers*. Or maybe you grew up marveling at him performing *Hi De Ho Man* with purple muppets on *Sesame Street*. If not, just call up his name on YouTube.com, and you will be rewarded.

🎬 IF YOU LIKED THIS, YOU'LL LIKE: *California Split*, director Robert Altman's 1974 caper film with Elliott Gould and George Segal. The third-best movie about poker.

SIGN OF THE TIMES: Sam Peckinpah was originally hired to direct *The Cincinnati Kid*. He was fired a week into production after shooting a nude scene (with an actress named Sharon Tate, who went on to both stardom and tragedy. She, too, was cut from this movie.). Producer Martin Ransohoff feared that nudity would destroy the movie's commercial appeal. Just a few years later, nude scenes became almost a requirement in Hollywood.

🎞 MY FAVORITE SPORTS MOVIE: Actor and celebrity poker player Gary Busey to the *Las Vegas Sun*: "As a person who loves good drama and loves playing cards, I consider *The Cincinnati Kid* to be a nearly perfect film."

77 HAPPY GILMORE (1996–PG-13)

SPORT: GOLF | STARS: ADAM SANDLER, CARL WEATHERS, CHRISTOPHER MCDONALD
DIRECTOR: DENNIS DUGAN

In the Hall of Comedy Genius, Adam Sandler does not stand near Charlie Chaplin. He's not up to the standards of W.C. Fields or Richard Pryor or Steve Martin or Eddie Murphy. He's no Jamie Foxx. No Bill Murray. No Robin Williams.

What he is, rather, is a modern-day version of the Three Stooges—an anarchic slapstick performer who trades on class warfare and frat-house humor to create films aiming right into the wheelhouse of the coveted 18-to-34-year-old male demographic.

Sometimes they work (*The Wedding Singer, Anger Management*), sometimes they don't (*Little Nicky, You Don't Mess With the Zohan*). Too often, Sandler gets caught up in his impish, man-child persona, sinking into a cutesy-pie voice (*The Waterboy*) and giggling too much at his own cleverness.

In *Happy Gilmore*, Sandler avoids the trap of self-adoration. Instead, he creates a funny, if uneven, story of a working-class slob who invades the pompous professional golf scene and ends up a national hero. All while winning the girl and saving his sweet grandmother's home.

The script here could have been written on a cocktail napkin, and probably was. Sandler's title character is a frustrated hockey player (he can fight but he cannot skate), who accidentally discovers that he can drive a golf ball 400 yards.

He has no interest in playing pro golf. But when his grandmother's house is repossessed for failure to pay $270,000 in back taxes, he figures this is his best way to earn quick cash—even though, of course, he has never played a round in his life, can't putt, has no short game, and uses every blown shot as an excuse to toss clubs, batter bystanders and curse like a longshoreman with Tourette's.

Happy's volcanic temper is the one-joke gag of the movie. On the one hand, it keeps threatening to get him tossed from the tour—like when a pin flag he launches like a javelin nearly decapitates a cameraman. On the other hand, it makes him an idol of the crowds. Apparently, golf has been missing a Dennis Rodman-like bad boy, and Happy's just the guy for the job.

"His behavior is completely unacceptable," says tour PR director (and eventual love interest) Virginia (Julie Bowen). "But, you know, golf has been waiting for a player like this—a colorful, emotional working-class hero."

VIRGINIA: "HIS BEHAVIOR IS COMPLETELY UNACCEPTABLE. BUT, YOU KNOW, GOLF HAS BEEN WAITING FOR A PLAYER LIKE THIS—A COLORFUL, EMOTIONAL, WORKING-CLASS HERO."

Happy plays the course in a Boston Bruins jersey and sweat pants. He wears construction boots rather than golf shoes, and uses white tube socks as head covers for the wooden-shaft clubs rescued from his grandfather's attic. His caddy is a homeless beggar who resembles Bigfoot and rinses his tighty-whities in the ball washer.

How could you not root for that guy? Well that, plus Happy's running-start drives that occasionally result in double-eagle holes-in-one. Suddenly, golf fandom is taken over by T-shirt-wearing, pro wrestling devotees, or, as TV announcer Verne Lundquist calls it, "quite a large and economically diverse crowd here today at the Buick Open."

Of course, slobs vs. snobs only succeeds as a theme if you've got an upper-crust worth despising. And actor Christopher McDonald, as tour money leader Shooter McGavin, plays the Judge Smails role to the hilt. He's an arrogant bully who fires his own caddies for laughs and aims to buy Happy's grandmother's house from the taxman just to ensure she stays on the street. When heckled by Happy's gallery, he shouts back, "Damn you people. Go back to your shanties."

One other actor worth noting is Carl Weathers, who devolves here from his role as Apollo Creed to Chubbs, the one-handed golf instructor (the prosthetic hand gag is not to the genius level of *Kingpin*, which also came out in 1996). Chubbs offers less on technique than he does on life lessons. He gets Gilmore to curb his anger by transporting his mind to a tranquilizing "happy place," in this case a world where Grandma gets silver dollars tumbling from the slot machines and the beautiful Virginia reclines on a sofa, wearing a bustier and hoisting two pitchers of beer.

Ahh, haven't we all been there?

🍺 **CHEERS:** There are some strong small performances here by talented skit comedians. *SNL* alum Kevin Nealon, *SCTV* star Joe Flaherty and an uncredited Ben Stiller all add to the mix.

🍺 **JEERS:** We're not sure how much the Subway sandwich chain paid for product placement, but it sure seems like an overt commercial—and we're not even counting Happy's endorsement deal.

✒ **WHAT THEY WROTE AT THE TIME:** "You probably skipped *Happy Gilmore* in theaters because it looked like just another Adam Sandler movie. But actually, it's a sort of Gen-X *Caddyshack*, with some good, punchy slapstick and delightfully sick twists. Sandler acts like a perfect jackass. And that's what he does best."—Michael Sauter, *Entertainment Weekly*

✔ **REALITY CHECK:** Seriously, the entire premise defies credibility. But, if we wanted to be sticklers, we could point out that some of the major golf tournaments in the movie appear to take place in a single day. Either that, or the participants just never change their clothes.

◎ **REPEATED WATCHING QUOTIENT:** Once a decade seems about right.

🎬 **PIVOTAL SCENE:** A goofball movie like this has no real pivotal scene, but the funniest moment has to be the pro-am tournament brawl between Happy and *The Price Is Right* host Bob Barker. It begins when Happy's game is crippled by a heckler ("Jackass!"), and Barker—who won the tourney the previous year—dismisses his struggling partner by suggesting, "There's no way that you could have been as bad at hockey as you are at golf."

Happy, still battling anger management issues, sucker punches the 72-year-old game show host. That prompts a three-minute smackdown that has the two men rolling down a hill, head butting each other and exchanging haymakers in a pond. It's not quite up there with *The Quiet Man* for best movie brawl, but you will laugh at Happy's premature victory cry of, "The price is *wrong*—bitch!"—as well as Barker's physical and verbal retort.

Barker told *Entertainment Weekly* that he initially declined a role in the movie—until he learned he would be duking it out with Sandler. "It seemed a good way for me to get out of character," he said.

☞ **DON'T FAIL TO NOTICE:** The first-date scene between Happy and Virginia takes place in an empty skating rink—either a tribute to or a direct copy from *Rocky*.

◀ **CASTING CALL:** Golf legend Lee Trevino keeps popping up throughout the movie, like some sort of club-carrying Zelig. And if you look closely among the players in the hockey tryout scene, the guy on the left is NHL all-star Joe Sakic. We can only assume he makes the squad.

★ **SPORTS-ACTION GRADE:** D-minus. But you're not watching this movie because it resembles real golf in any way.

👅 **BET YOU DIDN'T KNOW:** Seven-foot actor Richard Kiel—best remembered as "Jaws" in several *James Bond* films—plays an addled and menacing member of Happy's fan club (complete with a nine-inch nail sticking out of his head). Kiel is never seen walking or even standing unsupported in the movie. That's because he was in a serious car accident in 1992, which permanently damaged his balance.

👅 **BET YOU DIDN'T KNOW II:** At the 2008 Ryder Cup in Louisville, Ky., golfer Thomas "Boo" Weekley decided to loosen up his American teammates by galloping down the first fairway doing Sandler's "Happy Dance," riding his driver between his legs and whipping it like a quarter horse.

"That's one of the greatest things I've ever seen in my life," American captain Paul Azinger said of the *Happy Gilmore* tribute.

Perhaps not coincidentally, America trounced the Europeans.

💬 **BEST LINE:** Chubbs: "Golf is no different from hockey. It requires focus and self-discipline."

Happy: "Golf requires goofy pants and a fat ass. You should talk to my neighbor, the accountant. Huge ass."

👀 **"I KNOW THAT GUY":** Otto, Happy's hobo-turned-caddy, is portrayed by Allen Covert, who has been a friend of Sandler's since their student days at New York University. Covert has played a supporting role in 13 of Sandler's films and produced six of them. You might best recognize him as Sammy, the aging lounge lizard in *The Wedding Singer*.

SIGN OF THE TIMES: Check out the five-pound cell phone on Shooter. Hard to believe that as recently as 1996 cell phones were still the size of shoe boxes.

⊕ **IF YOU LIKED THIS, YOU'LL LIKE:** *The Waterboy*, Sandler's inane rip-off of this very film, in which a mentally challenged H$_2$O devotee becomes an unlikely college football sensation.

✍ **MY FAVORITE SPORTS MOVIE:** New York Mets third baseman David Wright: "I'm a big Adam Sandler fan. I have three brothers and it's great to be able to just laugh with them watching one of those movies. It's ridiculous stuff, totally out of the blue, but that's what's so funny, you don't expect it. I mean, he punches out Bob Barker. Who would do that?"

EVERYBODY'S ALL-AMERICAN
(1988–R)

SPORT: FOOTBALL | STARS: DENNIS QUAID, JESSICA LANGE, TIMOTHY HUTTON
DIRECTOR: TAYLOR HACKFORD

Everybody's All-American was originally a fine novel written by Frank Deford of *Sports Illustrated*, but screenwriter Thomas Rickman and director Taylor Hackford fumble in their attempt to bring Deford's story to the screen.

The film is good enough to hold your interest, and there are times when the travails of Gavin Grey (Dennis Quaid) are achingly real, but too often it is a plodding soap opera that can't decide whether it is about the fall of a football legend or the demise of the Old South. Hackford tries to tie the themes together, but he doesn't quite pull it off.

The story traces 25 years in the lives of Grey, better known as "The Grey Ghost," All-American halfback at Louisiana University (it's really LSU) and his beauty queen wife Babs (Jessica Lange). What begins as a fairy tale marriage crumbles over time as Grey's football skills decline and, suddenly, it's the bill collectors on the phone and not the fan clubs or the talk shows.

Everybody's All-American is at its best when it is dealing with those issues; that is, what happens to yesterday's hero? What happens to the great athlete when the applause dies and the stage goes dark? What happens when he awakens to discover the public has forgotten his name? This film makes you think about that.

There is a haunting scene late in the film when Grey's old team, the 1956 Sugar Bowl champion, is honored at the homecoming game. As Grey is introduced and walks on the field, the crowd stands and cheers. His smile widens and you can see him thinking "They *do* remember." Then he glances over his shoulder and sees the current varsity emerging from the tunnel. He realizes the cheer wasn't for him but for them. He doesn't say a word but the look of pain and embarrassment on his face is all-too-real.

It is a path most old jocks will travel. Some travel it more gracefully than others. Grey has a particularly difficult time. He goes from college superstar to All-Pro running back with the Washington Redskins to owner of a successful bar and restaurant. However, his old teammate Lawrence (John Goodman) who works at the bar has a gambling addiction that winds up putting the business in bankruptcy and getting him killed.

Grey, who was able to overcome any challenge on the football field, proves ill-equipped to deal with adversity in the real world. He tries an ill-fated comeback with the Denver Broncos—watching him peel the tape off his battered body will make you wince—and he picks up a few bucks at a country club, playing golf with the members and entertaining them with his war stories. That will make you wince, too.

"One time we were playing Baltimore and Unitas was kicking our ass," Grey says, beginning a tale he has told too many times. The tone of his voice is flat, bordering on sour.

"Oh, he tells this one real good," the boss says, patting him on the back.

The Grey Ghost has become a pathetic figure and he knows it.

Babs, who was once just a lovely ornament on her husband's arm, must find the strength to keep their family afloat. In college, Babs tells a friend she is majoring in "Gavin and me" and as long as the Grey Ghost is scoring touchdowns, she is content to play the role of Magnolia Queen. But with debts piling up and her husband a disillusioned prisoner of his past, she goes to work and proves to be a capable businesswoman.

This poses even more problems for Grey, who now has to deal with the fact that his wife is the success in the family. There are a lot of issues to resolve and Hackford almost gives himself a sports hernia trying to carry all that baggage to the finish line. The upbeat ending feels forced and the character of Cake (Timothy Hutton), the

Ghost's nephew who is meant to serve as the Nick Carraway to Gavin's Gatsby, never really registers.

🍺 **CHEERS:** Hackford does a good job evoking the feel of a college campus in the 1950s. The opening scene, a bonfire pep rally, is terrific.

🚩 **JEERS:** The film runs more than two hours, which is too long. It covers a lot of ground—including racism in the Old South—and while its heart is in the right place it would have been better served by keeping the focus on Gavin and Babs.

✔ **REALITY CHECK:** The winning touchdown in the Sugar Bowl—Grey scores after taking a pitch from Lawrence—should not have counted. If you look carefully, you'll see it is a forward lateral.

👊 **BET YOU DIDN'T KNOW:** Dennis Quaid suffered a broken collarbone filming one of the football scenes. "I volunteered to play full contact and that was not a good decision," Quaid said. "I gained 20 pounds for the role, but still. I was out there taking hits and on the very last day I had to re-create a play where (Grey) gets hit by the safety and his helmet goes flying off.

"We did the scene once and [former NFL safety] Tim Fox—who they called The Human Missile—runs up. He put his helmet on my collarbone and I hear a snap. It's all on film and that's the take they used. You see me, right there on the screen, in real agony."

☞ **DON'T FAIL TO NOTICE:** The Sugar Bowl scene was shot at LSU's Tiger Stadium in Baton Rouge during halftime of an LSU-Alabama game.

📢 **CASTING CALL:** The script for *Everybody's All-American* kicked around Hollywood for more than five years. Several stars read for the part of Gavin Grey, including Tommy Lee Jones, Robert Redford, Warren Beatty and Robert De Niro, but Hackford decided on the lesser-known Quaid.

💬 **BEST LINE:** Babs is watching Gavin's first game with the Redskins. She is taken aback at the violence of pro football. One of the other wives says, "Pro's a different game, honey. Not much rah-rah up here. Not like when you were homecoming queen in where was it?"

"Louisiana," Babs says. "I was Magnolia Queen."

"Most of us were the queen of something," the other wife says. "Now? We're just players' wives."

😎 **"I KNOW THAT GUY":** Frank Deford, who wrote the original novel and now is a regular correspondent on HBO's *Real Sports*, has a small role in the film playing a bigoted luncheonette owner.

☞ **ONE MORE THING:** It was widely speculated that Deford based the character of Gavin Grey on former LSU All-American Billy Cannon, who won the 1959 Heisman Trophy, played 11 seasons in the NFL and wound up going to prison after being found guilty of taking part in a counterfeiting scheme. Deford has always denied that Cannon was the inspiration for the Grey Ghost.

✎ **WHAT THEY WROTE AT THE TIME:** "Cake as the constant observer goes from a saucer-eyed student to a professor cringing with embarrassment over his uncle's decline."—Steve Wulf, *Sports Illustrated*

★ **SPORTS-ACTION GRADE:** C. Other than the Fox hit, the action is unconvincing and John Goodman hardly looks the part of an All-Conference lineman.

👁 **REPEATED WATCHING QUOTIENT:** Once is enough.

🎬 **MY FAVORITE SPORTS MOVIE:** Philadelphia Eagles broadcaster Merrill Reese, the longest-tenured play-by-play man in the NFL: "*Everybody's All-American* captures what happens to a star in the various stages of his life—and what can happen going through life's transitions—to a better extent than any other sports movie I've ever seen."

79 THE GREATEST GAME EVER PLAYED (2005–PG)

SPORT: GOLF | STARS: SHIA LABEOUF, STEPHEN DILLANE | DIRECTOR: BILL PAXTON

Watching *The Greatest Game Ever Played*, you'll be struck by three things:

1. Once upon a time, Americans were actually considered the scrappy underdogs to their European big brothers.

2. If you think golf is a snooty sport now, you should have seen it a century ago.

3. This story is so outrageous, it can't possibly be true. And if it is, how come you never heard about it before?

Last things first. *The Greatest Game Ever Played* tells the tale of the 1913 U.S. Open at The Country Club in Brookline, Ma. The tournament became a showdown between British pro Harry Vardon (Stephen Dillane), who was considered the world's best golfer, and amateur Francis Ouimet (Shia LaBeouf), a 20-year-old former caddy playing in his first major tournament.

Ouimet, as his World Golf Hall of Fame biography notes, "seemed to step from the pages of a Dickens novel." He grew up in a working-class home across the street from The Country Club and learned to play by tapping balls into tomato cans in his backyard. At 11, he began caddying on the famous course, and was invited into the Open—as the final participant with the longest odds—after he won the 1913 Massachusetts State Amateur Championship.

Sports history is rife with great upsets—1980 U.S. Olympic hockey team over the Soviets; Buster Douglas over Mike Tyson; the Giants over the Patriots in Super Bowl XLII. Each of those pales in comparison with this one. Imagine Tiger Woods, at the peak of his game, vanquishing all other opponents in a Grand Slam event, only to lose in an extra fifth round to a neighborhood kid making his debut. And just to make it more preposterous, stick the young upstart with a 10-year-old school-skipping caddy, barely bigger than the bags he must lug.

It really happened that way.

The story was largely lost to history until 2002, when author Mark Frost turned it into a best-selling book. Frost's work caught the attention of actor Bill Paxton (*Apollo 13, Twister*), who had himself grown up across the street from a golf course in Texas and whose dad had once played a round with Ouimet's former caddy. Paxton—who had previously directed the horror drama *Frailty*—sold the idea to Disney and hired Frost to turn his book into a screenplay.

The movie plays honest with the actual history—with a story this fantastic, why shouldn't it? In doing so, Paxton takes us back to a time when Brits thoroughly dominated the sport. This is before World War I, before America was a world power, a time when a young United States was just discovering its athletic muscles and still had somewhat of a little-brother complex. Indeed, Ouimet's shocking victory is still regarded as the single largest landmark moment in bringing golf into the mindset of American sports fans, and the 20-year-old became this country's first golf hero.

The Greatest Game Ever Played also succeeds in avoiding a common sports movie trap, which is casting the opponent as a one-dimensional villain—whether he be Ivan Drago, Warden Hazen or Judge Smails. Vardon, despite being the prohibitive favorite, remains a guy you can root for, in part because he shares Ouimet's underclass roots and must spend his life fighting the sport's upper-crust gatekeepers. One of the movie's best scenes shows a younger Vardon being interviewed at a posh English country club after winning an earlier U.S. Open. Vardon believes he is being asked to join as a member; turns out the snobs just want him to run the pro shop.

The movie follows the two men for a decade (including a brief encounter between them when Ouimet was a young lad), but most of its 120 minutes focuses on the five-round tournament. Golf is not the easiest sport to bring to film; the background may be pastoral, but the action falls closer to chess than it does to football. Paxton tries to speed things up with rapid-fire tee shots, undulating putts and Fourth of July crowd reaction shots.

"It's kind of like a fireworks show," Paxton said in an About.com interview shortly after the film's release. "We get into that final round, and it's the 'House of Flying Golf Balls' and everything else."

Sometimes that works, sometimes Paxton gets carried away with special effects. In one shot, we get "ball cam"—watching through the golf ball's vantage point as a seeing-eye shot makes its way through the woods. In another, a ladybug comes to alight on a ball, and, in close-up looks like a refugee from Pixar's *Toy Story*. Downright silly. What's next, the *Caddyshack* gopher?

That's a quibble. Generally, this is a story well told and well acted. And, most amazingly, it's true.

🏆 **CHEERS:** With golfers playing in ties and jackets, wooden-shafted mashers and brassies and balls with pimples rather than dimples, *The Greatest Game Ever Played* does a great job re-creating the sport as it was back in 1913.

🚩 **JEERS:** Eddie Lowery really was the 10-year-old caddy who helped Ouimet through the tournament and remained a lifelong friend. Great story. But Paxton allows young actor Josh Flitter to play the role with a little-kid-wise-guy approach usually reserved for WB Network sitcoms. Sometimes, we just wanted the wiser-than-his-years pipsqueak to shut his yap.

🎬 **PIVOTAL SCENE:** Ouimet is sailing along midway through the second round of the tournament when a friend informs him that he's tied with Vardon for second place. He begins to feel the pressure and flubs a tee shot when he notices that President Taft is present and watching him. He must collect himself, and with the sage words of his pint-sized caddy (okay, we didn't despise the kid *all* the time), recovers and pars the hole.

✒ **WHAT THEY WROTE AT THE TIME:** "Predictable though it is, the picture is rousing and well paced, and the final competition is effectively suspenseful.... This is not the greatest sports movie ever made, and it doesn't try to be. It aims for par, and makes it."—A.O. Scott, *New York Times*

☝ **DON'T FAIL TO NOTICE:** In the scene where 12-year-old Francis meets Vardon at a golf demonstration, the older man patiently instructs the boy on how to properly hold the club. The "Vardon Grip," with overlapping fingers, is still the preferred method of gripping the club today.

☺ **GOOFS:** Late in the final round, during a series of rapid-fire shots, Ouimet is shown taking one swing left-handed. We can only assume the film was flopped.

😀 **"I KNOW THAT GUY":** Graybeard pro shop proprietor Alec Campbell is played by Luke Askew, an older version of the 1960s-70s character actor who had great supporting roles in *Cool Hand Luke* (Boss Paul), *Easy Rider* (the stranger on the highway) and *Pat Garrett & Billy the Kid* (Eno). Look through the white hair and the stubble; you'll spot him.

✴ **IF YOU LIKED THIS, YOU'LL LIKE:** *The Legend of Bagger Vance*, a 2000 Robert Redford-directed film about a mystical caddy (Will Smith) who helps a down-and-out golfer (Matt Damon) rediscover his game.

SIGN OF THE TIMES: During the match, Vardon's ball comes to rest on the green directly between Ouimet's and the cup. Rather than have Vardon's ball marked—as became the rule in the 1950s—Ouimet must try to chip over it toward the hole. It would cost Ouimet a penalty stroke if he hit his opponent's ball while putting. Strategically blocking an opponent's shot was known as a stymie (hence the word "stymied.")

🎩 **BET YOU DIDN'T KNOW:** As an amateur, Ouimet could not collect the cash prize for winning the U.S. Open, so instead it went to runner-up Vardon. He collected a whopping $300.

🎞 **MY FAVORITE SPORTS MOVIE:** LPGA champion Lorena Ochoa to *LPGA.com*: "It's a beautiful example of how golfers should behave and how golf should be played."

STRIKE OUT!
THE WORST SPORTS-MOVIE CONCEPTS EVER PITCHED

FOR EVERY *BULL DURHAM*, THERE IS *SUMMER CATCH*. FOR EVERY *CADDYSHACK*, THERE IS *WHO'S YOUR CADDY*? AND, FOR EVERY *THE PRIDE OF THE YANKEES*, WHICH BEAUTIFULLY MEMORIALIZED LOU GEHRIG'S LIFE, THERE ARE—WELL, TWO VERSIONS OF BABE RUTH'S STORY INSULTING THE BAMBINO.

IN A BOOK DEDICATED TO THE GREATEST SPORTS FILMS EVER, LET'S TIP A CAP TO THE TRITE, THE UNBELIEVABLE, THE POORLY CAST—THE WORST SPORTS MOVIES EVER.

WE LEFT OUT SPORTS MOVIES AIMED AT KIDS BECAUSE, WELL, WE HAVE A MUCH LOWER STANDARD FOR THOSE.

1. *Summer Catch.* Blame it on 1988's *Bull Durham*, which more or less invented the successful genre of "sports movie/chick flick." Since then, the sports romance has been done well (*Jerry Maguire, Cinderella Man*) and poorly (*Fever Pitch, The Slugger's Wife*). It reached its nadir in 2001 with this other-side-of-the-tracks soaper about the rich girl (Jessica Biel) attracted to the poor-but-earnest lawn boy (Freddie Prinze Jr.). When they're not engaging in some wet tee-shirt canoodling in her swimming pool (a scene deftly edited to completely frustrate every male viewer), Prinze aims to catch on with the local Cape Cod summer league baseball team.

The relationship scenes may appeal to a 14-year-old middle school girl. Probably not. The clichéd baseball and locker room scenes are sort of a *"Bad News Bears for Dummies."* Says New York Mets pitcher John Maine: *"Summer Catch* was terrible for a lot of reasons, but a big part of the problem was that Freddie Prinze throws like a girl. It's a joke."

An unfunny joke. If you must watch, try to pass the time by debating which is worse, the baseball dialog or the romance dialog.

Baseball dialog: "Wood bats suck!"

Romance dialog: "Miles here thinks you have a nice pooper."

You decide.

2. *The Babe* and *The Babe Ruth Story.* Successful biopics have honored legends Lou Gehrig, Knute Rockne, Jim Thorpe . . . even schleppers like Rudy Ruettiger. So how come the two efforts to translate the most magnetic personality in sports history to the screen failed so miserably?

Start with dreadful casting. William Bendix, who plays the title role in 1948's *The Babe Ruth Story*, brings to the role the same blundering silliness he brought to *The Life of Riley* TV show. This Bambino is a milk-drinking dimwit, who enters the movie as a teenager in Bendix's 42-year-old body and appears frozen in some sort of sitcom stupor. You almost expect Bendix to roll out his catch phrase, "What a revoltin' development *this* is." Actually, that would have been an accurate review of the film.

John Goodman fares no better in *The Babe* (1992), but he does bring one great qualification to the role: He is fat. He can't swing a bat. He can't throw a pitch any better than nine out of 10 presidents on Opening Day. So why cast him? Mostly, well, he's got a gut.

"That movie is one of those things I wish I could go back and do over," Goodman told *Esquire.* "It's like being in that dream where you're in the subway with no clothes on."

You could live with the hoary clichés—such as Babe curing cancer by walking through a hospital ward—if either Bendix or Goodman brought any credibility to their roles. In truth, the best portrayal of Ruth was done by The Sultan of Swat himself in *The Pride of the Yankees.*

For what it's worth, the real Babe Ruth's last public appearance was at the premiere of the Bendix film. He died shortly after that.

We're just saying.

3. *Eddie.* For whatever reason, there seem to be more inane movies made about basketball in recent years than other sport. We don't have room here for *The Air Up There, Amazing Grace and Chuck, BASEketball, Celtic*

Pride, Juwanna Mann and *Semi-Pro*—all worthy contenders. So we'll let this implausible 1996 brick of a flick represent the sport.

Here's the plot in a nutshell: A trash-talking, limo-driving hoops fiend played by Whoopi Goldberg wins a rigged free-throw contest at halftime of a Knicks game, and somehow winds up as the team's new coach. It's a spoiled collection of underachievers, featuring the likes of John Salley, Dennis Rodman and Dwayne Schintzius, who manages to be more unimpressive on film than he was on the hardwood. Mostly, there's a lot of product placement so that it all ends up looking like an endless promo for ESPN.

Making it worse, Whoopi plays a whiney, dislikeable loudmouth—sort of like Spike Lee meets *The View*. So it's tough to root for her improbable success. We'll give her this much, however: As Knicks coach, she displays more basketball smarts than Isiah Thomas achieved over four-plus years with that franchise.

4. *MVP: Most Valuable Primate* and *Ed*. It's tough not to get laughs when you put a chimp in a movie, dress him up funny and make him do stupid human tricks. But these two efforts manage. *Ed* (1996) features an ape playing third base, and *MVP* (2000) is about a simian who shoots pucks.

And who could forget **Bedtime for Bonzo**? Now there was a movie that had a star who knew how to play off a funny monkey. I watched Ronald Reagan. I laughed at Ronald Reagan. Matt LeBlanc? He's no Ronald Reagan.

5. *The Fan*. This is an utterly creepy 1996 howler in which Robert De Niro gets one more chance to revise his patented role as a stalking psycho (*Taxi Driver, The King of Comedy, Cape Fear*) and Ellen Barkin gets another opportunity to show erect nipples through her shirt (*The Big Easy, Sea of Love, Bad Company*). We've enjoyed both such performances in the past but, hey, enough is enough.

Wesley Snipes plays a Willie Mays Hayes on steroids—a brooding, high-maintenance San Francisco Giants outfielder who is nasty to the press and distant from his teammates. Hmmm, we can't imagine whom he might have used for inspiration on that one.

It ends up with De Niro's character kidnapping Snipes's son and murdering another player who's wearing his favorite uniform number (John Kruk, who has a small role in this, once bought his number from a teammate for two cases of beer. That seems a better deal.).

The Fan is directed by Tony Scott—Ridley's kid brother—who did some great work in *True Romance* and *Top Gun*. It's his third sports-related movie (after *Days of Thunder* and *The Last Boy Scout*) and proof that some guys should just stay away from the athletic fields.

6. *Chairman of the Board*. This conversation apparently took place early in 1998:

Producer: "Here's the idea, boss. Carrot Top, the least funny man in America, stars as a lazy surfer dude who somehow inherits a Fortune 500 corporation. Lots of flatulence, belching, guys getting hit in the crotch and clumsy sight gags. Plus, more surfing."

Studio head: "Sounds great! Let's shoot it!"

We can only hope that someone at Trimark Pictures lost his job over this. Actually, the lead actress in this monstrosity, Courtney Thorne-Smith, deserves an Oscar. She was forced to make out with Carrot Top and manages to do so without barfing her lungs out. Who was her agent?

7. *Over the Top*. Here is our list of movies with the best arm-wrestling scenes ever:

1. *Predator*
2. *Titanic* (we're not endorsing the entire sob story of a film, just the scene where Leonardo's deceptive super-muscles win him boat passage.)
3. *Ensign Pulver*
4. *Revenge of the Nerds*

. . . . . .

53. *Paradise Alley* (Sylvester Stallone as wrestler Cosmo Carboni)
54. *Over the Top*

As we said earlier, we believe that Sly made a pact with the Devil back in the 1970s that allowed him to create the Oscar-winning *Rocky*, but forced him to wallow in artistic manure for the rest of his days. So he twice went to the trough of arm wrestling, the better to show off his sweaty HGH-enhanced python biceps.

In this 1987 drivel, Stallone plays Lincoln Hawk (sounds like a car model), a long-haul trucker trying to win back the love of his estranged son. Because the boy is a vegetarian wimp raised by his left-wing mom, Sly needs to teach him manly stuff—like sleeping in truck cabs and bending guys' arms backwards until they snap in half.

There are lots of pro wrestlers and bikers and sneering tough guys in this film, most of whom manage to keep a straight face as Stallone slaps them around. And there's dialog like this:

Hawk: "Tell you the truth, the truck is, uh, you know, the most important thing for me. I . . . I don't really . . . it doesn't matter if I, uh, become the champion or anything. That's, that's not the most important. . . . I . . . I need this truck."

Almost as inspiring as Rocky's night-before-the-fight heart-to-heart with Adrian, don't you think?

8. *Ladybugs.* For a guy who spent his career trying to get some respect, Rodney Dangerfield sure does nothing to earn it here. In what seems like a rejected script for a sitcom pilot, Rodney—glowing from the peroxide in his hair—plays a salesman who tries to butter up the boss by coaching his daughter's pathetic soccer team. How to win? Take an athletic boy and turn him into the team's 12-year-old "Tootsie."

Rodney's schtick, so brilliant when used to belittle the snobs in *Caddyshack*, seems misplaced on pre-teen girls. And it's sad to watch the boy-in-a-skirt played by Jonathan Brandis, a *Tiger Beat* heartthrob when this came out in 1992, who later hung himself. All in all, a very depressing experience.

9. *Johnny Be Good.* It is technically listed as a "comedy," but the only hilarious aspect about the 1988 movie is that they try to pass off 140-pound Anthony Michael Hall—so convincing as the nerdy brainiac in *The Breakfast Club* and *Sixteen Candles*—as a high school football hero.

The point, as much as we can figure, is to be a satire of college recruiting scandals, complete with willing cheerleaders, boosters in bad sports jackets and Jim McMahon posing in his underwear (how that relates to it all, we're not sure). Howard Cosell also plays himself, although not very convincingly. Jon Voight did it better in *Ali*.

The movie ends with a press conference scene, in which Hall's character, named Johnny Walker, is set to announce his choice of a college. The roomful of people, for some reason, end up in a massive brawl. It reminded us of the old *Three Stooges* two-reelers in which, when they ran out of script, they just let it devolve into a big pie fight.

One difference: The Stooges were funny.

10. *Who's Your Caddy?.* Intended as a *Caddyshack* rip-off for African-Americans, starring OutKast hip-hopper Antwan "Big Boi" Patton. The dialog boils down to this:

Hip black guys: "Wha's happenin', bro?"
Stuffy white guys: "Harumph!"
Repeat 246 times.
That, plus lots of farting.

80 SEARCHING FOR BOBBY FISCHER
(1993–PG)

SPORT: CHESS | STARS: JOE MANTEGNA, JOAN ALLEN, BEN KINGSLEY
DIRECTOR: STEVEN ZAILLIAN

For a brief moment, back in the Cold War year of 1972, chess was the hottest sport in America. A prodigy named Bobby Fischer went to Iceland and wrestled the world championship away from the Soviets in an event that made the gangly New Yorker an unlikely national hero and foreshadowed the 1980 Olympic Miracle on Ice.

Fischer is regarded as the greatest chess player of the 20th Century. As a boy, he defeated many of the world's grandmasters and prevailed in public displays, taking on as many as 50 top players simultaneously. He was initially indulged as a quirky personality practicing gamesmanship by complaining about the lighting, the size of

the board, even whining that the view from his hotel was "too nice."

Eventually, quirky became paranoid, and Fischer disappeared. He emerged occasionally to emit anti-Semitic outbursts and swear allegiance to religious cults. He renounced his citizenship, won one more competitive match in 1992 and died in exile in Iceland in 2008 at age 64.

There has never been another like him. But in the movie *Searching for Bobby Fischer*, a seven-year-old Manhattan boy suddenly appears to be the Next One.

Josh Waitzkin (Max Pomeranc) is that normal boy

who loves baseball and dinosaurs. One day he stumbles upon the hustlers playing three-minute speed chess at Washington Square Park, and he is hooked. Standing there for five minutes, he absorbs the intricacies of the game in a way that is invisible to even brilliant adults.

His parents are skeptical at first, but quickly convinced when Josh—sitting on two phone books to reach the board—disposes of anyone put against him. Josh's father, Fred (Joe Mantegna), a sportswriter, sees his own competitive juices stirred by his son's success. His mother (Joan Allen) is more concerned about how Josh can enjoy his talent without losing his right to enjoy childhood. The movie does a great job of juggling the blessing and curse that a special gift presents.

Beyond his parents, Josh has two influences: His coach Bruce Pandolfini (Ben Kingsley), who recognizes the youngster's brilliance but wants him to develop a winner's mean streak; and a wizened player from the park named Vinnie (Laurence Fishburne), who wants Josh to enjoy the game for what it is.

This is the kind of story that could be told about any individual sport where young phenoms excel—tennis, gymnastics, figure skating. For a parent, there is a battle between developing the talent to its fullest and letting the child lead a normal life. For the child, there is pressure and the risk of burnout by high school.

"Maybe it's better not to be the best," Josh says to his father early on. "Then you can lose and it's still okay."

Max Pomeranc, who plays Josh, was picked for the role not just for his acting ability (this was his debut), but also because he was ranked among the 100 best child chess players in America. Good choice. It's clear in how he moves the pieces and studies the board that the little boy isn't just faking it.

Presenting chess on film isn't exactly like presenting football. There isn't much action to make it exciting. But director Steve Zaillian, more known as a script writer (*Gangs of New York, American Gangster*) than a director, does as best as is possible. Pawns fly off the board, kings are toppled, little hands pound the speed clocks. This is chess as if it were shot by NFL Films. Indeed, it won the 1993 Oscar for best cinematography.

Throughout the movie, grainy black-and-white video footage of Fischer keeps popping up, with young Josh telling the story of Fischer's genius and frailties. It is as if the ghost lurks over the boy, to the point where in one scene, Josh sits under a photo of Fischer's haunting eyes.

Searching for Bobby Fischer is based on a true story and was adapted from a book written by Fred Waitzkin, Josh's true-life father. It is good to know that Josh survived his childhood, went on to win two U.S. Junior Chess championships in his teens and now, in his thirties, has moved on to become a martial arts champion.

"I consider myself a happy and balanced man," he said in a 2003 interview.

The same could never be said of the real Bobby Fischer.

👍 **CHEERS:** This is a superbly acted movie. Beyond the powerful leads, there's a terrific supporting cast. Small roles are aptly played by William H. Macy, David Paymer and Dan Hedaya. And make sure to catch Laura Linney's brilliant humiliation when, as Josh's skeptical school teacher, she is publicly dressed down by his father, who tells her, "He's better at this 'chess thing' than you'll ever be at anything."

👎 **JEERS:** Children: all good. Parents: all overbearing. Okay, we get it already.

✏ **WHAT THEY WROTE AT THE TIME:** "The real star is screenwriter and director Steve Zaillian [who] introduces us to a world we've never seen before, an arcane universe full of lifelong contenders, exalted winners, madly obsessive parents, and over-motivated youth missing out on the golden years of normal childhood. Never were the emotions this roundly affected—around a simple board game."—Desson Howe, *Washington Post*

🎬 **PIVOTAL SCENE:** Ranked No. 1 at the New York State children's tournament, Josh tanks his first match against an obviously inferior opponent. Fred Waitzkin is furious and, outside in the rain, berates him. Why did you lose, he demands to know. Did you drop your focus? Did you bring out your queen too early?

Josh absorbs it all, his legs tucked into his chest as rain falls on his head. Finally, he looks up at his enraged father and asks, "Why are you standing so far away from me?"

In an instant, Fred Waitzkin realizes that the winning has become more important to him than to his son. The pressure he has applied has made chess a burden and driven a wedge between them.

◀ **CASTING CALL:** Many of the world's great chess players have cameo roles—including the real Josh Waitzkin and Bruce Pandolfini. We'll give you extra credit for spotting Roman Dzindzichashvili. Or spelling his name.

★ **SPORTS-ACTION GRADE:** D. C'mon, this is chess after all. The closest we get to real action is watching Josh's father, a sportswriter, covering a Yankees-Blue Jays game from the press box. Plus, we get a scene of Little League ball.

✔ **REALITY CHECK:** In that Little League scene, the seven-year-old catcher flashes a two-finger sign to the seven-year-old pitcher. What, was he gonna throw the slider?

🍎 **BET YOU DIDN'T KNOW:** The seemingly cold-blooded, but ultimately sad character of Jonathan Poe—Josh's young rival—is based on real-life prodigy Jeff Sarwer. In real life, Sarwer went on to win the World Under-10 Championships. Soon afterward he and his sister were taken from the custody of their father, who had his children living in a car, not attending school and driving around from tournament to tournament.

🟥 **BEST LINE:** In his efforts to make his prodigy more coldblooded, coach Pandolfini explains that he needs to develop "contempt" for his opponents.

Pandolfini: "It means to hate them. You have to hate them, Josh. They hate you."

Josh: "But I don't hate them."

Pandolfini: "Well, you'd better start. Bobby Fischer held the world in contempt."

Josh: "I'm not him."

Pandolfini: "You're telling me."

🍎 **BET YOU DIDN'T KNOW II:** When the movie came out, Fischer briefly emerged from hiding to denounce it as part of the Jewish conspiracy against him and an attempt just to make money off his name.

😵 **"I KNOW THAT GUY":** The bearded and wonkish chess player whom Josh disposes of within minutes during his visit to the Metropolitan Chess Club is future *Monk* star Tony Shalhoub.

🎞 **IF YOU LIKED THIS, YOU'LL LIKE:** *Finding Forrester*, the 2000 Sean Connery vehicle about a reclusive author's friendship with a teenaged writing prodigy.

👁 **REPEATED WATCHING QUOTIENT:** Once every few years or so, whenever you need a reminder that children ought to be allowed to enjoy their childhood.

81 REBOUND: THE LEGEND OF EARL "THE GOAT" MANIGAULT

(1996–R)

SPORT: BASKETBALL | STARS: DON CHEADLE, JAMES EARL JONES, FOREST WHITAKER, ERIQ LA SALLE | DIRECTOR: ERIQ LA SALLE

Rebound, one of HBO's better docudramas, opens with two powerful scenes. First, we visit the actual retirement ceremony of Kareem Abdul-Jabbar. The NBA's all-time scoring leader smiles in an oversized rocking chair presented as a gift, and then answers questions from Los Angeles Lakers broadcasting legend Chick Hearn.

"Who," Hearn wants to know, "was the best player you ever faced?"

"Well," ponders Jabbar, "if I was limited to one—that would have to be The Goat."

Quick cut to a Harlem street, where a drug-addled man stumbles in pain before passing out in the middle of an intersection. A crowd gathers.

"Did you hit him?" a woman asks the closest motorist. "Is he dead? Who is he?"

"Just another junkie," says the dismissive driver, getting back into his car.

The junkie, of course, is the very same "Goat"—Earl Manigault—of whom Jabbar speaks reverentially. And the plotline is quickly established: How did Manigault devolve from a 1960s playground legend to a desperate drug addict in less than a decade?

Consider it a cautionary tale. *Rebound* is a story of poor choices and wasted talent. And, in the end—almost in epilogue form—of redemption. The movie has some plot holes and hoary clichés, but ranks behind only *Hoop Dreams* and *He Got Game* in showing the seduction and exploitation of aspiring inner-city players. It also has some terrific acting turns, most notably by Don Cheadle as The Legend himself.

We first meet Earl Manigault as a 14-year-old who practices hoops all day wearing ankle weights. He quickly shocks the older playground stars with his abil-

ity to grab a coin off the backboard rim, as well as perform a double dunk—catching his first jam and stuffing it back in the net before hitting the ground. In a brilliant casting move, the shy teen is played by Colin Cheadle—Don's brother—who looks, well, exactly like a younger version of the star actor.

The older ballplayers lure the kid into their lifestyle. He experiments with drugs and winds up being expelled from Benjamin Franklin High the day before his team is to play for the city championship. That sets up the movie for Rescue No. 1, in which playground director Holcombe Rucker (Forest Whitaker)—the founder of the now-famous pro-am tournament that takes place in Harlem every summer—sees potential in the kid and moves to protect him. Rucker steers The Goat to a South Carolina prep school, where he morphs from Colin to Don Cheadle. He also learns to read, knot a tie and impregnate Evonne (Monica Calhoun), the prettiest girl in school.

The Goat boasts of scholarship offers from Indiana and North Carolina. But the prep school headmaster (James Earl Jones) pushes him to tiny Johnson C. Smith College because, we later find out, that is where he graduated. So The Goat ends up laboring in a tiny Southern gym for a *Hoosiers*-style "pass-it-four-times" coach (Clarence Williams III), who aims to cure him of his "schoolyard n——r" hot dogging.

Needless to say, this does not work out. And so begins the descent—as The Goat quits the team by heaving the ball deep into the stands—into hell. He returns to Harlem and, within six months, is a full-fledged heroin addict, begging and stealing to support his habit.

The back half of the movie is painful to watch. The

Goat's pal Diego (Eriq La Salle)—who has returned from Vietnam with no hands—ODs and dies in his arms. In another scene, he hides from wife Evonne and his young son, not wanting them to see him as a junkie. Finally, he is arrested. In a wrenching scene, he goes cold turkey behind prison bars.

And here comes Rescue No. 2. A kindly cop, recognizing The Goat from his playground days, hands him a copy of Pete Axthelm's great book, *The City Game*, which lauds Manigault as Harlem's best-ever street player, but also as "the one star who didn't go on." Reading the book aloud on his cell floor, crying, Manigault becomes inspired to give his failed life another shot.

Ten months later he is out. He confronts neighborhood drug kingpin Legrand (Michael Beach), challenging him to remove the dealers and dice players from Rucker Playground. The Goat, back in his favorite element, starts a youth league and begins his new life.

The rise seems abrupt and a little too easy. *Rebound* is a bit of a roller coaster—straight up, then straight down, then up again. But even if the redemption didn't go quite that smoothly, it is based on a true story. And it leaves you wondering what might have been if Manigault had made better choices along the way.

The final moments of *Rebound* show the real Earl Manigault in 1996. He is smiling at his playground, directing kids, running the "Goat Walk Away from Drugs Tournament." Sadly, two years later, Manigault died from congestive heart failure. Doctors said his system was weakened by the years of drug abuse.

📖 **CHEERS:** There's a terrific soundtrack running through the movie that reflects the time period, starting with early-60s Motown and ending with Stevie Wonder's "A Place in the Sun."

🚩 **JEERS:** Too much here fails the credibility test. A hardened drug dealer would listen to a former junkie and walk away from his territory? Not in any world we've ever seen.

✍ **WHAT THEY WROTE AT THE TIME:** "With its TV-movie-of-the-week style, *Rebound* is painful to watch, and never takes you anywhere every other true-life drug-tragedy film hasn't. Still, any fan interested in the mythology of the game will find it irresistible."—Joe Tarr, *Knoxville Metro Pulse*

☺ **GOOFS:** It's pretty obvious that all the basketball rims have been moved down to eight feet to allow actors to appear able to dunk.

✓ **REALITY CHECK:** In the first scene, as we noted, Kareem Abdul-Jabbar cites Manigault as the best he has ever faced. And then, as the movie goes on, they never actually play against each other. Goat was suspended from his high school team the day before it was to meet Alcindor's (at that time Abdul-Jabbar was still known as Lew Alcindor) Power Memorial High for the 1965 New York City championship.

BROADCASTER:

"WHO WAS THE BEST PLAYER YOU EVER FACED?"

KAREEM ABDUL-JABBAR:

"IF I WAS LIMITED TO ONE, THAT WOULD HAVE TO BE THE GOAT."

REPEATED WATCHING QUOTIENT: Only worth multiple viewings if you're trying to scare someone away from drugs.

PIVOTAL SCENE: The Goat, as a college freshman, is chafing under the tough treatment of his coach, who preaches, "Basketball is a team sport, not a personal showcase." At halftime of one game, he is visited by his prep school headmaster, who has come to tell The Goat that his mentor, Mr. Rucker, has died back home in Harlem. The kid is crestfallen.

Moments later, the college coach signals The Goat off the bench, sending him in with the warning, "This is college ball, not one of those Rucker jive-ass tournaments." Of course, the kid goes wild, twisting and dunking and performing every street trick he can. He is immediately pulled, tosses the ball into the seats and quits.

That was the end of Manigault's brief college career and, ultimately, his hopes of turning pro.

CASTING CALL: That's Kevin Garnett as Wilt Chamberlain and Joe Smith playing Connic Hawkins.

"I KNOW THAT GUY": Glynn Turman, who plays the coach who originally recruits The Goat to Johnson C. Smith, went on to portray corrupt Baltimore Mayor Clarence Royce in HBO's *The Wire*.

SPORTS-ACTION GRADE: B-minus. You've seen these schoolyard hoops scenes before, most probably in *White Men Can't Jump*. Too many low angle shots looking up at guys catching the ball and dunking.

BEST LINE: In his first game against grown men, 14-year-old Earl stuns them with his talent.
Legrand: "What's your name, schoolboy?"
Earl: "Earl. Earl Manigault."
Legrand: "Did he say Nanny Goat? Okay, Nanny Goat."
And thus was the nickname born.

BET YOU DIDN'T KNOW: Actor Daryl Mitchell, who portrays Earl's playground buddy (and future NBA player) Dean Meminger, was paralyzed from the waist down in a 2001 motorcycle accident. He has continued his career, most notably as the wheelchair-bound bowling alley manager in the TV series *Ed*.

IF YOU LIKED THIS, YOU'LL LIKE: *Hooked: The Legend of Demetrius "Hook" Mitchell*, a 2003 documentary on another fallen playground star. While you're at it, we recommend you pick up Axthelm's book, *The City Game: Basketball from The Garden to the Playgrounds*.

Perhaps there are still neighborhoods where all the kids gather every day to play baseball from dawn until dusk. Where the joy of the sport is so overriding that no one even bothers to keep score. Where there is no talk of steroids or salary arbitration; not even aluminum bats.

We would love that place.

That utopia does exist in writer/director David M. Evans' *The Sandlot*, a childhood memoir where baseball means everything to a pack of pre-teens. If you grew up—or wish you had—in a world of tree houses and amusement parks, of oiling up a glove and playing a night game under the glare of Fourth of July fireworks, this movie will take you to that balmy, reassuring place.

The story focuses on Scotty Smalls (Tom Guiry), a boy who is uprooted from somewhere in Middle America to a dusty Los Angeles suburb in the summer of 1962. In a neighborhood of baseball-centric boys, he can't fit in. Scotty doesn't know how to play and doesn't know the sport's history (he thinks Babe Ruth was a woman).

Those shortcomings ostracize him from the sandlot gang, until Benjamin Franklin Rodriguez (Mike Vitar), the star and leader of the group of eight, discreetly teaches him how to catch, throw and hit—as well as the difference between The Bambino and Bambi. The outsider egghead kid becomes one of the crew, headed for the best summer of his life. And eight players conveniently becomes a team of nine.

It takes a huge suspension of critical analysis to believe that Scotty could graduate from nerdy klutz-boy to competent ballplayer within weeks. But *The Sandlot* expects you not to ask too many questions. The movie is told from the perspective of a child (Scotty, as a grownup, serves as narrator), and is full of awe and hyperbole. At its best moments, *The Sandlot* aims to be a warm weather version of *A Christmas Story*. It doesn't quite reach those heights, but some of the better scenes will remind you of that Jean Shepherd memory of childhood or Bill Bryson's great fifties memoir, *The Life and Times of the Thunderbolt Kid*.

The best scene actually has nothing to do with baseball. On a day too hot to play, the boys travel to the municipal pool, where they splash around too much and gawk at chesty lifeguard Wendy Peffercorn (Marley Shelton) in her drop-dead red bathing suit. They all dream of kissing her, but how?

The ballsiest of the boys—marvelously named Squints Palledorous (a dead ringer, you *Nick at Nite* fans, for Ernie from the old *My Three Sons* show), sinks to the bottom of the pool and feigns drowning. Which begins to verge on actual drowning. Wendy dives in, pulls his skinny 12-year-old body out and begins to administer mouth-to-mouth. Soon enough, the kiss of life turns into the kiss of *his* life, earning Squints a slap and, later, an admiring wink from Miss Peffercorn. (We learn at the end of the movie that, some day, scrawny Squints will marry Wendy and she will bear him nine children. That may be the furthest stretch of reality in the entire film.)

Adolescent fantasies and all-day baseball games make for a pretty good summer. But the fun ends when the boys' last ball is smacked out of the sandlot into a fenced junkyard inhabited by "The Beast"—a fearsome dog that, in some scenes, looks like an escapee from *Jurassic Park* (again, you have to buy the exaggeration). The legend, passed down over the years, is that the snarling, slobbering animal has eaten 173 boys. No one is quite sure, but no one wants to become No. 174.

Scotty, always trying to fit in, runs home to grab a new ball. This time, he becomes the batter who swats it over the fence, right into the waiting jaws of The Beast. Turns out, that baseball, swiped from his stepdad's trophy case, was a prized possession—autographed by the real Babe Ruth. If not recovered, as Scotty recalls in the narration, "My life was over. I had hit a chunk of priceless history into the mouth of a monster."

The back end of the movie focuses on the boys' ingenious ways of trying to rescue the keepsake ball. It concludes with a surprising and poignant meeting with James Earl Jones, who plays the mysterious owner of the junkyard and its larger-than-life canine.

🍺 **CHEERS:** Given that the movie is a memoir of childhood, Evans does a nice job of leaving intrusive adults out of the story. The boys play sandlot ball without grownup coaches ruining the fun, as it should be. Only Jones—whose brief role is critical to the plot—has much impact. Karen Allen and Denis Leary, who play Scotty Smalls' parents, are little more than background characters.

🍺 **JEERS:** Truth be told, most of the kids in the movie couldn't act their way into the junior high school play.

✏️ **WHAT THEY WROTE AT THE TIME:** "Yearning to be *The Natural* of the *Stand By Me* set, it falls short. But it's in there pitching, and in ways you can't hate even as you wish it had thrown a few more high hard ones."—Jay Carr, *Boston Globe*

✔️ **REALITY CHECK:** The film is set in Los Angeles, yet all of the boys are obsessed with Babe Ruth—including details of the 1932 called shot and The Sultan of Swat's odd mannerisms. Something tells us that young Los Angeles baseball fans in 1962 would be more fixated on Don Drysdale and Maury Wills.

"I KNOW THAT GAL": Shelton, every adolescent boy's dream as lifeguard Wendy Peffercorn, grew up to be every man's dream as Dr. Dakota Block in the Quentin Tarantino-Robert Rodriguez 2007 anthology film *Grindhouse*.

☝️ **DON'T FAIL TO NOTICE:** Benny has a dream, where the ghost of Babe Ruth tells him how to recover the priceless baseball. At the end of the scene, as Ruth prepares to leave, he pauses and scoops a baseball card off the shelf. "I don't know why," he asks Benny, "but can I have this?" It happens to be a 1961 Topps card of Hank Aaron, the man who would go on to break Ruth's career home run mark.

★ **SPORTS-ACTION GRADE:** C-minus. Hey, it's Little League-age kids. How good can it get?

🍎 **BET YOU DIDN'T KNOW:** Actor Pablo P. Vitar, who briefly portrays the grown-up Benny Rodriguez as a player for the Dodgers, is the real-life brother of actor Mike Vitar, who portrays Benny as a child.

☺ **GOOFS:** Wooden bats are used throughout the movie, but the "ping" sound effect is clearly that of aluminum bats.

✴️ **IF YOU LIKED THIS, YOU'LL LIKE:** The 1990s ABC show *Boy Meets World*. Five of the nine members of *The Sandlot's* baseball team had recurring roles on that series at some point during its eight-season run.

👁 **REPEATED WATCHING QUOTIENT:** Not worth it, unless you need to find a way to kill 101 minutes with a 10-year-old who stops by your house.

83 THE LIFE AND TIMES OF HANK GREENBERG (1999–PG)

SPORT: BASEBALL | STARS: HANK GREENBERG, CHARLIE GEHRINGER, WALTER MATTHAU
DIRECTOR: AVIVA KEMPNER

Aviva Kempner spent 13 years researching, editing and writing *The Life and Times of Hank Greenberg.* That is a long time to spend immersed in one story, but this is quite a story and Kempner tells it extremely well in this meticulously constructed documentary.

Greenberg was a power-hitting first baseman with the Detroit Tigers through the 1930s and '40s. He was also Jewish, which made him a symbol of hope for some and target of hate for others.

When most people think of bigotry in baseball, they think of Jackie Robinson, who broke the color line in 1947, but Greenberg faced many of the same issues more than a decade earlier.

There was rampant anti-Semitism in the 1930s, and it was not uncommon for Jewish people, especially those involved in sports, to change their names. Greenberg, a strapping six-foot-four, 210-pounder from the Bronx, refused to do so. He maintained his name—Henry Benjamin Greenberg—and his pride in his ethnic identity made him a hero in the Jewish community.

Greenberg understood the responsibility that rested on his shoulders. He did not resent it. Rather, he said, it made him work harder. "If I failed," he said, "I wasn't a bum, I was a Jewish bum." He would not allow that to happen.

Greenberg compiled a .313 batting average in 13 major league seasons. He won four home run titles and was the American League's Most Valuable Player in 1935 and 1940. He made the first serious run at Babe Ruth's single season home run record, banging out 58 homers in 1938. He may have broken the mark of 60 if opposing teams did not stop pitching to him late in the season.

The film suggests the strategy was motivated—at least in part—by anti-Semitism. Greenberg, in an interview recorded before his death in 1986, shrugs off the idea. He says he had a fair shot at The Babe's mark and just fell short. He says he didn't think that much about hitting home runs. He felt the more important statistic was runs batted in and he took pride in the fact that he led the major leagues in that category three times.

"I liked being the guy who comes up in the clutch, changes the ball game, makes all the difference," says Greenberg, who had a career-high 183 RBIs in 1937.

Kempner establishes the context for Greenberg's story through interviews with former teammates and opponents, broadcasters and journalists, and assorted celebrities who bring their own perspective to the film. Some documentaries err in using actors and politicians as talking heads simply for their star power. Kempner uses her celebrities very selectively and effectively. They all have something to say about Greenberg and they say it well.

Actor Walter Matthau says, "Growing up in the Bronx in the '30s, you thought of nothing but baseball and Hank Greenberg." Matthau says after he became a success in Hollywood he joined the Beverly Hills Tennis Club, not because he wanted to play tennis, but because he wanted to have lunch with Greenberg, who often dined there.

Attorney Alan Dershowitz talks about Greenberg's style of play, his imposing physical stature, and the power he displayed on the field. "He was," Dershowitz says, "what they said Jews could never be." Hammering Hank's success was shared by Jewish people of all ages who still were trying to fit in. "Baseball was our way of showing that we were as American as anyone else," he says.

As Senator Carl Levin says: "Because [Greenberg] was a hero, I was a little bit of a hero, too."

Actor Michael Moriarty, the grandson of a former major league umpire, talks about his grandfather telling stories about the bigotry he saw directed at Greenberg, the taunts of "sheenie" and "kike" coming from the bleachers and the opposing dugout. Greenberg never complained and never responded except to lash out a few more hits and help the Tigers to four World Series.

Kempner's film shows Greenberg to be a gentle and modest man who loved baseball, loved his country (he served in the Army during World War II and missed three seasons right in the prime of his career) and left the game with no regrets.

A highlight of the film is a moment from the 1947 season, Greenberg's final season in baseball. He is playing with Pittsburgh in the National League as Jackie Robinson is in his rookie year with the Brooklyn Dodgers. The scene shows Greenberg, who is on his way out, encouraging Robinson, who is just breaking in, to ignore the bigotry and play his game. It is as if a torch is being passed.

🍺 **CHEERS:** Kempner opens the film with "Take Me Out to the Ball Game" sung in Yiddish.

🍺 **JEERS:** There is very little to criticize. It follows the traditional documentary structure, there are not a lot of bells and whistles, but it suits the times and the subject.

✒ **WHAT THEY WROTE AT THE TIME:** "One would hardly think a baseball documentary could say so much about the nature of heroism and the nature of America. But the joyous, moving *The Life and Times of Hank Greenberg* is exceptional on both counts."—Peter Stack, *The San Francisco Chronicle*

💬 **BEST LINE:** Walter Matthau: "Hank Greenberg was part of my dreams, part of my aspirations. I wanted to be Hank Greenberg."

🍎 **BET YOU DIDN'T KNOW:** Greenberg's other nickname was "Hankus Spankus."

☞ **DON'T FAIL TO NOTICE:** Greenberg was a five-time All Star and two-time MVP in an era when two other legendary first basemen—Lou Gehrig of the Yankees and Jimmy Foxx of the Philadelphia A's—were still in the league. As Bill James notes in the *Historical Baseball Abstract*: "That is probably the most remarkable concentration of talent at one position in one league that there has ever been."

★ **SPORTS-ACTION GRADE:** A-minus. It is black and white footage, most of it shot from the press box. So it isn't sexy, but, boy, that Greenberg swing is sweet.

DOCUMENTARY FILMS: KEEPING IT REAL

The beauty of sports documentaries is that, unlike traditional Hollywood films, there is no one stacking the deck. There is no writer scripting the big game, there is no director telling the other team to miss tackles.

It is reality filmmaking which means the producers, like the fans, are not guaranteed a happy ending. They roll the cameras and take their chances.

When Steve James, Peter Gilbert and Fred Marx began chronicling basketball prodigies William Gates and Arthur Agee for *Hoop Dreams*, they had no way of knowing where their stories would lead or how they would end. Cutting down the nets at the Final Four? Signing a million dollar contract in the NBA? Or perhaps blowing out a knee and seeing those dreams evaporate?

No matter how it turned out, the filmmakers knew that in 250 hours of videotape shot over four years, they would have a compelling story. It might be a story of triumph, it might be a story of disappointment, but it would be a story nonetheless. It would be real, not some screenwriter's fantasy.

Few sports documentaries are released as theatrical films. Why? They are not money-makers. *Hoop Dreams* surpassed Michael Moore's *Roger & Me* as the highest-grossing non-musical documentary, but it still took in only $8 million at the box office. The 2005 film *Murderball*, the story of a wheelchair rugby team, was acclaimed by critics but made just $1.5 million in theaters.

One of the greatest sports documentaries ever made, *Olympia* was never shown in the United States—but that was due to politics. *Olympia* was a four-hour film about the 1936 Summer Olympics in Berlin produced and directed by Leni Riefenstahl. Because Riefenstahl was linked to the Nazi Party, *Olympia* was widely characterized as a propaganda film, not a sports film.

When Riefenstahl came to the United States in 1938 to promote the film, protestors marched outside her hotel and Hollywood heavyweights Walt Disney and Gary Cooper cancelled meetings with her. She had one private screening of *Olympia* for a few studio people and while everyone agreed the film was a masterpiece, no U.S. distributor would touch it. With the world on the brink of war, Nazis were a tough sell.

Viewed today, *Olympia* does not seem particularly political. It is certainly not on a level with *Triumph of the Will*, her 1935 film about the Nuremberg rally which romanticized many of the ideas Adolf Hitler put forth in his book *Mein Kampf*. Author Susan Sontag described *Triumph of the Will* as "the most purely propagandistic film ever made." *Olympia*, by contrast, is much more about the athletes and the competition.

Riefenstahl pioneered some new techniques including mounting a camera on a rail so it could move with the runners in track events, and having photographers leap off the high board with the divers to film them all the way to the water. She also was the first to use a blimp for overhead shots. Her airship was the Hindenburg, which later crashed in flames in Lakehurst, N.J.

Riefenstahl had 60 cameramen who shot more than 1.3 million feet of film. While *Olympia* celebrated the German athletes, Riefenstahl also devoted a great deal of time to American gold medal winner Jesse Owens, who was shunned by Hitler because he was black. If Riefenstahl was truly making a propaganda film, she would have left Owens on the cutting room floor.

"This picture is a triumph of the camera and an epic of the screen," wrote the *Los Angeles Times* in 1938. "Contrary to rumor, it is in no way a propaganda movie and as propaganda for any nation its effect is definitely zero."

Steve Sabol, president of NFL Films, considers *Olympia* the finest sports documentary ever made.

"The diving sequence awakened in me the mythic nature of sport," Sabol said. "The innovative camera angles, the editorial selection and flow, the orchestral music and the background of puffy clouds turned this athletic competition into an abstract but compelling work of art. I insist that every new cameraman and filmmaker at NFL Films take the time to study this six-minute sequence."

We included four modern documentaries among our top 100 films: *Hoop Dreams, When We Were Kings, Murderball* and *The Life and Times of Hank Greenberg*. All four were theatrical releases and *When We Were Kings*, a film about the 1974 Muhammad Ali-George Foreman fight known as "The Rumble in the Jungle," won the Academy Award for Best Documentary in 1996.

We compiled a list of 11 more outstanding sports documentaries, some of which were made for television. They are listed in order of release.

The Violent World of Sam Huff (1960). A documentary produced for the CBS series *The Twentieth Century*. The show, hosted by Walter Cronkite, normally focused on issues such as space exploration and global politics. But in 1960, the network turned its eye to pro football, which was just achieving national prominence.

They put a microphone on New York Giants linebacker Sam Huff and followed him through a week of training camp. People saw the inner workings of pro football: the classroom study, the dorm life, the reality of playing with pain. What they remember most is the sound of the hitting. It is a staple of NFL Films today, but no one had heard it back then. The ferocious collisions made a lasting impression.

"To this day, people still ask me about that show," Huff said in a 2006 interview. "It helped put the NFL on the map."

The Endless Summer (1966). Bruce Brown made several films about surfing, but this is the one that made the biggest splash. It came out at a time when most Americans were just becoming aware of surfing. Thanks to the Beach Boys, and Jan and Dean, even kids in Iowa were talking about "catching a wave" and "hanging ten." They were ready to see a film about the real thing.

Endless Summer follows two surfers, Mike Hynson

and Robert August, as they travel the world in search of the perfect wave. The photography is spectacular, especially the scenes in Australia, and the dialog between the surfer dudes as they get all spiritual and ponder the meaning of life is an amusing slice of the "Wow, this is heavy, man" Sixties.

Pro Football, Pottstown, Pa. (1971). NFL Films has done many compelling pieces, but none better than this loving study of minor league football. It was supposed to be a five-minute feature for the *NFL Today*, but it grew into a one-hour CBS special that follows the Pottstown Firebirds of the Atlantic Coast Football League through the 1970 season.

The players earn $100 a game, live in an old boarding house and play their games on a dusty high school field. Most have dreams of one day making it to the NFL. A receiver named Jack Dolbin sits on a cinder block (he has no furniture) and talks about putting medical school on hold in hopes of making the big time. It is a great scene made even better by the fact that Dolbin later signed with the Denver Broncos and played on their first Super Bowl team.

The film was written and produced by Phil Tuckett, who was a wide receiver for the minor league Las Vegas Cowboys before playing for the San Diego Chargers in 1968. Steve Sabol did most of the camera work.

Baseball: A Film by Ken Burns (1994). A nine-part series broadcast on PBS, it uses the same storytelling techniques as Burns' films on the Civil War and Jazz. It is divided into nine "innings", each one exploring a different theme with vintage photographs, film footage and interviews with players, poets and politicians.

The series does a fine job tracing the history of the game: the heroes, the scoundrels, the triumphs, the scandals. It does not shy away from discussing the shame of major league owners refusing to sign black players prior to Jackie Robinson. The series is at its best when it profiles players such as Babe Ruth and Walter Johnson and reminds us just how great they really were.

"Baseball is a game in which every player is measured against the ghosts who have gone before," Burns says in the script. He makes the point very eloquently.

Dogtown and Z-Boys (2001). This documentary about daredevil skateboarders (Z-Boys) from a depressed section of Venice Beach, Ca. (Dogtown), was called "radically stylish" by *Newsweek's* David Ansen. Even if you have no interest in skateboarding—and frankly, we don't—this film has enough energy and attitude to keep you entertained.

The Z-Boys are the Zephyr Skating Team and their freestyle acrobatics are the basis for today's X-Games. The film laments the sport "selling out" to the corporate sponsors who are only interested in making a buck. The original Z-Boys were in it for the thrills and it is with a note of sadness they acknowledge the boarders' loss of innocence.

With narration by Sean Penn and music by Black Sabbath, *Dogtown and Z-Boys* is a film intent on standing apart from the mainstream.

Do You Believe in Miracles? (2002). The story of the United States hockey team's stunning gold medal performance at the 1980 Winter Olympics has been told many times, including the Disney film *Miracle*, which made our top 100. But this HBO documentary is worth watching because it provides a fresh perspective.

There are interviews with the U.S. players and coach Herb Brooks (the show was done shortly before his death) and that's fine, but it is particularly interesting to hear from the Soviet players and learn what they were thinking as they watched the Americans roll around the ice celebrating their upset victory.

"We were so used to winning," defenseman Zinetula Bilyaletdinov says. "We watched how emotional they were and we had forgotten that. I was almost jealous of their emotions."

Dale (2007). This portrait of racing legend Dale Earnhardt Sr. played in theaters on the Nextel (now Sprint) Cup circuit. Earnhardt rarely talked about himself, but here he is interviewed while he fishes in a lake near his home. Away from the track, Earnhardt is relaxed and open. Asked what drives him, he says it is fear. Not fear of death on the track, but fear of failure. It is a surprising admission coming from the man known as "The Intimidator."

There is a touching moment when a girl in a wheelchair gives Earnhardt a penny for luck at the 1998 Daytona 500. He kisses her on the cheek, then goes out and wins Daytona for the first time in his career.

***The First Saturday in May* (2007).** That is the day the Kentucky Derby is run each year, but this film is about how the horses *get to* the starting gate at Churchill Downs. Brothers John and Brad Hennegan shot 500 hours of film during the 2005-06 racing season tracing the path of six horses, all considered Derby contenders.

The film introduces you to the horses, the owners and the trainers, and over the course of two hours you get to know them all. There are tender moments, such as watching Jazil nuzzle the hand of his trainer. It is heartbreaking to see Alex Matz, son of trainer Michael Matz, petting the magnificent Barbaro knowing what would happen to the horse later that season.

"You try not to get too close," says trainer Dan Hendricks, feeding a carrot to his horse Brother Derek. "But some horses just touch you."

Some films do, too. This is one of them.

***Bigger, Stronger, Faster* (2008).** Morgan Spurlock was praised for a 2004 documentary called *Super Size Me.* Christopher Bell took a different approach to the same idea. Where Spurlock grew by wolfing down Big Macs and fries, Bell's subjects used steroids. His film is a revealing study of the juicer's world.

This is Bell's first documentary and his technique is influenced by Oscar-winner Michael Moore. Like Moore, Bell does his own on-camera interviews and with his bulky frame, khaki shorts and baseball cap, he seems almost cartoonish, but you soon realize this is a smart guy who knows his stuff.

Bell doesn't condemn the use of steroids nor does he condone it. He offers views on both sides and, more than anything, puts it in context and allows the viewer to arrive at his or her own conclusions. Good interviews with people on both sides of the issue make this a documentary that both informs and entertains.

***Black Magic* (2008).** This four-hour documentary aired over two nights on ESPN during the NCAA basketball tournament, reminding young and old that before the days of March Madness there was a time when the sport was as racially segregated as major league baseball.

The film profiles coaches and players who excelled at so-called black colleges such as Winston-Salem State, Tennessee State and Fisk. It tells the story of those who achieved fame, such as Earl "The Pearl" Monroe (who co-produced the film) and Dick Barnett. It also tells of players such as Delano Middleton, who had just as much promise but fell victim to the times. Middleton, a high school standout who planned to attend South Carolina State, was shot and killed at a civil rights demonstration in 1968.

There is fascinating footage from the 1940s of Coach John McLendon directing his team, North Carolina College for Negroes, in the four-corners offense, the same offense Dean Smith later used to win an NCAA Championship at North Carolina. It makes the point that the small schools played a brand of basketball that was ahead of its time.

***Harvard Beats Yale, 29-29* (2008).** Called "preposterously entertaining" by Manohla Dargis of the *New York Times*, this film by Kevin Rafferty (a Harvard grad) succeeds on many levels.

First, it reconstructs the most famous game in the storied Harvard-Yale rivalry, a 1968 contest in which an underdog Harvard team rallies to tie Yale (which was unbeaten and ranked 16th in the nation) by scoring 16 points in the final 42 seconds. Hence the title, which is borrowed from the front page headline in the *Harvard Crimson.*

But what separates this film from other sports documentaries is the way Rafferty puts the game in the context of the tumultuous '60s. It adds another layer to the story knowing that on the Harvard team, a Vietnam veteran (safety Pat Conway) is lining up next to a member of the radical Students for a Democratic Society (middle guard Alex MacLean). Says MacLean: "We put all that aside."

There are amusing anecdotes such as now-famous-actor Tommy Lee Jones, a Harvard lineman, talking about his roommate Al Gore playing "Dixie" on the touch-tone phone in the dorms. Also, Bob Levin, the Yale fullback, talks about dating Meryl Streep, who was then a shy sophomore at Vassar.

84 TIN CUP (1996–R)

SPORT: GOLF | STARS: KEVIN COSTNER, RENE RUSSO, CHEECH MARIN
DIRECTOR: RON SHELTON

Eight years after *Bull Durham*, Kevin Costner and writer-director Ron Shelton teamed up again in *Tin Cup*. But while the original film was a tape-measure home run, the follow-up dies on the warning track.

This time the sport is golf. Shelton again tries for a quirky romantic comedy, but it doesn't work as well. Costner is a dissipated rascal named Roy "Tin Cup" McAvoy, who once was a promising golfer but now runs a broken-down driving range. McAvoy is similar to Crash Davis, the minor league catcher and philosopher Costner played in *Bull Durham*. He just isn't as much fun.

"Greatness courts failure," McAvoy says, explaining why he is content to live in a Winnebago with friend and part-time caddy Romeo (Cheech Marin) rather than pursue a career on the PGA tour. McAvoy has enough game to play with the big boys—and Costner's sweet swing makes you believe it—but he is an undisciplined and none-too-bright screw-up who refuses to play it safe even when it is the right thing to do.

"The word 'normal' and him don't often collide in the same sentence," explains one of McAvoy's cronies. No one says why, exactly. We're just left to wonder.

McAvoy is perfectly content hanging out at the driving range, drinking beer and counting armadillos until one day when Dr. Molly Griswold (Rene Russo) shows up asking for a golf lesson. She is blonde and willowy and, oh yes, she's dating David Simms (Don Johnson), who just happens to be a star on the PGA tour and McAvoy's former college teammate and nemesis.

Naturally, McAvoy falls for Molly. In an effort to prove he isn't a loser, he cleans himself up and enters the sectional qualifying for the U.S. Open. He makes it into the tournament and quicker than you can say "You Da Man," he is on the leaderboard, shooting a 62—the lowest score in Open history.

That's the problem with *Tin Cup*: Shelton takes ideas that worked in *Bull Durham* and inflates them to the point where you don't buy them anymore. In *Bull Durham*, Crash Davis sets a minor league home run record; in *Tin Cup*, McAvoy turns in the best round ever in a major championship. In *Bull Durham*, Susan Sarandon, the brainy love interest, is a teacher. Here, Sheldon ups the ante by making Molly a psychiatrist. In *Bull Durham*, Crash's romantic rival is a dim-witted teammate. This time his rival is a millionaire stud, exactly the kind of neatly packaged, corporate-sponsored, play-it-by-the-book pro McAvoy despises. So guess who winds up playing together in the final twosome at the Open? Guess who Molly roots for? It's all just a little much.

At the end, McAvoy and Simms are side by side in the 18th fairway, each man knowing a par will give him a tie for the lead. Simms chooses to play it safe. He decides to hit short of the water hazard and play for par. McAvoy sneers as Simms reaches for an iron.

"Fifteen years on the tour and you're still a fucking pussy," McAvoy says.

"Thirteen years on the driving range and you still think this game is about your testosterone count," Simms replies.

McAvoy, ever the thick-headed gambler, grabs his three wood. His shot hits the green 240 yards away, but it rolls back into the water. Rather than accept the two-stroke penalty and take a drop, McAvoy hits the three wood again from the same spot with the same result. He tries again. And again. Five shots in all, each one ending up in the water.

Finally on the sixth try, McAvoy not only clears the water but knocks the ball in the hole. The crowd goes wild, McAvoy walks onto the green to a standing ovation. Any sane person is thinking, "Why?" His score for the hole is a 12. He has just thrown away a chance to win the U.S. Open.

How, exactly, is this heroic?

It's not. Frankly, it is dumb.

Tin Cup has some fun moments, but for a Costner-Shelton collaboration it spends a lot of time in the rough.

CHEERS: Cheech Marin, half of the Cheech and Chong comedy team, is quite entertaining as McAvoy's wisecracking sidekick.

JEERS: The film plays slower than Phil Mickelson on Quaaludes. "At 2 hours and 13 minutes, *Tin Cup* is easily 30 minutes too long," said Robin Clifford of *Reeling Reviews*. "It takes a good 100 minutes to get to the film's point. I started to lose interest. I nearly lost consciousness, too."

WHAT THEY WROTE AT THE TIME: "Costner is back from his *Waterworld* shenanigans, acting in a scruffy *Bull Durham* style. No cowboy hats. No action hero stunts. Just an ordinary schlub who's gone beyond fallible to totally fallen."—Peter Stack, *San Francisco Chronicle*

BET YOU DIDN'T KNOW: The older couple whom Simms (Johnson) berates for asking for an autograph are actually Bill and Sharon Costner, Kevin's parents. The boy who is with them is Joe, Kevin's son.

SIGN OF THE TIMES: McAvoy is seen reading *Ring Magazine*. The cover story is: "Can Anyone Beat Mike Tyson?" I think we have learned the answer to that question.

CASTING CALL: John Leguizamo was considered for the part of Romeo, but the jaded and jowly Marin was a better choice.

BEST LINE: McAvoy: "Sex and golf are the two things you can enjoy even if you're not good at them."

SPORTS-ACTION GRADE: C. A number of PGA pros appear as themselves (Craig Stadler, Mickelson and Peter Jacobsen, among others) but the scenes drag on too long.

REPEATED WATCHING QUOTIENT: Once is enough.

MY FAVORITE SPORTS MOVIE: Dave Robinson, former Penn State linebacker and All-Pro with the Green Bay Packers: "The final scene where Kevin Costner hits five straight balls in the water reminds me of me. I would've done the same thing. It seems crazy, but as an athlete, you never want to give in."

85 ANY GIVEN SUNDAY (1999–R)

SPORT: FOOTBALL | STARS: AL PACINO, CAMERON DIAZ, JAMIE FOXX
DIRECTOR: OLIVER STONE

The term "any given Sunday" originated with Bert Bell, the NFL's commissioner from 1946 until his death in 1959. Bell said his goal was to create enough competitive balance that "on any given Sunday" the worst team in the NFL could knock off the best.

If Bell could see the NFL today, he would be pleased, because that's how things are in this era of parity. But he would have a heck of a time figuring out what's going on in the film that hijacks his famous phrase. *Any Given Sunday* isn't for old-school football guys.

One of the team owners is a gorgeous blonde (Cameron Diaz) who strolls through the locker room coolly surveying the prime cuts of beefcake. The team doctor is an evil snake (James Woods) who sends players onto the field with injuries that likely will cripple them for life. The players themselves are hopped-up sociopaths who live by a code that is somewhere between Caligula and Scarface.

And speaking of Scarface, the head coach is Al Pacino minus Tony Montana's white suit and machine-gun, but still in a wild-eyed rage, tossing F-bombs in every direction.

Welcome to the world of professional football as seen by director Oliver Stone.

Anyone familiar with Stone's filmography—*Platoon, Wall Street, The Doors, JFK, Natural Born Killers*, etc.—knows his work is provocative, political and often brutal. That's why the NFL refused to give this film its official blessing, which meant Stone could not use the names or uniforms of real NFL teams. He was forced to create his own league, but since the film is fiction it didn't really matter.

Any Given Sunday focuses on the Miami Sharks, a team owned by Christina Pagniacci (Diaz) and coached by Tony D'Amato (Pacino). She inherited the team from her late father, who was in it for the love of the game. Christina is as different from her father as Jimmy Choos are from Chuck Taylors. She is an ice-cold business-woman who is into making money.

Christina's father loved Tony, who was his coach and general manager, but she thinks Tony is a fossil whose time has passed. She hires a new offensive coordinator—a whiz kid named Nick Crozier (Aaron Eckhart) who calls plays from his laptop—and it is clear she is grooming him to be the next head coach. Tony sees the writing on the wall.

The clashes between Christina and Tony have the ring of truth. In today's NFL, with new owners taking over and old-timers trying to hang on, such friction is common. Tony tells Christina her father wouldn't approve of the way she is running things. She snaps, "Why the hell do you think my father put me in charge, you bullheaded moron?"

When the film opens, the Sharks are on their way to their third consecutive loss. Veteran quarterback Cap Rooney (Dennis Quaid) is injured and replaced by his untested backup, Willie Beamen (Jamie Foxx). Beamen is so nervous he throws up in the huddle, a scene Stone replays for us several times, including once in slow-motion.

But Beamen recovers to play well. He plays so well, in fact, he becomes an overnight sensation, "Steamin' " Willie Beamen. He is on magazine covers and partying in South Beach with groupies tugging at his Armani sleeves. He gets caught up in his fame, which puts him at odds with his coach and teammates.

"You're the goddamn quarterback," Tony tells him. "You know what that means? It's the top spot, kid. It's the guy who takes the fall. It's the guy everybody's looking at first, the leader of a team who will support you when they understand you, who'll break their ribs and their necks for you because they believe, because you make them believe."

Cap, of course, is that kind of quarterback. He and Tony have been together for years. They won a title with the Sharks, but that was years ago. Tony is faced with a tough decision: Does he put Cap back in the lineup or does he stay with Beamen, whose hot streak carried the

Sharks to the playoffs? What will it be, Tony, loyalty or winning?

Any Given Sunday has the familiar Oliver Stone touches—some call them conceits—such as shots cut so fast and in such bizarre fashion they feel like an LSD trip. (We're still trying to figure out how the Ben-Hur chariot race figures into the Sharks season.)

Opinions on the film break down along generational lines. Most establishment types pan it. Two-time Super Bowl-winning coach Mike Shanahan, who allowed Pacino to shadow him to prepare for his role, said, "I think [Pacino] is great, but I thought the movie was horrible."

Younger audiences, including current NFL players, like it. New Orleans Saints running back Reggie Bush calls *Any Given Sunday* "The most realistic and up-to-date football movie I've seen." Veteran running back Rudi Johnson said, "This movie gives you a different look at football. It covers a lot of angles about what it's really like to be a player, on and off the field."

Mike Leach, head coach at Texas Tech, is somewhere in the middle. "The opening scene did a great job of showing what it's like on the sideline during a game," Leach said. "The emotion, the confusion, the coach trying to keep it together, that's how it is. I didn't care for the movie as a whole—it went off in too many tangents—but those first few minutes my hair was standing up, it felt so real."

🍷 **CHEERS:** Two of the best performances are delivered by Pro Football Hall of Famers Jim Brown, who plays a coach, and Lawrence Taylor, who plays an aging All-Pro.

🍺 **JEERS:** The uniforms worn by the Dallas Knights look like leftovers from the Crusades.

🏈 **BET YOU DIDN'T KNOW:** Jamie Foxx gained 15 pounds pumping iron preparing to play quarterback Willie Beamen. He was bench-pressing more than 300 pounds.

☝ **DON'T FAIL TO NOTICE:** Cap Rooney's posh digs. It is the home of Dan Marino, the Miami Dolphins Hall of Fame quarterback.

✒ **WHAT THEY WROTE AT THE TIME:** "A rambunctious, hyperkinetic, testosterone and adrenaline-drenched look at that American obsession, professional football."—Todd McCarthy, *Variety*

🔊 **CASTING CALL:** Sean "P. Diddy" Combs was originally cast as Beamen, but dropped out due to a scheduling conflict.

👀 **"I KNOW THAT GUY":** If the coach of the Dallas Knights looks familiar, he should. It is Hall of Fame quarterback Johnny Unitas.

🎬 **PIVOTAL SCENE:** Tony (Pacino) delivers an emotional speech before the final game and pulls the fractured elements of his team together.

"Life is a game of inches and so is football," he says. "On this team, we fight for that inch. On this team we tear ourselves to pieces for that inch. . . . Because we know when you add up all those inches, that's gonna make the difference between winning and losing, between living and dying."

⭐ **SPORTS-ACTION GRADE:** C-plus. Some of the action, shown from the players' point of view, effectively captures the speed and violence. But Stone's editing is so choppy, it is often hard to follow.

👁 **REPEATED WATCHING QUOTIENT:** With a running time of 156 minutes, it feels like an entire season.

🎞 **MY FAVORITE SPORTS MOVIE:** Basketball Hall of Famer Charles Barkley: "I thought it was the most honest movie about what it's like in professional sports today. It showed how teams are made up of guys with different agendas. There was the old guy trying to hang on, the injured guy who wants to keep playing, the free agent guy who's playing for his stats and the young guy who's the threat to take somebody's job.

"That's how it is in sports. The biggest myth is that [players] are playing to win. Most of the time, it's a bunch of guys with their own agendas. They are worried about how much other guys are making, how much they're playing. The movie showed how hard it is for a coach to get beyond that and make those individuals play together."

86 BEST IN SHOW (2000–PG-13)

SPORT: DOG SHOW | STARS: CHRISTOPHER GUEST, CATHERINE O'HARA, EUGENE LEVY
DIRECTOR: CHRISTOPHER GUEST

Some people will ask why a satire about dog shows is included in a book about sports movies. Well, dog shows are competitions. Most newspapers run the results in the sports section alongside the baseball box scores and the racing form.

Big events, such as the Westminster Kennel Club show at Madison Square Garden, are nationally televised and the highlights are shown on ESPN's *SportsCenter*. Well-known sportscasters like Joe Garagiola call the action. For all those reasons, we feel *Best in Show* belongs in the book.

OK, there's another reason. *Best in Show* made us laugh. So sue us.

It is a breezy 89-minute spoof from the same folks who produced the faux documentaries *This is Spinal Tap,*

Waiting for Guffman and *A Mighty Wind*. This time director Christopher Guest turns his Second City ensemble loose in the dog show world with all of its brushing and fussing, and the results are predictably amusing.

As in his other films, Guest provides the actors with just the sketchiest of scripts. For *Best in Show,* Guest drew up a 15-page outline describing the characters and their assorted quirks, then he put the actors together with the dogs and let them wing it while the cameras rolled. Only the most gifted improv performers could make it work, but like a great coach, Guest knows his players and this is what they do best.

The first part of the film introduces the owners and dogs that will compete at the Mayflower Dog Show in Philadelphia. There is Harlan Pepper (Guest), a fishing shop owner from Pine Nut, N.C., and his bloodhound, Hubert; Stefan Vanderhoof (Michael McKean) and Scott Donlan (John Michael Higgins), a gay couple from New York and their prized Shih Tzu, Agnes; and Gerry and Cookie Fleck (Eugene Levy and Catherine O'Hara) from Fern City, FL, and their Norwich terrier, Winky.

The Flecks are the most fun. Gerry is an uptight clothing salesman who was born (literally) with two left feet. "When I was a kid, they called me 'Loopy' because I walked in little loops," he says. Cookie is a past-her-prime party girl with a trail of old boyfriends who keep popping up with tales of wild escapades ("Remember when we did it on the roller coaster?"). Of course, that makes poor Gerry squirm.

All of this is just building to the big dog show, which Guest stages very well. To make it authentic he insisted the actors take dog handling classes so when they walk the dogs around the ring, they move with the ease and assurance of professionals. The parading and posing for the judges, the primping and perfuming backstage, it all looks like the real thing.

A running gag is the clueless commentary of TV host Buck Laughlin (Fred Willard). The character is loosely based on Garagiola, the former baseball announcer who worked the Westminster show for several years. Laughlin turns the ex-jock into a macho buffoon who often leaves his strait-laced partner Trevor Beckwith (Jim Piddock) appalled and exasperated.

Laughlin blurts out things like: "And to think that in some countries these dogs are eaten."

Speaking of poodles, he wonders aloud, "How do they miniaturize dogs anyway?" When the bloodhound enters the ring, Laughlin says, "Why don't they put a Sherlock Holmes hat on him and stick a pipe in his mouth? That would get the crowd going." Beckwith replies dryly, "I don't think so."

Before the finals, Cookie sprains her ankle so Gerry has to take Winky into the ring. Laughlin says, "Am I nuts? Something's wrong with his feet. He's got two left feet." Beckwith says, "I never thought I'd find myself saying this, but you're right."

Gerry and Winky walk off with the blue ribbon. Improbable, sure, but we were having so much fun at that point, we didn't care.

CHEERS: Willard is hilarious doing a riff on his character from the TV series *Fernwood 2Night*. He won the Boston Society of Film Critics Award for Best Supporting Actor.

JEERS: Parker Posey grates on the nerves in her role as a yuppie lawyer. If any scenery was chewed, it wasn't by the dogs, it was by Posey.

BEST LINE: Laughlin asks Beckwith: "We have French dogs, German dogs, Chinese dogs. Tell me, do they all bark the same?"

WHAT THEY WROTE AT THE TIME: "Some may dis *Best* as too slapdash and inconsequential to warrant a feature length film. Bite me. Waggish fun like this is too good to miss."—Peter Travers, *Rolling Stone*

BET YOU DIDN'T KNOW: *Best in Show* was voted one of the 50 Greatest Comedies of All-Time by *Premiere Magazine*.

"I KNOW THAT GUY": John Michael Higgins, who plays the outrageously gay dog handler, came to prominence playing David Letterman in the TV movie *The Late Shift*.

SPORTS-ACTION GRADE: C. It is a dog show, after all.

REPEATED WATCHING QUOTIENT: If you are in need of a laugh, go to the end and wait for Buck Laughlin to set the scene. ("After all the petting and all the drooling, here we are at the finals.")

87 GLORY ROAD (2006–PG)

SPORT: BASKETBALL | STARS: JOSH LUCAS, JON VOIGHT, DEREK LUKE
DIRECTOR: JAMES GARTNER

The most surprising thing about *Glory Road* is that it took so long to make this momentous event into a movie. It was 1966 when Texas Western became the first school to win the NCAA Tournament with an all-black starting five. The Miners' win—over an all-white Kentucky squad—is often cited as *the* landmark moment in advancing the integration of college sports, particularly in the South.

So why did it take 40 years to put the Earth-changing event onto film? We're not sure. But we've got another problem. With four decades to get the story right, how did producer Jerry Bruckheimer and first-time director James Gartner manage to get so many things so wrong?

Listen, we're not quibblers. We realize that many of our favorite historical movies– *Miracle*, *Chariots of Fire*, *Eight Men Out*—take small liberties for dramatic purposes. We can live with Vince Papale being moved from the suburbs to South Philadelphia in *Invincible* because, hey, what's the difference? Maybe Jim Morris wasn't discovered exactly as *The Rookie* lays out, but that's not the important part.

But Disney's *Glory Road* takes a compelling—and significant—story, and performs more renovations than *Extreme Makeover: Home Edition*. In the process, it becomes just another decent sports movie—entertaining, yes, with well-choreographed game scenes and capable acting. Good enough to make this book. But the potential here was for a Top 20 finish. And the bigger sin is that any moviegoer who doesn't know the facts will likely accept what's laid out over 118 minutes in *Glory Road* as a historical document.

Among the more glaring errors:

• The movie portrays Texas Western (now Texas-El Paso) winning the national championship in Coach Don Haskins' first season. In fact, Haskins arrived five years before the 1966 title. Why change that fact?

• *Glory Road* asserts that Haskins (Josh Lucas) broke barriers by recruiting black players. In fact, the school began recruiting blacks in 1956. One player Haskins inherited in 1961 was point guard Nolan Richardson, who went on to become an NCAA Tournament-winning coach himself at Arkansas.

• The movie shows Haskins telling the team of his decision—as a political statement—to start five black players and only use his seven blacks (and not the three whites) in the title game against Adolph Rupp's Kentucky Wildcats. Wrong! Haskins often started an all-black lineup that season and the seven who played that game happened to be his seven best players. (Beyond that, there were five non-black players on the squad—not three as the movie showed.) Haskins has always insisted it did not occur to him he used an all-black rotation until people told him afterward. "I wasn't trying to send a message," he said. "I was trying to win a game."

We've got other misgivings, including the portrayal of Kentucky's players as sore losers (by all accounts they were gracious) and the hip-hop basketball supposedly played by Texas Western when, in fact, Haskins engineered a numbing, slow-down style. It all adds up to one big enchilada of complaints.

On the other hand. . . .

There's enough to like in *Glory Road*. The movie takes a look at 1960s American racism through the prism of sports, much as *Remember the Titans* did six years earlier—upbeat Motown music and all. One of Haskins' players gets beat up in a men's room; others have their motel rooms trashed while the team is on the road. Most viewers of this film will be too young to recall days when episodes like those really happened, and they are certainly worth remembering.

The story, while predictable, builds well. The game scenes work—especially the famous moment in the Midwest regional final when the Miners appear to lose as Kansas star Jo Jo White hits a jumper with seconds left in the first overtime. The referee rules that White's foot was touching the out-of-bounds line. The moment is well shot and dramatic.

The acting here is better than par. Derek Luke, terrific in *Friday Night Lights* and *Antwone Fisher*, once again shows himself as a powerful young actor as player Bobby Joe Hill. And Jon Voight, in a small but critical role as Rupp, portrays a nasty coach without falling into an angry caricature. Our only problem is the prosthetic nose and ears Voight wears, which make him appear more like Ross Perot than "The Baron of the Bluegrass." If you thought Voight looked silly in a Howard Cosell mask in *Ali*, wait until you get a load of this.

CHEERS: The *Glory Road* DVD has good extras and interviews. Make sure you catch the conversation with former NBA coach Pat Riley, who starred for that losing Kentucky team and proclaims that Haskins and Texas Western "wrote the Emancipation Proclamation of 1966."

JEERS: This movie badly needed a fact checker.

WHAT THEY WROTE AT THE TIME: "The film's political simplicity may help make it a hit with a teen crowd that needs its politics and history spelled out on flash cards. Nor will it hurt that the basketball scenes are edited with an MTV-style rhythm; the one-thing-at-a-time style of basketball that was played in the mid-1960s would probably have young fans of today laughing in the aisles."—Allen Barra, *New York Sun*

SPORTS-ACTION GRADE: B-minus. As Barra wrote, that's not how they really played back then. But there are rousing moments during the games.

REPEATED WATCHING QUOTIENT: Not high. *Hoosiers*, *Seabiscuit*, *Miracle* and many other movies in this book tell the same basic story—and tell it better.

DON'T FAIL TO NOTICE: The scene where Haskins pulls into the gas station and is asked by the attendant, "Hey, you want me to fill this thing up?" The gas jockey happens to be the real-life Don Haskins.

CASTING CALL: Ben Affleck was first hired to play Haskins, but pulled out because of scheduling conflicts.

BEST LINE: Haskins, while trying out recruit Orsten Artis: "Brother, without a little work, I don't think you can get past an old timer like me."

Artis: "Get past you? I will go past you, through you, over you, under you, around you. As a matter of fact I will spin you like a top, twist you in a pretzel, eat your lunch, steal your girl and kick your dog at the same time."

BET YOU DIDN'T KNOW: Many of the basketball scenes were filmed at a high school in suburban New Orleans that had been devastated by Hurricane Katrina. The gym at Chalmette High was rebuilt prior to shooting the movie.

"I KNOW THAT GUY": Red West, who plays trainer Ross Moore, is a veteran character actor once best known for being Elvis Presley's close friend. You've probably seen him as the grieving dad in *The Rainmaker*, or the Southern wag in *Road House* who gets to utter that movie's best line: "I got married to an ugly woman. Don't ever do that. It just takes the energy right out of you. She left me, though. Found somebody even uglier than she was."

IF YOU LIKED THIS, YOU'LL LIKE: The hour-long 2003 ESPN *Game of the Week* documentary focusing on Texas Western's journey. The show occasionally re-airs on ESPN Classic.

MY FAVORITE SPORTS MOVIE: Ryan Howard, 2006 National League MVP: "I didn't know the story. I just knew it was a basketball movie. When I saw it and realized the historical importance of what happened, I was, like, wow. You think about the barriers that were broken down and how it contributed to the growth of the game. It was very uplifting, very inspirational."

88 THE STRATTON STORY (1949–NR)

SPORT: BASEBALL | STARS: JAMES STEWART, JUNE ALLYSON | DIRECTOR: SAM WOOD

When MGM announced it was making a movie about the life of Monty Stratton, some of Hollywood's biggest stars expressed an interest. Gregory Peck and Van Johnson read for the part. Ronald Reagan wanted the role, but he was under contract to Warner Brothers and they would not let him work for another studio.

It is easy to see why so many actors wanted the part. It is the true story of a shy country boy who becomes a star pitcher with the Chicago White Sox, only to have his career cut short by a hunting accident which results in the loss of his leg. Outfitted with a prosthesis, Stratton comes back to pitch winning baseball again, albeit in the minor leagues.

It is an inspiring tale, it had a solid script (writer Douglas Morrow won the Oscar) and it was directed by Sam Wood, who had success with similar material in *The Pride of the Yankees*, the Lou Gehrig story which was nominated for five Academy Awards in 1942.

The real Monty Stratton was technical advisor on the film and he wanted Jimmy Stewart to play him. He had nothing against the other actors; he just thought the lanky, soft-spoken Stewart was a better fit. Once Stewart tested for the role, the producers agreed. It was a wise decision.

Johnson and Reagan weren't the right body type to play the spindly 6-5, 180-pound Stratton. Peck was lean enough, but he was too urbane. Stewart, with his scarecrow physique and aw-shucks manner, was perfect. He didn't throw the ball like a big league all-star, which Stratton was, but moviegoers weren't sticklers for that sort of thing back then.

The result is a satisfying little film that launched the on-screen partnership of Stewart and leading lady June Allyson. They paired so effectively as Monty and Ethel Stratton, they later were cast as husband and wife in *The Glenn Miller Story* (1953) and *Strategic Air Command* (1955). In the latter film, Stewart plays a major leaguer recalled to active duty with the Air Force. He wears his baseball cap while piloting his plane.

When we first see Monty Stratton (Stewart), he is pitching semi-pro baseball in Texas for three dollars a game. A broken-down old scout who happens to be riding a freight train through town spots Stratton and takes him to the White Sox spring training camp for a tryout. Manager Jimmy Dykes (playing himself) works him out and signs him to a contract.

In reality, Stratton bounced back and forth between the White Sox and the minors for the better part of three seasons, but in the film, he has a much faster rise to stardom. He is shown getting rocked in his major league debut and being sent down to Omaha, but when he rejoins the White Sox, he immediately starts mowing down the best hitters in the American League.

Stratton did not really hit his stride until 1937, his fourth season, but when he did, he was very good. That year, he was 15-5 with a 2.40 ERA, second in the American League behind only Lefty Gomez (2.33) of the Yankees. Stratton had five shutouts and 14 complete games in his 21 starts. He was named to the American League All-Star team and at age 25, he had a bright future.

The film makes that point. In one scene, Dykes is watching from the dugout and says,"I wouldn't trade him for any pitcher in baseball."

Stratton returns to his Texas farm in the off-season. One day while hunting rabbits, he stumbles and accidentally shoots himself in the leg. The wound becomes infected and the doctors are forced to amputate. Ethel (Allyson) is shown agonizing as she is asked to sign the paper giving the permission to operate.

"We have to remove the leg to save his life," the doctor says.

"His legs are his life," she replies.

She signs the paper, knowing she has ended her husband's major league career. When the doctor leaves the room, she puts her head on the desk and cries.

When Stratton returns to the farm, he is bitter and self-pitying. Ethel brings him a stack of get-well messages and he pushes them away, saying, "If you like 'em so much, you read 'em." When their baby boy takes his first step, Monty snaps, "What's so wonderful about that? He's got two legs, doesn't he?"

With Ethel's steadfast support, Monty slowly comes around. He agrees to put his crutches away and wear the prosthesis, which he has resisted. One day she coaxes him into having a catch. Pretty soon, he is throwing strikes into a bucket he nailed to the barn. Without telling anyone, he arranges to pitch in a minor league all-star game just to see if he can still do it. He wins the game even though the opposing team tries to take advantage of his bad leg by bunting on him.

The film ends with Stratton throwing out the final hitter and walking off as the crowd cheers and the narrator says, "Monty Stratton has won an even greater victory. He has shown what a man can do when he refuses to admit defeat."

It was true in Monty Stratton's case. He actually returned to pitching in the minor leagues and in 1946, eight years after losing his leg, he won 18 games for Sherman in the Class C East Texas League.

CHEERS: Jimmy Stewart is well cast as Monty Stratton and he is convincing in his struggling attempts to walk after his injury.

JEERS: The dialog is clunky in spots. For example, it's hard to imagine the real Monty Stratton telling his wife after the accident, "Looks like I shot the wrong rabbit."

✔ **REALITY CHECK:** Stratton's comeback game was not a minor league all-star game. It was an exhibition between the White Sox and Cubs with the proceeds going to Monty's family to help cover his medical bills.

BET YOU DIDN'T KNOW: Stratton rejoined the White Sox as a coach for several years before returning to his home in Texas.

WHAT THEY WROTE AT THE TIME: "A touching, human story of triumph over crushing odds with a warmth and sensitive appreciation for sentiment."—*New York Times*

★ **SPORTS-ACTION GRADE:** C. Stewart has a gawky throwing motion, but there are enough big leaguers in cameos (Bill Dickey and Gene Bearden among them) that the overall look of the film is passable.

89 VARSITY BLUES (1999–R)

SPORT: FOOTBALL | STARS: JAMES VAN DER BEEK, JON VOIGHT, AMY SMART
DIRECTOR: BRIAN ROBBINS

Varsity Blues is *Friday Night Lights* made for the MTV audience. It takes the same slice of American life (Texas high school football) and the same point of view (the values are corrupt, the kids are exploited) but it adds more booze, sex and rock and roll. It also rolls back the intelligence factor by half.

Friday Night Lights had the advantage of being a true story with real characters who were first introduced in Buzz Bissinger's best-selling book. The coaches and players from the dusty back roads of Odessa, Tex., had the feel of authenticity. The characters in *Varsity Blues* are fictional, but that isn't the problem. Fictional characters can feel real. Rocky Balboa, Norman Dale, Happy Gilmore. Well, maybe not Happy Gilmore, but you get the idea.

In *Varsity Blues*, the characters are more like a checklist. Stud quarterback, check. Vixen cheerleader, check. Nasty coach, check. Fat, dumb lineman, check. Let's see, did we miss anything? Oh yeah, we need some clueless parents who are still living out their own high school fantasies through their children. Got 'em. Check and double check.

In *Varsity Blues*, the only interesting character is Jonathan "Mox" Moxon (James Van Der Beek) but he is enough to keep you involved. In football-crazed West Canaan, Mox is unusual—heretical, almost—in that he is ambivalent about the game. He likes to play, but he is smart enough to realize coach Bud Kilmer (Jon Voight) has taken his win-at-all-costs philosophy to unhealthy extremes.

Kilmer is a living legend in West Canaan, thanks to his 23 district championships. The high school stadium bears his name and there is a statue of him behind the end zone. He has coached several generations of West Canaan Coyotes, which means he coached most of the fathers of the kids who are playing for him now. Mox's father (Thomas F. Duffy) is one of them, and he remains a loyal disciple who believes the coach can do no wrong.

Mox is the second-string quarterback buried behind all-state superstar Lance Harbor (Paul Walker), which means he has virtually no chance of ever taking a snap. He is so detached, he sits on the bench reading novels that he hides inside a playbook. You see, Mox is a brain who hopes to attend Brown University on an academic scholarship.

which offer a welcome surprise or two. For one thing, Mox finds that he likes the perks of being a star. He is a nice guy—in fact, his teammates tease him about being a goody-goody—and with his Ivy League brainpower, he should be above it all, but when girls start covering his car windshield with rollouts that say "Mox is a fox," well, he kind of digs it. He even takes a few teammates out for a night of shots and beers at the local strip joint. For awhile, you actually wonder if he is going over to the other side.

Van Der Beek, who became a star on the TV series *Dawson's Creek*, is quite effective portraying a kid who suddenly finds himself pulled in a lot of unexpected directions. His girlfriend Jules (Amy Smart) serves as his conscience, although she is more than a little judgmen-

COACH KILMER: "**NEVER SHOW WEAKNESS. THE ONLY PAIN THAT MATTERS IS THE PAIN YOU INFLICT.**"

But all that changes when Lance goes down with a knee injury and suddenly Mox has to put down *Slaughterhouse-Five* (yes, he was reading Kurt Vonnegut while the game was going on), pick up his helmet and save the season. Kilmer doesn't like Mox. He has seen the flicker of skepticism in his eyes and, besides, he gets all A's in class. Shoot, who can trust a kid like that? Not Bud Kilmer, that's for dang sure.

Mox confirms Kilmer's worst fears. He pulls out the victory, but he does it with a razzle-dazzle play he improvises in the huddle. While the team and fans mob Mox, Kilmer gives him the evil eye. You can see where this is headed. Mox is good enough to keep the team winning, but he and Kilmer are headed for a showdown. And given the nature of the film, you know Mox will win out (which he does).

But director Brian Robbins tosses in a few wrinkles

tal. One night after leading the team to a 66-3 victory, Mox is stopped by a radio reporter. Jules rolls her eyes as Mox does the interview.

"You're enjoying this, aren't you?" she says.

"Well, yeah," he says.

She offers a chilly "Look, I gotta go" and takes off, leaving Mox standing there, feeling like he should apologize but not quite sure what he is apologizing for. We get her point. Their quiet, down-to-earth, boy-girl dynamic is being intruded upon, but, geez, the guy is entitled to enjoy his success a little bit, isn't he?

One scene tells you all you need to know about Mox. The night Lance suffers his knee injury, Mox drives Lance's girlfriend, bombshell cheerleader Darcy Sears (Ali Larter) home. She starts flirting with Mox in the car and later comes on to him wearing a bikini made of whipped cream. With Lance's football career shot, Darcy is looking for another ticket out of town.

Mox pulls away, saying: "I can't do this."

Darcy is crushed. "Great, now I can look forward to a life working at the Wal-Mart," she says.

Such are the career options in West Canaan.

🍺 **CHEERS:** Van Der Beek is a likeable actor who brings credibility to a film where most of the characters are made out of cardboard.

👎 **JEERS:** The final game is totally phony. Mox leads a revolt in which the players refuse to follow Kilmer out of the locker room. Kilmer walks off alone and the players, specifically the injured Lance Harbor, coach themselves to victory. What happened to the assistant coaches? Did they all leave? If all the coaches are gone, who's Lance talking to on the headset?

☝ **DON'T FAIL TO NOTICE:** Mox wears uniform No. 4. That's because James Van Der Beek's favorite NFL player was Brett Favre.

✒ **WHAT THEY WROTE AT THE TIME:** "Somewhere between a John Hughes coming-of-age film and a Super Bowl beer commercial lies *Varsity Blues*. [It] can be enjoyable if you check your brain at the popcorn stand. There is no deep meaning, but there is some harmless fun to be had."—Tom Bennett, *Film Journal International*

✔ **REALITY CHECK:** Billy Bob (Ron Lester) faints at the line and allows a blitzer to come through untouched. In a game, if an offensive lineman fell out of his stance, it would be called a false start and the play would be whistled dead. There never would have been the devastating hit that ended Lance's career.

💬 **BEST LINE:** Coach Kilmer talking to Mox: "You got to be the dumbest smart kid I know."

🤓 **"I KNOW THAT GUY":** Scott Caan, who plays wide receiver and party animal Charlie Tweeder, is Turk Malloy in the *Ocean's 11* series. He is the son of actor James Caan and there are times when he's in his football gear that he bears an uncanny resemblance to his father in *Brian's Song*.

⭐ **SPORTS-ACTION GRADE:** C-minus. None of it is convincing, but in particular the final play. The whole season is on the line, and they call a hook and lateral play with the ball being pitched to Billy Bob, the 400-pound lineman, who has to catch it and carry it to the end zone. Sure, that makes sense.

👁 **REPEATED WATCHING QUOTIENT:** Teenage boys—and perhaps a father or two—will rerun the whipped cream bikini scene endlessly.

🖐 **MY FAVORITE SPORTS MOVIE:** All-pro defensive tackle Warren Sapp: "It reminded me of my days at Apopka [Fl.] High School. The team in the movie even wore our colors, blue and white. Our coach was like the coach in the movie [Jon Voight]. He coached at the school forever. He coached all the men in my family. He coached all the men in the town, practically. The only thing missing was the statue in the end zone.

"What I really liked was how the movie showed the effect the high school team had on the town. That's how it was in Apopka. On Friday night, when we played, the town closed down and everybody came to the game. Even the McDonalds closed down. You couldn't get anything to eat until the game was over. Seeing that movie brought back memories."

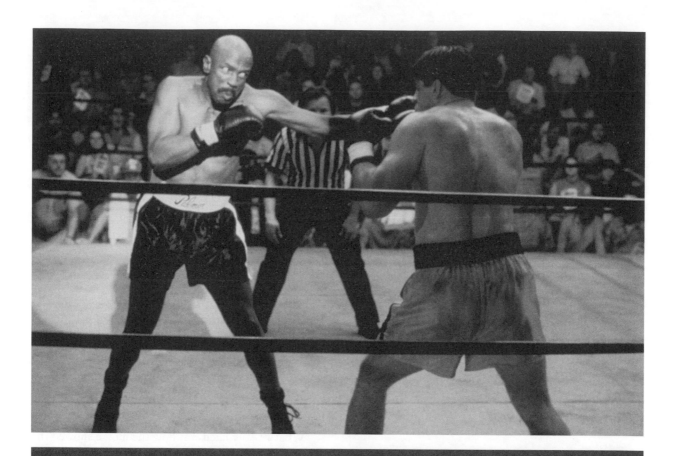

90 DIGGSTOWN (1992–R)

SPORT: BOXING | STARS: JAMES WOODS, LOUIS GOSSETT, JR., BRUCE DERN
DIRECTOR: MICHAEL RITCHIE

Director Michael Ritchie has a hit-and-miss history with sports movies. He started with two good ones (*Downhill Racer* and *The Bad News Bears*) but stumbled badly with the next two (*Semi-Tough* and *Wildcats*). His fifth effort, *Diggstown*, falls somewhere in between.

A combination boxing and caper film, *Diggstown* has an interesting premise and at times it is on the verge of being terrific, but there are too many shifts in tone and too many layers to the con.

Other sports films balance comedy and drama effectively—*The Longest Yard* is a good example—and that's what Ritchie tries to do here, but he's only partly successful. *Diggstown* veers from slapstick humor to ugly violence and back again, and it does so in a way that is hurried and often jarring.

Still, James Woods is very funny as con man Gabriel Caine and Louis Gossett Jr. brings just the right note of "here-we-go-again" cynicism to his role as "Honey" Roy Palmer, who supplies the muscle for Caine's latest scam.

The film opens in prison where Caine is about to be released. He has pocketed a cool $50 grand during his time behind bars, arranging (and betting on) fights among the prisoners. Caine is one of those 24/7 hustlers who talks fast and knows how to work an angle.

Caine's cellmate, Wolf Forrester (boxer Randall "Tex" Cobb), tells him about Diggstown, a little hamlet in Georgia where they hold what are known as "cash fights." There is no TV or newspaper coverage, no records kept.

These fights exist for one reason: betting. They are the equivalent of cockfights, except with people. It is a nasty business, but it is made to order for a sharpie like Caine.

Diggstown is controlled by John Gillon (Bruce Dern), a rich guy who loves the action and does whatever is necessary to win. Gillon got control of the town by fixing the last fight of Charles Diggs—the boxer for whom the town was named—and betting against him. To insure his bet, Gillon doped Diggs, which resulted in a savage beating that left Diggs in a vegetative state. He now sits in a wheelchair staring into space while Gillon runs the town.

Flush with his prison money, Caine heads for Diggstown with a card shark named Fitz (Oliver Platt). They offer Gillon a bet: they will find a boxer who will meet and defeat 10 Diggstown men in a 24-hour period. Caine already has a boxer in mind—Palmer (Gossett), a heavyweight who fought for Caine in the past. The trouble is it was the distant past. He is now 48 years old, and he hasn't fought in more than a decade.

Palmer is appropriately skeptical when Caine tries to enlist him in the scheme. But talking is what Caine does best, and he's able to convince Palmer that the town is full of hicks with no real boxing ability, which means they'll be easy pickings for a professional, even a rusty one such as Palmer. Of course, Caine knows Gillon will have a trick or two up his sleeve, so the real question is: which hustler gets hustled?

The early bouts are played mostly for laughs. Palmer knocks off the first few opponents with little difficulty. Gossett has just the right look: He isn't in his prime, but he's still an imposing figure in a pair of trunks and he's clearly too much for the ham-and-eggers who normally fight in Diggstown.

As Palmer piles up the wins, the maneuvering starts between Caine and Gillon. Caine wants to raise the ante, Gillon wants to change the rules. Soon they are discussing what, exactly, is a Diggstown man? Did he have to be born there? Live there? What if he just happens to show up that day? Yes, we're talking ringers. (You get the feeling Gillon has Lennox Lewis on speed dial.)

"Do I look stupid to you?" Fitz asks as Gillon tries to expand the boundaries of Diggstown to include roughly two-thirds of North America. "Or have you people been breeding too close to the gene pool again?"

The battle of wits between Caine and Gillon becomes the real heavyweight struggle, with each man trying to outfox the other. Gillon does succeed in back-loading his lineup card so Palmer's opponents get progressively bigger and tougher. Bleeding and sucking wind, Palmer starts looking his age and Caine has to do some fast thinking to save the day.

In a movie full of twists, Ritchie saves the best for last, so we don't want to ruin it. Stick with *Diggstown* to the end and you'll be rewarded. It is one of the better double-crosses you are likely to see.

CHEERS: Ritchie, a director known for his keen eye, really delivers the look and feel of a small town fight club. The visual elements make up for some of the weak spots in the narrative.

JEERS: The Charles Diggs subplot and the cutaways of his tragic character is one of the things that makes the movie—which is mostly humorous and often raunchy—feel uneven.

WHAT THEY WROTE AT THE TIME: "A funny and vulgar fable . . . it moves with such speed and cheerful nerviness that it's almost as irresistible as its fast-talking hero is reputed to be."— Vincent Canby, *New York Times*

BEST LINE: Caine gives the tiring Palmer a pep talk before one of his later bouts.

"This guy is bigger than you," Caine says. "He's younger than you and he hasn't fought 22 rounds today like you have. But remember this, you're black."

Palmer shoots him a look through his swollen eye.

"What the hell is that supposed to mean?" he asks.

"I don't know, I'm trying to inspire you," Caine says. "It's a *Roots* kind of thing."

It's also an inside joke. Gossett was in the cast of the *Roots* TV series.

SPORTS-ACTION GRADE: C. Gossett is fine as the ex-heavyweight, but some of his opponents take the clumsy country boy thing to extremes.

91 THE CLUB (1980–NR)

SPORT: AUSTRIALIAN RULES FOOTBALL | STARS: JACK THOMPSON, GRAHAM KENNEDY, FRANK WILSON | DIRECTOR: BRUCE BERESFORD

The Club, a film about Australian Rules Football, is next-to-impossible to find in the United States, but if you can track down a VHS copy, you will be rewarded with an entertaining trip to the Land Down Under.

Think *North Dallas Forty* with an Aussie accent. *The Club* is a look inside the lives of the coaches and players, the bickering and backstabbing of the front office, the jealousies that destroy teams regardless of sport or hemisphere. It is well-acted—especially by Jack Thompson, who plays the idealistic coach Laurie Holden—and it is often very funny.

Americans will be amused to see star players holding out for more money, owners meddling with coaches and coaches telling players, "The sportswriters say we're a lot of hacks and has-beens. Let's make them eat their words." Gee, it's all so familiar.

There are semantic differences. When the star player tells off the coach, he says, "Get stuffed." That's Aussie for, well, you know. The film was made for Australian audiences, so they don't bother to explain the rules of the game, but that's OK. An American viewer won't have trouble following the action. It's a cross between soccer and rugby.

The Club spends a fictional season with Collingwood, a real club in the Victorian Football League. The owner, Ted Parker, (Graham Kennedy) signs Geoff Hayward (John Howard), a highly touted player from Tasmania without ever consulting Holden, the head coach.

Holden is irritated by Parker's actions and the other players are resentful of Hayward's fat contract. In the first game, Hayward whiffs on his first few scoring opportunities and Holden benches him. Enraged, Parker leaves his box to confront the coach, who tells him to take a hike.

"I won't be told how to run my team by the owner of a meat pie factory who never played a game of football in his life," Holden tells Gerry Cooper (Alan Cassell), a member of the executive committee.

Collingwood loses its first five games, and the committee—a nasty basket of vipers—begins plotting to dump Holden. Jock Riley (Frank Wilson) is Holden's most vocal critic. He has resented Holden ever since Holden succeeded him as coach. Riley believes Holden went behind his back to get the job, which isn't true, but the old timer has held a grudge ever since.

It doesn't help that Riley and Holden are the two most celebrated players in Collingwood history. Riley holds the club record for most games played (282). Holden was on his way to breaking the mark when a knee injury ended his career. "I wasn't sorry to see it," Riley says with a wicked smile.

Unlike Riley, Holden is a decent fellow who loves and honors the game. He is infuriated by Hayward, who comes late to practices and shows up stoned for a game. When Holden confronts him, Hayward blows him off, saying he doesn't care about football. "It's a lot of macho bullshit," he says.

Holden has seen glimpses of the kid's talent and he is determined to unlock his potential. When Hayward says, "Football bores me," the coach tells him he's full of it.

"You know what you are? You're scared," Holden says. "You were a star in Tasmania. Big deal. Anyone who's not cross-eyed or bandy-kneed could be a star in Tasmania. You're in the big leagues now, Geoff, and you're scared. You're scared that you're not half the player you thought you were."

The message gets through and Hayward commits to Holden and the team. The coach demonstrates his confidence by putting Hayward at center and moving the aging team captain Danny Rowe (Harold Hopkins) to the backline. Hayward begins to play like an all-star and Collingwood becomes unstoppable, advancing to the championship game.

The Club was originally a successful play that debuted on the Melbourne stage in 1977. When it was made into a film, it reunited Thompson and director Bruce Beresford, who were coming off the hit *Breaker Morant*. That courtroom drama set in the Boer War was Australia's entry in the 1980 Cannes Film Festival and earned honors for both Thompson (Best Supporting Actor) and Beresford (nominated for Best Director).

It seemed like a can't-miss: a popular story, a hot actor, a talented director. Yet *The Club* flopped on the big screen. It brought in less than $900,000 during a brief run in Australia, but it attracted a cult following when it aired on American TV. It isn't easy to follow all the dialog—the Aussie accents are thick—but the theme of why athletes devote their lives to a sport, and each other, comes through very clearly.

TED:

"DO YOU REMEMBER YOUR FIRST GAME?"

LAURIE:

"NOT ALL THAT WELL."

TED:

"I DO. I WAS THERE AND WE ALL KNEW WE WERE SEEING OUR NEXT GREAT STAR."

🍺 **CHEERS:** There is a very funny scene in which Jock visits Geoff to discuss his poor play. Geoff is rolling a joint, but Jock thinks it's tobacco. Geoff offers him one and the clueless Jock accepts. As the old man gets high as a kite, Geoff explains that his football problems are the result of impotence.

He tells a graphic—and totally fabricated—tale of having sexual relations with both his mother and his younger sister. One night, Geoff says, his father came home unexpectedly and caught them in bed together. The poor guy shot himself in the head. "I've been impotent ever since," Geoff says.

"No bloody wonder," an ashen-faced Jock says.

🚩 **JEERS:** Sorry, but the scene where Geoff—stoned out of his mind—stops in the middle of a game to watch a seagull fly over the stadium takes his hippie jock too far.

🎬 **PIVOTAL SCENE:** Laurie Holden tells Jock Riley that he saw Riley's last game as a player. He was standing a few feet away when Riley deliberately slammed his knee into the face of a defenseless opponent.

"They said you retired out of remorse," Holden says, "but I know the truth. All the other teams said if you ever stepped on the field again, you'd be lucky to get off alive."

"It didn't scare me," Riley says.

"Not much it didn't," Holden replies.

"No one's ever called me a coward," Riley snaps.

"I'm calling you one now," Holden says.

✏️ **WHAT THEY WROTE AT THE TIME:** "Using a screenplay by David Williamson, Beresford has made a vigorous and funny film which preserves the warmth and ruefulness of the play." —Sandra Hall, *The (Melbourne) Bulletin*

💬 **BEST LINE:** Gerry Cooper: "You can't embarrass Ted Parker. I called him a cunning little rodent and he took it as a compliment."

⭐ **SPORTS-ACTION GRADE:** D. Beresford tries inter-cutting real game action with staged action involving the actors and it doesn't work. The difference between real players and actors trying to execute the same moves is obvious even to the untrained American eye.

92 COACH CARTER (2005–PG-13)

SPORT: BASKETBALL | STARS: SAMUEL L. JACKSON, ROB BROWN, ROBERT RI'CHARD
DIRECTOR: THOMAS CARTER

It is hardly an original story: the idealistic teacher/coach takes on a classroom/team full of problem kids and with a firm hand and an open mind turns their lives around. We've seen it in *Blackboard Jungle* (1955), *To Sir, with Love* (1967), *Stand and Deliver* (1988), *Lean on Me* (1989) and *Dangerous Minds* (1995)—just to name a few.

The film plays out the same way every time: Teacher/coach is appalled by the apathy of the school administration, which is prepared to write the kids off as a hopeless cause. The teacher/coach vows to whip the students/players into shape. His/her tough-love methods are met with hostility. There is a physical confrontation in which the teacher/coach prevails and the kids have that "Uh oh, Teach is a former Green Beret" epiphany.

Next thing you know, it is graduation day and all the kids who once appeared headed for the slammer are in their caps and gowns, thanking the teacher/coach for putting them on the right path. It doesn't matter if the film is based on a true story or if it is fiction, the dramatic arc and moral are always the same.

So what distinguishes the good ones? The lead, mostly.

Michelle Pfeiffer (*Dangerous Minds*) in a karate pose doesn't work. Sidney Poitier (*To Sir, with Love*) in boxing gloves? That doesn't work either. But Samuel L. Jackson slamming a Latino gang-banger against the gym wall? Yeah, that works. And for that reason, so does *Coach Carter*.

The film is not without its flaws. For one thing, it is much too long at two hours and 16 minutes. Also, there are too many subplots and secondary storylines. Each time the film builds up a little momentum, director Thomas Carter veers off in another direction and it seems to take forever getting underway again. But when Jackson is on the screen, *Coach Carter* comes to life.

"Jackson is the ideal star to deliver a lecture with fire, brimstone and panache, which he's demonstrated in everything from his DJ in *Do The Right Thing* and reformed hit man in *Pulp Fiction* to the besieged teacher in *187*," wrote Wesley Morris in the *Boston Globe*. "In *Coach Carter*, he delivers a castigating speech on the problem with kids who use the 'n' word on each other. Any owner of *Jackie Brown* will recognize the powerful irony in that."

Coach Carter is based on the true story of Ken Carter, a former hoops star who returns to his old high school in Oakland to rebuild the basketball program. The real Carter earned national publicity with his discipline, which included forcing players to sign a "contract" calling for them to maintain a 2.3 GPA (higher than the required 2.0), sit in the front row of class and wear a jacket and tie to every game.

At first, the players—all inner city kids with major attitudes—sneer at his rules. They aren't impressed by the fact he was the school's last All-American and still holds the record for points, assists and steals. But when Carter puts the mouthy Timo Cruz (Rick Gonzalez) up against the wall and announces, "I'm not a teacher, I'm the new basketball coach," they realize he means business.

Conducting tougher practices—with pushups and sprints as punishment for showing up late or talking back—Carter gets astonishing results. A team that was 4-22 the previous season becomes unbeatable. But with the newfound success comes arrogance. Players begin cutting class and skipping tests. When Carter finds out, he literally locks the gym and shuts down the basketball program, resulting in the forfeiture of several games.

Parents accuse Carter of ruining their sons' chances for a college scholarship. Even school administrators feel Carter has gone too far. The team was undefeated and bringing the mostly black and Hispanic community a welcome measure of pride. The school board votes to end the lockout, sending Carter into a rage.

"You need to consider the message you're sending the boys by ending the lockout," Carter says in the film. "It's the same message that we as a culture send to our professional athletes, and that is they are above the law. If these boys cannot honor the simple rules of a basketball contract, how long do you think it will be before they're out there breaking the law?

"I played ball here at Richmond High 30 years ago. It was the same thing then. Some of my teammates went to prison, some of them even ended up dead. If you vote to end the lockout, you won't have to terminate me. I'll quit."

When Carter returns to the school to clean out his office, he finds that although the administration has unlocked the gym, the players will not practice. Instead, they have turned the gym into a study hall. The same kids who were cutting class are now sitting with tutors doing algebra and reading *Beowulf.*

"Sir, they can cut the chains off the door, but they can't make us play," says Jason Lyle (Channing Tatum).

"We've decided we're going to finish what you started, sir," says Damien Carter (Robert Ri'chard), who transferred from a private school to Richmond High to play for his father.

Heartened by the team's support, Carter stays on as coach and leads the team to the state championship game.

"I came to coach basketball players and you became students," he says. "I came to teach boys and you became men."

It's the kind of cornball line that could have fallen flat, but the cool and commanding Jackson sells it big-time.

🏆 **CHEERS:** The closing credits include an epilogue saying six of the Richmond basketball players went on to college, five on basketball scholarships. As Roger Ebert of the *Chicago Sun-Times* writes: "Lives, not games, were won."

🚩 **JEERS:** The film is at least 30 minutes too long.

🍎 **BET YOU DIDN'T KNOW:** *Coach Carter* has the highest opening weekend of any MTV film release, $24.1 million. Its total box office was a solid $67.1 million.

🎬 **PIVOTAL SCENE:** Carter kicks point guard Timo Cruz

off the team. When Cruz asks for a second chance, Carter says he will consider it if Cruz does 2,500 pushups and 1,000 sprints.

Cruz falls short by 500 pushups and 100 sprints. As he is leaving the gym, another player says, "I'll do some." He drops to the floor and starts doing pushups. Several other players join in. Soon the whole team is doing pushups and sprints to help pay off Cruz's debt.

Carter's message of "team" is finally getting through.

☞ **DON'T FAIL TO NOTICE:** Pop singer Ashanti makes her acting debut as Kyra, the pregnant girlfriend of the star player.

✒ **WHAT THEY WROTE AT THE TIME:** "Samuel L. Jackson's wonderfully nuanced, witty performance and a few unexpected plot turns give *Coach Carter* a subtext that helps complicate such knee-jerk oversimplifications, redeeming the role with energetic humor and a loose-limbed grace."—Ken Tucker, *New York*

★ **SPORTS-ACTION GRADE:** C-plus. It gets a little repetitive after the 300th lob pass followed by a slam dunk.

🎞 **MY FAVORITE SPORTS MOVIE:** Seven-time NBA All-Star Tracy McGrady: "Samuel L. Jackson is a great actor, so I like just about every major movie he's been in. I like the sports movies that are based on true events and this movie also sent a good message about what it means to stay true to your word—as Coach Carter did in the movie."

93 LAGAAN: ONCE UPON A TIME IN INDIA (2001–PG)

SPORT: CRICKET | STARS: AAMIR KHAN, GRACY SINGH, PAUL BLACKTHORNE, RACHEL SHELLEY | DIRECTOR: ASHUTOSH GOWARIKER

A 224-minute movie about cricket in British colonial India is, pardon the phrase, not everyone's cup of tea. You must be willing to accept subtitles (unless you speak the three distinct Hindi dialects in the film) and a different acting style (melodramatic to say the least), and you must appreciate that most Indian movies come with lengthy singing and dancing scenes appearing to have little to do with the script.

Here's hoping that doesn't chase you away. Because if you can embrace (or at least cope with) the cultural differences in a movie out of Bollywood, Mumbai's version of Hollywood, you'll be rewarded with a rich, textured epic—part drama, part comedy—that meshes sports, politics and romance. It's a period piece (uh-oh, we're risking losing audience again) that's as beautifully shot as anything out of Hollywood in years.

The story centers on an Indian village in 1893. The residents are impoverished by a drought but still forced to pay a steep land tax (or "lagaan") to their British overlords. When brash young Bhuvan (Aamir Khan) implores for a break from the levy, he is goaded by the bullying English Capt. Andrew Russell (Paul Blackthorne) into a bet—if the Indians can beat the Brits in a game of cricket, they will be excused from the tax for three years. If not, they must pay triple.

Problem is, the natives have never played the game. So Bhuvan must assemble a ragtag squad of villagers that includes a mentally disturbed semi-feral fortune teller, a Sikh mercenary with a nasty grudge against the British Army and an Untouchable with a gimpy arm that allows him to throw a breaking ball better than Daisuke Matsuzaka. Rudyard Kipling could have written these characters.

Hopeless as it seems, there are a few athletes among the group. And Capt. Russell's sister (Rachel Shelley), appalled by his sadistic treatment of the Indians, sneaks away to teach them the sport. The underdogs start to believe. It's the same basic plot we've seen before—in *Rocky*, *Hoosiers* and dozens of other movies in this book—but it works here as it works in those.

Along the way, there are subplots involving a romantic triangle and a double agent. Plus singing. Lots of singing. And dancing. We've come to learn that moviegoers in India can't get enough of the Busby Berkeley stuff, and that they also like to get their money's worth at the theater. Hence the nearly four-hour length.

Indeed, it takes more than two hours before we get to the dramatic cricket match, and that lasts nearly 90 minutes itself (in the plot it covers a full three days!). We'll be honest and tell you that we don't understand the intricacies of the sport—when the score stood "295 for 6" we thought it was looking hopeless for the locals. We were wrong.

But you know what? Even if cricket is foreign to you, it's fun for a sports fan to watch. There's a batter and a pitcher (one of the meaner Brits will remind you of vintage Goose Gossage) and fielders. They might just be called by other names.

Lagaan was a huge box office success worldwide, but did poorly in the United States, grossing just over $1 million. We invite you to add to that total.

🍺 **CHEERS:** To the training scene where the villagers run up stairs and chase down chickens. Wait a second, haven't we seen that somewhere before?

🍺 **JEERS:** To some of the lyrics in the interminable songs. In one, during training, they sing, "Whiteys wear shorts and call it cricket. We wear loin clothes and call it gilli danda." Not exactly "My Heart Will Go On" from *Titanic*.

✒ **WHAT THEY WROTE AT THE TIME:** "A rippingly good, old-fashioned movie epic that takes the best of Bollywood cinema—unabashed romance, kitschy musical numbers, a fervent urge to entertain—and elevates it for an international audience. But not by too much."—Edward Guthmann, *San Francisco Chronicle*

☺ **GOOFS:** About 15 minutes into the movie, what appears to be an orange plastic fence looms in the background. That would be improbable in Nineteenth Century India.

☞ **DON'T FAIL TO NOTICE:** While filming the cricket match, actor Ben Nealon, who plays Lt. Smith, tripped while running. He landed on his bat and dislocated his left shoulder. The scene was left in the movie.

❞ **BEST LINE:** When the angry villager Guran comes to bat he shouts at his opponents, "You tea drinkers! Flea bags! Boot wearers! Tormentors of the weak—beware, you will pay!"

We'd love to see someone try shouting that at Josh Beckett.

👓 **"I KNOW THAT GUY":** Blackthorne, the sneeringly evil Capt. Russell, knows how to do the bad guy. He moved on to play Stephen Saunders, the British intelligence officer-turned terrorist in Season 3 of *24*.

👒 **BET YOU DIDN'T KNOW:** The small village where the movie was shot, named Bhuj, was destroyed by an earthquake six months after filming.

🎞 **IF YOU LIKED THIS, YOU'LL LIKE:** *Iqbal,* a three-hour saga about a deaf-and-dumb aspiring cricket player and his cricket-hating father, Go ahead, rent it. We dare you.

◉ **REPEATED WATCHING QUOTIENT:** As we said, it's 224 minutes long.

LOST TREASURES

MIKE TOMLIN WAS THE INSPIRATION FOR THIS CHAPTER. WHEN ASKED FOR HIS FAVORITE SPORTS MOVIE, THE PITTSBURGH STEELERS COACH THOUGHT FOR A MOMENT. "WELL, I HAVE A FAVORITE," HE SAID, "BUT I'M SURE YOU NEVER HEARD OF IT. IT'S A LOST TREASURE."

THE MOVIE IS *RUNNING BRAVE*, A 1983 FILM BASED ON THE LIFE OF BILLY MILLS, A NATIVE AMERICAN WHO OVERCAME LONG ODDS TO WIN THE 10,000 METER RUN AT THE 1964 TOKYO OLYMPICS. THE FILM, WHICH STARRED ROBBY BENSON AS MILLS, WAS FINANCED IN PART BY THE CREE INDIAN TRIBE AND PLAYED IN RELATIVELY FEW THEATERS. IT WAS SOLD TO THE VIDEO MARKET AND FORGOTTEN IN A MATTER OF WEEKS. GOOD LUCK TRYING TO FIND IT.

BUT TOMLIN SAW IT WHEN HE WAS IN GRAMMAR SCHOOL AND NEVER FORGOT IT. HE HAS SEEN DOZENS OF OTHER SPORTS MOVIES, INCLUDING ALL THE BIG ONES WITH THE GLAMOROUS CASTS, BUT HE STILL CONSIDERS *RUNNING BRAVE* THE BEST.

"IT CAPTURED MY HEART," TOMLIN SAID. "THIS GUY (MILLS) WAS AN AFTERTHOUGHT. HE GREW UP ON AN INDIAN RESERVATION AND RAN IN BORROWED SHOES. HE GOT A TRACK SCHOLARSHIP (KANSAS) BUT HE WAS LIKE A FISH OUT OF WATER. HE DIDN'T GET ALONG WITH HIS COACH, HE COULDN'T FIT IN ON CAMPUS, BUT HE STUCK IT OUT AND FINALLY PREVAILED.

"THE MOVIE HAS A GREAT MESSAGE," TOMLIN SAID. "IT'S A SHAME MORE PEOPLE HAVEN'T SEEN IT."

SO WE WONDERED HOW MANY OTHER LOST TREASURES WERE OUT THERE, QUALITY FILMS THAT HAVE ALL BUT DISAPPEARED EITHER BECAUSE THEY WERE MADE LONG AGO, OR THEY ONLY PLAYED ON TV, OR, LIKE *RUNNING BRAVE*, THEY RECEIVED A LIMITED RELEASE. HERE ARE SOME OTHER FILMS THAT WE WOULD PUT ON THAT LIST, IN THEIR ORDER OF RELEASE.

Million Dollar Legs (1932). This is a funny spoof of the Olympics starring W.C. Fields and Jack Oakie. Fields plays the president of Klopstokia, a tiny nation where all the citizens are superior athletes. Babies high-jump six feet, adults run the mile in just a few seconds. Oakie is a traveling salesman who discovers this mother lode of talent and convinces Fields to enter a team in the 1932 Summer Olympics in Los Angeles.

There are dozens of hilarious sight gags. One of the best is Fields winning the gold medal in weightlifting when his opponent tries to hoist 1,000 pounds and winds up falling through the earth.

The Jackie Robinson Story (1950). The Brooklyn Dodgers star does a credible job playing himself in this biography, which details his struggle to break the color line in major league baseball. Actress Ruby Dee plays his wife, Rachel, and Minor Watson is very good as Brooklyn general manager Branch Rickey.

"My Dad was a big Jackie Robinson fan," said Dusty Baker, who starred for the Los Angeles Dodgers and now manages Cincinnati. "As an African-American, of course I identified with the story. That movie motivated me. My Dad used to say when I screwed up, 'What would Jackie do?' So that movie really inspired me. Jackie was a model."

Trouble Along the Way (1953). John Wayne plays a football coach who is hired by a small Catholic college to put a winning team on the field and bring in more revenue so the school can stay afloat. Wayne bends a few rules and brings in a bunch of ringers to fill out the squad. Overnight, tiny St. Anthony's College is knocking off the big schools and people start getting suspicious.

The film is played mostly for laughs with Wayne as a football lifer who feels more at home in a pool hall or a card game than in chapel. Look for Chuck Connors, TV's *Rifleman,* in a small role as one of the school's assistant coaches.

Go, Man, Go (1954). This was the second—and better—of two films about the Harlem Globetrotters (the other was called, simply, *The Harlem Globetrotters*). Dane Clark stars as promoter Abe Saperstein, who forms the team and barnstorms across the country, taking on hostile crowds, crooked refs and racist opponents.

The real Globetrotters play themselves. The only actor on the team was Sidney Poitier. The film was directed by James Wong Howe, the famed cinematographer who shot the boxing scenes in the original *Body and Soul.*

Blood Sport (1973). This made-for-TV movie was really the first *Friday Night Lights.* Gary Busey plays a Texas high school football star driven to succeed by an overbearing father (Ben Johnson) and a sadistic coach (Larry Hagman). Busey was five years away from his breakout role in *The Buddy Holly Story,* but he shows great promise in his portrayal of all-state quarterback David Lee Birdsong.

The film effectively illustrates the pressure that is put on high school athletes by parents, coaches and recruiters. Birdsong visits a college on a recruiting trip. There he bumps into four other all-state quarterbacks who have been sold the same bill of goods by the coach. The "Gee, I-thought-I-was-his-Number-One" look on Birdsong's face is very believable.

The Deadliest Season (1977). Another made-for-TV movie which served as a stinging commentary on hockey violence. This was *Slap Shot* without the laughs. Michael Moriarty is a hockey player who is sent to the minor leagues because he isn't aggressive enough. Desperate to get back to the top, Moriarty starts fighting and playing dirty. Sure enough, he is recalled to the big club.

But Moriarty's goon tactics result in a fatal injury to another player, who also happens to be a friend, and he is brought to trial on manslaughter charges. An intelligent look at a complex issue, the film makes you think. Moriarty is excellent as the player who doesn't want to fight, but feels he must to keep his job.

The Miracle of Kathy Miller (1981). Yet another made-for-TV film, this one stars a young Helen Hunt in the true story of an Arizona teenager who is critically injured in a car accident. She is in a coma for 10 weeks, and when she awakens, she is unable to walk, talk, read or write. The doctors say she has no hope for recovery, but her parents refuse to accept the diagnosis.

After eight months of intense physical and mental therapy, Kathy—who was a track and cross-country champion in high school—is able to compete in a six-mile race. Hunt is excellent in the title role. Frank Converse and Sharon Gless play her parents. (Kathy's father, Larry Miller, was a pitcher with the Los Angeles Dodgers and New York Mets).

Girlfight (2000). This small indie was a sleeper hit at the Sundance Film Festival where it shared the Grand Jury Prize. Writer-director Karyn Kusama, a protege of John Sayles, makes a strong impression with her first film, the story of Latina teenager Diana Guzman (Michelle Rodriguez) who effectively channels her anger into the sport of boxing.

Rodriguez trained in a Brooklyn gym for four months to prepare for the role and she is totally convincing. Richard Corliss of *Time* magazine called Rodriguez "The young Brando womanized." Indeed, there is a smoldering Brando-like intensity in her face as she fights for—and earns—her respect in a macho world..

Undisputed (2002). Ralph Wiley, writing for ESPN.com, called this film "an eye-popping, soul-catching, neck-snapping knockout of a boxing film." Wiley said, "If *Undisputed* is not quite *Raging Bull*, it is not all that far away."

We won't go so far as to compare *Undisputed* to *Raging Bull*, but this film, directed by Walter Hill (who also directed *Hard Times*), is darn good. It tells the story of George "Iceman" Chambers (Ving Rhames), the undefeated heavyweight champion of the world who is sent to prison for rape. Hmmm, who might he be modeled after? Anyway, there he meets Monroe Hutchen (Wesley Snipes), a lifer who is unbeaten in 67 prison bouts. It's only a matter of time before they meet to settle who is the real heavyweight champ.

The Heart of the Game (2005). This is an entertaining documentary about a girls basketball team at Roosevelt High School in Seattle. The film focuses on two subjects: Coach Bill Resler, an impish tax professor who also happens to be a hoops junkie, and star player Darnellia Russell, who has plenty of game and a personality to match.

Coach Resler is a fascinating character who motivates his players by urging them to play like a pack of wolves one day and wreak havoc like a tropical storm the next. His parting words as the players break the huddle are, "Draw blood, have fun." We don't see any blood on the court, but we do see the Roosevelt players having a lot of fun. The film is narrated by rapper Chris "Ludacris" Bridges.

Pride (2007). The true story of Jim Ellis, who builds a state championship swimming team with inner-city kids in Philadelphia. The film marked the directorial debut of Sunu Gonera, a South African who obviously related strongly to the themes of segregation and discrimination. Terrence Howard, who earned an Oscar nomination for his role as a rapping pimp in the film *Hustle & Flow*, takes on a far different character here as the stern but caring coach. Bernie Mac plays the janitor who becomes Howard's assistant.

The film is predictable in many ways—the city tries to close down the pool, drug dealers try to corrupt the kids, the white swimmers make fun of the black kids (until they start kicking their preppie butts)—but *Pride* has a lot of heart and Howard's fine performance pulls it all together. When he tells the kids, "My life is way too short for me to spend my time around people who don't care about nothing," you believe him. And when he cries after the big meet, well, you might, too.

94 GRAND PRIX (1966–PG)

SPORT: AUTO RACING | STARS: JAMES GARNER, EVA MARIE SAINT, YVES MONTAND, JESSICA WALTER | DIRECTOR: JOHN FRANKENHEIMER

Grand Prix was an expensive and not particularly successful venture for MGM. The film was shot on the Formula One circuit during the 1965 season and cost a fortune, with director John Frankenheimer and his crew (which included every existing Panavision 65mm camera) traveling across Europe and North America.

It was marketed as a Cinerama film, which meant it could only play in theaters with oversized screens and surround sound. It also was three hours long (including an intermission) which meant many locations could show it only twice a day. The result was higher ticket prices and that, along with mixed reviews, discouraged business.

From a technical standpoint, *Grand Prix* is a triumph. Frankenheimer mounted cameras on the cars, allowing the audience to see the race from the driver's seat. This perspective—the tight turns on the streets of Monte Carlo, the open road flashing by in Belgium, the terrify-

ing vibration on the banked track in Italy—had theatergoers clutching their seats and, in some cases, dashing for the bathroom.

When the movie leaves the race track, however, it slows to a crawl. The soap opera plot follows four drivers—one American (James Garner), one Corsican (Yves Montand), one Englishman (Brian Bedford) and one Sicilian (Antonio Sabato)—as they compete for the world championship.

Naturally, they all have romantic issues that threaten to distract them at the worst possible time—for example, when Pete Aron (Garner) and Scott Stoddard (Bedford) are coming down the final straightaway. They look at each other and realize not only are they dueling for the Grand Prix title but they also slept with the same woman in the last reel. And, well, that's a lot to sort out at 180 miles per hour.

Stoddard has a decent back-story—he is trying to escape the shadow of his older brother who was world champion before he was killed—and the suave Jean-Pierre Sarti (Montand) is likable enough, but every time the actors start talking, we're looking at our watches wondering when they are going to get back in their cars and stomp on the gas.

For Frankenheimer, who also directed classics like *Birdman of Alcatraz* and *The Manchurian Candidate*, this was his first venture into color. He uses multiple images, taking a mundane shot (say, a wrench tightening a bolt), then dividing the screen into rows of smaller boxes until there are dozens of wrenches tightening dozens of bolts and, suddenly, what was mundane isn't mundane anymore.

Frankenheimer also uses a split screen to show a driver talking while at the same time steering his car around the track. One of the better moments is seeing Nino Barlini (Sabato) drive his Ferrari through a blinding rain while he tells an interviewer, "These cars, you sit in a box, a coffin, gasoline all around you. It is like being inside a bomb."

🍺 **CHEERS:** The action photography is spectacular, in particular the crash in Monte Carlo where Stoddard's car bursts into flames and Aron's car flips into the Mediterranean.

🚩 **JEERS:** The romantic subplots are tedious. It is hard to work up much sympathy for a wife (Jessica Walter) who leaves her husband (Bedford) while he is unconscious in a hospital and begins an affair with the man (Garner) who caused the accident that put him there.

✒ **WHAT THEY WROTE AT THE TIME:** "The same old story with the same types we've seen flying planes and riding horses in dozens of fast, cheap hour-and-a-quarter movies."—Pauline Kael, *The New Yorker*

🍎 **BET YOU DIDN'T KNOW:** Of the 32 Formula One drivers who make cameo appearances in the film, 10 would lose their lives on the track over the next 12 years.

◎ **REPEATED WATCHING QUOTIENT:** Fast forward to the racing scenes. Skip everything in-between.

◀ **CASTING CALL:** Steve McQueen was the first choice to play Pete Aron, but after a testy interview with producer Edward Lewis, he bowed out. Five years later, McQueen starred in another racing film, *Le Mans*. Robert Redford also passed on the part of Aron, opening the door for Garner.

🎬 **PIVOTAL SCENE:** Sarti begins to question his involvement in the sport. He tells his lover, Louise (Eva Marie Saint), "I've begun to see the absurdity of it. All of us, proving what? That we can go faster and perhaps remain alive?"

At that point, you know Jean-Pierre is a goner.

❞ **BEST LINE:** Surrounded by gawking spectators and paparazzi, Louise holds up her hands, which are covered with Sarti's blood, and cries, "Is this what you want? This is what you came for, isn't it?"

😎 **"I KNOW THAT GUY":** The driver with the British accent and the dashing mustache is Graham Hill, a Grand Prix champion in real life. He plays a character named Bob Turner in the film.

★ **SPORTS-ACTION GRADE:** A. The driving scenes are breathtaking, heightened by the fact that Frankenheimer resists the urge to add music to the soundtrack. During most of the races, the only sound is the roar of the engines. In other words, you are hearing what the drivers hear, which makes it feel like the real thing.

In addition, the site in the movie where Sarti meets his fiery demise—Italy's Monza—was actually the scene of the most horrific crash in Formula One history. In 1961, Wolfgang Von Trips of Germany lost control of his car and spun into the crowd. Sixteen people, including Von Trips, were killed.

🏎 **MY FAVORITE SPORTS MOVIE:** Dario Franchitti, Indianapolis 500 champion: "I think it's amazing. I was watching the movie three or four weeks ago in my motor home and I saw a friend of mine, Bernard Kaiyea [a journalist from France], in the credits. So I phoned him in France and said, 'Hey, what are you doing in *Grand Prix*?' It's a terrific movie."

95 WIND (1992–PG 13)

SPORT: SAILING | STARS: MATTHEW MODINE, JENNIFER GREY
DIRECTOR: CARROLL BALLARD

We're not America's Cup guys. Truth be told, we wouldn't know a spinnaker from a winch. Sailboats are for catching sunrays and studying bikinis—not so much for racing.

Nor are we chick-flick guys. Our idea of romance is Crash Davis breaking down Annie Savoy's defenses with The Speech—you know, "I believe in the sweet spot, soft-core pornography. . . . "

But somehow, despite our best instincts, we were drawn in by this little movie about the men who race 12-meter yachts and the women who love them (or, in some cases, race better than them). In fact, it wasn't the plot line, the characters or the romance that got us. Definitely not the romance, which seems like something lifted right off the Lifetime Network. Rather, it was the spectacular racing scenes. Who knew that a bunch of snooty, zinc-oxide-wearing bluebloods on boats could create some of the most intense sports action we've seen?

Wind centers on the story of young Will Parker (Matthew Modine), a talented sailor intent on winning the America's Cup. In case your sports interests lie elsewhere, the America's Cup is a 150-year-old competition among the world's top yachtsmen, most of whom appear attracted to ascots and silly hats. Up through the 1990s the United States has dominated the event.

Anyway, Will tries out for the crew of the legendary Morgan Weld (Cliff Robertson), who's kind of a combination of Howard Hughes and Robert Shaw's Quint from *Jaws*. He gets the nod to skipper Weld's yacht, but is told he must send home his sassy girlfriend, Kate Bass (Jennifer Grey), even though she's clearly the best sailor in the movie. So Will dumps the girl. Then he blows the race and loses the America's Cup to Australia. Bad month.

Flash forward six months. Will tracks down Kate on the salt flats of Utah (not exactly sailing country), where she's living with her new boyfriend, an aircraft designer named Joe (played by the always annoying Stellan Skarsgard). In a bit of a leap of faith, Will persuades them both

to help him design a revolutionary yacht that might win back the Cup. To make things more unlikely, their chief financial backer is Weld's nutty daughter, Abigail (Rebecca Miller), who likes to dance to *Madame Butterfly* while seducing a bag of Fritos.

Yeesh, this is starting to sound like the fall plotline of *The Young and the Restless*. Unfortunately, *Wind* loses its energy during all of the on-land sequences. But once we get into the water—wow, suddenly we have a heart-pounding thriller.

The racing scenes are absolutely invigorating. We witness head-on crashes, spectacularly torn sails and one moment when a crewman ends up strung helplessly upside down from the mast during a critical competition. This is not serene ocean sailing; these are real athletes—sweating, grunting, fighting fatigue to be the best in the world at their sport.

Give credit to director Carroll Ballard, who has shown a great visual sense in *The Black Stallion* and *Fly Away Home*. And give credit to cinematographer John Toll, whose daredevil camera shots—above, below, beside the yachts—put you right in the crashing waves.

The payoff here is the final race in Freemantle, Australia—the "Game Seven," if you will, between Will and Jack Neville (smartly played by Aussie Jack Thompson). Ballard devotes a full 21 minutes to the contest and you won't be bored for a second. Pay attention to the sound effects—creaking masts, crashing hulls, splashing water—which add to the tension. And notice how you keep inching forward in your chair as the tight race moves along. This is good stuff, comparable to *Raging Bull*, *Friday Night Lights* or any other brilliantly shot sports action.

🍺 **CHEERS:** Realizing that most audience members probably know little about sailing, Ballard was wise to work in explainers throughout the film. You'll learn what "stealing a boat's wind" means, and feel a little smarter for it.

JEERS: At 126 minutes, *Wind* starts becoming windbaggish. All of the boy-wins-girl, boy-loses-girl stuff could have been condensed to make this a 90-minute thriller.

WHAT THEY WROTE AT THE TIME: "Of all the sporting contests I've seen at the movies—bike races, boxing matches—I'm not sure there has ever been one more spectacular than the America's Cup sailing final that comes early on in Carroll Ballard's *Wind*. Ballard doesn't transform sailing into an etherealized daydream. He captures the physical and intellectual excitement of the sport—the aggressive athleticism and split-second decision making that turn competitive sailing into refined warfare."—Owen Gleiberman, *Entertainment Weekly*

REALITY CHECK: It appears that the total amount of time needed to design a yacht from scratch (by a first-time designer, no less), build it and train a crew to sail it to victory in the America's Cup is about five months.

REPEATED WATCHING QUOTIENT: If you skip all the on-land stuff and fast-forward right to the climactic race, it sustains through multiple viewings.

PIVOTAL SCENE: In the penultimate America's Cup race, the American and Australian boats crash. Both skippers blame each other. But at a post-race news conference, Will—who earlier insisted he would do *anything* to win—suddenly gets a pang of conscience. He admits the truth: it was his poor sailing that caused the accident. He even offers to lend the Aussies an extra mast to replace the one his yacht busted.

"We're almost there and you betray us with your principles," Abigail screams at him. But to Will, winning the right way is the only way.

CASTING CALL: The commentator for all the big races is New Zealander Peter Montgomery, known in the yachting world as the "Voice of the America's Cup." We're also told that Montgomery is regarded as the John Madden of cricket.

DON'T FAIL TO NOTICE: Jennifer Grey underwent her infamous rhinoplasty after filming for *Wind* had wrapped. Unfortunately, several scenes needed to be re-shot, making this the first movie since *Pinocchio* where a character's nose grows and shrinks throughout.

SPORTS-ACTION GRADE: A. And trust us, we never expected to say that about a yachting movie.

BEST LINE: Morgan Weld: "Tradition has it that the first American skipper to ever lose the Cup will replace it with his own head in the trophy case. Gentlemen, my head is in your hands. Please be careful, I've become attached to it."

"I KNOW THAT GUY": Weld's henchman, George, is played by James Rebhorn, who specializes in stiff upper lip. You may recognize him as Robert De Niro's doctor pal, Larry Banks, from *Meet the Parents* (the jackass who can't believe that Greg Focker is actually a nurse), or as District Attorney Norwalk from *Carlito's Way*. We also spotted him as the prosecutor who puts Jerry, George, Elaine and Kramer away on the final episode of *Seinfeld*.

96 VISION QUEST (1985–R)

SPORT: HIGH SCHOOL WRESTLING | **STARS:** MATTHEW MODINE, LINDA FIORENTINO
DIRECTOR: HAROLD BECKER

Vision Quest is the all-too-familiar tale of a teenager from a working class town trying to prove his mettle (and win the girl) by taking on a near-impossible athletic challenge. We saw the same story on bikes in *Breaking Away*, and on the mat in *The Karate Kid*.

Here, the venue shifts to high school wrestling. And while *Vision Quest* breaks no new ground in the coming-of-age sports genre, it succeeds for two reasons: First, the sport translates well onto film, with all of its rituals and practice methods and the easy-to-shoot action.

Second, and more importantly, *Vision Quest* works because you get to a watch a talented young cast of actors before they became famous. Matthew Modine stars as 17-year-old Louden Swain, two years before his breakout role in *Full Metal Jacket*. Linda Fiorentino, making her first movie appearance, displays the same icy sexiness (and no, that's not an oxymoron in this case) that she would later perfect in *The Last Seduction*. And that nightclub singer with the teased up hair and finger-less black gloves? That's Madonna, also in her screen debut (well, not counting any soft-core porn indie movies she may or may not have made).

Daphne Zuniga, a future star of *Melrose Place*, and Forest Whitaker, the future Oscar winner for his role as Idi Amin, also have small roles here. Whitaker doesn't get to say much, but his character's name—Balldozer—is worth a few laughs.

The story centers on Louden, a smart and quirky high school senior who can pin most anyone as a 190-pound wrestler. But that doesn't interest him. He wants a tougher challenge, so he decides to cut all the way down to 168 pounds to battle the nastiest monster in Spokane, WA, the undefeated Brian Shute. (It may be unrealistic to believe that any 168 pounder would be tougher than the wrestlers in Louden's weight class, but, hey, that's the movies.)

Shute (Frank Jasper) is kind of like Ivan Drago in a singlet. When we first meet him, he is running up rows of stadium bleachers carrying a log on his back the size of a telephone pole. When Louden goes to scout him, Shute humiliates a highly ranked opponent in 12 seconds.

Clearly, this is craziness. Everyone tries to talk Louden out of his folly—his coach (Charles Hallahan), who worries that he risks losing a college scholarship; his dad (Ronny Cox), who grows alarmed when Louden's quest to drop 22 pounds leads to fainting spells and constant nosebleeds; his teammates, who are all panic-stricken by the Mighty Shute. "I hear when he pins a guy, his coach has to stop him from biting the guy's throat open," says one.

The only support comes from two people. Louden's best friend, Kuch (Michael Schoeffling), a self-proclaimed half-Native American, touts Louden's goal as a "vision quest," an Inuit rite where a young man goes on a personal, spiritual endeavor. Kuch explains that Louden will be guided by the "Everywhere Spirit," although the first few times he says it in the film, it sure sounds like the "Underwear Spirit."

Louden's other ally is Carla (Fiorentino), a 20-year-old drifter who—at first—doesn't take him too seriously, but winds up falling for his boyish optimism. Suffice it to say, Louden earns his victory in bed before he ever gets to the match against Shute.

It leads up to an all-too-predictable finish, which would leave you flat if *Vision Quest* didn't have such full characters and a fine cast. Instead, this is a fun, well-written film that's worth the 105 minutes it asks you to invest.

CHEERS: There's an amusing subplot about Louden's ambition to grow up to become—yes—a gynecologist so, as he explains, "I can see what's inside women to find the power they have over me." He writes a story for the school newspaper on, well, the most intimate part of a woman's anatomy.

"You've broken new ground, Louden," says student editor Margie (Daphne Zuniga). "Where do you get your ideas?"

"Well, I've been thinking a lot about that stuff lately."

🎌 **JEERS:** Did the chunky middle-aged coach really need to wear a skin-hugging singlet during the practice scenes? Yo, Coach, put a pair of shorts on over that, would you?

✔ **REALITY CHECK:** Louden's constant nosebleeds become a problem when he starts leaking from the proboscis late in a match that he is winning. Louden's coach wipes his nose with a towel and then, when the flow doesn't immediately stop, passively accepts a medical forfeiture. Hey, having been through high school wrestling, we know that coaches and competitors would have tried a whole lot more than a measly dish rag to staunch a nosebleed—to the point of breaking off Q-Tips in our nostrils and instructing us to breathe through our mouths.

📷 **PIVOTAL SCENE:** When he discovers that Carla has skipped town right before his big match, Louden considers ditching his whole dream. He seeks solace at the home of his friend, short-order cook Elmo (J.C. Quinn). Louden discovers, to his amazement, that Elmo plans to skip work that night and attend the meet.

"Why bother?" asks a dejected Louden. "It's only six minutes."

Elmo, struggling to knot his only tie, launches into a pep talk about how he once stumbled upon a soccer game on TV and saw Pele score an amazing goal that left him in tears.

"That's right, I started crying," says Elmo. "Because another human being, a species that I happen to belong to, could kick a ball, and lift himself—and the rest of us sad-assed human beings—up to a better place, if only for a minute. Let me tell you kid, it was pretty goddamned glorious. It ain't the six minutes—it's what happens in those six minutes. Anyway, that's why I'm getting dressed up and giving up a night's pay for this."

Quick cut to the next scene: Louden sprinting to get to his pre-match weigh-in on time.

⭐ **SPORTS-ACTION GRADE:** B. Real wrestling (as opposed to the spectacle that is pro wrestling) adapts well to film because the action is quick, the matches are brief and there are just two competitors. We just wish we hadn't had to wait 90 minutes into *Vision Quest* to see the first real battle.

🗨 **BEST LINE:** Louden: "Do you know that sexual intercourse burns up 200 calories a shot?"

Carla: "That's one way to look at it."

✏ **WHAT THEY SAID AT THE TIME:** "The script is adapted from a very successful book by Darryl Ponicsan, who wrote one of my favorite films, *The Last Detail*, and he's done it again.... It's so fresh that it enlivens the formula. It was good writing that helped launch the *Rocky* series. I just wish they'd had the guts to go for a different kind of ending. That could have launched this into the stratosphere."—Gene Siskel, *Siskel and Ebert at the Movies*

🔘 **REPEATED WATCHING QUOTIENT:** It's worth catching the final battle or the Madonna performance if you happen to stumble upon it. Other than that, once is enough.

🎩 **BET YOU DIDN'T KNOW:** Modine said in later interviews that he believes the movie's poor box office showing ($13 million) stemmed from an inapt title. "It sounds more like a science fiction film than anything else," he told *Entertainment Weekly*.

👓 **"I KNOW THAT GUY":** That's veteran character actor James Gammon as the drunken and violently tempered dad of Louden's friend, Kuch. Gammon later brought his gravelly voice (but lost his rage) to play Cleveland Indians manager Lou Brown in *Major League*.

🎞 **IF YOU LIKED THIS, YOU'LL LIKE:** *Take Down*, a 1979 Disney film—starring Lorenzo Lamas and Stephen Furst—about a down-and-out bunch of high school seniors who form a wrestling team to take one last shot at glory before what they envision as a life of defeat.

97 COOL RUNNINGS (1993–PG)

SPORT: BOBSLEDDING | STARS: JOHN CANDY, LEON
DIRECTOR: JON TURTELTAUB

Silly as it sounds, there really is a Jamaican bobsled team. In 1988, the tropical nation best known for reggae and ganja amused the world by sending a four-man crew to the Winter Olympics. The team crashed and finished last, but it delighted the crowds in Calgary, Canada, and more than earned its way home by selling souvenir T-shirts.

Since then, the country that has never seen a flake of snow has tried out for each Olympics. In 1994, in Lille-hammer, Norway, Jamaica's four-man sled finished in 14th place—ahead of both American crews. These days, the team maintains a training base in Wyoming, which must create a good deal of culture shock for both locals and visitors.

All of which makes you ask: How does a tiny speck in the Atlantic—where the average daily temperature is 82 degrees—get involved in this most winterish of winter sports?

There's a good tale here, told—although not especially accurately—in the 1993 comedy *Cool Runnings*. In the movie, disgraced American bobsled coach Irv Blitzer (John Candy) recruits three Jamaican sprinters and their pushcart racing buddy (more about that in a second) to form a sledding team after they fail to qualify to run in the Summer Olympics. With no funds, no support and no training facilities, they practice by lugging a rickety go-kart up and down hills laden with palm trees.

In real life, two Americans with business ties to Jamaica witnessed the annual Pushcart Derby in Kingston, in which street vendors race their carts down steep roads at speeds reaching 60 miles per hour. They signed up the champion racer, enlisted three soldiers from the Jamaican Army, and moved the operation north to Canada, where they received top-flight training. Their coach, Howard Siler, was one of the best in the world and certainly not a pariah to the sport, as Candy's character portrayal would have us believe.

In the movie, the Jamaicans are met with ridicule and

hostility at Calgary. This leads to the inevitable bar brawl between our naive dreadlocked Rastas and the evil East German bobsled team, led by a Josef Grool, the nastiest movie Teuton this side of Hans Gruber. (On a side note, we've lost much of our interest in the Olympics since the Communist empire crumbled. It was more fun when you could root against the baddies from the GDR and USSR. Who's the enemy now? Until Iran forms a hockey team, we're boycotting the Winter Games.)

In real life, the Jamaicans became somewhat of a pet to the other competitors, who offered them everything from coaching tips to extra clothing to survive the minus-10 chill of Alberta. No one tried at the last minute to have them barred from the Games, as the movie suggests. No one considered them an embarrassment to the sport.

But, hey, that's Hollywood. "The movie accurately depicted the spirit of the team," original team member Devon Harris told *Entertainment Weekly*. "For purposes of entertainment, they portrayed us with far more color, let us say."

Okay, so it's not exactly *Hoop Dreams* on ice. But *Cool Runnings* is an upbeat, entertaining movie that's very appealing to kids and at least palatable for adults. While it uses every underdog movie cliché, you will find yourself attracted to the characters and, ultimately cheering their *Rocky*-like finish in Calgary. We won't give that ending away, except to say it, too, wasn't exactly true to real life.

CHEERS: The quartet of Jamaican sledders—played by actors Doug E. Doug, Leon, Rawle D. Lewis and Usain Bolt look-alike Malik Yoba—are an engaging, likeable crew. They fit every TV stereotype so well (the goofy one, the angry young man, the earnest guy, the rich kid struggling for his own identity) that we're surprised they weren't later cast together in a recurring sitcom.

JEERS: John Candy was one of the great comic actors of the past half century, at his best playing a mixture of sweetness and pathos. But as Irv Blitzer, he's just an unfunny, wise-cracking grouch. Where's that vulnerability that served him so well in *Planes, Trains & Automobiles* and *National Lampoon's Vacation*?

WHAT THEY WROTE AT THE TIME: "The title, *Cool Runnings*, is doubly apt. In Jamaica it's an expression meaning "peaceful journey"—and that's clearly what director Jon Turteltaub has in mind. His Jamaica is family-sitcom clean—no poverty, no ganja, not even a ganja joke."—Richard Harrington, *Washington Post*

REALITY CHECK: Well, they do appear to go from complete novices to Olympic qualifiers in about one week.

DON'T FAIL TO NOTICE: In an apparent money-grabbing nod to product placement, there are many Red Stripe beer bottles shown throughout the movie. But given that this is a Disney production, no one is ever seen actually drinking the beer.

SPORTS-ACTION GRADE: C-minus. Bobsledding is the kind of sport that could easily be made to appear thrilling through use of multiple cameras and sharp editing. Not so much here.

BET YOU DIDN'T KNOW: At the 1998 Olympics in Nagano, Japan, the Jamaican team crashed again. The driver suffered a concussion and for several days could not remember the last 11 years of his life. His brother, who was also on the team, had to inform him that he was married and had two children.

BEST LINE: Coach Blitzer giving his pep talk: "Always remember, your bones will not break in a bobsled. No, they will shatter. So, who wants in?"

IF YOU LIKED THIS, YOU'LL LIKE: Two James Bond movies feature bobsledding scenes, with the usual 007 mix of action and humor. *On Her Majesty's Secret Service* (1969) is George Lazenby's only appearance as Bond, while *For Your Eyes Only* (1981) stars Roger Moore and former figure skater Lynn-Holly Johnson. Stick with Sir Roger.

REPEATED WATCHING QUOTIENT: Once every presidential administration.

98 YOUNGBLOOD (1986–R)

SPORT: HOCKEY | STARS: ROB LOWE, PATRICK SWAYZE
DIRECTOR: PETER MARKLE

Some movies set out with great ambitions. They have a social conscience and their goal is to make people think. Those are the movies that are celebrated at Sundance and maybe win an Oscar.

Then there are movies like *Youngblood*.

The producers knew they weren't going to impress the critics with this film, and they didn't really care. They weren't worried about satisfying hardcore hockey fans who would take note of certain details, such as Rob Lowe's wobbly skating. *Youngblood* wasn't made for purists, either artistic or athletic.

This is the kind of movie a bunch of guys watch together with a few beers. It's the kind of movie women will enjoy because it's full of hunky guys who spend a lot

of time in the locker room getting undressed. There is no great message here. It's like a fast food meal: it goes down easy, and while it doesn't offer much in the way of nutrition, it tastes pretty good.

Parts of the film are downright hilarious, some intentionally, some not. For example, there is the moment the Hamilton Mustangs goalie appears and you realize, "Hey, that's Keanu Reeves." Then he begins talking in a mangled French-Canadian accent and you are on the floor laughing.

Also, there is the scene where Dean Youngblood (Lowe) shows up at his boarding house and is greeted by a landlady who looks like she just slid off a pole at the local gentlemen's club. When she knocks on Dean's door and says she has his afternoon tea, we know the room service won't stop there. The bewildered "Is-this-included-in-my-room-and-board?" look on Lowe's face is priceless.

Youngblood is the story of a hotshot teenage hockey player (Lowe) from upstate New York who is invited to try out for a junior team in Hamilton, Ontario, where he hopes to impress the pro scouts. His older brother Kelly (Jim Youngs) had the same dream, but his career ended when an opponent's high stick left him blind in one eye.

As they sit in the car outside the rink in Hamilton, Kelly tells Dean, "Don't take any shit from them Canucks. To them, you're just another wetback crossing the border to play their game."

"They'll never catch me," Dean says.

"Oh, they'll catch you," Kelly says, speaking from experience.

The Mustangs are looking to fill one roster spot, and Racki skating in warm-ups with the Thunder Bay Bombers, Hamilton's opponent in the Memorial Cup Playoffs. He caught on with the Bombers after Chadwick decided to let him go.

When Racki casts an evil stare in the direction of the Hamilton bench, you know it's only a matter of time before he lowers the boom on one of the Mustangs. It's no surprise when Racki drops Sutton on his mullet and sends him off the ice on a stretcher.

So much for Derek's hockey career. Guess he'll have to settle for being a dance instructor in the Catskills. Oh wait, that's another movie.

At this point, *Youngblood* lapses into melodrama and suffers for it. Dean is so sickened by Derek's injury that he quits the team and returns to the family farm. His brother can't believe it.

DEREK:

"THANK GOD THERE IS A SPORT FOR MIDDLE-SIZED WHITE BOYS."

coach Murray Chadwick (Ed Lauter) narrows the candidates down to Dean and a bearded tough guy named Carl Racki (George J. Finn). Chadwick picks Dean, even though Racki punches him out during a scrimmage.

Dean goes through the ritual of proving himself to his teammates, surviving a hazing and a drunken night on the town, but eventually the other players decide he's okay, even though he is an American and he looks, well, like Rob Lowe. Dean bonds with team captain Derek Sutton (Patrick Swayze), who also has his eyes on a pro career.

"I want to go No. 1 in the draft and sign the biggest contract I can," Sutton says. "I've been busting my ass in this league for four years and I'm gonna get what's coming to me."

That's a tip-off to what's coming. So is the sight of

"With one eye, I begged them to let me play," he says. "Would you rather spread manure or play hockey in Madison Square Garden?"

"Spread manure," Dean says.

"You candy-ass," his brother growls.

But soon Dean is in the barn smacking a punching bag and he is on the pond practicing his slap shot. It is clear he is planning to rejoin his team. One night Dean is on the ice and his father (former NHL star Eric Nesterenko) comes out to join him.

"You can learn to punch in the barn," the father says, "but you gotta learn to survive on the ice."

Dad shows Dean how to win a hockey fight (just wondering, but why didn't he give him this lesson *before* he went to Canada?) and just like that, he's headed back to

Hamilton. In real life, an old-school coach like Chadwick would have slammed the locker room door in Dean's face. He wouldn't have let the kid fool around with his precious daughter (Cynthia Gibb) either, but that's a different story.

But Chadwick allows Dean to dress for the deciding game. The movie tries for the big finish, but it turns out to be the weakest part of the film because so much of it doesn't make sense (See *Jeers*).

🍺 **CHEERS:** *Youngblood* was filmed in Hamilton, so you get a feel for life on the junior hockey circuit.

⚑ **JEERS:** In the final game, Dean scores two goals in the last ten seconds (one on a penalty shot) to win the series. And if that isn't enough, he squares off with the evil Racki and punches his lights out. All of a sudden, he's Wayne Gretzky and Bruce Lee all rolled into one. We know it's just a movie, but still. . . .

99 **BEST LINE:** Racki inviting Dean to drop the gloves: "Wanna go, pretty boy?"

✎ **WHAT THEY WROTE AT THE TIME:** "When the film sends [Lowe] back to the farm so as to create a dewy montage of him handling the barnyard chores, it seems to have gone entirely off the deep end. Whatever it is that Rob Lowe ought to be doing on the screen, pitching hay is not the answer."—Janet Maslin, *New York Times*

😎 **"I KNOW THAT GUY":** Longtime NHL players Peter Zezel and Steve Thomas are two of Lowe's Hamilton teammates.

🏒 **BET YOU DIDN'T KNOW:** Keanu Reeves played goalie on his high school hockey team, De La Salle in Toronto. We're not kidding.

★ **SPORTS-ACTION GRADE:** C. The hockey scenes are slightly less convincing than those in *The Mighty Ducks*.

🏒 **MY FAVORITE SPORTS MOVIE:** Cy Young Award winner Eric Gagne: "I played junior hockey in Canada until I was 18, so I really related to *Youngblood*. The rough stuff, the fighting—I went through all that. I liked hockey better than baseball. I get emotional when I compete and in hockey I can use that emotion by hitting people. I still play in a beer league in the off-season."

99 VICTORY (1981–PG)

SPORT: SOCCER | STARS: MICHAEL CAINE, SYLVESTER STALLONE | DIRECTOR: JOHN HUSTON

John Huston won an Academy Award as best director for *The Treasure of the Sierra Madre*. He was nominated for an Oscar for his work in other classic films, such as *The Asphalt Jungle*, *The African Queen* and *The Man Who Would Be King*.

So why did he sign on to direct *Victory*, a rather far-fetched tale of soccer and World War II?

"I only make pictures if I like the story, or they offer me a lot of money," Huston said, "and in this case it happened to be both."

Producer Freddie Fields wanted to hire Brian G. Hutton, who directed two other hit films about World War II: *Where Eagles Dare* and *Kelly's Heroes*. But Sylvester Stallone, one of *Victory*'s co-stars, persuaded Fields to hire the 74-year-old Huston.

Vincent Canby of the *New York Times* saw *Victory* as a lark for Huston. Canby said the film "represents [Huston] in an expansive and almost carefree mood. It's as if Mr. Huston—having just directed two of the most imaginative and difficult films of his long career, *The Man Who Would Be King* and *Wise Blood*—had decided to work on something more conventional and less demanding."

Victory was shot entirely on location in Hungary. It cost $15 million to produce and it earned just $10 million at the box office. Most critics dismissed it—Canby said the film "is not meant to be taken too seriously"—and soccer purists laughed at Stallone as a goalkeeper even if he did drop 40 pounds of his *Rocky* weight to look the part.

But *Victory* developed a cult following among the DVD crowd because it does have some enjoyable elements. The soccer action—we know, that seems like a contradiction in terms—is actually entertaining. It helps that eight goals are scored in the big game. That's seven more than are scored in most soccer games. And while Michael Caine doesn't look like David Beckham, his acting helps the script overcome its rough spots.

The film begins in an Allied POW camp where the prisoners, most of them British, pass the time by playing soccer. John Colby (Caine) is a former World Cup player now held captive by the Nazis. Major Karl Von Steiner (Max von Sydow) is a former German soccer star who recognizes Colby. Von Steiner proposes an exhibition match between the POWs and the German National team.

The Germans intend to use the game as a propaganda vehicle. They will play the game in Paris and show the world how well they are treating the POWs—"Look, we let them play soccer and everything"—then, of course, the Germans will win the game and wave the banner of Aryan superiority.

The Allies have a different agenda. Their plan is to use the game as a means to escape. Robert Hatch (Stallone), an American POW, breaks out of the prison camp, makes his way to Paris to meet with the French Resistance and plan the big escape. Hatch allows himself to be re-captured by the Nazis—hey, we said this is far-fetched—so that he can be returned to the POW camp where he tells Colby and the others what the French have in mind.

This all works out a little too conveniently. As Canby notes, Hatch escapes the camp and gets to Paris "all with less difficulty than your average journey to and from East Hampton via railroad." And how does an American POW find the Resistance in Paris? Is it listed in the Yellow Pages? Also when Hatch allows himself to be re-captured, how can he be sure the Nazis will return him to the camp? Suppose they just shoot him on the spot?

The same thoughts probably occurred to John Huston and then he decided: "Aw, the hell with it. Let's just get to the soccer game." Good idea.

Think *The Longest Yard* meets *Stalag 17*—that's *Victory*. The ending doesn't make a lot of sense—one critic called it "egregiously silly"—but it is fun in a shamelessly rah-rah kind of way. And the slow-motion shot of the legendary Brazilian soccer star Pele (he is one of the Allied POWs) executing his famous bicycle kick is one that will amaze even non-soccer fans.

🍺 **CHEERS:** The photography is often stunning, in particular the first shot of the POW camp. It is shown from a distance and the camp looks like a barbed wire cage set in the middle of nowhere. It really conveys the feeling of isolation and loneliness.

🍺 **JEERS:** In the big game, the Allies score a goal and Von Steiner, the German officer, applauds. It is meant to show that Von Steiner is a sportsman who appreciates the artistry of the well-played shot. It is one of those silly "only-in-the-movies" moments. If a real German officer was caught cheering for the Allies, he'd get more than a dirty look from the SS. He'd get a one-way ticket to the Russian front.

✐ **WHAT THEY WROTE AT THE TIME:** "*Victory* amounts to a frankly old-fashioned World War II morality play, hinging on soccer as a civilized metaphor for the game of war."—*Variety*

☞ **DON'T FAIL TO NOTICE:** The music score sounds very *Rocky*-like. That's because it was written by Bill Conti, who did the original theme for *Rocky*.

★ **SPORTS-ACTION GRADE:** C. There are a number of world class soccer players on the Allied team, including Bobby Moore, the captain of England's 1966 World Cup team, and the great Pele, but Stallone and Caine are the leads and they are woefully out of place on a soccer field.

☺ **GOOFS:** In the crowd scenes at the big game, many of the fans are wearing clothes and hair styles that are clearly from the 1980s, not the 1940s.

❋ **IF YOU LIKED THIS, YOU'LL LIKE:** Two very good POW films: *The Great Escape* with Steve McQueen and James Garner heading an all-star cast, and *Von Ryan's Express* with Frank Sinatra. Trust us, both are better than *Victory*.

100 THE FISH THAT SAVED PITTSBURGH (1979–PG)

SPORT: BASKETBALL | STARS: JULIUS ERVING, JONATHAN WINTERS, MEADOWLARK LEMON | DIRECTOR: GILBERT MOSES

The Fish That Saved Pittsburgh is by no means a great movie. It is not even considered by critics to be a good movie. The script is inane, the acting barely passable, the directing spotty. But if you give it a chance, *Fish* proves to be a campy period piece that prompts you to smile nostalgically at times and guffaw out loud at others. Just set aside any rational disbelief and let the movie wash over you. A beer or two wouldn't hurt.

We'll call it a guilty pleasure, a quirky film with enough redeeming value that we recommend it, warts and all. (See the next chapter for more guilty pleasures.)

Take the plot. (Please.) The Pittsburgh Pythons, led by selfish star Moses Guthrie (Julius Erving) are the worst team in pro basketball. When Guthrie's teammates all walk out in protest, the 12-year-old towel boy (James Bond III) convinces the addle-brained owner (Jonathan Winters) to hold open tryouts. The one requirement is that only players sharing Guthrie's astrological sign are selected.

And then it gets weird.

The team, which now resembles the Village People and is renamed the "Pisces," is guided by an astrologist, Miss Mona Mondieu (a slumming Stockard Channing), whose game plans have more to do with Jupiter rising than Dr. J dunking. And, of course, the team starts winning every game.

We are not making this up.

It all culminates with a kidnapping by the owner's evil twin, a showdown against Kareem Abdul-Jabbar and a lot of disco dancing in platform shoes. What's not to like?

If you're too young to remember the 1970s, *Fish* will take you to a time of huge Afros and pastel clothes, of breakdancing to a disco beat. Somehow, between the turbulence of the 60s and the greed of the 80s, there was this decade of totally fun nonsense.

It was also a decade of fun basketball. Much of the joy here is seeing Erving—an iconic figure of the era—lope his way through the game scenes and also try to look serious reacting to dialog like, "The man is only interested in playing for the bucks—the spending kind."

Leroy Burrell, the 1992 Olympic Gold-Medal sprinter who once held the title of world's fastest human, said, "I grew up in the Philadelphia area, Doctor J was my favorite athlete, I love basketball and I'm a Pisces. How could I not love that movie?"

An enjoyable sidelight here is spotting all the NBA players who show up for anonymous cameos as opposing players. Some are easy—Connie Hawkins, Bob Lanier, Spencer Haywood—but others will challenge your hoops memory. Isn't that Chris Ford in a Detroit uniform? Hey, did Cornbread Maxwell just pass the ball to Kevin Stacom? We were able to count 20 of Doc's old colleagues who dropped in for a scene or two. Perhaps you'll spot more.

🍺 **CHEERS:** To one of the underrated original soundtracks of history. The songs are not just thrown together—they're about that particular scene in the movie. The Spinners, Doc Severinsen, The Four Tops, Loretta Lynn—you name a candidate for a VH1 *I Love the 70s* special, and he or she performs here.

🚩 **JEERS:** Early in the movie, a quite naked Moses Guthrie emerges from the whirlpool before putting on a towel. Let's just say we know more about the Doctor than we ever intended.

✏ **WHAT THEY WROTE AT THE TIME:** "What you see in *Fish* smells. I cry for the honorable municipality of Pittsburgh, the noble city of champions, that its good name should be so violated. . . . People in the theater where I saw *Fish* loved the dunks, as they loved the disco, as they no doubt would be entertained by hockey thugs. Disco is obviously a fad, and I doubt that dunk ball can survive for long, either. *Fish* shows that, like punching people on ice skates, no matter how proficient you are at it, the dunk becomes horribly monotonous after a while."—Frank Deford, *Sports Illustrated*

(Well, he was correct about disco, anyway.)

✔ **REALITY CHECK:** What an awe-inspiring laser introduction for Abdul-Jabbar and his Los Angeles Fever teammates in the final game. Too bad the contest was being played in Pittsburgh, and no road team would receive that kind of pyrotechnic welcome.

◀ **CASTING CALL:** Beyond the many NBA stars of the day, don't miss the young, pre-toupeed Marv Albert and the disembodied voice of Chick Hearn as announcers here. And Cher was originally cast as the astrologist, but backed out at the last minute.

🎬 **PIVOTAL SCENE:** Well, with a plot this dopey, it's hard to say anything is pivotal. But the funniest scene has to be the Pisces open tryout scene, which resembles the intergalactic bar scene in *Star Wars*.

🍎 **BET YOU DIDN'T KNOW:** Erving, perhaps being modest, ranks this as his second-favorite film of all time, behind *The Great Escape*. Shaquille O'Neal said it is the one movie he would love to star in if it were remade.

99 **BEST LINE:** Moses: "I had to learn to walk and lean on air. I had to learn to listen to the rhythm inside my body. I had to learn to push myself, to see how far I can go. I have my dream."

Not exactly James Earl Jones's "Baseball" speech from *Field of Dreams*. But, hey, it does win the girl.

👓 **"I KNOW THAT GUY":** The chain-smoking, wise-cracking trainer? That's Michael V. Gazzo, most famously remembered as Frankie "Five Angels" Pentangeli from *The Godfather II*. In his 40-year career, Gazzo made 26 crime movies, usually playing a Mafioso; alas, just one sports movie.

★ **SPORTS-ACTION GRADE:** B+. At times, Doc appears to be going through the motions, but it's still a pleasure to watch him swoop and slam. And Harlem Globetrotters great Meadowlark Lemon, cast as teammate Rev. Grady Jackson, performs as only Meadowlark Lemon could perform.

👁 **REPEATED WATCHING QUOTIENT:** Only if you're stoned.

📖 **MY FAVORITE SPORTS MOVIE:** Quarterback Donovan McNabb: "*The Fish That Saved Pittsburgh* was an inspirational movie that showed how diverse individuals can be very compatible. It's proven not just by their talents and goals in life to be the best at what they do, but also in their minds. Believing is everything. It all starts with a little star in the sky that attracts the eyes of some, but not all."

Hmm, and we thought it was just a goofy movie.

***Idol of the Crowds* (1937).** John Wayne made 147 films during his 50-year acting career. Next to *The Conqueror*—a radioactively bad cult movie in which he portrays Genghis Khan—this one may be the least credible of them all. The Duke plays Johnny Hansen—the original "Hanson Brother"—a retired hockey player living out his dream as a Maine chicken farmer. He needs some scratch to keep the farm going, so he agrees to play one more season for the New York Panthers. The plot gets tough to follow from there, but there's a brush with cliché-spouting gangsters, an attempt on our hero's life and, of course, a B-movie finale that ends with Wayne getting the girl.

If you're a hockey fan, you'll enjoy *Idol* because, well, there just aren't many hockey movies. If you're a John Wayne fan, you'll enjoy watching him skate around on the insides of his ankles and shoot the puck like a guy sweeping out his garage. Let's just say it's a good thing for his career that Wayne learned how to ride a horse.

***Kid Galahad* (1962).** Speaking of which, it's good that Elvis Presley learned to play the guitar, because he wouldn't have made it as a prize fighter. He plays one here, however, or at least attempts to. In a plot that seems eerily similar to *Idol of the Crowds*, Elvis plays an ex-GI aiming for the dream of becoming a car mechanic. Instead, he's lured into becoming a boxer, and ends up as a top contender and crowd favorite. And, once again, here comes to mob trying to muscle in on his success.

You'll enjoy Elvis in satin trunks and gloves, enjoy the great Charles Bronson as his loyal trainer and—of course—enjoy the sound track, which includes six tunes by Elvis (none, however, one of his classics). How he strums that guitar while wearing boxing gloves is beyond belief.

Best line? Elvis as Walter Gulick to sleazy manager Willy Grogan (Gig Young): "Don't push me, Willy. I'm a grease monkey that won't slide so easily."

***Kansas City Bomber* (1972).** No one under age 40 is likely to remember Raquel Welch as anything more than a violent diva from the famous 1997 "The Summer of George" episode of *Seinfeld*. Trust us, once upon a time, she was Pamela Anderson—without the silicone. Likewise, no one under 40 is likely to remember when Roller Derby was a staple of local UHF programming on weekend afternoons.

Damn shame, because both Raquel and Roller Derby were fun eye candy. They combine in this sometimes laughable flick about a star skater trying to balance her shaky personal life (watch for Jodie Foster as her 10-year-old daughter) and her barbaric professional world. There are occasional ham-handed early women's liberation references, but mostly there's a lot of cleavage heaving and cat fights. Extra points to anyone who recognizes Judy Arnold, former Philadelphia Warrior, as the one doing Ms. Welch's dirty work as a stunt double.

***Death Race 2000* (1975).** The ultimate in cult flicks, starring a pre-*Rocky* Sylvester Stallone, Louisa Moritz's crowd-pleasing breasts and David Carradine as a cyborg-like character named Frankenstein in a leather suit resembling The Gimp from *Pulp Fiction*. All with cool cars and a 1970s porn-style soundtrack in the background. What's not to enjoy?

The setup here is a futuristic national sport/television series in the so-called United Provinces of America, in which cross-country drivers gain points for running over pedestrians. ("The big score: anyone, any sex, over 75 years old, has been upped to 100 points!"). There are rivalries, soap operas and sexcapades among the drivers, but, mostly, innocent fools getting flattened on the highway.

It all sounds ridiculous, until you turn on most contemporary reality shows, or take a peek at video games like *Grand Theft Auto*. But, hey, we don't want to get preachy. Where else do you get dialog like, "Well America, there you have it, Frankenstein has just been attacked by the French Air Force and he's whipped their derrieres." Occasionally, well after midnight, Turner Classic Movies will run the uncut version of *Death Race 2000*. Be there.

And don't bother with the version remade in 2008, starring Jason Statham and Ian McShane. It's not as sexy or as campy.

Brewster's Millions (1985).

Any movie starring both Richard Pryor and John Candy has to be a hoot and this one does not disappoint. Pryor plays minor-league pitcher Monty Brewster, who comes into a huge inheritance—with a catch. He must spend (waste, actually) $30 million in 30 days. If successful, he'll inherit $300 million; if not, he gets nothing. And, of course, Brewster can't tell anyone about the deal. That includes Candy, his catcher and goofy sidekick, who helps Brewster by spending too much money on a gold-plated catcher's mask once owned by Johnny Bench.

The best sports scene comes when Brewster pays to stage an exhibition game between his low-level club and the New York Yankees. The best waste of money comes when he spends $1.25 million on a valuable stamp and then uses it to send a letter. But, really, the best part of the movie is the chemistry between Pryor and Candy—two comic masters who left the stage too early.

Bloodsport (1988).

Jean-Claude Van Damme's pantheon movie, narrowly edging *Sudden Death* (in which the Belgian badass somehow ends up as the Pittsburgh Penguins goalie). In this classic, J.C.V.D. plays U.S. Army soldier Frank Dux, who goes AWOL to compete in a mysterious martial arts tournament, where, we keep being reminded, "Death is a single punch away." Or kick.

We don't want to say the movie plays to old-time stereotypes, but it seems that every Asian character was cast by the same Hollywood folks who produced those World War II propaganda films. Many of the cast members speak no English, which leaves the bulk of the dialog to the Shakespearean Van Damme. Like, "I ain't your pal, dickface."

It's all about as dumb as a 1980s martial arts shlockfest can be, complete with a lame love interest (Leah Ayres) and some of the greatest fighting scenes ever choreographed. Overall, it's wonderful mindless fun.

Men With Brooms (2002).

The best curling movie ever made. Actually, the only curling movie ever made. An all-Canadian cast—including a slumming Leslie Neilsen (in what aims to be a serious role) and the popular Ontario rock band The Tragically Hip—tell the story of a small-town team that reunites in the wake of its coach's death and tries to win the Golden Broom, curling's version of the Stanley Cup. All while making gags about beavers and frozen groins and drinking lots of Molson Ale.

Montreal Mirror critic Matthew Hays dismissed *Men With Brooms* as "a movie that's clearly meant to have everything in it: romance, comedy, pathos, suspense [who will win that final curling match?—stay tuned!], etc. You'll laugh, you'll cry, you know the drill. Sadly, everything about the film feels clumsy in that ultra-Canadian way."

We don't know about that. We didn't even know that Canadians were ultra-clumsy. (Take that, Sidney Crosby!) We'll just argue that this movie is so bad that it's good. Just make sure to bring the Molson Ale.

Dodgeball: A True Underdog Story (2004).

A great cast, led by Vince Vaughn and Ben Stiller, would seem to promise a great film about that junior high school gym staple that allowed bullies to terrorize glasses-wearing eggheads for decades. But *Dodgeball* doesn't quite get there. It's a funny concept—the owner of a gym perfectly named "Average Joe's" tries to save the shabby place by entering his clients into a $50,000 dodgeball tournament. But a funny concept doesn't always make for 92 minutes of on-screen entertainment.

Still, it has its moments. Stiller is hysterical as the mullet-wearing owner of the rival macho-man training spa. He's the guy who fights off his own little-man complex by surrounding himself with steroid-addled bodybuilders and wearing an inflatable crotch under his gym shorts. Vaughn aims to play the same wiseguy role he perfected in *Old School*—but doesn't quite get there. The movie is stolen by Rip Torn as Patches O'Houlihan, a legendary former dodgeballer (we didn't know dodgeball had legends) who reinvents himself as a sadistic, wrench-throwing coach.

***Nacho Libre* (2006).** Jack Black's ode to Mexican professional wrestling is kind of a cross between *Wrestlemania IV* and *Napoleon Dynamite*. We're not saying that the movie was made under the influence of drugs but, well, since Black has referred to himself as a modern-day Jeff Spicoli, we can't really rule it out, either.

Black plays Brother Ignacio, a monk living in the outposts of Mexico, who tends after impoverished orphans. He wants to give them better food than the slop he's providing, so he begins a second career as a *luchador*, or masked wrestler, in the sport of *Lucha Libre*, a freestyle form of wrestling that makes what you see on American cable resemble *Wall Street Week* in comparison. Brother Ignacio also spends a lot of time inappropriately lusting after Sister Encarnacion, played by the incredibly beautiful Ana de la Reguera. You'll share his lust. You'll also share a few laughs. You may also share a bong, but we advise against it.

***Talladega Nights: The Ballad of Ricky Bobby* (2006).** We happen to think that Will Ferrell is a talented comic—first for his work on *Saturday Night Live*, and later for the aforementioned *Old School* and *Anchorman: The Legend of Ron Burgundy*. His attempts at sports comedies, however, have largely fallen flat. *Blades of Glory*? Weird, but not amusing. *Semi-Pro*? A great script idea (focusing on the old American Basketball Association) that proved to be a snoozer. *Kicking & Screaming*? That's how we'll react if ever forced to watch that youth soccer nonsense again.

The best of the bunch, and the only Ferrell-inspired sports movie worth seeing, is *Talladega Nights*. Ferrell lets 'er rip as Ricky Bobby, a proudly dumb race driver from North Carolina. John C. Reilly, who can do lowbrow with the best of them, is his best bud, Cal. There's a white trash wife, some bratty kids and a tasteless (but funny) homage to the Baby Jesus. And then, unfortunately, director Adam McKay tries to get fluffy and sentimental with the ending. Take it from us—watch the first 90 minutes and then turn off your DVD player. You'll have a few laughs and won't miss a thing.

MY FAVORITE SPORTS MOVIE: Orlando Magic center Dwight Howard: "I just love *Dodgeball* because Ben Stiller is completely funny. Like he says in the movie: 'Nobody makes me drink my own blood. Nobody.' I use that line all the time."

S

Sabathia, CC, 234
Sabato, Antonio, 318
Sabol, Steve, 82, 292, 293
Safe at Home!, 249
Saint, Eva Marie, 318–19
Sakic, Joe, 274
Salinger, J.D., 63, 65
Salley, John, 280
Salon.com, 103, 170
Salter, James, 131–33
Sampson, Kelvin, 135
Sampson, Will, 157
Samson (*The Longest Yard*), 235
San Diego Chargers, 293
San Diego State, 246
San Francisco 49ers, 158
San Francisco Chronicle, 86, 182, 237, 291, 296, 315
San Francisco Examiner, 102
San Francisco Giants, 280
Sand Pebbles, The, 271
Sanders, Barry, 82
Sanders, Deion, 50
Sandler, Adam, 11, 47–48, 167, 195, 236, 246, 247, 272–74
Sandlot, The, 40, 175, 288–89
Sands, Billy, 18
Santos, Miguel "Sugar", 207–8
Saperstein, Abe, 316
Sapp, Warren, 307
Sarandon, Susan, 17, 36–39, 119, 296
Sarasota Herald-Tribune, 208
Sarris, Andrew, 71
Sarti, Jenan-Pierre, 319
Sarwer, Jeff, 284
Satan, 255
Saturday Evening Post, The, 205
Saturday Night Live (SNL), 55, 57, 216, 247, 273, 335
Saturday's Hero, 234
Saunders, Stephen, 315
Sauter, Michael, 273
Saving Private Ryan, 186, 224
Savoy, Annie, 37–39, 119, 190, 320
Sayers, Gale, 80–82
Sayles, John, 163–65, 317
Sayre, Nora, 45, 48
Scarborough, Nate, 47, 195
Scarface, 297
Schaaf, Ernie, 183
Schembechler, Bo, 233
Schenkel, Chris, 216
Schickel, Richard, 43
Schier, Ernest, 31, 132, 133

Schilling, Curt, 128
Schintzius, Dwayne, 280
Schneider, Billy, 86
Schneider, Buzz, 86
Schnell, Dutch, 127–28
Schoeffling, Michael, 322
Scholz, Jackson, 89
Schoonmaker, Thelma, 29, 31
Schram, Bitty, 105
Schramm, Tex, 59
Schroder, Rick, 11, 52
Schulberg, Budd, 202
Schwartzwalder, Ben, 264–66, 267
Schwarzenegger, Arnold, 231, 245, 246, 249
Scioscia, Mike, 65
Scool of Rock, The, 111
Scorsese, Martin, 28–31, 69, 93, 160
Scott, A.O., 278
Scott, George C., 49–52, 269
Scott, Ridley, 160, 280
Scott, Stuart, 240
Scott, Tony, 280
Scott, Wendell, 149
Scout, The, 40
Screen Actors Guild awards, 70
Scully, Vin, 257
Sea of Love, 280
Seabiscuit, 139, 177–79, 182, 302
Seabiscuit (Hillenbrand), 177
Seabiscuit, 139, 140, 177–79
Seaboard Football League, 225
Seals & Croft, 257
seanbaby.com, 240
Searching for Bobby Fischer, 282–84
Sears, Darcy, 306–7
Seattle Seahawks, 247
Seaver, Tom, 40, 128
Segal, George, 137, 271
Seger, Bob, 218
Seinfeld, 147, 321, 333
Seinfeld, Jerry, 321
Seldes, Gilbert, 251
Selig, Bud, 122, 197
Selleck, Tom, 34, 40, 67, 259
Sellers, Peter, 231
Semi-Pro, 12, 67, 280, 335
Semi-Tough, 41, 172, 308
Serling, Rod, 137
Serpico, 147
Sersen, Fred, 197
Sesame Street, 244, 271
Set-Up, The, 116–18
Severson, Jeff, 59
Sex and the City, 263
Sextette, 196
Sexual Malice, 194
Shaddock, O.W., 60, 235

Shafer, Robert, 255
Shalhoub, Tony, 284
Shanahan, Mike, 298
Shapiro, Dana Adam, 168–70
Shattered Glass (Bissinger), 112
Shavers, Earnie, 147
Shaw, Robert, 158, 320
Shaw, Stan, 155
Shea, Frank "Spec", 35
Sheed, Wilfrid, 33
Sheen, Charlie, 40, 67, 119–20, 121, 163–65, 196
Sheffer, Craig, 232–34
Shelley, Rachel, 314–15
Shelton, Marley, 288, 289
Shelton, Ron, 11, 36–37, 39, 206, 239–40, 243, 295–96
Shemp, 196
Shephard, Jack, 252
Shepherd, Jean, 288
Sheridan, Jim, 237–38
Shine, 216
Shire, Talia, 14–18
Shoeless Joe (Kinsella), 65. *see also* Jackson, Shoeless Joe
"Shoeless Joe" (song), 255
Shokner (*The Longest Yard*), 154
Shooter (*The Cincinnati Kid*), 270
Shore, Eddie, 41
Shore, Pauly, 195
Shor's Toots, 222
Shorty (*Body and Soul*), 91, 92
Show Boat, 245
Shrevie (*Diner*), 99
Shue, Elisabeth, 189, 193, 194
Shula, Don, 94, 253
Shulzhoffer, Donnie, 211
Shute, Brian, 322
Shuttlesworth, Jake, 134–36
Shuttlesworth, Jesus, 134–36
Shyamalan, M. Night, 83
SI.com, 213
Sideways, 70, 190
Siegel, Robert D., 114
Siler, Howard, 324
Silverado, 24
Simmons, Bill, 62, 186
Simmons, Roy, Sr., 266
Simms, David, 295–96
Simms, Phil, 12
Simon, Neil, 205
Simon, Sam, 206
Simon and Garfunkel, 216
Simon Sez, 247
Simpson, O.J., 248, 259
Simpson, Vernon, 40, 197–98
Sin City, 113
Sinatra, Frank, 51, 196, 330
Sinbad, 235

Singh, Gracy, 314–15
Sirius Satellite Radio, 224
Siskel, Gene, 38, 323
Siskel and Ebert at the Movies, 323
Sist, Sibby, 35
Sisto, Jeremy, 201
Sixkiller, Sonny, 46, 48
Sixteen Candles, 281
Skarsgard, Stellan, 320
Slamball, 195
Slap Shot, 41–44, 154, 190, 205, 253, 262, 316
Slap Shot 2: Breaking the Ice, 195
Slaughterhouse-Five (Vonnegut), 306
Sling Blade, 110
Slugger's Wife, The, 217, 279
Slumdog Millionaire, 99
Smails, Judge, 54–55, 273, 277
Smalls, Leonare, 247
Smalls, Scotty, 288–89
Smart, Amy, 305–7
Smile, 172
Smith, Bruce, 175
Smith, Dean, 23, 135, 294
Smith, Emmitt, 129, 175
Smith, Joe, 287
Smith, Kyle, 28, 226
Smith, Lt., 315
Smith, Noland, 158
Smith, Red, 28, 31
Smith, Russell, 238, 247
Smith, Shirley Wheeler, 197
Smith, Tom, 178, 179
Smith, Will, 94, 278
Smyth, Ryan, 22
Sneak Previews, 38
Snipes, Wesley, 40, 66, 239–40, 280, 317
Snow, Charlie, 155
Snow Job, 133
Soares, Andre, 29
Soares, Joe, 168–70
Somebody Up There Likes Me, 93, 118, 204
Something for Joey, 82
Somewhere in Georgia, 245
Sontag, Susan, 39, 292
Soprano, Carmela, 187
Sopranos, The, 39, 187, 226
Soto, Algenis Perez, 207–8
Sound of Music, The, 118
"Sounds of Silence, The" (song), 216
South Bend Blue Sox, 104
Soylent Green, 246
Space Jam, 176, 239, 262
Spackler, Carl, 53–56
Spartacus, 245